SELECTED CORPORATION AND PARTNERSHIP STATUTES, REGULATIONS AND FORMS

1982 EDITION

ST. PAUL, MINN.

WEST PUBLISHING CO.

1982

PREFACE

This selection of corporation and partnership statutes, regulations, and forms is intended to supplement existing and future casebooks and other teaching materials for courses in business organizations and contains only the text of the act or statute that normally would be used in a business associations course.

Frequent revisions are planned not only to maintain the materials on a current basis but to serve better the needs of teachers and students in the subject matter areas. Suggestions of users and prospective users are requested. All will be carefully considered.

Our special thanks to Professor Harry G. Henn, editor of the first edition of this pamphlet, for his continued editorial assistance with this edition.

In the process of selecting and editing the materials helpful suggestions were received from Professors of Law Richard M. Buxbaum, University of California, Berkeley, Richard W. Jennings, University of California, Berkeley, Donald E. Schwartz, Georgetown University, Lewis D. Solomon, George Washington University, Russell B. Stevenson, Jr., George Washington University. The size of this supplement is evidence of our inclusion of their ideas.

Adoption of this supplement should alleviate the need for publishing lengthy casebook appendices, which become increasingly outdated over the life of a book, and for separate but similar statutory supplements for different books.

THE PUBLISHER

St. Paul
April, 1982

TABLE OF CONTENTS

SELECTED CORPORATION AND PARTNERSHIP STATUTES, REGULATIONS, AND FORMS

I. CORPORATIONS

A. MODEL BUSINESS CORPORATION ACT *

(As amended to April 1, 1982)

Contents

* Arabic paragraph numbers correspond to the Arabic paragraph numbers of the amendments. The 1979 revisions resulted in the elimination of a number of sections [§§ 21, 46, 66, 67, 68, 69, and 70]. For ease of historical reference, sections have not been renumbered but will be shown in the Model Act as "repealed in 1979". "Changes in the Model Business Corporation Act— Amendments to Financial Provisions", 34 Bus.Law. 1867, 1878 (footnote) (1979). See also "Changes in the Model Business Corporation Act Affecting Indemnification of Corporate Personnel," 34 Bus. Law. 1595 (1979).

1

CORPORATIONS

MODEL BUSINESS CORPORATION ACT

FORMATION OF CORPORATIONS

AMENDMENT

MERGER AND CONSOLIDATION

SALE OF ASSETS

CORPORATIONS

DISSOLUTION

MODEL BUSINESS CORPORATION ACT

................* BUSINESS

CORPORATION ACT

§ 1. Short Title

This Act shall be known and may be cited as the "......*
Business Corporation Act."

§ 2. Definitions

As used in this Act, unless the context otherwise requires, the term:

(a) "Corporation" or "domestic corporation" means a corporation for profit subject to the provisions of this Act, except a foreign corporation.

(b) "Foreign corporation" means a corporation for profit organized under laws other than the laws of this State for a purpose or purposes for which a corporation may be organized under this Act.

(c) "Articles of incorporation" means the original or restated articles of incorporation or articles of consolidation and all amendments thereto including articles of merger.

(d) "Shares" means the units into which the proprietary interests in a corporation are divided.

(e) "Subscriber" means one who subscribes for shares in a corporation, whether before or after incorporation.

(f) "Shareholder" means one who is a holder of record of shares in a corporation. If the articles of incorporation or the by-laws so provide, the board of directors may adopt by resolution a procedure whereby a shareholder of the corporation may certify in writing to the corporation that all or a portion of the shares registered in the name of such shareholder are held for the account of a specified person or persons. The resolution shall set forth (1) the classification of shareholder who may certify, (2) the purpose or purposes for which the certification may be made, (3) the form of certification and information to be contained therein, (4) if the certification is with respect to a record date or closing of the stock transfer books within which the certification must be received by the corporation and (5) such other provisions with respect to the procedure as are deemed necessary or desirable. Upon receipt by the corporation of a certification complying with the

* Supply name of State.

procedure, the persons specified in the certification shall be deemed, for the purpose or purposes set forth in the certification, to be the holders of record of the number of shares specified in place of the shareholder making the certification.

(g) "Authorized shares" means the shares of all classes which the corporation is authorized to issue.

(h) "Employee" includes officers but not directors. A director may accept duties which make him also an employee.

(i) "Distribution" means a direct or indirect transfer of money or other property (except its own shares) or incurrence of indebtedness, by a corporation to or for the benefit of any of its shareholders in respect of any of its shares, whether by dividend or by purchase, redemption or other acquisition of its shares, or otherwise.

SUBSTANTIVE PROVISIONS

§ 3. Purposes

Corporations may be organized under this Act for any lawful purpose or purposes, except for the purpose of banking or insurance.

§ 4. General Powers

Each corporation shall have power:

(a) To have perpetual succession by its corporate name unless a limited period of duration is stated in its articles of incorporation.

(b) To sue and be sued, complain and defend, in its corporate name.

(c) To have a corporate seal which may be altered at pleasure, and to use the same by causing it, or a facsimile thereof, to be impressed or affixed or in any other manner reproduced.

(d) To purchase, take, receive, lease, or otherwise acquire, own, hold, improve, use and otherwise deal in and with, real or personal property, or any interest therein, wherever situated.

(e) To sell, convey, mortgage, pledge, lease, exchange, transfer and otherwise dispose of all or any part of its property and assets.

(f) To lend money and use its credit to assist its employees.

(g) To purchase, take, receive, subscribe for, or otherwise acquire, own, hold, vote, use, employ, sell, mortgage, lend, pledge, or otherwise dispose of, and otherwise use and deal in and with, shares or other interests in, or obligations of, other domestic or foreign corporations, associations, partnerships or individuals, or direct or indirect obligations of the United States or of any other government, state, territory, governmental district or municipality or of any instrumentality thereof.

(h) To make contracts and guarantees and incur liabilities, borrow money at such rates of interest as the corporation may determine, issue its notes, bonds, and other obligations, and secure any of its obligations by mortgage or pledge of all or any of its property, franchises and income.

(i) To lend money for its corporate purposes, invest and reinvest its funds, and take and hold real and personal property as security for the payment of funds so loaned or invested.

(j) To conduct its business, carry on its operations and have offices and exercise the powers granted by this Act, within or without this State.

(k) To elect or appoint officers and agents of the corporation, and define their duties and fix their compensation.

(*l*) To make and alter by-laws, not inconsistent with its articles of incorporation or with the laws of this State, for the administration and regulation of the affairs of the corporation.

(m) To make donations for the public welfare or for charitable, scientific or educational purposes.

(n) To transact any lawful business which the board of directors shall find will be in aid of governmental policy.

(*o*) To pay pensions and establish pension plans, pension trusts, profit sharing plans, stock bonus plans, stock option plans and other incentive plans for any or all of its directors, officers and employees.

(p) To be a promoter, partner, member, associate, or manager of any partnership, joint venture, trust or other enterprise.

(q) To have and exercise all powers necessary or convenient to effect its purposes.

§ 5. Indemnification of Directors and Officers

(a) As used in this section:

(1) "Director" means any person who is or was a director of the corporation and any person who, while a director of the corporation, is or was serving at the request of the corporation as a director, officer, partner, trustee, employee or agent of another

foreign or domestic corporation, partnership, joint venture, trust, other enterprise or employee benefit plan.

(2) "Corporation" includes any domestic or foreign predecessor entity of the corporation in a merger, consolidation or other transaction in which the predecessor's existence ceased upon consummation of such transaction.

(3) "Expenses" include attorneys' fees.

(4) "Official capacity" means

(A) when used with respect to a director, the office of director in the corporation, and

(B) when used with respect to a person other than a director, as contemplated in subsection (i), the elective or appointive office in the corporation held by the officer or the employment or agency relationship undertaken by the employee or agent in behalf of the corporation,

but in each case does not include service for any other foreign or domestic corporation or any partnership, joint venture, trust, other enterprise, or employee benefit plan.

(5) "Party" includes a person who was, is, or is threatened to be made, a named defendant or respondent in a proceeding.

(6) "Proceeding" means any threatened, pending or completed action, suit or proceeding, whether civil, criminal, administrative or investigative.

(b) A corporation shall have power to indemnify any person made a party to any proceeding by reason of the fact that he is or was a director if

(1) he conducted himself in good faith; and

(2) he reasonably believed

(A) in the case of conduct in his official capacity with the corporation, that his conduct was in its best interests, and

(B) in all other cases, that his conduct was at least not opposed to its best interests; and

(3) in the case of any criminal proceeding, he had no reasonable cause to believe his conduct was unlawful.

Indemnification may be made against judgments, penalties, fines, settlements and reasonable expenses, actually incurred by the person in connection with the proceeding; except that if the proceeding was by or in the right of the corporation, indemnification may be made only against such reasonable expenses and shall not be made in respect of any proceeding in which the person shall have been adjudged to be liable to the corporation. The termination of any proceeding by judgment, order, settlement, conviction, or upon a plea of nolo contendere or its equivalent, shall not, of itself, be determinative that the person did not meet the requisite standard of conduct set forth in this subsection (b).

(c) A director shall not be indemnified under subsection (b) in respect of any proceeding charging improper personal benefit to him, whether or not involving action in his official capacity, in which he shall have been adjudged to be liable on the basis that personal benefit was improperly received by him.

(d) Unless limited by the articles of incorporation,

(1) a director who has been wholly successful, on the merits or otherwise, in the defense of any proceeding referred to in subsection (b) shall be indemnified against reasonable expenses incurred by him in connection with the proceeding; and

(2) a court of appropriate jurisdiction, upon application of a director and such notice as the court shall require, shall have authority to order indemnification in the following circumstances:

(A) if it determines a director is entitled to reimbursement under clause (1), the court shall order indemnification, in which case the director shall also be entitled to recover the expenses of securing such reimbursement; or

(B) if it determines that the director is fairly and reasonably entitled to indemnification in view of all the relevant circumstances, whether or not he has met the standard of conduct set forth in subsection (b) or has been adjudged liable in the circumstances described in subsection (c), the court may order such indemnification as the court shall deem proper, except that indemnification with respect to any proceeding by or in the right of the corporation or in which liability shall have been adjudged in the circumstances described in subsection (c) shall be limited to expenses.

A court of appropriate jurisdiction may be the same court in which the proceeding involving the director's liability took place.

(e) No indemnification under subsection (b) shall be made by the corporation unless authorized in the specific case after a determination has been made that indemnification of the director is permissible in the circumstances because he has met the standard of conduct set forth in subsection (b). Such determination shall be made:

(1) by the board of directors by a majority vote of a quorum consisting of directors not at the time parties to the proceeding; or

(2) if such a quorum cannot be obtained, then by a majority vote of a committee of the board, duly designated to act in the

matter by a majority vote of the full board (in which designation directors who are parties may participate), consisting solely of two or more directors not at the time parties to the proceeding; or

(3) by special legal counsel, selected by the board of directors or a committee thereof by vote as set forth in clauses (1) or (2) of this subsection (e), or, if the requisite quorum of the full board cannot be obtained therefor and such committee cannot be established, by a majority vote of the full board (in which selection directors who are parties may participate); or

(4) by the shareholders.

Authorization of indemnification and determination as to reasonableness of expenses shall be made in the same manner as the determination that indemnification is permissible, except that if the determination that indemnification is permissible is made by special legal counsel, authorization of indemnification and determination as to reasonableness of expenses shall be made in a manner specified in clause (3) in the preceding sentence for the selection of such counsel. Shares held by directors who are parties to the proceeding shall not be voted on the subject matter under this subsection (c).

(f) Reasonable expenses incurred by a director who is a party to a proceeding may be paid or reimbursed by the corporation in advance of the final disposition of such proceeding upon receipt by the corporation of

(1) a written affirmation by the director of his good faith belief that he has met the standard of conduct necessary for indemnification by the corporation as authorized in this section, and

(2) a written undertaking by or on behalf of the director to repay such amount if it shall ultimately be determined that he has not met such standard of conduct, and

after a determination that the facts then known to those making the determination would not preclude indemnification under this section. The undertaking required by clause (2) shall be an unlimited general obligation of the director but need not be secured and may be accepted without reference to financial ability to make repayment. Determinations and authorizations of payments under this subsection (f) shall be made in the manner specified in subsection (c).

(g) No provision for the corporation to indemnify or to advance expenses to a director who is made a party to a proceeding, whether contained in the articles of incorporation, the bylaws, a resolution of shareholders or directors, an agreement or otherwise (except as contemplated by subsection (j)), shall be valid unless consistent with this section or, to the extent that indemnity hereunder is limited by the articles of incorporation, consistent therewith. Nothing contained in this section shall limit the corporation's power to pay or reimburse expenses incurred by a director in connection with his appearance as a witness in a proceeding at a time when he has not been made a named defendant or respondent in the proceeding.

(h) For purposes of this section, the corporation shall be deemed to have requested a director to serve an employee benefit plan whenever the performance by him of his duties to the corporation also imposes duties on, or otherwise involves services by, him to the plan or participants or beneficiaries of the plan; excise taxes assessed on a director with respect to an employee benefit plan pursuant to applicable law shall be deemed "fines"; and action taken or omitted by him with respect to an employee benefit plan in the performance of his duties for a purpose reasonably believed by him to be in the interest of the participants and beneficiaries of the plan shall be deemed to be for a purpose which is not opposed to the best interests of the corporation.

(i) Unless limited by the articles of incorporation,

(1) an officer of the corporation shall be indemnified as and to the same extent provided in subsection (d) for a director and shall be entitled to the same extent as a director to seek indemnification pursuant to the provisions of subsection (d);

(2) a corporation shall have the power to indemnify and to advance expenses to an officer, employee or agent of the corporation to the same extent that it may indemnify and advance expenses to directors pursuant to this section; and

(3) a corporation, in addition, shall have the power to indemnify and to advance expenses to an officer, employee or agent who is not a director to such further extent, consistent with law, as may be provided by its articles of incorporation, by-laws, general or specific action of its board of directors, or contract.

(j) A corporation shall have power to purchase and maintain insurance on behalf of any person who is or was a director, officer, employee or agent of the corporation, or who, while a director, officer, employee or agent of the corporation, is or was serving at the request of the corporation as a director, officer, partner, trustee, employee or agent of another foreign or domestic corporation, partnership, joint venture, trust, other enterprise or employee benefit plan, against any liability asserted against him and incurred by him in any such capacity or arising out of his status as such, whether or not the corporation would have the power to indemnify him against such liability under the provisions of this section.

12

(k) Any indemnification of, or advance of expenses to, a director in accordance with this section, if arising out of a proceeding by or in the right of the corporation, shall be reported in writing to the shareholders with or before the notice of the next shareholders' meeting.

§ 6. Power of Corporation to Acquire Its Own Shares

A corporation shall have the power to acquire its own shares. All of its own shares acquired by a corporation shall, upon acquisition, constitute authorized but unissued shares, unless the articles of incorporation provide that they shall not be reissued, in which case the authorized shares shall be reduced by the number of shares acquired.

If the number of authorized shares is reduced by an acquisition, the corporation shall, not later than the time it files its next annual report under this Act with the Secretary of State, file a statement of cancellation showing the reduction in the authorized shares. The statement of cancellation shall be executed in duplicate by the corporation by its president or a vice president and by its secretary or an assistant secretary, and verified by one of the officers signing such statement, and shall set forth:

(a) The name of the corporation.

(b) The number of acquired shares cancelled, itemized by classes and series.

(c) The aggregate number of authorized shares, itemized by classes and series, after giving effect to such cancellation.

Duplicate originals of such statement shall be delivered to the Secretary of State. If the Secretary of State finds that such statement conforms to law, he shall, when all fees and franchise taxes have been paid as in this Act prescribed:

(1) Endorse on each of such duplicate originals the word "Filed", and the month, day and year of the filing thereof.

(2) File one of such duplicate originals in his office.

(3) Return the other duplicate original to the corporation or its representative.

§ 7. Defense of Ultra Vires

No act of a corporation and no conveyance or transfer of real or personal property to or by a corporation shall be invalid by reason of the fact that the corporation was without capacity or power to do such act or to make or receive such conveyance or transfer, but such lack of capacity or power may be asserted:

(a) In a proceeding by a shareholder against the corporation to enjoin the doing of any act or the transfer of real or personal property by or to the corporation. If the unauthorized act or transfer sought to be enjoined is being, or is to be, performed or made pursuant to a contract to which the corporation is a party, the court may, if all of the parties to the contract are parties to the proceeding and if it deems the same to be equitable, set aside and enjoin the performance of such contract, and in so doing may allow to the corporation or to the other parties to the contract, as the case may be, compensation for the loss or damage sustained by either of them which may result from the action of the court in setting aside and enjoining the performance of such contract, but anticipated profits to be derived from the performance of the contract shall not be awarded by the court as a loss or damage sustained.

(b) In a proceeding by the corporation, whether acting directly or through a receiver, trustee, or other legal representative, or through shareholders in a representative suit, against the incumbent or former officers or directors of the corporation.

(c) In a proceeding by the Attorney General, as provided in this Act, to dissolve the corporation, or in a proceeding by the Attorney General to enjoin the corporation from the transaction of unauthorized business.

§ 8. Corporate Name

The corporate name:

(a) Shall contain the word "corporation," "company," "incorporated" or "limited," or shall contain an abbreviation of one of such words.

(b) Shall not contain any word or phrase which indicates or implies that it is organized for any purpose other than one or more of the purposes contained in its articles of incorporation.

(c) Shall not be the same as, or deceptively similar to, the name of any domestic corporation existing under the laws of this State or any foreign corporation authorized to transact business in this State, or a name the exclusive right to which is, at the time, reserved in the manner provided in this Act, or the name of a corporation which has in effect a registration of its corporate name as provided in this Act, except that this provision shall not apply if the applicant files with the Secretary of State either of the following: (1) the written consent of such other corporation or holder of a reserved or registered name to use the same or deceptively similar name and one or more words are added to make such name distinguishable from such other name, or (2) a certified copy of a final decree of a court of competent jurisdiction establishing the prior right of the applicant to the use of such name in this State.

A corporation with which another corporation, domestic or foreign, is merged, or which is formed by the reorganization or consolidation of one or more domestic or foreign corporations or upon a sale, lease or other disposition to or exchange with, a domestic corporation of all or substantially all the assets of another corporation, domestic or foreign, including its name, may have the same name as that used in this State by any of such corporations if such other corporation was organized under the laws of, or is authorized to transact business in, this State.

§ 9. Reserved Name

The exclusive right to the use of a corporate name may be reserved by:

(a) Any person intending to organize a corporation under this Act.

(b) Any domestic corporation intending to change its name.

(c) Any foreign corporation intending to make application for a certificate of authority to transact business in this State.

(d) Any foreign corporation authorized to transact business in this State and intending to change its name.

(e) Any person intending to organize a foreign corporation and intending to have such corporation make application for a certificate of authority to transact business in this State.

The reservation shall be made by filing with the Secretary of State an application to reserve a specified corporate name, executed by the applicant. If the Secretary of State finds that the name is available for corporate use, he shall reserve the same for the exclusive use of the applicant for a period of one hundred and twenty days.

The right to the exclusive use of a specified corporate name so reserved may be transferred to any other person or corporation by filing in the office of the Secretary of State a notice of such transfer, executed by the applicant for whom the name was reserved, and specifying the name and address of the transferee.

§ 10. Registered Name

Any corporation organized and existing under the laws of any state or territory of the United States may register its corporate name under this Act, provided its corporate name is not the same as, or deceptively similar to, the name of any domestic corporation existing under the laws of this State, or the name of any foreign corporation authorized to transact business in this State, or any corporate name reserved or registered under this Act.

Such registration shall be made by:

(a) Filing with the Secretary of State (1) an application for registration executed by the corporation by an officer thereof, setting forth the name of the corporation, the state or territory under the laws of which it is incorporated, the date of its incorporation, a statement that it is carrying on or doing business, and a brief statement of the business in which it is engaged, and (2) a certificate setting forth that such corporation is in good standing under the laws of the state or territory wherein it is organized, executed by the Secretary of State of such state or territory or by such other official as may have custody of the records pertaining to corporations, and

(b) Paying to the Secretary of State a registration fee in the amount of .... for each month, or fraction thereof, between the date of filing such application and December 31st of the calendar year in which such application is filed.

Such registration shall be effective until the close of the calendar year in which the application for registration is filed.

§ 11. Renewal of Registered Name

A corporation which has in effect a registration of its corporate name, may renew such registration from year to year by annually filing an application for renewal setting forth the facts required to be set forth in an original application for registration and a certificate of good standing as required for the original registration and by paying a fee of ....
A renewal application may be filed between the first day of October and the thirty-first day of December in each year, and shall extend the registration for the following calendar year.

§ 12. Registered Office and Registered Agent

Each corporation shall have and continuously maintain in this State:

(a) A registered office which may be, but need not be, the same as its place of business.

(b) A registered agent, which agent may be either an individual resident in this State whose business office is identical with such registered office, or a domestic corporation, or a foreign corporation authorized to transact business in this State, having a business office identical with such registered office.

§ 13.   Change of Registered Office or Registered Agent

A corporation may change its registered office or change its registered agent, or both, upon filing in the office of the Secretary of State a statement setting forth:

(a) The name of the corporation.

(b) The address of its then registered office.

(c) If the address of its registered office is to be changed, the address to which the registered office is to be changed.

(d) The name of its then registered agent.

(e) If its registered agent is to be changed, the name of its successor registered agent.

(f) That the address of its registered office and the address of the business office of its registered agent, as changed, will be identical.

(g) That such change was authorized by resolution duly adopted by its board of directors.

Such statement shall be executed by the corporation by its president, or a vice president, and verified by him, and delivered to the Secretary of State. If the Secretary of State finds that such statement conforms to the provisions of this Act, he shall file such statement in his office, and upon such filing the change of address of the registered office, or the appointment of a new registered agent, or both, as the case may be, shall become effective.

Any registered agent of a corporation may resign as such agent upon filing a written notice thereof, executed in duplicate, with the Secretary of State, who shall forthwith mail a copy thereof to the corporation at its registered office. The appointment of such agent shall terminate upon the expiration of thirty days after receipt of such notice by the Secretary of State.

If a registered agent changes his or its business address to another place within the same ....*, he or it may change such address and the address of the registered office of any corporation of which he or it is registered agent by filing a statement as required above except that it need be signed only by the registered agent and need not be responsive to (e) or (g) and must recite that a copy of the statement has been mailed to the corporation.

§ 14.   Service of Process on Corporation

The registered agent so appointed by a corporation shall be an agent of such corporation upon whom any process, notice or

* Supply designation of jurisdiction, such as county, etc., in accordance with local practice.

demand required or permitted by law to be served upon the corporation may be served.

Whenever a corporation shall fail to appoint or maintain a registered agent in this State, or whenever its registered agent cannot with reasonable diligence be found at the registered office, then the Secretary of State shall be an agent of such corporation upon whom any such process, notice, or demand may be served. Service on the Secretary of State of any such process, notice, or demand shall be made by delivering to and leaving with him, or with any clerk having charge of the corporation department of his office, duplicate copies of such process, notice or demand. In the event any such process, notice or demand is served on the Secretary of State, he shall immediately cause one of the copies thereof to be forwarded by registered mail, addressed to the corporation at its registered office. Any service so had on the Secretary of State shall be returnable in not less than thirty days.

The Secretary of State shall keep a record of all processes, notices and demands served upon him under this section, and shall record therein the time of such service and his action with reference thereto.

Nothing herein contained shall limit or affect the right to serve any process, notice or demand required or permitted by law to be served upon a corporation in any other manner now or hereafter permitted by law.

§ 15. Authorized Shares

Each corporation shall have power to create and issue the number of shares stated in its articles of incorporation. Such shares may be divided into one or more classes with such designations, preferences, limitations, and relative rights as shall be stated in the articles of incorporation. The articles of incorporation may limit or deny the voting rights of or provide special voting rights for the shares of any class to the extent not inconsistent with the provisions of this Act.

Without limiting the authority herein contained, a corporation, when so provided in its articles of incorporation, may issue shares of preferred or special classes:

(a) Subject to the right of the corporation to redeem any of such shares at the price fixed by the articles of incorporation for the redemption thereof.

(b) Entitling the holders thereof to cumulative, noncumulative or partially cumulative dividends.

(c) Having preference over any other class or classes of shares as to the payment of dividends.

(d) Having preference in the assets of the corporation over any other class or classes of shares upon the voluntary or involuntary liquidation of the corporation.

(e) Convertible into shares of any other class or into shares of any series of the same or any other class, except a class having prior or superior rights and preferences as to dividends or distribution of assets upon liquidation.

§ 16. Issuance of Shares of Preferred or Special Classes in Series

If the articles of incorporation so provide, the shares of any preferred or special class may be divided into and issued in series. If the shares of any such class are to be issued in series, then each series shall be so designated as to distinguish the shares thereof from the shares of all other series and classes. Any or all of the series of any such class and the variations in the relative rights and preferences as between different series may be fixed and determined by the articles of incorporation, but all shares of the same class shall be identical except as to the following relative rights and preferences, as to which there may be variations between different series:

(A) The rate of dividend.

(B) Whether shares may be redeemed and, if so, the redemption price and the terms and conditions of redemption.

(C) The amount payable upon shares in event of voluntary and involuntary liquidation.

(D) Sinking fund provisions, if any, for the redemption or purchase of shares.

(E) The terms and conditions, if any, on which shares may be converted.

(F) Voting rights, if any.

If the articles of incorporation shall expressly vest authority in the board of directors, then, to the extent that the articles of incorporation shall not have established series and fixed and determined the variations in the relative rights and preferences as between series, the board of directors shall have authority to divide any or all of such classes into series and, within the limitations set forth in this section and in the articles of incorporation, fix and determine the relative rights and preferences of the shares of any series so established.

In order for the board of directors to establish a series, where authority so to do is contained in the articles of incorporation, the board of directors shall adopt a resolution setting forth the designation of the series and fixing and determining the relative rights and preferences thereof, or so much thereof as shall not be fixed and determined by the articles of incorporation.

Prior to the issue of any shares of a series established by resolution adopted by the board of directors, the corporation shall file in the office of the Secretary of State a statement setting forth:

(a) The name of the corporation.

(b) A copy of the resolution establishing and designating the series, and fixing and determining the relative rights and preferences thereof.

(c) The date of adoption of such resolution.

(d) That such resolution was duly adopted by the board of directors.

Such statement shall be executed in duplicate by the corporation by its president or a vice president and by its secretary or an assistant secretary, and verified by one of the officers signing such statement, and shall be delivered to the Secretary of State. If the Secretary of State finds that such statement conforms to law, he shall, when all franchise taxes and fees have been paid as in this Act prescribed:

(1) Endorse on each of such duplicate originals the word "Filed," and the month, day, and year of the filing thereof.

(2) File one of such duplicate originals in his office.

(3) Return the other duplicate original to the corporation or its representative.

Upon the filing of such statement by the Secretary of State, the resolution establishing and designating the series and fixing and determining the relative rights and preferences thereof shall become effective and shall constitute an amendment of the articles of incorporation.

§ 17. Subscriptions for Shares

A subscription for shares of a corporation to be organized shall be irrevocable for a period of six months, unless otherwise provided by the terms of the subscription agreement or unless all of the subscribers consent to the revocation of such subscription.

Unless otherwise provided in the subscription agreement, subscriptions for shares, whether made before or after the organization of a corporation, shall be paid in full at such time, or in such installments and at such times, as shall be determined by the board of directors. Any call made by the board of directors for payment on subscriptions shall be uniform as to all shares of the same class or as to all shares of the same series, as the case may be. In case of default in the payment of any installment or call when such payment is due, the corporation may proceed to collect the amount due in the same manner as any debt due the corporation. The by-laws may prescribe other penalities for failure to pay installments or calls that may become due, but no penalty working a forfeiture of a subscription, or of the amounts paid thereon, shall be declared as against any subscriber unless the amount due thereon shall remain unpaid for a period of twenty days after written demand has been made therefor. If mailed, such written demand shall be deemed to be made when deposited in the United States mail in a sealed envelope addressed to the subscriber at his last post-office address known to the corporation, with postage thereon prepaid. In the event of the sale of any shares by reason of any forfeiture, the excess of proceeds realized over the amount due and unpaid on such shares shall be paid to the delinquent subscriber or to his legal representative.

§ 18. Issuance of Shares

Subject to any restrictions in the articles of incorporation:

(a) Shares may be issued for such consideration as shall be authorized by the board of directors establishing a price (in money or other consideration) or a minimum price or general formula or method by which the price will be determined; and

(b) Upon authorization by the board of directors, the corporation may issue its own shares in exchange for or in conversion of its outstanding shares, or distribute its own shares, pro rata to its shareholders or the shareholders of one or more classes or series, to effectuate stock dividends or splits, and any such transaction shall not require consideration; provided, that no such issuance of shares of any class or series shall be made to the holders of shares of any other class or series unless it is either expressly provided for in the articles of incorporation, or is authorized by an affirmative vote or the written consent of the holders of at least a majority of the outstanding shares of the class or series in which the distribution is to be made.

§ 19. Payment for Shares

The consideration for the issuance of shares may be paid, in whole or in part, in money, in other property, tangible or intangible, or in labor or services actually performed for the corporation. When payment of the consideration for which shares are to be issued shall have been received by the corporation, such shares shall be nonassessable.

Neither promissory notes nor future services shall constitute payment or part payment for the issuance of shares of a corporation.

In the absence of fraud in the transaction, the judgment of the board of directors or the shareholders, as the case may be, as to the value of the consideration received for shares shall be conclusive.

§ 20. Stock Rights and Options

Subject to any provisions in respect thereof set forth in its articles of incorporation, a corporation may create and issue, whether or not in connection with the issuance and sale of any of its shares or other securities, rights or options entitling the holders thereof to purchase from the corporation shares of any class or classes. Such rights or options shall be evidenced in such manner as the board of directors shall approve and, subject to the provisions of the articles of incorporation, shall set forth the terms upon which, the time or times within which and the price or prices at which such shares may be purchased from the corporation upon the exercise of any such right or option. If such rights or options are to be issued to directors, officers or employees as such of the corporation or of any subsidiary thereof, and not to the shareholders generally, their issuance shall be approved by the affirmative vote of the holders of a majority of the shares entitled to vote thereon or shall be authorized by and consistent with a plan approved or ratified by such a vote of shareholders. In the absence of fraud in the transaction, the judgment of the board of directors as to the adequacy of the consideration received for such rights or options shall be conclusive.

§ 21. Determination of Amount of Stated Capital

[*Repealed in 1979*].

§ 22. Expenses of Organization, Reorganization and Financing

The reasonable charges and expenses of organization or reorganization of a corporation, and the reasonable expenses of and compensation for the sale or underwriting of its shares, may be paid or allowed by such corporation out of the consideration received by it in payment for its shares without thereby rendering such shares assessable.

§ 23. Shares Represented by Certificates and Uncertificated Shares

The shares of a corporation shall be represented by certificates or shall be uncertificated shares. Certificates shall be signed by the chairman or vice-chairman of the board of directors or the president or a vice president and by the treasurer or an assistant treasurer or the secretary or an assistant secretary of the corporation, and may be sealed with the seal of the corporation or a fascimile thereof. Any of or all the signatures upon a certificate may be a facsimile. In case any officer, transfer agent or registrar who has signed or whose facsimile signature has been placed upon such certificate shall have ceased to be such officer, transfer agent or registrar before such certificate is issued, it may be issued by the corporation with the same effect as if he were such officer, transfer agent or registrar at the date of its issue.

Every certificate representing shares issued by a corporation which is authorized to issue shares of more than one class shall set forth upon the face or back of the certificate, or shall state that the corporation will furnish to any shareholder upon request and without charge, a full statement of the designations, preferences, limitations, and relative rights of the shares of each class authorized to be issued, and if the corporation is authorized to issue any preferred or special class in series, the variations in the relative rights and preferences between the shares of each such series so far as the same have been fixed and determined and the authority of the board of directors to fix and determine the relative rights and preferences of subsequent series.

Each certificate representing shares shall state upon the face thereof:

(a) That the corporation is organized under the laws of this State.

(b) The name of the person to whom issued.

(c) The number and class of shares, and the designation of the series, if any, which such certificate represents.

(d) The par value of each share represented by such certificate, or a statement that the shares are without par value.

No certificate shall be issued for any share until such share is fully paid.

Unless otherwise provided by the articles of incorporation or by-laws, the board of directors of a corporation may provide by resolution that some or all of any or all classes and series of its shares shall be uncertificated shares, provided that such resolution shall not apply to shares represented by a certificate until such certificate is surrendered to the corporation. Within a reasonable time after the issuance or transfer of uncertificated shares, the corporation shall send to the registered owner thereof a written notice containing the information required to be set forth or stated on certificates pursuant to the second and third paragraphs of this section. Except as otherwise expressly provided by law, the rights and obligations of the holders of uncertificated shares and the rights and obligations of the holders of certificates representing shares of the same class and series shall be identical.

§ 24. Fractional Shares

A corporation may (1) issue fractions of a share, either represented by a certificate or uncertificated, (2) arrange for the disposition of fractional interests by those entitled thereto, (3) pay in money the fair value of fractions of a share as of a time when those entitled to receive such fractions are determined, or (4) issue scrip in registered or bearer form which shall entitle the holder to receive a certificate for a full share or an uncertificated full share upon the surrender of such scrip aggregating a full share. A certificate for a fractional share or an uncertificated fractional share shall, but scrip shall not unless otherwise provided therein, entitle the holder to exercise voting rights, to receive dividends thereon, and to participate in any of the assets of the corporation in the event of liquidation. The board of directors may cause scrip to be issued subject to the condition that it shall become void if not exchanged for certificates representing full shares or uncertificated full shares before a specified date, or subject to the condition that the shares for which scrip is exchangeable may be sold by the corporation and the proceeds thereof distributed to the holders of scrip, or subject to any other conditions which the board of directors may deem advisable.

§ 25. Liability of Subscribers and Shareholders

A holder of or subscriber to shares of a corporation shall be under no obligation to the corporation or its creditors with respect to such shares other than the obligation to pay to the corporation the full consideration for which such shares were issued or to be issued.

Any person becoming an assignee or transferee of shares or of a subscription for shares in good faith and without knowledge or notice that the full consideration therefor has not been paid shall not be personally liable to the corporation or its creditors for any unpaid portion of such consideration.

An executor, administrator, conservator, guardian, trustee, assignee for the benefit of creditors, or receiver shall not be personally liable to the corporation as a holder of or subscriber to shares of a corporation but the estate and funds in his hands shall be so liable.

No pledgee or other holder of shares as collateral security shall be personally liable as a shareholder.

§ 26. Shareholders' Preemptive Rights

The shareholders of a corporation shall have no preemptive right to acquire unissued shares of the corporation, or securities of the corporation convertible into or carrying a right to subscribe to or acquire shares, except to the extent, if any, that such right is provided in the articles of incorporation.

§ 26A. Shareholders' Preemptive Rights [Alternative]

Except to the extent limited or denied by this section or by the articles of incorporation, shareholders shall have a preemptive right to acquire unissued shares or securities convertible into such shares or carrying a right to subscribe to or acquire shares.

Unless otherwise provided in the articles of incorporation,

(a) No preemptive right shall exist

(1) to acquire any shares issued to directors, officers or employees pursuant to approval by the affirmative vote of the holders of a majority of the shares entitled to vote thereon or when authorized by and consistent with a plan theretofore approved by such a vote of shareholders; or

(2) to acquire any shares sold otherwise than for money.

(b) Holders of shares of any class that is preferred or limited as to dividends or assets shall not be entitled to any preemptive right.

(c) Holders of shares of common stock shall not be entitled to any preemptive right to shares of any class that is preferred or limited as to dividends or assets or to any obligations, unless convertible into shares of common stock or carrying a right to subscribe to or acquire shares of common stock.

(d) Holders of common stock without voting power shall have no preemptive right to shares of common stock with voting power.

(e) The preemptive right shall be only an opportunity to acquire shares or other securities under such terms and conditions as the board of directors may fix for the purpose of providing a fair and reasonable opportunity for the exercise of such right.

§ 27. By-Laws

The initial by-laws of a corporation shall be adopted by its board of directors. The power to alter, amend or repeal the bylaws or adopt new by-laws, subject to repeal or change by action of the shareholders, shall be vested in the board of directors unless reserved to the shareholders by the articles of incorporation. The by-laws may contain any provisions for the regulation and management of the affairs of the corporation not inconsistent with law or the articles of incorporation.

§ 27A. By-Laws and Other Powers in Emergency [Optional]

The board of directors of any corporation may adopt emergency by-laws, subject to repeal or change by action of the shareholders, which shall, notwithstanding any different provision elsewhere in this Act or in the articles of incorporation or by-laws, be operative during any emergency in the conduct of the business of the corporation resulting from an attack on the United States or any nuclear or atomic disaster. The emergency by-laws may make any provision that may be practical and necessary for the circumstances of the emergency, including provisions that:

(a) A meeting of the board of directors may be called by any officer or director in such manner and under such conditions as shall be prescribed in the emergency by-laws;

(b) The director or directors in attendance at the meeting, or any greater number fixed by the emergency by-laws, shall constitute a quorum; and

(c) The officers or other persons designated on a list approved by the board of directors before the emergency, all in such order of priority and subject to such conditions, and for such period of time (not longer than reasonably necessary after the termination of the emergency) as may be provided in the emergency by-laws or in the resolution approving the list shall, to the extent required to provide a quorum at any meeting of the board of directors, be deemed directors for such meeting.

The board of directors, either before or during any such emergency, may provide, and from time to time modify, lines of succession in the event that during such an emergency any or all officers or agents of the corporation shall for any reason be rendered incapable of discharging their duties.

The board of directors, either before or during any such emergency, may, effective in the emergency, change the head office or designate several alternative head offices or regional offices, or authorize the officers so to do.

To the extent not inconsistent with any emergency by-laws so adopted, the by-laws of the corporation shall remain in effect during any such emergency and upon its termination the emergency by-laws shall cease to be operative.

Unless otherwise provided in emergency by-laws, notice of any meeting of the board of directors during any such emergency may be given only to such of the directors as it may be feasible to reach at the time and by such means as may be feasible at the time, including publication or radio.

To the extent required to constitute a quorum at any meeting of the board of directors during any such emergency, the officers of the corporation who are present shall, unless otherwise provided in emergency by-laws, be deemed, in order of rank and within the same rank in order of seniority, directors for such meeting.

No officer, director or employee acting in accordance with any emergency by-laws shall be liable except for willful misconduct. No officer, director or employee shall be liable for any action taken by him in good faith in such an emergency in furtherance of the ordinary business affairs of the corporation even though not authorized by the by-laws then in effect.

§ 28. Meetings of Shareholders

Meetings of shareholders may be held at such place within or without this State as may be stated in or fixed in accordance with the by-laws. If no other place is stated or so fixed, meetings shall be held at the registered office of the corporation.

An annual meeting of the shareholders shall be held at such time as may be stated in or fixed in accordance with the by-laws. If the annual meeting is not held within any thirteen-month period the Court of .... may, on the application of any shareholder, summarily order a meeting to be held.

Special meetings of the shareholders may be called by the board of directors, the holders of not less than one-tenth of all the shares entitled to vote at the meeting, or such other persons as may be authorized in the articles of incorporation or the by-laws.

§ 29. Notice of Shareholders' Meetings

Written notice stating the place, day and hour of the meeting and, in case of a special meeting, the purpose or purposes for which the meeting is called, shall be delivered not less than ten nor more than fifty days before the date of the meeting, either personally or by mail, by or at the direction of the president, the secretary, or the officer or persons calling the meeting, to each shareholder of record entitled to vote at such meeting. If mailed, such notice shall be deemed to be delivered when deposited in the United States mail addressed to the shareholder at his address as it appears on the stock transfer books of the corporation, with postage thereon prepaid.

§ 30. Closing of Transfer Books and Fixing Record Date

For the purpose of determining shareholders entitled to notice of or to vote at any meeting of shareholders or any adjournment thereof, or entitled to receive payment of any dividend, or in order to make a determination of shareholders for any other proper purpose, the board of directors of a corporation may provide that the stock transfer books shall be closed for a stated period but not to exceed, in any case, fifty days. If the stock transfer books shall be closed for the purpose of determining shareholders entitled to notice of or to vote at a meeting of shareholders, such books shall be closed for at least ten days immediately preceding such meeting. In lieu of closing the stock transfer books, the by-laws, or in the absence of an applicable by-law the board of directors, may fix in advance a date as the record date for any such determination of shareholders, such date in any case to be not more than fifty days and, in case of a meeting of shareholders, not less than ten days prior to the date on which the particular action, requiring such determination of shareholders, is to be taken. If the stock transfer books are not closed and no record date is fixed for the determination of shareholders entitled to notice of or to vote at a meeting of shareholders, or shareholders entitled to receive payment of a dividend, the date on which notice of the meeting is mailed or the date on which the resolution of the board of directors declaring such dividend is adopted, as the case may be, shall be the record date for such determination of shareholders. When a determination of shareholders entitled to vote at any meeting of shareholders has been made as provided in this section, such determination shall apply to any adjournment thereof.

§ 31. Voting Record

The officer or agent having charge of the stock transfer books for shares of a corporation shall make a complete record of the shareholders entitled to vote at such meeting or any adjournment thereof, arranged in alphabetical order, with the address of and the number of shares held by each. Such record shall be produced and kept open at the time and place of the meeting and shall be subject to the inspection of any shareholder during the whole time of the meeting for the purposes thereof.

Failure to comply with the requirements of this section shall not affect the validity of any action taken at such meeting.

An officer or agent having charge of the stock transfer books who shall fail to prepare the record of shareholders, or produce and keep it open for inspection at the meeting, as provided in this section, shall be liable to any shareholder suffering damage on account of such failure, to the extent of such damage.

§ 32. Quorum of Shareholders

Unless otherwise provided in the articles of incorporation, a majority of the shares entitled to vote, represented in person or by proxy, shall constitute a quorum at a meeting of shareholders, but in no event shall a quorum consist of less than one-third of the shares entitled to vote at the meeting. If a quorum is present, the affirmative vote of the majority of the shares represented at the meeting and entitled to vote on the subject matter shall be the act of the shareholders, unless the vote of a greater number or voting by classes is required by this Act or the articles of incorporation or by-laws.

§ 33. Voting of Shares

Each outstanding share, regardless of class, shall be entitled to one vote on each matter submitted to a vote at a meeting of shareholders, except as may be otherwise provided in the articles of incorporation. If the articles of incorporation provide for more or less than one vote for any share, on any matter, every reference in this Act to a majority or other proportion of shares shall refer to such a majority or other proportion of votes entitled to be cast.

Shares held by another corporation if a majority of the shares entitled to vote for the election of directors of such other corporation is held by the corporation, shall not be voted at any meeting or counted in determining the total number of outstanding shares at any given time.

A shareholder may vote either in person or by proxy executed in writing by the shareholder or by his duly authorized attorney-in-fact. No proxy shall be valid after eleven months from the date of its execution, unless otherwise provided in the proxy.

[Either of the following prefatory phrases may be inserted here: "The articles of incorporation may provide that" or "Unless the articles of incorporation otherwise provide"] . . . at each election for directors every shareholder entitled to vote at such election shall have the right to vote, in person or by proxy, the number of shares owned by him for as many persons as there are directors to be elected and for whose election he has a right to vote, or to cumulate his votes by giving one candidate as many votes as the number of such directors multiplied by the number of his shares shall equal, or by distributing such votes on the same principle among any number of such candidates.

Shares standing in the name of another corporation, domestic or foreign, may be voted by such officer, agent or proxy as the by-laws of such other corporation may prescribe, or, in the absence of such provision, as the board of directors of such other corporation may determine.

Shares held by an administrator, executor, guardian or conservator may be voted by him, either in person or by proxy, without a transfer of such shares into his name. Shares standing in the name of a trustee may be voted by him, either in person or by proxy, but no trustee shall be entitled to vote shares held by him without a transfer of such shares into his name.

Shares standing in the name of a receiver may be voted by such receiver, and shares held by or under the control of a receiver may be voted by such receiver without the transfer thereof into his name if authority so to do be contained in an appropriate order of the court by which such receiver was appointed.

A shareholder whose shares are pledged shall be entitled to vote such shares until the shares have been transferred into the name of the pledgee, and thereafter the pledgee shall be entitled to vote the shares so transferred.

On and after the date on which written notice of redemption of redeemable shares has been mailed to the holders thereof and a sum sufficient to redeem such shares has been deposited with a bank or trust company with irrevocable instruction and authority to pay the redemption price to the holders thereof upon surrender of certificates therefor, such shares shall not be entitled to vote on any matter and shall not be deemed to be outstanding shares.

§ 34. Voting Trusts and Agreements Among Shareholders

Any number of shareholders of a corporation may create a voting trust for the purpose of conferring upon a trustee or trustees the right to vote or otherwise represent their shares, for a period of not to exceed ten years, by entering into a written voting trust agreement specifying the terms and conditions of the voting trust, by depositing a counterpart of the agreement with the corporation at its registered office, and by transferring their shares to such trustee or trustees for the purposes of the agreement. Such trustee or trustees shall keep a record of the holders of voting trust certificates evidencing a beneficial interest in the voting trust, giving the names and addresses of all such holders and the number and class of the shares in respect of which the voting trust certificates held by each are issued, and shall deposit a copy of such record with the corporation at its registered office. The counterpart of the voting trust agreement and the copy of such record so deposited with the corporation shall be subject to the same right of examination by a shareholder of the corporation, in person or by agent or attorney, as are the books and records of the corporation, and such counterpart and such copy of such record shall be subject to examination by any holder of record of voting trust certificates, either in person or by agent or attorney, at any reasonable time for any proper purpose.

Agreements among shareholders regarding the voting of their shares shall be valid and enforceable in accordance with their terms. Such agreements shall not be subject to the provisions of this section regarding voting trusts.

§ 35. Board of Directors

All corporate powers shall be exercised by or under authority of, and the business and affairs of a corporation shall be managed under the direction of, a board of directors except as may be otherwise provided in this Act or the articles of incorporation. If any such provision is made in the articles of incorporation, the powers and duties conferred or imposed upon the board of directors by this Act shall be exercised or performed to such extent and by such person or persons as shall be provided in the articles of incorporation. Directors need not be residents of this State or shareholders of the corporation unless the articles of incorporation or by-laws so require. The articles of incorporation or by-laws may prescribe other qualifications for directors. The board of directors shall have authority to fix the compensation of directors unless otherwise provided in the articles of incorporation.

A director shall perform his duties as a director, including his duties as a member of any committee of the board upon which he may serve, in good faith, in a manner he reasonably believes to be in the best interests of the corporation, and with such care as an ordinarily prudent person in a like position would use under similar circumstances. In performing his duties, a director shall be entitled to rely on information, opinions, reports or statements, including financial statements and other financial data, in each case prepared or presented by:

    (a) one or more officers or employees of the corporation whom the director reasonably believes to be reliable and competent in the matters presented,

   (b) counsel, public accountants or other persons as to matters which the director reasonably believes to be within such person's professional or expert competence, or

   (c) a committee of the board upon which he does not serve, duly designated in accordance with a provision of the articles of incorporation or the by-laws, as to matters within its designated authority, which committee the director reasonably believes to merit confidence,

but he shall not be considered to be acting in good faith if he has knowledge concerning the matter in question that would cause such reliance to be unwarranted. A person who so performs his duties shall have no liability by reason of being or having been a director of the corporation.

A director of a corporation who is present at a meeting of its board of directors at which action on any corporate matter is taken shall be presumed to have assented to the action taken unless his dissent shall be entered in the minutes of the meeting or unless he shall file his written dissent to such action with the secretary of the meeting before the adjournment thereof or shall forward such dissent by registered mail to the secretary of the corporation immediately after the adjournment of the meeting. Such right to dissent shall not apply to a director who voted in favor of such action.

§ 36. Number and Election of Directors

The board of directors of a corporation shall consist of one or more members. The number of directors shall be fixed by, or in the manner provided in, the articles of incorporation or the by-laws, except as to the number constituting the initial board of directors, which number shall be fixed by the articles of incorporation. The number of directors may be increased or decreased from time to time by amendment to, or in the manner provided in, the articles of incorporation or the by-laws, but no decrease shall have the effect of shortening the term of any incumbent director. In the absence of a by-law providing for the number of directors, the number shall be the same as that provided for in the articles of incorporation. The names and addresses of the members of the first board of directors shall be stated in the articles of incorporation. Such persons shall hold office until the first annual meeting of shareholders, and until their successors shall have been elected and qualified. At the first annual meeting of shareholders and at each annual meeting thereafter the shareholders shall elect directors to hold office until the next succeeding annual meeting, except in case of the classification of directors as permitted by this Act. Each director shall hold office for the term for which he is elected and until his successor shall have been elected and qualified.

§ 37. Classification of Directors

When the board of directors shall consist of nine or more members, in lieu of electing the whole number of directors annually, the articles of incorporation may provide that the directors be divided into either two or three classes, each class to be as nearly equal in number as possible, the term of office of directors of the first class to expire at the first annual meeting of shareholders after their election, that of the second class to expire at the second annual meeting after their election, and that of the third class, if any, to expire at the third annual meeting after their election. At each annual meeting after such classification the number of directors equal to the number of the class whose term expires at the time of such meeting shall be elected to hold office until the second succeeding annual meeting, if there be two classes, or until the third succeeding annual meeting, if there be three classes. No classification of directors shall be effective prior to the first annual meeting of shareholders.

§ 38. Vacancies

Any vacancy occurring in the board of directors may be filled by the affirmative vote of a majority of the remaining directors though less than a quorum of the board of directors. A director elected to fill a vacancy shall be elected for the unexpired term of his predecessor in office. Any directorship to be filled by reason of an increase in the number of directors may be filled by the board of directors for a term of office continuing only until the next election of directors by the shareholders.

§ 39. Removal of Directors

At a meeting of shareholders called expressly for that purpose, directors may be removed in the manner provided in this section. Any director or the entire board of directors may be removed, with or without cause, by a vote of the holders of a majority of the shares then entitled to vote at an election of directors.

In the case of a corporation having cumulative voting, if less than the entire board is to be removed, no one of the directors may be removed if the votes cast against his removal would be sufficient to elect him if then cumulatively voted at an election of the entire board of directors, or, if there be classes of directors, at an election of the class of directors of which he is a part.

Whenever the holders of the shares of any class are entitled to elect one or more directors by the provisions of the articles of incorporation, the provisions of this section shall apply, in respect to the removal of a director or directors so elected, to the vote of the holders of the outstanding shares of that class and not to the vote of the outstanding shares as a whole.

§ 40. Quorum of Directors

A majority of the number of directors fixed by or in the manner provided in the by-laws or in the absence of a by-law fixing or providing for the number of directors, then of the number stated in the articles of incorporation, shall constitute a quorum for the transaction of business unless a greater number is required by the articles of incorporation or the by-laws. The act of the majority of the directors present at a meeting at which a quorum is present shall be the act of the board of directors, unless the act of a greater number is required by the articles of incorporation or the by-laws.

§ 41. Director Conflicts of Interest

No contract or other transaction between a corporation and one or more of its directors or any other corporation, firm, association or entity in which one or more of its directors are directors or officers or are financially interested, shall be either void or voidable because of such relationship or interest or because such director or directors are present at the meeting of the board of directors or a committee thereof which authorizes, approves or ratifies such contract or transaction or because his or their votes are counted for such purpose, if:

(a) the fact of such relationship or interest is disclosed or known to the board of directors or committee which authorizes, approves or ratifies the contract or transaction by a vote or consent sufficient for the purpose without counting the votes or consents of such interested directors; or

(b) the fact of such relationship or interest is disclosed or known to the shareholders entitled to vote and they authorize, approve or ratify such contract or transaction by vote or written consent; or

(c) the contract or transaction is fair and reasonable to the corporation.

Common or interested directors may be counted in determining the presence of a quorum at a meeting of the board of directors or a committee thereof which authorizes, approves or ratifies such contract or transaction.

§ 42. Executive and Other Committees

If the articles of incorporation or the by-laws so provide, the board of directors, by resolution adopted by a majority of the full board of directors, may designate from among its members an executive committee and one or more other committees each of which, to the extent provided in such resolution or in the articles of incorporation or the by-laws of the corporation, shall have and may exercise all the authority of the board of directors, *except that* no such committee shall have authority to (i) authorize distributions, (ii) approve or recommend to shareholders actions or proposals required by this Act to be approved by shareholders, (iii) designate candidates for the office of director, for purposes of proxy solicitation or otherwise, or fill vacancies on the board of directors or any committee thereof, (iv) amend the by-laws, (v) approve a plan of merger not requiring shareholder approval, (vi) authorize or approve the reacquisition of shares unless pursuant to a general formula or method specified by the board of directors, or (vii) authorize or approve the issuance or sale of, or any contract to issue or sell, shares or designate the terms of a series of a class of shares, provided that the board of directors, having acted regarding general authorization for the issuance or sale of shares, or any contract, therefor, and, in the case of a series, the designation thereof, may, pursuant to a general formula or method specified by the board by resolution or by adoption of a stock option or other plan, authorize a committee to fix the terms of any contract for the sale of the shares and to fix the terms upon which such shares may be issued or sold, including, without limitation, the price, the dividend rate, provisions for redemption, sinking fund, conversion, voting or preferential rights, and provisions for other features of a class of shares, or a series of a class of shares, with full power in such committee to adopt any final resolution setting forth all the terms thereof and to authorize the statement of the terms of a series for filing with the Secretary of State under this Act.

Neither the designation of any such committee, the delegation thereto of authority, nor action by such committee pursuant to such authority shall alone constitute compliance by any member of the board of directors, not a member of the committee in question, with his responsibility to act in good faith, in a manner he reasonably believes to be in the best interests of the corporation, and with such care as an ordinarily prudent person in a like position would use under similar circumstances.

§ 43. Place and Notice of Directors' Meetings; Committee Meetings

Meetings of the board of directors, regular or special, may be held either within or without this State.

Regular meetings of the board of directors or any committee designated thereby may be held with or without notice as prescribed in the by-laws. Special meetings of the board of directors or any committee designated thereby shall be held upon such notice as is prescribed in the by-laws. Attendance of a director at a meeting shall constitute a waiver of notice of such meeting, except where a director attends a meeting for the express purpose of objecting to the transaction of any business because the meeting is not lawfully called or convened. Neither the business to be transacted at, nor the purpose of, any regular or special meeting of the board of directors or any committee designated thereby need be specified in the notice or waiver of notice of such meeting unless required by the by-laws.

Except as may be otherwise restricted by the articles of incorporation or by-laws, members of the board of directors or any committee designated thereby may participate in a meeting of such board of committee by means of a conference telephone or similar communications equipment by means of which all persons participating in the meeting can hear each other at the same time and participation by such means shall constitute presence in person at a meeting.

§ 44. Action by Directors Without a Meeting

Unless otherwise provided by the articles of incorporation or by-laws, any action required by this Act to be taken at a meeting of the directors of a corporation, or any action which may be taken at a meeting of the directors or of a committee, may be taken without a meeting if a consent in writing, setting forth the action so taken, shall be signed by all of the directors, or all of the members of the committee, as the case may be. Such consent shall have the same effect as a unanimous vote.

§ 45. Distributions to Shareholders

Subject to any restrictions in the articles of incorporation, the board of directors may authorize and the corporation may make distributions, except that no distribution may be made if, after giving effect thereto, either:

(a) the corporation would be unable to pay its debts as they become due in the usual course of its business; or

(b) the corporation's total assets would be less than the sum of its total liabilities and (unless the articles of incorporation otherwise permit) the maximum amount that then would be payable, in any liquidation, in respect of all outstanding shares having preferential rights in liquidation.

Determinations under subparagraph (b) may be based upon (i) financial statements prepared on the basis of accounting practices and principles that are reasonable in the circumstances, or (ii) a fair valuation or other method that is reasonable in the circumstances.

In the case of a purchase, redemption or other acquisition of a corporation's shares, the effect of a distribution shall be measured as of the date money or other property is transferred or debt is incurred by the corporation, or as of the date the shareholder ceases to be a shareholder of the corporation with respect to such shares, whichever is earlier. In all other cases, the effect of a distribution shall be measured as of the date of its authorization if payment occurs 120 days or less following the date of authorization, or as of the date of payment if payment occurs more than 120 days following the date of authorization.

Indebtedness of a corporation incurred or issued to a shareholder in a distribution in accordance with this Section shall be on a parity with the indebtedness of the corporation to its general unsecured creditors except to the extent subordinated by agreement.

§ 46. Distributions from Capital Surplus

[*Repealed in 1979*].

§ 47. Loans to Employees and Directors

A corporation shall not lend money to or use its credit to assist its directors without authorization in the particular case by its shareholders, but may lend money to and use its credit to assist any employee of the corporation or of a subsidiary, including any such employee who is a director of the corporation, if the board of directors decides that such loan or assistance may benefit the corporation.

§ 48. Liabilities of Directors in Certain Cases

In addition to any other liabilities, a director who votes for or assents to any distribution contrary to the provisions of this Act or contrary to any restrictions contained in the articles of incorporation, shall, unless he complies with the standard provided in this Act for the performance of the duties of directors, be liable to the corporation, jointly and severally with all other directors so voting or assenting, for the amount of such dividend which is paid or the value of such distribution in excess of the amount of such distribution which could have been made without a violation of the provisions of this Act or the restrictions in the articles of incorporation.

Any director against whom a claim shall be asserted under or pursuant to this section for the making of a distribution and who shall be held liable thereon, shall be entitled to contribution from the shareholders who accepted or received any such distribution, knowing such distribution to have been made in violation of this Act, in proportion to the amounts received by them.

Any director against whom a claim shall be asserted under or pursuant to this section shall be entitled to contribution from any other director who voted for or assented to the action upon which the claim is asserted and who did not comply with the standard provided in this Act for the performance of the duties of directors.

§ 49. Provisions Relating to Actions by Shareholders

No action shall be brought in this State by a shareholder in the right of a domestic or foreign corporation unless the plaintiff was a holder of record of shares or of voting trust certificates therefor at the time of the transaction of which he complains, or his shares or voting trust certificates thereafter devolved upon him by operation of law from a person who was a holder of record at such time.

In any action hereafter instituted in the right of any domestic or foreign corporation by the holder or holders of record of shares of such corporation or of voting trust certificates therefor, the court having jurisdiction, upon final judgment and a finding that the action was brought without reasonable cause, may require the plaintiff or plaintiffs to pay to the parties named as defendant the reasonable expenses, including fees of attorneys, incurred by them in the defense of such action.

In any action now pending or hereafter instituted or maintained in the right of any domestic or foreign corporation by the holder or holders of record of less than five per cent of the outstanding shares of any class of such corporation or of voting trust certificates therefor, unless the shares or voting trust certificates so held have a market value in excess of twenty-five thousand dollars, the corporation in whose right such action is brought shall be entitled at any time before final judgment to require the plaintiff or plaintiffs to give security for the reasonable expenses, including fees of attorneys, that may be incurred by it in connection with such action or may be incurred by other parties named as defendant for which it may become legally liable. Market value shall be determined as of the date that the plaintiff institutes the action or, in the case of an intervenor, as of the date that he becomes a party to the action. The amount of such security may from time to time be increased or decreased, in the discretion of the court, upon showing that the security provided has or may become inadequate or is excessive. The corporation shall have recourse to such security in such amount as the court having jurisdiction shall determine upon the termination of such action, whether or not the court finds the action was brought without reasonable cause.

§ 50. Officers

The officers of a corporation shall consist of a president, one or more vice presidents as may be prescribed by the by-laws, a secretary, and a treasurer, each of whom shall be elected by the board of directors at such time and in such manner as may be prescribed by the by-laws. Such other officers and assistant officers and agents as may be deemed necessary may be elected or appointed by the board of directors or chosen in such other manner as may be prescribed by the by-laws. Any two or more offices may be held by the same person, except the offices of president and secretary.

All officers and agents of the corporation, as between themselves and the corporation, shall have such authority and perform such duties in the management of the corporation as may be provided in the by-laws, or as may be determined by resolution of the board of directors not inconsistent with the by-laws.

§ 51. Removal of Officers

Any officer or agent may be removed by the board of directors whenever in its judgment the best interests of the corporation will be served thereby, but such removal shall be without prejudice to the contract rights, if any, of the person so removed. Election or appointment of an officer or agent shall not of itself create contract rights.

§ 52. Books and Records: Financial Reports to Shareholders; Examination of Records

Each corporation shall keep correct and complete books and records of account and shall keep minutes of the proceedings of its shareholders and board of directors and shall keep at its registered office or principal place of business, or at the office of its transfer agent or registrar, a record of its shareholders, giving the names and addresses of all shareholders and the number and class of the shares held by each. Any books, records and minutes may be in written form or in any other form capable of being converted into written form within a reasonable time.

Any person who shall have been a holder of record of shares or of voting trust certificates therefor at least six months immediately preceding his demand or shall be the holder of record of, or the holder of record of voting trust certificates for, at least five per cent of all the outstanding shares of the corporation, upon written demand stating the purpose thereof, shall have the right to examine, in person, or by agent or attorney, at any reasonable time or times, for any proper purpose its relevant books and records of account, minutes, and record of shareholders and to make extracts therefrom.

Any officer or agent who, or a corporation which, shall refuse to allow any such shareholder or holder of voting trust certificates, or his agent or attorney, so to examine and make extracts from its books and records of account, minutes, and record of shareholders, for any proper purpose, shall be liable to such shareholder or holder of voting trust certificates in a penalty of ten per cent of the value of the shares owned by such shareholder, or in respect of which such voting trust certificates are issued, in addition to any other damages or remedy afforded him by law. It shall be a defense to any action for penalties under this section that the person suing therefor has within two years sold or offered for sale any list of shareholders or of holders of voting trust certificates for shares of such corporation or any other corporation or has aided or abetted any person in procuring any list of shareholders or of holders of voting trust certificates for any such purpose, or has improperly used any information secured through any prior examination of the books and records of account, or minutes, or record of shareholders or of holders of voting trust certificates for shares of such corporation or any other corporation, or was not acting in good faith or for a proper purpose in making his demand.

Nothing herein contained shall impair the power of any court of competent jurisdiction, upon proof by a shareholder or holder of voting trust certificates of proper purpose, irrespective of the period of time during which such shareholder or holder of voting trust certificates shall have been a shareholder of record or a holder of record of voting trust certificates, and irrespective of the number of shares held by him or represented by voting trust certificates held by him, to compel the production for examination by such shareholder or holder of voting trust certificates of the books and records of account, minutes and record of shareholders of a corporation.

Each corporation shall furnish to its shareholders annual financial statements, including at least a balance sheet as of the end of each fiscal year and a statement of income for such fiscal year, which shall be prepared on the basis of generally accepted accounting principles, if the corporation prepares financial statements for such fiscal year on that basis for any purpose, and may be consolidated statements of the corporation and one or more of its subsidiaries. The financial statements shall be mailed by the corporation to each of its shareholders within 120 days after the close of each fiscal year and, after such mailing and upon written request, shall be mailed by the corporation to any shareholder (or holder of a voting trust certificate for its shares) to whom a copy of the most recent annual financial statements has not previously been mailed. In the case of statements audited by a public accountant, each copy shall be accompanied by a report setting forth his opinion thereon; in other cases, each copy shall be accompanied by a statement of the president or the person in charge of the corporation's financial accounting records (1) stating his reasonable belief as to whether or not the financial statements were prepared in accordance with generally accepted accounting principles and, if not, describing the basis of presentation, and (2) describing any respects in which the financial statements were not prepared on a basis consistent with those prepared for the previous year.

FORMATION OF CORPORATIONS

§ 53. Incorporators

One or more persons, or a domestic or foreign corporation, may act as incorporator or incorporators of a corporation by signing and delivering in duplicate to the Secretary of State articles of incorporation for such corporation.

§ 54. Articles of Incorporation

The articles of incorporation shall set forth:

(a) The name of the corporation.

(b) The period of duration, which may be perpetual.

(c) The purpose or purposes for which the corporation is organized which may be stated to be, or to include, the transaction of any or all lawful business for which corporations may be incorporated under this Act.

(d) The aggregate number of shares which the corporation shall have authority to issue and, if such shares are to be divided into classes, the number of shares of each class.

(e) If the shares are to be divided into classes, the designation of each class and a statement of the preferences, limitations and relative rights in respect of the shares of each class.

41

(f) If the corporation is to issue the shares of any preferred or special class in series, then the designation of each series and a statement of the variations in the relative rights and preferences as between series insofar as the same are to be fixed in the articles of incorporation, and a statement of any authority to be vested in the board of directors to establish series and fix and determine the variations in the relative rights and preferences as between series.

(g) If any preemptive right is to be granted to shareholders, the provisions therefor.

(h) The address of its initial registered office, and the name of its initial registered agent at such address.

(i) The number of directors constituting the initial board of directors and the names and addresses of the persons who are to serve as directors until the first annual meeting of shareholders or until their successors be elected and qualify.

(j) The name and address of each incorporator.

In addition to provisions required therein, the articles of incorporation may also contain provisions not inconsistent with law regarding:

(1) the direction of the management of the business and the regulation of the affairs of the corporation;

(2) the definition, limitation and regulation of the powers of the corporation, the directors, and the shareholders, or any class of the shareholders, including restrictions on the transfer of shares;

(3) the par value of any authorized shares or class of shares;

(4) any provision which under this Act is required or permitted to be set forth in the by-laws.

It shall not be necessary to set forth in the articles of incorporation any of the corporate powers enumerated in this Act.

§ 55. Filing of Articles of Incorporation

Duplicate originals of the articles of incorporation shall be delivered to the Secretary of State. If the Secretary of State finds that the articles of incorporation conform to law, he shall, when all fees have been paid as in this Act prescribed:

(a) Endorse on each of such duplicate originals the word "Filed," and the month, day and year of the filing thereof.

(b) File one of such duplicate originals in his office.

(c) Issue a certificate of incorporation to which he shall affix the other duplicate original.

The certificate of incorporation, together with the duplicate original of the articles of incorporation affixed thereto by the Secretary of State, shall be returned to the incorporators or their representative.

§ 56. Effect of Issuance of Certificate of Incorporation

Upon the issuance of the certificate of incorporation, the corporate existence shall begin, and such certificate of incorporation shall be conclusive evidence that all conditions precedent required to be performed by the incorporators have been complied with and that the corporation has been incorporated under this Act, except as against this State in a proceeding to cancel or revoke the certificate of incorporation or for involuntary dissolution of the corporation.

§ 57. Organization Meeting of Directors

After the issuance of the certificate of incorporation an organization meeting of the board of directors named in the articles of incorporation shall be held, either within or without this State, at the call of a majority of the directors named in the articles of incorporation, for the purpose of adopting by-laws, electing officers and transacting such other business as may come before the meeting. The directors calling the meeting shall give at least three days' notice thereof by mail to each director so named, stating the time and place of the meeting.

AMENDMENT

§ 58. Right to Amend Articles of Incorporation

A corporation may amend its articles of incorporation, from time to time, in any and as many respects as may be desired, so long as its articles of incorporation as amended contain only such provisions as might be lawfully contained in original articles of incorporation at the time of making such amendment, and, if a change in shares or the rights of shareholders, or an exchange, reclassification or cancellation of shares or rights of shareholders is to be made, such provisions as may be necessary to effect such change, exchange, reclassification or cancellation.

In particular, and without limitation upon such general power of amendment, a corporation may amend its articles of incorporation, from time to time, so as:

(a) To change its corporate name.

(b) To change its period of duration.

(c) To change, enlarge or diminish its corporate purposes.

(d) To increase or decrease the aggregate number of shares, or shares of any class, which the corporation has authority to issue.

(e) To provide, change or eliminate any provision with respect to the par value of any shares or class of shares.

(f) To exchange, classify, reclassify or cancel all or any part of its shares, whether issued or unissued.

(g) To change the designation of all or any part of its shares, whether issued or unissued, and to change the preferences, limitations, and the relative rights in respect of all or any part of its shares, whether issued or unissued.

(h) To change the shares of any class, whether issued or unissued [sic] into a different number of shares of the same class or into the same or a different number of shares of other classes.

(i) To create new classes of shares having rights and preferences either prior and superior or subordinate and inferior to the shares of any class then authorized, whether issued or unissued.

(j) To cancel or otherwise affect the right of the holders of the shares of any class to receive dividends which have accrued but have not been declared.

(k) To divide any preferred or special class of shares, whether issued or unissued, into series and fix and determine the designations of such series and the variations in the relative rights and preferences as between the shares of such series.

(l) To authorize the board of directors to establish, out of authorized but unissued shares, series of any preferred or special class of shares and fix and determine the relative rights and preferences of the shares of any series so established.

(m) To authorize the board of directors to fix and determine the relative rights and preferences of the authorized but unissued shares of series theretofore established in respect of which either the relative rights and preferences have not been fixed and determined or the relative rights and preferences theretofore fixed and determined are to be changed.

(n) To revoke, diminish, or enlarge the authority of the board of directors to establish series out of authorized but unissued shares of any preferred or special class and fix and determine the relative rights and preferences of the shares of any series so established.

(o) To limit, deny or grant to shareholders of any class the preemptive right to acquire additional shares of the corporation, whether then or thereafter authorized.

§ 59. Procedure to Amend Articles of Incorporation

Amendments to the articles of incorporation shall be made in the following manner:

(a) The board of directors shall adopt a resolution setting forth the proposed amendment and, if shares have been issued, directing that it be submitted to a vote at a meeting of shareholders, which may be either the annual or a special meeting. If no shares have been issued, the amendment shall be adopted by resolution of the board of directors and the provisions for adoption by shareholders shall not apply. If the corporation has only one class of shares outstanding, an amendment solely to change the number of authorized shares to effectuate a split of, or stock dividend in, the corporation's own shares, or solely to do so and to change the number of authorized shares in proportion thereto, may be adopted by the board of directors; and the provisions for adoption by shareholders shall not apply, unless otherwise provided by the articles of incorporation. The resolution may incorporate the proposed amendment in restated articles of incorporation which contain a statement that except for the designated amendment the restated articles of incorporation correctly set forth without change the corresponding provisions of the articles of incorporation as theretofore amended, and that the restated articles of incorporation together with the designated amendment supersede the original articles of incorporation and all amendments thereto.

(b) Written notice setting forth the proposed amendment or a summary of the changes to be effected thereby shall be given to each shareholder of record entitled to vote thereon within the time and in the manner provided in this Act for the giving of notice of meetings of shareholders. If the meeting be an annual meeting, the proposed amendment of such summary may be included in the notice of such annual meeting.

(c) At such meeting a vote of the shareholders entitled to vote thereon shall be taken on the proposed amendment. The proposed amendment shall be adopted upon receiving the affirmative vote of the holders of a majority of the shares entitled to vote thereon, unless any class of shares is entitled to vote thereon as a class, in which event the proposed amendment shall be adopted upon receiving the affirmative vote of the holders of a majority of the shares of each class of shares entitled to vote thereon as a class and of the total shares entitled to vote thereon.

Any number of amendments may be submitted to the shareholders, and voted upon by them, at one meeting.

§ 60. Class Voting on Amendments

The holders of the outstanding shares of a class shall be entitled to vote as a class upon a proposed amendment, whether or not entitled to vote thereon by the provisions of the articles of incorporation, if the amendment would:

(a) Increase or decrease the aggregate number of authorized shares of such class.

(b) Effect an exchange, reclassification or cancellation of all or part of the shares of such class.

(c) Effect an exchange, or create a right of exchange, of all or any part of the shares of another class into the shares of such class.

(d) Change the designations, preferences, limitations or relative rights of the shares of such class.

(e) Change the shares of such class into the same or a different number of shares of the same class or another class or classes.

(f) Create a new class of shares having rights and preferences prior and superior to the shares of such class, or increase the rights and preferences or the number of authorized shares, of any class having rights and preferences prior or superior to the shares of such class.

(g) In the case of a preferred or special class of shares, divide the shares of such class into series and fix and determine the designation of such series and the variations in the relative rights and preferences between the shares of such series, or authorize the board of directors to do so.

(h) Limit or deny any existing preemptive rights of the shares of such class.

(i) Cancel or otherwise affect dividends on the shares of such class which have accrued but have not been declared.

§ 61. Articles of Amendment

The articles of amendment shall be executed in duplicate by the corporation by its president or a vice president and by its secretary or an assistant secretary, and verified by one of the officers signing such articles, and shall set forth:

(a) The name of the corporation.

(b) The amendments so adopted.

(c) The date of the adoption of the amendment by the shareholders, or by the board of directors where no shares have been issued.

(d) The number of shares outstanding, and the number of shares entitled to vote thereon, and if the shares of any class are entitled to vote thereon as a class, the designation and number of outstanding shares entitled to vote thereon of each such class.

(e) The number of shares voted for and against such amendment, respectively, and, if the shares of any class are entitled to vote thereon as a class, the number of shares of each such class voted for and against such amendment, respectively, or if no shares have been issued, a statement to that effect.

(f) If such amendment provides for an exchange, reclassification or cancellation of issued shares, and if the manner in which the same shall be effected is not set forth in the amendment, then a statement of the manner in which the same shall be effected.

§ 62.   Filing of Articles of Amendment

Duplicate originals of the articles of amendment shall be delivered to the Secretary of State. If the Secretary of State finds that the articles of amendment conform to law, he shall, when all fees and franchise taxes have been paid as in this Act prescribed:

(a) Endorse on each of such duplicate originals the word "Filed," and the month, day and year of the filing thereof.

(b) File one of such duplicate originals in his office.

(c) Issue a certificate of amendment to which he shall affix the other duplicate original.

The certificate of amendment, together with the duplicate original of the articles of amendment affixed thereto by the Secretary of State, shall be returned to the corporation or its representative.

§ 63.   Effect of Certificate of Amendment

Upon the issuance of the certificate of amendment by the Secretary of State, the amendment shall become effective and the articles of incorporation shall be deemed to be amended accordingly.

No amendment shall affect any existing cause of action in favor of or against such corporation, or any pending suit to which such corporation shall be a party, or the existing rights of persons other than shareholders; and, in the event the corporate name shall be changed by amendment, no suit brought by or against such corporation under its former name shall abate for that reason.

§ 64. Restated Articles of Incorporation

A domestic corporation may at any time restate its articles of incorporation as theretofore amended, by a resolution adopted by the board of directors.

Upon the adoption of such resolution, restated articles of incorporation shall be executed in duplicate by the corporation by its president or a vice president and by its secretary or assistant secretary and verified by one of the officers signing such articles and shall set forth all of the operative provisions of the articles of incorporation as theretofore amended together with a statement that the restated articles of incorporation correctly set forth without change the corresponding provisions of the articles of incorporation as theretofore amended and that the restated articles of incorporation supersede the original articles of incorporation and all amendments thereto.

Duplicate originals of the restated articles of incorporation shall be delivered to the Secretary of State. If the Secretary of State finds that such restated articles of incorporation conform to law, he shall, when all fees and franchise taxes have been paid as in this Act prescribed:

(1) Endorse on each of such duplicate originals the word "Filed," and the month, day and year of the filing thereof.

(2) File one of such duplicate originals in his office.

(3) Issue a restated certificate of incorporation, to which he shall affix the other duplicate original.

The restated certificate of incorporation, together with the duplicate original of the restated articles of incorporation affixed thereto by the Secretary of State, shall be returned to the corporation or its representative.

Upon the issuance of the restated certificate of incorporation by the Secretary of State, the restated articles of incorporation shall become effective and shall supersede the original articles of incorporation and all amendments thereto.

§ 65. Amendment of Articles of Incorporation in Reorganization Proceedings

Whenever a plan of reorganization of a corporation has been confirmed by decree or order of a court of competent jurisdiction in proceedings for the reorganization of such corporation, pursuant to the provisions of any applicable statute of the United States relating to reorganizations of corporations, the articles of incorporation of the corporation may be amended, in the manner provided in this section, in as many respects as may be necessary to carry out the plan and put it into effect, so long as the articles of incorporation as amended contain only such provisions as might be lawfully contained in original articles of incorporation at the time of making such amendment.

In particular and without limitation upon such general power of amendment, the articles of incorporation may be amended for such purpose so as to:

(A) Change the corporate name, period of duration or corporate purposes of the corporation;

(B) Repeal, alter or amend the by-laws of the corporation;

(C) Change the aggregate number of shares or shares of any class, which the corporation has authority to issue;

(D) Change the preferences, limitations and relative rights in respect of all or any part of the shares of the corporation, and classify, reclassify or cancel all or any part thereof, whether issued or unissued;

(E) Authorize the issuance of bonds, debentures or other obligations of the corporation, whether or not convertible into shares of any class or bearing warrants or other evidences of optional rights to purchase or subscribe for shares of any class, and fix the terms and conditions thereof; and

(F) Constitute or reconstitute and classify or reclassify the board of directors of the corporation, and appoint directors and officers in place of or in addition to all or any of the directors or officers then in office.

Amendments to the articles of incorporation pursuant to this section shall be made in the following manner:

(a) Articles of amendment approved by decree or order of such court shall be executed and verified in duplicate by such person or persons as the court shall designate or appoint for the purpose, and shall set forth the name of the corporation, the amendments of the articles of incorporation approved by the court, the date of the decree or order approving the articles of amendment, the title of the proceedings in which the decree or order was entered, and a statement that such decree or order was entered by a court having jurisdiction of the proceedings for the reorganization of the corporation pursuant to the provisions of an applicable statute of the United States.

(b) Duplicate originals of the articles of amendment shall be delivered to the Secretary of State. If the Secretary of State finds that the articles of amendment conform to law, he shall, when all fees and franchise taxes have been paid as in this Act prescribed:

(1) Endorse on each of such duplicate originals the word "Filed," and the month, day and year of the filing thereof.

(2) File one of such duplicate originals in his office.

(3) Issue a certificate of amendment to which he shall affix the other duplicate original.

The certificate of amendment, together with the duplicate original of the articles of amendment affixed thereto by the Secretary of State, shall be returned to the corporation or its representative.

Upon the issuance of the certificate of amendment by the Secretary of State, the amendment shall become effective and the articles of incorporation shall be deemed to be amended accordingly, without any action thereon by the directors or shareholders of the corporation and with the same effect as if the amendments had been adopted by unanimous action of the directors and shareholders of the corporation.

§ 66. Restriction on Redemption or Purchase of Redeemable Shares

[*Repealed in 1979*].

§ 67. Cancellation of Redeemable Shares by Redemption or Purchase

[*Repealed in 1979*].

§ 68. Cancellation of Other Reacquired Shares

[*Repealed in 1979*].

§ 69. Reduction of Stated Capital in Certain Cases

[*Repealed in 1979*].

§ 70. Special Provisions Relating to Surplus and Reserves

[*Repealed in 1979*].

MERGER AND CONSOLIDATION

§ 71. Procedure for Merger

Any two or more domestic corporations may merge into one of such corporations pursuant to a plan of merger approved in the manner provided in this Act.

The board of directors of each corporation shall, by resolution adopted by each such board, approve a plan of merger setting forth:

(a) The names of the corporations proposing to merge, and the name of the corporation into which they propose to merge, which is hereinafter designated as the surviving corporation.

(b) The terms and conditions of the proposed merger.

(c) The manner and basis of converting the shares of each corporation into shares, obligations or other securities of the surviving corporation or of any other corporation or, in whole or in part, into cash or other property.

(d) A statement of any changes in the articles of incorporation of the surviving corporation to be effected by such merger.

(e) Such other provisions with respect to the proposed merger as are deemed necessary or desirable.

§ 72. Procedure for Consolidation

Any two or more domestic corporations may consolidate into a new corporation pursuant to a plan of consolidation approved in the manner provided in this Act.

The board of directors of each corporation shall, by a resolution adopted by each such board, approve a plan of consolidation setting forth:

(a) The names of the corporations proposing to consolidate, and the name of the new corporation into which they propose to consolidate, which is hereinafter designated as the new corporation.

(b) The terms and conditions of the proposed consolidation.

(c) The manner and basis of converting the shares of each corporation into shares, obligations or other securities of the new corporation or of any other corporation or, in whole or in part, into cash or other property.

(d) With respect to the new corporation, all of the statements required to be set forth in articles of incorporation for corporations organized under this Act.

(e) Such other provisions with respect to the proposed consolidation as are deemed necessary or desirable.

§ 72A. Procedure for Share Exchange

All the issued or all the outstanding shares of one or more classes of any domestic corporation may be acquired through the exchange of all such shares of such class or classes by another domestic or foreign corporation pursuant to a plan of exchange approved in the manner provided in this Act.

The board of directors of each corporation shall, by resolution adopted by each such board, approve a plan of exchange setting forth:

(a) The name of the corporation the shares of which are proposed to be acquired by exchange and the name of the corporation to acquire the shares of such corporation in the exchange, which is hereinafter designated as the acquiring corporation.

(b) The terms and conditions of the proposed exchange.

(c) The manner and basis of exchanging the shares to be acquired for shares, obligations or other securities of the acquiring corporation or any other corporation, or, in whole or in part, for cash or other property.

(d) Such other provisions with respect to the proposed exchange as are deemed necessary or desirable.

The procedure authorized by this section shall not be deemed to limit the power of a corporation to acquire all or part of the shares of any class or classes of a corporation through a voluntary exchange or otherwise by agreement with the shareholders.

§ 73. Approval by Shareholders

(a) The board of directors of each corporation in the case of a merger or consolidation, and the board of directors of the corporation the shares of which are to be acquired in the case of an exchange, upon approving such plan of merger, consolidation or exchange, shall, by resolution, direct that the plan be submitted to a vote at a meeting of its shareholders, which may be either an annual or a special meeting. Written notice shall be given to each shareholder of record, whether or not entitled to vote at such meeting, not less than twenty days before such meeting, in the manner provided in this Act for the giving of notice of meetings of shareholders, and, whether the meeting be an annual or a special meeting, shall state that the purpose or one of the purposes is to consider the proposed plan of merger, consolidation or exchange. A copy or a summary of the plan of merger, consolidation or exchange, as the case may be, shall be included in or enclosed with such notice.

(b) At each such meeting, a vote of the shareholders shall be taken on the proposed plan. The plan shall be approved upon receiving the affirmative vote of the holders of a majority of the shares entitled to vote thereon of each such corporation, unless any class of shares of any such corporation is entitled to vote thereon as a class, in which event, as to such corporation, the plan shall be approved upon receiving the affirmative vote of the holders of a majority of the shares of each class of shares entitled to vote thereon as a class and of the total shares entitled to vote thereon. Any class of shares of any such corporation shall be entitled to vote as a class if any such plan contains any provision which, if contained in a proposed amendment to articles of incorporation, would entitle such class of shares to vote as a class and, in the case of an exchange, if the class is included in the exchange.

(c) After such approval by a vote of the shareholders of each such corporation, and at any time prior to the filing of the articles of merger, consolidation or exchange, the merger, consolidation or exchange may be abandoned pursuant to provisions therefor, if any, set forth in the plan.

(d) (1) Notwithstanding the provisions of subsections (a) and (b), submission of a plan of merger to a vote at a meeting of shareholders of a surviving corporation shall not be required if:

(i) the articles of incorporation of the surviving corporation do not differ except in name from those of the corporation before the merger,

(ii) each holder of shares of the surviving corporation which were outstanding immediately before the effective date of the merger is to hold the same number of shares with identical rights immediately after,

(iii) the number of voting shares outstanding immediately after the merger, plus the number of voting shares issuable on conversion of other securities issued by virtue of the terms of the merger and on exercise of rights and warrants so issued, will not exceed by more than 20 percent the number of voting shares outstanding immediately before the merger, and

(iv) the number of participating shares outstanding immediately after the merger, plus the number of participating shares issuable on conversion of other securities issued by virtue of the terms of the merger and on exercise of rights and warrants so issued, will not exceed by more than 20 percent the number of participating shares outstanding immediately before the merger.

(2) As used in this subsection:

(i) "voting shares" means shares which entitle their holders to vote unconditionally in elections of directors;

(ii) "participating shares" means shares which entitle their holders to participate without limitation in distribution of earnings or surplus.

§ 74. Articles of Merger, Consolidation or Exchange

(a) Upon receiving the approvals required by sections 71, 72 and 73, articles of merger or articles of consolidation shall be executed in duplicate by each corporation by its president or a vice president and by its secretary or an assistant secretary, and verified by one of the officers of each corporation signing such articles, and shall set forth:

(1) The plan of merger or the plan of consolidation;

(2) As to each corporation, either (i) the number of shares outstanding, and, if the shares of any class are entitled to vote as a class, the designation and number of outstanding shares of each such class, or (ii) a statement that the vote of shareholders is not required by virtue of subsection 73(d);

(3) As to each corporation the approval of whose shareholders is required, the number of shares voted for and against such plan, respectively, and, if the shares of any class are entitled to vote as a class, the number of shares of each such class voted for and against such plan, respectively.

(b) Duplicate originals of the articles of merger, consolidation or exchange shall be delivered to the Secretary of State. If the Secretary of State finds that such articles conform to law, he shall, when all fees and franchise taxes have been paid as in this Act prescribed:

(1) Endorse on each of such duplicate originals the word "Filed," and the month, day and year of the filing thereof.

(2) File one of such duplicate originals in his office.

(3) Issue a certificate of merger, consolidation or exchange to which he shall affix the other duplicate original.

(c) The certificate of merger, consolidation or exchange together with the duplicate original of the articles affixed thereto by the Secretary of State, shall be returned to the surviving, new or acquiring corporation, as the case may be, or its representative.

§ 75. Merger of Subsidiary Corporation

Any corporation owning at least ninety per cent of the outstanding shares of each class of another corporation may merge such other corporation into itself without approval by a vote of the shareholders of either corporation. Its board of directors shall, by resolution, approve a plan of merger setting forth:

(A) The name of the subsidiary corporation and the name of the corporation owning at least ninety per cent of its shares, which is hereinafter designated as the surviving corporation.

(B) The manner and basis of converting the shares of the subsidiary corporation into shares, obligations or other securities of the surviving corporation or of any other corporation or, in whole or in part, into cash or other property.

A copy of such plan of merger shall be mailed to each shareholder of record of the subsidiary corporation.

Articles of merger shall be executed in duplicate by the surviving corporation by its president or a vice president and by its secretary or an assistant secretary, and verified by one of its officers signing such articles, and shall set forth:

(a) The plan of merger;

(b) The number of outstanding shares of each class of the subsidiary corporation and the number of such shares of each class owned by the surviving corporation; and

(c) The date of the mailing to shareholders of the subsidiary corporation of a copy of the plan of merger.

On and after the thirtieth day after the mailing of a copy of the plan of merger to shareholders of the subsidiary corporation or upon the waiver thereof by the holders of all outstanding shares duplicate originals of the articles of merger shall be delivered to the Secretary of State. If the Secretary of State finds that such articles conform to law, he shall, when all fees and franchise taxes have been paid as in this Act prescribed:

(1) Endorse on each of such duplicate originals the word "Filed," and the month, day and year of the filing thereof,

(2) File one of such duplicate originals in his office, and

(3) Issue a certificate of merger to which he shall affix the other duplicate original.

The certificate of merger, together with the duplicate original of the articles of merger affixed thereto by the Secretary of State, shall be returned to the surviving corporation or its representative.

§ 76. Effect of Merger, Consolidation or Exchange

Upon the issuance of the certificate of merger or the certificate of consolidation by the Secretary of State, the merger or consolidation shall be effected.

When such merger or consolidation has been effected:

(a) The several corporations parties to the plan of merger or consolidation shall be a single corporation, which, in the case of a merger, shall be that corporation designated in the plan of merger as the surviving corporation, and, in the case of a consolidation, shall be the new corporation provided for in the plan of consolidation.

(b) The separate existence of all corporations parties to the plan of merger or consolidation, except the surviving or new corporation, shall cease.

(c) Such surviving or new corporation shall have all the rights, privileges, immunities and powers and shall be subject to all the duties and liabilities of a corporation organized under this Act.

(d) Such surviving or new corporation shall thereupon and thereafter possess all the rights, privileges, immunities, and franchises, of a public as well as of a private nature, of each of the merging or consolidating corporations; and all property, real, personal and mixed, and all debts due on whatever account, including subscriptions to shares, and all other choses in action, and all and every other interest of or belonging to or due to each of the corporations so merged or consolidated, shall be taken and deemed to be transferred to and vested in such single corporation without further act or deed; and the title to any real estate, or any interest therein, vested in any of such corporations shall not revert or be in any way impaired by reason of such merger or consolidation.

(e) Such surviving or new corporation shall thenceforth be responsible and liable for all the liabilities and obligations of each of the corporations so merged or consolidated; and any claim existing or action or proceeding pending by or against any of such corporations may be prosecuted as if such merger or consolidation had not taken place, or such surviving or new corporation may be substituted in its place. Neither the rights of creditors nor any liens upon the property of any such corporation shall be impaired by such merger or consolidation.

(f) In the case of a merger, the articles of incorporation of the surviving corporation shall be deemed to be amended to the extent, if any, that changes in its articles of incorporation are stated in the plan of merger; and, in the case of a consolidation, the statements set forth in the articles of consolidation and which are required or permitted to be set forth in the articles of incorporation of corporations organized under this Act shall be deemed to be the original articles of incorporation of the new corporation.

§ 77. Merger, Consolidation or Exchange of Shares Between Domestic and Foreign Corporations

One or more foreign corporations and one or more domestic corporations may be merged or consolidated in the following manner, if such merger or consolidation is permitted by the laws of the state under which each such foreign corporation is organized:

(a) Each domestic corporation shall comply with the provisions of this Act with respect to the merger or consolidation, as the case may be, of domestic corporations and each foreign corporation shall comply with the applicable provisions of the laws of the state under which it is organized.

(b) If the surviving or new corporation, as the case may be, is to be governed by the laws of any state other than this State, it shall comply with the provisions of this Act with respect to foreign corporations if it is to transact business in this State, and in every case it shall file with the Secretary of State of this State:

(1) An agreement that it may be served with process in this State in any proceeding for the enforcement of any obligation of any domestic corporation which is a party to such merger or consolidation and in any proceeding for the enforcement of the rights of a dissenting shareholder of any such domestic corporation against the surviving or new corporation;

(2) An irrevocable appointment of the Secretary of State of this State as its agent to accept service of process in any such proceeding; and

(3) An agreement that it will promptly pay to the dissenting shareholders of any such domestic corporation the amount, if any, to which they shall be entitled under the provisions of this Act with respect to the rights of dissenting shareholders.

The effect of such merger or consolidation shall be the same as in the case of the merger or consolidation of domestic corporations, if the surviving or new corporation is to be governed by the laws of this State. If the surviving or new corporation is to be governed by the laws of any state other than this State, the effect of such merger or consolidation shall be the same as in the case of the merger or consolidation of domestic corporations except insofar as the laws of such other state provide otherwise.

At any time prior to the filing of the articles of merger or consolidation, the merger or consolidation may be abandoned pursuant to provisions therefor, if any, set forth in the plan of merger or consolidation.

SALE OF ASSETS

§ 78. Sale of Assets in Regular Course of Business and Mortgage or Pledge of Assets

The sale, lease, exchange, or other disposition of all, or substantially all, the property and assets of a corporation in the usual and regular course of its business and the mortgage or pledge of any or all property and assets of a corporation whether or not in the usual and regular course of business may be made upon such terms and conditions and for such consideration, which may consist in whole or in part of cash or other property, including shares, obligations or other securities of any other corporation, domestic or foreign, as shall be authorized by its board of directors; and in any such case no authorization or consent of the shareholders shall be required.

§ 79. Sale of Assets Other Than in Regular Course of Business

A sale, lease, exchange, or other disposition of all, or substantially all, the property and assets, with or without the good will, of a corporation, if not in the usual and regular course of its business, may be made upon such terms and conditions and for such consideration, which may consist in whole or in part of cash or other property, including shares, obligations or other securities of any other corporation, domestic or foreign, as may be authorized in the following manner:

(a) The board of directors shall adopt a resolution recommending such sale, lease, exchange, or other disposition and directing the submission thereof to a vote at a meeting of shareholders, which may be either an annual or a special meeting.

(b) Written notice shall be given to each shareholder of record, whether or not entitled to vote at such meeting, not less than twenty days before such meeting, in the manner provided in this Act for the giving of notice of meetings of shareholders, and, whether the meeting be an annual or a special meeting, shall state that the purpose, or one of the purposes is to consider the proposed sale, lease, exchange, or other disposition.

(c) At such meeting the shareholders may authorize such sale, lease, exchange, or other disposition and may fix, or may authorize the board of directors to fix, any or all of the terms and conditions thereof and the consideration to be received by the corporation therefor. Such authorization shall require the affirmative vote of the holders of a majority of the shares of the corporation entitled to vote thereon, unless any class of shares is entitled to vote thereon as a class, in which event such authorization shall require the affirmative vote of the holders of a majority of the shares of each class of shares entitled to vote as a class thereon and of the total shares entitled to vote thereon.

(d) After such authorization by a vote of shareholders, the board of directors nevertheless, in its discretion, may abandon such sale, lease, exchange, or other disposition of assets, subject to the rights of third parties under any contracts relating thereto, without further action or approval by shareholders.

§ 80. Right of Shareholders to Dissent and Obtain Payment for Shares

(a) Any shareholder of a corporation shall have the right to dissent from, and to obtain payment for his shares in the event of, any of the following corporate actions:

(1) Any plan of merger or consolidation to which the corporation is a party, except as provided in subsection (c);

(2) Any sale or exchange of all or substantially all of the property and assets of the corporation not made in the usual or regular course of its business, including a sale in dissolution, but not including a sale pursuant to an order of a court having jurisdiction in the premises or a sale for cash on terms requiring that all or substantially all of the net proceeds of sale be distributed to the shareholders in accordance with their respective interests within one year after the date of sale;

(3) Any plan of exchange to which the corporation is a party as the corporation the shares of which are to be acquired;

(4) Any amendment of the articles of incorporation which materially and adversely affects the rights appurtenant to the shares of the dissenting shareholder in that it:

　(i) alters or abolishes a preferential right of such shares;

　(ii) creates, alters or abolishes a right in respect of the redemption of such shares, including a provision respecting a sinking fund for the redemption or repurchase of such shares;

　(iii) alters or abolishes a preemptive right of the holder of such shares to acquire shares or other securities;

　(iv) excludes or limits the right of the holder of such shares to vote on any matter, or to cumulate his votes, except as such right may be limited by dilution through the issuance of shares or other securities with similar voting rights; or

(5) Any other corporate action taken pursuant to a shareholder vote with respect to which the articles of incorporation, the bylaws, or a resolution of the board of directors directs that dissenting shareholders shall have a right to obtain payment for their shares.

(b) (1) A record holder of shares may assert dissenters' rights as to less than all of the shares registered in his name only if he dissents with respect to all the shares beneficially owned by any one person, and discloses the name and address of the person or persons on whose behalf he dissents. In that event, his rights shall be determined as if the shares as to which he has dissented and his other shares were registered in the names of different shareholders.

(2) A beneficial owner of shares who is not the record holder may assert dissenters' rights with respect to shares held on his behalf, and shall be treated as a dissenting shareholder under the terms of this section and section 31 if he submits to the corpora-

tion at the time of or before the assertion of these rights a written consent of the record holder.

(c) The right to obtain payment under this section shall not apply to the shareholders of the surviving corporation in a merger if a vote of the shareholders of such corporation is not necessary to authorize such merger.

(d) A shareholder of a corporation who has a right under this section to obtain payment for his shares shall have no right at law or in equity to attack the validity of the corporate action that gives rise to his right to obtain payment, nor to have the action set aside or rescinded, except when the corporate action is unlawful or fraudulent with regard to the complaining shareholder or to the corporation.

§ 81.   Procedures for Protection of Dissenters' Rights

(a) As used in this section:

(1) "Dissenter" means a shareholder or beneficial owner who is entitled to and does assert dissenters' rights under section 80, and who has performed every act required up to the time involved for the assertion of such rights.

(2) "Corporation" means the issuer of the shares held by the dissenter before the corporate action, or the successor by merger or consolidation of that issuer.

(3) "Fair value" of shares means their value immediately before the effectuation of the corporate action to which the dissenter objects, excluding any appreciation or depreciation in anticipation of such corporate action unless such exclusion would be inequitable.

(4) "Interest" means interest from the effective date of the corporate action until the date of payment, at the average rate currently paid by the corporation on its principal bank loans, or, if none, at such rate as is fair and equitable under all the circumstances.

(b) If a proposed corporate action which would give rise to dissenters' rights under section 80(a) is submitted to a vote at a meeting of shareholders, the notice of meeting shall notify all shareholders that they have or may have a right to dissent and obtain payment for their shares by complying with the terms of this section, and shall be accompanied by a copy of sections 80 and 81 of this Act.

(c) If the proposed corporate action is submitted to a vote at a meeting of shareholders, any shareholder who wishes to dissent and obtain payment for his shares must file with the corporation, prior to the vote, a written notice of intention to demand that he be paid fair compensation for his shares if the proposed action is effectuated, and shall refrain from voting his shares in approval of such action. A shareholder who fails in either respect shall acquire no right to payment for his shares under this section or section 80.

(d) If the proposed corporate action is approved by the required vote at a meeting of shareholders, the corporation shall mail a further notice to all shareholders who gave due notice of intention to demand payment and who refrained from voting in favor of the proposed action. If the proposed corporate action is to be taken without a vote of shareholders, the corporation shall send to all shareholders who are entitled to dissent and demand payment for their shares a notice of the adoption of the plan of corporate action. The notice shall (1) state where and when a demand for payment must be sent and certificates of certificated shares must be deposited in order to obtain payment, (2) inform holders of uncertificated shares to what extent transfer of shares will be restricted from the time that demand for payment is received, (3) supply a form for demanding payment which includes a request for certification of the date on which the shareholder, or the person on whose behalf the shareholder dissents, acquired beneficial ownership of the shares, and (4) be accompanied by a copy of sections 80 and 81 of this Act. The time set for the demand and deposit shall be not less than 30 days from the mailing of the notice.

(e) A shareholder who fails to demand payment, or fails (in the case of certificated shares) to deposit certificates, as required by a notice pursuant to subsection (d) shall have no right under this section or section 80 to receive payment for his shares. If the shares are not represented by certificates, the corporation may restrict their transfer from the time of receipt of demand for payment until effectuation of the proposed corporate action, or the release of restrictions under the terms of subsection (f). The dissenter shall retain all other rights of a shareholder until these rights are modified by effectuation of the proposed corporate action.

(f)(1) Within 60 days after the date set for demanding payment and depositing certificates, if the corporation has not effectuated the proposed corporate action and remitted payment for shares pursuant to paragraph (3), it shall return any certificates that have been deposited, and release uncertificated shares from any transfer restrictions imposed by reason of the demand for payment.

(2) When uncertificated shares have been released from transfer restrictions, and deposited certificates have been returned,

the corporation may at any later time send a new notice conforming to the requirements of subsection (d), with like effect.

(3) Immediately upon effectuation of the proposed corporate action, or upon receipt of demand for payment if the corporate action has already been effectuated, the corporation shall remit to dissenters who have made demand and (if their shares are certificated) have deposited their certificates the amount which the corporation estimates to be the fair value of the shares, with interest if any has accrued. The remittance shall be accompanied by:

> (i) the corporation's closing balance sheet and statement of income for a fiscal year ending not more than 16 months before the date of remittance, together with the latest available interim financial statements;

> (ii) a statement of the corporation's estimate of fair value of the shares; and

> (iii) a notice of the dissenter's right to demand supplemental payment, accompanied by a copy of sections 80 and 81 of this Act.

(g) (1) If the corporation fails to remit as required by subsection (f), or if the dissenter believes that the amount remitted is less than the fair value of his shares, or that the interest is not correctly determined, he may send the corporation his own estimate of the value of the shares or of the interest, and demand payment of the deficiency.

(2) If the dissenter does not file such an estimate within 30 days after the corporation's mailing of its remittance, he shall be entitled to no more than the amount remitted.

(h) (1) Within 60 days after receiving a demand for payment pursuant to subsection (g), if any such demands for payment remain unsettled, the corporation shall file in an appropriate court a petition requesting that the fair value of the shares and interest thereon be determined by the court.

(2) An appropriate court shall be a court of competent jurisdiction in the county of this state where the registered office of the corporation is located. If, in the case of a merger or consolidation or exchange of shares, the corporation is a foreign corporation without a registered office in this state, the petition shall be filed in the county where the registered office of the domestic corporation was last located.

(3) All dissenters, wherever residing, whose demands have not been settled shall be made parties to the proceeding as in an action against their shares. A copy of the petition shall be served on each such dissenter; if a dissenter is a nonresident, the copy

may be served on him by registered or certified mail or by publication as provided by law.

(4) The jurisdiction of the court shall be plenary and exclusive. The court may appoint one or more persons as appraisers to receive evidence and recommend a decision on the question of fair value. The appraisers shall have such power and authority as shall be specified in the order of their appointment or in any amendment thereof. The dissenters shall be entitled to discovery in the same manner as parties in other civil suits.

(5) All dissenters who are made parties shall be entitled to judgment for the amount by which the fair value of their shares is found to exceed the amount previously remitted, with interest.

(6) If the corporation fails to file a petition as provided in paragraph (1) of this subsection, each dissenter who made a demand and who has not already settled his claim against the corporation shall be paid by the corporation the amount demanded by him, with interest, and may sue therefor in an appropriate court.

(i) (1) The costs and expenses of any proceeding under subsection (h), including the reasonable compensation and expenses of appraisers appointed by the court, shall be determined by the court and assessed against the corporation, except that any part of the costs and expenses may be apportioned and assessed as the court may deem equitable against all or some of the dissenters who are parties and whose action in demanding supplemental payment the court finds to be arbitrary, vexatious, or not in good faith.

(2) Fees and expenses of counsel and of experts for the respective parties may be assessed as the court may deem equitable against the corporation and in favor of any or all dissenters if the corporation failed to comply substantially with the requirements of this section, and may be assessed against either the corporation or a dissenter, in favor of any other party, if the court finds that the party against whom the fees and expenses are assessed acted arbitrarily, vexatiously, or not in good faith in respect to the rights provided by this section and section 80.

(3) If the court finds that the services of counsel for any dissenter were of substantial benefit to other dissenters similarly situated, and should not be assessed against the corporation, it may award to these counsel reasonable fees to be paid out of the amounts awarded to the dissenters who were benefitted.

(j) (1) Notwithstanding the foregoing provisions of this section, the corporation may elect to withhold the remittance required by subsection (f) from any dissenter with respect to shares of which the dissenter (or the person on whose behalf the dissenter acts) was not the beneficial owner on the date of the first announcement to news media or to shareholders of the terms of the proposed corporate action. With respect to such shares, the corporation shall, upon effectuating the corporate action, state to each dissenter its estimate of the fair value of the shares, state the rate of interest to be used (explaining the basis thereof), and offer to pay the resulting amounts on receiving the dissenter's agreement to accept them in full satisfaction.

(2) If the dissenter believes that the amount offered is less than the fair value of the shares and interest determined according to this section, he may within 30 days after the date of mailing of the corporation's offer, mail the corporation his own estimate of fair value and interest, and demand their payment. If the dissenter fails to do so, he shall be entitled to no more than the corporation's offer.

(3) If the dissenter makes a demand as provided in paragraph (2), the provisions of subsections (h) and (i) shall apply to further proceedings on the dissenter's demand.

DISSOLUTION
§ 82. Voluntary Dissolution by Incorporators

A corporation which has not commenced business and which has not issued any shares, may be voluntarily dissolved by its incorporators at any time in the following manner:

(a) Articles of dissolution shall be executed in duplicate by a majority of the incorporators, and verified by them, and shall set forth:

(1) The name of the corporation.

(2) The date of issuance of its certificate of incorporation.

(3) That none of its shares has been issued.

(4) That the corporation has not commenced business.

(5) That the amount, if any, actually paid in on subscriptions for its shares, less any part thereof disbursed for necessary expenses, has been returned to those entitled thereto.

(6) That no debts of the corporation remain unpaid.

(7) That a majority of the incorporators elect that the corporation be dissolved.

(b) Duplicate originals of the articles of dissolution shall be delivered to the Secretary of State. If the Secretary of State finds that the articles of dissolution conform to law, he shall, when all fees and franchise taxes have been paid as in this Act prescribed:

(1) Endorse on each of such duplicate originals the word "Filed," and the month, day and year of the filing thereof.

MODEL BUSINESS CORPORATION ACT § 84

(2) File one of such duplicate originals in his office.

(3) Issue a certificate of dissolution to which he shall affix the other duplicate original.

The certificate of dissolution, together with the duplicate original of the articles of dissolution affixed thereto by the Secretary of State, shall be returned to the incorporators or their representative. Upon the issuance of such certificate of dissolution by the Secretary of State, the existence of the corporation shall cease.

§ 83. Voluntary Dissolution by Consent of Shareholders

A corporation may be voluntarily dissolved by the written consent of all of its shareholders.

Upon the execution of such written consent, a statement of intent to dissolve shall be executed in duplicate by the corporation by its president or a vice president and by its secretary or an assistant secretary, and verified by one of the officers signing such statement, which statement shall set forth:

(a) The name of the corporation.

(b) The names and respective addresses of its officers.

(c) The names and respective addresses of its directors.

(d) A copy of the written consent signed by all shareholders of the corporation.

(e) A statement that such written consent has been signed by all shareholders of the corporation or signed in their names by their attorneys thereunto duly authorized.

§ 84. Voluntary Dissolution by Act of Corporation

A corporation may be dissolved by the act of the corporation, when authorized in the following manner:

(a) The board of directors shall adopt a resolution recommending that the corporation be dissolved, and directing that the question of such dissolution be submitted to a vote at a meeting of shareholders, which may be either an annual or a special meeting.

(b) Written notice shall be given to each shareholder of record entitled to vote at such meeting within the time and in the manner provided in this Act for the giving of notice of meetings of shareholders, and, whether the meeting be an annual or special meeting, shall state that the purpose, or one of the purposes, of such meeting is to consider the advisability of dissolving the corporation.

(c) At such meeting a vote of shareholders entitled to vote thereat shall be taken on a resolution to dissolve the corporation.

Such resolution shall be adopted upon receiving the affirmative vote of the holders of a majority of the shares of the corporation entitled to vote thereon, unless any class of shares is entitled to vote thereon as a class, in which event the resolution shall be adopted upon receiving the affirmative vote of the holders of a majority of the shares of each class of shares entitled to vote thereon as a class and of the total shares entitled to vote thereon.

(d) Upon the adoption of such resolution, a statement of intent to dissolve shall be executed in duplicate by the corporation by its president or a vice president and by its secretary or an assistant secretary, and verified by one of the officers signing such statement, which statement shall set forth:

(1) The name of the corporation.

(2) The names and respective addresses of its officers.

(3) The names and respective addresses of its directors.

(4) A copy of the resolution adopted by the shareholders authorizing the dissolution of the corporation.

(5) The number of shares outstanding, and, if the shares of any class are entitled to vote as a class, the designation and number of outstanding shares of each such class.

(6) The number of shares voted for and against the resolution, respectively, and, if the shares of any class are entitled to vote as a class, the number of shares of each such class voted for and against the resolution, respectively.

§ 85.   Filing of Statement of Intent to Dissolve

Duplicate originals of the statement of intent to dissolve, whether by consent of shareholders or by act of the corporation, shall be delivered to the Secretary of State. If the Secretary of State finds that such statement conforms to law, he shall, when all fees and franchise taxes have been paid as in this Act prescribed:

(a) Endorse on each of such duplicate originals the word "Filed," and the month, day and year of the filing thereof.

(b) File one of such duplicate originals in his office.

(c) Return the other duplicate original to the corporation or its representative.

§ 86.   Effect of Statement of Intent to Dissolve

Upon the filing by the Secretary of State of a statement of intent to dissolve, whether by consent of shareholders or by act of the corporation, the corporation shall cease to carry on its business, except insofar as may be necessary for the winding up thereof, but its corporate existence shall continue until a certificate of dissolution has been issued by the Secretary of State or until a decree dissolving the corporation has been entered by a court of competent jurisdiction as in this Act provided.

§ 87. Procedure after Filing of Statement of Intent to Dissolve

After the filing by the Secretary of State of a statement of intent to dissolve:

(a) The corporation shall immediately cause notice thereof to be mailed to each known creditor of the corporation.

(b) The corporation shall proceed to collect its assets, convey and dispose of such of its properties as are not to be distributed in kind to its shareholders, pay, satisfy and discharge its liabilities and obligations and do all other acts required to liquidate its business and affairs, and, after paying or adequately providing for the payment of all its obligations, distribute the remainder of its assets, either in cash or in kind, among its shareholders according to their respective rights and interests.

(c) The corporation, at any time during the liquidation of its business and affairs, may make application to a court of competent jurisdiction within the state and judicial subdivision in which the registered office or principal place of business of the corporation is situated, to have the liquidation continued under the supervision of the court as provided in this Act.

§ 88. Revocation of Voluntary Dissolution Proceedings by Consent of Shareholders

By the written consent of all of its shareholders, a corporation may, at any time prior to the issuance of a certificate of dissolution by the Secretary of State, revoke voluntary dissolution proceedings theretofore taken, in the following manner:

Upon the execution of such written consent, a statement of revocation of voluntary dissolution proceedings shall be executed in duplicate by the corporation by its president or a vice president and by its secretary or an assistant secretary, and verified by one of the officers signing such statement, which statement shall set forth:

(a) The name of the corporation.

(b) The names and respective addresses of its officers.

(c) The names and respective addresses of its directors.

(d) A copy of the written consent signed by all shareholders of the corporation revoking such voluntary dissolution proceedings.

(e) That such written consent has been signed by all shareholders of the corporation or signed in their names by their attorneys thereunto duly authorized.

§ 89. Revocation of Voluntary Dissolution Proceedings by Act of Corporation

By the act of the corporation, a corporation may, at any time prior to the issuance of a certificate of dissolution by the Secretary of State, revoke voluntary dissolution proceedings theretofore taken, in the following manner:

(a) The board of directors shall adopt a resolution recommending that the voluntary dissolution proceedings be revoked, and directing that the question of such revocation be submitted to a vote at a special meeting of shareholders.

(b) Written notice, stating that the purpose or one of the purposes of such meeting is to consider the advisability of revoking the voluntary dissolution proceedings, shall be given to each shareholder of record entitled to vote at such meeting within the time and in the manner provided in this Act for the giving of notice of special meetings of shareholders.

(c) At such meeting a vote of the shareholders entitled to vote thereat shall be taken on a resolution to revoke the voluntary dissolution proceedings, which shall require for its adoption the affirmative vote of the holders of a majority of the shares entitled to vote thereon.

(d) Upon the adoption of such resolution, a statement of revocation of voluntary dissolution proceedings shall be executed in duplicate by the corporation by its president or a vice president and by its secretary or an assistant secretary, and verified by one of the officers signing such statement, which statement shall set forth:

(1) The name of the corporation.

(2) The names and respective addresses of its officers.

(3) The names and respective addresses of its directors.

(4) A copy of the resolution adopted by the shareholders revoking the voluntary dissolution proceedings.

(5) The number of shares outstanding.

(6) The number of shares voted for and against the resolution, respectively.

§ 90. Filing of Statement of Revocation of Voluntary Dissolution Proceedings

Duplicate originals of the statement of revocation of voluntary dissolution proceedings, whether by consent of shareholders or by act of the corporation, shall be delivered to the Secretary of State. If the Secretary of State finds that such statement conforms to law, he shall, when all fees and franchise taxes have been paid as in this Act prescribed:

(a) Endorse on each of such duplicate originals the word "Filed," and the month, day and year of the filing thereof.

(b) File one of such duplicate originals in his office.

(c) Return the other duplicate original to the corporation or its representative.

§ 91. Effect of Statement of Revocation of Voluntary Dissolution Proceedings

Upon the filing by the Secretary of State of a statement of revocation of voluntary dissolution proceedings, whether by consent of shareholders or by act of the corporation, the revocation of the voluntary dissolution proceedings shall become effective and the corporation may again carry on its business.

§ 92. Articles of Dissolution

If voluntary dissolution proceedings have not been revoked, then when all debts, liabilities and obligations of the corporation have been paid and discharged, or adequate provision has been made therefor, and all of the remaining property and assets of the corporation have been distributed to its shareholders, articles of dissolution shall be executed in duplicate by the corporation by its president or a vice president and by its secretary or an assistant secretary, and verified by one of the officers signing such statement, which statement shall set forth:

(a) The name of the corporation.

(b) That the Secretary of State has theretofore filed a statement of intent to dissolve the corporation, and the date on which such statement was filed.

(c) That all debts, obligations and liabilities of the corporation have been paid and discharged or that adequate provision has been made therefor.

(d) That all the remaining property and assets of the corporation have been distributed among its shareholders in accordance with their respective rights and interests.

(e) That there are no suits pending against the corporation in any court, or that adequate provision has been made for the satisfaction of any judgment, order or decree which may be entered against it in any pending suit.

§ 93. Filing of Articles of Dissolution

Duplicate originals of such articles of dissolution shall be delivered to the Secretary of State. If the Secretary of State finds that such articles of dissolution conform to law, he shall, when all fees and franchise taxes have been paid as in this Act prescribed:

(a) Endorse on each of such duplicate originals the word "Filed," and the month, day and year of the filing thereof.

(b) File one of such duplicate originals in his office.

(c) Issue a certificate of dissolution to which he shall affix the other duplicate original.

The certificate of dissolution, together with the duplicate original of the articles of dissolution affixed thereto by the Secretary of State, shall be returned to the representative of the dissolved corporation. Upon the issuance of such certificate of dissolution the existence of the corporation shall cease, except for the purpose of suits, other proceedings and appropriate corporate action by shareholders, directors and officers as provided in this Act.

§ 94. Involuntary Dissolution

A corporation may be dissolved involuntarily by a decree of the .... court in an action filed by the Attorney General when it is established that:

(a) The corporation has failed to file its annual report within the time required by this Act, or has failed to pay its franchise tax on or before the first day of August of the year in which such franchise tax becomes due and payable; or

(b) The corporation procured its articles of incorporation through fraud; or

(c) The corporation has continued to exceed or abuse the authority conferred upon it by law; or

(d) The corporation has failed for thirty days to appoint and maintain a registered agent in this State; or

(e) The corporation has failed for thirty days after change of its registered office or registered agent to file in the office of the Secretary of State a statement of such change.

§ 95. Notification to Attorney General

The Secretary of State, on or before the last day of December of each year, shall certify to the Attorney General the names of all corporations which have failed to file their annual reports or to pay franchise taxes in accordance with the provisions of this Act, together with the facts pertinent thereto. He shall also certify, from time to time, the names of all corporations which have given other cause for dissolution as provided in this Act, together with the facts pertinent thereto. Whenever the Secretary of State shall certify the name of a corporation to the Attorney General as having given any cause for dissolution, the Secretary of State shall concurrently mail to the corporation at its registered office a notice that such certification has been made. Upon the receipt of such certification, the Attorney General shall file an action in the name of the State against such corporation for its dissolution. Every such certificate from the Secretary of State to the Attorney General pertaining to the failure of a corporation to file an annual report or pay a franchise tax shall be taken and received in all courts as prima facie evidence of the facts therein stated. If, before action is filed, the corporation shall file its annual report or pay its franchise tax, together with all penalties thereon, or shall appoint or maintain a registered agent as provided in this Act, or shall file with the Secretary of State the required statement of change of registered office or registered agent, such fact shall be forthwith certified by the Secretary of State to the Attorney General and he shall not file an action against such corporation for such cause. If, after action is filed, the corporation shall file its annual report or pay its franchise tax, together with all penalties thereon, or shall appoint or maintain a registered agent as provided in this Act, or shall file with the Secretary of State the required statement of change of registered office or registered agent, and shall pay the costs of such action, the action for such cause shall abate.

§ 96. Venue and Process

Every action for the involuntary dissolution of a corporation shall be commenced by the Attorney General either in the .... court of the county in which the registered office of the corporation is situated, or in the .... court of .... county. Summons shall issue and be served as in other civil actions. If process is returned not found, the Attorney General shall cause publication to be made as in other civil cases in some newspaper published in the county where the registered office of the corporation is situated, containing a notice of the pendency of such action, the title of the court, the title of the action, and the date on or after which default may be entered. The Attorney General may include in one notice the names of any number of corporations against which actions are then pending in the same court. The Attorney General shall cause a copy of such notice to be mailed to the corporation at its registered office within ten days after the first publication thereof. The certificate of the Attorney General of the mailing of such notice shall be prima facie evidence thereof. Such notice shall be published at least once each week for two successive weeks, and the first publication thereof may begin at any time after the summons has been returned. Unless a corporation shall have been served with summons, no default shall be taken against it earlier than thirty days after the first publication of such notice.

§ 97. Jurisdiction of Court to Liquidate Assets and Business of Corporation

The .... courts shall have full power to liquidate the assets and business of a corporation:

(a) In an action by a shareholder when it is established:

(1) That the directors are deadlocked in the management of the corporate affairs and the shareholders are unable to break the deadlock, and that irreparable injury to the corporation is being suffered or is threatened by reason thereof; or

(2) That the acts of the directors or those in control of the corporation are illegal, oppressive or fraudulent; or

(3) That the shareholders are deadlocked in voting power, and have failed, for a period which includes at least two consecutive annual meeting dates, to elect successors to directors whose terms have expired or would have expired upon the election of their successors; or

(4) That the corporate assets are being misapplied or wasted.

(b) In an action by a creditor:

(1) When the claim of the creditor has been reduced to judgment and an execution thereon returned unsatisfied and it is established that the corporation is insolvent; or

(2) When the corporation has admitted in writing that the claim of the creditor is due and owing and it is established that the corporation is insolvent.

(c) Upon application by a corporation which has filed a statement of intent to dissolve, as provided in this Act, to have its liquidation continued under the supervision of the court.

(d) When an action has been filed by the Attorney General to dissolve a corporation and it is established that liquidation of its business and affairs should precede the entry of a decree of dissolution.

Proceedings under clause (a), (b) or (c) of this section shall be brought in the county in which the registered office or the principal office of the corporation is situated.

It shall not be necessary to make shareholders parties to any such action or proceeding unless relief is sought against them personally.

§ 98.   Procedure in Liquidation of Corporation by Court

In proceedings to liquidate the assets and business of a corporation the court shall have power to issue injunctions, to appoint a receiver or receivers pendente lite, with such powers and duties as the court, from time to time, may direct, and to take such other proceedings as may be requisite to preserve the corporate assets wherever situated, and carry on the business of the corporation until a full hearing can be had.

After a hearing had upon such notice as the court may direct to be given to all parties to the proceedings and to any other parties in interest designated by the court, the court may appoint a liquidating receiver or receivers with authority to collect the assets of the corporation, including all amounts owing to the corporation by subscribers on account of any unpaid portion of the consideration for the issuance of shares.   Such liquidating receiver or receivers shall have authority, subject to the order of the court, to sell, convey and dispose of all or any part of the assets of the corporation wherever situated, either at public or private sale.   The assets of the corporation or the proceeds resulting from a sale, conveyance or other disposition thereof shall be applied to the expenses of such liquidation and to the payment of the liabilities and obligations of the corporation, and any remaining assets or proceeds shall be distributed among its shareholders according to their respective rights and interests.   The order appointing such liquidating receiver or receivers shall state their powers and duties.   Such powers and duties may be increased or diminished at any time during the proceedings.

The court shall have power to allow from time to time as expenses of the liquidation compensation to the receiver or receivers and to attorneys in the proceeding, and to direct the payment thereof out of the assets of the corporation or the proceeds of any sale or disposition of such assets.

A receiver of a corporation appointed under the provisions of this section shall have authority to sue and defend in all courts in his own name as receiver of such corporation.   The court appointing such receiver shall have exclusive jurisdiction of the corporation and its property, wherever situated.

§ 99.   Qualifications of Receivers

A receiver shall in all cases be a natural person or a corporation authorized to act as receiver, which corporation may be a domestic corporation or a foreign corporation authorized to transact business in this State, and shall in all cases give such bond as the court may direct with such sureties as the court may require.

§ 100. Filing of Claims in Liquidation Proceedings

In proceedings to liquidate the assets and business of a corporation the court may require all creditors of the corporation to file with the clerk of the court or with the receiver, in such form as the court may prescribe, proofs under oath of their respective claims. If the court requires the filing of claims it shall fix a date, which shall be not less than four months from the date of the order, as the last day for the filing of claims, and shall prescribe the notice that shall be given to creditors and claimants of the date so fixed. Prior to the date so fixed, the court may extend the time for the filing of claims. Creditors and claimants failing to file proofs of claim on or before the date so fixed may be barred, by order of court, from participating in the distribution of the assets of the corporation.

§ 101. Discontinuance of Liquidation Proceedings

The liquidation of the assets and business of a corporation may be discontinued at any time during the liquidation proceedings when it is established that cause for liquidation no longer exists. In such event the court shall dismiss the proceedings and direct the receiver to redeliver to the corporation all its remaining property and assets.

§ 102. Decree of Involuntary Dissolution

In proceedings to liquidate the assets and business of a corporation, when the costs and expenses of such proceedings and all debts, obligations and liabilities of the corporation shall have been paid and discharged and all of its remaining property and assets distributed to its shareholders, or in case its property and assets are not sufficient to satisfy and discharge such costs, expenses, debts and obligations, all the property and assets have been applied so far as they will go to their payment, the court shall enter a decree dissolving the corporation, whereupon the existence of the corporation shall cease.

§ 103. Filing of Decree of Dissolution

In case the court shall enter a decree dissolving a corporation, it shall be the duty of the clerk of such court to cause a certified copy of the decree to be filed with the Secretary of State. No fee shall be charged by the Secretary of State for the filing thereof.

§ 104. Deposit with State Treasurer of Amount Due Certain Shareholders

Upon the voluntary or involuntary dissolution of a corporation, the portion of the assets distributable to a creditor or shareholder who is unknown or cannot be found, or who is under disability and there is no person legally competent to receive such distributive portion, shall be reduced to cash and deposited with the State Treasurer and shall be paid over to such creditor or shareholder or to his legal representative upon proof satisfactory to the State Treasurer of his right thereto.

§ 105. Survival of Remedy after Dissolution

The dissolution of a corporation either (1) by the issuance of a certificate of dissolution by the Secretary of State, or (2) by a decree of court when the court has not liquidated the assets and business of the corporation as provided in this Act, or (3) by expiration of its period of duration, shall not take away or impair any remedy available to or against such corporation, its directors, officers, or shareholders, for any right or claim existing, or any liability incurred, prior to such dissolution if action or other proceeding thereon is commenced within two years after the date of such dissolution. Any such action or proceeding by or against the corporation may be prosecuted or defended by the corporation in its corporate name. The shareholders, directors and officers shall have power to take such corporate or other action as shall be appropriate to protect such remedy, right or claim. If such corporation was dissolved by the expiration of its period of duration, such corporation may amend its articles of incorporation at any time during such period of two years so as to extend its period of duration.

FOREIGN CORPORATIONS

§ 106. Admission of Foreign Corporation

No foreign corporation shall have the right to transact business in this State until it shall have procured a certificate of authority so to do from the Secretary of State. No foreign corporation shall be entitled to procure a certificate of authority under this Act to transact in this State any business which a corporation organized under this Act is not permitted to transact. A foreign corporation shall not be denied a certificate of authority by reason of the fact that the laws of the state or country under which such corporation is organized governing its organization and internal affairs differ from the laws of this State, and nothing in this Act contained shall be construed to authorize this State to regulate the organization or the internal affairs of such corporation.

Without excluding other activities which may not constitute transacting business in this State, a foreign corporation shall not be considered to be transacting business in this State, for the purposes of this Act, by reason of carrying on in this State any one or more of the following activities:

(a) Maintaining or defending any action or suit or any administrative or arbitration proceeding, or effecting the settlement thereof or the settlement of claims or disputes.

(b) Holding meetings of its directors or shareholders or carrying on other activities concerning its internal affairs.

(c) Maintaining bank accounts.

(d) Maintaining offices or agencies for the transfer, exchange and registration of its securities, or appointing and maintaining trustees or depositaries with relation to its securities.

(e) Effecting sales through independent contractors.

(f) Soliciting or procuring orders, whether by mail or through employees or agents or otherwise, where such orders require acceptance without this State before becoming binding contracts.

(g) Creating as borrower or lender, or acquiring, indebtedness or mortgages or other security interests in real or personal property.

(h) Securing or collecting debts or enforcing any rights in property securing the same.

(i) Transacting any business in interstate commerce.

(j) Conducting an isolated transaction completed within a period of thirty days and not in the course of a number of repeated transactions of like nature.

§ 107. Powers of Foreign Corporation

A foreign corporation which shall have received a certificate of authority under this Act shall, until a certificate of revocation or of withdrawal shall have been issued as provided in this Act, enjoy the same, but no greater, rights and privileges as a domestic corporation organized for the purposes set forth in the application pursuant to which such certificate of authority is issued; and, except as in this Act otherwise provided, shall be subject to the same duties, restrictions, penalties and liabilities now or hereafter imposed upon a domestic corporation of like character.

§ 108. Corporate Name of Foreign Corporation

No certificate of authority shall be issued to a foreign corporation unless the corporate name of such corporation:

(a) Shall contain the word "corporation," "company," "incorporated," or "limited," or shall contain an abbreviation of one of such words, or such corporation shall, for use in this State, add at the end of its name one of such words or an abbreviation thereof.

(b) Shall not contain any word or phrase which indicates or implies that it is organized for any purpose other than one or more of the purposes contained in its articles of incorporation or that it is authorized or empowered to conduct the business of banking or insurance.

(c) Shall not be the same as, or deceptively similar to, the name of any domestic corporation existing under the laws of this State or any foreign corporation authorized to transact business in this State, or a name the exclusive right to which is, at the time, reserved in the manner provided in this Act, or the name of a corporation which has in effect a registration of its name as provided in this Act except that this provision shall not apply if the foreign corporation applying for a certificate of authority files with the Secretary of State any one of the following:

(1) a resolution of its board of directors adopting a fictitious name for use in transacting business in this State which fictitious name is not deceptively similar to the name of any domestic corporation or of any foreign corporation authorized to transact business in this State or to any name reserved or registered as provided in this Act, or

(2) the written consent of such other corporation or holder of a reserved or registered name to use the same or deceptively similar name and one or more words are added to make such name distinguishable from such other name, or

(3) a certified copy of a final decree of a court of competent jurisdiction establishing the prior right of such foreign corporation to the use of such name in this State.

§ 109. Change of Name by Foreign Corporation

Whenever a foreign corporation which is authorized to transact business in this State shall change its name to one under which a certificate of authority would not be granted to it on application therefor, the certificate of authority of such corporation shall be suspended and it shall not thereafter transact any business in this State until it has changed its name to a name which is available to it under the laws of this State or has otherwise complied with the provisions of this Act.

§ 110. Application for Certificate of Authority

A foreign corporation, in order to procure a certificate of authority to transact business in this State, shall make application therefor to the Secretary of State, which application shall set forth:

(a) The name of the corporation and the state or country under the laws of which it is incorporated.

(b) If the name of the corporation does not contain the word "corporation," "company," "incorporated," or "limited," or does not contain an abbreviation of one of such words, then the name of the corporation with the word or abbreviation which it elects to add thereto for use in this State.

(c) The date of incorporation and the period of duration of the corporation.

(d) The address of the principal office of the corporation in the state or country under the laws of which it is incorporated.

(e) The address of the proposed registered office of the corporation in this State, and the name of its proposed registered agent in this State at such address.

(f) The purpose or purposes of the corporation which it proposes to pursue in the transaction of business in this State.

(g) The names and respective addresses of the directors and officers of the corporation.

(h) A statement of the aggregate number of shares which the corporation has authority to issue, itemized by classes and series, if any, within a class.

(i) A statement of the aggregate number of issued shares, itemized by class and by series, if any, within each class.

(j) An estimate, expressed in dollars, of the value of all property to be owned by the corporation for the following year, wherever located, and an estimate of the value of the property of the corporation to be located within this State during such year, and an estimate, expressed in dollars of the gross amount of business which will be transacted by the corporation during such year, and an estimate of the gross amount thereof which will be transacted by the corporation at or from places of business in this State during such year.

(k) Such additional information as may be necessary or appropriate in order to enable the Secretary of State to determine whether such corporation is entitled to a certificate of authority to transact business in this State and to determine and assess the fees and franchise taxes payable as in this Act prescribed.

Such application shall be made on forms prescribed and furnished by the Secretary of State and shall be executed in duplicate by the corporation by its president or a vice president and by its secretary or an assistant secretary, and verified by one of the officers signing such application.

§ 111. Filing of Application for Certificate of Authority

Duplicate originals of the application of the corporation for a certificate of authority shall be delivered to the Secretary of State, together with a copy of its articles of incorporation and all amendments thereto, duly authenticated by the proper officer of the state or country under the laws of which it is incorporated.

If the Secretary of State finds that such application conforms to law, he shall, when all fees and franchise taxes have been paid as in this Act prescribed:

(a) Endorse on each of such documents the word "Filed," and the month, day and year of the filing thereof.

(b) File in his office one of such duplicate originals of the application and the copy of the articles of incorporation and amendments thereto.

(c) Issue a certificate of authority to transact business in this State to which he shall affix the other duplicate original application.

The certificate of authority, together with the duplicate original of the application affixed thereto by the Secretary of State, shall be returned to the corporation or its representative.

§ 112. Effect of Certificate of Authority

Upon the issuance of a certificate of authority by the Secretary of State, the corporation shall be authorized to transact business in this State for those purposes set forth in its application, subject, however, to the right of this State to suspend or to revoke such authority as provided in this Act.

§ 113. Registered Office and Registered Agent of Foreign Corporation

Each foreign corporation authorized to transact business in this State shall have and continuously maintain in this State:

(a) A registered office which may be, but need not be, the same as its place of business in this State.

(b) A registered agent, which agent may be either an individual resident in this State whose business office is identical with such registered office, or a domestic corporation, or a foreign corporation authorized to transact business in this State, having a business office identical with such registered office.

§ 114. Change of Registered Office or Registered Agent of Foreign Corporation

A foreign corporation authorized to transact business in this State may change its registered office or change its registered agent, or both, upon filing in the office of the Secretary of State a statement setting forth:

(a) The name of the corporation.

(b) The address of its then registered office.

(c) If the address of its registered office be changed, the address to which the registered office is to be changed.

(d) The name of its then registered agent.

(e) If its registered agent be changed, the name of its successor registered agent.

(f) That the address of its registered office and the address of the business office of its registered agent, as changed, will be identical.

(g) That such change was authorized by resolution duly adopted by its board of directors.

Such statement shall be executed by the corporation by its president or a vice president, and verified by him, and delivered to the Secretary of State. If the Secretary of State finds that such statement conforms to the provisions of this Act, he shall file such statement in his office, and upon such filing the change of address of the registered office, or the appointment of a new registered agent, or both, as the case may be, shall become effective.

Any registered agent of a foreign corporation may resign as such agent upon filing a written notice thereof, executed in duplicate, with the Secretary of State, who shall forthwith mail a copy thereof to the corporation at its principal office in the state or country under the laws of which it is incorporated. The appointment of such agent shall terminate upon the expiration of thirty days after receipt of such notice by the Secretary of State.

If a registered agent changes his or its business address to another place within the same _____*, he or it may change such address and the address of the registered office of any corporation of which he or it is registered agent by filing a statement as required above except that it need be signed only by the registered agent and need not be responsive to (e) or (g) and must recite that a copy of the statement has been mailed to the corporation.

* Supply designation of jurisdiction
such as county, etc., in accordance
with local practice.

§ 115. Service of Process on Foreign Corporation

The registered agent so appointed by a foreign corporation authorized to transact business in this State shall be an agent of such corporation upon whom any process, notice or demand required or permitted by law to be served upon the corporation may be served.

Whenever a foreign corporation authorized to transact business in this State shall fail to appoint or maintain a registered agent in this State, or whenever any such registered agent cannot with reasonable diligence be found at the registered office, or whenever the certificate of authority of a foreign corporation shall be suspended or revoked, then the Secretary of State shall be an agent of such corporation upon whom any such process, notice, or demand may be served. Service on the Secretary of State of any such process, notice or demand shall be made by delivering to and leaving with him, or with any clerk having charge of the corporation department of his office, duplicate copies of such process, notice or demand. In the event any such process, notice or demand is served on the Secretary of State, he shall immediately cause one of such copies thereof to be forwarded by registered mail, addressed to the corporation at its principal office in the state or country under the laws of which it is incorporated. Any service so had on the Secretary of State shall be returnable in not less than thirty days.

The Secretary of State shall keep a record of all processes, notices and demands served upon him under this section, and shall record therein the time of such service and his action with reference thereto.

Nothing herein contained shall limit or affect the right to serve any process, notice or demand, required or permitted by law to be served upon a foreign corporation in any other manner now or hereafter permitted by law.

§ 116. Amendment to Articles of Incorporation of Foreign Corporation

Whenever the articles of incorporation of a foreign corporation authorized to transact business in this State are amended, such foreign corporation shall, within thirty days after such amendment becomes effective, file in the office of the Secretary of State a copy of such amendment duly authenticated by the proper officer of the state or country under the laws of which it is incorporated; but the filing thereof shall not of itself enlarge or alter the purpose or purposes which such corporation is authorized to pursue in the transaction of business in this State, nor authorize such corporation to transact business in this State under any other name than the name set forth in its certificate of authority.

§ 117. Merger of Foreign Corporation Authorized to Transact Business in This State

Whenever a foreign corporation authorized to transact business in this State shall be a party to a statutory merger permitted by the laws of the state or country under the laws of which it is incorporated, and such corporation shall be the surviving corporation, it shall, within thirty days after such merger becomes effective, file with the Secretary of State a copy of the articles of merger duly authenticated by the proper officer of the state or country under the laws of which such statutory merger was effected; and it shall not be necessary for such corporation to procure either a new or amended certificate of authority to transact business in this State unless the name of such corporation be changed thereby or unless the corporation desires to pursue in this State other or additional purposes than those which it is then authorized to transact in this State.

§ 118. Amended Certificate of Authority

A foreign corporation authorized to transact business in this State shall procure an amended certificate of authority in the event it changes its corporate name, or desires to pursue in this State other or additional purposes than those set forth in its prior application for a certificate of authority, by making application therefor to the Secretary of State.

The requirements in respect to the form and contents of such application, the manner of its execution, the filing of duplicate originals thereof with the Secretary of State, the issuance of an amended certificate of authority and the effect thereof, shall be the same as in the case of an original application for a certificate of authority.

§ 119. Withdrawal of Foreign Corporation

A foreign corporation authorized to transact business in this State may withdraw from this State upon procuring from the Secretary of State a certificate of withdrawal. In order to procure such certificate of withdrawal, such foreign corporation shall deliver to the Secretary of State an application for withdrawal, which shall set forth:

(a) The name of the corporation and the state or country under the laws of which it is incorporated.

(b) That the corporation is not transacting business in this State.

(c) That the corporation surrenders its authority to transact business in this State.

(d) That the corporation revokes the authority of its registered agent in this State to accept service of process and consents that service of process in any action, suit or proceeding based upon any cause of action arising in this State during the time the corporation was authorized to transact business in this State may thereafter be made on such corporation by service thereof on the Secretary of State.

(e) A post-office address to which the Secretary of State may mail a copy of any process against the corporation that may be served on him.

(f) A statement of the aggregate number of shares which the corporation has authority to issue, itemized by class and series, if any, within each class, as of the date of such application.

(g) A statement of the aggregate number of issued shares, itemized by class and series, if any, within each class, as of the date of such application.

(h) Such additional information as may be necessary or appropriate in order to enable the Secretary of State to determine and assess any unpaid fees or franchise taxes payable by such foreign corporation as in this Act prescribed.

The application for withdrawal shall be made on forms prescribed and furnished by the Secretary of State and shall be executed by the corporation by its president or a vice president and by its secretary or an assistant secretary, and verified by one of the officers signing the application, or, if the corporation is in the hands of a receiver or trustee, shall be executed on behalf of the corporation by such receiver or trustee and verified by him.

§ 120. Filing of Application for Withdrawal

Duplicate originals of such application for withdrawal shall be delivered to the Secretary of State. If the Secretary of State finds that such application conforms to the provisions of this Act, he shall, when all fees and franchise taxes have been paid as in this Act prescribed:

(a) Endorse on each of such duplicate originals the word "Filed," and the month, day and year of the filing thereof.

(b) File one of such duplicate originals in his office.

(c) Issue a certificate of withdrawal to which he shall affix the other duplicate original.

The certificate of withdrawal, together with the duplicate original of the application for withdrawal affixed thereto by the

Secretary of State, shall be returned to the corporation or its representative. Upon the issuance of such certificate of withdrawal, the authority of the corporation to transact business in this State shall cease.

§ 121.　Revocation of Certificate of Authority

The certificate of authority of a foreign corporation to transact business in this State may be revoked by the Secretary of State upon the conditions prescribed in this section when:

(a) The corporation has failed to file its annual report within the time required by this Act, or has failed to pay any fees, franchise taxes or penalties prescribed by this Act when they have become due and payable; or

(b) The corporation has failed to appoint and maintain a registered agent in this State as required by this Act; or

(c) The corporation has failed, after change of its registered office or registered agent, to file in the office of the Secretary of State a statement of such change as required by this Act; or

(d) The corporation has failed to file in the office of the Secretary of State any amendment to its articles of incorporation or any articles of merger within the time prescribed by this Act; or

(e) A misrepresentation has been made of any material matter in any application, report, affidavit, or other document submitted by such corporation pursuant to this Act.

No certificate of authority of a foreign corporation shall be revoked by the Secretary of State unless (1) he shall have given the corporation not less than sixty days' notice thereof by mail addressed to its registered office in this State, and (2) the corporation shall fail prior to revocation to file such annual report, or pay such fees, franchise taxes or penalties, or file the required statement of change of registered agent or registered office, or file such articles of amendment or articles of merger, or correct such misrepresentation.

§ 122.　Issuance of Certificate of Revocation

Upon revoking any such certificate of authority, the Secretary of State shall:

(a) Issue a certificate of revocation in duplicate.

(b) File one of such certificates in his office.

(c) Mail to such corporation at its registered office in this State a notice of such revocation accompanied by one of such certificates.

Upon the issuance of such certificate of revocation, the authority of the corporation to transact business in this State shall cease.

§ 123. Application to Corporations Heretofore Authorized to Transact Business in This State

Foreign corporations which are duly authorized to transact business in this State at the time this Act takes effect, for a purpose or purposes for which a corporation might secure such authority under this Act, shall, subject to the limitations set forth in their respective certificates of authority, be entitled to all the rights and privileges applicable to foreign corporations procuring certificates of authority to transact business in this State under this Act, and from the time this Act takes effect such corporations shall be subject to all the limitations, restrictions, liabilities, and duties prescribed herein for foreign corporations procuring certificates of authority to transact business in this State under this Act.

§ 124. Transacting Business Without Certificate of Authority

No foreign corporation transacting business in this State without a certificate of authority shall be permitted to maintain any action, suit or proceeding in any court of this State, until such corporation shall have obtained a certificate of authority. Nor shall any action, suit or proceeding be maintained in any court of this State by any successor or assignee of such corporation on any right, claim or demand arising out of the transaction of business by such corporation in this State, until a certificate of authority shall have been obtained by such corporation or by a corporation which has acquired all or substantially all of its assets.

The failure of a foreign corporation to obtain a certificate of authority to transact business in this State shall not impair the validity of any contract or act of such corporation, and shall not prevent such corporation from defending any action, suit or proceeding in any court of this State.

A foreign corporation which transacts business in this State without a certificate of authority shall be liable to this State, for the years or parts thereof during which it transacted business in this State without a certificate of authority, in an amount equal to all fees and franchise taxes which would have been imposed by this Act upon such corporation had it duly applied for and received a certificate of authority to transact business in this State as required by this Act and thereafter filed all reports required by this Act, plus all penalties imposed by this

Act for failure to pay such fees and franchise taxes. The Attorney General shall bring proceedings to recover all amounts due this State under the provisions of this Section.

ANNUAL REPORTS
§ 125. Annual Report of Domestic and Foreign Corporations

Each domestic corporation, and each foreign corporation authorized to transact business in this State, shall file, within the time prescribed by this Act, an annual report setting forth:

(a) The name of the corporation and the state or country under the laws of which it is incorporated.

(b) The address of the registered office of the corporation in this State, and the name of its registered agent in this State at such address, and, in case of a foreign corporation, the address of its principal office in the state or country under the laws of which it is incorporated.

(c) A brief statement of the character of the business in which the corporation is actually engaged in this State.

(d) The names and respective addresses of the directors and officers of the corporation.

(e) A statement of the aggregate number of shares which the corporation has authority to issue, itemized by class and series, if any, within each class.

(f) A statement of the aggregate number of issued shares, itemized by class and series, if any, within each class.

(g) A statement, expressed in dollars, of the value of all the property owned by the corporation, wherever located, and the value of the property of the corporation located within this State, and a statement, expressed in dollars, of the gross amount of business transacted by the corporation for the twelve months ended on the thirty-first day of December preceding the date herein provided for the filing of such report and the gross amount thereof transacted by the corporation at or from places of business in this State. If, on the thirty-first day of December preceding the time herein provided for the filing of such report, the corporation had not been in existence for a period of twelve months, or in the case of a foreign corporation had not been authorized to transact business in this State for a period of twelve months, the statement with respect to business transacted shall be furnished for the period between the date of incorporation or the date of its authorization to transact business in this State, as the case may be, and such thirty-first day of December. If all the property of the corporation is located in this State and all of its business is transacted at or from places of business in this State, then the information required by this subparagraph need not be set forth in such report.

(h) Such additional information as may be necessary or appropriate in order to enable the Secretary of State to determine and assess the proper amount of franchise taxes payable by such corporation.

Such annual report shall be made on forms prescribed and furnished by the Secretary of State, and the information therein contained shall be given as of the date of the execution of the report, except as to the information required by subparagraphs (g) and (h) which shall be given as of the close of business on the thirty-first day of December next preceding the date herein provided for the filing of such report. It shall be executed by the corporation by its president, a vice president, secretary, an assistant secretary, or treasurer, and verified by the officer executing the report, or, if the corporation is in the hands of a receiver or trustee, it shall be executed on behalf of the corporation and verified by such receiver or trustee.

§ 126. Filing of Annual Report of Domestic and Foreign Corporations

Such annual report of a domestic or foreign corporation shall be delivered to the Secretary of State between the first day of January and the first day of March of each year, except that the first annual report of a domestic or foreign corporation shall be filed between the first day of January and the first day of March of the year next succeeding the calendar year in which its certificate of incorporation or its certificate of authority, as the case may be, was issued by the Secretary of State. Proof to the satisfaction of the Secretary of State that prior to the first day of March such report was deposited in the United States mail in a sealed envelope, properly addressed, with postage prepaid, shall be deemed a compliance with this requirement. If the Secretary of State finds that such report conforms to the requirements of this Act, he shall file the same. If he finds that it does not so conform, he shall promptly return the same to the corporation for any necessary corrections, in which event the penalties hereinafter prescribed for failure to file such report within the time hereinabove provided shall not apply, if such report is corrected to conform to the requirements of this Act and returned to the Secretary of State within thirty days from the date on which it was mailed to the corporation by the Secretary of State.

FEES, FRANCHISE TAXES AND CHARGES

§ 127. Fees, Franchise Taxes and Charges to be Collected by Secretary of State

The Secretary of State shall charge and collect in accordance with the provisions of this Act:

(a) Fees for filing documents and issuing certificates.

(b) Miscellaneous charges.

(c) License fees.

(d) Franchise taxes.

§ 128. Fees for Filing Documents and Issuing Certificates

The Secretary of State shall charge and collect for:

(a) Filing articles of incorporation and issuing a certificate of incorporation, ... dollars.

(b) Filing articles of amendment and issuing a certificate of amendment, ... dollars.

(c) Filing restated articles of incorporation, ... dollars.

(d) Filing articles of merger or consolidation and issuing a certificate of merger or consolidation, ... dollars.

(e) Filing an application to reserve a corporate name, ... dollars.

(f) Filing a notice of transfer of a reserved corporate name, ... dollars.

(g) Filing a statement of change of address of registered office or change of registered agent or both, ... dollars.

(h) Filing a statement of the establishment of a series of shares, ... dollars.

(i) Filing a statement of intent to dissolve, ... dollars.

(j) Filing a statement of revocation of voluntary dissolution proceedings, ... dollars.

(k) Filing articles of dissolution, ... dollars.

(*l*) Filing an application of a foreign corporation for a certificate of authority to transact business in this State and issuing a certificate of authority, ... dollars.

(m) Filing an application of a foreign corporation for an amended certificate of authority to transact business in this State and issuing an amended certificate of authority, ... dollars.

(n) Filing a copy of an amendment to the articles of incorporation of a foreign corporation holding a certificate of authority to transact business in this State, ... dollars.

(*o*) Filing a copy of articles of merger of a foreign corporation holding a certificate of authority to transact business in this State, ... dollars.

(p) Filing an application for withdrawal of a foreign corporation and issuing a certificate of withdrawal, ... dollars.

(q) Filing any other statement or report, except an annual report, of a domestic or foreign corporation, ... dollars.

§ 129. Miscellaneous Charges

The Secretary of State shall charge and collect:

(a) For furnishing a certified copy of any document, instrument, or paper relating to a corporation, ... cents per page and ...... dollars for the certificate and affixing the seal thereto.

(b) At the time of any service of process on him as resident agent of a corporation, ... dollars, which amount may be recovered as taxable costs by the party to the suit or action causing such service to be made if such party prevails in the suit or action.

§ 130. License Fees Payable by Domestic Corporations

The Secretary of State shall charge and collect from each domestic corporation license fees, based upon the number of shares which it will have authority to issue or the increase in the number of shares which it will have authority to issue, at the time of:

(a) Filing articles of incorporation;

(b) Filing articles of amendment increasing the number of authorized shares; and

(c) Filing articles of merger or consolidation increasing the number of authorized shares which the surviving or new corporation, if a domestic corporation, will have the authority to issue above the aggregate number of shares which the constituent domestic corporations and constituent foreign corporations authorized to transact business in this State had authority to issue.

The license fees shall be at the rate of ...... cents per share up to and including the first 10,000 authorized shares, ... cents per share for each authorized share in excess of 10,000 shares up to and including 100,000 shares, and ...... cents per share for each authorized share in excess of 100,000 shares.

The license fees payable on an increase in the number of authorized shares shall be imposed only on the increased number of shares, and the number of previously authorized shares shall be taken into account in determining the rate applicable to the increased number of authorized shares.

§ 131.   License Fees Payable by Foreign Corporations

The Secretary of State shall charge and collect from each foreign corporation license fees, based upon the proportion represented in this State of the number of shares which it has authority to issue or the increase in the number of shares which it has authority to issue, at the time of:

(a) Filing an application for a certificate of authority to transact business in this State;

(b) Filing articles of amendment which increased the number of authorized shares; and

(c) Filing articles of merger or consolidation which increased the number of authorized shares which the surviving or new corporation, if a foreign corporation, has authority to issue above the aggregate number of shares which the constituent domestic corporations and constituent foreign corporations authorized to transact business in this State had authority to issue.

The license fees shall be at the rate of . . . . . . cents per share up to and including the first 10,000 authorized shares represented in this State, ... cents per share for each authorized share in excess of 10,000 shares up to and including 100,000 shares represented in this State, and . . . . . . cents per share for each authorized share in excess of 100,000 shares represented in this State.

The license fees payable on an increase in the number of authorized shares shall be imposed only on the increased number of such shares represented in this State, and the number of previously authorized shares represented in this State shall be taken into account in determining the rate applicable to the increased number of authorized shares.

The number of authorized shares represented in this State shall be that proportion of its total authorized shares which the sum of the value of its property located in this State and the gross amount of business transacted by it at or from places of business in this State bears to the sum of the value of all of its property, wherever located, and the gross amount of its business, wherever transacted. Such proportion shall be determined from information contained in the application for a certificate of authority to transact business in this State until the filing of an annual report and thereafter from information contained in the latest annual report filed by the corporation.

§ 132. Franchise Taxes Payable by Domestic Corporations

The Secretary of State shall charge and collect from each domestic corporation an initial franchise tax at the time of filing its articles of incorporation at the rate of one-twelfth of one-half of the license fee payable by such corporation under the provisions of this Act at the time of filing its articles of incorporation, for each calendar month, or fraction thereof, between the date of the issuance of the certificate of incorporation by the Secretary of State and the first day of July of the next succeeding calendar year.

The Secretary of State shall charge and collect from each domestic corporation an annual franchise tax, payable in advance for the period from July 1 in each year to July 1 in the succeeding year, beginning July 1 in the calendar year in which such corporation is required to file its first annual report under this Act, (Alternative 1: at the rate of ...... of ...... per cent of the amount represented in this State of the stated capital of the corporation, as determined in accordance with accounting practices and principles that are reasonable in the circumstances, as disclosed by the latest report filed by the corporation with the Secretary of State) (Alternative 2: at the rate of ...... cents per share up to and including the first 10,000 issued and outstanding shares, and ...... cents per share for each issued and outstanding share in excess of 10,000 shares up to and including 100,000 shares, and ...... cents per share for each issued and outstanding share in excess of 100,000 shares).

*[If Alternative 2 is enacted, the following
paragraph should be deleted.]*

The amount represented in this State of the stated capital of the corporation shall be that proportion of its stated capital which the sum of the value of its property located in this State and the gross amount of business transacted by it at or from places of business in this State bears to the sum of the value of all of its property, wherever located, and the gross amount of its business, wherever transacted.

§ 133. Franchise Taxes Payable by Foreign Corporations

The Secretary of State shall charge and collect from each foreign corporation authorized to transact business in this State an initial franchise tax at the time of filing its application for a certificate of authority at the rate of one-twelfth of one-half of the license fee payable by such corporation under the provisions of this Act at the time of filing such application, for each month, or fraction thereof, between the date of the issuance of the certificate of authority by the Secretary of State and the first day of July of the next succeeding calendar year.

The Secretary of State shall charge and collect from each foreign corporation authorized to transact business in this State an annual franchise tax, payable in advance for the period from July 1 in each year to July 1 in the succeeding year, beginning July 1 in the calendar year in which such corporation is required to file its first annual report under this Act, (Alternative 1: at the rate of . . . . . per cent of the amount represented in this State of the stated capital of the corporation, as determined in accordance with accounting practices and principles that are reasonable in the circumstances, as disclosed by the latest annual report filed by the corporation with the Secretary of State) (Alternative 2: at a rate of . . . . . . cents per share up to and including the first 10,000 issued and outstanding shares represented in this State, and . . . . . . cents per share for each issued and outstanding share in excess of 10,000 shares up to and including 100,000 shares represented in this State, and . . . . . . cents per share for each issued and outstanding share in excess of 100,000 shares represented in this State).

*[If Alternative 2 is enacted, the following
paragraph should be deleted.]*

The amount represented in this State of the stated capital of the corporation shall be that proportion of its stated capital which the sum of the value of its property located in this State and the gross amount of business transacted by it at or from places of business in this State bears to the sum of the value of all of its property, wherever located, and the gross amount of its business, wherever transacted.

§ 134. Assessment and Collection of Annual Franchise Taxes

It shall be the duty of the Secretary of State to collect all annual franchise taxes and penalties imposed by, or assessed in accordance with, this Act.

Between the first day of March and the first day of June of each year, the Secretary of State shall assess against each corporation, domestic and foreign, required to file an annual report in such year, the franchise tax payable by it for the period from July 1 of such year to July 1 of the succeeding year in accordance with the provisions of this Act, and, if it has failed to file its annual report within the time prescribed by this Act, the penalty imposed by this Act upon such corporation for its failure so to do; and shall mail a written notice to each corporation against which such tax is assessed, addressed to such corporation at its registered office in this State, notifying the corporation (1) of the amount of franchise tax assessed against it for the ensuing year and the amount of penalty, if any, assessed against it for failure to file its annual report; (2) that objections, if any, to such assessment will be heard by the officer making the assessment on or before the fifteenth day of June of such year, upon receipt of a request from the corporation; and (3) that such tax and penalty shall be payable to the Secretary of State on the first day of July next succeeding the date of the notice. Failure to receive such notice shall not relieve the corporation of its obligation to pay the tax and any penalty assessed, or invalidate the assessment thereof.

The Secretary of State shall have power to hear and determine objections to any assessment of franchise tax at any time after such assessment and, after hearing, to change or modify any such assessment. In the event of any adjustment of franchise tax with respect to which a penalty has been assessed for failure to file an annual report, the penalty shall be adjusted in accordance with the provisions of this Act imposing such penalty.

All annual franchise taxes and all penalties for failure to file annual reports shall be due and payable on the first day of July of each year. If the annual franchise tax assessed against any corporation subject to the provisions of this Act, together with all penalties assessed thereon, shall not be paid to the Secretary of State on or before the thirty-first day of July of the year in which such tax is due and payable, the Secretary of State shall certify such fact to the Attorney General on or before the fifteenth day of November of such year, whereupon the Attorney General may institute an action against such corporation in the name of this State, in any court of competent jurisdiction, for the recovery of the amount of such franchise tax and penalties, together with the cost of suit, and prosecute the same to final judgment.

For the purpose of enforcing collection, all annual franchise taxes assessed in accordance with this Act, and all penalties assessed thereon and all interest and costs that shall accrue in connection with the collection thereof, shall be a prior and first lien on the real and personal property of the corporation from and including the first day of July of the year when such franchise taxes become due and payable until such taxes, penalties, interest, and costs shall have been paid.

PENALTIES

§ 135. Penalties Imposed Upon Corporations

Each corporation, domestic or foreign, that fails or refuses to file its annual report for any year within the time prescribed by this Act shall be subject to a penalty of ten per cent of the amount of the franchise tax assessed against it for the period beginning July 1 of the year in which such report should have been filed. Such penalty shall be assessed by the Secretary of State at the time of the assessment of the franchise tax. If the amount of the franchise tax as originally assessed against such corporation be thereafter adjusted in accordance with the provisions of this Act, the amount of the penalty shall be likewise adjusted to ten per cent of the amount of the adjusted franchise tax. The amount of the franchise tax and the amount of the penalty shall be separately stated in any notice to the corporation with respect thereto.

If the franchise tax assessed in accordance with the provisions of this Act shall not be paid on or before the thirty-first day of July, it shall be deemed to be delinquent, and there shall be added a penalty of one per cent for each month or part of month that the same is delinquent, commencing with the month of August.

Each corporation, domestic or foreign, that fails or refuses to answer truthfully and fully within the time prescribed by this Act interrogatories propounded by the Secretary of State in accordance with the provisions of this Act, shall be deemed to be guilty of a misdemeanor and upon conviction thereof may be fined in any amount not exceeding five hundred dollars.

§ 136. Penalties Imposed Upon Officers and Directors

Each officer and director of a corporation, domestic or foreign, who fails or refuses within the time prescribed by this Act to answer truthfully and fully interrogatories propounded to him by the Secretary of State in accordance with the provisions of this Act, or who signs any articles, statement, report, application or other document filed with the Secretary of State which is known to such officer or director to be false in any material respect, shall be deemed to be guilty of a misdemeanor, and upon conviction thereof may be fined in any amount not exceeding ...... dollars.

MISCELLANEOUS PROVISIONS

§ 137. Interrogatories by Secretary of State

The Secretary of State may propound to any corporation, domestic or foreign, subject to the provisions of this Act, and to any officer or director thereof, such interrogatories as may be reasonably necessary and proper to enable him to ascertain whether such corporation has complied with all the provisions of this Act applicable to such corporation. Such interrogatories shall be answered within thirty days after the mailing thereof, or within such additional time as shall be fixed by the Secretary of State, and the answers thereto shall be full and complete and shall be made in writing and under oath. If such interrogatories be directed to an individual they shall be answered by him, and if directed to a corporation they shall be answered by the president, vice president, secretary or assistant secretary thereof. The Secretary of State need not file any document to which such interrogatories relate until such interrogatories be answered as herein provided, and not then if the answers thereto disclose that such document is not in conformity with the provisions of this Act. The Secretary of State shall certify to the Attorney General, for such action as the Attorney General may deem appropriate, all interrogatories and answers thereto which disclose a violation of any of the provisions of this Act.

§ 138. Information Disclosed by Interrogatories

Interrogatories propounded by the Secretary of State and the answers thereto shall not be open to public inspection nor shall the Secretary of State disclose any facts or information obtained therefrom except insofar as his official duty may require the same to be made public or in the event such interrogatories or the answers thereto are required for evidence in any criminal proceedings or in any other action by this State.

§ 139. Powers of Secretary of State

The Secretary of State shall have the power and authority reasonably necessary to enable him to administer this Act efficiently and to perform the duties therein imposed upon him.

§ 140. Appeal from Secretary of State

If the Secretary of State shall fail to approve any articles of incorporation, amendment, merger, consolidation or dissolution, or any other document required by this Act to be approved by the Secretary of State before the same shall be filed in his office, he shall, within ten days after the delivery thereof to him, give written notice of his disapproval to the person or corporation, domestic or foreign, delivering the same, specifying the reasons therefor. From such disapproval such person or corporation may appeal to the ...... court of the county in which the registered office of such corporation is, or is proposed to be, situated by filing with the clerk of such court a petition setting forth a copy of the articles or other documents sought to be filed and a copy of the written disapproval thereof by the Secretary of State; whereupon the matter shall be tried de novo by the court, and the court shall either sustain the action of the Secretary of State or direct him to take such action as the court may deem proper.

If the Secretary of State shall revoke the certificate of authority to transact business in this State of any foreign corporation, pursuant to the provisions of this Act, such foreign corporation may likewise appeal to the ...... court of the county where the registered office of such corporation in this State is situated, by filing with the clerk of such court a petition setting forth a copy of its certificate of authority to transact business in this State and a copy of the notice of revocation given by the Secretary of State; whereupon the matter shall be tried de novo by the court, and the court shall either sustain the action of the Secretary of State or direct him to take such action as the court may deem proper.

Appeals from all final orders and judgments entered by the ...... court under this section in review of any ruling or decision of the Secretary of State may be taken as in other civil actions.

§ 141. Certificates and Certified Copies to be Received in Evidence

All certificates issued by the Secretary of State in accordance with the provisions of this Act, and all copies of documents filed in his office in accordance with the provisions of this Act when certified by him, shall be taken and received in all courts, public offices, and official bodies as prima facie evidence of the facts therein stated. A certificate by the Secretary of State under the great seal of this State, as to the existence or non-existence of the facts relating to corporations shall be taken and received in all courts, public offices, and official bodies as prima facie evidence of the existence or non-existence of the facts therein stated.

§ 142. Forms to be Furnished by Secretary of State

All reports required by this Act to be filed in the office of the Secretary of State shall be made on forms which shall be prescribed and furnished by the Secretary of State. Forms for all other documents to be filed in the office of the Secretary of State shall be furnished by the Secretary of State on request therefor, but the use thereof, unless otherwise specifically prescribed in this Act, shall not be mandatory.

§ 143. Greater Voting Requirements

Whenever, with respect to any action to be taken by the shareholders of a corporation, the articles of incorporation require the vote or concurrence of the holders of a greater proportion of the shares, or of any class or series thereof, than required by this Act with respect to such action, the provisions of the articles of incorporation shall control.

§ 144. Waiver of Notice

Whenever any notice is required to be given to any shareholder or director of a corporation under the provisions of this Act or under the provisions of the articles of incorporation or by-laws of the corporation, a waiver thereof in writing signed by the person or persons entitled to such notice, whether before or after the time stated therein, shall be equivalent to the giving of such notice.

§ 145. Action by Shareholders Without a Meeting

Any action required by this Act to be taken at a meeting of the shareholders of a corporation, or any action which may be taken at a meeting of the shareholders, may be taken without a meeting if a consent in writing, setting forth the action so taken, shall be signed by all of the shareholders entitled to vote with respect to the subject matter thereof.

Such consent shall have the same effect as a unanimous vote of shareholders, and may be stated as such in any articles or document filed with the Secretary of State under this Act.

§ 146. Unauthorized Assumption of Corporate Powers

All persons who assume to act as a corporation without authority so to do shall be jointly and severally liable for all debts and liabilities incurred or arising as a result thereof.

§ 147. Application to Existing Corporations

The provisions of this Act shall apply to all existing corporations organized under any general act of this State providing for the organization of corporations for a purpose or purposes for which a corporation might be organized under this Act, where the power has been reserved to amend, repeal or modify the act under which such corporation was organized and where such act is repealed by this Act.

§ 148. Application to Foreign and Interstate Commerce

The provisions of this Act shall apply to commerce with foreign nations and among the several states only insofar as the same may be permitted under the provisions of the Constitution of the United States.

§ 149. Reservation of Power

The   ....* shall at all times have power to prescribe such regulations, provisions and limitations as it may deem ad-

* Insert name of legislative body.

visable, which regulations, provisions and limitations shall be binding upon any and all corporations subject to the provisions of this Act, and the .... * shall have power to amend, repeal or modify this Act at pleasure.

§ 150.   Effect of Repeal of Prior Acts

The repeal of a prior act by this Act shall not affect any right accrued or established, or any liability or penalty incurred, under the provisions of such act, prior to the repeal thereof.

§ 151.   Effect of Invalidity of Part of this Act

If a court of competent jurisdiction shall adjudge to be invalid or unconstitutional any clause, sentence, paragraph, section or part of this Act, such judgment or decree shall not affect, impair, invalidate or nullify the remainder of this Act, but the effect thereof shall be confined to the clause, sentence, paragraph, section or part of this Act so adjudged to be invalid or unconstitutional.

§ 152.   Exclusivity of Certain Provisions [Optional]

In circumstances to which section 45 and related sections of this Act are applicable, such provisions supersede the applicability of any other statutes of this state with respect to the legality of distributions.

§ 153.   Repeal of Prior Acts
(Insert appropriate provisions) ....

SPECIAL COMMENT—CLOSE CORPORATIONS

In view of the increasing importance of close corporations, both for the small family business and for the larger undertakings conducted by some small number of other corporations, this liberalizing trend has now been followed by the 1969 Amendments to the Model Act. The first sentence of section 35, providing that the business of the corporation shall be managed by a board of directors, was supplemented by a new clause "except as may be otherwise provided in the articles of incorporation." This permits the shareholders to take over and exercise the functions of the directors by appropriate provision to that effect in the articles, or to allocate functions between the directors and shareholders in such manner as may be desired. Taken with other provisions of the Model Act, which are here enumerated for convenience, this rounds out the adaptability of the Model Act for all the needs of a close corporation:

1. By section 4(*l*) the by-laws may make any provision for the regulation of the affairs of the corporation that is not inconsistent with the articles or the laws of the incorporating state.

* Insert name of legislative body.

2. By section 15 shares may be divided into several classes and the articles may limit or deny the voting rights of or provide special voting rights for the shares of any class to the extent not inconsistent with the Model Act. The narrow limits of this exception are revealed by section 33 which provides that each outstanding share, regardless of class, shall be entitled to one vote on each matter submitted to a vote at a meeting of the shareholders "except as may be otherwise provided in the articles of incorporation," thus expressly authorizing more than one vote per share or less than one vote per share, either generally or in respect to particular matters.

3. By section 16 item (F) the shares of any preferred or special class may be issued in series and there may be variations between different series in numerous respects, including specifically the matter of voting rights, if any.

4. By section 32 the articles may reduce a quorum of shareholders to not less than one-third of the shares entitled to vote, or leave the quorum at the standard of a majority or, as confirmed by section 143, increase the number to any desired point.

5. By section 34 agreements among shareholders regarding the voting of their shares are made valid and enforceable in accordance with their terms without limitation in time. These could relate to the election or compensation of directors or officers or the creation of various types of securities for new financing or the conduct of business of various kinds or dividend policy or mergers and consolidations or other transactions without limit.

6. The flexibility permitted by the revision of section 35 in the distribution or reallocation of authority among directors and stockholders has already been mentioned.

7. Under section 36 the number of directors may be fixed by the by-laws at one or such greater number as may best serve the interests of the shareholders and that number may be increased or decreased from time to time by amendment to, or in the manner provided in, the articles or the by-laws, subject to any limiting provision adopted pursuant to law, such as an agreed requirement for a unanimous vote by directors for any such change or a requirement that amendments to the by-laws be made by shareholder vote. Similarly, under section 53, the incorporation may be effected by a single incorporator or by more as may be desired.

8. By section 37 directors may be classified. While this relates to directors classified in such manner that the term of office of a specified proportion terminates in each year, the Model Act does not forbid the election of separate directors by separate classes of stock.

9. Section 40 permits the articles or the by-laws to require more than a majority of the directors to constitute a quorum for the transaction of business and also permits the articles or by-laws to require the act of a greater number than a majority of those present at a meeting where a quorum is present before any specified business may be transacted. Or a unanimous vote of all directors may be required. This may be utilized to confer a right of veto on any designated class in order to protect its special interests.

10. By section 50 the authority and duties of the respective officers and agents of the corporation may be tailored and prescribed in the by-laws, or consistently with the by-laws, in such manner as the needs of the shareholders may indicate.

11. By section 54 the articles may include any desired provision for the regulation of the internal affairs of the corporation, including, in particular, "any provision restricting the transfer of shares." This expressly validates agreements for prior offering of shares to the corporation or other shareholders. All such restrictions must, of course, be clearly shown on the stock certificate as required by the Uniform Commercial Code. A similarly broad provision for the contents of the by-laws is contained in section 27.

12. By sections 60, 73 and 79, respectively, a class vote may be required for an amendment to the articles, for any merger or consolidation or for a sale of assets other than in the regular course of business.

13. Section 143 permits the articles to require, for any particular action by the shareholders, the vote or concurrence of the holders of a greater proportion of the shares, or of any class or series thereof, than the Model Act itself requires.

14. Section 44 permits action by directors without a meeting and section 145 permits the same for shareholders, while section 144 contains a broad provision on waiver of notice. Thus the formality of meetings may, where desired, be eliminated in whole or in part, except for the annual meeting required by section 28.

Under these provisions protection may be afforded for a great diversity of interests. By way of illustration, the shares may be divided into different classes with different voting rights and each class may be permitted to elect a different director. Or some classes may be permitted to vote on certain transactions, but not all. Even more drastically, some classes may be denied all voting rights whatever. Thus a family could provide for equal participation in the profits of the venture, but restrict the power of management to selected members. The advantages of having a known group of business associates may be safeguarded by restrictions on the transfer of shares. Most commonly this takes the form of a requirement for *pro rata* offering to the other shareholders before selling to an outsider. Or the other shareholders may be given an option, in the event of death or a proposed transfer, to buy the stock *pro rata*. The same option may be given to the corporation. The purchase price may be fixed by any agreed formula, such as adjusted book value or some multiple of recent earnings. Or stockholder agreements may be used to assure that, at least for a limited number of years, all shares will be voted for certain directors and officers, or in a certain way on other corporate matters. Cumulative voting may be provided for, by which each shareholder has a number of votes equal to the number of his shares multiplied by the number of directors to be elected, with the privilege of casting all of his votes for a single candidate, or dividing them as he may wish. This helps minorities obtain representation on the board of directors. Thus the holder of one-fourth of the shares voting, plus one share, is sure of electing one of three directors. The preemptive right is another important protection in the case of close corporations, since it assures each stockholder a right to maintain his proportionate interest. Still more definite protection is afforded by provisions in the articles that prohibit particular transactions except with the assent of a specified percentage of all outstanding shares or of each class of shares. Much the same protection can sometimes be obtained by requiring a specially large quorum for the election of directors, or a specially large vote, or even unanimous vote, by directors for the authorization of particular transactions. Quite the opposite situation exists if one of the participants is to be an inactive investor, for whom non-voting preferred stock, with its prior right to a return from earnings, may be sufficient. But even here he may require a veto power over major transactions, such as the issuance of debt, the issuance of additional preferred shares or mergers or consolidations. Or the preferred shareholders may be given as a class the right to elect one or more of the directors, particularly in the event that dividends should be in arrears.

These possibilities are listed merely as illustrations and not in any sense as exhausting the variations permissible under the Model Act.

B. MODEL PROFESSIONAL CORPORATION ACT

(As of January 1, 1982)

Contents

––––––––––––[1] PROFESSIONAL CORPORATION ACT

§ 1. Short Title [§ 1][2]

This Act shall be known and may be cited as the "_____ Professional Corporation Act."

[1] Supply name of State as required throughout the act.

[2] Bracketed references are to the parallel provisions in the Model Business Corporation Act.

Comment [3]

This model professional corporation act is designed as a supplement to the Model Business Corporation Act. Section 27 provides that the state's business corporation act shall apply to professional corporations except to the extent its provisions are inconsistent with the supplemental act. Accordingly, the supplement must be read in conjunction with the Model Business Corporation Act which it closely parallels in structure and semantics. With appropriate modifications, however, this model act may readily be adapted for use as a supplement to other business corporation acts.

§ 2. Definitions [§ 2]

As used in this Act, unless the context otherwise requires, the term:

(1) "Professional service" means any service which may lawfully be rendered only by persons licensed under the provisions of a licensing law of this State and may not lawfully be rendered by a corporation organized under the _____ Business Corporation Act.

(2) "Licensing authority" means the officer, board, agency, court or other authority in this State which has the power to issue a license or other legal authorization to render a professional service.

(3) "Professional corporation" or "domestic professional corporation" means a corporation for profit subject to the provisions of this Act, except a foreign professional corporation.

(4) "Foreign professional corporation" means a corporation for profit organized for the purpose of rendering professional services under a law other than the law of this State.

(5) "Qualified person" means a natural person, general partnership, or professional corporation [4] which is eligible under this Act to own shares issued by a professional corporation.

(6) "Disqualified person" means any natural person, corporation, partnership, fiduciary, trust, association, government agency, or other entity which for any reason is or becomes ineligible under this Act to own shares issued by a professional corporation.

---

[3] Only the more significant Comments have been reprinted.

[4] Delete "professional corporation" if alternate 2 or 3 of Section 11(d) is adopted.

Comment

Paragraph (1).   The definition of "professional service" limits and describes the purposes for which corporations may be organized under Section 3.

As a general proposition, corporations may not be formed under business corporation acts for the purpose of practicing a profession.   In the absence of any statutory definition of the word "profession," the courts have held that, although a licensing requirement is characteristic of the professions, all licensed services are not necessarily professional services which may not be rendered by corporations.   Accordingly, the determination as to whether particular licensed services may be rendered by corporations has been made on a case by case basis based upon construction of the state business corporation law or the applicable licensing law.

Some of the existing state statutes under which professional persons are permitted to incorporate cover all licensed services. Statutes of this type are not restricted to persons who are prohibited from incorporating under the business corporation law. Other existing state statutes limit those who may incorporate to specific professions described in a single statute or in a series of similar statutes each applicable to one profession.   The definition of "professional service" in paragraph (1) has the effect of restricting the use of the act to the practice of the professions. Rather than listing designated professions, however, the model act follows the precedent set by many existing state statutes of defining professional services as those licensed services which may not be rendered by a corporation organized under the business corporation law.

Paragraph (2).   See Section 26 with respect to jurisdiction of the licensing authority over professional corporations.

Paragraphs (5) and (6).   See comment following Section 9.

§ 3.   Purposes [§ 3]

(a) Except as hereinafter provided in this section professional corporations may be organized under this Act only for the purpose of rendering professional services and services ancillary thereto within a single profession.

(b) A professional corporation may be incorporated for the purpose of rendering professional services within two or more professions and for any purpose or purposes for which corporations may be organized under the _____ Business Corporation Act to the extent that such combination of professional purposes or of professional and business purposes is permitted by the licensing laws of this State applicable to such professions and rules or regulations thereunder.

Comment

Apparently most state legislatures have felt that it was necessary to limit the purposes of a professional corporation to the practice of a single profession, and subsection (a) follows the large majority of existing state statutes in this respect. However, the ethical proscriptions of the various professions are not uniform in restricting the activities of a professional group to a single professional field. Some professional groups such as engineers and architects are permitted to carry on joint practice, and in other fields, such as the field of medicine and allied health professions, the extent to which professional practices may be combined is an evolving subject. Accordingly, subsection (b) shifts the responsibility for determining the extent to which two or more professions may combine and the extent to which a professional corporation may engage in business activities to the licensing statutes and regulations governing each profession where variations in public policy and ethical requirements of the various professions may be properly treated.

§ 4. Prohibited Activities

A professional corporation shall not engage in any profession or business other than the profession or professions and businesses permitted by its articles of incorporation, except that a professional corporation may invest its funds in real estate, mortgages, stocks, bonds or any other type of investment.

§ 5. General Powers [§ 4]

A professional corporation shall have the powers enumerated in the _____ Business Corporation Act, except that a professional corporation may be a promoter, general partner, member, associate, or manager only of a partnership, joint venture, trust or other enterprise engaged only in rendering professional services or carrying on business permitted by the articles of incorporation of the corporation.

§ 6. Rendering Professional Services

A professional corporation, domestic or foreign, may render professional services in this State only through natural persons permitted to render such services in this State; but nothing in this Act shall be construed to require that any person who is employed by a professional corporation be licensed to perform services for which no license is otherwise required or to prohibit the rendering of professional services by a licensed natural person acting in his individual capacity, notwithstanding such person may be a shareholder, director, officer, employee or agent of a professional corporation, domestic or foreign.

§ 7. Right of Corporation to Acquire Its Own Shares [§ 6]

A professional corporation may purchase its own shares from a disqualified person without regard to the availability of capital or surplus for such purchase; however, no purchase of or payment for its own shares shall be made at a time when the corporation is insolvent or when such purchase or payment would make it insolvent.

Comment

Nearly all professional corporation statutes require that shareholders be licensed professional persons, and to implement this requirement most statutes require that the corporation repurchase shares which have become the property of unlicensed persons through operation of law. The usual business corporation law restriction against impairment of capital by purchase of the corporation's own shares may conflict with this statutory requirement for the purchase of shares of a professional corporation. Section 7 of the model act resolves the conflict by removing the Model Business Corporation Act limitation on purchase of shares to the extent of available earned surplus or capital surplus while retaining the insolvency test of Section 6 of the Model Business Corporation Act.[4a] Section 10(a) of the professional corporation supplement requires the corporation to repurchase shares "to the extent of funds which may be legally made available for such purchase." Thus the requirements of Section 10 that the professional corporation repurchase the shares of a disqualified person will be subject to the insolvency restriction against repurchase but will not be subject to the capital and surplus restriction.

§ 8. Corporate Name [§§ 8, 108]

The name of a domestic professional corporation or of a foreign professional corporation authorized to transact business in this State:

(1) shall contain the words "professional corporation" or the abbreviation "P.C.";

(2) shall not contain any word or phrase which indicates or implies that it is organized for any purpose other than the purposes contained in its articles of incorporation;

[4a] For current Model Business Corporation Act limitations, see §§ 2(i), 45, supra pages 7, and 36–37.

(3) shall not be the same as, or deceptively similar to, the name of any domestic corporation existing under the laws of this State or any foreign corporation authorized to transact business in this State, or a name the exclusive right to which is, at the time, reserved in the manner provided in the _____ Business Corporation Act, or the name of a corporation which has in effect a registration of its corporate name as provided in the _____ Business Corporation Act; except that this provision shall not apply if:

(i) such similarity results from the use in the corporate name of personal names of its shareholders or former shareholders or of natural persons who were associated with a predecessor entity; or

(ii) the applicant files with the Secretary of State either of the following: (A) the written consent of such other corporation or holder of a reserved or registered name to use the same or deceptively similar name and one or more words are added to make such name distinguishable from such other name, or (B) a certified copy of a final decree of a court of competent jurisdiction establishing the prior right of the applicant to the use of such name in this State; and

(4) shall otherwise conform to any rule promulgated by a licensing authority having jurisdiction of a professional service described in the articles of incorporation of such corporation.

Comment

Existing state statutes vary in the selection of terms required in the corporate name as corporate designators. To encourage uniformity and avoid confusion the model act approves and requires only the term "professional corporation" or its abbreviation. The Model Business Corporation Act corporate name provision is further modified in paragraph (3)(i) to permit similarity of names if the similarity results from the use of personal names of persons associated with the organization. Paragraph (4) authorizes the licensing authority to impose by rule additional requirements appropriate to a particular profession.

§ 9. Issuance and Transfer of Shares; Share Certificates [§§ 15, 20, 23, 24]

(a) A professional corporation may issue shares, fractional shares, and rights or options to purchase shares only to:

(1) natural persons who are authorized by law in this State or in any other state or territory of the United States or the District of Columbia to render a professional service permitted by the articles of incorporation of the corporation;

(2) general partnerships in which all the partners are qualified persons with respect to such professional corporation and in which at least one partner is authorized by law in this State to render a professional service permitted by the articles of incorporation of the corporation; and

(3) professional corporations, domestic or foreign, authorized by law in this State to render a professional service permitted by the articles of incorporation of the corporation.[5]

(b) Where deemed necessary by the licensing authority for any profession in order to prevent violations of the ethical standards of such profession, the licensing authority may by rule further restrict, condition, or abridge the authority of professional corporations to issue shares but no such rule shall, of itself, have the effect of causing a shareholder of a professional corporation at the time such rule becomes effective to become a disqualified person. All shares issued in violation of this section or any rule hereunder shall be void.

(c) A shareholder of a professional corporation may transfer or pledge shares, fractional shares, and rights or options to purchase shares of the corporation only to natural persons, general partnerships and professional corporations [6] qualified hereunder to hold shares issued directly to them by such professional corporation. Any transfer of shares in violation of this provision shall be void; however, nothing herein contained shall prohibit the transfer of shares of a professional corporation by operation of law or court decree.

(d) Every certificate representing shares of a professional corporation shall state conspicuously upon its face that the shares represented thereby are subject to restrictions on transfer imposed by this Act and are subject to such further restrictions on transfer as may be imposed by the licensing authority from time to time pursuant to this Act.

Comment

The model act departs from existing state statutes in permitting shares of a professional corporation to be issued to persons licensed outside the state of incorporation and to partnerships and other professional corporations authorized to render a professional service permitted by the articles of incorporation of the corporation.

Pennsylvania also permits a professional corporation to issue shares to persons licensed in another state, but existing statutes

[5] Delete paragraph (3) of subsection (a) if 2 or 3 of Section 11(d) is adopted.

[6] Delete "professional corporation" if alternate 2 or 3 of Section 11(d) is adopted.

generally restrict shareholders to natural persons. If shareholders are not liable for debts of the corporation, however, there is no policy reason to prohibit the issuance of shares to another corporation which is subject to the same professional corporation requirements, and under Section 9 of the model act professional corporations may be given the same flexibility in planning the corporate structure as business corporations. If shareholders are personally liable for the performance of professional services rendered on behalf of the corporation, however, as they may be under either alternate 2 or 3 of Section 11(d), then the holding company device may be used to avoid personal liability, and accordingly, paragraph (3) of subsection (a) should be deleted if alternate 2 or 3 of Section 11(d) is adopted.

§ 10. Death or Disqualification of a Shareholder [§ 81]

(a) Upon the death of a shareholder of a professional corporation or if a shareholder of a professional corporation becomes a disqualified person or if shares of a professional corporation are transferred by operation of law or court decree to a disqualified person, the shares of such deceased shareholder or of such disqualified person may be transferred to a qualified person and, if not so transferred, shall be purchased or redeemed by the corporation to the extent of funds which may be legally made available for such purchase.

(b) If the price for such shares is not fixed by the articles of incorporation or by-laws of the corporation or by private agreement, the corporation, within six months after such death or thirty days after such disqualification or transfer, as the case may be, shall make a written offer to pay for such shares at a specified price deemed by such corporation to be the fair value thereof as of the date of such death, disqualification or transfer. Such offer shall be given to the executor or administrator of the estate of a deceased shareholder or to the disqualified shareholder or transferee and shall be accompanied by a balance sheet of the corporation, as of the latest available date and not more than twelve months prior to the making of such offer, and a profit and loss statement of such corporation for the twelve months' period ended on the date of such balance sheet.

(c) If within thirty days after the date of such written offer from the corporation the fair value of such shares is agreed upon between such disqualified person and the corporation, payment therefor shall be made within sixty days, or such other period as the parties may fix by agreement, after the date of such offer, upon surrender of the certificate or certificates representing such shares. Upon payment of the agreed value the disqualified persons shall cease to have any interest in such shares.

(d) If within such period of thirty days the disqualified person and the corporation do not so agree, then the corporation, within thirty days after receipt of written demand from the disqualified person given within sixty days after the date of the corporation's written offer shall, or at its election at any time within such period of sixty days may, file a petition in any court of competent jurisdiction in the county in this State where the registered office of the corporation is located requesting that the fair value of such shares be found and determined. If the corporation shall fail to institute the proceeding as herein provided, the disqualified person may do so within sixty days after delivery of such written demand to the corporation. The disqualified person, wherever residing, shall be made a party to the proceeding as an action against his shares quasi in rem. A copy of the petition shall be served on the disqualified person, if a resident of this State, and shall be served by registered or certified mail on the disqualified person, if a nonresident. Service on nonresidents shall also be made by publication as provided by law. The jurisdiction of the court shall be plenary and exclusive. The disqualified person shall be entitled to judgment against the corporation for the amount of the fair value of his shares as of the date of death, disqualification or transfer upon surrender to the corporation of the certificate or certificates representing such shares. The court may, at its discretion, order that the judgment be paid in such installments as the court may determine. The court may, if it so elects, appoint one or more persons as appraisers to receive evidence and recommend a decision on the question of fair value. The appraisers shall have such power and authority as shall be specified in the order of their appointment or an amendment thereof.

(e) The judgment shall include an allowance for interest at such rate as the court may find to be fair and equitable in all the circumstances, from the date of death, disqualification or transfer.

(f) The costs and expenses of any such proceeding shall be determined by the court and shall be assessed against the corporation, but all or any part of such costs and expenses may be apportioned and assessed as the court may deem equitable against the disqualified person if the court shall find that the action of such disqualified person in failing to accept such offer was arbitrary or vexatious or not in good faith. Such expenses shall include reasonable compensation for and reasonable expenses of the appraisers, but shall exclude the fees and expenses of counsel for and experts employed by any party; but if the fair value of the shares as determined materially exceeds the amount which the corporation offered to pay therefor, or if no offer was made, the court in its discretion may award to the disqualified person such sum as the court may determine to be reasonable compensation to any expert or experts employed by the disqualified person in the proceeding.

(g) If a purchase, redemption, or transfer of the shares of a deceased or disqualified shareholder or of a transferee who is a disqualified person is not completed within ten months after the death of the deceased shareholder or five months after the disqualification or transfer, as the case may be, the corporation shall forthwith cancel the shares on its books and the disqualified person shall have no further interest as a shareholder in the corporation other than his right to payment for such shares under this section.

(h) Shares acquired by a corporation pursuant to payment of the agreed value therefor or to payment of the judgment entered therefor, as in this section provided, may be held and disposed of by such corporation as in the case of other treasury shares.

(i) This section shall not be deemed to require the purchase of shares of a disqualified person where the period of such disqualification is for less than five months from the date of disqualification or transfer.

(j) Any provision regarding purchase, redemption or transfer of shares of a professional corporation contained in the articles of incorporation, by-laws or any private agreement shall be specifically enforceable in the courts of this State.

(k) Nothing herein contained shall prevent or relieve a professional corporation from paying pension benefits or other deferred compensation for services rendered to or on behalf of a former shareholder as otherwise permitted by law.

Comment

Existing state statutes generally require that the shares of a deceased or disqualified shareholder be transferred to a qualified shareholder or purchased by the corporation within a specified period of time following the shareholder's death or disqualification. The model act requires payment of fair value for such shares if the corporation does not establish an alternative method, and the procedure for determining fair value set forth in subsections (b) through (f) parallels the procedure set forth in Section 81 of the Model Business Corporation Act with respect to the determination of rights of dissenting shareholders. Shares of a deceased or disqualified shareholder that have not been transferred or purchased within the time limits specified in sub-section (g) are cancelled, and the shareholder's interest becomes a creditor's claim under this section.

One of the troublesome aspects of the requirement that a shareholder of a professional corporation be licensed to practice the profession is the disposition of the corporation entity of a deceased sole practitioner. Under Section 33 of the Model Business Corporation Act the executor of the estate of a sole practitioner may vote the decedent's shares in his professional corporation. See comment following Section 13. Accordingly, if the shares of a deceased shareholder are not transferred, the executor may vote the shares to dissolve the corporation or to amend the articles of incorporation to change its purposes to those of a business corporation. If the executor elects to dissolve, a licensed member of the profession must act as director and president during the winding up of the corporation's affairs. If the executor elects to amend the articles, he may do so himself by signing and filing articles of amendment pursuant to Section 15.

See comment following Section 7 concerning the effect of statutory restrictions against purchases by a corporation of its own shares resulting in impairment of capital or insolvency. To further reduce the possibility of conflict between the insolvency restriction of Section 7 and the requirement for purchase of shares under Section 10 in the event of a judicial determination of fair value, the court is expressly authorized in subsection (d) to order that the judgment be paid in installments.

§ 11. Responsibilities for Professional Services [§ 25]

(a) Any reference to a corporation in this section shall include both domestic and foreign corporations.

(b) Every individual who renders professional services as an employee of a professional corporation shall be liable for any negligent or wrongful act or omission in which he personally participates to the same extent as if he rendered such services as a sole practitioner. An employee of a professional corporation shall not be liable for the conduct of other employees unless he is at fault in appointing, supervising, or cooperating with them.

(c) Every corporation whose employees perform professional services within the scope of their employment or of their apparent authority to act for the corporation shall be liable to the same extent as its employees.

(d) (Alternate 1) Except as otherwise provided by statute, the personal liability of a shareholder of a professional corporation shall be no greater in any respect than that of a shareholder of a corporation organized under the _____ Business Corporation Act.

(d) (Alternate 2) Except as otherwise provided by statute, if any corporation is liable under the provisions of subsection (c) of this section, every shareholder of the corporation shall be liable to the same extent as though he were a partner in a partnership and the services giving rise to liability had been rendered on behalf of the partnership.

(d) (Alternate 3) (1) Except as otherwise provided by statute, if any corporation is liable under the provisions of subsection (c) of this section, every shareholder of that corporation shall be liable to the same extent as though he were a partner in a partnership and the services giving rise to liability had been rendered on behalf of the partnership, unless the corporation has provided security for professional responsibility as provided in paragraph (2) of this subsection and the liability is satisfied to the extent contemplated by the insurance or bond which effectuates the security.

(2) A professional corporation, domestic or foreign, may provide security for professional responsibility by procuring insurance or a surety bond issued by an insurance company, or a combination thereof, as the corporation may elect. The minimum amount of security and requirements as to the form and coverage provided by the insurance policy or surety bond may be established for each profession by the licensing authority for the profession, and the minimum amount may be set to vary with the number of shareholders, the type of practice, or other variables deemed appropriate by the licensing authority. If no effective determination by the licensing authority is in effect, the minimum amount of professional responsibility security for the professional corporation shall be the product of _____[7] dollars multiplied by the number of shareholders of the professional corporation.

Comment

Although all existing state statutes include some provision concerning professional liability or professional responsibility, most statutes are silent as to the vicarious liability of shareholders leaving this question to be determined by the business corporation law. Several statutes clearly provide that shareholder liability is limited as in a business corporation. A few expressly state that shareholders shall be jointly and severally liable for debts of the corporation. And a few, either by statute or rule

[7] A minimum amount to be determined by state legislature.

of practice, condition limited liability for some professions on maintenance of professional liability insurance. A majority of the statutes contain simply a provision to the effect that the statute does not modify any law applicable to the relationship between a person furnishing professional services and a person receiving such services including liability arising out of such professional services. * * * Accordingly, it seems that shareholders of professional corporations have limited liability under existing statutes in most states.

Section 11 of the model act states affirmatively the rules for liability of the professional corporation, its employees, and its shareholders resulting from negligence in the performance of professional services. Consistent with the common law doctrine of respondeat superior, subsection (b) limits liability of a professional employee to his personal negligence, and subsection (c) imposes liability on the corporation for conduct of professional employees within the scope of their employment or of their apparent authority.

Three alternative provisions as to liability of shareholders are proposed in subsection (d): limited liability as in a business corporation, vicarious personal liability as in a partnership, and personal liability limited in amount conditioned upon financial responsibility in the form of insurance or a surety bond. Alternate 3 would permit the licensing authority for each profession to establish the minimum amount of security required as a condition for limiting liability of shareholders and to impose requirements as to the coverage provided by the policy or bond representing the security. The minimum amount of security designated in alternate 3 would apply to any profession only if no minimum has been fixed by the licensing authority for the profession, but no attempt is made in the model act to specify minimum coverage requirements. Each alternate recognizes by the introductory phrase, "Except as otherwise provided by statute," that more specific rules as to shareholder liability may be enacted with respect to a particular profession or professions, but the formulation of statutory requirements as to either the minimum amount of security or coverage for particular professions is beyond the scope of this model act.

Limited liability of shareholders has historically been considered by the courts and by the Internal Revenue Service as one of several characteristics that distinguish the corporation from the partnership. It should be noted, therefore, that the choice of alternates in subsection (d) may affect the tax status of professional corporations formed pursuant to the act.

§ 12. Professional Relationships; Privileged Communications

(a) The relationship between an individual performing professional services as employee of a professional corporation, domestic or foreign, and a client or patient shall be the same as if the individual performed such services as a sole practitioner.

(b) The relationship between a professional corporation, domestic or foreign, performing professional services and the client or patient shall be the same as between the client or patient and the individual performing the services.

(c) Any privilege applicable to communications between a person rendering professional services and the person receiving such services recognized under the laws of this State, whether statutory or deriving from common law, shall remain inviolate and shall extend to a professional corporation, domestic or foreign, and its employees in all cases in which it shall be applicable to communications between a natural person rendering professional services on behalf of the corporation and the person receiving such services.

§ 13. Voting of Shares [§§ 33, 34]

No proxy for shares of a professional corporation shall be valid unless it shall be given to a qualified person. A voting trust with respect to shares of a professional corporation shall not be valid [unless all the trustees and beneficiaries thereof are qualified persons, except that a voting trust may be validly continued for a period of ten months after the death of a deceased beneficiary or for a period of five months after a beneficiary has become a disqualified person].[8]

Comment

Section 13 of the model act requires that the holder of a proxy and the parties to a voting trust agreement be qualified to own shares in the corporation. If shareholders may be personally liable for the performance of professional services rendered on behalf of the corporation, voting trusts should be prohibited to prevent their use to avoid personal liability. See comment following Section 9. With regard to other types of agreements regarding voting of shares, Section 34 of the Model Business Corporation Act providing that agreements among shareholders regarding voting shall be valid and enforceable is unchanged by the professional corporation supplement.

[8] Delete the bracketed clause if alternate 2 or 3 of Section 11(d) is adopted.

Pursuant to Section 33 of the Model Business Corporation Act the shares of a professional corporation held by an administrator, executor, guardian or conservator may be voted without a transfer of such shares, and shares held by a receiver may be voted by the receiver without transfer if such authority is contained in the order of a court by which the receiver was appointed. Upon the death or insolvency of a major shareholder, it may be necessary to dissolve the corporation or amend its articles by changing its purposes to those of a business corporation. The interest of the shareholder's estate will be protected by permitting the holder of his shares to vote on such proposals. In view of the requirement of Section 14 that one-half the directors and the principal officers of a corporation be qualified shareholders, there is no significant risk that an unqualified person may exercise control over the professional practice of the corporation during the period that shares of the corporation may be owned by the estate or receiver of a shareholder under Section 10. Accordingly, the model act does not modify the provisions of the Model Business Corporation Act regarding voting by administrators and receivers.

§ 14. Directors and Officers [§§ 35, 50]

Not less than one-half the directors of a professional corporation and all the officers other than the secretary and the treasurer shall be qualified persons with respect to the corporation.

Comment

Section 14 requires that no less than one-half the directors and the officers other than the secretary and treasurer of a professional corporation be licensed professionals. The professional corporation statute of many states require that all directors be licensed while others require less than all. Most existing statutes also prohibit unlicensed persons from serving as officers with variations as to whether all or only certain designated offices are subject to the requirement.

§ 15. Amendments to Articles of Incorporation [§§ 59, 61]

An administrator, executor, guardian, conservator, or receiver of the estate of a shareholder of a professional corporation who holds all of the outstanding shares of the corporation may amend the articles of incorporation by signing a written consent to such amendment. Articles of amendment so adopted shall be executed in duplicate by the corporation by such administrator, executor, guardian, conservator, or receiver and by the secretary or assistant secretary of the corporation, and verified by one of the persons signing such articles, and shall set forth:

(1) the name of the corporation;

(2) the amendments so adopted;

(3) the date of adoption of the amendment by the administrator, executor, guardian, conservator, or receiver;

(4) the number of shares outstanding; and

(5) the number of shares held by the administrator, executor, guardian, conservator, or receiver.

Comment

Section 15 enables the professional corporation of the sole practitioner to continue in existence following the death of its shareholder and simplifies the procedure for amendment of articles set forth in the Model Business Corporation Act. Without some modification of the Model Business Corporation Act procedure, the executor of the deceased shareholder's estate would be required to find another member of the profession to serve as director and president for the purpose of adopting and filing articles of amendment.

§ 16. Merger and Consolidation [§§ 71, 72, 77]

(a) A professional corporation may merge or consolidate with another corporation, domestic or foreign, only if every shareholder of each corporation is qualified to be a shareholder of the surviving or new corporation.

(b) Upon the merger or consolidation of a professional corporation, if the surviving or new corporation, as the case may be, is to render professional services in this state, it shall comply with the provisions of this Act.

Comment

Section 16 permits mergers and consolidations among professional corporations and business corporations to the extent that professional and business purposes may be combined under Section 3. Many existing professional corporation statutes limit mergers and consolidations to domestic professional corporations incorporated for the purpose of rendering the same professional service. Such a limitation would be inconsistent with Section 3 of this Act permitting a broader statement of purposes and Section 19 providing for admission of foreign professional corporations.

117

§ 17. Termination of Professional Activities

If a professional corporation shall cease to render professional services, it shall amend its articles of incorporation to delete from its stated purposes the rendering of professional services and to conform to the requirements of the _____ Business Corporation Act regarding its corporate name. The corporation may then continue in existence as a corporation under the _____ Business Corporation Act and shall no longer be subject to the provisions of this Act.

Comment

Section 17 resolves any question as to the power of a professional corporation to continue in existence under the business corporation act after it has ceased to render professional services and avoids the forced dissolution of a corporation whose shareholders have died or become disqualified. See comment following Section 10. A corporation which has ceased to render professional services and does not dissolve is required to amend its articles to comply with the business corporation law.

§ 18. Involuntary Dissolution [§§ 94, 95]

A professional corporation may be dissolved involuntarily by a decree of the _____ Court in an action filed by the Attorney General when it is established that the corporation has failed to comply with any provision of this Act applicable to it within sixty days after receipt of written notice of noncompliance. Each licensing authority in this State and the Secretary of State shall certify to the Attorney General, from time to time, the names of all corporations which have given cause for dissolution as provided in this Act, together with the facts pertinent thereto. Whenever the Secretary of State or any licensing authority shall certify the name of a corporation to the Attorney General as having given any cause for dissolution, the Secretary of State or such licensing authority, as the case may be, shall concurrently mail to the corporation at its registered office a notice that such certification has been made. Upon the receipt of such certification, the Attorney General shall file an action in the name of the State against such corporation for its dissolution.

§ 19. Admission of Foreign Professional Corporations [§ 106]

(a) A foreign professional corporation shall be entitled to procure a certificate of authority to transact business in this State only if:

(1) the name of the corporation meets the requirements of this Act;

(2) the corporation is organized only for purposes for which a professional corporation organized under this Act may be organized; and

(3) all the shareholders, not less than one-half the directors, and all the officers other than the secretary and treasurer of the corporation are qualified persons with respect to the corporation.

(b) No foreign professional corporation shall be required to obtain a certificate of authority to transact business in this State unless it shall maintain an office in this State for the conduct of business or professional practice.

Comment

Many small as well as large professional practices are conducted in more than one state by individuals licensed to practice in more than one state or by partnerships whose members are licensed to practice in various states. A serious defect in many existing state statutes is the absence of any provision concerning foreign professional corporations, although several statutes do specifically provide for admission of foreign professional corporations.

Under the foreign corporation provisions of state business corporation laws, foreign corporations are generally admitted with few if any restrictions other than restrictions as to the use of corporate names. In order to prevent a professional corporation from avoiding the professional corporation laws of the state in which it carries on its practice by incorporating in a state with more lenient professional corporation requirements, Section 19 requires that foreign corporations comply with the domestic state law requirements concerning corporate purposes and qualification of shareholders, directors and officers. Under Section 6 a foreign corporation may render professional services only through persons permitted to render such services in the state. Section 11 concerning responsibility for professional services and security for professional responsibility is applicable to foreign corporations as well as domestic corporations; and foreign corporations are subject to regulation by the licensing authority to the same extent as domestic corporations under Section 26.

Section 19(b) requires that a professional corporation obtain a certificate of authority only if the corporation maintains an office in the state. This provision would permit foreign professional corporations greater freedom in rendering professional services in the state without complying with foreign corporation law requirements than is permitted in the case of business corporations.

119

§ 20. Application for Certificate of Authority [§ 110]

The application of a foreign professional corporation for a certificate of authority for the purpose of rendering professional services shall include a statement that all the shareholders, not less than one-half the directors, and all the officers other than the secretary and treasurer are licensed in one or more states or territories of the United States or the District of Columbia to render a professional service described in the statement of purposes of the corporation.

§ 21. Revocation of Certificate of Authority [§ 121]

The certificate of authority of a foreign professional corporation may be revoked by the Secretary of State if the corporation fails to comply with any provision of this Act applicable to it. Each licensing authority in this State shall certify to the Secretary of State, from time to time, the names of all foreign professional corporations which have given cause for revocation as provided in this Act, together with the facts pertinent thereto. Whenever a licensing authority shall certify the name of a corporation to the Secretary of State as having given cause for dissolution, the licensing authority shall concurrently mail to the corporation at its registered office in this State a notice that such certification has been made. No certificate of authority of a foreign professional corporation shall be revoked by the Secretary of State unless he shall have given the corporation not less than sixty days' notice thereof and the corporation shall fail prior to revocation to correct such noncompliance.

§ 22. Annual Report of Domestic and Foreign Professional Corporations [§ 125]

(a) The annual report of each domestic professional corporation, and each foreign professional corporation authorized to transact business in this State, filed with the Secretary of State pursuant to the _____ Business Corporation Act shall include a statement that all the shareholders, not less than one-half the directors, and all the officers other than the secretary and treasurer of the corporation are qualified persons with respect to the corporation.

(b) Financial information contained in the annual report of a professional corporation, other than the amount of stated capital of the corporation, shall not be open to public inspection nor shall the licensing authority disclose any facts or information obtained therefrom except insofar as its official duty may require the same to be made public or in the event such information is required for evidence in any criminal proceedings or in any other action by this State.

§ 23. Annual Statement of Qualification of Domestic and Foreign Professional Corporations

(a) Each domestic professional corporation, and each foreign professional corporation, authorized to transact business in this State, shall file annually before March 1 with each licensing authority having jurisdiction over a professional service of a type described in its articles of incorporation a statement of qualification setting forth the names and respective addresses of the directors and officers of the corporation and such additional information as the licensing authority may by rule prescribe as appropriate in determining whether such corporation is complying with the provisions of this Act and rules promulgated hereunder.

(b) The licensing authority shall charge and collect a fee of _____ dollars for filing a statement of qualification pursuant to this Act.

Comment

Many existing professional corporation statutes require the filing of an annual report with the Secretary of State or licensing authority setting forth the names and addresses of all shareholders of the corporation. The model act requires that a professional corporation file an annual statement with the licensing authority setting forth the names and addresses of directors and officers and authorizes the licensing authority to require additional information which might include names and addresses of shareholders.

§ 24. Interrogatories by Licensing Authority [§§ 137, 138]

(a) Each licensing authority of this State may propound to any professional corporation, domestic or foreign, organized to practice a profession within the jurisdiction of such licensing authority, and to any officer or director thereof, such interrogatories as may be reasonably necessary and proper to enable the licensing authority to ascertain whether such corporation has complied with all the provisions of this Act applicable to such corporation. Such interrogatories shall be answered within thirty days after the mailing thereof, or within such additional time as shall be fixed by the licensing authority, and the answers thereto shall be full and complete and shall be made in writing and under oath. If such interrogatories be directed to an individual they shall be answered by him, and if directed to a corporation they shall be answered by the president, vice president, secretary or assistant secretary thereof. The licensing authority shall certify to the Attorney General, for such action as the

Attorney General may deem appropriate, all interrogatories and answers thereto which disclose a violation of any of the provisions of this Act.

(b) Interrogatories propounded by a licensing authority and the answers thereto shall not be open to public inspection nor shall the licensing authority disclose any facts or information obtained therefrom except insofar as its official duty may require the same to be made public or in the event such interrogatories or the answers thereto are required for evidence in any criminal proceedings or in any other action by this State.

§ 25. Penalties [§§ 135, 136]

(a) Each professional corporation, domestic or foreign, that fails or refuses to answer truthfully within the time prescribed by this Act interrogatories propounded in accordance with the provisions of this Act by the licensing authority having jurisdiction of a type of professional service described in the articles of incorporation of such corporation, shall be deemed to be guilty of a misdemeanor and upon conviction thereof may be fined in any amount not exceeding five hundred dollars.

(b) Each officer and director of a professional corporation, domestic or foreign, who fails or refuses within the time prescribed by this Act to answer truthfully and fully interrogatories propounded to him in accordance with the provisions of this Act by the licensing authority having jurisdiction of a type of professional service described in the articles of incorporation of such corporation, or who signs any articles, statement, report, application or other document filed with such licensing authority which is known to such officer or director to be false in any material respect, shall be deemed to be guilty of a misdemeanor, and upon conviction thereof may be fined in any amount not exceeding _____ dollars.

§ 26. Regulation of Professional Corporations

No professional corporation, domestic or foreign, shall begin to render professional services in this State until it has filed a copy of its articles of incorporation with each licensing authority having jurisdiction of a type of professional service described in its articles of incorporation. Each licensing authority in this State is hereby authorized to promulgate rules in accordance with the provisions of this Act which specifically provide for the issuance of rules to the extent consistent with the public interest or required by the public health or welfare or by generally recognized standards of professional conduct. Nothing in this Act shall restrict or limit in any manner the authority or duty of a licensing authority with respect to natural persons rendering a professional service within the jurisdiction of the licensing authority, or any law, rule or regulation pertaining to standards of professional conduct.

§ 27. Application of Business Corporation Act

The provisions of the _____ Business Corporation Act shall apply to professional corporations, domestic and foreign, except to the extent such provisions are inconsistent with the provisions of this Act.

§ 28. Application to Existing Corporations [§ 147]

(a) The provisions of this Act shall apply to all existing corporations organized under any general act of this State which is repealed by this Act. Every such existing corporation which shall be required to amend its corporate name or purposes to comply with this Act shall deliver duly executed duplicate originals of articles of amendment or restated articles of incorporation containing such amendments to the Secretary of State within ninety days after the effective date of this Act.

(b) Any corporation organized under any act of this State which is not repealed hereby may become subject to the provisions of this Act by delivering to the Secretary of State duly executed duplicate originals of articles of amendment or restated articles of incorporation stating that the corporation elects to become subject to this Act and containing such amendment of its corporate name or purposes as may be required to comply with this Act.

(c) The provisions of this Act shall not apply to any corporation now in existence or hereafter organized under any act of this State which is not repealed hereby unless such corporation voluntarily becomes subject to this Act as herein provided, and nothing contained in this Act shall alter or affect any existing or future right or privilege permitting or not prohibiting performance of professional services through the use of any other form of business organization.

Comment

While most states have adopted a single general professional corporation law applicable to all covered professions, several states have adopted a series of professional corporation laws applicable to individual professions. Section 28 of the model act sets forth procedures with respect to existing corporations which include mandatory provisions applicable to corporations incorporated under a repealed act and also provisions for voluntary compliance with this act by corporations organized under acts which may not be repealed.

§ 29.   Reservation of Power [§ 149]

The _____[9] shall at all times have power to prescribe such regulations, provisions and limitations as it may deem advisable, which regulations, provisions and limitations shall be binding upon any and all corporations subject to the provisions of this Act, and the _____[10] shall have power to amend, repeal or modify this Act at pleasure.

§ 30.   Effect of Repeal of Prior Acts [§ 150]

The repeal of a prior act by this Act shall not affect any right accrued or established, or any liability or penalty incurred, under the provisions of such act, prior to the repeal thereof.

§ 31.   Effect of Invalidity of Part of this Act [§ 151]

If a court of competent jurisdiction shall adjudge to be invalid or unconstitutional any clause, sentence, paragraph, section or part of this Act, such judgment or decree shall not affect, impair, invalidate or nullify the remainder of this Act, but the effect thereof shall be confined to the clause, sentence, paragraph, section or part of this Act so adjudged to be invalid or unconstitutional.

§ 32.   Repeal of Prior Acts [§ 152]

[*Insert appropriate provisions*]

*   *   *

Blue Sky Law Exemption

In most states the interest of a partner in a professional partnership is exempted by definition or otherwise from the application of the state securities law. A few states have exempted shares of a professional corporation, but many states have ignored this problem in enacting professional corporation laws. Because the "one subject" requirement of state constitutions may prohibit amendment of the state securities law in a professional corporation act, the model act does not create a securities law exemption for shares of professional corporations. It is recommended, however, that shares of professional corporations be exempted from the state securities law by appropriate amendment of that law.

---

[9] Insert name of legislative body.   [10] Insert name of legislative body.

C. CALIFORNIA GENERAL CORPORATION LAW
(Selected Sections)
Contents

CHAPTER 1.   GENERAL PROVISIONS
AND DEFINITIONS

§ 158.   Close corporation

(a) "Close corporation" means a corporation whose articles contain, in addition to the provisions required by Section 202, a provision that all of the corporation's issued shares of all classes shall be held of record by not more than a specified number of persons, not exceeding 10, and a statement "This corporation is a close corporation."

(b) The special provisions referred to in subdivision (a) may be included in the articles by amendment, but if such amendment is adopted after the issuance of shares only by the affirmative vote of all of the issue and outstanding shares of all classes.

(c) The special provisions referred to in subdivision (a) may be deleted from the articles by amendment, or the number of shareholders specified may be changed by amendment, but if such amendment is adopted after the issuance of shares only by the affirmative vote of at least two-thirds of each class of the outstanding shares; provided, however, that the articles may provide for a lesser vote, but not less than a majority of the outstanding shares, or may deny a vote to any class, or both.

§ 160.   Control

(a) Except as provided in subdivision (b), "control" means the possession, direct or indirect, of the power to direct or cause the direction of the management and policies of a corporation.

(b) "Control" in Sections 181, 1001 and 1200 means the ownership directly or indirectly of shares possessing more than 50 percent of the voting power.

§ 166.   Distribution to its shareholders

"Distribution to its shareholders" means the transfer of cash or property by a corporation to its shareholders without consideration, whether by way of dividend or otherwise, except a dividend in shares of the corporation, or the purchase or redemption of its shares for cash or property, including such transfer, purchase or redemption by a subsidiary of the corporation. The time of any distribution by way of dividend shall be the date of declaration thereof and the time of any distribution by purchase or redemption of shares shall be the date cash or property is transferred by the corporation, whether or not pursuant to a contract of an earlier date; provided, that where a negotiable debt security (as defined in subdivision (1) of Section 8102 of the Commercial Code) is issued in exchange for shares the time of the distribution is the date when the corporation acquires the shares in such exchange. In the case of a sinking fund payment, cash or property is transferred within the meaning of this section at the time that it is delivered to a trustee for the holders of preferred shares to be used for the redemption of such shares or physically segregated by the corporation in trust for that purpose.

§ 172. Liquidation price; liquidation preference

"Liquidation price" or "liquidation preference" means amounts payable on shares of any class upon voluntary or involuntary dissolution, winding up or distribution of the entire assets of the corporation, including any cumulative dividends accrued and unpaid, in priority to shares of another class or classes.

§ 181. Reorganization

"Reorganization" means:

(a) A merger pursuant to Chapter 11 (commencing with Section 1100) other than a short-form merger (a "merger reorganization");

(b) The acquisition by one corporation in exchange in whole or in part for its equity securities (or the equity securities of a corporation which is in control of the acquiring corporation) of shares of another corporation if, immediately after the acquisition, the acquiring corporation has control of such other corporation (an "exchange reorganization"); or

(c) The acquisition by one corporation in exchange in whole or in part for its equity securities (or the equity securities of a corporation which is in control of the acquiring corporation) or for its debt securities (or debt securities of a corporation which is in control of the acquiring corporation) which are not adequately secured and which have a maturity date in excess of five years after the consummation of the reorganization, or both, of all or substantially all of the assets of another corporation (a "sale-of-assets reorganization").

§ 186. Shareholders' agreement

"Shareholders' agreement" means a written agreement among all of the shareholders of a close corporation, or if a close corporation has only one shareholder between such shareholder and the corporation, as authorized by subdivision (b) of Section 300.

CHAPTER 2. ORGANIZATION AND BYLAWS

§ 204. Articles of incorporation; optional provisions

The articles of incorporation may set forth:

(a) Any or all of the following provisions, which shall not be effective unless expressly provided in the articles:

(1) Granting, with or without limitations, the power to levy assessments upon the shares or any class of shares;

(2) Granting to shareholders preemptive rights to subscribe to any or all issues of shares or securities;

(3) Special qualifications of persons who may be shareholders;

(4) A provision limiting the duration of the corporation's existence to a specified date;

(5) A provision requiring, for any or all corporate actions (except as provided in Section 303, subdivision (c) of Section 708 and Section 1900) the vote of a larger proportion or of all of the shares of any class or series, or the vote or quorum for taking action of a larger proportion or of all of the directors, than is otherwise required by this division;

(6) A provision limiting or restricting the business in which the corporation may engage or the powers which the corporation may exercise or both;

(7) A provision conferring upon the holders of any evidences of indebtedness, issued or to be issued by the corporation, the right to vote in the election of directors and on any other matters on which shareholders may vote;

(8) A provision conferring upon shareholders the right to determine the consideration for which shares shall be issued.

(9) A provision requiring the approval of the shareholders (Section 153) or the approval of the outstanding shares (Section 152) for any corporate action, even though not otherwise required by this division.

Notwithstanding this subdivision, in the case of a close corporation any of the provisions referred to above may be validly included in a shareholders' agreement. Notwithstanding this subdivision, bylaws may require for all or any actions by the board the affirmative vote of a majority of the authorized number of directors. Nothing contained in this subdivision shall affect the enforceability, as between the parties thereto, of any lawful agreement not otherwise contrary to public policy.

(b) Reasonable restrictions upon the right to transfer or hypothecate shares of any class or classes or series, but no restriction shall be binding with respect to shares issued prior to the adoption of the restriction unless the holders of such shares voted in favor of the restriction.

(c) The names and addresses of the persons appointed to act as initial directors.

(d) Any other provision, not in conflict with law, for the management of the business and for the conduct of the affairs of the corporation, including any provision which is required or permitted by this division to be stated in the bylaws.

§ 212. Bylaws; contents

(a) The bylaws shall set forth (unless such provision is contained in the articles, in which case it may only be changed by an amendment of the articles) the number of directors of the corporation; or that the number of directors shall be not less than a stated minimum nor more than a stated maximum (which in no case shall be greater than two times the stated minimum minus one), with the exact number of directors to be fixed, within the limits specified, by approval of the board or the shareholders (Section 153) in the manner provided in the bylaws, subject to paragraph (5) of subdivision (a) of Section 204. The number or minimum number of directors shall not be less than three; provided, however, that (1) before shares are issued, the number may be one, (2) before shares are issued, the number may be two, (3) so long as the corporation has only one shareholder, the number may be one, (4) so long as the corporation has only one shareholder, the number may be two, and (5) so long as the corporation has only two shareholders, the number may be two. After the issuance of shares, a bylaw specifying or changing a fixed number of directors or the maximum or minimum number or changing from a fixed to a variable board or vice versa may only be adopted by approval of the outstanding shares (Section 152); provided, however, that a bylaw or amendment of the articles reducing the fixed number or the minimum number of directors to a number less than five cannot be adopted if the votes cast against its adoption at a meeting or the shares not consenting in the case of action by written consent are equal to more than 16⅔ percent of the outstanding shares entitled to vote.

(b) The bylaws may contain any provision, not in conflict with law or the articles for the management of the business and for the conduct of the affairs of the corporation, including but not limited to:

(1) Any provision referred to in subdivision (b), (c) or (d) of Section 204.

(2) The time, place and manner of calling, conducting and giving notice of shareholders', directors' and committee meetings.

(3) The manner of execution, revocation and use of proxies.

(4) The qualifications, duties and compensation of directors; the time of their annual election; and the requirements of a quorum for directors' and committee meetings.

(5) The appointment and authority of committees of the board.

(6) The appointment, duties, compensation and tenure of officers.

(7) The mode of determination of holders of record of its shares.

(8) The making of annual reports and financial statements to the shareholders.

CHAPTER 3. DIRECTORS AND MANAGEMENT

§ 300. Powers of board; delegation; close corporations; shareholders' agreements; validity; liability; failure to observe formalities

(a) Subject to the provisions of this division and any limitations in the articles relating to action required to be approved by the shareholders (Section 153) or by the outstanding shares (Section 152), the business and affairs of the corporation shall be managed and all corporate powers shall be exercised by or under the direction of the board. The board may delegate the management of the day-to-day operation of the business of the corporation to a management company or other person provided that the business and affairs of the corporation shall be managed and all corporate powers shall be exercised under the ultimate direction of the board.

(b) Notwithstanding subdivision (a) or any other provision of this division, but subject to subdivision (c), no shareholders' agreement, which relates to any phase of the affairs of a close corporation, including but not limited to management of its business, division of its profits or distribution of its assets on liquidation, shall be invalid as between the parties thereto on the ground that it so relates to the conduct of the affairs of the corporation as to interfere with the discretion of the board or that it is an attempt to treat the corporation as if it were a partnership or to arrange their relationships in a manner that would be appropriate only between partners. A transferee of shares covered by such an agreement which is filed with the secretary of the corporation for inspection by any prospective purchaser of shares, who has actual knowledge thereof or notice thereof by a notation on the certificate pursuant to Section 418, is bound by its provisions and is a party thereto for the purposes of subdivision (d). Original issuance of shares by the corporation to a new shareholder who does not become a party to the agreement terminates the agreement, except that if the agreement so provides it shall continue to the extent it is enforceable apart from this subdivision. The agreement may not be modified, extended or revoked without the consent of such a transferee, subject to any provision of the agreement permitting modification, extension or revocation by less than unanimous agreement of the parties. A transferor of shares covered by such an agreement ceases to be a party thereto upon ceasing to be a shareholder of the corporation unless the transferor is a party thereto other than as a shareholder. An agreement made pursuant to this subdivision shall terminate when the corporation ceases to be a close corporation, except that if the agreement so provides it shall continue to the extent it is enforceable apart from this subdivision. This subdivision does not apply to an agreement authorized by subdivision (a) of Section 706.

(c) No agreement entered into pursuant to subdivision (b) may alter or waive any of the provisions of Sections 158, 417, 418, 500, 501, and 1111, subdivision (e) of Section 1201, Sections 2009, 2010, and 2011, or of Chapters 15 (commencing with Section 1500), 16 (commencing with Section 1600), 18 (commencing with Section 1800), and 22 (commencing with Section 2200). All other provisions of this division may be altered or waived as between the parties thereto in a shareholders' agreement, except the required filing of any document with the Secretary of State.

(d) An agreement of the type referred to in subdivision (b) shall, to the extent and so long as the discretion or powers of the board in its management of corporate affairs is controlled by such agreement, impose upon each shareholder who is a party thereto liability for managerial acts performed or omitted by such person pursuant thereto that is otherwise imposed by this division upon directors, and the directors shall be relieved to that extent from such liability.

(e) The failure of a close corporation to observe corporate formalities relating to meetings of directors or shareholders in connection with the management of its affairs, pursuant to an agreement authorized by subdivision (b), shall not be considered a factor tending to establish that the shareholders have personal liability for corporate obligations.

§ 301. Directors; election; term

(a) At each annual meeting of shareholders, directors shall be elected to hold office until the next annual meeting. The articles may provide for the election of one or more directors by the holders of the shares of any class or series voting as a class or series.

(b) Each director, including a director elected to fill a vacancy, shall hold office until the expiration of the term for which elected and until a successor has been elected and qualified.

§ 303. Directors; removal without cause

(a) Any or all of the directors may be removed without cause if such removal is approved by the outstanding shares (Section 152), subject to the following:

(1) No director may be removed (unless the entire board is removed) when the votes cast against removal, or not consenting in writing to such removal, would be sufficient to elect such director if voted cumulatively at an election at which the same total number of votes were cast (or, if such action is taken by written consent, all shares entitled to vote were voted) and the entire number of directors authorized at the time of the director's most recent election were then being elected; and

(2) When by the provisions of the articles the holders of the shares of any class or series, voting as a class or series, are entitled to elect one or more directors, any director so elected may be removed only by the applicable vote of the holders of the shares of that class or series.

(b) Any reduction of the authorized number of directors does not remove any director prior to the expiration of such director's term of office.

(c) Except as provided in this section and Sections 302 and 304, a director may not be removed prior to the expiration of such director's term of office.

§ 307. Meetings

(a) Unless otherwise provided in the articles or (subject to paragraph (5) of subdivision (a) of Section 204) in the bylaws:

(1) Meetings of the board may be called by the chairman of the board or the president or any vice president or the secretary or any two directors.

(2) Regular meetings of the board may be held without notice if the time and place of such meetings are fixed by the bylaws or the board. Special meetings of the board shall be held upon four days' notice by mail or 48 hours' notice delivered personally or by telephone or telegraph. The articles or bylaws

may not dispense with notice of a special meeting. A notice, or waiver of notice, need not specify the purpose of any regular or special meeting of the board.

(3) Notice of a meeting need not be given to any director who signs a waiver of notice or a consent to holding the meeting or an approval of the minutes thereof, whether before or after the meeting, or who attends the meeting without protesting, prior thereto or at its commencement, the lack of notice to such director. All such waivers, consents and approvals shall be filed with the corporate records or made a part of the minutes of the meeting.

(4) A majority of the directors present, whether or not a quorum is present, may adjourn any meeting to another time and place. If the meeting is adjourned for more than 24 hours, notice of any adjournment to another time or place shall be given prior to the time of the adjourned meeting to the directors who were not present at the time of the adjournment.

(5) Meetings of the board may be held at any place within or without the state which has been designated in the notice of the meeting or, if not stated in the notice or there is no notice, designated in the bylaws or by resolution of the board.

(6) Members of the board may participate in a meeting through use of conference telephone or similar communications equipment, so long as all members participating in such meeting can hear one another. Participation in a meeting pursuant to this subdivision constitutes presence in person at such meeting.

(7) A majority of the authorized number of directors constitutes a quorum of the board for the transaction of business. The articles or bylaws may not provide that a quorum shall be less than one-third the authorized number of directors or less than two, whichever is larger, unless the authorized number of directors is one, in which case one director constitutes a quorum.

(8) Every act or decision done or made by a majority of the directors present at a meeting duly held at which a quorum is present is the act of the board, subject to the provisions of Section 310 and subdivision (e) of Section 317. The articles or bylaws may not provide that a lesser vote than a majority of the directors present at a meeting is the act of the board. A meeting at which a quorum is initially present may continue to transact business notwithstanding the withdrawal of directors, if any action taken is approved by at least a majority of the required quorum for such meeting.

(b) Any action required or permitted to be taken by the board may be taken without a meeting, if all members of the board shall individually or collectively consent in writing to such action. Such written consent or consents shall be filed with the minutes of the proceedings of the board. Such action by written consent shall have the same force and effect as a unanimous vote of such directors.

(c) The provisions of this section apply also to committees of the board and incorporators and action by such committees and incorporators, mutatis mutandis.

§ 309. Performance of duties by director; liability

(a) A director shall perform the duties of a director, including duties as a member of any committee of the board upon which the director may serve, in good faith, in a manner such director believes to be in the best interests of the corporation and with such care, including reasonable inquiry, as an ordinarily prudent person in a like position would use under similar circumstances.

(b) In performing the duties of a director, a director shall be entitled to rely on information, opinions, reports or statements, including financial statements and other financial data, in each case prepared or presented by:

(1) One or more officers or employees of the corporation whom the director believes to be reliable and competent in the matters presented,

(2) Counsel, independent accountants or other persons as to matters which the director believes to be within such person's professional or expert competence, or

(3) A committee of the board upon which the director does not serve, as to matters within its designated authority, which committee the director believes to merit confidence,

so long as, in any such case, the director acts in good faith, after reasonable inquiry when the need therefor is indicated by the circumstances and without knowledge that would cause such reliance to be unwarranted.

(c) A person who performs the duties of a director in accordance with subdivisions (a) and (b) shall have no liability based upon any alleged failure to discharge the person's obligations as a director.

§ 310. Contracts in which director has material financial interest; validity

(a) No contract or other transaction between a corporation and one or more of its directors, or between a corporation and any corporation, firm or association in which one or more of its directors has a material financial interest, is either void or voidable because such director or directors or such other corporation, firm or association are parties or because such director or directors are present at the meeting of the board or a committee thereof which authorizes, approves or ratifies the contract or transaction, if

(1) The material facts as to the transaction and as to such director's interest are fully disclosed or known to the shareholders and such contract or transaction is approved by the shareholders (Section 153) in good faith, with the shares owned by the interested director or directors not being entitled to vote thereon, or

(2) The material facts as to the transaction and as to such director's interest are fully disclosed or known to the board or committee, and the board or committee authorizes, approves or ratifies the contract or transaction in good faith by a vote sufficient without counting the vote of the interested director or directors and the contract or transaction is just and reasonable as to the corporation at the time it is authorized, approved or ratified, or

(3) As to contracts or transactions not approved as provided in paragraph (1) or (2) of this subdivision, the person asserting the validity of the contract or transaction sustains the burden of proving that the contract or transaction was just and reasonable as to the corporation at the time it was authorized, approved or ratified.

A mere common directorship does not constitute a material financial interest within the meaning of this subdivision. A director is not interested within the meaning of this subdivision in a resolution fixing the compensation of another director as a director, officer or employee of the corporation, notwithstanding the fact that the first director is also receiving compensation from the corporation.

(b) No contract or other transaction between a corporation and any corporation or association of which one or more of its directors are directors is either void or voidable because such director or directors are present at the meeting of the board or a committee thereof which authorizes, approves or ratifies the contract or transaction, if

(1) The material facts as to the transaction and as to such director's other directorship are fully disclosed or known to the board or committee, and the board or committee authorizes, approves or ratifies the contract or transaction in good faith by a vote sufficient without counting the vote of the common director or directors or the contract or transaction is approved by the shareholders (Section 153) in good faith, or

(2) As to contracts or transactions not approved as provided in paragraph (1) of this subdivision, the contract or transaction is just and reasonable as to the corporation at the time it is authorized, approved or ratified.

This subdivision does not apply to contracts or transactions covered by subdivision (a).

(c) Interested or common directors may be counted in determining the presence of a quorum at a meeting of the board or a committee thereof which authorizes, approves or ratifies a contract or transaction.

§ 313. Instrument in writing and assignment or endorsement thereof; signatures; validity

Subject to the provisions of subdivision (a) of Section 208, any note, mortgage, evidence of indebtedness, contract, share certificate, conveyance or other instrument in writing, and any assignment or endorsement thereof, executed or entered into between any corporation and any other person, when signed by the chairman of the board, the president or any vice president and the secretary, any assistant secretary, the chief financial officer or any assistant treasurer of such corporation, is not invalidated as to the corporation by any lack of authority of the signing officers in the absence of actual knowledge on the part of the other person that the signing officers had no authority to execute the same.

§ 317. Indemnification of agent of corporation in proceedings or actions

(a) For the purposes of this section, "agent" means any person who is or was a director, officer, employee or other agent of the corporation, or is or was serving at the request of the corporation as a director, officer, employee or agent of another foreign or domestic corporation, partnership, joint venture, trust or other enterprise, or was a director, officer, employee or agent of a foreign or domestic corporation which was a predecessor corporation of the corporation or of another enterprise at the request of such predecessor corporation; "proceeding" means any threatened, pending or completed action or proceeding, whether civil, criminal, administrative or investigative; and "expenses" includes without limitation attorneys' fees and any expenses of establishing a right to indemnification under subdivision (d) or paragraph (3) of subdivision (e).

(b) A corporation shall have power to indemnify any person who was or is a party or is threatened to be made a party to any proceeding (other than an action by or in the right of the corporation to procure a judgment in its favor) by reason of the fact that such person is or was an agent of the corporation, against expenses, judgments, fines, settlements and other amounts actually and reasonably incurred in connection with such proceeding if such person acted in good faith and in a manner such person reasonably believed to be in the best interests of the corporation and, in the case of a criminal proceeding, had no reasonable cause to believe the conduct of such person was unlawful. The termination of any proceeding by judgment, order, settlement, conviction or upon a plea of nolo contendere or its equivalent shall not, of itself, create a presumption that the person did not act in good faith and in a manner which the person reasonably believed to be in the best interests of the corporation or that the person had reasonable cause to believe that the person's conduct was unlawful.

(c) A corporation shall have power to indemnify any person who was or is a party or is threatened to be made a party to any threatened, pending or completed action by or in the right of the corporation to procure a judgment in its favor by reason of the fact that such person is or was an agent of the corporation, against expenses actually and reasonably incurred by such person in connection with the defense or settlement of such action if such person acted in good faith, in a manner such person believed to be in the best interests of the corporation and with such care, including reasonable inquiry, as an ordinarily prudent person in a like position would use under similar circumstances. No indemnification shall be made under this subdivision (c):

(1) In respect of any claim, issue or matter as to which such person shall have been adjudged to be liable to the corporation in the performance of such person's duty to the corporation, unless and only to the extent that the court in which such proceeding is or was pending shall determine upon application that, in view of all the circumstances of the case, such person is fairly and reasonably entitled to indemnity for the expenses which such court shall determine;

(2) Of amounts paid in settling or otherwise disposing of a threatened or pending action, with or without court approval; or

(3) Of expenses incurred in defending a threatened or pending action which is settled or otherwise disposed of without court approval.

(d) To the extent that an agent of a corporation has been successful on the merits in defense of any proceeding referred to in subdivision (b) or (c) or in defense of any claim, issue or matter therein, the agent shall be indemnified against expenses actually and reasonably incurred by the agent in connection therewith.

(e) Except as provided in subdivision (d), any indemnification under this section shall be made by the corporation only if authorized in the specific case, upon a determination that indemnification of the agent is proper in the circumstances because the agent has met the applicable standard of conduct set forth in subdivision (b) or (c), by:

(1) A majority vote of a quorum consisting of directors who are not parties to such proceeding;

(2) Approval of the shareholders (Section 153), with the shares owned by the person to be indemnified not being entitled to vote thereon; or

(3) The court in which such proceeding is or was pending upon application made by the corporation or the agent or the attorney or other person rendering services in connection with the defense, whether or not such application by the agent, attorney or other person is opposed by the corporation.

(f) Expenses incurred in defending any proceeding may be advanced by the corporation prior to the final disposition of such proceeding upon receipt of an undertaking by or on behalf of the agent to repay such amount unless it shall be determined ultimately that the agent is entitled to be indemnified as authorized in this section.

(g) No provision made by a corporation to indemnify its or its subsidiary's directors or officers for the defense of any proceeding, whether contained in the articles, bylaws, a resolution of shareholders or directors, an agreement or otherwise, shall be valid unless consistent with this section. Nothing contained in this section shall affect any right to indemnification to which persons other than such directors and officers may be entitled by contract or otherwise.

(h) No indemnification or advance shall be made under this section, except as provided in subdivision (d) or paragraph (3) of subdivision (e), in any circumstance where it appears:

(1) That it would be inconsistent with a provision of the articles, bylaws, a resolution of the shareholders or an agreement in effect at the time of the accrual of the alleged cause of action asserted in the proceeding in which the expenses were incurred or other amounts were paid, which prohibits or otherwise limits indemnification; or

(2) That it would be inconsistent with any condition expressly imposed by a court in approving a settlement.

(i) A corporation shall have power to purchase and maintain insurance on behalf of any agent of the corporation against any liability asserted against or incurred by the agent in such capacity or arising out of the agent's status as such whether or not the corporation would have the power to indemnify the agent against such liability under the provisions of this section.

(j) This section does not apply to any proceeding against any trustee, investment manager or other fiduciary of an employee benefit plan in such person's capacity as such, even though such person may also be an agent as defined in subdivision (a) of the employer corporation. A corporation shall have power to indemnify such a trustee, investment manager or other fiduciary to the extent permitted by subdivision (f) of Section 207.

CHAPTER 4. SHARES AND SHARE CERTIFICATES

§ 409. Issuance of shares; consideration; liability to call; determination by shareholders; valuation of property other than money by board resolution

(a) Shares may be issued:

(1) For such consideration as is determined from time to time by the board, or by the shareholders if the articles so provide, consisting of any or all of the following: money paid; labor done; services actually rendered to the corporation or for its benefit or in its formation or reorganization; debts or securities canceled; and tangible or intangible property actually received either by the issuing corporation or by a wholly owned subsidiary; but neither promissory notes of the purchaser (unless adequately secured by collateral other than the shares acquired or unless permitted by Section 408) nor future services shall constitute payment or part payment for shares of the corporation; or

(2) As a share dividend or upon a stock split, reverse stock split, reclassification of outstanding shares into shares of another class, conversion of outstanding shares into shares of another class, exchange of outstanding shares for shares of another class or other change affecting outstanding shares.

(b) Except as provided in subdivision (d), shares issued as provided in this section or Section 408 shall be declared and taken to be fully paid stock and not liable to any further call nor shall the holder thereof be liable for any further payments under the provisions of this division. In the absence of fraud in the transaction, the judgment of the directors as to the value of the consideration for shares shall be conclusive.

(c) If the articles reserve to the shareholders the right to determine the consideration for the issue of any shares, such determination shall be made by approval of the outstanding shares (Section 152).

(d) A corporation may issue the whole or any part of its shares as partly paid and subject to call for the remainder of the consideration to be paid therefor. On the certificate issued to represent any such partly paid shares the total amount of the consideration to be paid therefor and the amount paid thereon shall be stated. Upon the declaration of any dividend on fully paid shares, the corporation shall declare a dividend upon partly paid shares of the same class, but only upon the basis of the percentage of the consideration actually paid thereon.

(e) The board shall state by resolution its determination of the fair value to the corporation in monetary terms of any consideration other than money for which shares are issued. This subdivision does not affect the accounting treatment of any transaction, which shall be in conformity with generally accepted accounting principles.

§ 410. Liability for full agreed consideration; time of payment

(a) Every subscriber to shares and every person to whom shares are originally issued is liable to the corporation for the full consideration agreed to be paid for the shares.

(b) The full agreed consideration for shares shall be paid prior to or concurrently with the issuance thereof, unless the shares are issued as partly paid pursuant to subdivision (d) of Section 409, in which case the consideration shall be paid in accordance with the agreement of subscription or purchase.

§ 414. Creditor's remedy to reach liability due corporation on shares

(a) No action shall be brought by or on behalf of any creditor to reach and apply the liability, if any, of a shareholder to the corporation to pay the amount due on such shareholder's shares unless final judgment has been rendered in favor of the creditor against the corporation and execution has been returned unsatisfied in whole or in part or unless such proceedings would be useless.

* * *

CHAPTER 5. DIVIDENDS AND REACQUISITIONS OF SHARES

§ 500. Distribution; retained earnings or assets remaining after completion

Neither a corporation nor any of its subsidiaries shall make any distribution to the corporation's shareholders (Section 166) unless:

(a) The amount of the retained earnings of the corporation immediately prior thereto equals or exceeds the amount of the proposed distribution; or

(b) Immediately after giving effect thereto:

(1) The sum of the assets of the corporation (exclusive of goodwill, capitalized research and development expenses and deferred charges) would be at least equal to 1¼ times its liabilities (not including deferred taxes, deferred income and other deferred credits); and

(2) The current assets of the corporation would be at least equal to its current liabilities or, if the average of the earnings of the corporation before taxes on income and before interest expense for the two preceding fiscal years was less than the average of the interest expense of the corporation for such fiscal years, at least equal to 1¼ times its current liabilities; provided, however, that in determining the amount of the assets of the corporation profits derived from an exchange of assets shall not be included unless the assets received are currently realizable in cash; and provided, further, that for the purpose of this subdivision "current assets" may include net amounts which the board has determined in good faith may reasonably be expected to be received from customers during the 12-month period used in calculating current liabilities pursuant to existing contractual relationships obligating such customers to make fixed or periodic payments during the term of the contract or, in the case of public utilities, pursuant to service connections with customers, after in each case giving effect to future costs not then included in current liabilities but reasonably expected to be incurred by the corporation in performing such contracts or providing service to utility customers. The amount of any distribution payable in property shall, for the purpose of this chapter, be determined on the basis of the value at which such property is carried on the corporation's financial statements in accordance with generally accepted accounting principles. Paragraph (2) of subdivision (b) is not applicable to a corporation which does not classify its assets into current and fixed under generally accepted accounting principles.

§ 501. Inability to meet liabilities as they mature; prohibition of distribution

Neither a corporation nor any of its subsidiaries shall make any distribution to the corporation's shareholders (Section 166) if the corporation or the subsidiary making the distribution is, or as a result thereof would be, likely to be unable to meet its liabilities (except those whose payment is otherwise adequately provided for) as they mature.

§ 502.   Distribution to junior shares if excess of assets over liabilities less than liquidation preference of senior shares; prohibition

Neither a corporation nor any of its subsidiaries shall make any distribution to the corporation's shareholders (Section 166) on any shares of its stock of any class or series which are junior to outstanding shares of any other class or series with respect to distribution of assets on liquidation if, after giving effect thereto, the excess of its assets (exclusive of goodwill, capitalized research and development expenses and deferred charges) over its liabilities (not including deferred taxes, deferred income and other deferred credits) would be less than the liquidation preference of all shares having a preference on liquidation over the class or series to which the distribution is made.

§ 503.   Retained earnings necessary to allow distribution to junior shares

Neither a corporation nor any of its subsidiaries shall make any distribution to the corporation's shareholders (Section 166) on any shares of its stock of any class or series which are junior to outstanding shares of any other class or series with repsect to payment of dividends unless the amount of the retained earnings of the corporation immediately prior thereto equals or exceeds the amount of the proposed distribution plus the aggregate amount of the cumulative dividends in arrears on all shares having a preference with respect to payment of dividends over the class or series to which the distribution is made.

§ 506.   Receipt of prohibited dividend; liability of shareholder; suit by creditors or other shareholders

(a) Any shareholder who receives any distribution prohibited by this chapter with knowledge of facts indicating the impropriety thereof is liable to the corporation for the benefit of all of the creditors or shareholders entitled to institute an action under subdivision (b) for the amount so received by such shareholder with interest thereon at the legal rate on judgments until paid, but not exceeding the liabilities of the corporation owed to nonconsenting creditors at the time of the violation and the injury suffered by nonconsenting shareholders, as the case may be.

(b) Suit may be brought in the name of the corporation to enforce the liability (1) to creditors arising under subdivision (a) for a violation of Section 500 or 501 against any or all shareholders liable by any one or more creditors of the corporation whose debts or claims arose prior to the time of the distribution to shareholders and who have not consented thereto, whether or not they have reduced their claims to judgment, or

(2) to shareholders arising under subdivision (a) for a violation of Section 502 or 503 against any or all shareholders liable by any one or more holders of preferred shares outstanding at the time of the distribution who have not consented thereto, without regard to the provisions of Section 800.

(c) Any shareholder sued under this section may implead all other shareholders liable under this section and may compel contribution, either in that action or in an independent action against shareholders not joined in that action.

(d) Nothing contained in this section affects any liability which any shareholder may have under Sections 3439 to 3439.12, inclusive, of the Civil Code.

CHAPTER 6. SHAREHOLDERS' MEETINGS AND CONSENTS

§ 604. Proxies or written consents; contents; form

(a) Any form of proxy or written consent distributed to 10 or more shareholders of a corporation with outstanding shares held of record by 100 or more persons shall afford an opportunity on the proxy or form of written consent to specify a choice between approval and disapproval of each matter or group of related matters intended to be acted upon at the meeting for which the proxy is solicited or by such written consent, other than elections to office, and shall provide, subject to reasonable specified conditions, that where the person solicited specifies a choice with respect to any such matter the shares will be voted in accordance therewith.

(b) In any election of directors, any form of proxy in which the directors to be voted upon are named therein as candidates and which is marked by a shareholder "withhold" or otherwise marked in a manner indicating that the authority to vote for the election of directors is withheld shall not be voted for the election of a director.

(c) Failure to comply with this section shall not invalidate any corporate action taken, but may be the basis for challenging any proxy at a meeting and the superior court may compel compliance therewith at the suit of any shareholder.

(d) This section does not apply to any corporation with an outstanding class of securities registered under Section 12 of the Securities Exchange Act of 1934 or whose securities are exempted from such registration by Section 12(g)(2) of that act.

CHAPTER 7. VOTING OF SHARES

§ 705. Proxies; validity; expiration; revocation; irrevocable proxies

(a) Every person entitled to vote shares may authorize another person or persons to act by proxy with respect to such shares. Any proxy purporting to be executed in accordance with the provisions of this division shall be presumptively valid.

(b) No proxy shall be valid after the expiration of 11 months from the date thereof unless otherwise provided in the proxy. Every proxy continues in full force and effect until revoked by the person executing it prior to the vote pursuant thereto, except as otherwise provided in this section. Such revocation may be effected by a writing delivered to the corporation stating that the proxy is revoked or by a subsequent proxy executed by the person executing the prior proxy and presented to the meeting, or as to any meeting by attendance at such meeting and voting in person by the person executing the proxy. The dates contained on the forms of proxy presumptively determine the order of execution, regardless of the postmark dates on the envelopes in which they are mailed.

(c) A proxy is not revoked by the death or incapacity of the maker unless, before the vote is counted, written notice of such death or incapacity is received by the corporation.

(d) Except when other provision shall have been made by written agreement between the parties, the recordholder of shares which such person holds as pledgee or otherwise as security or which belong to another shall issue to the pledgor or to the owner of such shares, upon demand therefor and payment of necessary expenses thereof, a proxy to vote or take other action thereon.

(e) A proxy which states that it is irrevocable is irrevocable for the period specified therein (notwithstanding subdivision (c)) when it is held by any of the following or a nominee of any of the following:

(1) A pledgee;

(2) A person who has purchased or agreed to purchase or holds an option to purchase the shares or a person who has sold a portion of such person's shares in the corporation to the maker of the proxy;

(3) A creditor or creditors of the corporation or the shareholder who extended or continued credit to the corporation or the shareholder in consideration of the proxy if the proxy states that it was given in consideration of such extension or continua-

tion of credit and the name of the person extending or continuing credit;

(4) A person who has contracted to perform services as an employee of the corporation, if a proxy is required by the contract of employment and if the proxy states that it was given in consideration of such contract of employment, the name of the employee and the period of employment contracted for; or

(5) A person designated by or under an agreement under Section 706.

(6) A beneficiary of a trust with respect to shares held by the trust.

Notwithstanding the period of irrevocability specified, the proxy becomes revocable when the pledge is redeemed, the option or agreement to purchase is terminated or the seller no longer owns any shares of the corporation or dies, the debt of the corporation or the shareholder is paid, the period of employment provided for in the contract of employment has terminated, the agreement under Section 706 has terminated, or the person ceases to be a beneficiary of the trust. In addition to the foregoing clauses (1) through (5), a proxy may be made irrevocable (notwithstanding subdivision (c)) if it is given to secure the performance of a duty or to protect a title, either legal or equitable, until the happening of events which, by its terms, discharge the obligations secured by it.

(f) A proxy may be revoked, notwithstanding a provision making it irrevocable by a transferee of shares without knowledge of the existence of the provision unless the existence of the proxy and its irrevocability appears on the certificate representing such shares.

§ 706. Agreement between two or more shareholders of close corporation; voting trust agreements

(a) Notwithstanding any other provision of this division, an agreement between two or more shareholders of a close corporation, if in writing and signed by the parties thereto, may provide that in exercising any voting rights the shares held by them shall be voted as provided by the agreement, or as the parties may agree or as determined in accordance with a procedure agreed upon by them, and the parties may transfer the shares covered by such an agreement to a third party or parties with authority to vote them in accordance with the terms of the agreement. Such an agreement shall not be denied specific performance by a court on the ground that the remedy at law is adequate or on other grounds relating to the jurisdiction of a court of equity. An agreement made pursuant to this subdivision between shareholders of a close corporation shall terminate when the corporation ceases to be a close corporation, except that if the agreement so provides it shall continue to the extent it is enforceable apart from this subdivision.

(b) Shares in any corporation may be transferred by written agreement to trustees in order to confer upon them the right to vote and otherwise represent the shares for such period of time, not exceeding 10 years, as may be specified in the agreement. The validity of a voting trust agreement, otherwise lawful, shall not be affected during a period of 10 years from the date when it was created or last extended as hereinafter provided by the fact that under its terms it will or may last beyond such 10-year period. At any time within two years prior to the time of expiration of any voting trust agreement as originally fixed or as last extended as provided in this subdivision, one or more beneficiaries under the voting trust agreement may, by written agreement and with the written consent of the voting trustee or trustees, extend the duration of the voting trust agreement with respect to their shares for an additional period not exceeding 10 years from the expiration date of the trust as originally fixed or as last extended as provided in this subdivision. A duplicate of the voting trust agreement and any extension thereof shall be filed with the secretary of the corporation and shall be open to inspection by a shareholder, a holder of a voting trust certificate or the agent of either, upon the same terms as the record of shareholders of the corporation is open to inspection.

(c) No agreement made pursuant to subdivision (a) shall be held to be invalid or unenforceable on the ground that it is a voting trust which does not comply with subdivision (b).

(d) This section shall not invalidate any voting or other agreement among shareholders or any irrevocable proxy complying with subdivision (e) of Section 705, which agreement or proxy is not otherwise illegal.

CHAPTER 8. SHAREHOLDER DERIVATIVE ACTIONS

§ 800. Conditions; security; motion for order; determination

(a) As used in this section, "corporation" includes an unincorporated association; "board" includes the managing body of an unincorporated association; "shareholder" includes a member of an unincorporated association; and "shares" includes memberships in an unincorporated association.

(b) No action may be instituted or maintained in right of any domestic or foreign corporation by any holder of shares or of voting trust certificates of such corporation unless both of the following conditions exist:

(1) The plaintiff alleges in the complaint that plaintiff was a shareholder, of record or beneficially, or the holder of voting trust certificates at the time of the transaction or any part thereof of which plaintiff complains or that plaintiff's shares or voting trust certificates thereafter devolved upon plaintiff by operation of law from a holder who was a holder at the time of the transaction or any part thereof complained of; provided, that any shareholder who does not meet such requirements may nevertheless be allowed in the discretion of the court to maintain such action on a preliminary showing to and determination by the court, by motion and after a hearing, at which the court shall consider such evidence, by affidavit or testimony, as it deems material, that (i) there is a strong prima facie case in favor of the claim asserted on behalf of the corporation, (ii) no other similar action has been or is likely to be instituted, (iii) the plaintiff acquired the shares before there was disclosure to the public or to the plaintiff of the wrongdoing of which plaintiff complains, (iv) unless the action can be maintained the defendant may retain a gain derived from defendant's willful breach of a fiduciary duty, and (v) the requested relief will not result in unjust enrichment of the corporation or any shareholder of the corporation; and

(2) The plaintiff alleges in the complaint with particularity plaintiff's efforts to secure from the board such action as plaintiff desires, or the reasons for not making such effort, and alleges further that plaintiff has either informed the corporation or the board in writing of the ultimate facts of each cause of action against each defendant or delivered to the corporation or the board a true copy of the complaint which plaintiff proposes to file.

(c) In any action referred to in subdivision (b), at any time within 30 days after service of summons upon the corporation or upon any defendant who is an officer or director of the corporation, or held such office at the time of the acts complained of, the corporation or such defendant may move the court for an order, upon notice and hearing, requiring the plaintiff to furnish security as hereinafter provided. The motion shall be based upon one or both of the following grounds:

(1) That there is no reasonable possibility that the prosecution of the cause of action alleged in the complaint against the moving party will benefit the corporation or its shareholders.

(2) That the moving party, if other than the corporation, did not participate in the transaction complained of in any capacity.

The court on application of the corporation or any defendant may, for good cause shown, extend the 30-day period for an additional period or periods not exceeding 60 days.

(d) At the hearing upon any motion pursuant to subdivision (c), the court shall consider such evidence, written or oral, by witnesses or affidavit, as may be material (1) to the ground or grounds upon which the motion is based, or (2) to a determination of the probable reasonable expenses, including attorneys' fees, of the corporation and the moving party which will be incurred in the defense of the action. If the court determines, after hearing the evidence adduced by the parties, that the moving party has established a probability in support of any of the grounds upon which the motion is based, the court shall fix the nature and amount of security, not to exceed fifty thousand dollars ($50,000), to be furnished by the plaintiff for reasonable expenses, including attorneys' fees, which may be incurred by the moving party and the corporation in connection with the action, including expenses for which the corporation may become liable pursuant to Section 317. A ruling by the court on the motion shall not be a determination of any issue in the action or of the merits thereof. The amount of the security may thereafter be increased or decreased in the discretion of the court upon a showing that the security provided has or may become inadequate or is excessive, but the court may not in any event increase the total amount of the security beyond fifty thousand dollars ($50,000) in the aggregate for all defendants. If the court, upon any such motion, makes a determination that security shall be furnished by the plaintiff as to any one or more defendants, the action shall be dismissed as to such defendant or defendants, unless the security required by the court shall have been furnished within such reasonable time as may be fixed by the court. The corporation and the moving party shall have recourse to the security in such amount as the court shall determine upon the termination of the action.

(e) If the plaintiff shall, either before or after a motion is made pursuant to subdivision (c), or any order or determination pursuant to such motion, post good and sufficient bond or bonds in the aggregate amount of fifty thousand dollars ($50,000) to secure the reasonable expenses of the parties entitled to make the motion, the plaintiff has complied with the requirements of this section and with any order for security theretofore made pursuant hereto, and any such motion then pending shall be dismissed and no further or additional bond or other security shall be required.

(f) If a motion is filed pursuant to subdivision (c), no pleadings need be filed by the corporation or any other defendant and the prosecution of the action shall be stayed until 10 days after the motion has been disposed of.

CHAPTER 10. SALES OF ASSETS

§ 1001. Sale, lease, exchange, etc.; of property or assets; approval; abandonment; terms, conditions and consideration

* * *

(d) If the buyer in a sale of assets pursuant to subdivision (a) of this section or subdivision (g) of Section 2001 is in control of or under common control with the seller, the principal terms of the sale must be approved by at least 90 percent of the voting power unless the sale is to a domestic or foreign corporation in consideration of the nonredeemable common shares of the purchasing corporation or its parent.

* * *

CHAPTER 11. MERGER

§ 1101. Agreement of merger; approval of boards; contents

* * *

Each share of the same class or series of any constituent corporation (other than the cancellation of shares held by a constituent corporation or its parent or a wholly owned subsidiary of either in another constituent corporation) shall, unless all shareholders of the class or series consent and except as provided in Section 407, be treated equally with respect to any distribution of cash, property, rights or securities. Notwithstanding subdivision (d), except in a short-form merger, and in the merger of a corporation into its subsidiary in which it owns at least 90 percent of the outstanding shares of each class, the nonredeemable common shares of a constituent corporation may be converted only into nonredeemable common shares of the surviving corporation or a parent party if a constituent corporation or its parent owns, directly or indirectly, shares of another constituent corporation representing more than 50 percent of the voting power of the other constituent corporation prior to the merger, unless all of the shareholders of the class consent and except as provided in Section 407.

CHAPTER 12. REORGANIZATIONS

§ 1200. Approval by board

A reorganization (Section 181) shall be approved by the board of:

(a) Each constituent corporation in a merger reorganization;

(b) The acquiring corporation in an exchange reorganization;

(c) The acquiring corporation and the corporation whose property and assets are acquired in a sale-of-assets reorganization; and

(d) The corporation in control of any constituent or acquiring corporation under subdivision (a), (b) or (c) and whose equity securities are issued or transferred in the reorganization (a "parent party").

§ 1201. Approval of shareholders; abandonment by board; actions to attack validity if party directly or indirectly controlled by other party

(a) The principal terms of a reorganization shall be approved by the outstanding shares (Section 152) of each class of each corporation the approval of whose board is required under Section 1200, except as provided in subdivision (b) and except that (unless otherwise provided in the articles) no approval of any class of outstanding preferred shares of the surviving or acquiring corporation or parent party shall be required if the rights, preferences, privileges and restrictions granted to or imposed upon such class of shares remain unchanged (subject to the provisions of subdivision (c)). For the purpose of this subdivision, two classes of common shares differing only as to voting rights shall be considered as a single class of shares.

(b) No approval of the outstanding shares (Section 152) is required by subdivision (a) in the case of any corporation if such corporation, or its shareholders immediately before the reorganization, or both, shall own (immediately after the reorganization) equity securities, other than any warrant or right to subscribe to or purchase such equity securities, of the surviving or acquiring corporation or a parent party (subdivision (d) of Section 1200) possessing more than five-sixths of the voting power of the surviving or acquiring corporation or parent party. In making the determination of ownership by the shareholders of a corporation, immediately after the reorganization, of equity securities pursuant to the preceding sentence, equity securities which they owned immediately before the reorganization as shareholders of another party to the transaction shall be disregarded. For the purpose of this section only, the voting power of a corporation shall be calculated by asssuming the conversion of all equity securities convertible (immediately or at some future time) into shares entitled to vote but not assuming the exercise of any warrant or right to subscribe to or purchase such shares.

(c) Notwithstanding the provisions of subdivision (b), a reorganization shall be approved by the outstanding shares (Section 152) of the surviving corporation in a merger reorganization if any amendment is made to its articles which would otherwise require such approval.

(d) Notwithstanding the provisions of subdivision (b) a reorganization shall be approved by the outstanding shares (Section 152) of any class of a corporation which is a party to a merger or sale-of-assets reorganization if holders of shares of that class receive shares of the surviving or acquiring corporation or parent party having different rights, preferences, privileges or restrictions than those surrendered. Shares in a foreign corporation received in exchange for shares in a domestic corporation have different rights, preferences, privileges and restrictions within the meaning of the preceding sentence.

(e) Notwithstanding the provisions of subdivisions (a) and (b), a reorganization shall be approved by the affirmative vote of at least two-thirds of each class of the outstanding shares of any close corporation if the reorganization would result in their receiving shares of a corporation which is not a close corporation; provided, however, that the articles may provide for a lesser vote, but not less than a majority of the outstanding shares of each class.

(f) Any approval required by this section may be given before or after the approval by the board. Notwithstanding approval required by this section, the board may abandon the proposed reorganization without further action by the 'shareholders, subject to the contractual rights, if any, of third parties.

CHAPTER 13. DISSENTERS' RIGHTS

§ 1300. Reorganization or short-form merger; dissenting shares; corporate purchase at fair market value; definitions

(a) If the approval of the outstanding shares (Section 152) of a corporation is required for a reorganization under subdivisions (a) and (b) or subdivision (e) of Section 1201, each shareholder of such corporation and each shareholder of a disappearing corporation in a short-form merger may, by complying with this chapter, require the corporation in which the shareholder holds shares to purchase for cash at their fair market value the shares owned by the shareholder which are dissenting shares as defined in subdivision (b). The fair market value shall be determined as of the day before the first announcement of the terms of the proposed reorganization or short-form merger, excluding any appreciation or depreciation in consequence of the proposed action, but adjusted for any stock split, reverse stock split or share dividend which becomes effective thereafter.

(b) As used in this chapter, "dissenting shares" means shares which come within all of the following descriptions:

(1) Which were not immediately prior to the reorganization or short-form merger either (i) listed on any national securities exchange certified by the Commissioner of Corporations under subdivision (o) of Section 25100 or (ii) listed on the list of OTC margin stocks issued by the Board of Governors of the Federal Reserve System, and the notice of meeting of shareholders to act upon the reorganization summarizes the provisions of this section and Sections 1301, 1302, 1303 and 1304; provided, however, that this provision does not apply to any shares with respect to which there exists any restriction on transfer imposed by the corporation or by any law or regulation; and provided, further, that this provision does not apply to any class of shares described in clause (i) or (ii) if demands for payment are filed with respect to 5 percent or more of the outstanding shares of that class.

(2) Which were outstanding on the date for the determination of shareholders entitled to vote on the reorganization and (i) were not voted in favor of the reorganization or, (ii) if described in clause (i) or (ii) of paragraph (1) (without regard to the provisos in that paragraph), were voted against the reorganization, or which were held of record on the effective date of a short-form merger; provided, however, that clause (i) rather than clause (ii) of this paragraph applies in any case where the approval required by Section 1201 is sought by written consent rather than at a meeting.

(3) Which the dissenting shareholder has demanded that the corporation purchase at their fair market value, in accordance with Section 1301.

(4) Which the dissenting shareholder has submitted for endorsement, in accordance with Section 1302.

(c) As used in this chapter, "dissenting shareholder" means the recordholder of dissenting shares and includes a transferee of record.

§ 1312. **Right of dissenting shareholder to attack, set aside or rescind merger or reorganization; restraining order or injunction; conditions**

(a) No shareholder of a corporation who has a right under this chapter to demand payment of cash for the shares held by the shareholder shall have any right at law or in equity to attack the validity of the reorganization or short-form merger, or to have the reorganization or short-form merger set aside or rescinded, except in an action to test whether the number of shares required to authorize or approve the reorganization have been legally voted in favor thereof; but any holder of shares of a class whose terms and provisions specifically set forth the amount to be paid in respect to them in the event of a reorganization or short-form merger is entitled to payment in accordance with those terms and provisions.

(b) If one of the parties to a reorganization or short-form merger is directly or indirectly controlled by, or under common control with, another party to the reorganization or short-form merger, subdivision (a) shall not apply to any shareholder of such party who has not demanded payment of cash for such shareholder's shares pursuant to this chapter; but if the shareholder institutes any action to attack the validity of the reorganization or short-form merger or to have the reorganization or short-form merger set aside or rescinded, the shareholder shall not thereafter have any right to demand payment of cash for the shareholder's shares pursuant to this chapter. The court in any action attacking the validity of the reorganization or short-form merger or to have the reorganization or short-form merger set aside or rescinded shall not restrain or enjoin the consummation of the transaction except upon 10-days prior notice to the corporation and upon a determination by the court that clearly no other remedy will adequately protect the complaining shareholder or the class of shareholders of which such shareholder is a member.

(c) If one of the parties to a reorganization or short-form merger is directly or indirectly controlled by, or under common control with, another party to the reorganization or short-form merger, in any action to attack the validity of the reorganization or short-form merger or to have the reorganization or short-form merger set aside or rescinded, (1) a party to a reorganization or short-form merger which controls another party to the reorganization or short-form merger shall have the burden of proving that the transaction is just and reasonable as to the shareholders of the controlled party, and (2) a person who controls two or more parties to a reorganization shall have the burden of proving that the transaction is just and reasonable as to the shareholders of any party so controlled.

CHAPTER 21. FOREIGN CORPORATIONS

§ 2115. Foreign corporations subject to corporate laws of state; tests to determine subject corporations; laws applicable; time of application

(a) A foreign corporation (other than a foreign association or foreign nonprofit corporation but including a foreign parent corporation even though it does not itself transact intrastate business) is subject to this section if the average of the property factor, the payroll factor and the sales factor (as defined in Sections 25129, 25132 and 25134 of the Revenue and Taxation Code) with respect to it is more than 50 percent during its latest full income year and if more than one-half of its outstanding voting securities are held of record by persons having addresses in this state. The property factor, payroll factor and sales factor shall be those used in computing the portion of its income allocable to this state in its franchise tax return or, with respect to corporations the allocation of whose income is governed by special formulas or which are not required to file separate or any tax returns, which would have been so used if they were governed by such three-factor formula. The determination of these factors with respect to any parent corporation shall be made on a consolidated basis, including in a unitary computation (after elimination of intercompany transactions) the property, payroll and sales of the parent and all of its subsidiaries in which it owns directly or indirectly more than 50 percent of the outstanding shares entitled to vote for the election of directors, but deducting a percentage of such property, payroll and sales of any subsidiary equal to the percentage minority ownership, if any, in such subsidiary. For the purpose of this subdivision, any securities held to the knowledge of the issuer in the names of broker-dealers or nominees for broker-dealers shall not be considered outstanding.

(b) The following chapters and sections of this division shall apply to a foreign corporation subject to this section (to the exclusion of the law of the jurisdiction in which it is incorporated):

Chapter 1 (general provisions and definitions), to the extent applicable to the following provisions;

Section 301 (annual election of directors);

Section 303 (removal of directors without cause);

Section 304 (removal of directors by court proceedings);

Section 305, subdivision (c) (filing of director vacancies where less than a majority in office elected by shareholders);

Section 309 (directors' standard of care);

Section 316 (excluding paragraph (3) of subdivision (a) and paragraph (3) of subdivision (f)) (liability of directors for unlawful distributions);

Section 317 (indemnification of directors, officers and others);

Sections 500 to 505, inclusive (limitations on corporate distributions in cash or property);

Section 506 (liability of shareholder who receives unlawful distribution);

Section 600, subdivisions (b) and (c) (requirement for annual shareholders' meeting and remedy if same not timely held);

Section 708, subdivisions (a), (b) and (c) (shareholder's right to cumulate votes at any election of directors);

Section 1001, subdivision (d) (limitations on sale of assets);

Section 1101 (provisions following subdivision (e)) (limitations on mergers);

Chapter 12 (commencing with Section 1200) (reorganizations);

Chapter 13 (commencing with Section 1300) (dissenters' rights);

Sections 1500 and 1501 (records and reports);

Section 1508 (action by Attorney General);

Chapter 16 (commencing with Section 1600) (rights of inspection).

(c) Subdivision (a) shall become applicable to any foreign corporation only upon the first day of the first income year of the corporation commencing on or after the 30th day after the filing by it of the report pursuant to Section 2108 showing that the tests referred to in subdivision (a) have been met or on or after the entry of a final order by a court of competent jurisdiction declaring that such tests have been met.

(d) Subdivision (a) shall cease to be applicable at the end of any income year during which a report pursuant to Section 2108 shall have been filed showing that at least one of the tests referred to in subdivision (a) is not met or a final order shall have been entered by a court of competent jurisdiction declaring that one of such tests is not met, provided that such filing or order shall be ineffective if a contrary report or order shall be made or entered before the end of such income year.

(e) This section does not apply to any corporation with outstanding securities listed on any national securities exchange certified by the Commissioner of Corporations under subdivision (o) of Section 25100, or to any corporation if all of its voting shares (other than directors' qualifying shares) are owned directly or indirectly by a corporation or corporations not subject to this section.

D. DELAWARE GENERAL CORPORATION LAW

(Selected Sections)

Contents

DELAWARE GENERAL CORPORATION LAW

SUBCHAPTER VI. STOCK TRANSFERS

SUBCHAPTER VII. MEETINGS, ELECTIONS, VOTING AND NOTICE

SUBCHAPTER VIII. AMENDMENT OF CERTIFICATE OF INCORPORATION; CHANGES IN CAPITAL AND CAPITAL STOCK

SUBCHAPTER IX. MERGER OR CONSOLIDATION

SUBCHAPTER X. SALE OF ASSETS, DISSOLUTION AND WINDING UP

SUBCHAPTER XII. RENEWAL, REVIVAL, EXTENSION AND RESTORATION OF CERTIFICATE OF INCORPORATION OR CHARTER

CORPORATIONS

SUBCHAPTER XIV. CLOSE CORPORATIONS; SPECIAL PROVISIONS

SUBCHAPTER I. FORMATION

§ 101. Incorporators; how corporation formed; purposes

(a) Any person, partnership, association or corporation, singly or jointly with others, and without regard to his or their residence, domicile or state of incorporation, may incorporate or organize a corporation under this chapter by filing with the Secretary of State a certificate of incorporation which shall be executed, acknowledged, filed and recorded in accordance with section 103 of this title.

(b) A corporation may be incorporated or organized under this chapter to conduct or promote any lawful business or purposes, except as may otherwise be provided by the constitution or other law of this State.

(c) Corporations for constructing, maintaining and operating public utilities, whether in or outside of this State, may be organized under this chapter, but corporations for constructing, maintaining and operating public utilities within this State shall be subject to, in addition to the provisions of this chapter, the special provisions and requirements of Title 26 applicable to such corporations.

§ 102. Certificate of incorporation; contents

(a) The certificate of incorporation shall set forth—

(1) The name of the corporation which shall contain one of the words "association", "company", "corporation", "club", "foundation", "fund", "incorporated", "institute", "society", "union", "syndicate", or "limited", or one of the abbreviations ["co.", "corp.", "inc.", "ltd."], or words or abbreviations of like import in other languages (provided they are written in Roman characters or letters), and which shall be such as to distinguish it upon the records in the office of the Secretary of State from the names of other corporations organized, reserved or registered as a foreign corporation under the laws of this State;

(2) The address (which shall include the street, number, city and county) of the corporation's registered office in this State, and the name of its registered agent at such address;

(3) The nature of the business or purposes to be conducted or promoted. It shall be sufficient to state, either alone or with other businesses or purposes, that the purpose of the corporation is to engage in any lawful act or activity for which corporations may be organized under the General Corporation Law of Delaware, and by such statement all lawful acts and activities shall be within the purposes of the corporation, except for express limitations, if any.

(4) If the corporation is to be authorized to issue only one class of stock, the total number of shares of stock which the corporation shall have authority to issue and the par value of each of such shares, or a statement that all such shares are to be without par value. If the corporation is to be authorized to issue more than one class of stock, the certificate of incorporation shall set forth the total number of shares of all classes of stock which the corporation shall have authority to issue and the number of shares of each class that are to have a par value and the par value of each share of each such class, the number of shares of each class that are to be without par value, and a statement of the designations and the powers, preferences and rights, and the qualifications, limitations or restrictions thereof, which are permitted by section 151 of this title in respect of any class or classes of stock or any series of any class of stock of the corporation and the fixing of which by the certificate of incorporation is desired, and an express grant of such authority as it may then be desired to grant to the board of directors to fix by resolution or resolutions any thereof that may be desired but which shall not be fixed by the certificate of incorporation. The foregoing provisions of this paragraph shall not apply to corporations which are not organized for profit and which are not to have authority to issue capital stock. In the case of such corporations, the fact that they are not to have authority to issue capital stock shall be stated in the certificate of incorporation. The conditions of membership of such corporations shall likewise be stated in the certificate of incorporation or the certificate may provide that the conditions of membership shall be stated in the by-laws.

(5) The name and mailing address of the incorporator or incorporators;

(6) If the powers of the incorporator or incorporators are to terminate upon the filing of the certificate of incorporation, the names and mailing addresses of the persons who are to serve as directors until the first annual meeting of stockholders or until their successors are elected and qualify.

(b) In addition to the matters required to be set forth in the certificate of incorporation by subsection (a) of this section, the certificate of incorporation may also contain any or all of the following matters—

(1) Any provision for the management of the business and for the conduct of the affairs of the corporation, and

any provision creating, defining, limiting and regulating the powers of the corporation, the directors, and the stockholders, or any class of the stockholders, or the members of a non-stock corporation; if such provisions are not contrary to the laws of this State. Any provision which is required or permitted by any section of this chapter to be stated in the by-laws may instead be stated in the certificate of incorporation;

(2) The following provisions, in haec verba, viz.—

"Whenever a compromise or arrangement is proposed between this corporation and its creditors or any class of them and/or between this corporation and its stockholders or any class of them, any court of equitable jurisdiction within the State of Delaware may, on the application in a summary way of this corporation or of any creditor or stockholder thereof or on the application of any receiver or receivers appointed for this corporation under the provisions of section 291 of Title 8 of the Delaware Code or on the application of trustees in dissolution or of any receiver or receivers appointed for this corporation under the provisions of section 279 of Title 8 of the Delaware Code order a meeting of the creditors or class of creditors, and/or of the stockholders or class of stockholders of this corporation, as the case may be, to be summoned in such manner as the said court directs. If a majority in number representing three-fourths in value of the creditors or class of creditors, and/or of the stockholders or class of stockholders of this corporation, as the case may be, agree to any compromise or arrangement and to any reorganization of this corporation as consequence cf such compromise or arrangement, the said compromise or arrangement and the said reorganization shall, if sanctioned by the court to which the said application has been made, be binding on all the creditors or class of creditors, and/or on all the stockholders or class of stockholders, of this corporation, as the case may be, and also on this corporation;"

(3) Such provisions as may be desired granting to the holders of the stock of the corporation, or the holders of any class or series of a class thereof, the preemptive right to subscribe to any or all additional issues of stock of the corporation of any or all classes or series thereof, or to any securities of the corporation convertible into such stock. No stockholder shall have any preemptive right to subscribe to an additional issue of stock or to any security convertible into such stock unless, and except to the extent that, such right is expressly granted to him in the certificate of in-

corporation. All such rights in existence on July 3, 1967, shall remain in existence unaffected by this paragraph (3) unless and until changed or terminated by appropriate action which expressly provides for such change or termination.

(4) Provisions requiring for any corporate action, the vote of a larger portion of the stock or of any class or series thereof, or of any other securities having voting power, or a larger number of the directors, than is required by this chapter;

(5) A provision limiting the duration of the corporation's existence to a specified date; otherwise, the corporation shall have perpetual existence;

(6) A provision imposing personal liability for the debts of the corporation on its stockholders or members to a specified extent and upon specified conditions; otherwise, the stockholders or members of a corporation shall not be personally liable for the payment of the corporation's debts except as they may be liable by reason of their own conduct or acts;

(c) It shall not be necessary to set forth in the certificate of incorporation any of the powers conferred on corporations by this chapter.

SUBCHAPTER III. REGISTERED OFFICE AND REGISTERED AGENT

§ 131. Registered office in State; principal office or place of business in State

(a) Every corporation shall have and maintain in this State a registered office which may, but need not be, the same as its place of business.

(b) Whenever the term "corporation's principal office or place of business in this State" or "principal office or place of business of the corporation in this State", or other term of like import, is or has been used in a corporation's certificate of incorporation, or in any other document, or in any statute, it shall be deemed to mean and refer to, unless the context indicates otherwise, the corporation's registered office required by this section; and it shall not be necessary for any corporation to amend its certificate of incorporation or any other document to comply with this section.

§ 132. Registered agent in State; resident agent

(a) Every corporation shall have and maintain in this State a registered agent, which agent may be either an individual resident in this State whose business office is identical with the corporation's registered office, or a domestic corporation (which may be itself), or a foreign corporation authorized to transact business in this State, having a business office identical with such registered office.

(b) Whenever the term "resident agent" or "resident agent in charge of a corporation's principal office or place of business in this State", or other term of like import which refers to a corporation's agent required by statute to be located in this State, is or has been used in a corporation's certificate of incorporation, or in any other document, or in any statute, it shall be deemed to mean and refer to, unless the context indicates otherwise, the corporation's registered agent required by this section; and it shall not be necessary for any corporation to amend its certificate of incorporation or any other document to comply with this section.

§ 133. Change of location of registered office; change of registered agent

Any corporation may, by resolution of its board of directors, change the location of its registered office in this State to any other place in this State. By like resolution, the registered agent of a corporation may be changed to any other person or corporation including itself. In either such case, the resolution shall be as detailed in its statement as is required by section 102(a) (2) of this title. Upon the adoption of such a resolution, a certificate certifying the change shall be executed, acknowledged, and filed in accordance with section 103 of this title; and a certified copy shall be recorded in the office of the Recorder for the county in which the new office is located; and, if such new office is located in a county other than that in which the former office was located, a certified copy of such certificate shall also be recorded in the office of the Recorder for the county in which such former office was located.

§ 134. Change of address of registered agent

A registered agent may change the address of the registered office of the corporation or corporations for which he is registered agent to another address in this State by filing with the Secretary of State a certificate, executed and acknowledged by such registered agent, setting forth the names of all the corporations represented by such registered agent, and the address at which such registered agent has maintained the registered office for each of such corporations, and further certifying to the new address to which each such registered office will be changed on a given day, and at which new address such registered agent will thereafter maintain the registered office for each of the corporations recited in the certificate. Upon the filing of such certificate, the Secretary of State shall furnish a certified copy of the same under his hand and seal of office, and the certified copy shall be recorded in the office of the Recorder of the county where the registered office of the corporation is located in this State, and thereafter, or until further change of address, as authorized by law, the registered office in this State of each of the corporations recited in the certificate shall be located at the new address of the registered agent thereof as given in the certificate. If the location of such office shall be changed from one county to another county, a certified copy of such certificate shall also be recorded in the office of the Recorder for the county in which such office was formerly located.

§ 135. Resignation of registered agent coupled with appointment of successor

The registered agent of one or more corporations may resign and appoint a successor registered agent by filing a certificate with the Secretary of State, stating the name and address of the successor agent, in accordance with section 102(a) (2) of this title. There shall be attached to such certificate a statement of each affected corporation ratifying and approving such change of registered agent. Each such statement shall be executed and acknowledged in accordance with section 103 of this title. Upon such filing, the successor registered agent shall become the registered agent of such corporations as have ratified and approved such substitution and the successor registered agent's address, as stated in such certificate, shall become the address of each such corporation's registered office in this state. The Secretary of State shall then issue his certificate that the successor registered agent has become the registered agent of the corporations so ratifying and approving such change, and setting out the names of such corporations. The certificate of the Secretary of State shall be recorded in accordance with section 103 of this title, and the Recorder shall forthwith make a note of the change of registered office and registered agent on the margin of the record of the certificates of incorporation of those corporations which have ratified and approved such change. If the location of such office shall be changed from one county to another county, a certified copy of such certificate shall also be recorded in the office of the Recorder for the county in which such office will thereafter be located.

§ 136. Resignation of registered agent not coupled with appointment of successor

(a) The registered agent of one or more corporations may resign without appointing a successor by filing a certificate with the Secretary of State; but such resignation shall not become effective until 60 days after the certificate is filed. There shall be attached to such certificate, in duplicate, an affidavit of such registered agent, if an individual, or of the president, a vice president or the secretary thereof, if a corporation, that at least 30 days prior to the date of the filing of said certificate, due notice was sent by certified or registered mail to the corporation for which such registered agent was acting, at the principal office thereof outside the State, if known to such registered agent or, if not, to the last known address of the attorney or other individual at whose request such registered agent was appointed for such corporation, of the resignation of such registered agent.

(b) Upon the filing of such certificate of resignation with the Secretary of State, the Secretary of State shall then notify the Recorder for the county in which the certificate of incorporation of such corporation is recorded of the resignation of its registered agent as set forth in such certificate and the Recorder shall forthwith make a note of the resignation of such registered agent on the margin of the record of the certificate of incorporation of such corporation.

(c) After receipt of the notice of the resignation of its registered agent, provided for in subsection (a) of this section, the corporation for which such registered agent was acting shall obtain and designate a new registered agent to take the place of the registered agent so resigning in the same manner as provided in section 133 of this title for change of registered agent. If such corporation being a corporation of this State, fails to obtain and designate a new registered agent as aforesaid prior to the expiration of the period of 60 days after the filing by the registered agent of the certificate of resignation, the Secretary of State shall declare the charter of such corporation forfeited. If such corporation, being a foreign corporation, fails to obtain and designate a new registered agent as aforesaid prior to the expiration of the period of 60 days after the filing by the registered agent of the certificate of resignation, the Secretary of State shall forfeit its authority to do business in this State.

(d) After the resignation of the registered agent shall have become effective as provided in this section and if no new registered agent shall have been obtained and designated in the time and manner aforesaid, service of legal process against the corporation for which the resigned registered agent had been acting shall thereafter be upon the Secretary of State in accordance with section 321 of this title.

SUBCHAPTER V. STOCK AND DIVIDENDS

§ 152. **Issuance of stock; lawful consideration; fully paid stock**

The consideration, as determined pursuant to subsections (a) and (b) of Section 153 of this title, for subscriptions to, or the purchase of, the capital stock to be issued by a corporation shall be paid in such form and in such manner as the board of directors shall determine. In the absence of actual fraud in the transaction, the judgment of the directors as to the value of such consideration shall be conclusive. The capital stock so issued shall be deemed to be fully paid and nonassessable stock, if: (1) the entire amount of such consideration has been received by the corporation in the form of cash, services rendered, personal property, real property, leases of real property, or a combination thereof; or (2) not less than the amount of the consideration determined to be capital pursuant to Section 154 of this title has been received by the corporation in such form and the corporation has received a binding obligation of the subscriber or purchaser to pay the balance of the subscription or purchase price; provided, however, nothing contained herein shall prevent the board of directors from issuing partly paid shares under Section 156 of this title.

§ 153. **Consideration for stock**

(a) Shares of stock with par value may be issued for such consideration, having a value not less than the par value thereof, as is determined from time to time by the board of directors, or by the stockholders if the certificate of incorporation so provides.

(b) Shares of stock without par value may be issued for such consideration as is determined from time to time by the board of directors, or by the stockholders if the certificate of incorporation so provides.

(c) Treasury shares may be disposed of by the corporation for such consideration as may be determined from time to time by the board of directors, or by the stockholders if the certificate of incorporation so provides.

(d) If the certificate of incorporation reserves to the stockholders the right to determine the consideration for the issue of any shares, the stockholders shall, unless the certificate requires a greater vote, do so by a vote of a majority of the outstanding stock entitled to vote thereon.

§ 154. Determination of amount of capital; capital, surplus and net assets defined

Any corporation may, by resolution of its board of directors, determine that only a part of the consideration which shall be received by the corporation for any of the shares of its capital stock which it shall issue from time to time shall be capital; but, in case any of the shares issued shall be shares having a par value, the amount of the part of such consideration so determined to be capital shall be in excess of the aggregate par value of the shares issued for such consideration having a par value, unless all the shares issued shall be shares having a par value, in which case the amount of the part of such consideration so determined to be capital need be only equal to the aggregate par value of such shares. In each such case the board of directors shall specify in dollars the part of such consideration which shall be capital. If the board of directors shall not have determined (1) at the time of issue of any shares of the capital stock of the corporation issued for cash or (2) within 60 days after the issue of any shares of the capital stock of the corporation issued for property other than cash what part of the consideration for such shares shall be capital, the capital of the corporation in respect of such shares shall be an amount equal to the aggregate par value of such shares having a par value, plus the amount of the consideration for such shares without par value. The amount of the consideration so determined to be capital in respect of any shares without par value shall be the stated capital of such shares. The capital of the corporation may be increased from time to time by resolution of the board of directors directing that a portion of the net assets of the corporation in excess of the amount so determined to be capital be transferred to the capital account. The board of directors may direct that the portion of such net assets so transferred shall be treated as capital in respect of any shares of the corporation of any designated class or classes. The excess, if any, at any given time, of the net assets of the corporation over the amount so determined to be capital shall be surplus. Net assets means the amount by which total assets exceed total liabilities. Capital and surplus are not liabilities for this purpose.

§ 160. Corporation's powers respecting ownership, voting, etc., of its own stock; rights of stock called for redemption

(a) Every corporation may purchase, redeem, receive, take or otherwise acquire, own and hold, sell, lend, exchange, transfer or otherwise dispose of, pledge, use and otherwise deal in and with its own shares; provided, however, that no corporation shall—

1. Purchase or redeem its own shares of capital stock for cash or other property when the capital of the corporation is impaired or when such purchase or redemption would cause any impairment of the capital of the corporation, except that a corporation may purchase or redeem out of capital any of its own shares which are entitled upon any distribution of its assets, whether by dividend or in liquidation, to a preference over another class or series of its stock if such shares will be retired upon their acquisition and the capital of the corporation reduced in accordance with Sections 243 and 244 of this title. Nothing in this subsection shall invalidate or otherwise affect a note, debenture or other obligation of a corporation given by it as consideration for its acquisition by purchase, redemption or exchange of its shares of stock if at the time such note, debenture or obligation was delivered by the corporation its capital was not then impaired or did not thereby become impaired;

2. Purchase, for more than the price at which they may then be redeemed, any of its shares which are redeemable at the option of the corporation; or,

3. Redeem any of its shares unless their redemption is authorized by Section 151(b) of this title and then only in accordance with such Section and the certificate of incorporation.

(b) Nothing in this section limits or affects a corporation's right to resell any of its shares theretofore purchased or redeemed out of surplus and which have not been retired,

170

for such consideration as shall be fixed by the board of directors.

(c) Shares of its own capital stock belonging to the corporation or to another corporation, if a majority of the shares entitled to vote in the election of directors of such other corporation is held, directly or indirectly, by the corporation, shall neither be entitled to vote nor be counted for quorum purposes. Nothing in this section shall be construed as limiting the right of any corporation to vote stock, including but not limited to its own stock, held by it in a fiduciary capacity.

(d) Shares which have been called for redemption shall not be deemed to be outstanding shares for the purpose of voting or determining the total number of shares entitled to vote on any matter on and after the date on which written notice of redemption has been sent to holders thereof and a sum sufficient to redeem such shares has been irrevocably deposited or set aside to pay the redemption price to the holders of the shares upon surrender of certificates therefor.

§ 162. Liability of stockholder or subscriber for stock not paid in full

(a) When the whole of the consideration payable for shares of a corporation has not been paid in, and the assets shall be insufficient to satisfy the claims of its creditors, each holder of or subscriber for such shares shall be bound to pay on each share held or subscribed for by him the sum necessary to complete the amount of the unpaid balance of the consideration for which such shares were issued or to be issued by the corporation.

(b) The amounts which shall be payable as provided in subsection (a) of this section may be recovered as provided in section 325 of this title, after a writ of execution against the corporation has been returned unsatisfied as provided in that section.

(c) Any person becoming an assignee or transferee of shares or of a subscription for shares in good faith and without knowledge or notice that the full consideration therefor has not been paid shall not be personally liable for any unpaid portion of such consideration, but the transferor shall remain liable therefor.

(d) No person holding shares in any corporation as collateral security shall be personally liable as a stockholder but the person pledging such shares shall be considered the holder thereof and shall be so liable. No executor, administrator, guardian, trustee or other fiduciary shall be personally liable as a stockholder, but the estate or funds held by such executor, administrator, guardian, trustee or other fiduciary in such fiduciary capacity shall be liable.

(e) No liability under this section or under section 325 of this title shall be asserted more than six years after the issuance of the stock or the date of the subscription upon which the assessment is sought.

(f) In any action by a receiver or trustee of an insolvent corporation or by a judgment creditor to obtain an assessment under this section, any stockholder or subscriber for stock of the insolvent corporation may appear and contest the claim or claims of such receiver or trustee.

§ 163.   Payment for stock not paid in full

The capital stock of a corporation shall be paid for in such amounts and at such times as the directors may require. The directors may, from time to time, demand payment, in respect of each share of stock not fully paid, of such sum of money as the necessities of the business may, in the judgment of the board of directors, require, not exceeding in the whole the balance remaining unpaid on said stock, and such sum so demanded shall be paid to the corporation at such times and by such installments as the directors shall direct. The directors shall give written notice of the time and place of such payments, which notice shall be mailed at least 30 days before the time for such payment, to each holder of or subscriber for stock which is not fully paid at his last known postoffice address.

§ 164.   Failure to pay for stock; remedies

When any stockholder fails to pay any installment or call upon his stock which may have been properly demanded by the directors, at the time when such payment is due, the directors may collect the amount of any such installment or call or any balance thereof remaining unpaid, from the said stockholder by an action at law, or they shall sell at public sale such part of the shares of such delinquent stockholder as will pay all demands then due from him with interest and all incidental expenses, and shall transfer the shares so sold to the purchaser, who shall be entitled to a certificate therefor. Notice of the time and place of such sale and of the sum due on each share shall be given by advertisement at least one week before the sale, in a newspaper of the county in this State where such corporation's registered office is located, and such notice shall be mailed by the corporation to such delinquent stockholder at his last known postoffice address, at least 20 days before such sale. If no bidder can be had to pay the amount due on the stock, and if the amount is not collected by an action at law, which may be brought within the county where the corporation has its registered office, within one year from the date of the bringing of such action at law, the said stock and the amount previously paid in by the delinquent stockholder on the stock shall be forfeited to the corporation.

§ 169. Situs of ownership of stock

For all purposes of title, action, attachment, garnishment and jurisdiction of all courts held in this State, but not for the purpose of taxation, the situs of the ownership of the capital stock of all corporations existing under the laws of this State, whether organized under this chapter or otherwise, shall be regarded as in this State.

§ 170. Dividends; payment; wasting asset corporations

(a) The directors of every corporation, subject to any restrictions contained in its certificate of incorporation, may declare and pay dividends upon the shares of its capital stock either (1) out of its surplus, as defined in and computed in accordance with sections 154, 242 and 244 of this title, or (2) in case there shall be no such surplus, out of its net profits for the fiscal year in which the dividend is declared and/or the preceding fiscal year. If the capital of the corporation, computed in accordance with sections 154, 242 and 244 of this title, shall have been diminished by depreciation in the value of its property, or by losses, or otherwise, to an amount less than the aggregate amount of the capital represented by the issued and outstanding stock of all classes having a preference upon the distribution of assets, the directors of such corporation shall not declare and pay out of such net profits any dividends upon any shares of any classes of its capital stock until the deficiency in the amount of capital represented by the issued and outstanding stock of all classes having a preference upon the distribution of assets shall have been repaired.

(b) Subject to any restrictions contained in its certificate of incorporation, the directors of any corporation engaged in the exploitation of wasting assets (including but not limited to a corporation engaged in the exploitation of natural resources or other wasting assets, including patents, or engaged primarily in the liquidation of specific assets) may determine the net profits derived from the exploitation of such wasting assets or the net proceeds derived from such liquidation without taking into consideration the depletion of such assets resulting from lapse of time, consumption, liquidation or exploitation of such assets.

§ 171. Special purpose reserves

The directors of a corporation may set apart out of any of the funds of the corporation available for dividends a reserve or reserves for any proper purpose and may abolish any such reserve.

§ 172. Liability of directors as to dividends or stock redemption

A director shall be fully protected in relying in good faith upon the books of account or other records of the corporation or statements prepared by any of its officers or by independent public accountants or by an appraiser selected with reasonable care by the board of directors as to the value and amount of the assets, liabilities and/or net profits of the corporation, or any other facts pertinent to the existence and amount of surplus or other funds from which dividends might properly be declared and paid, or with which the corporation's stock might properly be purchased or redeemed.

§ 173. Declaration and payment of dividends

No corporation shall pay dividends except in accordance with the provisions of this chapter. Dividends may be paid in cash, in property, or in shares of the corporation's capital stock. If the dividend is to be paid in shares of the corporation's theretofore unissued capital stock the board of directors shall, by resolution, direct that there be transferred from surplus to the capital account in respect of such shares an amount which is not less than the aggregate par value of par value shares being declared as a dividend and, in the case of shares without par value being declared as a dividend, such amount as shall be determined by the board of directors. No transfer from surplus to capital shall be necessary if shares are being distributed by a corporation pursuant to a split-up or division of its stock rather than as payment of a dividend declared payable in stock of the corporation.

§ 174. **Liability of directors for unlawful payment of dividend or unlawful stock purchase or redemption; exoneration from liability; contribution among directors; subrogation**

(a) In case of any willful or negligent violation of the provisions of sections 160 or 173 of this title, the directors under whose administration the same may happen shall be jointly and severally liable, at any time within six years after paying such unlawful dividend or after such unlawful stock purchase or redemption, to the corporation, and to its creditors in the event of its dissolution or insolvency, to the full amount of the dividend unlawfully paid, or to the full amount unlawfully paid for the purchase or redemption of the corporation's stock, with interest from the time such liability accrued. Any director who may have been absent when the same was done, or who may have dissented from the act or resolution by which the same was done, may exonerate himself from such liability by causing his dissent to be entered on the books containing the minutes of the proceedings of the directors at the time the same was done, or immediately after he has notice of the same.

(b) Any director against whom a claim is successfully asserted under this section shall be entitled to contribution from the other directors who voted for or concurred in the unlawful dividend, stock purchase or stock redemption.

(c) Any director against whom a claim is successfully asserted under this section shall be entitled, to the extent of the amount paid by him as a result of such claim, to be subrogated to the rights of the corporation against stockholders who received the dividend on, or assets for the sale or redemption of, their stock with knowledge of facts indicating that such dividend, stock purchase or redemption was unlawful under this chapter, in proportion to the amounts received by such stockholders respectively.

SUBCHAPTER VI. STOCK TRANSFERS

§ 201. **Transfer of stock and stock certificate**

Except as otherwise provided in this chapter, the transfer of stock and the certificates of stock which represent the stock shall be governed by Article 8 of Title 6.

§ 202. **Restriction on transfer of securities**

(a) A written restriction on the transfer or registration of transfer of a security of a corporation, if permitted by this section and noted conspicuously on the security, may be enforced against the holder of the restricted security or any successor or transferee of the holder including an executor, administrator, trustee, guardian or other fiduciary entrusted with like responsibility for the person or estate of the holder. Unless noted conspicuously on the security, a restriction, even though permitted by this section, is ineffective except against a person with actual knowledge of the restriction.

(b) A restriction on the transfer or registration of transfer of securities of a corporation may be imposed either by the certificate of incorporation or by the by-laws or by an agreement among any number of security holders or among such holders and the corporation. No restriction so imposed shall be binding with respect to securities issued prior to the adoption of the restriction unless the holders of the securities are parties to an agreement or voted in favor of the restriction.

(c) A restriction on the transfer of securities of a corporation is permitted by this section if it:

(1) Obligates the holder of the restricted securities to offer to the corporation or to any other holders of securities of the corporation or to any other person or to any combination of the foregoing, a prior opportunity, to be exercised within a reasonable time, to acquire the restricted securities; or

(2) Obligates the corporation or any holder of securities of the corporation or any other person or any combination of the foregoing, to purchase the securities which are the subject of an agreement respecting the purchase and sale of the restricted securities; or

(3) Requires the corporation or the holders of any class of securities of the corporation to consent to any proposed transfer of the restricted securities or to approve the proposed transferee of the restricted securities; or

(4) Prohibits the transfer of the restricted securities to designated persons or classes of persons, and such designation is not manifestly unreasonable.

(d) Any restriction on the transfer of the shares of a corporation for the purpose of maintaining its status as an electing small business corporation under subchapter S of the United States Internal Revenue Code is conclusively presumed to be for a reasonable purpose.

(e) Any other lawful restriction on transfer or registration of transfer of securities is permitted by this section.

§ 203. Tender offers

(a) No offeror shall make a tender offer unless:

(1) Not less than 20 nor more than 60 days before the date the tender offer is to be made, the offeror shall deliver personally or by registered or certified mail to the corporation whose equity securities are to be subject to the tender offer, at its registered office in this State or at its principal place of business, a written statement of the offeror's intention to make the tender offer. The statement shall include the name and address of the offeror and of each director and principal officer of the offeror; a description of the equity securities to be purchased and the consideration to be offered; the duration of the offer; the date on which the offeror may first purchase tendered securities; the amount or number of equity securities to be purchased or the manner in which such number or amount will be determined; whether the offeror will unconditionally accept all or any part of the equity securities tendered and, if not, upon what conditions acceptance will be made; the number or amount of any equity securities of the corporation owned beneficially by the offeror and any associate of the offeror as of the date of the delivery of the statement; a description of any contract, agreement or understanding to which the offeror or any associate of the offeror is a party with respect to the ownership, voting rights or any other interest in any equity security of the corporation; and, if the offeror permits the purchase of less than all the outstanding equity securities issued by the corporation, copies of a balance sheet of the offeror as of the end of its last fiscal year and of its income statements for the three fiscal years preceding the offer:

(2) The tender offer shall remain open for a period of at least 20 days after it is first made to the holders of the equity securities, during which period any stockholder may withdraw any of the equity securities tendered to the offeror, and any revised or amended tender offer which changes the amount or type of consideration offered or the number of equity securities for which the offer is made shall remain open for an additional period of at least 10 days following the amendment; and

(3) The offeror and any associate of the offeror will not purchase or pay for any tendered equity security for a period of at least 20 days after the tender offer is first made to the holders of the equity securities, and no such purchase or payment shall be made within 10 days after an amended or revised tender offer if the amendment or revision changes the amount or type of consideration offered or the number of equity securities for which the offer is made. If during the period the tender offer must remain open pursuant to the provisions of this Section, a greater number of equity securities is tendered than the offeror is bound or willing to purchase, the equity securities shall be purchased pro rata, as nearly as may be, according to the number of shares tendered during such period by each equity security holder;

(b) Notwithstanding the foregoing:

(1) Whenever an offeror has delivered the statement required by subsection (a) (1) of this section, a subsequent offeror who shall also deliver the statement required by subsection (a) (1) of this section may thereafter make a tender offer for equity securities of the same class as in the original offer at or after the date this section permits the original offeror to make an offer.

(2) If the original offeror has made a tender offer in compliance with this section, the date upon which a subsequent offer for equity securities of the same class may close and the offeror purchase or pay for equity securities tendered thereunder may be the same as provided in the original offer at the date the subsequent offer is made.

(c) As used in this section, the term:

(1) 'Offeror' means any person, corporation, partnership, unincorporated association or other entity who makes a tender offer, and includes any two or more of the same who make a tender offer jointly or intend to exercise jointly or in concert any voting rights of the equity securities for which the tender offer is made;

(2) 'Tender offer' means any offer to purchase or invitation to tender equity securities for purchase made by an offeror to more than 30 of the holders of equity securities of any corporation organized under this chapter if, after the consummation thereof, the offeror and any associate of

the offeror would own beneficially, directly or indirectly, more than five percent of any class of the outstanding equity securities of the corporation, unless the offer is exempted by any other provision of this section;

(3) 'Tender offer' does not mean:

(i) An offer made by a corporation to purchase its own equity securities or equity securities of another corporation, if a majority of the shares entitled to vote in the election of directors of such corporation is held directly or indirectly by the offering corporation;

(ii) An offer to purchase equity securities to be effected by a registered broker-dealer on a stock exchange or in the over-the-counter market if the broker performs only the customary broker's function, and receives no more than the customary broker's commissions, and neither the principal nor the broker solicits or arranges for the solicitation of orders to sell such equity securities;

(4) A tender offer is 'made' when it is first published or sent or given to the holders of the equity securities;

(5) 'Equity security' means any stock, bond, or other obligation the holder of which has the right to vote, or any security convertible into, or any right, option or warrant to purchase, any such stock, bond or other obligation;

(6) 'Associate of the offeror' means:

(i) Any corporation or other organization of which the offeror is an officer, director or partner, or is, directly or indirectly, the beneficial owner of ten percent or more of any class of equity securities;

(ii) Any person who is an officer, director, partner or managing agent of an offeror, or who is, directly or indirectly, the beneficial owner of ten percent or more of any class of equity securities of the offeror;

(iii) Any trust or other estate in which the offeror has a substantial beneficial interest or as to which the offeror serves as trustee or in a similar fiduciary capacity; or

(iv) The spouse of the offeror, or any relative of the offeror or of such spouse who has the same home as the offeror;

(d) The certificate of incorporation of any corporation organized under this chapter may provide that tender offers for the purchase of its equity securities shall not be subject to the provisions of this section.

(e) The Court of Chancery is hereby vested with exclusive jurisdiction summarily to hear and determine alleged violations of the provisions of this section. The court may, in its discretion, award such relief as it may deem just and proper, including directing the corporation to refuse to transfer on its books and to refuse to recognize the vote with respect to any equity security acquired pursuant to a tender offer which does not comply with or is not exempt under the provisions of this section.

SUBCHAPTER VII. MEETINGS, ELECTIONS, VOTING AND NOTICE

§ 211. Meetings of stockholders

(a) Meetings of stockholders may be held at such place, either within or without this State, as may be designated by or in the manner provided in the by-laws or, if not so designated, at the registered office of the corporation in this State.

(b) An annual meeting of stockholders shall be held for the election of directors on a date and at a time designated by or in the manner provided in the by-laws. Any other proper business may be transacted at the annual meeting.

(c) A failure to hold the annual meeting at the designated time or to elect a sufficient number of directors to conduct the business of the corporation shall not affect otherwise valid corporate acts or work a forfeiture or dissolution of the corporation except as may be otherwise specifically provided in this chapter. If the annual meeting for election of directors is not held on the date designated therefor, the directors shall cause the meeting to be held as soon thereafter as convenient. If there be a failure to hold the annual meeting for a period of thirty days after the date designated therefor, or if no date has been designated, for a period of thirteen months after the organization of the corporation or after its last annual meeting, the Court of Chancery may summarily order a meeting to be held upon the application of any stockholder or director. The shares of stock represented at such meeting, either in person or by proxy, and entitled to vote thereat, shall constitute a quorum for the purpose of such meeting, notwithstanding any provision of the certificate of incorporation or by-laws to the contrary. The Court of Chancery may issue such orders as may be appropriate, including, without limitation, orders designating the time and place of such meeting, the record date for determination of stockholders entitled to vote, and the form of notice of such meeting.

(d) Special meetings of the stockholders may be called by the board of directors or by such person or persons as may be authorized by the certificate of incorporation or by the by-laws.

(e) All elections of directors shall be by written ballot, unless otherwise provided in the certificate of incorporation.

§ 212. Voting rights of stockholders; proxies; limitations

(a) Unless otherwise provided in the certificate of incorporation and subject to the provisions of section 213 of this title, each stockholder shall be entitled to one vote for each share of capital stock held by such stockholder. If the certificate of incorporation provides for more or less than one vote for any share, on any matter, every reference in this chapter to a majority or other proportion of stock shall refer to such majority or other proportion of the votes of such stock.

(b) Each stockholder entitled to vote at a meeting of stockholders or to express consent or dissent to corporate action in writing without a meeting may authorize another person or persons to act for him by proxy, but no such proxy shall be voted or acted upon after three years from its date, unless the proxy provides for a longer period.

(c) A duly executed proxy shall be irrevocable if it states that it is irrevocable and if, and only as long as, it is coupled with an interest sufficient in law to support an irrevocable power. A proxy may be made irrevocable regardless of whether the interest with which it is coupled is an interest in the stock itself or an interest in the corporation generally.

§ 214. Cumulative voting

The certificate of incorporation of any corporation may provide that at all elections of directors of the corporation, or at elections held under specified circumstances, each holder of stock or of any class or classes or of a series or series thereof shall be entitled to as many votes as shall equal the number of votes which (except for such provision as to cumulative voting) he would be entitled to cast for the election of directors with respect to his shares of stock multiplied by the number of directors to be elected by him, and that he may cast all of such votes for a single director or may distribute them among the number to be voted for, or for any two or more of them as he may see fit.

§ 218. Voting trusts and other voting agreements

(a) One or more stockholders may by agreement in writing deposit capital stock of an original issue with or transfer capital stock to any person or persons, or corporation or corporations authorized to act as trustee, for the purpose of vesting in such person or persons, corporation or corporations, who may be designated voting trustee, or voting trustees, the right to vote thereon for any period of time determined by such agreement, not exceeding ten years, upon the terms and conditions stated in such agreement. The agreement may contain any other lawful provisions not inconsistent with such purpose. After the filing of a copy of the agreement in the registered office of the corporation in this State, which copy shall be open to the inspection of any stockholder of the corporation or any beneficiary of the trust under the agreement daily during business hours, certificates of stock shall be issued to the voting trustee or trustees to represent any stock of an original issue so deposited with him or them, and any certificates of stock so transferred to the voting trustee or trustees shall be surrendered and cancelled and new certificates therefor shall be issued to the voting trustee or trustees. In the certificate so issued it shall be stated that they are issued pursuant to such agreement, and that fact shall also be stated in the stock ledger of the corporation. The voting trustee or trustees may vote the stock so issued or transferred during the period specified in the agreement. Stock standing in the name of the voting trustee or trustees may be voted either in person or by proxy, and in voting the stock, the voting trustee or trustees shall incur no responsibility as stockholder, trustee or otherwise, except for his or their own individual malfeasance. In any case where two or more persons are designated as voting trustees, and the right and method of voting any stock standing in their names at any meeting of the corporation are not fixed by the agreement appointing the trustees, the right to vote the stock and the manner of voting it at the meeting shall be determined by a majority of the trustees, or if they be equally divided as to the right and manner of voting the stock in any particular case, the vote of the stock in such case shall be divided equally among the trustees.

(b) At any time within two years prior to the time of expiration of any voting trust agreement as originally fixed or as last extended as provided in this subsection, one or more beneficiaries of the trust under the voting trust agreement may, by written agreement and with the written consent of the voting trustee or trustees, extend the duration of the voting trust agreement for an additional period not exceeding ten years from the expiration date of the trust as originally fixed or as last extended, as provided in this subsection. The voting trustee or trustees shall, prior to the time of expiration of any such voting trust agreement, as originally fixed or as previously extended, as the case may be, file in the registered office of the corporation in this State a copy of such extension agreement and of his or their consent thereto, and thereupon the duration of the voting trust agreement shall be extended for the period fixed in the extension agreement; but no such extension agreement shall affect the rights or obligations of persons not parties thereto.

(c) An agreement between two or more stockholders, if in writing and signed by the parties thereto, may provide that in exercising any voting rights, the shares held by them shall be voted as provided by the agreement, or as the parties may agree, or as determined in accordance with a procedure agreed upon by them. No such agreement shall be effective for a term of more than ten years, but, at any time within two years prior to the time of expiration of such agreement, the parties may extend its duration for as many additional periods, each not to exceed ten years, as they may desire.

(d) The validity of any such voting trust or other voting agreement, otherwise lawful, shall not be affected during a period of ten years from the date when it was created or last extended by the fact that under its terms it will or may last beyond such ten-year period.

(e) This section shall not be deemed to invalidate any voting or other agreement among stockholders or any irrevocable proxy which is not otherwise illegal.

§ 220. Stockholder's right of inspection

(a) As used in this section, "stockholder" means a stockholder of record.

(b) Any stockholder, in person or by attorney or other agent, shall, upon written demand under oath stating the purpose thereof, have the right during the usual hours for business to inspect for any proper purpose the corporation's stock ledger, a list of its stockholders, and its other books and records, and to make copies or extracts therefrom. A proper purpose shall mean a purpose reasonably related to such person's interest as a stockholder. In every instance where an attorney or other agent shall be the person who seeks the right to inspection, the demand under oath shall be accompanied by a power of attorney or such other writing which authorizes the attorney or other agent to so act on behalf of the stockholder. The demand under oath shall be directed to the corporation at its registered office in this State or at its principal place of business.

(c) If the corporation, or an officer or agent thereof, refuses to permit an inspection sought by a stockholder or attorney or other agent acting for the stockholder pursuant to sub-section (b) or does not reply to the demand within five business days after the demand has been made, the stockholder may apply to the Court of Chancery for an order to compel such inspection. The Court of Chancery is hereby vested with exclusive jurisdiction to determine whether or not the person seeking inspection is entitled to the inspection sought. The court may summarily order the corporation to permit the stockholder to inspect the corporation's stock ledger, an existing list of stockholders, and its other books and records, and to make copies or extracts therefrom; or the Court may order the corporation to furnish to the stockholder a list of its stockholders as of a specific date on condition that the stockholder first pay to the corporation the reasonable cost of obtaining and furnishing such list and on such other conditions as the Court deems appropriate. Where the stockholder seeks to inspect the corporation's books and records, other than its stock ledger or list of stockholders, he shall first establish (1) that he has complied with the provisions of this section respecting the form and manner of making demand for inspection of such document; and (2) that the inspection he seeks is for a proper purpose. Where the stockholder seeks to inspect the corporation's stock ledger or list of stockholders and he has complied with the provisions of this section respecting the form and manner of making demand for inspection of such documents, the burden of proof shall be upon the corporation to establish that the inspection he seeks is for an improper purpose. The court may, in its discretion, prescribe any limitations or conditions with reference to the inspection, or award such other or further relief as the court may deem just and proper. The court may order books, documents and records, pertinent extracts therefrom, or duly authenticated copies thereof, to be brought within this State and kept in this State upon such terms and conditions as the order may prescribe.

(d) Any director shall have the right to examine the corporation's stock ledger, a list of its stockholders and its other books and records for a purpose reasonably related to his position as a director. The Court of Chancery is hereby vested with the exclusive jurisdiction to determine whether a director is entitled to the inspection sought. The court may summarily order the corporation to permit the director to inspect any and all books and records, the stock ledger and the stock list and to make copies or extracts therefrom. The court may, in its discretion, prescribe any limitations or conditions with reference to the inspection, or award such other and further relief as the court may deem just and proper.

§ 226. Appointment of custodian or receiver of corporation on deadlock or for other cause

(a) The Court of Chancery, upon application of any stockholder, may appoint one or more persons to be custodians, and, if the corporation is insolvent, to be receivers, of and for any corporation when:

(1) At any meeting held for the election of directors the stockholders are so divided that they have failed to elect successors to directors whose terms have expired or would have expired upon qualification of their successors; or

(2) The business of the corporation is suffering or is threatened with irreparable injury because the directors are so divided respecting the management of the affairs of the corporation that the required vote for action by the board of directors cannot be obtained and the stockholders are unable to terminate this division; or

(3) The corporation has abandoned its business and has failed within a reasonable time to take steps to dissolve, liquidate or distribute its assets.

(b) A custodian appointed under this section shall have all the powers and title of a receiver appointed under section 291 of this title, but the authority of the custodian is to continue the business of the corporation and not to liquidate its affairs and distribute its assets, except when the Court shall otherwise order and except in cases arising under subparagraph (a) (3) of this section or section 352(a) (2) of this title. __

SUBCHAPTER VIII. AMENDMENT OF CERTIFICATE OF INCORPORATION; CHANGES IN CAPITAL AND CAPITAL STOCK

§ 242. Amendment of certificate of incorporation after receipt of payment for stock; non-stock corporations

(a) After a corporation has received payment for any of its capital stock, it may amend its certificate of incorporation, from time to time, in any and as many respects as may be desired, so long as its certificate of incorporation as amended would contain only such provisions as it would be lawful and proper to insert in an original certificate of incorporation filed at the time of the filing of the amendment; and, if a change in stock or the rights of stockholders, or an exchange, reclassification or cancellation of stock or rights of stockholders is to be made, such provisions as may be necessary to effect such change, exchange, reclassification or cancellation. In particular, and without limitation upon such general power of amendment, a corporation may amend its certificate of incorporation, from time to time, so as:

(1) To change its corporate name; or

(2) To change, substitute, enlarge or diminish the nature of its business or its corporate powers and purposes; or

(3) To increase or decrease its authorized capital stock or to reclassify the same, by changing the number, par value, designations, preferences, or relative, participating, optional, or other special rights of the shares, or the qualifications, limitations or restrictions of such rights, or by changing shares with par value into shares without par value, or shares without par value into shares with par value either with or without increasing or decreasing the number of shares; or

(4) To cancel or otherwise affect the right of the holders of the shares of any class to receive dividends which have accrued but have not been declared; or

(5) To create new classes of stock having rights and preferences either prior and superior or subordinate and inferior to the stock of any class then authorized, whether issued or unissued; or

(6) To change the period of its duration.

Any or all such changes or alterations may be effected by one certificate of amendment.

(b) If an amendment effects any change in the issued shares of the corporation, and if, when the amendment becomes effective the aggregate amount of capital represented by all issued shares immediately after the amendment will be less than the aggregate amount of capital represented by all issued shares immediately before the amendment, the certificate of amendment shall state that a certificate of reduction of capital pursuant to section 244(c) of this title is being filed with the certificate of amendment.

(c) Every amendment authorized by subsection (a) of this section shall be made and effected in the following manner—

(1) If the corporation has capital stock, its board of directors shall adopt a resolution setting forth the amendment proposed, declaring its advisability, and either calling a special meeting of the stockholders entitled to vote in respect thereof for the consideration of such amendment or directing that the amendment proposed be considered at the next annual meeting of the stockholders. Such special or annual meeting shall be called and held upon notice in accordance with section 222 of this title. The notice shall set forth such amendment in full or a brief summary of the changes to be effected thereby, as the directors shall deem advisable. At the meeting a vote of the stockholders entitled to vote thereon shall be taken for and against the proposed amendment. If a majority of the outstanding stock entitled to vote thereon, and a majority of the outstanding stock of each class entitled to vote thereon as a class has been voted in favor of the amendment, a certificate setting forth the amendment and certifying that such amendment has been duly adopted in accordance with the provisions of this section shall be executed, acknowledged, filed, and recorded, and shall become effective in accordance with section 103 of this title.

(2) The holders of the outstanding shares of a class shall be entitled to vote as a class upon a proposed amendment, whether or not entitled to vote thereon by the provisions of the certificate of incorporation, if the amendment would increase or decrease the aggregate number of authorized shares of such class, increase or decrease the par value of the shares of such class, or alter or change the powers, preferences or special rights of the shares of such class so as to affect them adversely. If any proposed amendment would alter or change the powers, preferences, or special rights of one or more series of any class so as to affect them adversely, but shall not so affect the entire class, then only the shares of the series so affected by the amendment shall be considered a separate class for the purposes of this paragraph. The number of authorized shares of any such class or classes of stock may be increased or decreased (but not below the number of shares thereof then outstanding) by the of the corporation entitled to vote irrespective of the provision of this paragraph (c) (2), if so provided in the original certificate of incorporation, in any amendment thereto which created such class or classes of stock or which was adopted prior to the issuance of any shares of such class or classes of stock, or in any amendment thereto which was authorized by a resolution or resolutions adopted by the affirmative vote of the holders of a majority of such class or classes of stock.

(3) If the corporation has no capital stock, then the governing body thereof shall adopt a resolution setting forth the amendment proposed and declaring its advisability. If at a subsequent meeting, held, on notice stating the purpose thereof, not earlier than 15 days and not later than 60 days from the meeting at which such resolution has been passed, a majority of all the members of the governing body, shall vote in favor of such amendment, a certificate thereof shall be executed, acknowledged, filed, recorded, and shall become effective in accordance with section 103 of this title. The certificate of incorporation of any such corporation without capital stock may contain a provision requiring any amendment thereto to be approved by a specified number or percentage of the members or of any specified class of members of such corporation in which event only one meeting of the governing body thereof shall be necessary, and such proposed amendment shall be submitted to the members or to any specified class of members of such corporation without capital stock in the same manner, so far as applicable, as is provided in this section for an amendment to the certifi-

cate of incorporation of a stock corporation; and in the event of the adoption thereof, a certificate evidencing such amendment shall be executed, filed, acknowledged, recorded and shall become effective in accordance with section 103 of this title.

(4) Whenever the certificate of incorporation shall require for action by the board of directors, by the holders of any class or series of shares or by the holders of any other securities having voting power the vote of a greater number or proportion than is required by any section of this title, the provision of the certificate of incorporation requiring such greater vote shall not be altered, amended or repealed except by such greater vote.

§ 244. Reduction of capital

(a) A corporation, by resolution of its board of directors, may reduce its capital in any of the following ways:

1. By reducing or eliminating the capital represented by shares of capital stock which have been retired;

2. By applying to an otherwise authorized purchase or redemption of outstanding shares of its capital stock some or all of the capital represented by the shares being purchased or redeemed, or any capital that has not been allocated to any particular class of its capital stock;

3. By applying to an otherwise authorized conversion or exchange of outstanding shares of its capital stock some or all of the capital represented by the shares being converted or exchanged, or some or all of any capital that has not been allocated to any particular class of its capital stock, or both, to the extent that such capital in the aggregate exceeds the total aggregate par value or the stated capital of any previously unissued shares issuable upon such conversion or exchange; or,

4. By transferring to surplus (i) some or all of the capital not represented by any particular class of its capital stock; (ii) some or all of the capital represented by issued shares of its par value capital stock, which capital is in excess of the aggregate par value of such shares; or (iii) some of the capital represented by issued shares of its capital stock without par value.

(b) Notwithstanding the other provisions of this section, no reduction of capital shall be made or effected unless the assets of the corporation remaining after such reduction shall be sufficient to pay any debts of the corporation for which payment has not been otherwise provided, and the certificate required by subsection (c) of this section shall so state. No reduction of capital shall release any liability of any stockholder whose shares have not been fully paid.

(c) Whenever capital of a corporation is to be reduced, such reduction shall not become effective until a certificate has been executed, acknowledged and filed and has become effective in accordance with section 103 of this title. Such certificate shall set forth the manner in and the extent to which the capital is to be reduced, including an identification of any shares of capital stock retired in connection with such reduction.

SUBCHAPTER IX. MERGER OR CONSOLIDATION

§ 251. Merger or consolidation of domestic corporations

(a) Any two or more corporations existing under the laws of this State may merge into a single corporation, which may be any one of the constituent corporations or may consolidate into a new corporation formed by the consolidation, pursuant to an agreement of merger or consolidation, as the case may be, complying and approved in accordance with this section.

(b) The board of directors of each corporation which desires to merge or consolidate shall adopt a resolution approving an agreement of merger or consolidation. The agreement shall state: (1) the terms and conditions of the merger or consolidation; (2) the mode of carrying the same into effect; (3) such amendments or changes in the certificate of incorporation of the surviving corporation as are desired to be effected by the merger or consolidation, or, if no such amendments or changes are desired, a statement that the certificate of incorporation of one of the constituent corporations shall be the certificate of incorporation of the surviving or resulting corporation; (4) the manner of converting the shares of each of the constituent corporations into shares or other securities of the corporation surviving or resulting from the merger or consolidation, and, if any shares of any of the constituent corporations are not to be converted solely into shares or other securities of the surviving or resulting corporation, the cash, property, rights or securities of any other corporation which the holders of such shares are to receive in exchange for, or upon conversion of such shares and the surrender of the certificates evidencing them, which cash, property, rights or securities of any other corporation may be in addition to or in lieu of shares or other securities of the surviving or resulting corporation; and (5) such other details or provisions as are deemed desirable, including, without limiting the generality of the foregoing, a provision for the payment of cash in lieu of the issuance or recognition of fractional shares, interests or rights, or for any other arrangement with respect thereto, consistent with the provisions of section 155 of this title. The agreement so adopted shall be executed in accordance with section 103 of this title. Any of the terms of the agreement of merger or consolidation may ne made dependent upon facts ascertainable outside of such agreement, provided that the manner in which such facts shall operate upon the terms of the agreement is clearly and expressly set forth in the agreement of merger or consolidation.

(c) The agreement required by subsection (b) shall be submitted to the stockholders of each constituent corporation at an annual or special meeting thereof for the purpose of acting on the agreement. Due notice of the time, place and purpose of the meeting shall be mailed to each holder of stock, whether voting or nonvoting, of the corporation at his address as it appears on the records of the corporation, at least 20 days prior to the date of the meeting. At the meeting the agreement shall be considered and a vote taken for its adoption or rejection. If a majority of the outstanding stock of the corporation entitled to vote thereon shall be voted for the adoption of the agreement, that fact shall be certified on the agreement by the secretary or assistant secretary of the corporation. If the agreement shall be so adopted and certified by each constituent corporation it shall then, in addition to the execution required by subsection (b) of this section, be executed, acknowledged and filed, and shall become effective, in accordance with section 103 of this title. It shall be recorded in the office of the Recorder of the County of this State in which the registered office of each such constituent corporation is located; or if any of the constitutent corporations shall have been specially created by a public act of the Legislature, then the agreement shall be recorded in the county where such corporation had its principal place of business in this State. In lieu of filing and recording the agreement or merger or consolidation, the surviving or resulting corporation may file a certificate of merger or consolidation, executed in accordance with section 103 of this title, which states (1) the name and state of incorporation of each of the constituent corporations, (2) that an agreement of merger or consolidation has been approved, adopted, certified, executed and acknowledged by each of the constituent corporations in accordance with this subsection, (3) the name of the surviving or resulting corporation, (4) the amendments or changes, if any, in the certificate of incorporation of the surviving corporation that are to be effected by merger or consolidation, or, if none, that the certificate of incorporation of one of the constituent corporations, naming it, shall be the certificate of incorporation of the surviving or resulting corporation, (5) that the executed agreement of consolidation or merger is on file at the principal place of business of the surviving corporation, stating the address thereof and (6) that a copy of the agreement of consolidation or merger will be furnished by the surviving corporation, on request and without cost, to any stockholder of any constituent corporation.

(d) Any agreement of merger or consolidation may contain a provision that at any time prior to the filing of the agreement with the Secretary of State, the agreement may be terminated by the board of directors of any constituent corporation notwithstanding approval of the agreement by the stockholders of all or any of the constituent corporations.

(e) In the case of a merger, the certificate of incorporation of the surviving corporation shall automatically be amended to the extent, if any, that changes in the certificate of incorporation are set forth in the agreement of merger.

(f) Notwithstanding the requirements of subsection (c), unless required by its certificate of incorporation, no vote of stockholders of a constituent corporation surviving a merger shall be necessary to authorize a merger if (1) the agreement of merger does not amend in any respect the certificate of incorporation of such constituent corporation, (2) each share of stock of such constituent corporation outstanding immediately prior to the effective date of the merger is to be an identical outstanding or treasury share of the surviving corporation after the effective date of the merger, and (3) either no shares of common stock of the surviving corporation and no shares, securities or obligations convertible into such stock are to be issued or delivered under the plan of merger, or the authorized unissued shares or the treasury shares of common stock of the surviving corporation to be issued or delivered under the plan of merger plus those initially issuable upon conversion of any other shares, securities or obligations to be issued or delivered under such plan do not exceed 20 percent of the shares of common stock of such constituent corporation outstanding immediately prior to the effective date of the merger. No vote of stockholders of a constituent corporation shall be necessary to authorize a merger or consolidation if no shares of the stock of such corporation shall have been issued prior to the adoption by the board of directors of the resolution approving the agreement of merger or consolidation. If an agreement of merger is adopted by the constituent corporation surviving the merger, by action of its board of directors and without any vote of its stockholders pursuant to this subsection, the secretary or assistant secretary of that corporation shall certify on the agreement, that the agreement has been adopted pursuant to this subsection and that, as of the date of such certificate, the outstanding shares of the corporation were such as to render this subsection applicable. The agreement so adopted and certified shall then be executed, acknowledged and filed and shall become effective, in accordance with section 103 of this title. Such filing shall constitute a representation by the person who executes the agreement that the facts stated in the certificate remain true immediately prior to such filing.

§ 253. Merger of parent corporation and subsidiary or subsidiaries

(a) In any case in which at least 90 percent of the outstanding shares of each class of the stock of a corporation or corporations is owned by another corporation and one of such corporations is a corporation of this State and the other or others are corporations of this State or of any other state or states or of the District of Columbia and the laws of such other state or states or of the District permit a corporation of such jurisdiction to merge with a corporation of another jurisdiction, the corporation having such stock ownership may either merge such other corporation or corporations into itself and assume all of its or their obligations, or merge itself, or itself and one or more of such other corporations, into one of such other corporations by executing, acknowledging and filing, in accordance with section 103 of this title, a certificate of such ownership and merger setting forth a copy of the resolution of its board of directors to so merge and the date of the adoption thereof; provided, however, that in case the parent corporation shall not own all the outstanding stock of all the subsidiary corporations, parties to a merger as aforesaid, the resolution of the board of directors of the parent corporation shall state the terms and conditions of the merger, including the securities, cash, property, or rights to be issued, paid, delivered or granted by the surviving corporation upon surrender of each share of the subsidiary corporation or corporations not owned by the parent corporation. If the parent corporation be not the surviving corporation, the resolution shall include provision for the pro rata issuance of stock of the surviving corporation to the holders of the stock of the parent corporation on surrender of the certificates therefor, and the certificate of ownership and merger shall state that the proposed merger has been approved by a majority of the outstanding stock of the parent corporation entitled to vote thereon at a meeting thereof duly called and held after 20 days' notice of the purpose of the meeting mailed to each such stockholder at his address as it appears on the records of the corporation. A certified copy of the certificate shall be recorded in the office of the Recorder of the County in this State in which the registered office of each constituent corporation which is a corporation of this State is located. If the surviving corporation exists under the laws of the District of Columbia or any state other than this State, the provisions of section 252(d) of this title shall also apply to a merger under this section.

(b) If the surviving corporation is a Delaware corporation, it may change its corporate name by the inclusion of a provision to that effect in the resolution of merger adopted by the directors of the parent corporation and set forth in the certificate of ownership and merger, and upon the effective date of the merger, the name of the corporation shall be so changed.

(c) The provisions of section 251(d) of this title shall apply to a merger under this section, and the provisions of section 251(e) shall apply to a merger under this section in which the surviving corporation is the subsidiary corporation and is a corporation of this State. Any merger which effects any changes other than those authorized by this section or made applicable by this subsection shall be accomplished under the provisions of section 251 or section 252 of this title. The provisions of section 262 of this title shall not apply to any merger effected under this section, except as provided in subsection (d) of this section.

(d) In the event all of the stock of a subsidiary Delaware corporation party to a merger effected under this section is not owned by the parent corporation immediately prior to the merger, the stockholders of the subsidiary Delaware corporation party to the merger shall have appraisal rights as set forth in section 262 of this Title.

(e) A merger may be effected under this section although one or more of the corporations parties to the merger is a corporation organized under the laws of a jurisdiction other than one of the United States; provided that the laws of such jurisdiction permit a corporation of such jurisdiction to merge with a corporation of another jurisdiction; and provided further that the surviving or resulting corporation shall be a corporation of this State.

* * *

§ 262. Payment for stock or membership of person objecting to merger or consolidation

(a) Any stockholder who has complied with the provisions of subsection (d) of this Section and has neither voted in favor of the merger or consolidation nor consented thereto in writing pursuant to Section 228 of this Chapter shall be entitled to an appraisal by the Court of Chancery of the fair value of his shares of stock under the circumstances described in subsections (b) and (c). As used in this Section, the word "stockholder" means a holder of record of stock in a stock corporation and also a member of record of a non-stock corporation; the words "stock" and "share" mean and include what is ordinarily meant by those words and also membership or membership interest of a member of a non-stock corporation.

(b) Appraisal rights shall be available for the shares of any class or series of stock of a constituent corporation in a merger to be effected pursuant to Sections 251, 252, 254, 257 or 258 of this Chapter;

(1) provided, however, that no appraisal rights under this Section shall be available for the shares of any class or series of stock which, at the record date fixed to determine the stockholders entitled to receive notice of and to vote at the meeting of stockholders to act upon the agreement of merger or consolidation, were either (i) listed on a national securities exchange or (ii) held of record by more than 2,000 stockholders; and further provided that no appraisal rights shall be available for any shares of stock of the constituent corporation surviving a merger if the merger did not require for its approval the vote of the stockholders of the surviving

corporation as provided in subsection (f) of Section 251 of this Chapter.

(2) Notwithstanding the provisions of subsection (b) (1) of this Section, appraisal rights under this Section shall be available for the shares of any class or series of stock of a constituent corporation if the holders are required by the terms of an agreement of merger or consolidation pursuant to Sections 251, 252, 254, 257 and 258 of this Chapter to accept for such stock anything except (i) shares of stock of the corporation surviving or resulting from such merger or consolidation; (ii) shares of stock of any other corporation which at the effective date of the merger *or* consolidation will be either listed on a national securities exchange or held of record by more than 2,000 stockholders; (iii) *cash* in lieu of fractional shares of the corporations described in the foregoing clauses (i) and (ii); or (iv) any combination of the shares of stock and cash in lieu of fractional shares described in the foregoing clauses (i), (ii) and (iii) of this subsection.

(3) In the event all of the stock of a subsidiary Delaware corporation party to a merger effected under Section 253 of this chapter is not owned by the parent corporation immediately prior to the merger, appraisal rights shall be available for the shares of the subsidiary Delaware corporation.

(c) Any corporation may provide in its certificate of incorporation that appraisal rights under this Section shall be available for the shares of any class or series of its stock as a result of an amendment to its certificate of incorporation, any merger or consolidation in which the corporation is a constituent corporation or the sale of all or substantially all of the assets of the corporation. In such event, the procedures of this Section, including those set forth in subsections (d) and (e), shall apply as nearly as is practicable.

(d) Appraisal rights shall be perfected as follows:

(1) If a proposed merger or consolidation for which appraisal rights are provided under this Section is to be submitted for approval at a meeting of stockholders, the corporation, not less than 20 days prior to the meeting, shall notify each of its stockholders entitled to such appraisal rights that appraisal rights are available for any or all of the shares of the constituent corporations, and shall include in such notice a copy of this Section. Each stockholder electing to demand the appraisal of his shares shall deliver to the corporation, before the taking of the vote on the merger or consolidation, a written demand for appraisal of his shares. Such demand will be sufficient if it reasonably informs the corporation

of the identity of the stockholder and that the stockholder intends thereby to demand the appraisal of his shares; provided, however, that such demand must be in addition to and separate from any proxy or vote against the merger. Within 10 days after the effective date of such merger or consolidation, the surviving corporation shall notify each stockholder of each constituent corporation who has complied with the provisions of this subsection and has not voted in favor of or consented to the merger or consolidation of the date that the merger or consolidation has become effective; or

(2) If the merger or consolidation was approved pursuant to Section 228 or Section 253 of this Chapter, the surviving corporation, either before the effective date of the merger or within 10 days thereafter, shall notify each of the stockholders entitled to appraisal rights of the effective date of the merger or consolidation and that appraisal rights are available for any or all of the shares of the constituent corporation, and shall include in such notice a copy of this Section. The notice shall be sent by certified or registered mail, return receipt requested, addressed to the stockholder at his address as it appears on the records of the corporation. Any stockholder entitled to appraisal rights may, within 20 days after the date of mailing of the notice, demand in writing from the surviving corporation the appraisal of his shares. Such demand will be sufficient if it reasonably informs the corporation of the identity of the stockholder and that the stockholder intends to demand the appraisal of his shares.

(e) Within 120 days after the effective date of the merger or consolidation, the corporation or any stockholder who has complied with the provisions of subsections (a) and (d) hereof and who is otherwise entitled to appraisal rights, may file a petition in the Court of Chancery demanding a determination of the value of the stock of all such stockholders. Notwithstanding the foregoing, at any time within 60 days after the effective date of the merger or consolidation, any stockholder shall have the right to withdraw his demand for appraisal and to accept the terms offered upon the merger or consolidation. Within 120 days after the effective date of the merger or consolidation, any stockholder who has complied with the requirements of subsections (a) and (d) hereof, upon written request, shall be entitled to receive from the corporation surviving the merger or consolidation a statement setting forth the aggregate number of shares not voted in favor of the merger and with respect to which demands for appraisal have been received and the aggregate number of holders of such shares. Such written statement shall be mailed to the stockholder within 10 days after his written request for such a statement is received by the corporation or within 10 days after expiration of the period for delivery of demands for appraisal under subsection (d) hereof, whichever is later.

(f) Upon the filing of any such petition by a stockholder, service of a copy thereof shall be made upon the corporation, which shall within 20 days after such service file in the office of the Register in Chancery in which the petition was filed a duly verified list containing the names and addresses of all stockholders who have demanded payment for their shares and with whom agreements as to the value of their shares have not been reached by the corporation. If the petition shall be filed by the corporation, the petition shall be accompanied by such a duly verified list. The Register in Chancery, if so ordered by the Court, shall give notice of the time and place fixed for the hearing of such petition by registered or certified mail to the corporation and to the stockholders shown on the list at the addresses therein stated. Such notice shall also be given by one or more publications at least one week before the day of the hearing, in a newspaper of general circulation published in the City of Wilmington, Delaware or such publication as the Court deems advisable. The forms of the notices by mail and by publication shall be approved by the Court, and the costs thereof shall be borne by the corporation.

(g) At the hearing on such petition, the Court shall determine the stockholders who have complied with the provisions of this Section and who have become entitled to appraisal rights. The Court may require the stockholders who have demanded in appraisal for their shares to submit their certificates of stock to the Register in Chancery for notation thereon of the pendency of the appraisal proceedings; and if any stockholder fails to comply with such direction, the Court may dismiss the proceedings as to such stockholder.

(h) After determining the stockholders entitled to an appraisal, the Court shall appraise the shares, determining their fair value exclusive of any element of value arising from the accomplishment or expectation of the merger, together with a fair rate of interest, if any, to be paid upon the amount determined to be the fair value. In determining such fair value, the Court shall taken into account all relevant factors. In determining the fair rate of interest, the Court may consider all relevant factors, including the rate of interest which the corporation would have had to pay to borrow money during the pendency of the proceeding. Upon application by the corporation or by any stockholder entitled to participate in the appraisal proceeding, the Court may, in its discretion, permit discovery or other pretrial proceedings and may proceed to trial upon the appraisal prior to the final determination of the stockholder entitled to an appraisal. Any stockholder whose name appears on the list filed by the corporation pursuant to subsection (f) of this Section and who has submitted his certificates of stock to the Register in Chancery, if such is required, may participate fully in all proceedings until it is finally determined that he is not entitled to appraisal rights under this Section.

(i) The Court shall direct the payment of the fair value of the shares, together with interest, if any, by the surviving or resulting corporation to the stockholders entitled thereto upon the surrender to the corporation of the certificates representing such stock. The Court's decree may be enforced as other decrees of the Court of Chancery may be enforced, whether such surviving or resulting corporation be a corporation of this State or of any other state.

(j) The costs of the proceeding may be determined by the Court and taxed upon the parties as the Court deems equitable in the circumstances. Upon application of a stockholder, the Court may order all or a portion of the expenses incurred by any stockholder in connection with the appraisal proceeding, including, without limitation, reasonable attorney's fees and the fees and expenses of experts, to be charged pro rata against the value of all of the shares entitled to an appraisal.

(k) From and after the effective date of the merger or consolidation, no stockholder who has demanded his appraisal rights as provided in subsection (d) of this Section shall be entitled to vote such stock for any purpose or to receive payment of dividends or other distributions on the stock (except dividends or other distributions payable to stockholders of record at a date which is prior to the effective date of the merger or consolidation), provided, however, that if no petition for an appraisal shall be filed within the time provided in subsection (e) of this Section, or if such stockholder shall deliver to the corporation a written withdrawal of his demand for an appraisal and an acceptance of the merger or consolidation, either within 60 days after the effective date of the merger or consolidation as provided in subsection (e) of this Section or thereafter with the written approval of the corporation, then the right of such stockholder to an appraisal shall cease. Notwithstanding the foregoing, no appraisal proceeding in the Court of Chancery shall be dismissed as to any stockholder without the approval of the Court, and such approval may be conditioned upon such terms as the Court deems just.

(*l*) The shares of the surviving or resulting corporation into which the shares of such objecting stockholders would have been converted had they assented to the merger or consolidation shall have the status of authorized and unissued shares of the surviving or resulting corporation.

SUBCHAPTER X.   SALE OF ASSETS, DISSOLUTION AND WINDING UP

§ 271.   Sale, lease or exchange of assets; consideration; procedure

(a) Every corporation may at any meeting of its board of directors sell, lease, or exchange all or substantially all of its property and assets, including its good will and its corporate franchises, upon such terms and conditions and for such consideration, which may consist in whole or in part of money or other property, including shares of stock in, and/or other securities of, any other corporation or corporations, as its board of directors deems expedient and for the best interests of the corporation, when and as authorized by a resolution adopted by a majority of the outstanding stock of the corporation entitled to vote thereon at a meeting thereof duly called upon at least 20 days notice. The notice of the meeting shall state that such a resolution will be considered.

(b) Notwithstanding stockholder authorization or consent to a proposed sale, lease or exchange of a corporation's property and assets, the board of directors may abandon such proposed sale, lease or exchange without further action by the stockholders, subject to the rights, if any, of third parties under any contract relating thereto.

§ 275.   Dissolution; procedure

(a) If it should be deemed advisable in the judgment of the board of directors of any corporation that it should be dissolved, the board, after the adoption of a resolution to that effect by a majority of the whole board at any meeting called for that purpose, shall cause notice to be mailed to each stockholder entitled to vote thereon of the adoption of the resolution and of a meeting of stockholders to take action upon the resolution.

(b) At the meeting a vote shall be taken for and against the proposed dissolution. If a majority of the outstanding stock of the corporation entitled to vote thereon shall vote for the proposed dissolution, a certificate stating that the dissolution has been authorized in accordance with the provisions of this section and setting forth the names and residences of the directors and officers shall be executed, acknowledged and filed, and shall become effective, in accordance with section 103 of this title. Upon such certificate becoming effective in accordance with section 103 of this title, the corporation shall be dissolved.

(c) Whenever all the stockholders entitled to vote on a dissolution shall consent in writing, either in person or by duly authorized attorney, to a dissolution, no meeting of directors or stockholders shall be necessary. The consent shall be filed and shall become effective in accordance with section 103 of this title. Upon such consent becoming effective in accordance with section 103 of this title, the corporation shall be dissolved. In the event that the consent is signed by an attorney, the original power of attorney or a photocopy thereof shall be attached to and filed with the consent. The consent filed with the Secretary of State shall have attached to it the affidavit of the secretary or some other officer of the corporation stating that the consent has been signed by or on behalf of all the stockholders entitled to vote on a dissolution; in addition there shall be attached to the consent a certification by the secretary or some other officer of the corporation setting forth the names and residences of the directors and officers of the corporation.

* * *

SUBCHAPTER XII. RENEWAL, REVIVAL, EXTENSION AND RESTORATION OF CERTIFICATE OF INCORPORATION OR CHARTER

§ 311. Revocation of voluntary dissolution

(a) At any time prior to the expiration of three years following the dissolution of a corporation pursuant to section 275 of this title, or, at any time prior to the expiration of such longer period as the Court of Chancery may have directed pursuant to section 278 of this title, a corporation may revoke the dissolution theretofore effected by it in the following manner—

(1) The board of directors shall adopt a resolution recommending that the dissolution be revoked and directing

that the question of the revocation be submitted to a vote at a special meeting of stockholders.

(2) Notice of the special meeting of stockholders shall be given in accordance with section 222 of this title to each stockholder whose shares were entitled to vote upon a proposed dissolution before the corporation was dissolved.

(3) At the meeting a vote of the stockholders shall be taken on a resolution to revoke the dissolution. If a majority of the stock of the corporation which was outstanding and entitled to vote upon a dissolution at the time of its dissolution shall be voted for the resolution, a certificate of revocation of dissolution shall be executed and acknowledged in accordance with section 103 of this title, which shall state:

(i) the name of the corporation;

(ii) the names and respective addresses of its officers;

(iii) the names and respective addresses of its directors;

(iv) that a majority of the stock of the corporation which was outstanding and entitled to vote upon a dissolution at the time of its dissolution have voted in favor of a resolution to revoke the dissolution; or, if it be the fact, that, in lieu of a meeting and vote of stockholders, the stockholders have given their written consent to the revocation in accordance with section 228 of this title.

(b) Upon the filing in the office of the Secretary of State of the certificate of revocation of dissolution, the Secretary of State, upon being satisfied that the requirements of this section have been complied with, shall issue his certificate that the dissolution has been revoked, and the certificate of the Secretary of State shall be recorded in the office of the Recorder of the county in which the registered office of the corporation was maintained. Upon the issuance of such certificate by the Secretary of State, the revocation of the dissolution shall become effective and the corporation may again carry on its business.

(c) If after the dissolution became effective any other corporation organized under the laws of this State shall have adopted the same name as the corporation, or shall have adopted a name so nearly similar thereto as not to distinguish it from the corporation, or any foreign corporation shall have qualified to do business in this State under the same name as the corporation or under a name so nearly similar thereto as not to distinguish it from the corporation, then, in such case, the corporation shall not be reinstated under the same name which it bore when its dissolution became effective, but shall adopt and be reinstated under some other name, and in such case the certificate to be filed under the provisions of this section shall set forth the name borne by the corporation at the time its dissolution became effective and the new name under which the corporation is to be reinstated.

(d) Nothing in this section shall be construed to affect the jurisdiction or power of the Court of Chancery under sections 279 or 280 of this title.

§ 312. Renewal, revival, extension and restoration of certificate of incorporation

(a) As used in this section, the term "certificate of incorporation" includes the charter of a corporation organized under any special act or any law of this State.

(b) Any corporation may, at any time before the expiration of the time limited for its existence and any corporation whose certificate of incorporation has become inoperative by law for non-payment of taxes and any corporation whose certificate of incorporation has been forfeited pursuant to section 136(c) of this title and any corporation whose certificate of incorporation has expired by reason of failure to renew it or whose certificate of incorporation has been renewed, but, through failure to comply strictly with the provisions of this chapter, the validity of whose renewal has been brought into question, may at any time procure an extension, restoration, renewal or revival of its certificate of incorporation, together with all the rights, franchises, privileges and immunities and subject to all of its duties, debts and liabilities which had been secured or imposed by its original certificate of incorporation and all amendments thereto.

(c) The extension, restoration, renewal or revival of the certificate of incorporation may be procured by executing, acknowledging, filing and recording a certificate in accordance with section 103 of this title.

(d) The certificate required by subsection (c) shall state—

(1) The name of the corporation, which shall be the existing name of the corporation or the name it bore when its

certificate of incorporation expired, except as provided in subsection (f) of this section;

(2) The address (which shall include the street, city and county) of the corporation's registered office in this State and the name of its registered agent at such address;

(3) Whether or not the renewal, restoration or revival is to be perpetual and if not perpetual the time for which the renewal, restoration or revival is to continue and, in case of renewal before the expiration of the time limited for its existence, the date when the renewal is to commence, which shall be prior to the date of the expiration of the old certificate of incorporation which it is desired to renew;

(4) That the corporation desiring to be renewed or revived and so renewing or reviving its certificate of incorporation was organized under the laws of this State;

(5) The date when the certificate of incorporation would expire, if such is the case, or such other facts as may show that the certificate of incorporation has been forfeited pursuant to section 136(c) of this title, or has become inoperative or void or that the validity of any renewal has been brought into question;

(6) That the certificate for renewal or revival is filed by authority of those who were directors or members of the governing body of the corporation at the time its certificate of incorporation expired or who were elected directors or members of the governing body of the corporation as provided in subsection (h) of this section.

(e) Upon the filing of the certificate in accordance with section 103 of this title the corporation shall be renewed and revived with the same force and effect as if its certificate of incorporation had not been forfeited pursuant to section 136(c) of this title, or inoperative and void, or had not expired by limitation. Such reinstatement shall validate all contracts, acts, matters and things made, done and performed within the scope of its certificate of incorporation by the corporation, its officers and agents during the time when its certificate of incorporation was forfeited pursuant to section 136(c) of this title, or was inoperative or void or after its expiration by limitation, with the same force and effect and to all intents and purposes as if the certificate of incorporation had at all times remained in full force and effect. All real and personal property, rights and credits, which belonged to the corporation at the time its certificate of incorporation became forfeited pursuant to section

136(c) of this title, or inoperative or void, or expired by limitation and which were not disposed of prior to the time of its revival or renewal shall be vested in the corporation, after its revival and renewal, as fully and amply as they were held by the corporation at and before the time its certificate of incorporation became forfeited pursuant to section 136(c) of this title, inoperative or void, or expired by limitation, and the corporation after its renewal and revival shall be as exclusively liable for all contracts, acts, matters and things made, done or performed in its name and on its behalf by its officers and agents prior to its reinstatement, as if its certificate of incorporation had at all times remained in full force and effect.

(f) If, since the certificate of incorporation became forfeited pursuant to Section 136(c) of this title, or inoperative or void for non-payment of taxes, or expired by limitation, any other corporation organized under the laws of this State shall have adopted the same name as the corporation sought to be renewed or revived or shall have adopted a name so nearly similar thereto as not to distinguish it from the corporation to be renewed or revived or any foreign corporation qualified in accordance with section 371 of this title shall have adopted the same name as the corporation sought to be renewed or revived or shall have adopted a name so nearly similar thereto as not to distinguish it from the corporation to be renewed or revived, then in such case the corporation to be renewed or revived shall not be renewed under the same name which it bore when its certificate of incorporation became forfeited pursuant to section 136(c) of this title, inoperative or void, or expired but shall adopt or be renewed under some other name and in such case the certificate to be filed under the provisions of this section shall set forth the name borne by the corporation at the time its certificate of incorporation became forfeited pursuant to section 136(c) of this title, inoperative or void, or expired and the new name under which the corporation is to be renewed or revived.

(g) Any corporation seeking to renew or revive its certificate of incorporation under the provisions of this chapter shall pay to this State a sum equal to all franchise taxes and penalties thereon due at the time its certificate of incorporation became forfeited pursuant to section 136(c) of this title, inoperative and void for non-payment of taxes, or expired by limitation or otherwise.

(h) If a sufficient number of the last acting officers of any corporation desiring to renew or revive its certificate of incorporation are not available by reason of death, unknown address or refusal or neglect to act, the directors of the corporation or those remaining on the board, even if only one, may elect successors to such officers. In any case where there shall be no directors of the corporation available for the purposes aforesaid, the stockholders may elect a full board of directors, as provided by the by-laws of the corporation, and the board shall then elect such officers as are provided by law, by the certificate of incorporation or by the by-laws to carry on the business and affairs of the corporation. A special meeting of the stockholders for the purposes of electing directors may be called by any officer, director or stockholder upon notice given in accordance with section 222 of this title.

(i) After a renewal or revival of the certificate of incorporation of the corporation shall have been effected (except where a special meeting of stockholders has been called in accordance with the provisions of subsection (h)), the officers who signed the certificate of renewal or revivals shall, jointly, forthwith call a special meeting of the stockholders of the corporation upon notice given in accordance with section 222 of this title, and at the special meeting the stockholders shall elect a full board of directors, which board shall then elect such officers as are provided by law, by the certificate of incorporation or the by-laws to carry on the business and affairs of the corporation.

(j) Whenever it shall be desired to renew or revive the certificate of incorporation of any corporation organized under this chapter not for profit and having no capital stock, the governing body shall perform all the acts necessary for the renewal or revival of the charter of the corporation which are performed by the board of directors in the case of a corporation having capital stock. The members of any corporation not for profit and having no capital stock who are entitled to vote for the election of members of its governing body, shall perform all the acts necessary for the renewal or revival of the certificate of incorporation of the corporation which are performed by the stockholders in the case of a corporation having capital stock. In all other respects, the procedure for the renewal or revival of the certificate of incorporation of a corporation not for profit or having no capital stock shall conform, as nearly as may be applicable, to the procedure prescribed in this section

206

for the renewal or revival of the certificate of incorporation of a corporation having capital stock.

§ 313. Renewal, etc. of certificate of incorporation or charter of religious, charitable, educational, etc. corporations

(a) Every religious corporation, and every purely charitable or educational association, and every company, association or society, which by its certificate of incorporation, had, at the time its certificate of incorporation or charter became void by operation of law, for its object the assistance of sick, needy, or disabled members, or the defraying of funeral expenses of deceased members, or to provide for the wants of the widows and families after death of its members, whose certificate of incorporation or charter has become inoperative and void, by operation of section 510 of this title for failure to file annual franchise tax reports required, and for failure to pay taxes or penalties from which it would have been exempt if the reports had been filed, shall be deemed to have filed all the reports and be relieved of all the taxes and penalties, upon satisfactory proof submitted to the Secretary of State of its right to be classified under any of the classifications set out in this subsection, and upon filing with the Secretary of State a certificate of renewal and revival in manner and form as required by section 312 of this title.

(b) Upon the filing by the corporation of the proof of classification as required in subsection (a) of this section, and the filing of the certificate of renewal and revival, and payment of the required filing fee, the Secretary of State shall issue a certificate that the corporation's certificate of incorporation or charter has been renewed and revived as of the date of the certificate, and upon the recording of the certificate of the Secretary of State in the office of the Recorder for the county in which the original certificate of incorporation or charter of the corporation was rcorded, the corporation shall be renewed and revived with the same force and effect as is provided in subsection (e) of section 312 of this title for other corporations.

(c) Nothing contained in this section relieves any corporation of any of the classifications set out in subsection (a) of this section from filing the annual report required by section 502 of this title.

§ 314. Status of corporation

Any corporation desiring to renew, extend and continue its corporate existence, shall upon complying with the provisions of sections 312 or 313 of this title, and with the provisions of section 2 of Article IX of the Constitution of this State, be and continue for the time stated in its certificate of renewal, a corporation and shall, in addition to the rights, privileges and immunities conferred by its charter, possess and enjoy all the benefits of this chapter, which are applicable to the nature of its business, and shall be subject to the restrictions and liabilities by this chapter imposed on such corporations.

SUBCHAPTER XIV. CLOSE CORPORATIONS; SPECIAL PROVISIONS

§ 341. Law applicable to close corporation

(a) This subchapter applies to all close corporations, as defined in section 342 of this title. Unless a corporation elects to become a close corporation under this subchapter in the manner prescribed in this subchapter, it shall be subject in all respects to the provisions of this chapter, except the provisions of this subchapter.

(b) All provisions of this chapter shall be applicable to all close corporations, as defined in section 342 of this title, except insofar as this subchapter otherwise provides.

§ 342. Close corporation defined; contents of certificate of incorporation

(a) A close corporation is a corporation organized under this chapter whose certificate of incorporation contains the provisions required by section 102 of this title and, in addition, provides that:

(1) All of the corporation's issued stock of all classes, exclusive of treasury shares, shall be held of record by not more than a specified number of persons, not exceeding thirty; and

(2) All of the issued stock of all classes shall be subject to one or more of the restrictions on transfer permitted by section 202 of this title; and

(3) The corporation shall make no offering of any of its stock of any class which would constitute a "public offering" within the meaning of the United States Securities Act of 1933, as it may be amended from time to time.

(b) The certificate of incorporation of a close corporation may set forth the qualifications of stockholders, either by specifying classes of persons who shall be entitled to be holders of record of stock of any class, or by specifying classes of persons who shall not be entitled to be holders of stock of any class or both.

(c) For purposes of determining the number of holders of record of the stock of a close corporation, stock which is held in joint or common tenancy or by the entireties shall be treated as held by one stockholder.

§ 343. Formation of a close corporation

A close corporation shall be formed in accordance with sections 101, 102 and 103 of this title, except that:

(a) Its certificate of incorporation shall contain a heading stating the name of the corporation and that it is a close corporation, and

(b) Its certificate of incorporation shall contain the provisions required by section 342 of this title.

§ 344. Election of existing corporation to become a close corporation

Any corporation organized under this chapter may become a close corporation under this subchapter by executing, acknowledging, filing and recording, in accordance with section 103 of this title, a certificate of amendment of its certificate of incorporation which shall contain a statement that it elects to become a close corporation, the provisions required by section 342 of this title to appear in the certificate of incorporation of a close corporation, and a heading stating the name of the corporation and that it is a close corporation. Such amendment shall be adopted in accordance with the requirements of section 241 or 242 of this title, except that it must be approved by a vote of the holders of record of at least two-thirds of the shares of each class of stock of the corporation which are outstanding.

§ 345. Limitations on continuation of close corporation status

A close corporation continues to be such and to be subject to this subchapter until:

(a) It files with the Secretary of State a certificate of amendment deleting from its certificate of incorporation the provisions required or permitted by section 342 of this title to be stated in the certificate of incorporation to qualify it as a close corporation, or

(b) Any one of the provisions or conditions required or permitted by section 342 of this title to be stated in a certificate of incorporation to qualify a corporation as a close corporation has in fact been breached and neither the corporation nor any of its stockholders takes the steps required by section 348 of this title to prevent such loss of status or to remedy such breach.

§ 346. Voluntary termination of close corporation status by amendment of certificate of incorporation; vote required

(a) A corporation may voluntarily terminate its status as a close corporation and cease to be subject to this subchapter by amending its certificate of incorporation to delete therefrom the additional provisions required or permitted by section 342 of this title to be stated in the certificate of incorporation of a close corporation. Any such amendment shall be adopted and shall become effective in accordance with section 242 of this title, except that it must be approved by a vote of the holders of record of at least two-thirds of the shares of each class of stock of the corporation which are outstanding.

(b) The certificate of incorporation of a close corporation may provide that on any amendment to terminate its status as a close corporation, a vote greater than two-thirds or a vote of all shares of any class shall be required; and if the certificate of incorporation contains such a provision, that provision shall not be amended, repealed or modified by any vote less than that required to terminate the corporation's status as a close corporation.

§ 347. Issuance or transfer of stock of a close corporation in breach of qualifying conditions

(a) If stock of a close corporation is issued or transferred to any person who is not entitled under any provision of the certificate of incorporation permitted by section 342(b) of this title to be a holder of record of stock of such corporation, and if the certificate for such stock conspicuously notes the qualifications of the persons entitled to be holders of record thereof, such person is conclusively presumed to have notice of the fact of his ineligibility to be a stockholder.

(b) If the certificate of incorporation of a close corporation states the number of persons, not in excess of thirty, who are entitled to be holders of record of its stock, and if the certificate for such stock conspicuously states such number, and if the issuance or transfer of stock to any person would cause the stock to be held by more than such number of persons, the person to whom such stock is issued or transferred is conclusively presumed to have notice of this fact.

(c) If a stock certificate of any close corporation conspicuously notes the fact of a restriction on transfer of stock of the corporation, and the restriction is one which is permitted by section 202 of this title, the transferee of the stock is conclusively presumed to have notice of the fact that he has acquired stock in violation of the restriction, if such acquisition violates the restriction.

(d) Whenever any person to whom stock of a close corporation has been issued or transferred has, or is conclusively presumed under this section to have, notice either (i) that he is a person not eligible to be a holder of stock of the corporation, or (ii) that transfer of stock to him would cause the stock of the corporation to be held by more than the number of persons permitted by its certificate of incorporation to hold stock of the corporation, or (iii) that the transfer of stock is in violation of a restriction on transfer of stock, the corporation may, at its option, refuse to register transfer of the stock into the name of the transferee.

(e) The provisions of subsection (d) shall not be applicable if the transfer of stock, even though otherwise contrary to subsections (a), (b) or (c), has been consented to by all the stockholders of the close corporation, or if the close corporation has amended its certificate of incorporation in accordance with section 346 of this title.

(f) The term "transfer," as used in this section, is not limited to a transfer for value.

(g) The provisions of this section do not in any way impair any rights of a transferee regarding any right to rescind the transaction or to recover under any applicable warranty express or implied.

§ 348. Involuntary termination of close corporation status; proceeding to prevent loss of status

(a) If any event occurs as a result of which one or more of the provisions or conditions included in a close corporation's certificate of incorporation pursuant to section 342 of this title to qualify it as a close corporation has been breached, the corporation's status as a close corporation under this subchapter shall terminate unless

(1) within thirty days after the occurrence of the event, or within thirty days after the event has been discovered, whichever is later, the corporation files with the Secretary of State a certificate, executed and acknowledged in accordance with section 103 of this title, stating that a specified provision or condition included in its certificate of incorporation pursuant to section 342 of this title to qualify it as a close corporation has ceased to be applicable, and furnishes a copy of such certificate to each stockholder, and

(2) the corporation concurrently with the filing of such certificate takes such steps as are necessary to correct the situation which threatens its status as a close corporation, including, without limitation, the refusal to register the transfer of stock which has been wrongfully transferred as provided by section 347 of this title, or a proceeding under subsection (b) of this section.

(b) The Court of Chancery, upon the suit of the corporation or any stockholder, shall have jurisdiction to issue all orders necessary to prevent the corporation from losing its status as a close corporation, or to restore its status as a close corporation by enjoining or setting aside any act or threatened act on the part of the corporation or a stockholder which would be inconsistent with any of the provisions or conditions required or permitted by section 342 of this title to be stated in the certificate of incorporation of a close corporation, unless it is an act approved in accordance with section 346 of this title. The Court of Chancery may enjoin or set aside any transfer or treatened transfer of stock of a close corporation which is contrary to the terms of its certificate of incorporation or of any transfer restriction permitted by section 202 of this title, and may enjoin any public offering, as defined in section 342 of this title, or threatened public offering of stock of the close corporation.

§ 349. Corporate option where a restriction on transfer of a security is held invalid

If a restriction on transfer of a security of a close corporation is held not to be authorized by section 202 of this title, the corporation shall nevertheless have an option, for a period of thirty days after the judgment setting aside the restriction becomes final, to acquire the restricted security at a price which is agreed upon by the parties, or if no agreement is reached as to price, then at the fair value as determined by the Court of Chancery. In order to determine fair value, the Court may appoint an appraiser to receive evidence and report to the Court his findings and recommendation as to fair value. The appraiser shall have such powers and shall proceed, so far as applicable, in the same manner as appraisers appointed under section 262 of this title.

§ 350. Agreements restricting discretion of directors

A written agreement among the stockholders of a close corporation holding a majority of the outstanding stock entitled to vote, whether solely among themselves or with a party not a stockholder, is not invalid, as between the parties to the agreement, on the ground that it so relates to the conduct of the business and affairs of the corporation as to restrict or interfere with the discretion or powers of the board of directors. The effect of any such agreement shall be to relieve the directors and impose upon the stockholders who are parties to the agreement the liability for managerial acts or omissions which is imposed on directors to the extent and so long as the discretion or powers of the board in its management of corporate affairs is controlled by such agreement.

§ 351. Management by stockholders

The certificate of incorporation of a close corporation may provide that the business of the corporation shall be managed by the stockholders of the corporation rather than by a board of directors. So long as this provision continues in effect,

(1) No meeting of stockholders need be called to elect directors;

(2) Unless the context clearly requires otherwise, the stockholders of the corporation shall be deemed to be directors for purposes of applying provisions of this chapter; and

(3) The stockholders of the corporation shall be subject to all liabilities of directors.

Such a provision may be inserted in the certificate of incorporation by amendment if all incorporators and subscribers or all holders of record of all of the outstanding stock, whether or not having voting power, authorize such a provision. An amendment to the certificate of incorporation to delete such a provision shall be adopted by a vote of the holders of a majority of all outstanding stock of the corporation, whether or not otherwise entitled to vote. If the certificate of incorporation contains a provision authorized by this section, the existence of such provision shall be noted conspicuously on the face or back of every stock certificate issued by such corporation.

§ 352. Appointment of custodian for close corporation

(a) In addition to the provisions of section 226 of this title respecting the appointment of a custodian for any corporation, the Court of Chancery, upon application of any stockholder, may appoint one or more persons to be custodians, and, if the corporation is insolvent, to be receivers, of any close corporation when:

(1) Pursuant to section 351 of this title the business and affairs of the corporation are managed by the stockholders and they are so divided that the business of the corporation is suffering or is threatened with irreparable injury and any remedy with respect to such deadlock provided in the certificate of incorporation or by-laws or in any written agreement of the stockholders has failed; or

(2) The petitioning stockholder has the right to the dissolution of the corporation under a provision of the certificate of incorporation permitted by section 355 of this title.

(b) In lieu of appointing a custodian for a close corporation under this section or section 226 of this title the Court of Chancery may appoint a provisional director, whose powers and status shall be as provided in section 353 of this title if the Court determines that it would be in the best interest of the corporation. Such appointment shall not preclude any subsequent order of the Court appointing a custodian for such corporation.

§ 353. Appointment of a provisional director in certain cases

(a) Notwithstanding any contrary provision of the certificate of incorporation or the by-laws or agreement of the stockholders, the Court of Chancery may appoint a provisional director for a close corporation if the directors are so divided respecting the management of the corporation's business and affairs that the votes required for action by the board of directors cannot be obtained with the consequence that the business and affairs of the corporation can no longer be conducted to the advantage of the stockholders generally.

(b) An application for relief under this section must be filed (1) by at least one-half of the number of directors then in office, (2) by the holders of at least one-third of all stock then entitled to elect directors, or, (3) if there be more than one class of stock then entitled to elect one or more directors, by the holders of two-thirds of the stock of any such class; but the certificate of incorporation of a close corporation may provide that a lesser proportion of the directors or of the stockholders or of a class of stockholders may apply for relief under this section.

(c) A provisional director shall be an impartial person who is neither a stockholder nor a creditor of the corporation or of any subsidiary or affiliate of the corporation, and whose further qualifications, if any, may be determined by the Court of Chancery. A provisional director is not a receiver of the corporation and does not have the title and powers of a custodian or receiver appointed under sections 226 and 291 of this title. A provisional director shall have all the rights and powers of a duly elected director of the corporation, including the right to notice of and to vote at meetings of directors, until such time as he shall be removed by order of the Court of Chancery or by the holders of a majority of all shares then entitled to vote to elect directors or by the holders of two-thirds of the shares of that class of voting shares which filed the application for appointment of a provisional director. His compensation shall be determined by agreement between him and the corporation subject to approval of the Court of Chancery, which may fix his compensation in the absence of agreement or in the event of disagreement between the provisional director and the corporation.

(d) Even though the requirements of subsection (b) of this section relating to the number of directors or stockholders who may petition for appointment of a provisional director are not satisfied, the Court of Chancery may nevertheless appoint a provisional director if permitted by subsection (b) of section 352 of this title.

§ 354. Operating corporation as partnership

No written agreement among stockholders of a close corporation, nor any provision of the certificate of incorporation or of the by-laws of the corporation, which agreement or provision relates to any phase of the affairs of such corporation, including but not limited to the management of its business or declaration and payment of dividends or other division of profits or the election of directors or officers or the employment of stockholders by the corporation or the arbitration of disputes, shall be invalid on the ground that it is an attempt by the parties to the agreement or by the stockholders of the corporation to treat the corporation as if it were a partnership or to arrange relations among the stockholders or between the stockholders and the corporation in a manner that would be appropriate only among partners.

§ 355. Stockholders' option to dissolve corporation

(a) The certificate of incorporation of any close corporation may include a provision granting to any stockholder, or to the holders of any specified number or percentage of shares of any class of stock, an option to have the corporation dissolved at will or upon the occurrence of any specified event or contingency. Whenever any such option to dissolve is exercised, the stockholders exercising such option shall give written notice thereof to all other stockholders. After the expiration of 30 days following the sending of such notice, the dissolution of the corporation shall proceed as if the required number of stockholders having voting power had consented in writing to dissolution of the corporation as provided by section 228 of this title.

(b) If the certificate of incorporation as originally filed does not contain a provision authorized by subsection (a), the certificate may be amended to include such provision if adopted by the affirmative vote of the holders of all the outstanding stock, whether or not entitled to vote, unless the certificate of incorporation specifically authorizes such an amendment by a vote which shall be not less than two-thirds of all the outstanding stock whether or not entitled to vote.

(c) Each stock certificate in any corporation whose certificate of incorporation authorizes dissolution as permitted by this section shall conspicuously note on the face thereof the existence of the provision. Unless noted conspicuously on the face of the stock certificate, the provision is ineffective.

§ 356. Effect of this subchapter on other laws

The provisions of this subchapter shall not be deemed to repeal any statute or rule of law which is or would be applicable to any corporation which is organized under the provisions of this chapter but is not a close corporation.

E. MARYLAND CLOSE CORPORATIONS LAW

Contents

SUBTITLE 1. DEFINITIONS; GENERAL PROVISIONS

§ 4-101. Definitions

(a) *In General.* In this title the following words have the meanings indicated.

(b) *Close Corporation.* "Close corporation" means a corporation which elects to be a close corporation in accordance with § 4-201 of this title.

(c) *Unanimous Stockholders' Agreement.* "Unanimous stockholders' agreement" means an agreement to which every stockholder of a close corporation actually has assented and which is contained in its charter or bylaws or in a written instrument signed by all the stockholders.

§ 4-102. Execution of documents

Notwithstanding any contrary provision of law, an individual who holds more than one office in a close corporation may act in more than one capacity to execute, acknowledge, or verify any instrument required to be executed, acknowledged, or verified by more than one officer.

SUBTITLE 2. ELECTION TO BE A CLOSE CORPORATION

§ 4-201. Statement of election

(a) *Statement to Be Contained in Charter.* A corporation may elect to be a close corporation under this title by including in its charter a statement that it is a close corporation.

(b) *Procedure.* The statement that a corporation is a close corporation shall be:

(1) Contained in the articles of incorporation originally filed with the Department; or

(2) Added to the charter by an amendment which is approved:

(i) Under the provisions of § 2-603 of this article, if at the time of the adoption of the amendment no stock of the corporation is either outstanding or subscribed for; or

(ii) By the affirmative vote of every stockholder and every subscriber for stock of the corporation.

§ 4-202. Required references to close corporation status

(a) *Clear Reference Required.* Clear reference to the fact that the corporation is a close corporation shall appear prominently:

(1) At the head of the charter document in which the election to be a close corporation is made;

(2) In each subsequent charter document of the corporation; and

(3) On each certificate representing outstanding stock of the corporation.

(b) *Absence of Reference.* The status of a corporation as a close corporation is not affected by the failure of any charter document or stock certificate to contain the reference required by this section.

§ 4-203. Removal of statement from charter

The charter of a close corporation may be amended to remove the statement of election to be a close corporation, but only by the affirmative vote of every stockholder and every subscriber for stock of the corporation.

SUBTITLE 3. BOARD OF DIRECTORS

§ 4-301. At least one director required initially

A close corporation shall have at least one director until an election by the corporation in its charter to have no board of directors becomes effective.

§ 4-302. Election to have no board of directors

(a) *Effective Time of Election.* An election to have no board of directors becomes effective at the later of:

(1) The time that the organization meeting of directors and the issuance of at least one share of stock of the corporation are completed;

(2) The time the charter document in which the election is made becomes effective; or

(3) The time specified in the charter document in which the election is made.

(b) *Cessation of Director's Status.* A director automatically ceases to be a director when an election to have no board of directors become effective.

§ 4-303. Effect of election to have no board of directors

If there is an election to have no board of directors:

(1) The stockholders may exercise all powers of directors, and the business and affairs of the corporation shall be managed under their direction;

(2) The stockholders of the corporation are responsible for taking any action required by law to be taken by the board of directors;

(3) Action by stockholders shall be taken by the voting of shares of stock as provided in this article;

(4) The stockholders may take any action for which this article otherwise would require both a resolution of directors and a vote of stockholders;

(5) By the affirmative vote of a majority of all the votes entitled to be cast, the stockholders may take any action for which this article otherwise would require a vote of a majority of the entire board of directors;

(6) A statement that the corporation is a close corporation which has no board of directors satisfies any requirement that an instrument filed with the Department contain a statement that a specified action was taken by the board of directors;

(7) The special liabilities imposed on directors by § 2–315(b), (c), and (d) of this article and the provisions of §§ 2–315(e) and (f) and 2–410 of this article applying to the stockholders of the corporation and, for this purpose, "present" in § 2–410 of this article means present in person or by proxy; and

(8) A stockholder is not liable for any action taken as a result of a vote of the stockholders, unless he was entitled to vote on the action.

SUBTITLE 4. STOCKHOLDERS

§ 4–401. Unanimous stockholders' agreement

(a) *Governing the Corporation.* Under an unanimous stockholders' agreement, the stockholders of a close corporation may regulate any aspect of the affairs of the corporation or the relations of the stockholders, including:

(1) The management of the business and affairs of the corporation;

(2) Restrictions on the transfer of stock;

(3) The right of one or more stockholders to dissolve the corporation at will or on the occurrence of a specified event or contingency;

(4) The exercise or division of voting power;

(5) The terms and conditions of employment of an officer or employee of the corporation, without regard to the period of his employment;

(6) The individuals who are to be directors and officers of the corporation; and

(7) The payment of dividends or the division of profits.

(b) *Amending Unanimous Stockholders' Agreement.* A unanimous stockholders' agreement may be amended, but only by the unanimous written consent of the stockholders then parties to the agreement.

(c) *Acquisition of Stock Subject to Unanimous Stockholders' Agreement.* A stockholder who acquires his stock after a unanimous stockholders' agreement becomes effective is considered to have actually assented to the agreement and is a party to it:

(1) Whether or not he has actual knowledge of the existence of the agreement at the time he acquires the stock, if acquired by gift or bequest from a person who was a party to the agreement; and

(2) If he has actual knowledge of the existence of the agreement at the time he acquires the stock, if acquired in any other manner.

(d) *Enforcement of Unanimous Stockholders' Agreement.*

(1) A court of equity may enforce a unanimous stockholders' agreement by injunction or by any other relief which the court in its discretion determines to be fair and appropriate in the circumstances.

(2) As an alternative to the granting of an injunction or other equitable relief, on motion of a party to the proceeding, the court may order dissolution of the corporation under the provisions of Subtitle 6 of this title.

(e) *Inapplicability of Section to Other Agreements.* This section does not affect any otherwise valid agreement among stockholders of a close corporation or of any other corporation.

§ 4–402. Stockholders' annual meeting

(d) *General Rule.* The bylaws of a close corporation shall provide for an annual meeting of stockholders in accordance with Title 2 of this article, but the meeting need not be held unless requested by a stockholder.

(b) *Written Request for Annual Meeting.* A request for an annual meeting shall be in writing and delivered to the president or secretary of the corporation:

(1) At least 30 days before the date specified in the bylaws for the meeting; or

(2) If the bylaws specify a period during which the date for the meeting may be set, at least 30 days before the beginning of that period.

§ 4–403. Stockholders' right of inspection

A stockholder of a close corporation or his agent may inspect and copy during usual business hours any records or documents of the corporation relevant to its business and affairs, including any:

(1) Bylaws;

(2) Minutes of the proceedings of the stockholders and directors;

(3) Annual statement of affairs;

(4) Stock ledger; and

(5) Books of account.

§ 4–404. Statement of affairs

(a) *Stockholders' Right to Request.* Once during each calendar year, each stockholder of a close corporation may present to any officer of the corporation a written request for a statement of its affairs.

(b) *Duty to Prepare and File; Verification.* Within 20 days after a request is made for a statement of a close corporation's affairs, the corporation shall prepare and have available on file at its principal office a statement verified under oath by its president or treasurer of one of its vice-presidents or assistant treasurers which sets forth in reasonable detail the corporation's assets and liabilities as of a reasonably current date.

SUBTITLE 5. STOCK RESTRICTIONS

§ 4–501. Restriction on issuance or sale of stock

If there is any stock of a close corporation outstanding, the corporation may not issue or sell any of its stock, including treasury stock, unless the issuance or sale is:

(1) Approved by the affirmative vote of the holders of all outstanding stock; or

(2) Permitted by a unanimous stockholders' agreement.

§ 4–502. Certain securities and stock options prohibited

A close corporation may not have outstanding any:

(1) Securities which are convertible into its stock;

(2) Voting securities other than stock; or

(3) Options, warrants, or other rights to subscribe for or purchase any of its stock, unless they are nontransferable.

§ 4–503. Restrictions on transfer of stock

(a) *"Transfer" Defined.* (1) In this section, "transfer" means the transfer of any interest in the stock of a close corporation, except:

(i) A transfer by operation of law to a personal representative, trustee in bankruptcy, receiver, guardian, or similar legal representative;

(ii) The acquisition of a lien or power of sale by an attachment, levy, or similar procedure; or

(iii) The creation or assignment of a security interest.

(2) A foreclosure sale or other transfer by a person who acquired his interest or power in a transaction described in paragraph (1) of this subsection is a transfer subject to all the provisions of this section. For purposes of the transfer, the person effecting the foreclosure sale or other transfer shall be treated as and have the rights of a holder of the stock under this section and § 4–602(b) of this title.

(b) *Enumeration of Restrictions.* A transfer of the stock of a close corporation is invalid unless:

(1) Every stockholder of the corporation consents to the transfer in writing within the 90 days before the date of the transfer; or

(2) The transfer is made under a provision of a unanimous stockholders' agreement permitting the transfer to the corporation or to or in trust for the principal benefit of:

(i) One or more of the stockholders or security holders of the corporation or their wives, children, or grandchildren; or

(ii) One or more persons names in the agreement.

§ 4–504.   Denial or restriction of voting rights; unanimous stockholder vote

(a) *Denial or Restriction of Voting Rights.* A close corporation may deny or restrict the voting rights of any of its stock as provided in this article. Notwithstanding any denial or restriction, all stock has voting rights on any matter required by this title to be authorized by the affirmative vote of every stockholder or every subscriber for stock of a close corporation.

(b) *Unanimous Stockholder Vote.* Notwithstanding the provisions of § 2–104(b)(5) of this article, the charter of a close corporation may not lower the proportion of votes required to approve any action for which this title requires the affirmative vote or assent of every stockholder or every subscriber for stock of the corporation.

SUBTITLE 6.   TERMINATION OF EXISTENCE

§ 4–601.   Consolidation, merger, share exchange, or transfer of assets

A consolidation, merger, share exchange, or transfer of assets of a close corporation shall be made in accordance with the provisions of Title 3 of this article. However, approval of a proposed consolidation or merger, a transfer of its assets, or an acquisition of its stock in a share exchange requires the affirmative vote of every stockholder of the corporation.

§ 4-602. Involuntary dissolution

(a) *Dissolution by Stockholder Generally.* Any stockholder of a close corporation may petition a court of equity for dissolution of the corporation on the grounds set forth in § 3-413 of this article or on the ground that there is such internal dissension among the stockholders of the corporation that the business and affairs of the corporation can no longer be conducted to the advantage of the stockholders generally.

(b) *Dissolution by Stockholder Desiring to Transfer Stock.*

(1) Unless a unanimous stockholders' agreement provides otherwise, a stockholder of a close corporation has the right to require dissolution of the corporation if:

(i) The stockholder made a written request for consent to a proposed bona fide transfer of his stock in accordance with the provisions of § 4-503(b)(1) of this title, specifying the proposed transferee and the consideration, and the consent was not received by him within 30 days after the date of the request; or

(ii) Another party to a unanimous stockholders' agreement defaulted in an obligation, set forth in or arising under the agreement, to purchase or cause to be purchased stock of the stockholder, and the default was not remedied within 30 days after the date for performance of the obligation.

(2) A petition for dissolution under this subsection shall be filed within 60 days after the date of the request or the default, as the case may be.

(c) *Proceeding to Be in Accordance with § 3-414.* A proceeding for dissolution authorized by this section shall be in accordance with the provisions of § 3-414 of this article.

§ 4-603. Avoidance of dissolution by purchase of petitioner's stock

(a) *Stockholder's Right to Avoid Dissolution.* Any one or more stockholders who desire to continue the business of a close corporation may avoid the dissolution of the corporation or the appointment of a receiver by electing to purchase the stock owned by the petitioner at a price equal to its fair value.

(b) *Court to Determine Fair Value of Stock.* (1) If a stockholder who makes the election is unable to reach an agreement with the petitioner as to the fair value of the stock, then, if the electing stockholder gives bond or other security sufficient to assure payment to the petitioner of the fair value of the stock, the court shall stay the proceeding and determine the fair value of the stock.

(2) Fair value shall be determined in accordance with the procedure set forth in Title 3, Subtitle 2 of this article, as of the close of business on the day on which the petition for dissolution was filed.

(c) *Court Order.* After the fair value of the stock is determined, the order of the court directing the purchase shall set the purchase price and the time within which payment shall be made. The court may order other appropriate terms and conditions of sale, including:

(1) Payment of the purchase price in installments; and

(2) The allocation of shares of stock among electing stockholders.

(d) *Interest on Purchase Price; Cessation of Other Rights.* The petitioner:

(1) Is entitled to interest on the purchase price of his stock from the date the petition is filed; and

(2) Ceases to have any other rights with respect to the stock, except the right to receive payment of its fair value.

(e) *Costs of Proceeding.* The costs of the proceeding, as determined by the court, shall be divided between the petitioner and the purchasing stockholder. The costs shall include the reasonable compensation and expenses of appraisers, but may not include fees and expenses of counsel or of other experts retained by a party.

(f) *Transfer of Stock.* The petitioner shall transfer his shares of stock to the purchasing stockholder:

(1) At a time set by the court; or

(2) If the court sets no time, at the time the purchase price is paid in full.

F. NEW YORK BUSINESS CORPORATION LAW

Contents

(Selected Sections)

ARTICLE 5. CORPORATE FINANCE

ARTICLE 6. SHAREHOLDERS

ARTICLE 7. DIRECTORS AND OFFICERS

ARTICLE 5. CORPORATE FINANCE

§ 504. Consideration and payment for shares

(a) Consideration for the issue of shares shall consist of money or other property, tangible or intangible, or labor or services actually received by or performed for the corporation or for its benefit or in its formation or reorganization, or a combination thereof. In the absence of fraud in the transaction, the judgment of the board or shareholders, as the case may be, as to the value of the consideration received for shares shall be conclusive.

* * *

§ 505. Rights and options to purchase shares; issue of rights and options to directors, officers and employees

(a) Except as otherwise provided in this section or in the certificate of incorporation, a corporation may create and issue, whether or not in connection with the issue and sale of any of its shares or bonds, rights or options entitling the holders thereof to purchase from the corporation, upon such consideration, terms and conditions as may be fixed by the board, shares of any class or series, whether authorized but unissued shares, treasury shares or shares to be purchased or acquired.

(b) The consideration for shares to be purchased under any such right or option shall comply with the requirements of section 504 (Consideration and payment for shares).

(c) The terms and conditions of such rights or options, including the time or times at or within which and the price or prices at which they may be exercised and any limitations upon transferability, shall be set forth or incorporated by reference in the instrument or instruments evidencing such rights or options.

(d) The issue of such rights or options to one or more directors, officers or employees of the corporation or a subsidiary or affiliate thereof, as an incentive to service or continued service with the corporation, a subsidiary or affiliate thereof, or to a trustee on behalf of such directors, officers or employees, shall be authorized at a meeting of shareholders by the vote of the holders of a majority of all outstanding shares entitled to vote thereon, or authorized by and consistent with a plan adopted by such vote of shareholders. If, under the certificate of incorporation, there are preemptive rights to any of the shares to be thus subject to rights or options to purchase, either such issue or such plan, if any shall also be approved by the vote or written consent of the holders of a majority of the shares entitled to exercise preemptive rights with respect to such shares and such vote or written consent shall operate to release the preemptive rights with respect thereto of the holders of all the shares that were entitled to exercise such preemptive rights.

In the absence of preemptive rights, nothing in this paragraph shall require shareholder approval for the issuance of rights or options to purchase shares of the corporation in substitution for, or upon the assumption of, rights or options issued by another corporation, if such substitution or assumption is in connection with such other corporation's merger or consolidation with, or the acquisition of its shares or all or part of its assets by, the corporation or its subsidiary.

(e) A plan adopted by the shareholders for the issue of rights or options to directors, officers or employees shall include the material terms and conditions upon which such rights or options are to be issued, such as, but without limitation thereof, any restrictions on the number of shares that eligible individuals may have the right or option to purchase, the method of administering the plan, the terms and conditions of payment for shares in full or in installments, the issue of certificates for shares to be paid for in installments, any limitations upon the transferability of such shares and the voting and dividend rights to which the holders of such shares may be entitled, though the full amount of the consideration therefor has not been paid; provided that under this section no certificate for shares shall be delivered to a shareholder, prior to full payment therefor, unless the fact that the shares are partly paid is noted conspicuously on the face or back of such certificate.

(f) If there is shareholder approval for the issue of rights or options to individual directors, officers or employees, but not under an approved plan under paragraph (e), the terms and conditions of issue set forth in paragraph (e) shall be permissible except that the grantees of such rights or options shall not be granted voting or dividend rights until the consideration for the shares to which they are entitled under such rights or options has been fully paid.

(g) If there is shareholder approval for the issue of rights and options, such approval may provide that the board is authorized by certificate of amendment under section 805 (Certificate of amendment; contents) to increase the authorized shares of any class or series to such number as will be sufficient, when added to the previously authorized but unissued shares of such class or series, to satisfy any such rights or options entitling the holders thereof to purchase from the corporation authorized but unissued shares of such class or series.

(h) In the absence of fraud in the transaction, the judgment of the board shall be conclusive as to the adequacy of the consideration, tangible or intangible, received or to be received by the corporation for the issue of rights or options for the purchase from the corporation of its shares.

(i) The provisions of this section are inapplicable to the rights of the holders of convertible shares or bonds to acquire shares upon the exercise of conversion privileges under section 519 (Convertible shares and bonds).

§ 510. Dividends or other distributions in cash or property

(a) A corporation may declare and pay dividends, or make other distributions in cash or its bonds or its property, including the shares or bonds of other corporations, on its outstanding shares, except when currently the corporation is insolvent or would thereby be made insolvent, or when the declaration, payment or distribution would be contrary to any restrictions contained in the certificate of incorporation.

(b) Dividends may be declared or paid and other distributions may be made out of surplus only, so that the net assets of the corporation remaining after such declaration, payment or distribution shall at least equal the amount of its stated capital; except that a corporation engaged in the exploitation of natural resources or other wasting assets, including patents, or formed primarily for the liquidation of specific assets, may declare and pay dividends or make other distributions in excess of its surplus, computed after taking due account of depletion and amortization to the extent that the cost of the wasting or specific assets has been recovered by depletion reserves, amortization or sale, if the net assets remaining after such dividends or distributions are sufficient to cover the liquidation preferences of shares having such preferences in involuntary liquidation.

(c) When any dividend is paid or any other distribution is made, in whole or in part, from sources other than earned surplus, it shall be accompanied by a written notice (1) disclosing the amounts by which such dividend or distribution affects stated capital, capital surplus and earned surplus, or (2) if such amounts are not determinable at the time of such notice, disclosing the approximate effect of such dividend or distribution upon stated capital, capital surplus and earned surplus and stating that such amounts are not yet determinable.

§ 513. Purchase or redemption by a corporation of its own shares

(a) A corporation, subject to any restrictions contained in its certificate of incorporation, may purchaase its own shares, or redeem its redeemable shares, out of surplus except when currently the corporation is insolvent or would thereby be made insolvent.

(b) A corporation may purchase its own shares out of stated capital except when currently the corporation is insolvent or would thereby be made insolvent, if the purchase is made for the purpose of:

(1) Eliminating fractions of shares;

(2) Collecting or compromising indebtedness to the corporation; or

(3) Paying shareholders entitled to receive payment for their shares under section 623 (Procedure to enforce shareholder's right to receive payment for shares).

(c) A corporation, subject to any restrictions contained in its certificate of incorporation, may redeem or purchase its redeemable shares out of stated capital except when currently the corporation is insolvent or would thereby be made insolvent and except when such redemption or purchase would reduce net assets below the stated capital remaining after giving effect to the cancellation of such redeemable shares.

(d) When its redeemable shares are purchased by a corporation within the period of redeemability, the purchase price thereof shall not exceed the applicable redemption price stated in the certificate of incorporation. Upon a call for redemption, the amount payable by the corporation for shares having a cumulative preference on dividends may include the stated redemption price plus accrued dividends to the next dividend date following the date of redemption of such shares.

§ 514. Agreements for purchase by a corporation of its own shares

(a) An agreement for the purchase by a corporation of its own shares shall be enforceable by the shareholder and the corporation to the extent such purchase is permitted at the time of purchase by section 513 (Purchase or redemption by a corporation of its own shares).

(b) The possibility that a corporation may not be able to purchase its shares under section 513 shall not be a ground for denying to either party specific performance of an agreement for the purchase by a corporation of its own shares, if at the time for performance the corporation can purchase all or part of such shares under section 513.

ARTICLE 6. SHAREHOLDERS

§ 601. By-laws

(a) The initial by-laws of a corporation shall be adopted by its incorporator or incorporators at the organization meeting. Thereafter, subject to section 613 (Limitations on right to vote), by-laws may be adopted, amended or repealed by vote of the holders of the shares at the time entitled to vote in the election of any directors. When so provided in the certificate of incorporation or a by-law adopted by the shareholders, by-laws may also be adopted, amended or repealed by the board by such vote as may be therein specified, which may be greater than the vote otherwise prescribed by this chapter, but any by-law adopted by the board may be amended or repealed by the shareholders entitled to vote thereon as herein provided. Any reference in this chapter to a "by-law adopted by the shareholders" shall include a by-law adopted by the incorporator or incorporators.

(b) If any by-law regulating an impending election of directors is adopted, amended or repealed by the board, there shall be set forth in the notice of the next meeting of shareholders for the election of directors the by-law so adopted, amended or repealed, together with a concise statement of the changes made.

(c) The by-laws may contain any provision relating to the business of the corporation, the conduct of its affairs, its rights or powers or the rights or powers of its shareholders, directors

or officers, not inconsistent with this chapter or any other statute of this state or the certificate of incorporation.

§ 609. Proxies

(a) Every shareholder entitled to vote at a meeting of shareholders or to express consent or dissent without a meeting may
authorize another person or persons to act for him by proxy.

(b) Every proxy must be signed by the shareholder or his attorney-in-fact. No proxy shall be valid after the expiration of
eleven months from the date thereof unless otherwise provided
in the proxy. Every proxy shall be recoverable at the pleasure
of the shareholder executing it, except as otherwise provided in
this section.

(c) The authority of the holder of a proxy to act shall not be
revoked by the incompetence or death of the shareholder who
executed the proxy unless, before the authority is exercised,
written notice of an adjudication of such incompetence or of
such death is received by the corporate officer responsible for
maintaining the list of shareholders.

(d) Except when other provision shall have been made by
written agreement between the parties, the record holder of
shares which he holds as pledgee or otherwise as security or
which belong to another, shall issue to the pledgor or to such
owner of such shares, upon demand therefor and payment of
necessary expenses thereof, a proxy to vote or take other action
thereon.

(e) A shareholder shall not sell his vote or issue a proxy to
vote to any person for any sum of money or anything of value,
except as authorized in this section and section 620 (Agreements
as to voting; provision in certificate of incorporation as to control of directors).

(f) A proxy which is entitled "irrevocable proxy" and which
states that it is irrevocable, is irrevocable when it is held by any
of the following or a nominee of any of the following:

(1) A pledgee;

(2) A person who has purchased or agreed to purchase the
shares;

(3) A creditor or creditors of the corporation who extend or
continue credit to the corporation in consideration of the proxy
if the proxy states that it was given in consideration of such extension or continuation of credit, the amount thereof, and the
name of the person extending or continuing credit;

(4) A person who has contracted to perform services as an
officer of the corporation, if a proxy is required by the contract

233

of employment, if the proxy states that it was given in consideration of such contract of employment, the name of the employee and the period of employment contracted for;

(5) A person designated by or under an agreement under paragraph (a) of section 620.

(g) Notwithstanding a provision in a proxy, stating that it is irrevocable, the proxy becomes revocable after the pledge is redeemed, or the debt of the corporation is paid, or the period of employment provided for in the contract of employment has terminated, or the agreement under paragraph (a) of section 620 has terminated; and, in a case provided for in subparagraphs (f)(3) or (4), becomes revocable three years after the date of the proxy or at the end of the period, if any, specified therein, whichever period is less, unless the period of irrevocability is renewed from time to time by the execution of a new irrevocable proxy as provided in this section. This paragraph does not affect the duration of a proxy under paragraph (b).

(h) A proxy may be revoked, notwithstanding a provision making it irrevocable, by a purchaser of shares without knowledge of the existence of the provision unless the existence of the proxy and its irrevocability is noted conspicuously on the face or back of the certificate representing such shares.

§ 616. Greater requirement as to quorum and vote of shareholders

(a) The certificate of incorporation may contain provisions specifying either or both of the following:

(1) That the proportion of shares, or the proportion of shares of any class or series thereof, the holders of which shall be present in person or by proxy at any meeting of shareholders, including a special meeting for election of directors under section 603 (Special meeting for election of directors), in order to constitute a quorum for the transaction of any business or of any specified item of business, including amendments to the certificate of incorporation, shall be greater than the proportion prescribed by this chapter in the absence of such provision.

(2) That the proportion of votes of the holders of shares, or of the holders of shares of any class or series thereof, that shall be necessary at any meeting of shareholders for the transaction of any business or of any specified item of business, including amendments to the certificate of incorporation, shall be greater than the proportion prescribed by this chapter in the absence of such provision.

(b) An amendment of the certificate of incorporation which adds a provision permitted by this section or which changes or strikes out such a provision, shall be authorized at a meeting of shareholders by vote of the holders of two-thirds of all outstanding shares entitled to vote thereon, or of such greater proportion of shares, or class or series of shares, as may be provided specifically in the certificate of incorporation for adding, changing or striking out a provision permitted by this section.

(c) If the certificate of incorporation of any corporation contains a provision authorized by this section, the existence of such provision shall be noted conspicuously on the face or back of every certificate for shares issued by such corporation.

§ 620. Agreements as to voting; provision in certificate of incorporation as to control of directors

(a) An agreement between two or more shareholders, if in writing and signed by the parties thereto, may provide that in exercising any voting rights, the shares held by them shall be voted as therein provided, or as they may agree, or as determined in accordance with a procedure agreed upon by them.

(b) A provision in the certificate of incorporation otherwise prohibited by law because it improperly restricts the board in its management of the business of the corporation, or improperly transfers to one or more shareholders or to one or more persons or corporations to be selected by him or them, all or any part of such management otherwise within the authority of the board under this chapter, shall nevertheless be valid:

(1) If all the incorporators or holders of record of all outstanding shares, whether or not having voting power, have authorized such provision in the certificate of incorporation or an amendment thereof; and

(2) If, subsequent to the adoption of such provision, shares are transferred or issued only to persons who had knowledge or notice thereof or consented in writing to such provision.

(c) A provision authorized by paragraph (b) shall be valid only so long as no shares of the corporation are listed on a national securities exchange or regularly quoted in an over-the-counter market by one or more members of a national or affiliated securities association.

(d) Except as provided in paragraph (e), an amendment to strike out a provision authorized by paragraph (b) shall be authorized at a meeting of shareholders by vote of the holders of two-thirds of all outstanding shares entitled to vote thereon or by the holders of such greater proportion of shares as may be required by the certificate of incorporation for that purpose.

(e) Alternatively, if a provision authorized by paragraph (b) shall have ceased to be valid under this section, the board may authorize a certificate of amendment under section 805 (Certificate of amendment; contents) striking out such provision. Such certificate shall set forth the event by reason of which the provision ceased to be valid.

(f) The effect of any such provision authorized by paragraph (b) shall be to relieve the directors and impose upon the shareholders authorizing the same or consenting thereto the liability for managerial acts or omissions that is imposed on directors by this chapter to the extent that and so long as the discretion or powers of the board in its management of corporate affairs is controlled by any such provision.

(g) If the certificate of incorporation of any corporation contains a provision authorized by paragraph (b), the existence of such provision shall be noted conspicuously on the face or back of every certificate for shares issued by such corporation.

§ 622. Preemptive rights

(a) As used in this section, the term:

(1) "Unlimited dividend rights" means the right without limitation as to amount either to all or to a share of the balance of current or liquidating dividends after the payment of dividends on any shares entitled to a preference.

(2) "Equity shares" means shares of any class, whether or not preferred as to dividends or assets, which have unlimited dividend rights.

(3) "Voting rights" means the right to vote for the election of one or more directors, excluding a right so to vote which is dependent on the happening of an event specified in the certificate of incorporation which would change the voting rights of any class of shares.

(4) "Voting shares" means shares of any class which have voting rights, but does not include bonds on which voting rights are conferred under section 518 (Corporate bonds).

(5) "Preemptive right" means the right to purchase shares or other securities to be issued or subjected to rights or options to purchase, as such right is defined in this section.

(b) Except as otherwise provided in the certificate of incorporation, and except as provided in this section, the holders of equity shares of any class, in case of the proposed issuance by the corporation of, or the proposed granting by the corporation of rights or options to purchase, its equity shares of any class or any shares or other securities convertible into or carrying rights or options to purchase its equity shares of any class, shall, if the issuance of the equity shares proposed to be issued or issuable upon exercise of such rights or options or upon conversion of such other securities would adversely affect the unlimited dividend rights of such holders, have the right during a reasonable time and on reasonable conditions, both to be fixed by the board, to purchase such shares or other securities in such proportions as shall be determnined as provided in this section.

(c) Except as otherwise provided in the certificate of incorporation, and except as provided in this section, the holders of voting shares of any class, in case of the proposed issuance by the corporation of, or the proposed granting by the corporation of rights or options to purchase, its voting shares of any class or any shares or other securities convertible into or carrying rights or options to purchase its voting shares of any class, shall, if the issuance of the voting shares proposed to be issued or issuable upon exercise of such rights or options or upon conversion of such other securities would adversely affect the voting rights of such holders, have the right during a reasonable time and on reasonable conditions, both to be fixed by the board, to purchase such shares or other securities in such proportions as shall be determined as provided in this section.

(d) The preemptive right provided for in paragraphs (b) and (c) shall entitle shareholders having such rights to purchase the shares or other securities to be offered or optioned for sale as nearly as practicable in such proportions as would, if such preemptive right were exercised, preserve the relative unlimited dividend rights and voting rights of such holders and at a price or prices not less favorable than the price or prices at which such shares or other securities are proposed to be offered for sale to others, without deduction of such reasonable expenses of and compensation for the sale, underwriting or purchase of such shares or other securities by underwriters or dealers as may lawfully be paid by the corporation. In case each of the shares entitling the holders thereof to preemptive rights does not confer the same unlimited dividend right or voting right, the board shall apportion the shares or other securities to be offered or optioned for sale among the shareholders having preemptive rights to purchase them in such proportions as in the opinion of the board shall preserve as far as practicable the relative unlimited dividend rights and voting rights of the holders at the time of such offering. The apportionment made by the board shall, in the absence of fraud or bad faith, be binding upon all shareholders.

(e) Unless otherwise provided in the certificate of incorporation, shares or other securities offered for sale or subjected to rights or options to purchase shall not be subject to preemptive rights if they:

(1) Are to be issued by the board to effect a merger or consolidation or offered or subjected to rights or options for consideration other than cash;

(2) Are to be issued or subjected to rights or options under paragraph (d) of section 505 (Rights and options to purchase shares; issue of rights and options to directors, officers and employees);

(3) Are to be issued to satisfy conversion or option rights theretofore granted by the corporation;

(4) Are treasury shares;

(5) Are part of the shares or other securities of the corporation authorized in its original certificate of incorporation and are issued, sold or optioned within two years from the date of filing such certificate; or

(6) Are to be issued under a plan of reorganization approved in a proceeding under any applicable act of congress relating to reorganization or corporations.

(f) Shareholders of record entitled to preemptive rights on the record date fixed by the board under section 604 (Fixing record date), or, if no record date is fixed, then on the record date determined under section 604, and no others shall be entitled to the right defined in this section.

(g) The board shall cause to be given to each shareholder entitled to purchase shares or other securities in accordance with this section, a notice directed to him in the manner provided in section 605 (Notice of meetings of shareholders) setting forth the time within which and the terms and conditions upon which the shareholder may purchase such shares or other securities and also the apportionment made of the right to purchase among the shareholders entitled to preemptive rights. Such notice shall be given personally or by mail at least fifteen days prior to the expiration of the period during which the shareholder shall have the right to purchase. All shareholders entitled to preemptive rights to whom notice shall have been given as aforesaid shall be deemed conclusively to have had a reasonable time in which to exercise their preemptive rights.

(h) Shares or other securities which have been offered to shareholders having preemptive rights to purchase and which have not been purchased by them within the time fixed by the board may thereafter, for a period of not exceeding one year following the expiration of the time during which shareholders might have exercised such preemptive rights, be issued, sold or subjected to rights or options to any other person or persons at a price, without deduction of such reasonable expenses of and compensation for the sale, underwriting or purchase of such shares by underwriters or dealers as may lawfully be paid by the corporation, not less than that at which they were offered to such shareholders. Any such shares or other securities not so issued, sold or subjected to rights or options to others during such one year period shall thereafter again be subject to the preemptive rights of shareholders.

(i) Except as otherwise provided in the certificate of incorporation and except as provided in this section, no holder of any shares of any class shall as such holder have any preemptive right to purchase any other shares or securities of any class which at any time may be sold or offered for sale by the corporation. Unless otherwise provided in the certificate of incorporation, holders of bonds on which voting rights are conferred under section 518 shall have no preemptive rights.

§ 624. Books and records; right of inspection, prima facie evidence

(a) Each corporation shall keep correct and complete books and records of account and shall keep minutes of the proceedings of its shareholders, board and executive committee, if any, and shall keep at the office of the corporation in this state or at the office of its transfer agent or registrar in this state, a record containing the names and addresses of all shareholders, the number and class of shares held by each and the dates when they respectively became the owners of record thereof. Any of the foregoing books, minutes or records may be in written form or in any other form capable of being converted into written form within a reasonable time.

(b) Any person who shall have been a shareholder of record of a corporation for at least six months immediately preceding his demand, or any person holding, or thereunto authorized in writing by the holders of, at least five percent of any class of the outstanding shares, upon at least five days' written demand shall have the right to examine in person or by agent or attorney, during usual business hours, its minutes of the proceedings of its shareholders and record of shareholders and to make extracts therefrom. Holders of voting trust certificates representing shares of the corporation shall be regarded as shareholders for the purpose of this section. If the corporation has failed to pay wages as defined in paragraph (b) of section 630 (Liability of shareholders for wages due to laborers, servants or employees), any person to whom a shareholder may be liable thereunder upon at least five days written demand shall have the right to examine in person or by agent or attorney during usual business hours, the record of shareholders and to make extracts therefrom.

(c) An inspection authorized by paragraph (b) may be denied to such shareholder or other person upon his refusal to furnish to the corporation, its transfer agent or registrar an affidavit that such inspection is not desired for a purpose which is in the interest of a business or object other than the business of the corporation and that he has not within five years sold or offered for sale any list of shareholders of any corporation of any type or kind, whether or not formed under the laws of this state, or aided or abetted any person in procuring any such record of shareholders for any such purpose. The enforcement of liability under section 630 shall not be an object other than the business of the corporation.

(d) Upon refusal by the corporation or by an officer or agent of the corporation to permit an inspection of the minutes of the proceedings of its shareholders or of the record of shareholders as herein provided, the person making the demand for inspection may apply to the supreme court in the judicial district where the office of the corporation is located, upon such notice as the court may direct, for an order directing the corporation, its officer or agent to show cause why an order should not be granted permitting such inspection by the applicant. Upon the return day of the order to show cause, the court shall hear the parties summarily, by affidavit or otherwise, and if it appears that the applicant is qualified and entitled to such inspection, the court shall grant an order compelling such inspection and awarding such further relief as to the court may seem just and proper.

(e) Upon the written request of any person who shall have been a shareholder of record for at least six months immediately preceding his request, or of any person holding, or thereunto authorized in writing by the holders of, at least five percent of any class of the outstanding shares, the corporation shall give or mail to such shareholder an annual balance sheet and profit and loss statement for the preceding fiscal year, and, if any interim balance sheet or profit and loss statement has been distributed to its shareholders or otherwise made available to the public, the most recent such interim balance sheet or profit and loss statement. The corporation shall be allowed a reasonable time to prepare such annual balance sheet and profit and loss statement.

(f) Nothing herein contained shall impair the power of courts to compel the production for examination of the books and records of a corporation.

(g) The books and records specified in paragraph (a) shall be prima facie evidence of the facts therein stated in favor of the plaintiff in any action or special proceeding against such corporation or any of its officers, directors or shareholders.

§ 625. Infant shareholders and bondholders

(a) A corporation may treat an infant who holds shares or bonds of such corporation as having capacity to receive and to empower others to receive dividends, interest, principal and other payments and distributions, to vote or express consent or dissent, in person or by proxy, and to make elections and exercise rights relating to such shares or bonds, unless, in the case of shares, the corporate officer responsible for maintaining the list of shareholders or the transfer agent of the corporation or, in the case of bonds, the treasurer or paying officer or agent has received written notice that such holder is an infant.

(b) An infant holder of shares or bonds of a corporation who has received or empowered others to receive payments or distributions, voted or expressed consent or dissent, or made an election or exercised a right relating thereto, shall have no right thereafter to disaffirm or avoid, as against the corporation, any such act on his part, unless prior to such receipt, vote, consent, dissent, election or exercise, as to shares, the corporate officer responsible for maintaining the list of shareholders or its transfer agent or, in the case of bonds, the treasurer or paying officer had received written notice that such holder was an infant.

(c) This section does not limit any other statute which authorizes any corporation to deal with an infant or limits the right of an infant to disaffirm his acts.

§ 626. Shareholders' derivative action brought in the right of the corporation to procure a judgment in its favor

(a) An action may be brought in the right of a domestic or foreign corporation to procure a judgment in its favor, by a holder of shares or of voting trust certificates of the corporation or of a beneficial interest in such shares or certificates.

(b) In any such action, it shall be made to appear that the plaintiff is such a holder at the time of bringing the action and that he was such a holder at the time of the transaction of which he complains, or that his shares or his interest therein devolved upon him by operation of law.

(c) In any such action, the complaint shall set forth with particularity the efforts of the plaintiff to secure the initiation of such action by the board or the reasons for not making such effort.

(d) Such action shall not be discontinued, compromised or settled, without the approval of the court having jurisdiction of the action. If the court shall determine that the interests of the shareholders or any class or classes thereof will be substantially affected by such discontinuance, compromise, or settlement, the court, in its discretion, may direct that notice, by publication or otherwise, shall be given to the shareholders or class or classes thereof whose interests it determines will be so affected; if notice is so directed to be given, the court may determine which one or more of the parties to the action shall bear the expense of giving the same, in such amount as the court shall determine and find to be reasonable in the circumstances, and the amount of such expense shall be awarded as special costs of the action and recoverable in the same manner as statutory taxable costs.

(e) If the action on behalf of the corporation was successful, in whole or in part, or if anything was received by the plaintiff or plaintiffs or a claimant or claimants as the result of a judgment, compromise or settlement of an action or claim, the court may award the plaintiff or plaintiffs, claimant or claimants, reasonable expenses, including reasonable attorney's fees, and shall direct him or them to account to the corporation for the remainder of the proceeds so received by him or them. This paragraph shall not apply to any judgment rendered for the benefit of injured shareholders only and limited to a recovery of the loss or damage sustained by them.

§ 627. Security for expenses in shareholders' derivative action brought in the right of the corporation to procure a judgment in its favor

In any action specified in section 626 (Shareholders' derivative action brought in the right of the corporation to procure a judgment in its favor), unless the plaintiff or plaintiffs hold five percent or more of any class of the outstanding shares or hold voting trust certificates or a beneficial interest in shares representing five percent or more of any class of such shares, or the shares, voting trust certificates and beneficial interest of such plaintiff or plaintiffs have a fair value in excess of fifty thousand dollars, the corporation in whose right such action is brought shall be entitled at any stage of the proceedings before final judgment to require the plaintiff or plaintiffs to give security for the reasonable expenses, including attorney's fees, which may be incurred by it in connection with such action and by the other parties defendant in connection therewith for which the corporation may become liable under this chapter, under any contract or otherwise under law, to which the corporation shall have recourse in such amount as the court having jurisdiction of such action shall determine upon the termination of such action. The amount of such security may thereafter from time to time be increased or decreased in the discretion of the court having jurisdiction of such action upon showing that the security provided has or may become inadequate or excessive.

§ 630. Liability of shareholders for wages due to laborers, servants or employees

(a) The ten largest shareholders, as determined by the fair value of their beneficial interest as of the beginning of the period during which the unpaid services referred to in this section are performed, of every corporation (other than an investment company registered as such under an act of congress entitled "Investment Company Act of 1940" [1]), no shares of which are listed on a national securities exchange or regularly quoted in an over-the-counter market by one or more members of a national or an affiliated securities association, shall jointly and severally be personally liable for all debts, wages or salaries due and owing to any of its laborers, servants or employees other than contractors, for services performed by them for such corporation. Before such laborer, servant or employee shall charge such shareholder for such services, he shall give notice in writing to such shareholder that he intends to hold him liable under this section. Such notice shall be given within ninety days after termination of such services, except that if, within such period, the laborer, servant or employee demands an examination of the record of shareholders under paragraph (b) of section 624 (Books and records; right of inspection, prima facie evidence), such notice may be given within sixty days after he has been given the opportunity to examine the record of shareholders. An action to enforce such liability shall be commenced within ninety days after the return of an execution unsatisfied against the corporation upon a judgment recovered against it for such services.

(b) For the purposes of this section, wages or salaries shall mean all compensation and benefits payable by an employer to or for the account of the employee for personal services rendered by such employee. These shall specifically include but not be limited to salaries, overtime, vacation, holiday and severance pay; employer contributions to or payments of insurance or welfare benefits; employer contributions to pension or annuity funds; and any other moneys properly due or payable for services rendered by such employee.

(c) A shareholder who has paid more than his pro rata share under this section shall be entitled to contribution pro rata from the other shareholders liable under this section with respect to the excess so paid, over and above his pro rata share, and may sue them jointly or severally or any number of them to recover the amount due from them. Such recovery may be had in a separate action. As used in this paragraph, "pro rata" means in proportion to beneficial share interest. Before a shareholder may claim contribution from other shareholders under this paragraph, he shall, unless they have been given notice by a laborer, servant or employee under paragraph (a), give them notice in writing that he intends to hold them so liable to him. Such notice shall be given by him within twenty days after the date that notice was given to him by a laborer, servant or employee under paragraph (a).

ARTICLE 7. DIRECTORS AND OFFICERS

§ 709. Greater requirement as to quorum and vote of directors

(a) The certificate of incorporation may contain provisions specifying either or both of the following:

(1) That the proportion of directors that shall constitute a quorum for the transaction of business or of any specified item of business shall be greater than the proportion prescribed by this chapter in the absence of such provision.

(2) That the proportion of votes of directors that shall be necessary for the transaction of business or of any specified item of business shall be greater than the proportion prescribed by this chapter in the absence of such provision.

(b) An amendment of the certificate of incorporation which adds a provision permitted by this section or which changes or strikes out such a provision, shall be authorized at a meeting of shareholders by vote of the holders of two-thirds of all outstanding shares entitled to vote thereon, or of such greater proportion of shares or class or series of shares, as may be provided specifically in the certificate of incorporation for adding, changing or striking out a provision permitted by this section.

(c) If the certificate of incorporation of any corporation contains a provision authorized by this section, the existence of such provision shall be noted conspicuously on the face or back of every certificate for shares issued by such corporation.

§ 713. Interested directors

(a) No contract or other transaction between a corporation and one or more of its directors, or between a corporation and any other corporation, firm, association or other entity in which one or more of its directors are directors or officers, or have a substantial financial interest, shall be either void or voidable for this reason alone or by reason alone that such director or directors are present at the meeting of the board, or of a committee thereof, which approves such contract or transaction, or that his or their votes are counted for such purpose:

(1) If the material facts as to such director's interest in such contract or transaction and as to any such common directorship, officership or financial interest are disclosed in good faith or known to the board or committee, and the board or committee approves such contract or transaction by a vote sufficient for such purpose without counting the vote of such interested director or, if the votes of the disinterested directors are insufficient to constitute an act of the board as defined in section 708 (Action by the board), by unanimous vote of the disinterested directors; or

(2) If the material facts as to such director's interest in such contract or transaction and as to any such common directorship, officership or financial interest are disclosed in good faith or known to the shareholders entitled to vote thereon, and such contract or transaction is approved by vote of such shareholders.

(b) If such good faith disclosure of the material facts as to the director's interest in the contract or transaction and as to any such common directorship, officership or financial interest is made to the directors or shareholders, or known to the board or committee or shareholders approving such contract or transaction, as provided in paragraph (a), the contract or transaction may not be avoided by the corporation for the reasons set forth in paragraph (a). If there was no such disclosure or knowledge, or if the vote of such interested director was necessary for the approval of such contract or transaction at a meeting of the board or committee at which it was approved, the corporation may avoid the contract or transaction unless the party or parties thereto shall establish affirmatively that the contract or transaction was fair and reasonable as to the corporation at the time it was approved by the board, a committee or the shareholders.

(c) Common or interested directors may be counted in determining the presence of a quorum at a meeting of the board or of a committee which approves such contract or transaction.

(d) The certificate of incorporation may contain additional restrictions on contracts or transactions between a corporation and its directors and may provide that contracts or transactions in violation of such restrictions shall be void or voidable by the corporation.

(e) Unless otherwise provided in the certificate of incorporation or the by-laws, the board shall have authority to fix the compensation of directors for services in any capacity.

§ 715. Officers

(a) The board may elect or appoint a president, one or more vice-presidents, a secretary and a treasurer, and such other officers as it may determine, or as may be provided in the by-laws.

(b) The certificate of incorporation may provide that all officers or that specified officers shall be elected by the shareholders instead of by the board.

(c) Unless otherwise provided in the certificate of incorporation or the by-laws, all officers shall be elected or appointed to hold office until the meeting of the board following the next annual meeting of shareholders or, in the case of officers elected by the shareholders, until the next annual meeting of shareholders.

(d) Each officer shall hold office for the term for which he is elected or appointed, and until his successor has been elected or appointed and qualified.

(e) Any two or more offices may be held by the same person, except the offices of president and secretary. When all of the issued and outstanding stock of the corporation is owned by one person, such person may hold all or any combination of offices.

(f) The board may require any officer to give security for the faithful performance of his duties.

(g) All officers as between themselves and the corporation shall have such authority and perform such duties in the management of the corporation as may be provided in the by-laws or, to the extent not so provided, by the board.

(h) An officer shall perform his duties as an officer in good faith and with that degree of care which an ordinarily prudent person in a like position would use under similar circumstances. In performing his duties, an officer shall be entitled to rely on information, opinions, reports or statements including financial statements and other financial data, in each case prepared or presented by:

(1) one or more other officers or employees of the corporation or of any other corporation of which at least fifty percentum of the outstanding shares of stock entitling the holders thereof to vote for the election of directors is owned directly or indirectly by the corporation, whom the officer believes to be reliable and competent in the matters presented, or

(2) counsel, public accounts or other persons as to matters which the officer believes to be within such person's professional or expert competence, so long as in so relying he shall be acting in good faith and with such degree of care, but he shall not be considered to be acting in good faith if he has knowledge con-

cerning the matter in question that would cause such reliance to be unwarranted. A person who so performs his duties shall have no liability by reason of being or having been an officer of the corporation.

§ 716. Removal of officers

(a) Any officer elected or appointed by the board may be removed by the board with or without cause. An officer elected by the shareholders may be removed, with or without cause, only by vote of the shareholders, but his authority to act as an officer may be suspended by the board for cause.

(b) The removal of an officer without cause shall be without prejudice to his contract rights, if any. The election or appointment of an officer shall not of itself create contract rights.

(c) An action to procure a judgment removing an officer for cause may be brought by the attorney-general or by the holders of ten percent of the outstanding shares, whether or not entitled to vote. The court may bar from re-election or reappointment any officer so removed for a period fixed by the court.

§ 719. Liability of directors in certain cases

(a) Directors of a corporation who vote for or concur in any of the following corporate actions shall be jointly and severally liable to the corporation for the benefit of its creditors or shareholders, to the extent of any injury suffered by such persons, respectively, as a result of such action:

(1) The declaration of any dividend or other distribution to the extent that it is contrary to the provisions of paragraphs (a) and (b) of section 510 (Dividends or other distributions in cash of property).

(2) The purchase of the shares of the corporation to the extent that it is contrary to the provisions of section 513 (Purchase or redemption by a corporation of its own shares).

(3) The distribution of assets to shareholders after dissolution of the corporation without paying or adequately providing for all known liabilities of the corporation, excluding any claims not filed by creditors within the time limit set in a notice given to creditors under articles 10 (Non-judicial dissolution) or 11 (Judicial dissolution).

(4) The making of any loan contrary to section 714 (Loans to directors).

(b) A director who is present at a meeting of the board, or any committee thereof, when action specified in paragraph (a) is taken shall be presumed to have concurred in the action unless his dissent thereto shall be entered in the minutes of the meeting, or unless he shall submit his written dissent to the person acting as the secretary of the meeting before the adjournment thereof, or shall deliver or send by registered mail such dissent to the secretary of the corporation promptly after the adjournment of the meeting. Such right to dissent shall not apply to a director who voted in favor of such action. A director who is absent from a meeting of the board, or any committee thereof, when such action is taken shall be presumed to have concurred in the action unless he shall deliver or send by registered mail his dissent thereto to the secretary of the corporation or shall cause such dissent to be filed with the minutes of the proceedings of the board or committee within a reasonable time after learning of such action.

(c) Any director against whom a claim is successfully asserted under this section shall be entitled to contribution from the other directors who voted for or concurred in the action upon which the claim is asserted.

(d) Directors against whom a claim is successfully asserted under this section shall be entitled, to the extent of the amounts paid by them to the corporation as a result of such claims:

(1) Upon payment to the corporation of any amount of an improper dividend or distribution, to be subrogated to the rights of the corporation against shareholders who received such dividend or distribution with knowledge of facts indicating that it was not authorized by section 510, in proportion to the amounts received by them respectively.

(2) Upon payment to the corporation of any amount of the purchase price of an improper purchase of shares, to have the corporation rescind such purchase of shares and recover for their benefit, but at their expense, the amount of such purchase price from any seller who sold such shares with knowledge of facts indicating that such purchase of shares by the corporation was not authorized by section 513.

(3) Upon payment to the corporation of the claim of any creditor by reason of a violation of subparagraph (a) (3), to be subrogated to the rights of the corporation against shareholders who received an improper distribution of assets.

(4) Upon payment to the corporation of the amount of any loan made contrary to section 714, to be subrogated to the rights of the corporation against a director who received the improper loan.

(e) A director shall not be liable under this section if, in the circumstances, he performed his duty to the corporation under section 717.

(f) This section shall not affect any liability otherwise imposed by law upon any director.

§ 720. Action againt directors and officers for misconduct

(a) An action may be brought against one or more directors or officers of a corporation to procure a judgment for the following relief:

(1) To compel the defendant to account for his official conduct in the following cases:

    (A) The neglect of, or failure to perform, or other violation of his duties in the management and disposition of corporate assets committed to his charge.

    (B) The acquisition by himself, transfer to others, loss or waste of corporate assets due to any neglect of, or failure to perform, or other violation of his duties.

(2) To set aside an unlawful conveyance, assignment or transfer of corporate assets, where the transferee knew of its unlawfulness.

(3) To enjoin a proposed unlawful conveyance, assignment or transfer of corporate assets, where there is sufficient evidence that it will be made.

(b) An action may be brought for the relief provided in this section, and in paragraph (a) of section 719 (Liability of directors in certain cases) by a corporation, or a receiver, trustee in bankruptcy, officer, director or judgment creditor thereof, or, under section 626 (Shareholders' derivative action brought in the right of the corporation to procure a judgment in its favor), by a shareholder, voting trust certificate holder, or the owner of a beneficial interest in shares thereof.

(c) This section shall not affect any liability otherwise imposed by law upon any director or officer.

§ 721. Exclusivity of statutory provisions for indemnification of directors and officers

No provision made to indemnify directors or officers for the defense of any civil or criminal action or proceeding, whether contained in the certificate of incorporation, the by-laws, a resolution of shareholders or directors, an agreement or otherwise, nor any award of indemnification by a court, shall be valid unless consistent with this article. Nothing contained in this article shall affect any rights to indemnification to which corporate personnel other than directors and officers may be entitled by contract or otherwise under law.

§ 722.   Authorization for indemnification of directors and officers in actions by or in the right of a corporation to procure a judgment in its favor

(a) A corporation may indemnify any person, made a party to an action by or in the right of the corporation to procure a judgment in its favor by reason of the fact that he, his testator or intestate, is or was a director or officer of the corporation, against the reasonable expenses, including attorneys' fees, actually and necessarily incurred by him in connection with the defense of such action, or in connection with an appeal therein, except in relation to matters as to which such director or officer is adjudged to have breached his duty to the corporation under section 717 (Duty of directors) or under paragraph (h) of section 715 (Officers).

(b) The indemnification authorized under paragraph (a) shall in no case include:

(1) Amounts paid in settling or otherwise disposing of a threatened action, or a pending action with or without court approval, or

(2) Expenses incurred in defending a threatened action, or a pending action which is settled or otherwise disposed of without court approval.

§ 723.   Authorization for indemnification of directors and officers in actions or proceedings other than by or in the right of a corporation to procure a judgment in its favor

(a) A corporation may indemnify any person, made, or threatened to be made, a party to an action or proceeding other than one by or in the right of the corporation to procure a judgment in its favor, whether civil or criminal, including an action by or in the right of any other corporation of any type or kind, domestic or foreign, or any partnership, joint venture, trust, employee benefit plan or other enterprise, which any director or officer of the corporation served in any capacity at the request of the corporation, by reason of the fact that he, his testator or intestate, was a director or officer of the corporation, or served such other corporation, partnership, joint venture, trust, employee benefit plan or other enterprise in any capacity, against judgments, fines, amounts paid in settlement and reasonable expenses, including attorneys' fees actually and necessarily incurred as a result of such action or proceeding, or any appeal therein, if such director or officer acted, in good faith, for a purpose which he reasonably believed to be in, or, in the case of service for any other corporation or any partnership, joint venture, trust, employee benefit plan or other enterprise, not opposed to, the best interests of the corporation and, in criminal actions or proceedings, in addition, had no reasonable cause to believe that his conduct was unlawful.

(b) The termination of any such civil or criminal action or proceeding by judgment, settlement, conviction or upon a plea of nolo contendere, or its equivalent, shall not in itself create a presumption that any such director or officer did not act, in good faith, for a purpose which he reasonably believed to be in, or, in the case of service for any other corporation or any partnership, joint venture, trust, employee benefit plan or other enterprise, not opposed to, the best interests of the corporation or that he had reasonable cause to believe that his conduct was unlawful.

(c) For the purpose of this section, a corporation shall be deemed to have requested a person to serve an employee benefit plan where the performance by such person of his duties to the corporation also imposes duties on, or otherwise involves services by, such person to the plan or participants or beneficiaries of the plan; excise taxes assessed on a person with respect to an employee benefit plan pursuant to applicable law shall be considered fines; and action taken or omitted by a person with respect to an employee benefit plan in the performance of such person's duties for a purpose reasonably believed by such person to be in the interest of the participants and beneficiaries of the plan shall be deemed to be for a purpose which is not opposed to the best interests of the corporation.

§ 724. Payment of indemnification other than by court award

(a) A person who has been wholly successful, on the merits or otherwise, in the defense of a civil or criminal action or proceeding of the character described in section 722 (Authorization for indemnification of directors and officers in actions by or in the right of a corporation to procure a judgment in its favor) or 723 (Authorization for indemnification of directors and officers in actions or proceedings other than by or in the right of a corporation to procure a judgment in its favor) shall be entitled to indemnification as authorized in such sections.

(b) Except as provided in paragraph (a), any indemnification under section 722 or 723, unless ordered by a court under section 725 (Indemnification of directors and officers by a court), shall be made by the corporation, only if authorized in the specific case:

(1) By the board acting by a quorum consisting of directors who are not parties to such action or proceeding upon a finding that the director or officer has met the standard of conduct set forth in section 722 or 723, as the case may be, or,

(2) If a quorum under subparagraph (1) is not obtainable with due diligence;

(A) By the board upon the opinion in writing of independent legal counsel that indemnification is proper in the circumstances because the applicable standard of conduct set forth in such sections has been met by such director or officer, or

(B) By the shareholders upon a finding that the director or officer has met the applicable standard of conduct set forth in such sections.

(c) Expenses incurred in defending a civil or criminal action or proceeding may be paid by the corporation in advance of the final disposition of such action or proceeding if authorized under paragraph (b).

§ **725.**   Indemnification of directors and officers by a court

(a) Notwithstanding the failure of a corporation to provide indemnification, and despite any contrary resolution of the board or of the shareholders in the specific case under section 724 (Payment of indemnification other than by court award), indemnification shall be awarded by a court to the extent authorized under sections 722 (Authorization for indemnification of directors and officers in actions by or in the right of a corporation to procure a judgment in its favor), 723 (Authorization for indemnification of directors and officers in actions or proceedings other than by or in the right of a corporation to procure a judgment in its favor), and paragraph (a) of section 724. Application therefor may be made, in every case, either:

(1) In the civil action or proceeding in which the expenses were incurred or other amounts were paid, or

(2) To the supreme court in a separate proceeding, in which case the application shall set forth the disposition of any previous application made to any court for the same or similar relief and also reasonable cause for the failure to make application for such relief in the action or proceeding in which the expenses were incurred or other amounts were paid.

(b) The application shall be made in such manner and form as may be required by the applicable rules of court or, in the absence thereof, by direction of a court to which it is made. Such application shall be upon notice to the corporation. The court may also direct that notice be given at the expense of the corporation to the shareholders and such other persons as it may designate in such manner as it may require.

(c) Where indemnification is sought by judicial action, the court may allow a person such reasonable expenses, including attorneys' fees, during the pendency of the litigation as are necessary in connection with his defense therein, if the court shall find that the defendant has by his pleadings or during the course of the litigation raised genuine issues of fact or law.

§ **726.**   Other provisions affecting indemnification of directors and officers

(a) All expenses incurred in defending a civil or criminal action or proceeding which are advanced by the corporation under paragraph (c) of section 724 (Payment of indemnification other than by court award) or allowed by a court under paragraph (c) of section 725 (Indemnification of directors and officers by a court) shall be repaid in case the person receiving such advancement or allowance is ultimately found, under the procedure set forth in this article, not to be entitled to indemnification or, where indemnification is granted, to the extent the expenses so advanced by the corporation or allowed by the court exceed the indemnification to which he is entitled.

(b) No indemnification, advancement or allowance shall be made under this article in any circumstance where it appears:

(1) That the indemnification would be inconsistent with the law of the jurisdiction of incorporation of a foreign corporation which prohibits or otherwise limits such indemnification;

(2) That the indemnification would be inconsistent with a provision of the certificate of incorporation, a by-law, a resolution of the board or of the shareholders, an agreement or other proper corporate action, in effect at the time of the accrual of the alleged cause of action asserted in the threatened or pending action or proceeding in which the expenses were incurred or other amounts were paid, which prohibits or otherwise limits indemnification; or

(3) If there has been a settlement approved by the court, that the indemnification would be inconsistent with any condition with respect to indemnification expressly imposed by the court in approving the settlement.

(c) If, under this article, any expenses or other amounts are paid by way of indemnification, otherwise than by court order or action by the shareholders, the corporation shall, not later than the next annual meeting of shareholders unless such meeting is held within three months from the date of such payment, and, in any event, within fifteen months from the date of such payment, mail to its shareholders of record at the time entitled to vote for the election of directors a statement specifying the persons paid, the amounts paid, and the nature and status at the time of such payment of the litigation or threatened litigation.

(d) The provisions of this article relating to indemnification of directors and officers and insurance therefor shall apply to domestic corporations and foreign corporations doing business in this state, except as provided in section 1320 (Exemption from certain provisions).

§ 727. Insurance for indemnification of directors and officers

(a) Subject to paragraph (b), a corporation shall have power to purchase and maintain insurance:

(1) To indemnify the corporation for any obligation which it incurs as a result of the indemnification of directors and officers under the provisions of this article, and

(2) To indemnify directors and officers in instances in which they may be indemnified by the corporation under the provisions of this article, and

(3) To indemnify directors and officers in instances in which they may not otherwise be indemnified by the corporation under the provisions of this article provided the contract of insurance covering such directors and officers provides, in a manner acceptable to the superintendent of insurance, for a retention amount and for co-insurance.

(b) No insurance under paragraph (a) may provide for any payment, other than cost of defense, to or on behalf of any director or officer.

(1) if a judgment or other final adjudication adverse to the insured director or officer establishes that his acts of active and deliberate dishonesty were material to the cause of action so adjudicated, or that he personally gained in fact a financial profit or other advantage to which he was not legally entitled, or

(2) in relation to any risk the insurance of which is prohibited under the insurance law of this state.

(c) Insurance under any or all subparagraphs of paragraph (a) may be included in a single contract or supplement thereto. Retrospective rated contracts are prohibited.

(d) The corporation shall, within the time and to the persons provided in paragraph (c) of section 726 (Other provisions affecting indemnification of directors or officers), mail a statement in respect of any insurance it has purchased or renewed under this section, specifying the insurance carrier, date of the contract, cost of the insurance, corporate positions insured, and a statement explaining all sums, not previously reported in a statement to shareholders, paid under any indemnification insurance contract.

(e) This section is the public policy of this state to spread the risk of corporate management, notwithstanding any other general or special law of this state or of any other jurisdiction including the federal government.

ARTICLE 10. NON–JUDICIAL DISSOLUTION

§ 1002. Dissolution under provision in certificate of incorporation

(a) The certificate of incorporation may contain a provision that any shareholder, or the holders of any specified number or proportion of shares, or of any specified number or proportion of shares of any class or series thereof, may require the dissolution of the corporation at will or upon the occurrence of a specified event. If the certificate of incorporation contains such a provision, a certificate of dissolution under section 1003 (Certificate of dissolution; contents) may be signed, verified and delivered to the department of state as provided in section 104 (Certificate; requirements, signing, filing, effectiveness) when authorized by a holder or holders of the number or proportion of shares specified in such provision, given in such manner as may be specified therein, or if no manner is specified therein, when authorized on written consent signed by such holder or holders; or such certificate may be signed, verified and delivered to the department by such holder or holders or by such of them as are designated by them.

(b) An amendment of the certificate of incorporation which adds a provision permitted by this section, or which changes or strikes out such a provision, shall be authorized at a meeting of shareholders by vote of all outstanding shares, whether or not otherwise entitled to vote on any amendment, or of such lesser proportion of shares and of such class or series of shares, but not less than a majority of all outstanding shares entitled to vote on any amendment, as may be provided specifically in the certificate of incorporation for adding, changing or striking out a provision permitted by this section.

(c) If the certificate of incorporation of any corporation contains a provision authorized by this section, the existence of such provision shall be noted conspicuously on the face or back of every certificate for shares issued by such corporation.

ARTICLE 11.　JUDICIAL DISSOLUTION

§ 1104.　Petition in case of deadlock among directors or shareholders

(a) Except otherwise provided in the certificate of incorporation under section 613 (Limitations on right to vote), the holders of one-half of all outstanding shares of a corporation entitled to vote in an election of directors may present a petition for dissolution on one or more of the following grounds:

(1) That the directors are so divided respecting the management of the corporation's affairs that the votes required for action by the board cannot be obtained.

(2) That the shareholders are so divided that the votes required for the election of directors cannot be obtained.

(3) That there is internal dissension and two or more factions of shareholders are so divided that dissolution would be beneficial to the shareholders.

(b) If the certificate of incorporation provides that the proportion of votes required for action by the board, or the proportion of votes of shareholders required for election of directors, shall be greater than that otherwise required by this chapter, such a petition may be presented by the holders of more than one-third of all outstanding shares entitled to vote on non-judicial dissolution under section 1001 (Authorization of dissolution).

(c) Notwithstanding any provision in the certificate of incorporation, any holder of shares entitled to vote at an election of directors of a corporation, may present a petition for its dissolution on the ground that the shareholders are so divided that they have failed, for a period which includes at least two consecutive annual meeting dates, to elect successors to directors whose terms have expired or would have expired upon the election and qualification of their successors.

§ 1104–a.　Petition for judicial dissolution under special circumstances

(a) The holders of twenty percent or more of all outstanding shares of a corporation, other than a corporation registered as an investment company under an act of congress entitled "Investment Company Act of 1940", no shares of which are listed on a national securities exchange or regularly quoted in an over-the-counter market by one or more members of a national or an affiliated securities association, who are entitled to vote in an election of directors may present a petition of dissolution on one or more of the following grounds:

(1) The directors or those in control of the corporation have been guilty of illegal, fraudulent or oppressive actions toward the complaining shareholders;

(2) The property or assets of the corporation are being looted, wasted, or diverted for non-corporate purposes by its directors, officers or those in control of the corporation.

(b) The court, in determining whether to proceed with involuntary dissolution pursuant to this section, shall take into account:

(1) Whether liquidation of the corporation is the only feasible means whereby the petitioners may reasonably expect to obtain a fair return on their investment; and

(2) Whether liquidation of the corporation is reasonably necessary for the protection of the rights and interests of any substantial number of shareholders or of the petitioners.

§ 1111. Judgment or final order of dissolution

(a) In an action or special proceeding under this article if, in the court's discretion, it shall appear that the corporation should be dissolved, it shall make a judgment or final order dissolving the corporation.

(b) In making its decision, the court shall take into consideration the following criteria:

(1) In an action brought by the attorney-general, the interest of the public is of paramount importance.

(2) In a special proceeding brought by directors or shareholders, the benefit to the shareholders of a dissolution is of paramount importance.

(3) In a special proceeding brought under section 1104 (Petition in case of deadlock among directors or shareholders) or section 1104–a (Petition for judicial dissolution under special circumstances) dissolution is not to be denied merely because it is found that the corporate business has been or could be conducted at a profit.

(c) If the judgment or final order shall provide for a dissolution of the corporation, the court may, in its discretion, provide therein for the distribution of the property of the corporation to those entitled thereto according to their respective rights.

(d) The clerk of the court or such other person as the court may direct shall transmit certified copies of the judgment or final order of dissolution to the department of state and to the clerk of the county in which the office of the corporation was located at the date of the judgment or order. Upon filing by the department of state, the corporation shall be dissolved.

(e) The corporation shall promptly thereafter transmit a certified copy of the judgment or final order to the clerk of each other county in which its certificate of incorporation was filed.

§ 1118. Purchase of petitioner's shares; valuation

(a) In any proceeding brought pursuant to section eleven hundred four-a of this chapter, any other shareholder or shareholders or the corporation may, at any time within ninety days after the filing of such petition or at such later time as the court in its discretion may allow, elect to purchase the shares owned by the petitioners at their fair value and upon such terms and conditions as may be approved by the court.

(b) If one or more shareholders or the corporation elect to purchase the shares owned by the petitioner but are unable to agree with the petitioner upon the fair value of such shares, the court, upon the application of such prospective purchaser or purchasers, shall stay the proceedings brought pursuant to section 1104–a of this chapter and determine the fair value of the petitioner's shares as of the day prior to the date on which such petition was filed, exclusive of any element of value arising from such filing.

ARTICLE 13. FOREIGN CORPORATIONS

§ 1317. Liabilities of directors and officers of foreign corporations

(a) Except as otherwise provided in this chapter, the directors and officers of a foreign corporation doing business in this state are subject, to the same extent as directors and officers of a domestic corporation, to the provisions of:

(1) Section 719 (Liability of directors in certain cases) except subparagraph (a)(3) thereof, and

(2) Section 720 (Action against directors and officers for misconduct.)

(b) Any liability imposed by paragraph (a) may be enforced in, and such relief granted by, the courts in this state, in the same manner as in the case of a domestic corporation.

§ 1318. Liability of foreign corporations for failure to disclose required information

(a) A foreign corporation doing business in this state shall, in the same manner as a domestic corporation, disclose to its shareholders of record who are residents of this state the information required under paragraph (c) of section 510 (Dividends or other distributions in cash or property), paragraphs (f) and (g) of section 511 (Share distributions and changes), paragraph

(d) of section 515 (Reacquired shares), paragraph (c) of section 516 (Reduction of stated capital in certain cases), subparagraph (a) (4) of section 517 (Special provisions relative to surplus and reserves) or paragraph (f) of section 519 (Convertible shares and bonds), and shall be liable as provided in section 520 (Liability for failure to disclose required information) for failure to comply in good faith with these requirements.

(b) For the purposes of this section, an authorized foreign corporation may by board action determine the amount of its earned surplus before the declaration of its first dividend after either (1) the effective date of this chapter or (2) the date of filing of its application for authority under this chapter, whichever is later; and such determination if made in good faith shall be conclusive. Thereafter such foreign corporation may determine the amount or availability of its earned surplus in the same manner as a domestic corporation.

§ 1319. Applicability of other provisions

(a) In addition to articles 1 (Short title; definitions; application; certificates; miscellaneous) and 3 (Corporate name and service of process) and the other sections of article 13, the following provisions, to the extent provided therein, shall apply to a foreign corporation doing business in this state, its directors, officers and shareholders:

(1) Section 623 (Procedure to enforce shareholder's right to receive payment for shares).

(2) Section 626 (Shareholders' derivative action brought in the right of the corporation to procure a judgment in its favor).

(3) Section 627 (Security for expenses in shareholders' derivative action brought in the right of the corporation to procure a judgment in its favor).

(4) Section 721 (Exclusivity of statutory provisions for indemnification of directors and officers) through 727 (Insurance for indemnification of directors and officers), inclusive.

(5) Section 808 (Reorganization under act of congress).

(6) Section 907 (Merger or consolidation of domestic and foreign corporations).

§ 1320. Exemption from certain provisions

(a) Notwithstanding any other provision of this chapter, a foreign corporation doing business in this state which is authorized under this article, its directors, officers and shareholders, shall be exempt from the provisions of paragraph (e) of section 1316 (Voting trust records), subparagraph (a)(1) of section 1317 (Liabilities of directors and officers of foreign corporations), section 1318 (Liability of foreign corporations for failure to disclose required information) and subparagraph (a)(4) of section 1319 (Applicability of other provisions) if when such provision would otherwise apply:

(1) Shares of such corporation were listed on a national securities exchange, or

(2) Less than one-half of the total of its business income for the preceding three fiscal years, or such portion thereof as the foreign corporation was in existence, was allocable to this state for franchise tax purposes under the tax law.

G. CORPORATION FORMS

Table of Forms

1. ARTICLES OF INCORPORATION

ARTICLES OF INCORPORATION OF
BUSINESS ENTERPRISES, INC.

The undersigned, acting as incorporator of a corporation under the Model Business Corporation Act, adopts the following Articles of Incorporation for such corporation:

FIRST: The name of the corporation is Business Enterprises, Inc.

SECOND: The period of its duration is perpetual.

THIRD: The purposes for which the corporation is organized are the transaction of any and all lawful business for which corporations may be incorporated.

FOURTH: The aggregate number of shares which the corporation shall have the authority to issue is 80,000 shares, divided into three classes, designated as follows:

20,000 "5% Cumulative Preferred Shares" ($100 par value); *
30,000 "Preference Shares" (without par value) (issuable in series); and
30,000 "Common Shares" ($10 par value).

The preferences, limitations and relative rights of the shares of each class shall be as follows:

The holders of the 5% Cumulative Preferred Shares shall be entitled to receive, when, as and if declared by the board of directors out of

---

* The Model Business Corporation Act no longer provides for par value shares.

funds legally available therefor, cumulative preferential dividends in cash at the rate of, but not exceeding, five percent (5%) of the par value per annum, payable quarterly on the first days of March, June, September and December in each year. Such dividends on each share of 5% Cumulative Preferred Shares shall commence to accrue and be cumulative, whether or not earned or declared, from and after the date of issue of such share. So long as any of the 5% Cumulative Preferred Shares remains outstanding, in no event shall any dividend whatever be paid upon or declared or set apart for the Preference Shares or the Common Shares, nor shall any Preference Shares or Common Shares be redeemed, purchased, retired or otherwise acquired by the corporation, unless and until all dividends on the then outstanding shares of 5% Cumulative Preferred Shares for all past quarterly dividend periods shall have been paid or declared and set apart for payment, but without interest, and the full dividends thereon for the then current quarterly dividend period shall have been concurrently paid or declared and set apart for payment. After such full dividends on the 5% Cumulative Preferred Shares shall have been so paid or declared and set apart for payment, then and not otherwise dividends may be declared and paid on the Preference Shares or the Common Shares when and as determined by the board of directors out of any funds legally available for dividends; provided, however, that if any of the Preference Shares is outstanding, in no event shall any dividend whatever be paid upon or declared or set apart for the Common Shares, nor shall any Common Shares be purchased, retired or otherwise acquired by the corporation, unless and until all dividends on the then outstanding Preference Shares, including unpaid dividends for all past quarterly dividend periods, as well as the full dividends thereon for the then current quarterly dividend period, to the extent, if any, that dividends thereon are fixed and determined as cumulative by the board of directors in the resolution establishing the same, shall have been paid or declared and set apart for payment. In case Preference Shares of more than one series are outstanding, dividends on the shares of all series shall be ratably in proportion to the full dividend to which such shares respectively are entitled.

In the event of any voluntary or involuntary liquidation, dissolution or winding up of the affairs of the corporation, the holders of the 5% Cumulative Preferred Shares shall be entitled to receive for each share thereof an amount equal to one hundred and five dollars ($105.00) plus five percent of the par value per annum for each year in which the share has been outstanding to the date of such payment, less the sum of any dividends paid thereon, without interest, before any distribution of the assets of the corporation shall be made to the holders of Preference Shares or Common Shares. After such payment shall have been made in full to the holders of the outstanding 5% Cumulative Preferred Shares or funds necessary for such payment shall have been set aside in trust for the account of the holders of the outstanding 5% Cumulative Preferred Shares so as to be and continue available therefor, the holders of the outstanding 5% Cumulative Preferred Shares shall be entitled to no further participation in such distribution of the assets of the corporation. Thereafter, if any of the Preference Shares are outstanding, the holders of the Preference Shares shall be entitled to receive all amounts payable thereon in the event of liquidation, dissolution or winding up. After such payment shall have been made in full to the holders of the outstanding Preference Shares or funds necessary for such payment shall have been set aside in trust for the account of the holders of the outstanding Preference Shares so as to be and continue available therefor, the remaining assets of the corporation shall be divided and distributed among the holders of the Common Shares then outstanding according to their respective shares. If, upon such liquidation, dissolution or winding up, the assets of the corporation distributable as aforesaid among the holders of the 5% Cumulative Preferred Shares shall be insufficient to permit the payment to them of all amounts payable thereon, the entire assets shall be distributed ratably among the holders of the 5% Cumulative Preferred Shares. If such assets shall be sufficient to permit the payment to the holders of the 5% Cumulative Preferred Shares of all amounts payable thereon but insufficient to permit the payment to the holder of the Preference Shares of all amounts payable on such Preference Shares, all of the assets remaining after the payment to the holders of the 5% Cumulative Preferred Shares of all amounts payable thereon shall be distributed among the holders of all outstanding shares of the Preference Shares of all series ratably in proportion to the full amounts to which they respectively are entitled. A consolidation or merger of the corporation, a sale or transfer of all or substantially all of its assets, or any purchase or redemption of shares of the corporation of any class or series, shall not be regarded as a "liquidation, dissolution, or winding up" within the meaning of this paragraph.

The corporation at the option of the board of directors may at any time or from time to time redeem all or any part of the 5% Cumulative Preferred Shares then outstanding upon notice duly given as hereinafter provided, by paying for each share thereof an amount equal to one hundred and five dollars ($105.00) plus five percent of the par value per annum for each year in which the share has been outstanding to the date fixed for redemption, less the sum of any dividends paid thereon, without interest. In case less than all of the outstanding shares of 5% Cumulative Preferred Shares are to be redeemed, the shares to be redeemed shall be selected pro rata or by lot or by such other equitable method as the board of directors may determine. Notice of redemption of any shares of 5% Cumulative Preferred Shares shall be mailed, postage prepaid, to the holders of record of the shares to be redeemed at their respective addresses then appearing on the record of shareholders of the corporation, not less than fifteen (15) nor more than sixty (60) days prior to the date designated for such redemption. If such notice of redemption shall have been duly given, and if on or before the redemption date named therein the funds necessary for such redemption shall have been set aside by the corporation in trust for the account of the holders of the 5% Cumulative Preferred Shares so called for redemption so as to be and continue available therefor, then, from and after the giving of such notice and the setting aside of such funds, notwithstanding that any certificate for shares of 5% Cumulative Preferred Shares so called for redemption shall not have been surrendered for cancellation, the shares represented thereby shall no longer be deemed outstanding, and the holders of such certificate or certificates shall have with respect to such shares no rights in or with respect to the corporation except the right to receive for each share thereof an amount equal to one hundred and five dollars ($105.00) plus five percent of the par value per annum for each year in which the share has been outstanding to the date fixed for redemption, less the sum of any dividends paid thereon, without interest, upon the surrender of such certificate or certificates.

The Preference Shares may be divided into and issued in series. Each series shall be so designated as to distinguish the shares thereof from the shares of all other series and classes. The board of directors is vested with authority to divide the Preference Shares into series and, within the limitations set forth in these Articles of Incorporation, fix and determine the relative rights and preferences of the shares of any series so established, but all shares of the same class shall be identical except as to the following relative rights and preferences, as to which there may be variations between different series:

(A) The rate of dividend;

(B) Whether shares may be redeemed and, if so, the redemption price and the terms and conditions of redemption;

(C) The amount payable upon shares in event of voluntary and involuntary liquidation;

(D) Sinking fund provisions, if any, for the redemption and purchase of shares;

(E) The terms and conditions, if any, on which shares may be converted;

(F) Voting rights, if any.

FIFTH: The address of the initial registered office of the corporation is 100 Main Street, Grand City, State of . . . ., and the name of its initial registered agent at such address is Corporation Service Company.

SIXTH: The number of directors constituting the initial board of directors of the corporation is three, and the names and addresses of the persons who are to serve as directors until the first annual meeting of shareholders or until their successors are elected and shall qualify are:

Name	Address
Gilbert C. Dee	27 Iroquois Street, Grand City, State of . . . .
R. Sullivan Dum	27 Iroquois Street, Grand City, State of . . . .
Robert P. Lawyer	10 Main Street, Grand City, State of . . . .

SEVENTH: The name and address of each incorporator is:

Name	Address
Robert P. Lawyer	10 Main Street, Grand City, State of . . . .

Dated . . . ., 19 . . . . . .

Robert P. Lawyer
. . . .
Incorporator

2. CERTIFICATE OF INCORPORATION

STATE OF ....
OFFICE OF THE SECRETARY OF STATE

CERTIFICATE OF INCORPORATION

OF

BUSINESS ENTERPRISES, INC.

The undersigned, as Secretary of State of the State of ....
.........., hereby certifies that duplicate originals of Articles of Incorporation for the incorporation of Business Enterprises, Inc., duly signed pursuant to the provisions of the ....
Business Corporation Act, have been received in this office and are found to conform to law.

ACCORDINGLY the undersigned, as such Secretary of State, and by virtue of the authority vested in him by law, hereby issues this Certificate of Incorporation of Business Enterprises, Inc., duplicate original of the Articles of Incorporation.

Dated ...., 19...

.... *John R. Alexander* ....
Secretary of State   [A7918]

3. BYLAWS

Model By-Laws—a Long Form

BY-LAWS
OF

BUSINESS ENTERPRISES, INC.

ARTICLE I. OFFICES

The principal office of the corporation in the State of ....
.... shall be located in the City of ...., County of
.... The corporation may have such other offices, either within or without the State of ...., as the board of directors may designate or as the business of the corporation may require from time to time

266

The registered office of the corporation, required by the ....
.... Business Corporation Act to be maintained in the
State of .... may be, but need not be, identical with
the principal office in the State of ...., and the address
of the registered office may be changed from time to time by the
board of directors. [§ 12] [§ 13, Clause (g)]*

ARTICLE II.   SHAREHOLDERS

Section 1. **Annual Meeting.** The annual meeting of the
shareholders shall be held on the .... in the month of
.... in each year, beginning with the year 19..., at
the hour of ...... o'clock .... M., or at such other time on such
other day within such month as shall be fixed by the board of
directors, for the purpose of electing directors and for the transaction of such other business as may come before the meeting.
If the day fixed for the annual meeting shall be a legal holiday
in the State of ...., such meeting shall be held on
the next succeeding business day. If the election of directors
shall not be held on the day designated herein for any annual
meeting of the shareholders, or at any adjournment thereof, the
board of directors shall cause the election to be held at a special
meeting of the shareholders as soon thereafter as conveniently
may be. [§ 28] [§ 36]

Section 2. **Special Meetings.** Special meetings of the shareholders, for any purpose or purposes, unless otherwise prescribed
by statute, may be called by the president or by the board of
directors, and shall be called by the president at the request of
the holders of not less than one-tenth of all outstanding shares
of the corporation entitled to vote at the meeting. [§ 28]

Section 3. **Place of Meeting.** The board of directors may
designate any place, either within or without the State of ......
........, as the place of meeting for any annual meeting or for
any special meeting called by the board of directors. A waiver
of notice signed by all shareholders entitled to vote at a meeting
may designate any place, either within or without the State of
..............., as the place for the holding of such meeting.
If no designation is made, or if a special meeting be otherwise
called, the place of meeting shall be the principal office of the
corporation in the State of .... [§ 28]

Section 4. **Notice of Meeting.** Written notice stating the
place, day and hour of the meeting and, in case of a special meeting, the purpose or purposes for which the meeting is called,

* Numbers in brackets are references to sections of the Model Act.
The form of Model Bylaws has not
been revised by the Committee on
Corporate Laws of the American
Bar Association to reflect the most
recent changes in the Model Act.

shall, unless otherwise prescribed by statute, be delivered not less than ten nor more than fifty days before the date of the meeting, either personally or by mail, by or at the direction of the president, or the secretary, or the officer or other persons calling the meeting, to each shareholder of record entitled to vote at such meeting. If mailed, such notice shall be deemed to be delivered when deposited in the United States mail, addressed to the shareholder at his address as it appears on the stock transfer books of the corporation, with postage thereon prepaid. [§ 29]

Section 5. **Closing of Transfer Books or Fixing of Record Date.** For the purpose of determining shareholders entitled to notice of or to vote at any meeting of shareholders or any adjournment thereof, or shareholders entitled to receive payment of any dividend, or in order to make a determination of shareholders for any other proper purpose, the board of directors of the corporation may provide that the stock transfer books shall be closed for a stated period but not to exceed, in any case, fifty days. If the stock transfer books shall be closed for the purpose of determining shareholders entitled to notice of or to vote at a meeting of shareholders, such books shall be closed for at least ten days immediately preceding such meeting. In lieu of closing the stock transfer books, the board of directors may fix in advance a date as the record date for any such determination of shareholders, such date in any case to be not more than fifty days and, in case of a meeting of shareholders, not less than ten days prior to the date on which the particular action, requiring such determination of shareholders, is to be taken. If the stock transfer books are not closed and no record date is fixed for the determination of shareholders entitled to notice of or to vote at a meeting of shareholders, or shareholders entitled to receive payment of a dividend, the date on which notice of the meeting is mailed or the date on which the resolution of the board of directors declaring such dividend is adopted, as the case may be, shall be the record date for such determination of shareholders. When a determination of shareholders entitled to vote at any meeting of shareholders has been made as provided in this section, such determination shall apply to any adjournment thereof. [§ 30]

Section 6. **Voting Record.** The officer or agent having charge of the stock transfer books for shares of the corporation shall make a complete record of the shareholders entitled to vote at each meeting of shareholders or any adjournment thereof, arranged in alphabetical order, with the address of and the number of shares held by each. Such record shall be produced and kept open at the time and place of the meeting and shall be subject to the inspection of any shareholder during the whole time of the meeting for the purposes thereof. [§ 31]

268

Section 7. **Quorum.** A majority of the outstanding shares of the corporation entitled to vote, represented in person or by proxy, shall constitute a quorum at a meeting of shareholders. If less than a majority of the outstanding shares are represented at a meeting, a majority of the shares so represented may adjourn the meeting from time to time without further notice. At such adjourned meeting at which a quorum shall be present or represented, any business may be transacted which might have been transacted at the meeting as originally noticed. The shareholders present at a duly organized meeting may continue to transact business until adjournment, notwithstanding the withdrawal of enough shareholders to leave less than a quorum. [§ 32]

Section 8. **Proxies.** At all meetings of shareholders, a shareholder may vote in person or by proxy executed in writing by the shareholder or by his duly authorized attorney in fact. Such proxy shall be filed with the secretary of the corporation before or at the time of the meeting. No proxy shall be valid after eleven months from the date of its execution, unless otherwise provided in the proxy. [§ 33]

Section 9. **Voting of Shares.** Subject to the provisions of Section 12 of this Article II, each outstanding share entitled to vote shall be entitled to one vote upon each matter submitted to a vote at a meeting of shareholders. [§ 33]

Section 10. **Voting of Shares by Certain Holders.** Shares standing in the name of another corporation may be voted by such officer, agent or proxy as the by-laws of such corporation may prescribe, or, in the absence of such provision, as the board of directors of such other corporation may determine. [§ 33]

Shares held by an administrator, executor, guardian or conservator may be voted by him, either in person or by proxy, without a transfer of such shares into his name. Shares standing in the name of a trustee may be voted by him, either in person or by proxy, but no trustee shall be entitled to vote shares held by him without a transfer of such shares into his name. [§ 33]

Shares standing in the name of a receiver may be voted by such receiver, and shares held by or under the control of a receiver may be voted by such receiver without the transfer thereof into his name if authority so to do be contained in an appropriate order of the court by which such receiver was appointed. [§ 33]

A shareholder whose shares are pledged shall be entitled to vote such shares until the shares have been transferred into the name of the pledgee, and thereafter the pledgee shall be entitled to vote the shares so transferred. [§ 33]

Neither treasury shares of its own stock held by the corporation, nor shares held by another corporation if a majority of the shares entitled to vote for the election of directors of such other corporation are held by the corporation, shall be voted at any meeting or counted in determining the total number of outstanding shares at any given time for purposes of any meeting. [§ 33]

Section 11. **Informal Action by Shareholders.** Any action required or permitted to be taken at a meeting of the shareholders may be taken without a meeting if a consent in writing, setting forth the action so taken, shall be signed by all of the shareholders entitled to vote with respect to the subject matter thereof. [§ 145]

[Optional Section.] Section 12. **Cumulative Voting.** At each election for directors every shareholder entitled to vote at such election shall have the right to vote, in person or by proxy, the number of shares owned by him for as many persons as there are directors to be elected and for whose election he has a right to vote, or to cumulate his votes by giving one candidate as many votes as the number of such directors multiplied by the number of his shares shall equal, or by distributing such votes on the same principle among any number of such candidates. [§ 33]

ARTICLE III. BOARD OF DIRECTORS

Section 1. **General Powers.** The business and affairs of the corporation shall be managed by its board of directors. [§ 35]

Section 2. **Number, Tenure and Qualifications.** The number of directors of the corporation shall be .... Each director shall hold office until the next annual meeting of shareholders and until his successor shall have been elected and qualified. Directors need not be residents of the State of .... or shareholders of the corporation. [§ 35] [§ 36]

Section 3. **Regular Meetings.** A regular meeting of the board of directors shall be held without other notice than this by-law immediately after, and at the same place as, the annual meeting of shareholders. The board of directors may provide, by resolution, the time and place, either within or without the State of ...., for the holding of additional regular meetings without other notice than such resolution. [§ 43]

Section 4. **Special Meetings.** Special meetings of the board of directors may be called by or at the request of the president or any two directors. The person or persons authorized to call special meetings of the board of directors may fix any place, either within or without the State of ...., as the place for holding any special meeting of the board of directors called by them. [§ 43]

Section 5. **Notice.** Notice of any special meeting shall be given at least two days previously thereto by written notice delivered personally or mailed to each director at his business address, or by telegram. If mailed, such notice shall be deemed to be delivered when deposited in the United States mail, so addressed, with postage thereon prepaid. If notice be given by telegram, such notice shall be deemed to be delivered when the telegram is delivered to the telegraph company. Any director may waive notice of any meeting. The attendance of a director at a meeting shall constitute a waiver of notice of such meeting, except where a director attends a meeting for the express purpose of objecting to the transaction of any business because the meeting is not lawfully called or convened. Neither the business to be transacted at, nor the purpose of, any regular or special meeting of the board of directors need be specified in the notice or waiver of notice of such meeting. [§ 43]

Section 6. **Quorum.** A majority of the number of directors fixed by Section 2 of this Article III shall constitute a quorum for the transaction of business at any meeting of the board of directors, but if less than such majority is present at a meeting, a majority of the directors present may adjourn the meeting from time to time without further notice. [§ 40]

Section 7. **Manner of Acting.** The act of the majority of the directors present at a meeting at which a quorum is present shall be the act of the board of directors. [§ 40]

Section 8. **Action Without a Meeting.** Any action required or permitted to be taken by the board of directors at a meeting may be taken without a meeting if a consent in writing, setting forth the action so taken, shall be signed by all of the directors. [§ 44]

Section 9. **Vacancies.** Any vacancy occurring in the board of directors may be filled by the affirmative vote of a majority of the remaining directors though less than a quorum of the board of directors. A director elected to fill a vacancy shall be elected for the unexpired term of his predecessor in office. Any directorship to be filled by reason of an increase in the number of directors may be filled by election by the board of directors for a term of office continuing only until the next election of directors by the shareholders. [§ 38]

Section 10. **Compensation.** By resolution of the board of directors, each director may be paid his expenses, if any, of at-

271

tendance at each meeting of the board of directors, and may be paid a stated salary as director or a fixed sum for attendance at each meeting of the board of directors or both. No such payment shall preclude any director from serving the corporation in any other capacity and receiving compensation therefor. [§ 35]

Section 11. **Presumption of Assent.** A director of the corporation who is present at a meeting of the board of directors at which action on any corporate matter is taken shall be presumed to have assented to the action taken unless his dissent shall be entered in the minutes of the meeting or unless he shall file his written dissent to such action with the person acting as the secretary of the meeting before the adjournment thereof or shall forward such dissent by registered mail to the secretary of the corporation immediately after the adjournment of the meeting. Such right to dissent shall not apply to a director who voted in favor of such action. [§ 48]

ARTICLE IV. OFFICERS

Section 1. **Number.** The officers of the corporation shall be a president, one or more vice-presidents (the number thereof to be determined by the board of directors), a secretary, and a treasurer, each of whom shall be elected by the board of directors. Such other officers and assistant officers as may be deemed necessary may be elected or appointed by the board of directors. Any two or more offices may be held by the same person, except the offices of president and secretary. [§ 50]

Section 2. **Election and Term of Office.** The officers of the corporation to be elected by the board of directors shall be elected annually by the board of directors at the first meeting of the board of directors held after each annual meeting of the shareholders. If the election of officers shall not be held at such meeting, such election shall be held as soon thereafter as conveniently may be. Each officer shall hold office until his successor shall have been duly elected and shall have qualified or until his death or until he shall resign or shall have been removed in the manner hereinafter provided. [§ 50]

Section 3. **Removal.** Any officer or agent may be removed by the board of directors whenever in its judgment the best interests of the corporation will be served thereby, but such removal shall be without prejudice to the contract rights, if any, of the person so removed. Election or appointment of an officer or agent shall not of itself create contract rights. [§ 51]

Section 4. **Vacancies.** A vacancy in any office because of death, resignation, removal, disqualification or otherwise, may be filled by the board of directors for the unexpired portion of the term.

Section 5. **President.** The president shall be the principal executive officer of the corporation and, subject to the control of the board of directors, shall in general supervise and control all of the business and affairs of the corporation. He shall, when present, preside at all meetings of the shareholders and of the board of directors. He may sign, with the secretary or any other proper officer of the corporation thereunto authorized by the board of directors, certificates for shares of the corporation and deeds, mortgages, bonds, contracts, or other instruments which the board of directors has authorized to be executed, except in cases where the signing and execution thereof shall be expressly delegated by the board of directors or by these By-Laws to some other officer or agent of the corporation, or shall be required by law to be otherwise signed or executed; and in general shall perform all duties incident to the office of president and such other duties as may be prescribed by the board of directors from time to time. [§ 23]

Section 6. **The Vice-Presidents.** In the absence of the president or in the event of his death, inability or refusal to act, the vice-president (or in the event there be more than one vice-president, the vice-presidents in the order designated at the time of their election, or in the absence of any designation, then in the order of their election) shall perform the duties of the president, and when so acting, shall have all the powers of and be subject to all the restrictions upon the president. Any vice-president may sign, with the secretary or an assistant secretary, certificates for shares of the corporation; and shall perform such other duties as from time to time may be assigned to him by the president or by the board of directors. [§ 23]

Section 7. **The Secretary.** The secretary shall: (a) keep the minutes of the proceedings of the shareholders and of the board of directors in one or more books provided for that purpose; (b) see that all notices are duly given in accordance with the provisions of these By-Laws or as required by law; (c) be custodian of the corporate records and of the seal of the corporation and see that the seal of the corporation is affixed to all documents the execution of which on behalf of the corporation under its seal is duly authorized; (d) keep a register of the postoffice address of each shareholder which shall be furnished to the secretary by such shareholder; (e) sign with the president, or a vice-president, certificates for shares of the corporation, the issuance of which shall have been authorized by resolution of the board of directors; (f) have general charge of the stock transfer books of the corporation; and (g) in general perform all duties incident to the office of secretary and such other duties as from time to time may be assigned to him by the president or by the board of directors. [§ 23]

Section 8. **The Treasurer.** The treasurer shall: (a) have charge and custody of and be responsible for all funds and securities of the corporation; (b) receive and give receipts for moneys due and payable to the corporation from any source whatsoever, and deposit all such moneys in the name of the corporation in such banks, trust companies or other depositaries as shall be selected in accordance with the provisions of Article V of these By-Laws; and (c) in general perform all of the duties incident to the office of treasurer and such other duties as from time to time may be assigned to him by the president or by the board of directors. If required by the board of directors, the treasurer shall give a bond for the faithful discharge of his duties in such sum and with such surety or sureties as the board of directors shall determine.

Section 9. **Assistant Secretaries and Assistant Treasurers.** The assistant secretaries, when authorized by the board of directors, may sign with the president or a vice-president certificates for shares of the corporation the issuance of which shall have been authorized by a resolution of the board of directors. The assistant treasurers shall respectively, if required by the board of directors, give bonds for the faithful discharge of their duties in such sums and with such sureties as the board of directors shall determine. The assistant secretaries and assistant treasurers, in general, shall perform such duties as shall be assigned to them by the secretary or the treasurer, respectively, or by the president or the board of directors. [§ 23]

Section 10. **Salaries.** The salaries of the officers shall be fixed from time to time by the board of directors and no officer shall be prevented from receiving such salary by reason of the fact that he is also a director of the corporation.

ARTICLE V. CONTRACTS, LOANS, CHECKS AND DEPOSITS

Section 1. **Contracts.** The board of directors may authorize any officer or officers, agent or agents, to enter into any contract or execute and deliver any instrument in the name of and on behalf of the corporation, and such authority may be general or confined to specific instances.

Section 2. **Loans.** No loans shall be contracted on behalf of the corporation and no evidences of indebtedness shall be issued in its name unless authorized by a resolution of the board of directors. Such authority may be general or confined to specific instances.

Section 3. **Checks, Drafts, etc.** All checks, drafts or other orders for the payment of money, notes or other evidences of indebtedness issued in the name of the corporation shall be signed by such officer or officers, agent or agents of the corporation and in such manner as shall from time to time be determined by resolution of the board of directors.

Section 4. **Deposits.** All funds of the corporation not otherwise employed shall be deposited from time to time to the credit of the corporation in such banks, trust companies or other depositaries as the board of directors may select.

ARTICLE VI.   CERTIFICATES FOR SHARES AND THEIR TRANSFER

Section 1. **Certificates for Shares.** Certificates representing shares of the corporation shall be in such form as shall be determined by the board of directors. Such certificates shall be signed by the president or a vice-president and by the secretary or an assistant secretary and sealed with the corporate seal or a facsimile thereof. The signatures of such officers upon a certificate may be facsimiles if the certificate is manually signed on behalf of a transfer agent or a registrar, other than the corporation itself or one of its employees. Each certificate for shares shall be consecutively numbered or otherwise identified. The name and address of the person to whom the shares represented thereby are issued, with the number of shares and date of issue, shall be entered on the stock transfer books of the corporation. All certificates surrendered to the corporation for transfer shall be cancelled and no new certificate shall be issued until the former certificate for a like number of shares shall have been surrendered and cancelled, except that in case of a lost, destroyed or mutilated certificate a new one may be issued therefor upon such terms and indemnity to the corporation as the board of directors may prescribe. [§ 23] [§ 52]

Section 2. **Transfer of Shares.** Transfer of shares of the corporation shall be made only on the stock transfer books of the corporation by the holder of record thereof or by his legal representative, who shall furnish proper evidence of authority to transfer, or by his attorney thereunto authorized by power of attorney duly executed and filed with the secretary of the corporation, and on surrender for cancellation of the certificate for such shares. The person in whose name shares stand on the books of the corporation shall be deemed by the corporation to be the owner thereof for all purposes.

CORPORATION FORMS

ARTICLE VII. FISCAL YEAR

The fiscal year of the corporation shall begin on the first day of January and end on the thirty-first day of December in each year.

ARTICLE VIII. DIVIDENDS

The board of directors may, from time to time, declare and the corporation may pay dividends on its outstanding shares in the manner and upon the terms and conditions provided by law and its Articles of Incorporation. [§ 45]

ARTICLE IX. CORPORATE SEAL

The board of directors shall provide a corporate seal which shall be circular in form and shall have inscribed thereon the name of the corporation and the state of incorporation and the words "Corporate Seal". [§ 4, Clause (c)]

ARTICLE X. WAIVER OF NOTICE

Whenever any notice is required to be given to any shareholder or director of the corporation under the provisions of these By-Laws or under the provisions of the Articles of Incorporation or under the provisions of the .... Business Corporation Act, a waiver thereof in writing signed by the person or persons entitled to such notice, whether before or after the time stated therein, shall be deemed equivalent to the giving of such notice. [§ 144]

ARTICLE XI. AMENDMENTS

These By-Laws may be altered, amended or repealed and new By-Laws may be adopted by the board of directors or by the shareholders at any regular or special meeting. [§ 27]

[Optional] ARTICLE XII. EXECUTIVE COMMITTEE

Section 1. **Appointment.** The board of directors by resolution adopted by a majority of the full board, may designate two or more of its members to constitute an executive committee. The designation of such committee and the delegation thereto of authority shall not operate to relieve the board of directors, or any member thereof, of any responsibility imposed by law. [§ 42]

Section 2. **Authority.** The executive committee, when the board of directors is not in session shall have and may exercise all of the authority of the board of directors except to the extent, if any, that such authority shall be limited by the resolution appointing the executive committee and except also that the executive committee shall not have the authority of the board of directors in reference to amending the articles of incorporation, adopting a plan of merger or consolidation, recommending to the shareholders the sale, lease or other disposition of all or substantially all of the property and assets of the corporation otherwise than in the usual and regular course of its business, recommending to the shareholders a voluntary dissolution of the corporation or a revocation thereof, or amending the By-Laws of the corporation. [§ 42]

Section 3. **Tenure and Qualifications.** Each member of the executive committee shall hold office until the next regular annual meeting of the board of directors following his designation and until his successor is designated as a member of the executive committee and is elected and qualified.

Section 4. **Meetings.** Regular meetings of the executive committee may be held without notice at such times and places as the executive committee may fix from time to time by resolution. Special meetings of the executive committee may be called by any member thereof upon not less than one day's notice stating the place, date and hour of the meeting, which notice may be written or oral, and if mailed, shall be deemed to be delivered when deposited in the United States mail addressed to the member of the executive committee at his business address. Any member of the executive committee may waive notice of any meeting and no notice of any meeting need be given to any member thereof who attends in person. The notice of a meeting of the executive committee need not state the business proposed to be transacted at the meeting.

Section 5. **Quorum.** A majority of the members of the executive committee shall constitute a quorum for the transaction of business at any meeting thereof, and action of the executive committee must be authorized by the affirmative vote of a majority of the members present at a meeting at which a quorum is present.

Section 6. **Action Without a Meeting.** Any action required or permitted to be taken by the executive committee at a meeting may be taken without a meeting if a consent in writing, setting forth the action so taken, shall be signed by all of the members of the executive committee. [§ 44]

Section 7. **Vacancies.** Any vacancy in the executive committee may be filled by a resolution adopted by a majority of the full board of directors.

Section 8. **Resignations and Removal.** Any member of the executive committee may be removed at any time with or without cause by resolution adopted by a majority of the full board of directors. Any member of the executive committee may resign from the executive committee at any time by giving written notice to the president or secretary of the corporation, and unless otherwise specified therein, the acceptance of such resignation shall not be necessary to make it effective.

Section 9. **Procedure.** The executive committee shall elect a presiding officer from its members and may fix its own rules of procedure which shall not be inconsistent with these By-Laws. It shall keep regular minutes of its proceedings and report the same to the board of directors for its information at the meeting thereof held next after the proceedings shall have been taken.

ARTICLE XIII. EMERGENCY BY-LAWS [§ 27–A]

The Emergency By-Laws provided in this Article XIII shall be operative during any emergency in the conduct of the business of the corporation resulting from an attack on the United States or any nuclear or atomic disaster, notwithstanding any different provision in the preceding Articles of the By-Laws or in the Articles of Incorporation of the corporation or in the . . . . Business Corporation Act. To the extent not inconsistent with the provisions of this Article, the By-Laws provided in the preceding Articles shall remain in effect during such emergency and upon its termination the Emergency By-Laws shall cease to be operative.

During any such emergency:

(a) A meeting of the board of directors may be called by any officer or director of the corporation. Notice of the time and place of the meeting shall be given by the person calling the meeting to such of the directors as it may be feasible to reach by any available means of communication. Such notice shall be given at such time in advance of the meeting as circumstances permit in the judgment of the person calling the meeting.

(b) At any such meeting of the board of directors, a quorum shall consist of . . . . [here insert the particular provisions desired].

(c) The board of directors, either before or during any such emergency, may provide, and from time to time modify, lines of succession in the event that during such an emergency any or all officers or agents of the corporation shall for any reason be rendered incapable of discharging their duties.

(d) The board of directors, either before or during any such emergency, may, effective in the emergency, change the head office or designate several alternative head offices or regional offices, or authorize the officers so to do.

No officer, director or employee acting in accordance with these Emergency By-Laws shall be liable except for willful misconduct.

These Emergency By-Laws shall be subject to repeal or change by further action of the board of directors or by action of the shareholders, but no such repeal or change shall modify the provisions of the next preceding paragraph with regard to action taken prior to the time of such repeal or change. Any amendment of these Emergency By-Laws may make any further or different provision that may be practical and necessary for the circumstances of the emergency.

4. SHARE CERTIFICATE

BUSINESS ENTERPRISES, INC.

INCORPORATED UNDER THE LAWS OF THE STATE OF

COMMON SHARES

THIS CERTIFIES THAT

is the owner of .... COMMON SHARES ($10 PAR VALUE) of BUSINESS ENTERPRISES, INC. fully paid and nonassessable, transferable only on the books of the Corporation by the holder hereof in person or by duly authorized Attorney upon surrender of this Certificate properly endorsed.

[Here, in the case of a corporation authorized to issue shares of more than one class, may be set forth that the corporation will furnish to any shareholder upon request and without charge a full statement of the designation, preferences, limitations, and relative rights of the shares of each class authorized to be issued by the corporation; in the case of a corporation authorized to issue any preferred or special class in series, the variations in the relative rights and preferences between the shares of each such series so far as the same have been fixed and determined and the authority of the board of directors to fix and determine the relative rights and preferences of subsequent series; and in the case of a close corporation, may be printed appropriate legends—although these are often set forth on the reverse of the share certificate.]

WITNESS the seal of the Corporation and the signatures of its duly authorized officers.

Dated ....

Gilbert C. Dee
President

Robert R. Lawper
Secretary

BUSINESS ENTERPRISES, INC.
CORPORATE SEAL
19—
STATE OF

CERTIFICATE

№

For .... Shares

Issued to

Dated 19

FROM WHOM TRANSFERRED

Dated 19

No. Original Certificate	No. Original Shares	No. of Shares Transferred

Received Certificate No. .... Shares

For ....

this .... day of 19

[REVERSE]

[Here may be printed appropriate legends, although these are sometimes printed on the face to make them more conspicuous.]

Abbreviations, when used in the inscription on the face of this certificate, shall be construed as though they were written out in full and when so construed shall be given the meaning ascribed by applicable laws or regulations.

FOR VALUE RECEIVED, _____ hereby sell, assign and transfer unto

_____
Please print or typewrite name and address of assignee

_____

_____ shares of the Common Shares represented by the within certificate, and do hereby irrevocably constitute and appoint _____ attorney, to transfer the said Common Shares on the books of the within-named corporation, with full power of substitution in the premises.

Dated _____

In presence of:

_____

_____

NOTICE: The signature to this assignment must correspond with the name as written upon the face of the Certificate, in every particular, without alteration or enlargement, or any change whatever.

[A7963]

5. MINUTES (AGENDA) OF ORGANIZATION MEETING OF DIRECTORS

FORM: MINUTES (AGENDA) OF ORGANIZATION MEETING OF DIRECTORS

Time and Place of Meeting. The organization meeting of the Board of Directors of Business Enterprises, Inc. was held at 27 Iroquois Street, Grand City, State of _____, on _____, 19__, at 4:00 p. m. pursuant to waiver of notice signed by all of the Directors.

Initial Directors Present. There were present Messrs. Gilbert C. Dee, R. Sullivan Dum, and Robert P. Lawyer, counsel, constituting all of the Directors.

Selection of Chairman and Secretary of Meeting. Upon motion duly made, seconded, and unanimously adopted, Mr. Dee was chosen Chairman and Mr. Lawyer was chosen Secretary of the meeting.

Waiver of Notice of Meeting. The Secretary presented the waiver of notice of the meeting signed by all the Directors. The Secretary was instructed to affix such waiver to the minutes.

Filing of Articles of Incorporation and Issuance of Certificate of Incorporation. Mr. Lawyer reported that Articles of Incorporation of the Corporation had been filed in the office of the Secre-

tary of State of _____ and its Certificate of Incorporation issued on _____, 19__. The Secretary was instructed to insert
the Certificate of Incorporation, with a duplicate original of the
Articles of Incorporation affixed thereto, in the minute book preceding the minutes.

Adoption of Bylaws. Mr. Lawyer presented proposed Bylaws.
After discussion and on motion duly made and seconded, the following resolution was unanimously adopted:

> RESOLVED, that the Bylaws submitted and read at this
> meeting be and are adopted as the Bylaws of this Corpora-
> tion, and that the Secretary is instructed to insert a copy of
> such Bylaws certified by him in the minute book imme-
> diately following the Certificate of Incorporation with af-
> fixed duplicate original of the Articles of Incorporation.

Election of Officers. The meeting then proceeded to the election of officers of the Corporation. Upon motion duly made,
seconded, and unanimously adopted, the following were duly elected to the offices stated beside their respective names to serve
during the pleasure of the Board of Directors:

Gilbert C. Dee	President
R. Sullivan Dum	Vice-President
R. Sullivan Dum	Treasurer
Robert P. Lawyer	Secretary

Salaries of Officers. There was discussion concerning salaries,
following which, on motion duly made, seconded, and unanimously
adopted, the following salaries were fixed to be paid until further
action by the Board of Directors:

Gilbert C. Dee, President	$1,500 per month
R. Sullivan Dum, Vice-President	$ 500 per month
R. Sullivan Dum, Treasurer	$1,000 per month
Robert P. Lawyer, Secretary	$ 300 per month

Fees for Legal Services. It was recognized that Mr. Lawyer
would not be expected to devote all of his time to the affairs of
the Corporation and that he would be entitled to submit to the
Corporation statements for legal services performed by him from
time to time for the Corporation.

Fidelity Bonds. After discussion and on motion, duly made, seconded, and unanimously adopted, the Treasurer was instructed to secure in behalf of the Corporation fidelity insurance protecting the Corporation against defalcations by any of its employees up to $25,000.

Approval of Forms of Share Certificates. The Secretary presented specimen share certificates to represent the 5% Cumulative Preferred Shares and Common Shares of the Corporation. After discussion and on motion duly made and seconded, the following resolution was unanimously adopted:

> RESOLVED, that the forms of certificates to represent the 5% Cumulative Preferred Shares and Common Shares presented at the meeting be and are approved, and that the Secretary is instructed to insert the specimens in the minute book.

Approval of Corporate Seal. The Secretary presented a form of seal for the Corporation. After discussion and on motion duly made and seconded, the following resolution was unanimously adopted:

> RESOLVED, that the seal, an impression of which is hereto affixed, be and is adopted as the corporate seal of the Corporation.

Designation of Depository of Corporate Funds. The President recommended that an account be established at The Grand City National Bank. After discussion and on motion duly made and seconded, the following resolution was unanimously adopted:

> RESOLVED, that The Grand City National Bank (hereinafter called the "Bank") be and hereby is designated a depository of the funds of the Corporation, and the President and Treasurer of the Corporation, jointly, are hereby authorized to sign, for and on behalf of the Corporation, any and all checks, drafts or other orders with respect to any funds at any time to the credit of the Corporation with the Bank and/or against any account(s) of the Corporation maintained at any time with the Bank, inclusive of any such checks, drafts or other orders in favor of any of the above-designated officers, and that the Bank be and hereby is authorized (a) to pay the same to the debit of any account of the Corporation then maintained with it; (b) to receive for deposit to the credit of the Corporation, and/or for collection for the account of the Corporation, any and all checks, drafts, notes or other instruments for the payment of money, whether or not endorsed by the Corporation, which

may be received by it for such deposit and/or collection, it being understood that each such item shall be deemed to have been unqualifiedly endorsed by the Corporation, and (c) to receive, as the act of the Corporation, reconcilements of accounts when signed by any one or more of the above-designated officers, or their appointees; and that the Bank may rely upon the authority conferred by this entire resolution until the receipt by the Bank of a certified copy of a resolution of the Board of Directors of the Corporation revoking or modifying the same.

After discussion and on motion duly made and seconded, the following resolutions were unanimously adopted:

Appointment of Resident Agent Within State; Designation of Registered Office Within State.

RESOLVED, the Corporation Service Company be and is appointed the resident agent of the Corporation in the State of _____ and the office of such agent at 100 Main Street, Grand City, _____, State of _____ be and is designated as the registered office of the Corporation in the State of _____.

Office of Corporation; Place of Meetings.

RESOLVED, that an office of the Corporation be established and maintained at 27 Iroquois Street, Grand City, _____, State of _____, and that until further action by the Board of Directors, meetings of the Board of Directors and shareholders shall be held at such office.

Admission as Foreign Corporation in Other Jurisdictions.

RESOLVED, that the officers of the Corporation be and are authorized and directed to qualify the Corporation as a foreign corporation authorized to conduct business in the States of _____ and in connection therewith to appoint all necessary agents or attorneys for service of process and to take all other action which any officer may deem appropriate.

Place and Time of Regular Meetings of Board of Directors.

RESOLVED, that regular meetings of the Board of Directors be held without notice at the Corporation's office at 27 Iroquois Street, Grand City, State of _____, at 2:00 p. m., Grand City time, on the second Monday in each month except May when the regular meeting shall be held immediately following the annual meeting of shareholders and at the place thereof.

MINUTES OF MEETING OF DIRECTORS

"Section 1244 Stock". The Treasurer discussed the advantages of qualifying the shares, to the extent possible, under Section 1244 of the Internal Revenue Code in order that any loss sustained on shares might receive ordinary loss deduction treatment, subject to the limitations prescribed by Section 1244. Upon motion duly made and seconded, the following resolution was unanimously adopted:

> RESOLVED, that the offer, sale, and issue of up to 30,000 Common Shares during a period ending not later than two years from the date hereof be carried out in such a manner that, in the hands of qualified shareholders, such shares will receive the benefits of Section 1244 of the Internal Revenue Code.

Fixing of Consideration for Shares Issued for Property. The Treasurer stated that J. B. Rich had offered in writing to sell to the Corporation all his right, title, and interest in and to the "J. B. Rich tract" for the sum of $500,000.00, to be paid for by the issuance to him as fully paid and nonassessable of 5,000 5% Cumulative Preferred Shares of the Corporation. Upon motion duly made and seconded, the following resolution was unanimously adopted:

> RESOLVED, that it is the judgment of the board of directors that the value of said property so offered, is the sum of $500,000.00, which is the sum stated in said offer, and that the Corporation accept this offer of J. B. Rich; that the President be and is authorized to accept said offer in writing on behalf of the Corporation; and that the officers of the Corporation be and are authorized and directed to cause to be issued to J. B. Rich certificates representing 5,000 5% Cumulative Preferred Shares upon receipt from J. B. Rich of all necessary documents transferring said property to the Corporation.

Fixing of Consideration for Shares Issued for Services. The Treasurer stated that A. B. Promoter had rendered services in the formation of the Corporation and had agreed to accept in payment for such services as fully paid and nonassessable 250 Common Shares of the Corporation. Upon motion duly made and seconded, the following resolution was unanimously adopted:

> RESOLVED, that said compensation is reasonable and that the officers of the Corporation be and are authorized and directed to cause to be issued to A. B. Promoter certifi-

cates representing 250 Common Shares in full payment for her services.

Acceptance of Share Subscriptions. The Treasurer stated that the Corporation had received the following offers to subscribe to shares of the Corporation:

Gilbert C. Dee:

10,000 Common Shares at $20 per share.

R. Sullivan Dum:

7,500 Common Shares at $20 per share.

Upon motion duly made, seconded, and unanimously adopted, said offers were accepted, and the officers of the Corporation were authorized and directed to cause to be issued to said subscribers certificates representing said shares upon receipt of the agreed subscription price therefor.

Retainer of Accountants; Fiscal Years. The President recommended that Ford, Slater & Co., certified public accountants, be retained as the Corporation's accountants. Upon motion duly made, seconded, and unanimously adopted, the President was authorized to retain said accounting firm to serve during the pleasure of the Board of Directors. The President further stated that Ford, Slater & Co. had recommended that the Corporation adopt the calendar year as its fiscal year. Upon motion duly made and seconded, the following resolution was unanimously adopted:

RESOLVED, that the fiscal year of the Corporation shall be from January 1 to December 31 in each year.

Organizational Expenses. The Treasurer reported that the fees and expenses involved in the incorporation and organization of the Corporation other than for the services of A. B. Promoter, amounted to $2,531.75. Upon motion duly made and seconded, the following resolution was unanimously adopted:

RESOLVED, that the Treasurer be and is authorized and directed to pay in cash all fees and expenses incurred in connection with the incorporation and organization of the Corporation, other than for the services of A. B. Promoter, and that such organizational expenditures, amounting to $2,531.-75, shall be amortized over such period of not less than 60 months as may be selected by the Corporation in accordance with Section 248 of the Internal Revenue Code.

Subchapter S Election. The Treasurer discussed the advantages of Subchapter S election by the Corporation and the requirements and procedures involved. Upon motion duly made and seconded, the following resolution was unanimously adopted:

> RESOLVED, that the Corporation elect under Section 1372(a) of the Internal Revenue Code, with the consent of all the shareholders, to be treated as a "small business corporation" for income tax purposes, and that the Treasurer be and is authorized to file such election and the shareholders' statement of consent.

Adjournment. There being no further business to come before the meeting, upon motion duly made, seconded, and unanimously adopted, the meeting was adjourned.

[*Signed*] Robert P. Lawyer

WAIVER OF NOTICE

The undersigned directors of Business Enterprises, Inc., hereby consent that the organization meeting of the Board of Directors of the Corporation be held at 27 Iroquois Street, Grand City, State of _____, on _____, 19__, at 4:00 p. m., for the purpose of adopting bylaws, electing officers, and the transaction of such other business as may come before the meeting, and waive notice of such meeting.

[*Signed*] Gilbert C. Dee

R. Sullivan Dum

Robert P. Lawyer

_____, 19__

6. WAIVER OF NOTICE

NOTICE OF WAIVER OF MEETING BY SHAREHOLDER

The undersigned, a shareholder of [name of corporation], does hereby waive notice of the annual [or special] meeting of the shareholders of said corporation and hereby consents that such meeting be held on the _____ day of _____, 19__, at _____, __. m. (_____ Time), or any adjournment or adjournments thereof, at No. _____ Street, City of _____, State of _____, and authorizes and approves any and all action that may be properly taken at such meeting.

287

The undersigned does further consent to the transaction of any business, in addition to the business noticed to be transacted, that may come before the meeting.

[*Signature*]

_____

Shareholder

[*or*]

[*Signature*]

_____

Shareholder

[*Signature*]

By _____

Attorney-in-fact

7. APPLICATION FOR CERTIFICATE OF AUTHORITY

APPLICATION FOR CERTIFICATE OF AUTHORITY
OF BUSINESS ENTERPRISES, INC.

To the Secretary of State
    of the State of _____:

Pursuant to the provisions of Section 110 of the _____ Business Corporation Act, the undersigned corporation hereby applies for a Certificate of Authority to transact business in your State, and for that purpose submits the following statement:

FIRST: The name of the corporation is BUSINESS ENTERPRISES, INC.

SECOND: The name which [it] elects to use in your State is BUSINESS ENTERPRISES, INC.

THIRD: It is incorporated under the laws of _____.

FOURTH: The date of its incorporation is _____ and the period of its duration is perpetual.

FIFTH: The address of its principal office in the state or country under the laws of which it is incorporated is 27 Iroquois Street, Grand City, State of _____.

SIXTH: The address of its proposed registered office in your State is 125 Court Street, Gotham City, State of _____, and the name of its proposed registered agent in your State at that address is Corporation Service Company.

SEVENTH: The purpose or purposes which it proposes to pursue in the transaction of business in your State are the transaction of any and all lawful business for which corporations may be incorporated.

CERTIFICATE OF AUTHORITY

EIGHTH: The names and respective addresses of its directors and officers are:

Name	Office	Address
Gilbert C. Dee	Director	27 Iroquois Street, Grand City, _____
R. Sullivan Dum	Director	27 Iroquois Street, Grand City, _____
Robert P. Lawyer	Director	10 Main Street, Grand City, _____
Gilbert C. Dee	President	27 Iroquois Street, Grand City, _____
R. Sullivan Dum	Vice-President	27 Iroquois Street, Grand City, _____
Robert P. Lawyer	Secretary	10 Main Street, Grand City, _____
R. Sullivan Dum	Treasurer	27 Iroquois Street, Grand City, _____

NINTH: The aggregate number of shares which it has authority to issue, itemized by classes, par value of shares, shares without par value, and series, if any, within a class, is:

Number of Shares	Class	Series	Par Value per Share or Statement that Shares are without Par Value
20,000	5% Cumulative Pre-ferred Shares	_____	$100 Par Value*
30,000	Preference Shares (issuable in series)		Without Par Value
30,000	Common Shares	_____	$10 Par Value

TENTH: The aggregate number of its issued shares itemized by classes, par value of shares, shares without par value, and series, if any, within a class, is:

Number of Shares	Class	Series	Par Value per Share or Statement that Shares are without Par Value
10,000	5% Cumulative Pre-ferred Shares	_____	$100 Par Value
–0–	Preference Shares	_____	Without Par Value
17,500	Common Shares	_____	$10 Par Value

ELEVENTH: The amount of its stated capital, as defined in the _____ Business Corporation Act, is $1,175,000.*

* The current Model Business Corporation Act has eliminated the concepts of par value and stated capital.

TWELFTH: An estimate of the value of all property to be owned by it for the following year, wherever located, is $16,-000,000.

THIRTEENTH: An estimate of the value of its property to be located within your State during such year is $2,500,000.

FOURTEENTH: An estimate of the gross amount of business to be transacted by it during such year is $200,000.

FIFTEENTH: An estimate of the gross amount of business to be transacted by it at or from places of business in your State during such year is $50,000.

SIXTEENTH: This Application is accompanied by a copy of its articles of incorporation and all amendments thereto, duly authenticated by the proper officer of the state or county under the laws of which it is incorporated.

Dated _____, 19__.

BUSINESS ENTERPRISES, INC.

By [s] Gilbert C. Dee
————————————————
Its President

and [s] Robert P. Lawyer
————————————————
Its Secretary

8. CERTIFICATE OF AUTHORITY

STATE OF _____

OFFICE OF THE SECRETARY OF STATE

CERTIFICATE OF AUTHORITY

OF

BUSINESS ENTERPRISES, INC.

The undersigned, as Secretary of State of the State of _____, hereby certifies that duplicate originals of an Application of BUSINESS ENTERPRISES, INC. for a Certificate of Authority to transact business in this State, duly signed and verified pursuant to the provisions of the _____ Business Corporation Act, have been received in this office and are found to conform to law.

ACCORDINGLY the undersigned, as such Secretary of State, and by virtue of the authority vested in him by law, hereby issues this Certificate of Authority to BUSINESS ENTERPRISES, INC. to transact business in this State under the name of BUSI-

PROXY

NESS ENTERPRISES, INC. and attaches hereto a duplicate original of the Application for such Certificate.

Dated _____, 19__.

Secretary of State
[*Signature*]

9. PROXY

[Front]

IBM **International Business Machines Corporation**
Armonk, New York

Proxy Solicited by the Board of Directors for the Annual Meeting of Stockholders
April 26, 1982

Punched in

this card

is the proxy

number used

for machine

sorting and

counting of

votes.

Shares: Account No.:

George B. Beitzel, Frank T. Cary, John R. Opel, and Paul J. Rizzo or any of them with power of substitution are hereby appointed Proxies of the undersigned to vote all stock of International Business Machines Corporation owned by the undersigned at the Annual Meeting of Stockholders to be held in the Civic Auditorium, Jacksonville, Florida, at 10:00 a.m. on Monday, April 26, 1982, or any adjournment thereof, upon such business as may properly come before the meeting, including the items on the reverse side of this card as set forth in the Notice of Meeting and the Proxy Statement.

(Shares cannot be voted unless this proxy card is signed and returned, or other specific arrangements are made to have the shares represented at the meeting.)

[Back]

IBM

Proxy No.

000 099
(((000
111111
222222
333333
444444
555555
666666
777777
888888
999999

IBM's directors recommend a vote for the proposals numbered 1 through 5 and against the stockholder proposals numbered 6 and 7 and SHARES WILL BE SO VOTED UNLESS OTHERWISE INDICATED:

1. FOR ☐ NOT FOR ☐ election of directors
S. D. Bechtel, Jr., G. B. Beitzel, H. Brown, J. E. Burke, F. T. Cary, W. T. Coleman, Jr., J. M. Fox, P. R. Harris, C. A. Hills, A. Houghton, Jr., J. N. Irwin, II, N. Katzenbach, T. V. Learson, R. W. Lyman, M. M. Moller, W. H. Moore, J. R. Munro, J. R. Opel, D. P. Phypers, P. J. Rizzo, W. W. Scranton, I. S. Shapiro, C. R. Vance, T. J. Watson, Jr.
except vote withheld from nominee(s) listed below:

_____

2. FOR ☐ AGAINST ☐ ABSTAIN ☐
   ratifying auditors appointment
3. FOR ☐ AGAINST ☐ ABSTAIN ☐
   adopting a new Stock Option Plan
4. FOR ☐ AGAINST ☐ ABSTAIN ☐
   amending Charter to increase authorized shares
5. FOR ☐ AGAINST ☐ ABSTAIN ☐
   amending Charter to eliminate preemptive rights

6. FOR ☐ AGAINST ☐ ABSTAIN ☐
   stockholder proposal on consultants (page 22)
7. FOR ☐ AGAINST ☐ ABSTAIN ☐
   stockholder proposal on South Africa (page 23)

X

PLEASE SIGN HERE AND RETURN PROMPTLY
Dated: , 1982
☐ Please send me a ticket for the Jacksonville meeting
                                        (C5035)

10. PROXY STATEMENT

INTERNATIONAL BUSINESS MACHINES CORPORATION

Armonk, New York 10504

March 17, 1982

Notice of Meeting

The Annual Meeting of Stockholders of International Business Machines Corporation will be held on Monday, April 26, 1982, at 10:00 a. m., local time, in the Civic Auditorium, Jacksonville, Florida.

The items of business are:

1. The election of twenty-four of the present directors for a term of one year.

2. The ratification of the appointment of auditors.

3. The adoption of a new five-year Stock Option Plan.

4. The amendment of the Certificate of Incorporation to increase the authorized capital stock from 650,000,000 to 750,000,000 shares to have sufficient shares for the proposed Stock Option Plan, and for other corporate purposes as may be determined by the Board of Directors.

5. The amendment of the Certificate of Incorporation to eliminate preemptive rights.

6. Such other matters, including two stockholder proposals, as may properly come before the meeting.

These items are more fully described in the following pages, which are hereby made a part of this Notice. Only stockholders of record at the close of business on March 8, 1982, are entitled to vote at the meeting. <u>Stockholders are reminded that shares cannot be voted unless the signed proxy card is returned or other arrangements are made to have the shares represented at the meeting.</u>

John H. Grady

John H. Grady
Secretary

If you have not received or had access to the 1981 IBM Annual Report, which includes financial statements, kindly notify the IBM Stockholder Relations Department, 717 Fifth Avenue, New York, N.Y. 10022, and a copy will be sent to you.

PROXY STATEMENT

1. Election of Directors

The Board proposes the election of twenty-four of the present directors of the Corporation for a term of one year. Following is information about each nominee, including biographical data for the last five years.

Should any one or more of these nominees become unavailable to accept nomination or election as a director, the proxy committee named in the enclosed proxy will vote the shares which they represent for the election of such other persons as the Board may recommend, unless the Board reduces the number of directors.

John R. Opel, 57, is President and Chief Executive Officer of IBM and a member of IBM's Executive Committee. He joined IBM in 1949, was elected Vice President, Corporate Finance and Planning in 1968, named Group Executive of the Data Processing Product Group in 1972, and elected President in 1974. He assumed the position of Chief Executive Officer at the beginning of 1981. He is a trustee of Westminster College, and the Institute for Advanced Study; a director of The Federal Reserve Bank of New York, and Pfizer, Inc.; a member of the Board of Governors of United Way of America, and the Wilson Council; and a member of The Business Council, and the Policy Committee of The Business Roundtable. He became an IBM director in 1972.

Irving S. Shapiro, 65, is a partner in the law firm of Skadden, Arps, Slate, Meagher & Flom. He retired as Chairman and Chief Executive Officer of E. I. du Pont de Nemours and Company in 1981, but continues as Chairman of its Finance Committee. He is a member of IBM's Executive, and Executive Compensation Committees. He is also a director of Citibank and Citicorp, Hospital Corporation of America, The Boeing Company, Continental American Life Insurance Company, The Seagram Company, Ltd., and Conoco, Inc.; a trustee of the Ford Foundation and the University of Pennsylvania; and a member of The Business Council, and the Policy Committee of The Business Roundtable. He became an IBM director in 1974.

General Information

Board of Directors

The Board of Directors is responsible for the overall affairs of the corporation. To assist it in carrying out its duties, the Board has delegated certain authority to several Committees.

The Board of Directors held 12 meetings during 1981. Overall attendance at Board and Committee meetings was over 92%.

Individual attendance was as follows: (Percentage of attendance for each director set forth).

Committees of the Board

The Executive Committee, the Audit Committee, the Executive Compensation Committee and the Finance Committee are the standing Committees of the Board of Directors. Membership is as follows: (Membership set forth).

Executive Committee

The responsibilities of the Executive Committee include: the administration of the IBM Employees Stock Purchase Plan; acquisition and disposal of real estate, and approval of construction expenditures; approval of contributions and memberships; and delegation of certain authority for execution of bids, proposals and contracts. The Committee held 13 meetings in 1981.

Acting as the Nominating Committee of the Board, the Executive Committee recommends qualified candidates for election as officers and directors of the Corporation, including the slate of directors which the Board proposes for election by stockholders at the Annual Meeting.

Stockholders wishing to nominate director candidates for consideration by the Committee may do so by writing to the Secretary of the Corporation, giving the candidate's name, biographical data and qualifications.

Audit Committee

The Audit Committee reviews the Company's financial results, has the responsibility of recommending the appointment of the Company's outside auditors, reviewing the scope and results of audits, reviewing internal accounting controls, and examining procedures for ensuring compliance with the Corporation's policies on conflict of interest. In addition, the Committee reviews the estimated fees and types of non-audit services for the coming year.

The Audit Committee is always composed of directors who are not officers or employees of IBM or its subsidiaries. The Committee held 5 meetings during 1981.

Executive Compensation Committee

The Executive Compensation Committee has the responsibility of administering and approving: salaries of all IBM corporate officers and of other employees of the Corporation and its subsidiaries above specified dollar levels; all awards and participation under the IBM Variable Compensation Plan; grants and actions related thereto under the provisions of the IBM Stock Option Plans; and changes in the IBM Retirement Plan primarily affecting IBM corporate officers.

Members of this Committee are always directors who are not officers or employees of IBM or its subsidiaries and are not eligible to participate in any of the plans or programs which it administers. The Committee held 8 meetings during 1981.

Finance Committee

The Finance Committee has the responsibility of administering the IBM Retirement Plans, including the selection of investment managers, determination of investment guidelines within which they operate, reviewing their performance, and amending the Plans. The Committee has delegated the responsibility for investment management of the Retirement Plan Trust Funds to professional investment managers, two of whom are full-time employees of the Corporation, but retains the right to modify or revoke such delegation. The Committee held 5 meetings in 1981.

Other Relationships

In 1981, the Corporation and its subsidiaries purchased services, supplies and equipment in the normal course of business from many suppliers, including the following:

Purchases from Johnson & Johnson, of which Mr. Burke is Chairman of the Board, amounted to approximately $872,000. Purchases from Corning Glass Works, of which Mr. Houghton, Jr., is Chairman of the Board, amounted to approximately $5,470,000. Purchases from E. I. du Pont de Nemours and Company, of which Mr. Shapiro was Chairman of the Board until he retired in May, 1981, amounted to approximately $45,993,000 for the year. Purchases, principally of advertising space in various publications, from Time, Inc., of which Mr. Munro is President, amounted to approximately $4,479,000. Purchases from SCA Services, Inc., of which Mr. Fox is Chairman of the Board, amounted to approximately $2,692,000. Airline tickets purchased by IBM in Europe from Maersk Air I/S, a subsidiary of A.P. Moller, of which Mr. Moller is Chief Executive, resulted in commissions of approximately $80,000 paid by the carriers to that firm. Other purchases from A.P. Moller amounted to approximately $16,000.

Legal fees of $1,441,891 were paid to the firm of O'Melveny & Myers, of which Mr. Coleman, Jr., is a partner, and fees of $372,925 were paid to the law firm of Patterson, Belknap, Webb & Tyler, to which Mr. Irwin II is Of Counsel.

At December 31, 1981, the Corporation's non-U.S. subsidiaries were indebted for amounts of $5,000,000 or more to certain banks which, during 1981, had common directors with IBM, as follows: Bankers Trust Company, ($9,170,000), G.B. Beitzel and W.H. Moore; Chase Manhattan Bank, ($22,382,000), W.T. Coleman, Jr., and R.W. Lyman; Citibank, $31,280,000), A. Houghton, Jr., and I.S. Shapiro; Morgan Guaranty Trust Company, ($13,726,000), F.T. Cary; Continental Illinois National Bank, ($20,460,000), P.J. Rizzo; Chemical Bank, ($17,712,000), T.V. Learson; Manufacturers Hanover Trust Co., ($7,089,000), C.R. Vance.

Since 1973, IBM has owned 20% of a 36-story office building in San Francisco in which Mr. Bechtel, Jr., has an indirect interest through a partnership with one-third ownership. Bechtel Group, Inc. companies and IBM occupy portions of the building.

IBM retains the services of many consultants, some of whom are retired officers and directors of the Corporation. During 1981, consulting fees of $1,077,376 were paid to 18 retired officers and directors. Mr. D.R. McKay, who retired as an IBM Senior Vice President on February 28, 1982, has been retained on a three-year consulting arrangement for a fee of $300,000 per year. In addition to continuation of travel accident insurance during this period, and of his survivors income benefit coverage until age 65, supplemental retirement payments will be made commencing at the expiration of the consulting agreement which will be the equivalent of the additional retirement income had the consulting fees been pensionable earnings.

Stock Ownership

The table which follows reflects beneficially owned shares of IBM capital stock as of December 31, 1981, and indicates whether voting and investment power is solely exercisable by the persons named or is shared with others.

Voting power includes the power to direct the voting of the shares held, and investment power includes the power to direct the disposition of shares held. Also shown are shares over which any person could have acquired such powers within 60 days. Since most shares appear under both the voting power and investment power columns, the individual columns will not add across to the total column.

Remuneration

The following table shows remuneration during 1981 for all employee directors, each of the five highest-paid executive officers and for all directors and officers as a group. Employee directors receive no additional compensation for service on the Board of Directors or Committees. Directors who are not employees receive an annual retainer of $15,000 and a fee for attended Board and Committee meetings of $500 ($700 for committee meetings on days when there is no Board meeting). Committee Chairmen receive an additional annual retainer of $4,000.

The amounts set forth in the table do not include amounts earned by officers and directors during periods when they were not serving in that capacity, or amounts paid under certain benefit plans, such as medical cost reimbursements.

Variable Compensation Plan

Under the Variable Compensation Plan adopted by stockholders, certain executives, designated as participants by the Executive Compensation Committee of the Board of Directors, are eligible to receive, in addition to a fixed salary, annual awards based upon their performance and that of the Company as a whole or a business unit thereof. The performance measurement for executives with overall corporate responsibilities is earnings-per-share growth, and for operating unit executives, a variety of factors encompassing business volume growth, and attainment of financial objectives. Special supplemental awards for extraordinary achievement may be made to any participant. During 1981, approximately 100 executives participated in the Plan. The Executive Compensation Committee is composed of directors who are not eligible to participate in this Plan. Awards may be in cash, capital stock of the Corporation, or both. The awards in aggregate may not exceed 1.5% of the Corporation's adjusted net earnings (i.e., consolidated net earnings after taxes less 10% of stockholders' equity at the end of the preceding year) for the year with respect to which the awards are made. Shares of stock awarded are valued at the average closing price on the New York Stock Exchange for the 30 calendar days prior to the award date.

Stock Option Plan

In 1956, stockholders first approved a Stock Option Plan designed to attract and retain key executives in the business. Subsequent Plans were approved by stockholders, most recently in 1978. Grants may now be made only under the 1978 Plan. The Board of Directors recommends approval of a new Stock Option Plan to replace the 1978 Plan, and if approved by stockholders no new grants will be made under the 1978 Plan. The new Plan is Item of Business Number 3, which is described starting on page 18. At December 31, 1981, options for 14,885,009 shares were held by 1,120 executives under the 1978 and predecessor Plans, at adjusted option prices averaging $62.-42 per share, and expiring during the period from January 7, 1982, to May 25, 1991.

Employees Stock Purchase Plan

The IBM Employees 1981 Stock Purchase Plan permits employees to purchase IBM stock through payroll deductions during five consecutive annual offerings. Eligible employees who are not participants in an IBM Stock Option Plan may purchase stock through payroll deductions of up to 10% of compensation. The price an employee pays is 85% of the market price on the date the employee has accumulated enough money to buy a share.

At the end of 1981, approximately 322,000 employees were eligible to participate, and approximately 142,000 were participating in the Plan. Under the Plan and predecessor Plans, employees purchased 33,403,381 shares, adjusted for the May 10, 1979, stock split, from January 1, 1977, to January 31, 1982. No directors or officers participated during that period.

2. Ratification of Appointment of Auditors

[Ratification of the selection of Price Waterhouse as independent accountants for 1982].

3. Adoption of a New Five-Year Stock Option Plan

The Board of Directors continues to believe that a stock option program is an important factor in retaining and motivating key executives. To keep IBM's stock option program competitive, the Board recommends adoption of a new 1982 Stock Option Plan incorporating the authority to grant Incentive Stock Options (ISOS) as permitted by the Economic Recovery Tax Act of 1981. Non-qualified options, as in the 1978 Plan, may also be granted. If approved by stockholders, 9,500,000 shares of authorized capital stock will be reserved for issuance under the proposed 1982 Stock Option Plan, and no new grants for additional shares, beyond those already granted, will be made under the 1978 Plan.

[Description of plan].

4. Amendment of the Certificate of Incorporation to Increase the Number of Authorized Shares

The Board of Directors recommends an amendment to the Certificate of Incorporation increasing the number of authorized shares of capital stock from the 650,000,000 currently authorized to 750,000,000 shares.

On January 31, 1982, there were 592,864,690 shares issued and outstanding. The proposed IBM Stock Option Plan may require up to 9,500,000 shares over its five-year term. Of the current authorized and unissued shares, an estimated 6,800,000 will not be required for existing plans and would be available for the new Plan.

The Board of Directors believes, however, it is prudent to have additional shares available for general corporate purposes, none of which is specifically known or planned at the present time. Such shares could be used for future financing arrangements requiring stock, issuance under the Dividend Reinvestment Plan, or acquisitions.

5. Amendment of the Certificate of Incorporation to Eliminate Preemptive Rights

Under the present Certificate of Incorporation, if the Company wishes to sell new common stock, or securities convertible into common stock, for cash, it must first offer such securities proportionately to the current holders of its common stock, except for employee stock plans approved by stockholders. This "preemptive rights" procedure involves considerable delay and substantial expense, and limits the Company's ability to take advantage of the lowest-cost financing that may become available in the rapidly changing financial markets. If underwriting is required, higher costs and fees to the Company may result from longer exposure to market risks.

Historically, preemptive rights originated when companies were small, had relatively few stockholders, and market liquidity was limited. Their purpose was to preserve the stockholder's proportionate interest. Today, however, there exists a broad base of company ownership and a ready market for its stock. Stockholders wishing to maintain or increase their holdings can do so through market purchases, or through the Company's Dividend Reinvestment Plan without paying brokerage commissions.

This amendment will also give the Company the option to use unissued stock for the Dividend Reinvestment Plan, instead of open-market purchases, and thus provide another vehicle for raising the capital necessary to expand the business.

In the last 15 years, the advantages of eliminating preemptive rights have been recognized by over 200 other companies listed on the New York Stock Exchange, and their stockholders have approved such action.

The Board of Directors believes the elimination of preemptive rights will be in the best interests of the Company for the reasons stated and recommends a vote in favor of this amendment.

Stockholder Proposals

The deadline for receipt of stockholder proposals for inclusion in IBM's 1983 proxy material is December 17, 1982.

Management carefully considers all proposals and suggestions from stockholders. When adoption is clearly in the best interests of the Company and the stockholders, and can be accomplished without stockholder approval, the proposal is implemented without inclusion in the proxy material.

Examples of stockholder proposals and suggestions that have been adopted over the years include stockholder ratification of the appointment of auditors, improved procedures involving dividend checks and stockholder publications, and changes or additions to the proxy material concerning such matters as abstentions from voting, appointment of alternative proxy and the privacy of proxy voting results.

However, management opposes the following proposals for the reasons stated after each proposal.

6. Stockholder Proposal on Consultants

Management has been advised that Mrs. Evelyn Y. Davis of 1127 Connecticut Avenue, N.W., Washington, D.C. 20036, the owner of 48 shares, intends to submit the following proposal and supporting reasons at the meeting.

RESOLVED: That the stockholders recommend that the Board of Directors take the necessary steps to disclose to all shareholders in each quarterly report the total fees paid to consultants (other than legal counsel and accountants), names of such firms involved, and names of individuals of such firms who performed such services, together with the fees to such firms, and/or individuals, description of services performed and who in the Company recommended hiring of such firms and/or individuals, and to disclose in the case of consultant university professors the total amount, if any, of charitable contributions received by such universities. And if no such firms were used in the U.S.A. or foreign countries, to disclose this to all shareholders in each quarterly report sent to all.

REASONS: All stockholders are entitled to receive FULL disclosure on these matters.

If you AGREE, please mark your proxy FOR this resolution, otherwise it is automatically cast against.

The IBM *Board of Directors recommends a vote* AGAINST *this proposal.*

The accumulation of the detailed information required by this proposal and its inclusion in each Stockholder Quarterly Report would involve considerable time and expense with no commensurate benefit to the stockholders. The number of persons and organizations retained by IBM in a wide variety of business activities that might qualify as "consultants" under this proposal would number in the thousands. The selection of consultants is based strictly on professional merit and cost effectiveness. The Company's conflict of interest policies are designed to prevent abuses in this area. In addition, existing business controls and audit procedures monitor the employment of consultants on a continuing basis. All significant transactions in which directors, officers or their immediate families have a material interest are required to be reported in the proxy statement. Therefore, the Board of Directors believes that stockholders' interests are already being safeguarded by existing procedures and that the additional expense and administrative burden this proposal would impose are unnecessary.

7. Stockholder Proposal on South Africa

Management has been advised that a number of church-related groups (names and addresses will be supplied upon oral or written request to the Secretary of the Corporation or the Securities and Exchange Commission), owners of 82,849 shares, intend to submit the following proposal and supporting reasons at the meeting.

WHEREAS: In South Africa apartheid systematically denies human rights to over 20 million blacks.

IBM is the U.S. computer company with the largest sales and investment in South Africa. IBM computers are in virtually every government department, and IBM sales are the largest among U.S. computer companies. We believe that IBM's presence in South Africa, its sales to the South African government and its agencies, taxes paid to that government, act to support apartheid and white minority rule. This support is not offset by IBM's limited employment of Africans, which totalled 203 in 1979.

We have not seen changes in South Africa leading to a sharing of power between blacks and whites, and therefore believe the time has come for strategic companies to disengage. This position is shared by many black South Africans, including Bishop Desmond Tutu, who stated before the United Nations in March 1980, that apartheid was "one of the most vicious systems since Nazism." He stated, "for the sake of our children, for the sake of the children of all South Africans, black or white, for God's sake, for the sake of world peace .   .   . take action .   .   . exert pressure on South Africa—political pressure, diplomatic pressure and above all economic pressure— that will persuade the South African authorities to come to the conference table before it is too late."

RESOLVED: The shareholders request the Directors to establish the following policy: IBM and any of its subsidiaries or affiliates shall terminate operations as expeditiously as possible and

301

make no new contracts in South Africa, unless the government commits itself to ending apartheid and takes meaningful steps toward the achievement of full political, legal and social rights for the majority population.

Supporting Statement: We believe IBM should begin to disengage from South Africa by making no new contracts to sell computers and by phasing our their operations there. We are aware this is a strong position to take. However IBM has refused repeated requests by Church stockholders to end sales to the South African government and its agencies. We believe a number of these IBM computers help run the apartheid system more efficiently. Management has argued as long as IBM has operations there, they must sell to the government and service their computer needs. A phasing out of operations seems justified in light of the extreme situation in South Africa. Despite the threat of imprisonment, numerous South African leaders and organizations have called for economic pressures against their country. In the USA numerous organizations including the NAACP, AFL–CIO, the State Legislature of Michigan, the National Council of Churches, have supported calls for economic pressures against South Africa as a means of encouraging peaceful change. South Africa faces growing racial unrest in the 1980's and this will affect the business climate. It may also be good business for IBM to phase out operations.

The IBM *Board of Directors recommends a vote* AGAINST *this proposal.*

Resolutions concerning IBM's business in South Africa have been submitted to stockholders by religious organizations in six of the last nine years, and in each case have been defeated by stockholders by more than 96 percent of the votes cast.

The stockholder resolution this year goes beyond the 1980 and 1981 proposals that IBM should expand the U.S. Government's embargo by refusing to do business with non-embargoed agencies of the South African Government. This proposal asks that IBM terminate all of its operations in South Africa, with both the public and private sectors, unless that government commits itself to ending apartheid. IBM complies fully with all United States regulations governing trade with foreign countries, including the South African embargo. We continue to believe that imposing a total embargo against a foreign government or country is engaging in foreign policy. The conduct of foreign policy should be reserved to the U.S. Government. If the proponents wish to expand the current embargo, the proper way to achieve that expansion is through the U.S. Government, not in a stockholder proposal to IBM.

PROXY STATEMENT

The Board of Directors and management join the proponei. s of this resolution in deploring racial discrimination in South Africa. We provide equal opportunity for all IBM employees there, as we do elsewhere in the world. We have steadily increased the percentage of black and other non-white employees. We have provided training and advancement for blacks and other non-whites in marketing, systems engineering, administration and finance. We have been a leader in developing and implementing education, training and housing assistance programs for blacks in South Africa. IBM makes substantial contributions to the community beyond the workplace, particularly for black education. Our progress and contributions in South Africa are a matter of record. A report on all these matters is available to stockholders upon request to the Secretary of the Company.

We believe our operations in South Africa are responsible and that it is appropriate to continue them.

Other Business

Management knows of no other matters which may properly be, or are likely to be, brought before the meeting. If other proper matters are introduced, the proxy committee named in the enclosed proxy will vote shares it represents as the Board recommends.

Proxies and Voting at the Meeting

The capital stock of the Corporation is its only class of voting security. Each stockholder of record at the close of business on March 8, 1982, is entitled to one vote for each share held. The proxy card indicates the number of shares to be voted, including any full shares held by the bank for participants in the IBM Dividend Reinvestment Plan. On February 28, 1982, there were 593,569,182 shares outstanding and entitled to be voted.

Directors are elected by a plurality of votes cast. An affirmative vote of a majority of shares outstanding on the record date is required to approve the Stock Option Plan, and the amendments to the Certificate of Incorporation to increase the authorized shares, and eliminate preemptive rights. A majority of the votes cast is required to ratify the appointment of auditors and to adopt the stockholder proposals.

All stockholder meeting proxies, ballots and tabulations that identify individual stockholders are kept private, and no such document shall be available for examination, nor shall the identity or the vote of any stockholder be disclosed except as may be necessary to meet legal requirements under the laws of New York State, IBM's state of incorporation.

Shares cannot be voted unless the signed proxy card is returned or other specific arrangements are made to have shares represented at the meeting. Any stockholder giving a proxy may revoke it at any time before it is voted. If a stockholder wishes to give a proxy to someone other than the management proxy committee, he or she may cross out the names appearing on the enclosed proxy card, insert the name of some other person, sign, and give the card to that person for use at the meeting.

A stockholder planning to attend the meeting, but choosing not to return the proxy card, should send a note requesting a ticket in the envelope provided.

In accordance with the Board of Director's recommendations, signed proxies returned by stockholders will be voted, if no contrary instruction is indicated, for the election of the 24 nominees described herein, for ratification of the appointment of auditors, for the Stock Option Plan, for the amendments to the Certificate of Incorporation to increase the authorized shares, and to eliminate preemptive rights, and against the stockholder proposals.

Solicitation of proxies is being made by management through the mail, in person, and by telegraph and telephone. The cost thereof will be borne by the Corporation.

By order of the Board of Directors

John H. Grady

John H. Grady
Secretary   March 17, 1982

H. MISCELLANEOUS

1. UNITED STATES CODE: TITLE 28—JUDICIARY & JUDICIAL PROCEDURE

Contents

§ 1332. Diversity of citizenship; amount in controversy; costs

(a) The district courts shall have original jurisdiction of all civil actions where the matter in controversy exceeds the sum or value of $10,000, exclusive of interest and costs, and is between—

(1) citizens of different States;

(2) citizens of a State and citizens or subjects of a foreign state;

(3) citizens of different States and in which citizens or subjects of a foreign state are additional parties; and

(4) a foreign state, defined in section 1603(a) of this title, as plaintiff and citizens of a State or of different States.

(b) Except when express provision therefor is otherwise made in a statute of the United States, where the plaintiff who files the case originally in the Federal courts is finally adjudged to be entitled to recover less than the sum or value of $10,000, computed without regard to any setoff or counterclaim to which the defendant may be adjudged to be entitled, and exclusive of interest and costs, the district court may deny costs to the plaintiff and, in addition, may impose costs on the plaintiff.

(c) For the purposes of this section and section 1441 of this title, a corporation shall be deemed a citizen of any State by which it has been incorporated and of the State where it has its principal place of business: *Provided further,* That in any direct action against the insurer of a policy or contract of liability insurance, whether incorporated or unincorporated, to which action the insured is not joined as a party-defendant, such insurer shall be deemed a citizen of the State of which the insured is a citizen, as well as of any State by which the insurer has been incorporated and of the State where it has its principal place of business.

(d) The word "States", as used in this section, includes the Territories, the District of Columbia, and the Commonwealth of Puerto Rico.

§ 1391. Venue generally

(a) A civil action wherein jurisdiction is founded only on diversity of citizenship may, except as otherwise provided by law, be brought only in the judicial district where all plaintiffs or all defendants reside, or in which the claim arose.

(b) A civil action wherein jurisdiction is not founded solely on diversity of citizenship may be brought only in the judicial district where all defendants reside, or in which the claim arose, except as otherwise provided by law.

(c) A corporation may be sued in any judicial district in which it is incorporated or licensed to do business or is doing business, and such judicial district shall be regarded as the residence of such corporation for venue purposes.

(d) An alien may be sued in any district.

(e) A civil action in which a defendant is an officer or employee of the United States or any agency thereof acting in his official capacity or under color of legal authority, or an agency of the United States, or the United States, may, except as otherwise provided by law, be brought in any judicial district in which (1) a defendant in the action resides, or (2) the cause of action arose, or (3) any real property involved in the action is situated, or (4) the plaintiff resides if no real property is involved in the action. Additional persons may be joined as parties to any such action in accordance with the Federal Rules of Civil Procedure and with such other venue requirements as would be applicable if the United States or one of its officers, employees, or agencies were not a party.

The summons and complaint in such an action shall be served as provided by the Federal Rules of Civil Procedure except that the delivery of the summons and complaint to the officer or agency as required by the rules may be made by certified mail beyond the territorial limits of the district in which the action is brought.

(f) A civil action against a foreign state as defined in section 1603(a) of this title may be brought—

(1) in any judicial district in which a substantial part of the events or omissions giving rise to the claim occurred, or a substantial part of property that is the subject of the action is situated;

(2) in any judicial district in which the vessel or cargo of a foreign state is situated, if the claim is asserted under section 1605(b) of this title;

(3) in any judicial district in which the agency or instrumentality is licensed to do business or is doing business, if the action is brought against an agency or instrumentality of a foreign state as defined in section 1603(b) of this title; or

(4) in the United States District Court for the District of Columbia if the action is brought against a foreign state or political subdivision thereof.

§ 1401. Stockholder's derivative action

Any civil action by a stockholder on behalf of his corporation may be prosecuted in any judicial district where the corporation might have sued the same defendants.

§ 1695. Stockholder's derivative action

Process in a stockholder's action in behalf of his corporation may be served upon such corporation in any district where it is organized or licensed to do business or is doing business.

2. FEDERAL RULES OF CIVIL PROCEDURE

Contents

Rule 23. Class Actions

(a) *Prerequisites to a class action.* One or more members of a class may sue or be sued as representative parties on behalf of all only if (1) the class is so numerous that joinder of all members is impracticable, (2) there are questions of law or fact common to the class, (3) the claims or defenses of the representative parties are typical of the claims or defenses of the class, and (4) the representative parties will fairly and adequately protect the interests of the class.

(b) *Class actions maintainable.* An action may be maintained as a class action if the prerequisites of subdivision (a) are satisfied, and in addition:

(1) the prosecution of separate actions by or against individual members of the class would create a risk of

(A) inconsistent or varying adjudications with respect to individual members of the class which would establish incompatible standards of conduct for the party opposing the class, or

(B) adjudications with respect to individual members of the class which would as a practical matter be dispositive of the interests of the other members not parties to the adjudications or substantially impair or impede their ability to protect their interests; or

(2) the party opposing the class has acted or refused to act on grounds generally applicable to the class, thereby making appropriate final injunctive relief or corresponding declaratory relief with respect to the class as a whole; or

(3) the court finds that the questions of law or fact common to the members of the class predominate over any questions affecting only individual members, and that a class action is superior to other available methods for the fair and efficient adjudication of the controversy.   The matters pertinent to the findings include: (A) the interest of members of the class in individually controlling the prosecution or defense of separate actions; (B) the extent and nature of any litigation concerning the controversy already commenced by or against members of the class; (C) the desirability or undesirability of concentrating the litigation of the claims in the particular forum; (D) the difficulties likely to be encountered in the management of a class action.

(c) *Determination by order whether class action to be maintained; notice; judgment; actions conducted partially as class actions.*

(1) As soon as practicable after the commencement of an action brought as a class action, the court shall determine by order whether it is to be so maintained.   An order under this subdivision may be conditional, and may be altered or amended before the decision on the merits.

(2) In any class action maintained under subdivision (b)(3), the court shall direct to the members of the class the best notice practicable under the circumstances, including individual notice to all members who can be identified through reasonable effort. The notice shall advise each member that (A) the court will exclude him from the class if he so requests by a specified date; (B) the judgment, whether favorable or not, will include all members who do not request exclusion; and (C) any member who does not request exclusion may, if he desires, enter an appearance through his counsel.

(3) The judgment in an action maintained as a class action under subdivision (b)(1) or (b)(2), whether or not favorable to the class, shall include and describe those whom the court finds to be members of the class.   The judgment in an action maintained as a class action under subdivision (b)(3), whether or not favorable to the class, shall include and specify or describe those

to whom the notice provided in subdivision (c) (2) was directed, and who have not requested exclusion, and whom the court finds to be members of the class.

(4) When appropriate (A) an action may be brought or maintained as a class action with respect to particular issues, or (B) a class may be divided into subclasses and each subclass treated as a class, and the provisions of this rule shall then be construed and applied accordingly.

(d) *Orders in conduct of actions.* In the conduct of actions to which this rule applies, the court may make appropriate orders: (1) determining the course of proceedings or prescribing measures to prevent undue repetition or complication in the presentation of evidence or argument; (2) requiring, for the protection of the members of the class or otherwise for the fair conduct of the action, that notice be given in such manner as the court may direct to some or all of the members of any step in the action, or of the proposed extent of the judgment, or of the opportunity of members to signify whether they consider the representation fair and adequate, to intervene and present claims or defenses, or otherwise to come into the action; (3) imposing conditions on the representative parties or on intervenors; (4) requiring that the pleadings be amended to eliminate therefrom allegations as to representation of absent persons, and that the action proceed accordingly; (5) dealing with similar procedural matters. The orders may be combined with an order under Rule 16, and may be altered or amended as may be desirable from time to time.

(e) *Dismissal or compromise.* A class action shall not be dismissed or compromised without the approval of the court, and notice of the proposed dismissal or compromise shall be given to all members of the class in such manner as the court directs.

Rule 23.1 Derivative Actions by Shareholders

In a derivative action brought by one or more shareholders or members to enforce a right of a corporation or of an unincorporated association, the corporation or association having failed to enforce a right which may properly be asserted by it, the complaint shall be verified and shall allege (1) that the plaintiff was a shareholder or member at the time of the transaction of which he complains or that his share or membership thereafter devolved on him by operation of law, and (2) that the action is not a collusive one to confer jurisdiction on a court of the United States which it would not otherwise have. The complaint shall also allege with particularity the efforts, if any, made by the plaintiff to obtain the action he desires from the directors or comparable authority and, if necessary, from the shareholders or members, and the reasons for his failure to obtain the action or for not making the effort. The derivative action may not be maintained if it appears that the plaintiff does not fairly and adequately represent the interests of the shareholders or members similarly situated in enforcing the right of the corporation or association. The action shall not be dismissed or compromised without the approval of the court, and notice of the proposed dismissal or compromise shall be given to shareholders or members in such manner as the court directs.

II. PARTNERSHIPS

A. UNIFORM PARTNERSHIP ACT, 1914

6 ULA 1 et seq. (1969)

UNIFORM PARTNERSHIP ACT

Table of Jurisdictions Wherein Act Has Been Adopted

Jurisdiction	Laws	Effective Date	Statutory Citation
Alabama	1971, No. 1513	1–1–1972	Code of Ala., 1975, §§ 10–8–1 to 10–8–103.
Alaska	1917, c. 69	5–3–1917*	AS 32.05.010 to 32.05.430.
Arizona	1954, c. 66	3–25–1954*	A.R.S. §§ 29–201 to 29–244.
Arkansas	1941, Act 263	3–26–1941*	Ark.Stats. §§ 65–101 to 65–143.
California	1949, p. 674	5–23–1949*	West's Ann.Corp.Code, §§ 15001 to 15045.
Colorado	1931, c. 129	4–17–1931*	C.R.S. '73, 7–60–101 to 7–60–143.
Connecticut	1961, No. 158	5–15–1961	C.G.S.A. §§ 34–39 to 34–82.
Delaware	1947, c. 229	4–8–1947*	6 Del.C. §§ 1501 to 1543.
Dist. of Columbia	1962, 76 Stat. 636	9–27–1962*	D.C.Code 1973, §§ 41–301 to 41–342.
Florida	1972, c. 72–108	1–1–1973	West's F.S.A. §§ 620.56 to 620.77.
Guam			Guam Civil Code, §§ 2395 to 2472.
Hawaii	1972, c. 17	1–1–1973	HRS §§ 425–101 to 425–143.
Idaho	1919, c. 154	1–1–1920	I.C. §§ 53–301 to 53–343.
Illinois	1917, p. 625	7–1–1917	S.H.A. ch. 106½, ¶¶ 1 to 43.
Indiana	1949, c. 114	1–1–1950	IC 23–4–1–1 to 23–4–1–43.
Iowa	1971, (64 G.A.) S.F. 460	7–1–1971	I.C.A. §§ 544.1 to 544.43.
Kansas	1972, c. 210	7–1–1972	K.S.A. 56–301 to 56–343.
Kentucky	1954, c. 38	3–24–1954*	KRS 362.150 to 362.360.
Maine	1973, c. 377	10–3–1973	31 M.R.S.A. §§ 281 to 323.
Maryland	1916, c. 175	6–1–1916	Code, Corporations and Associations, §§ 9–101 to 9–703.
Massachusetts	1922, c. 486	1–1–1923	M.G.L.A. c. 108A §§ 1 to 44.
Michigan	1917, No. 72	4–17–1917*	M.C.L.A. §§ 449.1 to 449.43n.
Minnesota	1921, c. 487	6–1–1921	M.S.A. §§ 323.01 to 323.43.
Mississippi	1976, c. 407	4–1–1977	Code 1972, §§ 79–12–1 to 79–12–85.
Missouri	1949, p. 506	8–9–1949*	V.A.M.S. §§ 358.010 to 358.430.
Montana	1947, c. 251	3–8–1947*	MCA 35–10–101 to 35–10–615.
Nebraska	1943, c. 143	5–25–1943*	R.R.S.1943, §§ 67–301 to 67–343.
Nevada	1931, c. 74	7–1–1931	N.R.S. 87.010 to 87.430.
New Hampshire	1973, c. 378	8–29–1973	RSA 304–A:1 to 304–A:43.
New Jersey	1919, c. 212	4–15–1919*	N.J.S.A. 42:1–1 to 42:1–43.
New Mexico	1947, c. 37	3–3–1947*	NMSA 1978, §§ 54–1–1 to 54–1–43.
New York	1919, c. 408	10–1–1919	McKinney's Partnership Law, §§ 1 to 74.
North Carolina	1941, c. 374	3–15–1941	G.S. §§ 59–31 to 59–73.
North Dakota	1959, c. 326	3–4–1959*	NDCC 45–05–01 to 45–09–15.
Ohio	1949, p. 329	9–14–1949	R.C. §§ 1775.01 to 1775.42.
Oklahoma	1955, p. 288	6–3–1955	54 Okl.St.Ann. §§ 201 to 244.
Oregon	1939, c. 550	3–31–1939	ORS 68.010 to 68.650.
Pennsylvania	1915, P.L. 18	7–1–1915	59 Pa.C.S.A. §§ 301 to 365.
Rhode Island	1957, c. 74	10–1–1957	Gen.Laws 1956, §§ 7–12–12 to 7–12–55.
South Carolina	1950, p. 1841	2–13–1950	Code 1976, §§ 33–41–10 to 33–4–1090.
South Dakota	1923, c. 296	3–12–1923	SDCL 48–1–1 to 48–5–56.

PARTNERSHIPS

Jurisdiction	Laws	Effective Date	Statutory Citation
Tennessee	1917, c. 140	7–1–1917	T.C.A. §§ 61–101 to 61–142.
Texas	1961, c. 158	1–1–1962	Vernon's Ann.Civ.St. art. 6132b.
Utah	1921, c. 89	5–10–1921	U.C.A.1953, 48–1–1 to 48–1–40.
Vermont	1941, No. 146	3–31–1941	11 V.S.A. §§ 1121 to 1335.
Virgin Islands	1957, Act, No. 160	9–1–1957	26 V.I.C. §§ 1 to 135.
Virginia	1918, c. 365	7–1–1918	Code 1950, §§ 50–1 to 50–43.
Washington	1955, c. 15	2–8–1955	West's RCWA 25.04.010 to 25.04.430.
West Virginia	1953, c. 139	3–13–1953	Code, 47–8A–1 to 47–8A–45.
Wisconsin	1915, c. 358	7–6–1915*	W.S.A. 178.01 to 178.39.
Wyoming	1917, c. 97	2–20–1917*	W.S.1977, §§ 17–13–101 to 17–13–615.

*Date of Approval.

UNIFORM PARTNERSHIP ACT

Contents

PART I. PRELIMINARY PROVISIONS

PART II. NATURE OF A PARTNERSHIP

PART III. RELATIONS OF PARTNERS TO PERSONS DEALING WITH THE PARTNERSHIP

PART IV. RELATIONS OF PARTNERS TO ONE ANOTHER

PART V. PROPERTY RIGHTS OF A PARTNER

PART VI. DISSOLUTION AND WINDING UP

Commissioners' Prefatory Note

The subject of a uniform law on partnership was taken up by the Conference of Commissioners on Uniform State Laws in 1902, and the Committee on Commercial Law was instructed to employ an expert and prepare a draft to be submitted to the next annual Conference. (See Am.Bar Assn.Report for 1902, p. 477.) At the meeting in 1903 the committee reported that it had secured the services of James Barr Ames, Dean of the Law School of Harvard University, as expert to draft the act. (See Am.Bar Assn.Report for 1903, p. 501.)

In 1905 the Committee on Commercial Law reported progress on this subject, and a resolution was passed by the Conference, directing that a draft be prepared upon the mercantile theory. (See Am.Bar Assn.Reports, 1905, pp. 731–738.) And in 1909 the committee reported that it had in its hands a draft of an act on this subject, which draft was recommitted to the committee for revision and amendment, with directions to report to the next Conference for discussion and action. (See Report, C.U. S.L., 1906, p. 40.)

In 1907 the matter was brought before the Conference and postponed until the 1908 meeting. (See Report, C.U.S.L., 1907, p. 93.) In 1908 the matter was discussed by the Conference. (See Am.Bar Assn.Reports, 1908, pp. 983, 1048.) And in 1909 the Second Tentative Draft of the Partnership Act was introduced and discussed. (See p. 1081 of Am.Bar Assn.Reports for 1909.)

In 1910 the committee reported that on account of the death of Dean Ames no progress had been made, but that Dr. Wm. Draper Lewis, then Dean and now Professor of Law at the Law School of the University of Pennsylvania, and Mr. James B. Lichtenberger, of the Philadelphia Bar, had prepared a draft of a partnership act on the so-called entity idea, with the aid of the various drafts and notes of Dean Ames, and that they had also submitted a draft of a proposed uniform act, embodying the theory that a partnership is an aggregate of individuals associated in business, which is that at present accepted in nearly all the states of the Union. (See Report C.U.S.L., 1910, p. 142.) Dean Lewis expressed his belief that with certain modifications the aggregate or common law theory should be adopted. A resolution was passed by the Conference that any action that might have theretofore been adopted by it, tending to limit the Committee on Commercial Law in its consideration of the partnership law to what is known as the entity theory, be rescinded and that the committee be allowed and directed to consider the subject of partnership at large as though no such resolution had been adopted by the Conference. (See p. 52.)

In the fall of 1910 the committee invited to a Conference, held in Philadelphia, all the teachers of, and writers on, partnerships, besides several other lawyers known to have made a special study of the subject. There was a large attendance. For two days the members of the committee and their guests discussed the theory on which the proposed act should be drawn. At the conclusion of the discussion the experts present recommended that the act be drawn on the aggregate or common law theory, with the modification that the partners be treated as owners of partnership property holding by a special tenancy which should be called tenancy in partnership. (See section 25 of the act recommended.) Accordingly, at the meeting of the Conference in the summer of 1911, the committee reported that, after hearing the discussion of experts, it had voted that Dean Lewis be requested to prepare a draft of a partnership act on the so-called common law theory. (See Report, C.U.S.L., 1911, p. 149.)

The committee reported another draft of the act to the Conference at its session in 1912, drawn on the aggregate or common law theory, with the modification referred to. At this session the Conference spent several days in the discussion of the act, again referring it to the Committee on Commercial Law for their further consideration. (See Report, C.U.S.L., 1912, p. 67.)

PARTNERSHIPS

The Committee on Commercial Law held a meeting in New York on March 29, 1913, and took up the draft of the act referred back to it by the Conference, and after careful consideration of the amendments suggested by the Conference, prepared their seventh draft, which was, at their annual session in the summer of 1913, submitted to the Conference. The Conference again spent several days in discussing the act and again referred it to the Committee on Commercial Law, this time mainly for protection in form.

The Committee on Commercial Law assembled in the City of New York, September 21, 1914, and had before them a new draft of the act, which had been carefully prepared by Dr. Wm. Draper Lewis with valuable suggestions submitted by Charles E. Shepard, Esq., one of the commissioners from the State of Washington, and others interested in the subject. The committee reported the Eighth Draft to the Conference which, on October 14, 1914, passed a resolution recommending the act for adoption to the legislatures of all the States.

Uniformity of the law of partnerships is constantly becoming more important, as the number of firms increases which not only carry on business in more than one state, but have among the members residents of different states.

It is however, proper here to emphasize the fact that there are other reasons, in addition to the advantages which will result from uniformity, for the adoption of the act now issued by the Commissioners. There is probably no other subject connected with our business law in which a greater number of instances can be found where, in matters of almost daily occurrence, the law is uncertain. This uncertainty is due, not only to conflict between the decisions of different states, but more to the general lack of consistency in legal theory. In several of the sections, but especially in those which relate to the rights of the partner and his separate creditors in partnership property, and to the rights of firm creditors where the personnel of the partnership has been changed without liquidation of partnership affairs, there exists an almost hopeless confusion of theory and practice, making the actual administration of the law difficult and often inequitable.

Another difficulty of the present partnership law is the scarcity of authority on matters of considerable importance in the daily conduct and in the winding up of partnership affairs. In any one state it is often impossible to find an authority on a matter of comparatively frequent occurrence, while not infrequently an exhaustive research of the reports of the decisions of all the states and the federal courts fails to reveal a single authority throwing light on the question. The existence of a statute stating in detail the rights of the partners inter se during the carrying on of the partnership business, and on the winding up of partnership affairs, will be a real practical advantage of moment to the business world.

The notes which are printed in connection with this edition of the Act were prepared by Dr. Wm. Draper Lewis, the draftsman. They are designed to point out the few changes in the law which the adoption of the act will effect, and the many confusions and uncertainties which it will end.

WALTER GEORGE SMITH
Chairman, Committee on Commercial Law

PART I

PRELIMINARY PROVISIONS

§ 1. Name of Act

This act may be cited as Uniform Partnership Act.

§ 2. Definition of Terms

In this act, "Court" includes every court and judge having jurisdiction in the case.

"Business" includes every trade, occupation, or profession.

"Person" includes individuals, partnerships, corporations, and other associations.

"Bankrupt" includes bankrupt under the Federal Bankruptcy Act or insolvent under any state insolvent act.

"Conveyance" includes every assignment, lease, mortgage, or encumbrance.

"Real property" includes land and any interest or estate in land.

§ 3. Interpretation of Knowledge and Notice

(1) A person has "knowledge" of a fact within the meaning of this act not only when he has actual knowledge thereof, but also when he has knowledge of such other facts as in the circumstances shows bad faith.

(2) A person has "notice" of a fact within the meaning of this act when the person who claims the benefit of the notice:

(a) States the fact to such person, or

(b) Delivers through the mail, or by other means of communication, a written statement of the fact to such person or to a proper person at his place of business or residence.

§ 4. Rules of Construction

(1) The rule that statutes in derogation of the common law are to be strictly construed shall have no application to this act.

(2) The law of estoppel shall apply under this act.

(3) The law of agency shall apply under this act.

(4) This act shall be so interpreted and construed as to effect its general purpose to make uniform the law of those states which enact it.

(5) This act shall not be construed so as to impair the obligations of any contract existing when the act goes into effect, nor to affect any action or proceedings begun or right accrued before this act takes effect.

§ 5. Rules for Cases Not Provided for in This Act

In any case not provided for in this act the rules of law and equity, including the law merchant, shall govern.

PART II

NATURE OF A PARTNERSHIP

§ 6. Partnership Defined

(1) A partnership is an association of two or more persons to carry on as co-owners a business for profit.

(2) But any association formed under any other statute of this state, or any statute adopted by authority, other than the authority of this state, is not a partnership under this act, unless such association would have been a partnership in this state prior to the adoption of this act; but this act shall apply to limited partnerships except in so far as the statutes relating to such partnerships are inconsistent herewith.

§ 7. Rules for Determining the Existence of a Partnership

In determining whether a partnership exists, these rules shall apply:

(1) Except as provided by section 16 persons who are not partners as to each other are not partners as to third persons.

(2) Joint tenancy, tenancy in common, tenancy by the entireties, joint property, common property, or part ownership does not of itself establish a partnership, whether such co-owners do or do not share any profits made by the use of the property.

(3) The sharing of gross returns does not of itself establish a partnership, whether or not the persons sharing them have a joint or common right or interest in any property from which the returns are derived.

(4) The receipt by a person of a share of the profits of a business is prima facie evidence that he is a partner in the business, but no such inference shall be drawn if such profits were received in payment:

(a) As a debt by installments or otherwise,

(b) As wages of an employee or rent to a landlord,

(c) As an annuity to a widow or representative of a deceased partner,

(d) As interest on a loan, though the amount of payment vary with the profits of the business,

(e) As the consideration for the sale of a good-will of a business or other property by installments or otherwise.

§ 8. Partnership Property

(1) All property originally brought into the partnership stock or subsequently acquired by purchase or otherwise, on account of the partnership, is partnership property.

(2) Unless the contrary intention appears, property acquired with partnership funds is partnership property.

(3) Any estate in real property may be acquired in the partnership name. Title so acquired can be conveyed only in the partnership name.

(4) A conveyance to a partnership in the partnership name, though without words of inheritance, passes the entire estate of the grantor unless a contrary intent appears.

PART III

RELATIONS OF PARTNERS TO PERSONS DEALING WITH THE PARTNERSHIP

§ 9. Partner Agent of Partnership as to Partnership Business

(1) Every partner is an agent of the partnership for the purpose of its business, and the act of every partner, including the execution in the partnership name of any instrument, for apparently carrying on in the usual way the business of the partnership of which he is a member binds the partnership, unless the partner so acting has in fact no authority to act for the partnership in the particular matter, and the person with whom he is dealing has knowledge of the fact that he has no such authority.

(2) An act of a partner which is not apparently for the carrying on of the business of the partnership in the usual way does not bind the partnership unless authorized by the other partners.

(3) Unless authorized by the other partners or unless they have abandoned the business, one or more but less than all the partners have no authority to:

(a) Assign the partnership property in trust for creditors or on the assignee's promise to pay the debts of the partnership,

(b) Dispose of the good-will of the business,

(c) Do any other act which would make it impossible to carry on the ordinary business of a partnership,

(d) Confess a judgment,

(e) Submit a partnership claim or liability to arbitration or reference.

(4) No act of a partner in contravention of a restriction on authority shall bind the partnership to persons having knowledge of the restriction.

§ 10. Conveyance of Real Property of the Partnership

(1) Where title to real property is in the partnership name, any partner may convey title to such property by a conveyance executed in the partnership name; but the partnership may recover such property unless the partner's act binds the partnership under the provisions of paragraph (1) of section 9, or unless such property has been conveyed by the grantee or a person claiming through such grantee to a holder for value without knowledge that the partner, in making the conveyance, has exceeded his authority.

(2) Where title to real property is in the name of the partnership, a conveyance executed by a partner, in his own name, passes the equitable interest of the partnership, provided the act is one within the authority of the partner under the provisions of paragraph (1) of section 9.

(3) Where title to real property is in the name of one or more but not all the partners, and the record does not disclose the right of the partnership, the partners in whose name the title stands may convey title to such property, but the partnership may recover such property if the partners' act does not bind the partnership under the provisions of paragraph (1) of section 9, unless the purchaser or his assignee, is a holder for value, without knowledge.

(4) Where the title to real property is in the name of one or more or all the partners, or in a third person in trust for the partnership, a conveyance executed by a partner in the partnership name, or in his own name, passes the equitable interest of the partnership, provided the act is one within the authority of the partner under the provisions of paragraph (1) of section 9.

(5) Where the title to real property is in the names of all the partners a conveyance executed by all the partners passes all their rights in such property.

§ 11. Partnership Bound by Admission of Partner

An admission or representation made by any partner concerning partnership affairs within the scope of his authority as conferred by this act is evidence against the partnership.

§ 12. Partnership Charged with Knowledge of or Notice to Partner

Notice to any partner of any matter relating to partnership affairs, and the knowledge of the partner acting in the particular matter, acquired while a partner or then present to his mind, and the knowledge of any other partner who reasonably could and should have communicated it to the acting partner, operate as notice to or knowledge of the partnership, except in the case of a fraud on the partnership committed by or with the consent of that partner.

§ 13. Partnership Bound by Partner's Wrongful Act

Where, by any wrongful act or omission of any partner acting in the ordinary course of the business of the partnership or with the authority of his co-partners, loss or injury is caused to any person, not being a partner in the partnership, or any penalty is incurred, the partnership is liable therefor to the same extent as the partner so acting or omitting to act.

§ 14. Partnership Bound by Partner's Breach of Trust

The partnership is bound to make good the loss:

(a) Where one partner acting within the scope of his apparent authority receives money or property of a third person and misapplies it; and

(b) Where the partnership in the course of its business receives money or property of a third person and the money or property so received is misapplied by any partner while it is in the custody of the partnership.

§ 15. Nature of Partner's Liability

All partners are liable

(a) Jointly and severally for everything chargeable to the partnership under sections 13 and 14.

(b) Jointly for all other debts and obligations of the partnership; but any partner may enter into a separate obligation to perform a partnership contract.

§ 16. Partner by Estoppel

(1) When a person, by words spoken or written or by conduct, represents himself, or consents to another representing him to any one, as a partner in an existing partnership or with one or more persons not actual partners, he is liable to any such person to whom such representation has been made, who has, on the faith of such representation, given credit to the actual or apparent partnership, and if he has made such representation or consented to its being made in a public manner he is liable to such person, whether the representation has or has not been made or communicated to such person so giving credit by or with the knowledge of the apparent partner making the representation or consenting to its being made.

(a) When a partnership liability results, he is liable as though he were an actual member of the partnership.

(b) When no partnership liability results, he is liable jointly with the other persons, if any, so consenting to the contract or representation as to incur liability, otherwise separately.

(2) When a person has been thus represented to be a partner in an existing partnership, or with one or more persons not actual partners, he is an agent of the persons consenting to such representation to bind them to the same extent and in the same manner as though he were a partner in fact, with respect to persons who rely upon the representation. Where all the members of the existing partnership consent to the representation, a partnership act or obligation results; but in all other cases it is the joint act or obligation of the person acting and the persons consenting to the representation.

§ 17. Liability of Incoming Partner

A person admitted as a partner into an existing partnership is liable for all the obligations of the partnership arising before his admission as though he had been a partner when such obligations were incurred, except that this liability shall be satisfied only out of partnership property.

PART IV

RELATIONS OF PARTNERS TO ONE ANOTHER

§ 18. Rules Determining Rights and Duties of Partners

The rights and duties of the partners in relation to the partnership shall be determined, subject to any agreement between them, by the following rules:

(a) Each partner shall be repaid his contributions, whether by way of capital or advances to the partnership property and share equally in the profits and surplus remaining after all liabilities, including those to partners, are satisfied; and must contribute towards the losses, whether of capital or otherwise, sustained by the partnership according to his share in the profits.

(b) The partnership must indemnify every partner in respect of payments made and personal liabilities reasonably incurred by him in the ordinary and proper conduct of its business, or for the preservation of its business or property.

(c) A partner, who in aid of the partnership makes any payment or advance beyond the amount of capital which he agreed to contribute, shall be paid interest from the date of the payment or advance.

(d) A partner shall receive interest on the capital contributed by him only from the date when repayment should be made.

(e) All partners have equal rights in the management and conduct of the partnership business.

(f) No partner is entitled to remuneration for acting in the partnership business, except that a surviving partner is entitled to reasonable compensation for his services in winding up the partnership affairs.

(g) No person can become a member of a partnership without the consent of all the partners.

(h) Any difference arising as to ordinary matters connected with the partnership business may be decided by a majority of the partners; but no act in contravention of any agreement between the partners may be done rightfully without the consent of all the partners.

§ 19. Partnership Books

The partnership books shall be kept, subject to any agreement between the partners, at the principal place of business of the partnership, and every partner shall at all times have access to and may inspect and copy any of them.

§ 20. Duty of Partners to Render Information

Partners shall render on demand true and full information of all things affecting the partnership to any partner or the legal resentative of any deceased partner or partner under legal disability.

§ 21. Partner Accountable as a Fiduciary

(1) Every partner must account to the partnership for any benefit, and hold as trustee for it any profits derived by him without the consent of the other partners from any transaction

connected with the formation, conduct, or liquidation of the partnership or from any use by him of its property.

(2) This section applies also to the representatives of a deceased partner engaged in the liquidation of the affairs of the partnership as the personal representatives of the last surviving partner.

§ 22. Right to an Account

Any partner shall have the right to a formal account as to partnership affairs:

(a) If he is wrongfully excluded from the partnership business or possession of its property by his co-partners,

(b) If the right exists under the terms of any agreement,

(c) As provided by section 21,

(d) Whenever other circumstances render it just and reasonable.

§ 23. Continuation of Partnership Beyond Fixed Term

(1) When a partnership for a fixed term or particular undertaking is continued after the termination of such term or particular undertaking without any express agreement, the rights and duties of the partners remain the same as they were at such termination, so far as is consistent with a partnership at will.

(2) A continuation of the business by the partners or such of them as habitually acted therein during the term, without any settlement or liquidation of the partnership affairs, is prima facie evidence of a continuation of the partnership.

PART V

PROPERTY RIGHTS OF A PARTNER

§ 24. Extent of Property Rights of a Partner

The property rights of a partner are (1) his rights in specific partnership property, (2) his interest in the partnership, and (3) his right to participate in the management.

§ 25. Nature of a Partner's Right in Specific Partnership Property

(1) A partner is co-owner with his partners of specific partnership property holding as a tenant in partnership.

(2) The incidents of this tenancy are such that:

(a) A partner, subject to the provisions of this act and to any agreement between the partners, has an equal right with his partners to possess specific partnership property for partnership purposes; but he has no right to possess such property for any other purpose without the consent of his partners.

(b) A partner's right in specific partnership property is not assignable except in connection with the assignment of rights of all the partners in the same property.

(c) A partner's right in specific partnership property is not subject to attachment or execution, except on a claim against the partnership. When partnership property is attached for a partnership debt the partners, or any of them, or the representatives of a deceased partner, cannot claim any right under the homestead or exemption laws.

(d) On the death of a partner his right in specific partnership property vests in the surviving partner or partners, except where the deceased was the last surviving partner, when his right in such property vests in his legal representative. Such surviving partner or partners, or the legal representative of the last surviving partner, has no right to possess the partnerhip property for any but a partnership purpose.

(e) A partner's right in specific partnership property is not subject to dower, curtesy, or allowances to widows, heirs, or next of kin.

§ 26. Nature of Partner's Interest in the Partnership

A partner's interest in the partnership is his share of the profits and surplus, and the same is personal property.

§ 27. Assignment of Partner's Interest

(1) A conveyance by a partner of his interest in the partnership does not of itself dissolve the partnership, nor, as against the other partners in the absence of agreement, entitle the assignee, during the continuance of the partnership, to interfere in the management or administration of the partnership business or affairs, or to require any information or account of partnership transactions, or to inspect the partnership books; but it merely entitles the assignee to receive in accordance with his contract the profits to which the assigning partner would otherwise be entitled.

(2) In case of a dissolution of the partnership, the assignee is entitled to receive his assignor's interest and may require an account from the date only of the last account agreed to by all the partners.

§ 28. Partner's Interest Subject to Charging Order

(1) On due application to a competent court by any judgment creditor of a partner, the court which entered the judgment, order, or decree, or any other court, may charge the interest of

the debtor partner with payment of the unsatisfied amount of such judgment debt with interest thereon; and may then or later appoint a receiver of his share of the profits, and of any other money due or to fall due to him in respect of the partnership, and make all other orders, directions, accounts and inquiries which the debtor partner might have made, or which the circumstances of the case may require.

(2) The interest charged may be redeemed at any time before foreclosure, or in case of a sale being directed by the court may be purchased without thereby causing a dissolution:

(a) With separate property, by any one or more of the partners, or

(b) With partnership property, by any one or more of the partners with the consent of all the partners whose interests are not so charged or sold.

(3) Nothing in this act shall be held to deprive a partner of his right, if any, under the exemption laws, as regards his interest in the partnership.

PART VI

DISSOLUTION AND WINDING UP

§ 29. Dissolution Defined

The dissolution of a partnership is the change in the relation of the partners caused by any partner ceasing to be associated in the carrying on as distinguished from the winding up of the business.

§ 30. Partnership not Terminated by Dissolution

On dissolution the partnership is not terminated, but continues until the winding up of partnership affairs is completed.

§ 31. Causes of Dissolution

Dissolution is caused:

(1) Without violation of the agreement between the partners,

(a) By the termination of the definite term or particular undertaking specified in the agreement,

(b) By the express will of any partner when no definite term or particular undertaking is specified,

(c) By the express will of all the partners who have not assigned their interests or suffered them to be charged for their separate debts, either before or after the termination of any specified term or particular undertaking,

(d) By the expulsion of any partner from the business bona fide in accordance with such a power conferred by the agreement between the partners;

(2) In contravention of the agreement between the partners, where the circumstances do not permit a dissolution under any other provision of this section, by the express will of any partner at any time;

(3) By any event which makes it unlawful for the business of the partnership to be carried on or for the members to carry it on in partnership;

(4) By the death of any partner;

(5) By the bankruptcy of any partner or the partnership;

(6) By decree of court under section 32.

§ 32.   Dissolution by Decree of Court

(1) On application by or for a partner the court shall decree a dissolution whenever:

(a) A partner has been declared a lunatic in any judicial proceeding or is shown to be of unsound mind,

(b) A partner becomes in any other way incapable of performing his part of the partnership contract,

(c) A partner has been guilty of such conduct as tends to affect prejudicially the carrying on of the business,

(d) A partner wilfully or persistently commits a breach of the partnership agreement, or otherwise so conducts himself in matters relating to the partnership business that it is not reasonably practicable to carry on the business in partnership with him,

(e) The business of the partnership can only be carried on at a loss,

(f) Other circumstances render a dissolution equitable.

(2) On the application of the purchaser of a partner's interest under sections 28 or 29 [should read 27 or 28];

(a) After the termination of the specified term or particular undertaking,

(b) At any time if the partnership was a partnership at will when the interest was assigned or when the charging order was issued.

§ 33.   General Effect of Dissolution on Authority of Partner

Except so far as may be necessary to wind up partnership affairs or to complete transactions begun but not then finished, dissolution terminates all authority of any partner to act for the partnership,

(1) With respect to the partners,

(a) When the dissoution is not by the act, bankruptcy or death of a partner; or

(b) When the dissolution is by such act, bankruptcy or death of a partner, in cases where section 34 so requires.

(2) With respect to persons not partners, as declared in section 35.

§ 34. Rights of Partner to Contribution from Co-partners after Dissolution

Where the dissolution is caused by the act, death or bankruptcy of a partner, each partner is liable to his co-partners for his share of any liability created by any partner acting for the partnership as if the partnership had not been dissolved unless

(a) The dissolution being by act of any partner, the partner acting for the partnership had knowledge of the dissolution, or

(b) The dissolution being by the death or bankruptcy of a partner, the partner acting for the partnership had knowledge or notice of the death or bankruptcy.

§ 35. Power of Partner to Bind Partnership to Third Persons after Dissolution

(1) After dissolution a partner can bind the partnership except as provided in Paragraph (3).

(a) By any act appropriate for winding up partnership affairs or completing transactions unfinished at dissolution;

(b) By any transaction which would bind the partnership if dissolution had not taken place, provided the other party to the transaction

(I) Had extended credit to the partnership prior to dissolution and had no knowledge or notice of the dissolution; or

(II) Though he had not so extended credit, had nevertheless known of the partnership prior to dissolution, and, having no knowledge or notice of dissolution, the fact of dissolution had not been advertised in a newspaper of general circulation in the place (or in each place if more than one) at which the partnership business was regularly carried on.

(2) The liability of a partner under Paragraph (1b) shall be satisfied out of partnership assets alone when such partner had been prior to dissolution

(a) Unknown as a partner to the person with whom the contract is made; and

(b) So far unknown and inactive in partnership affairs that the business reputation of the partnership could not be said to have been in any degree due to his connection with it.

(3) The partnership is in no case bound by any act of a partner after dissolution

(a) Where the partnership is dissolved because it is unlawful to carry on the business, unless the act is appropriate for winding up partnership affairs; or

(b) Where the partner has become bankrupt; or

(c) Where the partner has no authority to wind up partnership affairs; except by a transaction with one who

 (I) Had extended credit to the partnership prior to dissolution and had no knowledge or notice of his want of authority; or

 (II) Had not extended credit to the partnership prior to dissolution, and, having no knowledge or notice of his want of authority, the fact of his want of authority has not been advertised in the manner provided for advertising the fact of dissolution in Paragraph (1b II).

(4) Nothing in this section shall affect the liability under Section 16 of any person who after dissolution represents himself or consents to another representing him as a partner in a partnership engaged in carrying on business.

§ 36. Effect of Dissolution on Partner's Existing Liability

(1) The dissolution of the partnership does not of itself discharge the existing liability of any partner.

(2) A partner is discharged from any existing liability upon dissolution of the partnership by an agreement to that effect between himself, the partnership creditor and the person or partnership continuing the business; and such agreement may be inferred from the course of dealing between the creditor having knowledge of the dissolution and the person or partnership continuing the business.

(3) Where a person agrees to assume the existing obligations of a dissolved partnership, the partners whose obligations have been assumed shall be discharged from any liability to any creditor of the partnership who, knowing of the agreement, consents to a material alteration in the nature or time of payment of such obligations.

(4) The individual property of a deceased partner shall be liable for all obligations of the partnership incurred while he

was a partner but subject to the prior payment of his separate debts.

§ 37. Right to Wind Up

Unless otherwise agreed the partners who have not wrongfully dissolved the partnership or the legal representative of the last surviving partner, not bankrupt, has the right to wind up the partnership affairs; provided, however, that any partner, his legal representative or his assignee, upon cause shown, may obtain winding up by the court.

§ 38. Rights of Partners to Application of Partnership Property

(1) When dissolution is caused in any way, except in contravention of the partnership agreement, each partner, as against his co-partners and all persons claiming through them in respect of their interests in the partnership, unless otherwise agreed, may have the partnership property applied to discharge its liabilities, and the surplus applied to pay in cash the net amount owing to the respective partners. But if dissolution is caused by expulsion of a partner, bona fide under the partnership agreement and if the expelled partner is discharged from all partnership liabilities, either by payment or agreement under section 36(2), he shall receive in cash only the net amount due him from the partnership.

(2) When dissolution is caused in contravention of the partnership agreement the rights of the partners shall be as follows:

(a) Each partner who has not caused dissolution wrongfully shall have,

   I.   All the rights specified in paragraph (1) of this section, and

   II.   The right, as against each partner who has caused the dissolution wrongfully, to damages for breach of the agreement.

(b) The partners who have not caused the dissolution wrongfully, if they all desire to continue the business in the same name, either by themselves or jointly with others, may do so, during the agreed term for the partnership and for that purpose may possess the partnership property, provided they secure the payment by bond approved by the court, or pay to any partner who has caused the dissolution wrongfully, the value of his interest in the partnership at the dissolution, less any damages recoverable under clause (2a II) of this section, and in like manner indemnify him against all present or future partnership liabilities.

(c) A partner who has caused the dissolution wrongfully shall have:

I.   If the business is not continued under the provisions of paragraph (2b) all the rights of a partner under paragraph (1), subject to clause (2a II), of this section,

II.   If the business is continued under paragraph (2b) of this section the right as against his co-partners and all claiming through them in respect of their interests in the partnership, to have the value of his interest in the partnership, less any damages caused to his co-partners by the dissolution, ascertained and paid to him in cash, or the payment secured by bond approved by the court, and to be released from all existing liabilities of the partnership; but in ascertaining the value of the partner's interest the value of the good-will of the business shall not be considered.

§ 39.   Rights Where Partnership is Dissolved for Fraud or Misrepresentation

Where a partnership contract is rescinded on the ground of the fraud or misrepresentation of one of the parties thereto, the party entitled to rescind is, without prejudice to any other right, entitled,

(a) To a lien on, or a right of retention of, the surplus of the partnership property after satisfying the partnership liabilities to third persons for any sum of money paid by him for the purchase of an interest in the partnership and for any capital or advances contributed by him; and

(b) To stand, after all liabilities to third persons have been satisfied, in the place of the creditors of the partnership for any payments made by him in respect of the partnership liabilities; and

(c) To be indemnified by the person guilty of the fraud or making the representation against all debts and liabilities of the partnership.

§ 40.   Rules for Distribution

In settling accounts between the partners after dissolution, the following rules shall be observed, subject to any agreement to the contrary:

(a) The assets of the partnership are:

I.   The partnership property,

II.   The contributions of the partners necessary for the payment of all the liabilities specified in clause (b) of this paragraph.

331

(b) The liabilities of the partnership shall rank in order of payment, as follows:

I.   Those owing to creditors other than partners,

II. Those owing to partners other than for capital and profits,

III. Those owing to partners in respect of capital,

IV. Those owing to partners in respect of profits.

(c) The assets shall be applied in the order of their declaration in clause (a) of this paragraph to the satisfaction of the liabilities.

(d) The partners shall contribute, as provided by section 18 (a) the amount necessary to satisfy the liabilities; but if any, but not all, of the partners are insolvent, or, not being subject to process, refuse to contribute, the other partners shall contribute their share of the liabilities, and, in the relative proportions in which they share the profits, the additional amount necessary to pay the liabilities.

(e) An assignee for the benefit of creditors or any person appointed by the court shall have the right to enforce the contributions specified in clause (d) of this paragaph.

(f) Any partner or his legal representative shall have the right to enforce the contributions specified in clause (d) of this paragraph, to the extent of the amount which he has paid in excess of his share of the liability.

(g) The individual property of a deceased partner shall be liable for the contributions specified in clause (d) of this paragraph.

(h) When partnership property and the individual properties of the partners are in possession of a court for distribution, partnership creditors shall have priority on partnership property and separate creditors on individual property, saving the rights of lien or secured creditors as heretofore.

(i) Where a partner has become bankrupt or his estate is insolvent the claims against his separate property shall rank in the following order:

I.   Those owing to separate creditors,

II. Those owing to partnership creditors,

III. Those owing to partners by way of contribution.

§ 41. Liability of Persons Continuing the Business in Certain Cases

(1) When any new partner is admitted into an existing partnership, or when any partner retires and assigns (or the representative of the deceased partner assigns) his rights in partner-

332

ship property to two or more of the partners, or to one or more of the partners and one or more third persons, if the business is continued without liquidation of the partnership affairs, creditors of the first or dissolved partnership are also creditors of the partnership so continuing the business.

(2) When all but one partner retire and assign (or the representative of a deceased partner assigns) their rights in partnership property to the remaining partner, who continues the business without liquidation of partnership affairs, either alone or with others, creditors of the dissolved partnership are also creditors of the person or partnership so continuing the business.

(3) When any partner retires or dies and the business of the dissolved partnership is continued as set forth in paragraphs (1) and (2) of this section, with the consent of the retired partners or the representative of the deceased partner, but without any assignment of his right in partnership property, rights of creditors of the dissolved partnership and of the creditors of the person or partnership continuing the business shall be as if such assignment had been made.

(4) When all the partners or their representatives assign their rights in partnership property to one or more third persons who promise to pay the debts and who continue the business of the dissolved partnership, creditors of the dissolved partnership are also creditors of the person or partnership continuing the business.

(5) When any partner wrongfully causes a dissolution and the remaining partners continue the business under the provisions of section 38(2b), either alone or with others, and without liquidation of the partnership affairs, creditors of the dissolved partnership are also creditors of the person or partnership continuing the business.

(6) When a partner is expelled and the remaining partners continue the business either alone or with others, without liquidation of the partnership affairs, creditors of the dissolved partnership are also creditors of the person or partnership continuing the business.

(7) The liability of a third person becoming a partner in the partnership continuing the business, under this section, to the creditors of the dissolved partnership shall be satisfied out of partnership property only.

(8) When the business of a partnership after dissolution is continued under any conditions set forth in this section the creditors of the dissolved partnership, as against the separate creditors of the retiring or deceased partner or the representative of the deceased partner, have a prior right to any claim of

the retired partner or the representative of the deceased partner against the person or partnership continuing the business, on account of the retired or deceased partner's interest in the dissolved partnership or on account of any consideration promised for such interest or for his right in partnership property.

(9) Nothing in this section shall be held to modify any right of creditors to set aside any assignment on the ground of fraud.

(10) The use by the person or partnership continuing the business of the partnership name, or the name of a deceased partner as part thereof, shall not of itself make the individual property of the deceased partner liable for any debts contracted by such person or partnership.

§ 42. Rights of Retiring or Estate of Deceased Partner When the Business is Continued

When any partner retires or dies, and the business is continued under any of the conditions set forth in section 41(1, 2, 3, 5, 6), or section 38(2b) without any settlement of accounts as between him or his estate and the person or partnership continuing the business, unless otherwise agreed, he or his legal representative as against such persons or partnership may have the value of his interest at the date of dissolution ascertained, and shall receive as an ordinary creditor an amount equal to the value of his interest in the dissolved partnership with interest, or, at his option or at the option of his legal representative, in lieu of interest, the profits attributable to the use of his right in the property of the dissolved partnership; provided that the creditors of the dissolved partnership as against the separate creditors, or the representative of the retired or deceased partner, shall have priority on any claim arising under this section, as provided by section 41(8) of this act.

§ 43. Accrual of Actions

The right to an account of his interest shall accrue to any partner, or his legal representative, as against the winding up partners or the surviving partners or the person or partnership continuing the business, at the date of dissolution, in the absence of any agreement to the contrary.

PART VII

MISCELLANEOUS PROVISIONS

§ 44. When Act Takes Effect

This act shall take effect on the _____ day of _____ one thousand nine hundred and _____.

§ 45. Legislation Repealed

All acts or parts of acts inconsistent with this act are hereby repealed.

B. UNIFORM LIMITED PARTNERSHIP ACT, 1916

6 U.L.A. 559 et seq. (1969)

UNIFORM LIMITED PARTNERSHIP ACT

Table of Jurisdictions Wherein Act Has Been Adopted

Jurisdiction	Laws	Effective Date	Statutory Citation
Alabama	1971, No. 1512	1–1–1972	Code of Ala.1975, §§ 10–9–1 to 10–9–91.
Alaska	1917, c. 71	5–2–1917*	AS 32.10.010 to 32.10.290.
Arizona	1943, c. 60	3–19–1943*	A.R.S. §§ 29–301 to 29–329.
California	1949, p. 668	5–23–1949*	West's Ann.Corp.Code, §§ 15501 to 15531.
Colorado	1931, c. 128	4–11–1931*	C.R.S. '73 7–61–101 to 7–61–130.
Delaware	1973, c. 105	7–1–1973	6 Del.C. §§ 1701 to 1733.
Dist. of Columbia	1962, P.L. 87– 716, 76 Stat. 655	9–28–1962	D.C.Code 1973, §§ 41–401 to 41–429.
Florida	1943, c. 21887	5–31–1943	West's F.S.A. §§ 620.01 to 620.32.
Georgia	1952, p. 375	2–2–1952	Code, §§ 75–401 to 75–431.
Hawaii	1943, Act 162	5–12–1943	HRS §§ 425–21 to 425–52.
Idaho	1919, c. 151	1–1–1920	I.C. §§ 53–201 to 53–233.
Illinois	1917, p. 569	7–1–1917	S.H.A. ch. 106½, ¶¶ 44 to 73.
Indiana	1949, c. 121	9–10–1949	IC 23–4–2–1 to 23–4–2–30.
Iowa	40 Ex.G.A,H.F. 74, §§ 1–58.	1924	I.C.A. §§ 545.1 to 545.58.
Kansas	1967, c. 302	7–1–1967	K.S.A. 56–122 to 56–151.
Kentucky	1970, c. 97		KRS 362.410 to 362.700.
Maine	1969, c. 324	9–1–1969	31 M.R.S.A. §§ 151 to 181. 10–101 to 10–129.
Massachusetts	1923, c. 112	1–1–1924	M.G.L.A. c. 109 §§ 1 to 31.
Michigan	1931, No. 110	5–18–1931*	M.C.L.A. §§ 449.201 to 449.231.
Mississippi	1964, c. 271	4–22–1964*	Code 1972, §§ 79–13–1 to 79–13–57.
Missouri	1947, Vol. 2, p. 311	5–11–1947*	V.A.M.S. §§ 359.010 to 359.290.
Montana	1947, c. 252	3–8–1947*	MCA 35–12–101 to 35–12–403.
Nebraska	1939, c. 87	3–17–1939*	R.R.S.1943, §§ 67–201 to 67–232.
Nevada	1931, c. 73	7–1–1931	N.R.S. 88.010 to 88.310.
New Hampshire	1937, c. 101	5–12–1937*	RSA 305:1 to 305:30.
New Jersey	1919, c. 211	4–15–1919	N.J.S.A. 42:2–1 to 42:2–30.
New Mexico	1947, c. 120	3–19–1947*	NMSA 1978, §§ 54–2–1 to 54–2–30.
New York	1922, c. 640	4–13–1922	McKinney's Partnership Law, §§ 90 to 120l.
North Carolina	1941, c. 251	3–15–1941	G.S. §§ 59–1 to 59–30.
North Dakota	1959, c. 326	3–4–1959*	NDCC 45–10–01 to 45–12–04.
Ohio	1957, p. 447	9–14–1957	R.C. §§ 1781.01 to 1781.27.
Oklahoma	1951, p. 144	5–29–1951*	54 Okl.St.Ann. §§ 141 to 171.
Oregon	1971, c. 594	9–9–1971	ORS 69.150 to 69.470.
Pennsylvania	1917, P.L. 55	4–12–1917*	59 Pa.C.S.A. §§ 501 to 545.
Rhode Island	1930, c. 1571	4–1–1930	Gen.Laws 1956, §§ 7–13–1 to 7–13–31.
South Carolina	1960, p. 1970	5–24–1960	Code 1976, §§ 33–43–10 to 33–43–300.
South Dakota	1925, c. 251	3–5–1925*	SDCL 48–6–1 to 48–6–64.
Tennessee	1919, c. 120	1–1–1920	T.C.A. §§ 61–2–101 to 61–2–130.
Texas	1955, c. 133	4–30–1955	Vernon's Ann.Civ.St. art. 6132a.
Utah	1921, c. 88	5–10–1921	U.C.A.1953, 48–2–1 to 48–2–27.
Vermont	1941, No. 145	3–31–1941	11 V.S.A. §§ 1391 to 1419.
Virgin Islands	1957, Act, No. 160	9–1–1957	26 V.I.C. §§ 201 to 228.
Virginia	1918, c. 216	3–14–1918*	Code 1950, §§ 50–44 to 50–73.
Wisconsin	1919, c. 449	6–28–1919*	W.S.A. 179.01 to 179.30.

* Date of approval.

PARTNERSHIPS

Contents

Official Comment

The business reason for the adoption of acts making provisions for limited or special partners is that men in business often desire to secure capital from others. There are at least three classes of contracts which can be made with those from whom the capital is secured: One, the ordinary loan on interest; another, the loan where the lender, in lieu of interest, takes a share in the profits of the business; third, those cases in which the person advancing the capital secures, besides a share in the profits, some measure of control over the business.

At first, in the absence of statutes the courts, both in this country and in England, assumed that one who is interested in a business is bound by its obligations, carrying the application of this principle so far, that a contract where the only evidence of interest was a share in the profits made one who supposed himself a lender, and who was probably unknown to the creditors at the times they extended their credits, unlimitedly liable as a partner for the obligations of those actually conducting the business.

Later decisions have much modified the earlier cases. The lender who takes a share in the profits, except possibly in one or two of our jurisdictions, does not by reason of that fact run a risk of being held as a partner. If, however, his contract falls within the third class mentioned, and he has any measure of control over the business, he at once runs serious risk of being held liable for the debts of the business as a partner; the risk increasing as he increases the amount of his control.

The first Limited Partnership Act was adopted by New York in 1822; the other commercial states, during the ensuing 30 years, following her example. Most of the statutes follow the language of the New York statute with little material alteration. These statutes were adopted, and to a considerable degree interpreted by the courts, during that period when it was generally held that any interest in a business should make the person holding the interest liable for its obligations. As a result the courts usually assume in the interpretation of these statutes two principles as fundamental.

First: That a limited (or as he is also called a special) partner is a partner in all respects like any other partner, except that to obtain the privilege of a limitation on his liability, he has conformed to the statutory requirements in respect to filing a certificate and refraining from participation in the conduct of the business.

Second: The limited partner, on any failure to follow the requirements in regard to the certificate or any participation in the conduct of his business, loses his privilege of limited liability and becomes, as far as those dealing with the business are concerned, in all respects a partner.

The courts in thus interpreting the statutes, although they made an American partnership with limited members something very different from the French Societe en Commandite from which the idea of the original statutes was derived, unquestionably carried out the intent of those responsible for their adoption. This is shown by the very wording of the statutes themselves. For instance, all the statutes require that all partners, limited and general, shall sign the certificate, and nearly all state that: "If any false statement be made in such certificate all the persons interested in such partnership shall be liable for all the engagements thereof as general partners."

The practical result of the spirit shown in the language and in the interpretation of existing statutes, coupled with the fact that a man may now lend money to a partnership and take a share in the profits in lieu of interest without running serious danger of becoming bound for partnership obligations, has, to a very great extent, deprived the existing statutory provisions for limited partners of any practical usefulness. Indeed, apparently their use is largely confined to associations in which those who conduct the business have not more than one limited partner.

One of the causes forcing business into the corporate form, in spite of the fact that the corporate form is ill suited to many business conditions, is the failure of the existing limited partnership acts to meet the desire of the owners of a business to secure necessary capital under the existing limited partnership form of business association.

The draft herewith submitted proceeds on the following assumptions:

First: No public policy requires a person who contributes to the capital of a business, acquires an interest in the profits, and some degree of control over the conduct of the business, to become bound for the obligations of the business; provided creditors have no reason to believe at the times their credits were extended that such person was so bound.

Second: That persons in business should be able, while remaining themselves liable without limit for the obligations contracted in its conduct, to associate with themselves others who contribute to the capital and acquire rights of ownership, provided that such contributors do not compete with creditors for the assets of the partnership.

The attempt to carry out these ideas has led to the incorporation into the draft submitted of certain features, not found in, or differing from, existing limited partnership acts.

First: In the draft the person who contributes the capital, though in accordance with custom called a limited partner, is not in any sense a partner. He is, however, a member of the association (see Sec. 1.).

Second: As limited partners are not partners securing limited liability by filing a certificate, the association is formed when substantial compliance, in good faith, is had with the requirements for a certificate (Sec. 2(2)). This provision eliminates the difficulties which arise from the recognition of de facto associations, made necessary by the assumption that the association is not formed unless a strict compliance with the requirements of the act is had.

Third: The limited partner not being in any sense a principal in the business, failure to comply with the requirements of the act in respect to the certificate, while it may result in the nonformation of the association, does not make him a partner or liable as such. The exact nature of his ability in such cases is set forth in Sec. 11.

Fourth: The limited partner, while not as such in any sense a partner, may become a partner as any person not a member of the association may become a partner; and, becoming a partner, may nevertheless retain his rights as limited partner; this last provision enabling the entire capital embraced in the business to be divided between the limited partners, all the general partners being also limited partners (Sec. 12).

Fifth: The limited partner is not debarred from loaning money or transacting other business with the partnership as any other nonmember; provided he does not, in respect to such transactions, accept from the partnership collateral security, or receive from any partner or the partnership any payment, conveyance, or release from liability, if at the time the assets of the partnership are not sufficient to discharge its obligations to persons not general or limited partners. (Sec. 13).

Sixth: The substitution of a person as limited partner in place of an existing limited partner, or the withdrawal of a limited partner, or the addition of new limited partners, does not necessarily dissolve the association (Secs. 8, 16(2b)); no limited partner, however, can withdraw his contribution until all liabilities to creditors are paid (Sec. 16(1a)).

Seventh: As limited partners are not principals in transactions of the partnership, their liability, except for known false statements in the certificate (Sec. 6), is to the partnership, not to creditors of the partnership (Sec. 17). The general partners cannot, however, waive any liability of the limited partners to the prejudice of such creditors (Sec. 17(3)).

§ 1. Limited Partnership Defined

A limited partnership is a partnership formed by two or more persons under the provisions of Section 2, having as members one or more general partners and one or more limited partners. The limited partners as such shall not be bound by the obligations of the partnership.

§ 2. Formation

(1) Two or more persons desiring to form a limited partnership shall

(a) Sign and swear to a certificate, which shall state

    I.   The name of the partnership,

    II.   The character of the business,

    III.   The location of the principal place of business,

    IV.   The name and place of residence of each member; general and limited partners being respectively designated,

    V.   The term for which the partnership is to exist,

    VI.   The amount of cash and a description of and the agreed value of the other property contributed by each limited partner,

    VII.   The additional contributions, if any, agreed to be made by each limited partner and the times at which or events on the happening of which they shall be made,

    VIII.   The time, if agreed upon, when the contribution of each limited partner is to be returned,

    IX.   The share of the profits or the other compensation by way of income which each limited partner shall receive by reason of his contribution,

    X.   The right, if given, of a limited partner to substitute an assignee as contributor in his place, and the terms and conditions of the substitution,

    XI.   The right, if given, of the partners to admit additional limited partners,

    XII.   The right, if given, of one or more of the limited partners to priority over other limited partners, as to contributions or as to compensation by way of income, and the nature of such priority,

    XIII.   The right, if given, of the remaining general partner or partners to continue the business on the death, retirement or insanity of a general partner, and

    XIV.   The right, if given, of a limited partner to demand and receive property other than cash in return for his contribution.

(b) File for record the certificate in the office of [here designate the proper office].

(2) A limited partnership is formed if there has been substantial compliance in good faith with the requirements of paragraph (1).

§ 3. Business Which May Be Carried on

A limited partnership may carry on any business which a partnership without limited partners may carry on, except [here designate the business to be prohibited].

§ 4. Character of Limited Partner's Contribution

The contributions of a limited partner may be cash or other property, but not services.

§ 5. A Name Not to Contain Surname of Limited Partner; Exceptions

(1) The surname of a limited partner shall not appear in the partnership name, unless

(a) It is also the surname of a general partner, or

(b) Prior to the time when the limited partner became such the business had been carried on under a name in which his surname appeared.

(2) A limited partner whose name appears in a partnership name contrary to the provisions of paragraph (1) is liable as a general partner to partnership creditors who extend credit to the partnership without actual knowledge that he is not a general partner.

§ 6. Liability for False Statements in Certificate

If the certificate contains a false statement, one who suffers loss by reliance on such statement may hold liable any party to the certificate who knew the statement to be false.

(a) At the time he signed the certificate, or

(b) Subsequently, but within a sufficient time before the statement was relied upon to enable him to cancel or amend the certificate, or to file a petition for its cancellation or amendment as provided in Section 25(3).

§ 7. Limited Partner Not Liable to Creditors

A limited partner shall not become liable as a general partner unless, in addition to the exercise of his rights and powers as a limited partner, he takes part in the control of the business.

§ 8. Admission of Additional Limited Partners

After the formation of a limited partnership, additional limited partners may be admitted upon filing an amendment to the original certificate in accordance with the requirements of Section 25.

§ 9. Rights, Powers and Liabilities of a General Partner

(1) A general partner shall have all the rights and powers and be subject to all the restrictions and liabilities of a partner in a

partnership without limited partners, except that without the written consent or ratification of the specific act by all the limited partners, a general partner or all of the general partners have no authority to

(a) Do any act in contravention of the certificate,

(b) Do any act which would make it impossible to carry on the ordinary business of the partnership,

(c) Confess a judgment against the partnership,

(d) Possess partnership property, or assign their rights in specific partnership property, for other than a partnership purpose,

(e) Admit a person as a general partner,

(f) Admit a person as a limited partner, unless the right so to do is given in the certificate,

(g) Continue the business with partnership property on the death, retirement or insanity of a general partner, unless the right so to do is given in the certificate.

§ 10. Rights of a Limited Partner

(1) A limited partner shall have the same rights as a general partner to

(a) Have the partnership books kept at the principal place of business of the partnership, and at all times to inspect and copy any of them.

(b) Have on demand true and full information of all things affecting the partnership, and a formal account of partnership affairs whenever circumstances render it just and reasonable, and

(c) Have dissolution and winding up by decree of court.

(2) A limited partner shall have the right to receive a share of the profits or other compensation by way of income, and to the return of his contribution as provided in Sections 15 and 16.

§ 11. Status of Person Erroneously Believing Himself a Limited Partner

A person who has contributed to the capital of a business conducted by a person or partnership erroneously believing that he has become a limited partner in a limited partnership, is not, by reason of his exercise of the rights of a limited partner, a general partner with the person or in the partnership carrying on the business, or bound by the obligations of such person or partnership; provided that on ascertaining the mistake he promptly renounces his interest in the profits of the business, or other compensation by way of income.

§ 12. One Person Both General and Limited Partner

(1) A person may be a general partner and a limited partner in the same partnership at the same time.

(2) A person who is a general, and also at the same time a limited partner, shall have all the rights and powers and be subject to all the restrictions of a general partner; except that, in respect to his contribution, he shall have the rights against the other members which he would have had if he were not also a general partner.

§ 13. Loans and Other Business Transactions with Limited Partner

(1) A limited partner also may loan money to and transact other business with the partnership, and, unless he is also a general partner, receive on account of resulting claims against the partnership, with general creditors, a pro rata share of the assets. No limited partner shall in respect to any such claim

(a) Receive or hold as collateral security any partnership property, or

(b) Receive from a general partner or the partnership any payment, conveyance, or release from liability, if at the time the assets of the partnership are not sufficient to discharge partnership liabilities to persons not claiming as general or limited partners,

(2) The receiving of collateral security, or a payment, conveyance, or release in violation of the provisions of paragraph (1) is a fraud on the creditors of the partnership.

§ 14. Relation of Limited Partners Inter Se

Where there are several limited partners the members may agree that one or more of the limited partners shall have a priority over other limited partners as to the return of their contributions, as to their compensation by way of income, or as to any other matter. If such an agreement is made it shall be stated in the certificate, and in the absence of such a statement all the limited partners shall stand upon equal footing.

§ 15. Compensation of Limited Partner

A limited partner may receive from the partnership the share of the profits or the compensation by way of income stipulated for in the certificate; provided, that after such payment is made, whether from the property of the partnership or that of a general partner, the partnership assets are in excess of all liabilities of the partnership except liabilities to limited partners on account of their contributions and to general partners.

343

§ 16. Withdrawal or Reduction of Limited Partner's Contribution

(1) A limited partner shall not receive from a general partner or out of partnership property any part of his contribution until

(a) All liabilities of the partnership, except liabilities to general partners and to limited partners on account of their contributions, have been paid or there remains property of the partnership sufficient to pay them,

(b) The consent of all members is had, unless the return of the contribution may be rightfully demanded under the provisions of paragraph (2), and

(c) The certificate is cancelled or so amended as to set forth the withdrawal or reduction.

(2) Subject to the provisions of paragraph (1) a limited partner may rightfully demand the return of his contribution

(a) On the dissolution of a partnership, or

(b) When the date specified in the certificate for its return has arrived, or

(c) After he has given six months' notice in writing to all other members, if no time is specified in the certificate either for the return of the contribution or for the dissolution of the partnership,

(3) In the absence of any statement in the certificate to the contrary or the consent of all members, a limited partner, irrespective of the nature of his contribution, has only the right to demand and receive cash in return for his contribution.

(4) A limited partner may have the partnership dissolved and its affairs wound up when

(a) He rightfully but unsuccessfully demands the return of his contribution, or

(b) The other liabilities of the partnership have not been paid, or the partnership property is insufficient for their payment as required by paragraph (1a) and the limited partner would otherwise be entitled to the return of his contribution.

§ 17. Liability of Limited Partner to Partnership

(1) A limited partner is liable to the partnership

(a) For the difference between his contribution as actually made and that stated in the certificate as having been made, and

(b) For any unpaid contribution which he agreed in the certificate to make in the future at the time and on the conditions stated in the certificate.

(2) A limited partner holds as trustee for the partnership

(a) Specific property stated in the certificate as contributed by him, but which was not contributed or which has been wrongfully returned, and

(b) Money or other property wrongfully paid or conveyed to him on account of his contribution.

(3) The liabilities of a limited partner as set forth in this section can be waived or compromised only by the consent of all members; but a waiver or compromise shall not affect the right of a creditor of a partnership who extended credit or whose claim arose after the filing and before a cancellation or amendment of the certificate, to enforce such liabilities.

(4) When a contributor has rightfully received the return in whole or in part of the capital of his contribution, he is nevertheless liable to the partnership for any sum, not in excess of such return with interest, necessary to discharge its liabilities to all creditors who extended credit or whose claims arose before such return.

§ 18. Nature of Limited Partner's Interest in Partnership

A limited partner's interest in the partnership is personal property.

§ 19. Assignment of Limited Partner's Interest

(1) A limited partner's interest is assignable.

(2) A substituted limited partner is a person admitted to all the rights of a limited partner who has died or has assigned his interest in a partnership.

(3) An assignee, who does not become a substituted limited partner, has no right to require any information or account of the partnership transactions or to inspect the partnership books; he is only entitled to receive the share of the profits or other compensation by way of income, or the return of his contribution, to which his assignor would otherwise be entitled.

(4) An assignee shall have the right to become a substituted limited partner if all the members (except the assignor) consent thereto or if the assignor, being thereunto empowered by the certificate, gives the assignee that right.

(5) An assignee becomes a substituted limited partner when the certificate is appropriately amended in accordance with Section 25.

(6) The substituted limited partner has all the rights and powers, and is subject to all the restrictions and liabilities of his assignor, except those liabilities of which he was ignorant at the time he became a limited partner and which could not be ascertained from the certificate.

(7) The substitution of the assignee as a limited partner does not release the assignor from liability to the partnership under Sections 6 and 17.

§ 20. Effect of Retirement, Death or Insanity of a General Partner

The retirement, death or insanity of a general partner dissolves the partnership, unless the business is continued by the remaining general partners

(a) Under a right so to do stated in the certificate, or

(b) With the consent of all members.

§ 21. Death of Limited Partner

(1) On the death of a limited partner his executor or administrator shall have all the rights of a limited partner for the purpose of settling his estate, and such power as the deceased had to constitute his assignee a substituted limited partner.

(2) The estate of a deceased limited partner shall be liable for all his liabilities as a limited partner.

§ 22. Rights of Creditors of Limited Partner

(1) On due application to a court of competent jurisdiction by any judgment creditor of a limited partner, the court may charge the interest of the indebted limited partner with payment of the unsatisfied amount of the judgment debt; and may appoint a receiver, and make all other orders, directions, and inquiries which the circumstances of the case may require.

> In those states where a creditor on beginning an action can attach debts due the defendant before he has obtained a judgment against the defendant it is recommended that paragraph (1) of this section read as follows:

> On due application to a court of competent jurisdiction by any creditor of a limited partner, the court may charge the interest of the indebted limited partner with payment of the unsatisfied amount of such claim; and may appoint a receiver, and make all other orders, directions, and inquiries which the circumstances of the case may require.

(2) The interest may be redeemed with the separate property of any general partner, but may not be redeemed with partnership property.

(3) The remedies conferred by paragraph (1) shall not be deemed exclusive of others which may exist.

(4) Nothing in this act shall be held to deprive a limited partner of his statutory exemption.

§ 23. Distribution of Assets

(1) In settling accounts after dissolution the liabilities of the partnership shall be entitled to payment in the following order:

(a) Those to creditors, in the order of priority as provided by law, except those to limited partners on account of their contributions, and to general partners,

(b) Those to limited partners in respect to their share of the profits and other compensation by way of income on their contributions,

(c) Those to limited partners in respect to the capital of their contributions,

(d) Those to general partners other than for capital and profits,

(e) Those to general partners in respect to profits,

(f) Those to general partners in respect to capital.

(2) Subject to any statement in the certificate or to subsequent agreement, limited partners share in the partnership assets in respect to their claims for capital, and in respect to their claims for profits or for compensation by way of income on their contributions respectively, in proportion to the respective amounts of such claims.

§ 24. When Certificate Shall Be Cancelled or Amended

(1) The certificate shall be cancelled when the partnership is dissolved or all limited partners cease to be such.

(2) A certificate shall be amended when

(a) There is a change in the name of the partnership or in the amount or character of the contribution of any limited partner,

(b) A person is substituted as a limited partner,

(c) An additional limited partner is admitted,

(d) A person is admitted as a general partner,

(e) A general partner retires, dies or becomes insane, and the business is continued under Section 20,

(f) There is a change in the character of the business of the partnership,

(g) There is a false or erroneous statement in the certificate,

(h) There is a change in the time as stated in the certificate for the dissolution of the partnership or for the return of a contribution,

(i) A time is fixed for the dissolution of the partnership, or the return of a contribution, no time having been specified in the certificate, or

(j) The members desire to make a change in any other statement in the certificate in order that it shall accurately represent the agreement between them.

§ 25. Requirements for Amendment and for Cancellation of Certificate

(1) The writing to amend a certificate shall

(a) Conform to the requirements of Section 2(1a) as far as necessary to set forth clearly the change in the certificate which it is desired to make, and

(b) Be signed and sworn to by all members, and an amendment substituting a limited partner or adding a limited or general partner shall be signed also by the member to be substituted or, added, and when a limited partner is to be substituted, the amendment shall also be signed by the assigning limited partner.

(2) The writing to cancel a certificate shall be signed by all members.

(3) A person desiring the cancellation or amendment of a certificate, if any person designated in paragraphs (1) and (2) as a person who must execute the writing refuses to do so, may petition the [here designate the proper court] to direct a cancellation or amendment thereof.

(4) If the court finds that the petitioner has a right to have the writing executed by a person who refuses to do so, it shall order the [here designate the responsible official in the office designated in Section 2] in the office where the certificate is recorded to record the cancellation or amendment of the certificate; and where the certificate is to be amended, the court shall also cause to be filed for record in said office a certified copy of its decree setting forth the amendment.

(5) A certificate is amended or cancelled when there is filed for record in the office [here designate the office designated in Section 2] where the certificate is recorded

(a) A writing in accordance with the provisions of paragraph (1), or (2) or

(b) A certified copy of the order of court in accordance with the provisions of paragraph (4).

(6) After the certificate is duly amended in accordance with this section, the amended certificate shall thereafter be for all purposes the certificate provided for by this act.

§ 26. Parties to Actions

A contributor, unless he is a general partner, is not a proper party to proceedings by or against a partnership, except where the object is to enforce a limited partner's right against or liability to the partnership.

§ 27. Name of Act

This act may be cited as The Uniform Limited Partnership Act.

§ 28. Rules of Construction

(1) The rule that statutes in derogation of the common law are to be strictly construed shall have no application to this act.

(2) This act shall be so interpreted and construed as to effect its general purpose to make uniform the law of those states which enact it.

(3) This act shall not be so construed as to impair the obligations of any contract existing when the act goes into effect, nor to affect any action or proceedings begun or right accrued before this act takes effect.

§ 29. Rules for Cases Not Provided for in This Act

In any case not provided for in this act the rules of law and equity, including the law merchant, shall govern.

§ 30. Provisions for Existing Limited Partnerships

(1) A limited partnership formed under any statute of this state prior to the adoption of this act, may become a limited partnership under this act by complying with the provisions of Section 2; provided the certificate sets forth

(a) The amount of the original contribution of each limited partner, and the time when the contribution was made, and

(b) That the property of the partnership exceeds the amount sufficient to discharge its liabilities to persons not claiming as general or limited partners by an amount greater than the sum of the contributions of its limited partners.

(2) A limited partnership formed under any statute of this state prior to the adoption of this act, until or unless it becomes a limited partnership under this act, shall continue to be governed by the provisions of [here insert proper reference to the existing limited partnership act or acts], except that such partnership shall not be renewed unless so provided in the original agreement.

§ 31. Act (Acts) Repealed

Except as affecting existing limited partnerships to the extent set forth in Section 30, the act (acts) of [here designate the existing limited partnership act or acts] is (are) hereby repealed.

C. REVISED UNIFORM LIMITED PARTNERSHIP ACT, 1976 (WITH COMMISSIONERS' COMMENTS)

6 U.L.A. 1982 Pocket Part 159 et seq.

Adoptions

Table of Jurisdictions Wherein Act Has Been Adopted

Jurisdiction	Laws	Effective Date	Statutory Citation
Arkansas	1979, No. 657	7–1–1979	Ark.Stats. §§ 65–501 to 65–566.
Connecticut	1979, P.A. 440	6–14–1979*	C.G.S.A. §§ 34–9 to 34–38n.
Maryland	1981, c. 801	7–1–1982	Code, Corporations and Associations, §§ 10–101 to 10–1104.
Minnesota	1980, c. 582	4–16–1980 *	M.S.A. §§ 322A.01 to 322A.87.
Washington	1981, c. 51	1–1–1982	West's RCWA 25.10.010 to 25.10.690.
West Virginia	1981, c. 208	1–1–1982	Code, 47–9–1 to 47–9–63.
Wyoming	1979, c. 153	7–1–1979	W.S. 1977, §§ 17–14–201 to 17–14–1104.

*Date of approval.

Contents

ARTICLE 1. GENERAL PROVISIONS

ARTICLE 2. FORMATION; CERTIFICATE OF LIMITED PARTNERSHIP

ARTICLE 3. LIMITED PARTNERS

ARTICLE 11.   MISCELLANEOUS

Commissioners' Prefatory Note

The Revised Uniform Limited Partnership Act adopted by the National Conference of Commissioners on Uniform State Laws in August, 1976, was intended to modernize the prior uniform law while retaining the special character of limited partnerships as compared with corporations. The draftsman of a limited partnership agreement has a degree of flexibility in defining the relations among the partners that is not available in the corporate form. Moreover, the relationship among partners is consensual, and requires a degree of privity that forces the general partner to seek approval of the partners (sometimes unanimous approval) under circumstances that corporate management would find unthinkable. The limited partnership was not intended to be an alternative in all cases where corporate form is undesirable for tax or other reasons, and the new Act was not intended to make it so. The new Act clarifies many ambiguities and fills interstices in the prior uniform law by adding more detailed language and mechanics. In addition, some important substantive changes and additions have been made.

Article 1 provides a list of all of the definitions used in the Act, integrates the use of limited partnership names with corporate names and provides for an office and agent for service of process in the state of organization. All of these provisions are new. Article 2 collects in one place all provisions dealing with execution and filing of certificates of limited partnership and certificates of amendment and cancellation. Articles 1 and 2 reflect an important change in the statutory scheme: recognition that the basic document in any partnership, including a limited partnership, is the partnership agreement. The certificate of limited partnership is not a constitutive document (except in the sense that it is a statutory prerequisite to creation of the limited partnership), and merely reflects matters as to which creditors should be put on notice.

Article 3 deals with the single most difficult issue facing lawyers who use the limited partnership form of organization: the powers and potential liabilities of limited partners. Section 303

352

lists a number of activities in which a limited partner may engage without being held to have so participated in the control of the business that he assumes the liability of a general partner. Moreover, it goes on to confine the liability of a limited partner who merely steps over the line of participation in control to persons who actually know of that participation in control. General liability for partnership debts is imposed only on those limited partners who are, in effect, "silent general partners". With that exception, the provisions of the new Act that impose liability on a limited partner who has somehow permitted third parties to be misled to their detriment as to the limited partner's true status confine that liability to those who have actually been misled. The provisions relating to general partners are collected in Article 4.

Article 5, the finance section, makes some important changes from the prior uniform law. The contribution of services and promises to contribute cash, property or services are now explicitly permitted as contributions. And those who fail to perform promised services are required, in the absence of an agreement to the contrary, to pay the value of the services stated in the certificate of limited partnership.

A number of changes from the prior uniform law are made in Article 6, dealing with distributions from and the withdrawal of partners from the partnership. For example, Section 608 creates a statute of limitations on the right of a limited partnership to recover all or part of a contribution that has been returned to a limited partner, whether to satisfy creditors or otherwise.

The assignability of partnership interests is dealt with a considerable detail in Article 7. The provisions relating to dissolution appear in Article 8, which, among other things, imposes a new standard for seeking judicial dissolution of a limited partnership.

One of the thorniest questions for those who operate limited partnerships in more than one state has been the status of the partnership in a state other than the state of organization. Neither existing case law nor administrative practice makes it clear whether the limited partners continue to possess their limited liability and which law governs the partnership. Article 9 deals with this problem by providing for registration of foreign limited partnerships and specifying choice-of-law rules.

Finally, Article 10 of the new Act authorizes derivative actions to be brought by limited partners.

Caveat

At this time [May 1977], provisions of this Act have not been ruled upon by the Internal Revenue Service. We advise any state or interested party to monitor the

tax consequences carefully when considering it. Par-
ticularly, we suggest that a delayed effective date be
inserted in any bills introduced. A substantially delayed
effective date would permit an IRS ruling before that
date with respect to an enactment, and would preclude
any adverse consequences to those who might rely on
the Act's provisions.

ARTICLE 1

GENERAL PROVISIONS

§ 101. Definitions

As used in this Act, unless the context otherwise requires:

(1) "Certificate of limited partnership" means the certificate referred to in Section 201, and the certificate as amended.

(2) "Contribution" means any cash, property, services rendered, or a promissory note or other binding obligation to contribute cash or property or to perform services, which a partner contributes to a limited partnership in his capacity as a partner.

(3) "Event of withdrawal of a general partner" means an event that causes a person to cease to be a general partner as provided in Section 402.

(4) "Foreign limited partnership" means a partnership formed under the laws of any State other than this State and having as partners one or more general partners and one or more limited partners.

(5) "General partner" means a person who has been admitted to a limited partnership as a general partner in accordance with the partnership agreement and named in the certificate of limited partnership as a general partner.

(6) "Limited partner" means a person who has been admitted to a limited partnership as a limited partner in accordance with the partnership agreement and named in the certificate of limited partnership as a limited partner.

(7) "Limited partnership" and "domestic limited partnership" mean a partnership formed by 2 or more persons under the laws of this State and having one or more general partners and one or more limited partners.

(8) "Partner" means a limited or general partner.

(9) "Partnership agreement" means any valid agreement, written or oral, of the partners as to the affairs of a limited partnership and the conduct of its business.

(10) "Partnership interest" means a partner's share of the profits and losses of a limited partnership and the right to receive distributions of partnership assets.

(11) "Person" means a natural person, partnership, limited partnership (domestic or foreign), trust, estate, association, or corporation.

(12) "State" means a state, territory, or possession of the United States, the District of Columbia, or the Commonwealth of Puerto Rico.

Commissioners' Comment

The definitions in this section clarify a number of uncertainties in existing law and make certain changes.

Contribution: this definition makes it clear that a present contribution of services and a promise to make a future payment of cash, contribution of property or performance of services are permissible forms for a contribution. Accordingly, the present services or promise must be accorded a value in the certificate of limited partnership (Section 201(5)), and, in the case of a promise, that value may determine the liability of a partner who fails to honor his agreement (Section 502). Section 3 of the prior uniform law did not permit a limited partner's contribution to be in the form of services, although that inhibition did not apply to general partners.

Foreign limited partnership: the Act only deals with foreign limited partnerships formed under the laws of another "State" of the United States (see subdivision 12 of Section 101), and any adopting State that desires to deal by statute with the status of entities formed under the laws of foreign countries must make appropriate changes throughout the Act. The exclusion of such entities from the Act was not intended to suggest that their "limited partners" should not be accorded limited liability by the courts of a State adopting the Act. That question would be resolved by the choice-of-law rules of the forum State.

General partner: this definition recognizes the separate functions of the partnership agreement and the certificate of limited partnership. The partnership agreement establishes the basic grant of management power to the persons named as general partners; but because of the passive role played by the limited partners, the separate, formal step of embodying that grant of power in the certificate of limited partnership has been preserved to emphasize its importance.

Limited partner: as in the case of general partners, this definition provides for admission of limited partners through the partnership agreement and solemnization in the certificate of limited partnership. In addition, the definition makes it clear that being named in the certificate of limited partnership is a prerequisite to limited partner status. Failure to file does not, however, mean that the participant is a general partner or that he has general liability. See Sections 202(e) and 303.

Partnership agreement: the prior uniform law did not refer to the partnership agreement, assuming that all important matters affecting limited partners would be set forth in the certificate of limited partnership. Under modern practice, however, it has been common for the partners to enter into a comprehensive partnership agreement, only part of which was required to be included in the certificate of limited partnership. As reflected in Section 201, the certificate of limited partnership is confined principally to matters respecting the addition and withdrawal of partners and of capital, and other important issues are left to the partnership agreement.

Partnership interest: this definition is new and is intended to define what it is that is transferred when a partnership interest is assigned.

§ 102. Name

The name of each limited partnership as set forth in its certificate of limited partnership:

(1) shall contain without abbreviation the words "limited partnership";

(2) may not contain the name of a limited partner unless (i) it is also the name of a general partner or the corporate name of a corporate general partner, or (ii) the business of the limited partnership had been carried on under that name before the admission of that limited partner;

(3) may not contain any word or phrase indicating or implying that it is organized other than for a purpose stated in its certificate of limited partnership;

(4) may not be the same as, or deceptively similar to, the name of any corporation or limited partnership organized under the laws of this State or licensed or registered as a foreign corporation or limited partnership in this State; and

(5) may not contain the following words [here insert prohibited words].

Commissioners' Comment

Subdivision (2) of Section 102 has been carried over from Section 5 of the prior uniform law with certain editorial changes. The remainder of Section 102 is new and primarily reflects the intention to integrate the registration of limited partnership names with that of corporate names. Accordingly, Section 201 provides for central, State-wide filing of certificates of limited partnership, and subdivisions (3), (4) and (5) of Section 102 contain standards to be applied by the filing officer in determining whether the certificate should be filed. Subdivision (1) requires that the proper name of a limited partnership contain the words "limited partnership" in full.

§ 103. Reservation of Name

(a) The exclusive right to the use of a name may be reserved by:

(1) any person intending to organize a limited partnership under this Act and to adopt that name;

(2) any domestic limited partnership or any foreign limited partnership registered in this State which, in either case, intends to adopt that name;

(3) any foreign limited partnership intending to register in this State and adopt that name; and

(4) any person intending to organize a foreign limited partnership and intending to have it register in this State and adopt that name.

(b) The reservation shall be made by filing with the Secretary of State an application, executed by the applicant, to reserve a specified name. If the Secretary of State finds that the name is available for use by a domestic or foreign limited partnership, he shall reserve the name for the exclusive use of the applicant for a period of 120 days. Once having so reserved a name, the same applicant may not again reserve the same name until more than 60 days after the expiration of the last 120-day period for which that applicant reserved that name. The right to the exclusive use of a reserved name may be transferred to any other person by filing in the office of the Secretary of State a notice of the transfer, executed by the applicant for whom the name was reserved and specifying the name and address of the transferee.

Commissioners' Comment

Section 103 is new. The prior uniform law did not provide for registration of names.

§ 104. Specified Office and Agent

Each limited partnership shall continuously maintain in this State:

(1) an office, which may but need not be a place of its business in this State, at which shall be kept the records required by Section 105 to be maintained; and

(2) an agent for service of process on the limited partnership, which agent must be an individual resident of this State, a domestic corporation, or a foreign corporation authorized to do business in this State.

Commissioners' Comment

Section 104 is new. It requires that a limited partnership have certain minimum contacts with its State of organization, i. e., an office at which the constitutive documents and basic financial information is kept and an agent for service of process.

§ 105. Records to Be Kept

Each limited partnership shall keep at the office referred to in Section 104(1) the following: (1) a current list of the full name and last known business address of each partner set forth in alphabetical order, (2) a copy of the certificate of limited partnership and all certificates of amendment thereto, together with executed copies of any powers of attorney pursuant to which any certificate has been executed, (3) copies of the limited partnership's federal, state, and local income tax returns and reports, if any, for the 3 most recent years, and (4) copies of any then effective written partnership agreements and of any financial statements of the limited partnership for the 3 most recent years. Those records are subject to inspection and copying at the reasonable request, and at the expense, of any partner during ordinary business hours.

Commissioners' Comment

Section 105 is new. In view of the passive nature of the limited partner's position, it has been widely felt that limited partners are entitled to access to certain basic documents, including the certificate of limited partnership and any partnership agreement. In view of the great diversity among limited partnerships, it was thought inappropriate to require a standard form of financial report, and Section 105 does no more than require retention of tax returns and any other financial statements that are prepared. The names and addresses of the partners are made available to the general public.

§ 106. Nature of Business

A limited partnership may carry on any business that a partnership without limited partners may carry on except [here designate prohibited activities].

Commissioners' Comment

Section 106 is identical to Section 3 of the prior uniform law. Many states require that certain regulated industries, such as banking, may be carried on only by entities organized pursuant to special statutes, and it is contemplated that the prohibited activities would be confined to the matters covered by those statutes.

§ 107. Business Transactions of Partner With the Partnership

Except as provided in the partnership agreement, a partner may lend money to and transact other business with the limited partnership and, subject to other applicable law, has the same rights and obligations with respect thereto as a person who is not a partner.

Commissioners' Comment

Section 107 makes a number of important changes in Section 13 of the prior uniform law. Section 13, in effect, created a special fraudulent conveyance provision applicable to the making of secured loans by limited partners and the repayment by limited partnerships of loans from limited partners. Section 107 leaves that question to a State's general fraudulent conveyance statute. In addition, Section 107 eliminates the prohibition in former Section 13 against a general partner (as opposed to a limited partner) sharing pro rata with general creditors in the case of an unsecured loan. Of course, other doctrines developed under bankruptcy and insolvency laws may require the subordination of loans by partners under appropriate circumstances.

ARTICLE 2

FORMATION; CERTIFICATE OF LIMITED PARTNERSHIP

§ 201. Certificate of Limited Partnership

(a) In order to form a limited partnership two or more persons must execute a certificate of limited partnership. The certificate shall be filed in the office of the Secretary of State and set forth:

(1) the name of the limited partnership;

(2) the general character of its business;

(3) the address of the office and the name and address of the agent for service of process required to be maintained by Section 104;

(4) the name and the business address of each partner (specifying separately the general partners and limited partners);

(5) the amount of cash and a description and statement of the agreed value of the other property or services contributed by each partner and which each partner has agreed to contribute in the future;

(6) the times at which or events on the happening of which any additional contributions agreed to be made by each partner are to be made;

(7) any power of a limited partner to grant the right to become a limited partner to an assignee of any part of his partnership interest, and the terms and conditions of the power;

(8) if agreed upon, the time at which or the events on the happening of which a partner may terminate his membership in the limited partnership and the amount of, or the method of determining, the distribution to which he may be entitled respecting his partnership interest, and the terms and conditions of the termination and distribution;

(9) any right of a partner to receive distributions of property, including cash from the limited partnership;

(10) any right of a partner to receive, or of a general partner to make, distributions to a partner which include a return of all or any part of the partner's contribution;

(11) any time at which or events upon the happening of which the limited partnership is to be dissolved and its affairs wound up;

(12) any right of the remaining general partners to continue the business on the happening of an event of withdrawal of a general partner; and

(13) any other matters the partners determine to include therein.

(b) A limited partnership is formed at the time of the filing of the certificate of limited partnership in the office of the Secretary of State or at any later time specified in the certificate of limited partnership if, in either case, there has been substantial compliance with the requirements of this section.

Commissioners' Comment

The matters required to be set forth in the certificate of limited partnership are not different in kind from those required by Section 2 of the prior uniform law, although certain additions and deletions have been made and the description has been revised to conform with the rest of the Act. In general, the certificate is intended to serve two functions: first, to place creditors on notice of the facts concerning the capital of the partnership and the rules regarding additional contributions to and withdrawals from the partnership; second, to clearly delineate the time at which persons become general partners and limited partners. Subparagraph (b), which is based upon the prior uniform law, has been retained to make it clear that the existence of the limited partnership depends only upon compliance with this section. Its continued existence is not dependent upon compliance with other provisions of this Act.

§ 202. Amendment to Certificate

(a) A certificate of limited partnership is amended by filing a certificate of amendment thereto in the office of the Secretary of State. The certificate shall set forth:

(1) the name of the limited partnership;

(2) the date of filing of the certificate; and

(3) the amendment to the certificate.

(b) Within 30 days after the happening of any of the following events an amendment to a certificate of limited partnership reflecting the occurrence of the event or events shall be filed:

(1) a change in the amount or character of the contribution of any partner, or in any partner's obligation to make a contribution;

(2) the admission of a new partner;

(3) the withdrawal of a partner; or

(4) the continuation of the business under Section 801 after an event of withdrawal of a general partner.

(c) A general partner who becomes aware that any statement in a certificate of limited partnership was false when made or that any arrangements or other facts described have changed, making the certificate inaccurate in any respect, shall promptly amend the certificate, but an amendment to show a change of address of a limited partner need be filed only once every 12 months.

(d) A certificate of limited partnership may be amended at any time for any other proper purpose the general partners may determine.

(e) No person has any liability because an amendment to a certificate of limited partnership has not been filed to reflect the occurrence of any event referred to in subsection (b) of this Section if the amendment is filed within the 30-day period specified in subsection (b).

Commissioners' Comment

Section 202 makes substantial changes in Section 24 of the prior uniform law. Paragraph (b) lists the basic events—the addition or withdrawal of partners or capital or capital obligations—that are so central to the function of the certificate of limited partnership that they require prompt amendment. Paragraph (c) makes it clear, as it was not clear under subdivision (2)(g) of former Section 24, that the certificate of limited partnership is intended to be an accurate description of the facts to which it relates at all times and does not speak merely as of the date it is executed. Paragraph (e) provides a "safe harbor" against claims of creditors or others who assert that they have been misled by the failure to amend the certificate of limited partnership to reflect changes in any of the important facts referred to in paragraph (b); if the certificate of limited partnership is amended within 30 days of the occurrence of the event, no creditor or other person can recover for damages sustained during the interim. Additional protection is afforded by the provisions of Section 304.

§ 203. Cancellation of Certificate

A certificate of limited partnership shall be cancelled upon the dissolution and the commencement of winding up of the partnership or at any other time there are no limited partners. A certificate of cancellation shall be filed in the office of the Secretary of State and set forth:

(1) the name of the limited partnership;

(2) the date of filing of its certificate of limited partnership;

(3) the reason for filing the certificate of cancellation;

(4) the effective date (which shall be a date certain) of cancellation if it is not to be effective upon the filing of the certificate; and

(5) any other information the general partners filing the certificate determine.

Commissioners' Comment

Section 203 changes Section 24 of the prior uniform law by making it clear that the certificate of cancellation should be filed upon the commencement of winding up of the limited partnership. Section 24 provided for cancellation "when the partnership is dissolved".

§ 204. Execution of Certificates

(a) Each certificate required by this Article to be filed in the office of the Secretary of State shall be executed in the following manner:

(1) an original certificate of limited partnership must be signed by all partners named therein;

(2) a certificate of amendment must be signed by at least one general partner and by each other partner designated in the certificate as a new partner or whose contribution is described as having been increased; and

(3) a certificate of cancellation must be signed by all general partners;

(b) Any person may sign a certificate by an attorney-in-fact, but a power of attorney to sign a certificate relating to the admission, or increased contribution, of a partner must specifically describe the admission or increase.

(c) The execution of a certificate by a general partner constitutes an affirmation under the penalties of perjury that the facts stated therein are true.

Commissioners' Comment

Section 204 collects in one place the formal requirements for the execution of certificates which were set forth in Sections 2 and 25 of the prior uniform law. Those sections required that each certificate be signed by all partners, and there developed an unnecessarily cumbersome practice of having each limited partner sign powers of attorney to authorize the general partners to execute certificates of amendment on their behalf. Section 204 insures that each partner must sign a certificate when he becomes a partner or when the certificates reflect any increase in his obligation to make contributions. Certificates of amendment are required to be signed by only one general partner and all general partners must sign certificates of cancellation. Section 204 prohibits blanket powers of attorney for the execution of certificates in many cases, since those conditions under which a partner is required to sign have been narrowed to circumstances of special importance to that partner. The former requirement that all certificates be sworn has been confined to statements by the general partners, recognizing that the limited partner's role is a limited one.

§ 205. Amendment or Cancellation by Judicial Act

If a person required by Section 204 to execute a certificate of amendment or cancellation fails or refuses to do so, any other partner, and any assignee of a partnership interest, who is adversely affected by the failure or refusal, may petition the [here designate the proper court] to direct the amendment or cancellation. If the court finds that the amendment or cancellation is proper and that any person so designated has failed or refused to execute the certificate, it shall order the Secretary of State to record an appropriate certificate of amendment or cancellation.

Section 205 changes subdivisions (3) and (4) of Section 25 of the prior uniform law by confining the persons who have standing to seek judicial intervention to partners and to those assignees who are adversely affected by the failure or refusal of the appropriate persons to file a certificate of amendment or cancellation.

§ 206. Filing in Office of Secretary of State

(a) Two signed copies of the certificate of limited partnership and of any certificates of amendment or cancellation (or of any judicial decree of amendment or cancellation) shall be delivered to the Secretary of State. A person who executes a certificate as an agent or fiduciary need not exhibit evidence of his authority as a prerequisite to filing. Unless the Secretary of State finds that any certificate does not conform to law, upon receipt of all filing fees required by law he shall:

(1) endorse on each duplicate original the word "Filed" and the day, month, and year of the filing thereof;

(2) file one duplicate original in his office; and

(3) return the other duplicate original to the person who filed it or his representative.

(b) Upon the filing of a certificate of amendment (or judicial decree of amendment) in the office of the Secretary of State, the certificate of limited partnership shall be amended as set forth therein, and upon the effective date of a certificate of cancellation (or a judicial decree thereof), the certificate of limited partnership is cancelled.

Section 206 is new. In addition to providing mechanics for the central filing system, the second sentence of this section does away with the requirement, formerly imposed by some local filing officers, that persons who have executed certificates under a power of attorney exhibit executed copies of the power of attorney itself. Paragraph (b) changes subdivision (5) of Section 25 of the prior uniform law by providing that certificates of cancellation are effective upon their effective date under Section 203.

§ 207. Liability for False Statement in Certificate

If any certificate of limited partnership or certificate of amendment or cancellation contains a false statement, one who suffers loss by reliance on the statement may recover damages for the loss from:

(1) any person who executes the certificate, or causes another to execute it on his behalf, and knew, and any general partner who knew or should have known, the statement to be false at the time the certificate was executed; and

(2) any general partner who thereafter knows or should have known that any arrangement or other fact described in the cer-

tificate has changed, making the statement inaccurate in any respect within a sufficient time before the statement was relied upon reasonably to have enabled that general partner to cancel or amend the certificate, or to file a petition for its cancellation or amendment under Section 205.

Commissioners' Comment

Section 207 changes Section 6 of the prior uniform law by providing explicitly for the liability of persons who sign a certificate as agent under a power of attorney and by confining the obligation to amend a certificate of limited partnership in light of future events to general partners.

§ 208. Notice

The fact that a certificate of limited partnership is on file in the office of the Secretary of State is notice that the partnership is a limited partnership and the persons designated therein as limited partners are limited partners, but it is not notice of any other fact.

Commissioners' Comment

Section 208 is new. By stating that the filing of a certificate of limited partnership only results in notice of the limited liability of the limited partners, it obviates the concern that third parties may be held to have notice of special provisions set forth in the certificate. While this section is designed to preserve the limited liability of limited partners, the notice provided is not intended to change any liability of a limited partner which may be created by his action or inaction under the law of estoppel, agency, fraud, or the like.

§ 209. Delivery of Certificates to Limited Partners

Upon the return by the Secretary of State pursuant to Section 206 of a certificate marked "Filed," the general partners shall promptly deliver or mail a copy of the certificate of limited partnership and each certificate to each limited partner unless the partnership agreement provides otherwise.

Commissioners' Comment

This section is new.

ARTICLE 3

LIMITED PARTNERS

§ 301. Admission of Additional Limited Partners

(a) After the filing of a limited partnership's original certificate of limited partnership, a person may be admitted as an additional limited partner:

(1) in the case of a person acquiring a partnership interest directly from the limited partnership, upon the compliance with the partnership agreement or, if the partnership agreement does not so provide, upon the written consent of all partners; and

(2) in the case of an assignee of a partnership interest of a partner who has the power, as provided in Section 704, to grant the assignee the right to become a limited partner, upon the exercise of that power and compliance with any conditions limiting the grant or exercise of the power.

(b) In each case under subsection (a), the person acquiring the partnership interest becomes a limited partner only upon amendment of the certificate of limited partnership reflecting that fact.

Commissioners' Comment

Subdivision (1) of Section 301(a) adds to Section 8 of the prior uniform law an explicit recognition of the fact that unanimous consent of all partners is required for admission of new limited partners unless the partner-ship agreement provides otherwise. Subdivision (2) is derived from Section 19 of the prior uniform law but abandons the former terminology of "substituted limited partner".

§ 302. Voting

Subject to Section 303, the partnership agreement may grant to all or a specified group of the limited partners the right to vote (on a per capita or other basis) upon any matter.

Commissioners' Comment

Section 302 is new, and must be read together with subdivision (b)(5) of Section 303. Although the prior uniform law did not speak specifically of the voting powers of limited partners, it is not uncommon for partnership agreements to grant such power to limited partners. Section 302 is designed only to make it clear that the partnership agreement may grant such power to limited partners. If such powers are granted to limited partners beyond the "safe harbor" of Section 303(b)(5), a court may hold that, under the circumstances, the limited partners have participated in "control of the business" within the meaning of Section 303(a). Section 303(c) simply means that the exercise of powers beyond the ambit of Section 303(b) is not ipso facto to be taken as taking part in the control of the business.

§ 303. Liability to Third Parties

(a) Except as provided in subsection (d), a limited partner is not liable for the obligations of a limited partnership unless he is also a general partner or, in addition to the exercise of his rights and powers as a limited partner, he takes part in the control of the business. However, if the limited partner's participation in the control of the business is not substantially the same as the exercise of the powers of a general partner, he is liable only to persons who transact business with the limited partnership with actual knowledge of his participation in control.

(b) A limited partner does not participate in the control of the business within the meaning of subsection (a) solely by doing one or more of the following:

(1) being a contractor for or an agent or employee of the limited partnership or of a general partner;

365

(2) consulting with and advising a general partner with respect to the business of the limited partnership;

(3) acting as surety for the limited partnership;

(4) approving or disapproving an amendment to the partnership agreement; or

(5) voting on one or more of the following matters:

    (i) the dissolution and winding up of the limited partnership;

    (ii) the sale, exchange, lease, mortgage, pledge, or other transfer of all or substantially all of the assets of the limited partnership other than in the ordinary course of its business;

    (iii) the incurrence of indebtedness by the limited partnership other than in the ordinary course of its business;

    (iv) a change in the nature of the business; or

    (v) the removal of a general partner.

(c) The enumeration in subsection (b) does not mean that the possession or exercise of any other powers by a limited partner constitutes participation by him in the business of the limited partnership.

(d) A limited partner who knowingly permits his name to be used in the name of the limited partnership, except under circumstances permitted by Section 102(2)(i), is liable to creditors who extend credit to the limited partnership without actual knowledge that the limited partner is not a general partner.

Commissioners' Comment

Section 303 makes several important changes in Section 7 of the prior uniform law. The first sentence of Section 303(a) carries over the basic test from former Section 7—whether the limited partner "takes part in the control of the business"—in order to insure that judicial decisions under the prior uniform law remain applicable to the extent not expressly changed. The second sentence of Section 303(a) reflects a wholly new concept. Because of the difficulty of determining when the "control" line has been overstepped, it was thought it unfair to impose general partner's liability on a limited partner except to the extent that a third party had knowledge of his participation in control of the business. On the other hand, in order to avoid permitting a limited partner to exercise all of the powers of a general partner while avoiding any direct dealings with third parties, the "is not substantially the same as" test was introduced. Paragraph (b) is intended to provide a "safe harbor" by enumerating certain activities which a limited partner may carry on for the partnership without being deemed to have taken part in control of the business. Paragraph (d) is derived from Section 5 of the prior uniform law, but adds as a condition to the limited partner's liability the fact that a limited partner must have knowingly permitted his name to be used in the name of the limited partnership.

§ 304. Person Erroneously Believing Himself Limited Partner

(a) Except as provided in subsection (b), a person who makes a contribution to a business enterprise and erroneously but in good faith believes that he has become a limited partner in the enterprise is not a general partner in the enterprise and is not bound by its obligations by reason of making the contribution, receiving distributions from the enterprise, or exercising any rights of a limited partner, if, on ascertaining the mistake, he:

(1) causes an appropriate certificate of limited partnership or a certificate of amendment to be executed and filed; or

(2) withdraws from future equity participation in the enterprise.

(b) A person who makes a contribution of the kind described in subsection (a) is liable as a general partner to any third party who transacts business with the enterprise (i) before the person withdraws and an appropriate certificate is filed to show withdrawal, or (ii) before an appropriate certificate is filed to show his status as a limited partner and, in the case of an amendment, after expiration of the 30-day period for filing an amendment relating to the person as a limited partner under Section 202, but in either case only if the third party actually believed in good faith that the person was a general partner at the time of the transaction.

Commissioners' Comment

Section 304 is derived from Section 11 of the prior uniform law. The "good faith" requirement has been added in the first sentence of Section 304(a). The provisions of subdivision (2) of Section 304(a) are intended to clarify an ambiguity in the prior law by providing that a person who chooses to withdraw from the enterprise in order to protect himself from liability is not required to renounce any of his then current interest in the enterprise so long as he has no further participation as an equity participant. Paragraph (b) preserves the liability of the equity participant prior to withdrawal (and after the time for appropriate amendment in the case of a limited partnership) to any third party who has transacted business with the person believing in good faith that he was a general partner.

§ 305. Information

Each limited partner has the right to:

(1) inspect and copy any of the partnership records required to be maintained by Section 105; and

(2) obtain from the general partners from time to time upon reasonable demand (i) true and full information regarding the state of the business and financial condition of the limited partnership, (ii) promptly after becoming available, a copy of the limited partnership's federal, state, and local income tax returns for each year, and (iii) other information regarding the affairs of the limited partnership as is just and reasonable.

Commissioners' Comment

Section 305 changes and restates the rights of limited partners to information about the partnership formerly provided by Section 10 of the prior uniform law.

ARTICLE 4

GENERAL PARTNERS

§ 401. Admission of Additional General Partners

After the filing of a limited partnership's original certificate of limited partnership, additional general partners may be admitted only with the specific written consent of each partner.

Commissioners' Comment

Section 401 is derived from Section 9(1)(e) of the prior law and carries over the unwaivable requirement that all limited partners must consent to the admission of an additional general partner and that such consent must specifically identify the general partner involved.

§ 402. Events of Withdrawal

Except as approved by the specific written consent of all partners at the time, a person ceases to be a general partner of a limited partnership upon the happening of any of the following events:

(1) the general partner withdraws from the limited partnership as provided in Section 602;

(2) the general partner ceases to be a member of the limited partnership as provided in Section 702;

(3) the general partner is removed as a general partner in accordance with the partnership agreement;

(4) unless otherwise provided in the certificate of limited partnership, the general partner: (i) makes an assignment for the benefit of creditors; (ii) files a voluntary petition in bankruptcy; (iii) is adjudicated a bankrupt or insolvent; (iv) files a petition or answer seeking for himself any reorganization, arrangement, composition, readjustment, liquidation, dissolution, or similar relief under any statute, law, or regulation; (v) files an answer or other pleading admitting or failing to contest the material allegations of a petition filed against him in any proceeding of this nature; or (vi) seeks, consents to, or acquiesces in the appointment of a trustee, receiver, or liquidator of the general partner or of all or any substantial part of his properties;

(5) unless otherwise provided in the certificate of limited partnership, [120] days after the commencement of any proceeding against the general partner seeking reorganization, ar-

rangement, composition, readjustment, liquidation, dissolution, or similar relief under any statute, law, or regulation, the proceeding has not been dismissed, or if within [90] days after the appointment without his consent or acquiescence of a trustee, receiver, or liquidator of the general partner or of all or any substantial part of his properties, the appointment is not vacated or stayed, or within [90] days after the expiration of any such stay, the appointment is not vacated;

(6) in the case of a general partner who is a natural person,

(i) his death; or

(ii) the entry by a court of competent jurisdiction adjudicating him incompetent to manage his person or his estate;

(7) in the case of a general partner who is acting as a general partner by virtue of being a trustee of a trust, the termination of the trust (but not merely the substitution of a new trustee);

(8) in the case of a general partner that is a separate partnership, the dissolution and commencement of winding up of the separate partnership;

(9) in the case of a general partner that is a corporation, the filing of a certificate of dissolution, or its equivalent, for the corporation or the revocation of its charter; or

(10) in the case of an estate, the distribution by the fiduciary of the estate's entire interest in the partnership.

Commissioners' Comment

Section 402 expands considerably the provisions of Section 20 of the prior uniform law which provided for dissolution in the event of the retirement, death or insanity of a general partner. Subdivisions (1), (2) and (3) recognize, that the general partner's agency relationship is terminable at will, although it may result in a breach of the partnership agreement giving rise to an action for damages. Subdivisions (4) and (5) reflect a judgment that, unless the limited partners agree otherwise, they ought to have the power to rid themselves of a general partner who is in such dire financial straits that he is the subject of proceedings under the National Bankruptcy Act or a similar provision of law. Subdivisions (6) through (10) simply elaborate on the notion of death in the case of a general partner who is not a natural person. Of course, the addition of the words "and in the partnership agreement" was not intended to suggest that liabilities to third parties could be affected by provisions in the partnership agreement.

§ 403. General Powers and Liabilities

Except as provided in this Act or in the partnership agreement, a general partner of a limited partnership has the rights and powers and is subject to the restrictions and liabilities of a partner in a partnership without limited partners.

Section 403 is derived from Section 9(1) of the prior uniform law.

§ 404. Contributions by a General Partner

A general partner of a limited partnership may make contributions to the partnership and share in the profits and losses of, and in distributions from, the limited partnership as a general partner. A general partner also may make contributions to and share in profits, losses, and distributions as a limited partner. A person who is both a general partner and a limited partner has the rights and powers, and is subject to the restrictions and liabilities, of a general partner and, except as provided in the partnership agreement, also has the powers, and is subject to the restrictions, of a limited partner to the extent of his participation in the partnership as a limited partner.

Section 404 is derived from Section 12 of the prior uniform law and makes clear that the partnership agreement may provide that a general partner who is also a limited partner may exercise all of the powers of a limited partner.

§ 405. Voting

The partnership agreement may grant to all or certain identified general partners the right to vote (on a per capita or any other basis), separately or with all or any class of the limited partners, on any matter.

Section 405 is new and is intended to make it clear that the Act does not require that the limited partners have any right to vote on matters as a separate class.

ARTICLE 5

FINANCE

§ 501. Form of Contribution

The contribution of a partner may be in cash, property, or services rendered, or a promissory note or other obligation to contribute cash or property or to perform services.

As noted in the comment to Section 101, the explicit permission to make contributions of services expands Section 4 of the prior uniform law.

§ 502. Liability for Contributions

(a) Except as provided in the certificate of limited partnership, a partner is obligated to the limited partnership to perform any promise to contribute cash or property or to perform services, even if he is unable to perform because of death, disability or any other reason. If a partner does not make the required contribution of property or services, he is obligated at the option of the limited partnership to contribute cash equal to that portion of the value (as stated in the certificate of limited partnership) of the stated contribution that has not been made.

(b) Unless otherwise provided in the partnership agreement, the obligation of a partner to make a contribution or return money or other property paid or distributed in violation of this Act may be compromised only by consent of all the partners. Notwithstanding the compromise, a creditor of a limited partnership who extends credit, or whose claim arises, after the filing of the certificate of limited partnership or an amendment thereto which, in either case, reflects the obligation, and before the amendment or cancellation thereof to reflect the compromise, may enforce the original obligation.

Commissioners' Comment

Although Section 17(1) of the prior uniform law required a partner to fulfill his promise to make contributions, the addition of contributions in the form of a promise to render services means that a partner who is unable to perform those services because of death or disability as well as because of an intentional default is required to pay the cash value of the services unless the certificate of limited partnership provides otherwise. Subdivision (b) is derived from Section 17(3) of the prior uniform law.

§ 503. Sharing of Profits and Losses

The profits and losses of a limited partnership shall be allocated among the partners, and among classes of partners, in the manner provided in the partnership agreement. If the partnership agreement does not so provide, profits and losses shall be allocated on the basis of the value (as stated in the certificate of limited partnership) of the contributions made by each partner to the extent they have been received by the partnership and have not been returned.

Commissioners' Comment

Section 503 is new. The prior uniform law did not provide for the basis on which partners share profits and losses in the absence of agreement.

§ 504. Sharing of Distributions

Distributions of cash or other assets of a limited partnership shall be allocated among the partners, and among classes of partners, in the manner provided in the partnership agreement. If the partnership agreement does not so provide, distributions shall be made on the basis of the value (as stated in the certificate of limited partnership) of the contributions made by each partner to the extent they have been received by the partnership and have not been returned.

Commissioners' Comment

Section 504 is new. The prior uniform law did not provide for the basis on which partners share distributions in the absence of agreement. This section also recognizes that partners may choose to share in distribution on a different basis than they share in profits and losses.

ARTICLE 6

DISTRIBUTIONS AND WITHDRAWAL

§ 601. Interim Distributions

Except as provided in this Article, a partner is entitled to receive distributions from a limited partnership before his withdrawal from the limited partnership and before the dissolution and winding up thereof:

(1) to the extent and at the times or upon the happening of the events specified in the partnership agreement; and

(2) if any distribution constitutes a return of any part of his contribution under Section 608(c), to the extent and at the times or upon the happening of the events specified in the certificate of limited partnership.

Commissioners' Comment

Section 601 is new.

§ 602. Withdrawal of General Partner

A general partner may withdraw from a limited partnership at any time by giving written notice to the other partners, but if the withdrawal violates the partnership agreement, the limited partnership may recover from the withdrawing general partner damages for breach of the partnership agreement and offset the damages against the amount otherwise distributable to him.

Commissioners' Comment

Section 602 is new but is generally derived from Section 38 of the Uniform Partnership Act.

§ 603. Withdrawal of Limited Partner

A limited partner may withdraw from a limited partnership at the time or upon the happening of events specified in the certificate of limited partnership and in accordance with the partnership agreement. If the certificate does not specify the time or the events upon the happening of which a limited partner may withdraw or a definite time for the dissolution and winding up of the limited partnership, a limited partner may withdraw upon not less than 6 months' prior written notice to each general partner at his address on the books of the limited partnership at its office in this State.

Commissioners' Comment

Section 603 is derived from Section 16(c) of the prior uniform law.

§ 604. Distribution Upon Withdrawal

Except as provided in this Article, upon withdrawal any withdrawing partner is entitled to receive any distribution to which he is entitled under the partnership agreement and, if not otherwise provided in the agreement, he is entitled to receive, within a reasonable time after withdrawal, the fair value of his interest in the limited partnership as of the date of withdrawal based upon his right to share in distributions from the limited partnership.

Commissioners' Comment

Section 604 is new. It fixes the distributive share of a withdrawing partner in the absence of an agreement among the partners.

§ 605. Distribution in Kind

Except as provided in the certificate of limited partnership, a partner, regardless of the nature of his contribution, has no right to demand and receive any distribution from a limited partnership in any form other than cash. Except as provided in the partnership agreement, a partner may not be compelled to accept a distribution of any asset in kind from a limited partnership to the extent that the percentage of the asset distributed to him exceeds a percentage of that asset which is equal to the percentage in which he shares in distributions from the limited partnership.

Commissioners' Comment

The first sentence of Section 605 is derived from Section 16(3) of the prior uniform law. The second sentence is new, and is intended to protect a limited partner (and the remaining partners) against a distribution in kind of more than his share of particular assets.

§ 606. Right to Distribution

At the time a partner becomes entitled to receive a distribution, he has the status of, and is entitled to all remedies available to, a creditor of the limited partnership with respect to the distribution.

Section 606 is new and is intended to make it clear that the right of a partner to receive a distribution, as between the partners, is not subject to the equity risks of the enterprise. On the other hand, since partners entitled to distributions have creditor status, there did not seem to be a need for the extraordinary remedy of Section 16(4)(a) of the prior uniform law, which granted a limited partner the right to seek dissolution of the partnership if he was unsuccessful in demanding the return of his contribution. It is more appropriate for the partner to simply sue as an ordinary creditor and obtain a judgment.

§ 607. Limitations on Distribution

A partner may not receive a distribution from a limited partnership to the extent that, after giving effect to the distribution, all liabilities of the limited partnership, other than liabilities to partners on account of their partnership interests, exceed the fair value of the partnership assets.

Section 607 is derived from Section 16(1)(a) of the prior uniform law.

§ 608. Liability Upon Return of Contribution

(a) If a partner has received the return of any part of his contribution without violation of the partnership agreement or this Act, he is liable to the limited partnership for a period of one year thereafter for the amount of the returned contribution, but only to the extent necessary to discharge the limited partnership's liabilities to creditors who extended credit to the limited partnership during the period the contribution was held by the partnership.

(b) If a partner has received the return of any part of his contribution in violation of the partnership agreement or this Act, he is liable to the limited partnership for a period of 6 years thereafter for the amount of the contribution wrongfully returned.

(c) A partner receives a return of his contribution to the extent that a distribution to him reduces his share of the fair value of the net assets of the limited partnership below the value (as set forth in the certificate of limited partnership) of his contribution which has not been distributed to him.

Paragraph (a) is derived from Section 17(4) of the prior uniform law, but the one-year statute of limitations has been added. Paragraph (b) is derived from Section 17(2)(b) of the prior uniform law but, again, a statute of limitations has been added. Paragraph (c) is new. The provisions of former Section 17(2) that referred to the partner holding as "trustee" any money or specific property wrongfully returned to him have been eliminated.

ARTICLE 7

ASSIGNMENT OF PARTNERSHIP INTERESTS

§ 701. Nature of Partnership Interest
A partnership interest is personal property.

§ 702. Assignment of Partnership Interest
Except as provided in the partnership agreement, a partnership interest is assignable in whole or in part. An assignment of a partnership interest does not dissolve a limited partnership or entitle the assignee to become or to exercise any rights of a partner. An assignment entitles the assignee to receive, to the extent assigned, only the distribution to which the assignor would be entitled. Except as provided in the partnership agreement, a partner ceases to be a partner upon assignment of all his partnership interest.

Commissioners' Comment

Section 19(1) of the prior uniform law provided simply that "a limited partner's interest is assignable", raising a question whether *any* limitations on the right of assignment were permitted. While the first sentence of Section 702 recognizes that the power to assign may be restricted in the partnership agreement, there was no intention to affect in any way the usual rules regarding restraints on alienation of personal property. The second and third sentences of Section 702 are derived from Section 19(3) of the prior uniform law. The last sentence is new.

§ 703. Rights of Creditor
On application to a court of competent jurisdiction by any judgment creditor of a partner, the court may charge the partnership interest of the partner with payment of the unsatisfied amount of the judgment with interest. To the extent so charged, the judgment creditor has only the rights of an assignee of the partnership interest. This Act does not deprive any partner of the benefit of any exemption laws applicable to his partnership interest.

Commissioners' Comment

Section 703 is derived from Section 22 of the prior uniform law but has not carried over some provisions that were thought to be superfluous. For example, references in Section 22(1) to specific remedies have been omitted, as has a prohibition in Section 22(2) against discharge of the lien with partnership property. Ordinary rules governing the remedies available to a creditor and the fiduciary obligations of general partners will determine those matters.

§ 704. Right of Assignee to Become Limited Partner
(a) An assignee of a partnership interest, including an assignee of a general partner, may become a limited partner if and to the

375

extent that (1) the assignor gives the assignee that right in accordance with authority described in the certificate of limited partnership, or (2) all other partners consent.

(b) An assignee who has become a limited partner has, to the extent assigned, the rights and powers, and is subject to the restrictions and liabilities, of a limited partner under the partnership agreement and this Act.   An assignee who becomes a limited partner also is liable for the obligations of his assignor to make and return contributions as provided in Article 6.   However, the assignee is not obligated for liabilities unknown to the assignee at the time he became a limited partner and which could not be ascertained from the certificate of limited partnership.

(c) If an assignee of a partnership interest becomes a limited partner, the assignor is not released from his liability to the limited partnership under Sections 207 and 502.

Commissioners' Comment

Section 704 is derived from Section 19 of the prior uniform law, but paragraph (b) defines more narrowly than Section 19 the obligations of the assignor that are automatically assumed by the assignee.

§ 705. Power of Estate of Deceased or Incompetent Partner

If a partner who is an individual dies or a court of competent jurisdiction adjudges him to be incompetent to manage his person or his property, the partner's executor, administrator, guardian, conservator, or other legal representative may exercise all of the partner's rights for the purpose of settling his estate or administering his property, including any power the partner had to give an assignee the right to become a limited partner.   If a partner is a corporation, trust, or other entity and is dissolved or terminated, the powers of that partner may be exercised by its legal representative or successor.

Commissioners' Comment

Section 705 is derived from Section 21(1) of the prior uniform law. Former Section 21(2), making a deceased limited partner's estate liable for his liabilities as a limited partner was deleted as superfluous, with no intention of changing the liability of the estate.

ARTICLE 8

DISSOLUTION

§ 801. Nonjudicial Dissolution

A limited partnership is dissolved and its affairs shall be wound up upon the happening of the first to occur of the following:

(1) at the time or upon the happening of events specified in the certificate of limited partnership;

376

(2) written consent of all partners;

(3) an event of withdrawal of a general partner unless at the time there is at least one other general partner and the certificate of limited partnership permits the business of the limited partnership to be carried on by the remaining general partner and that partner does so, but the limited partnership is not dissolved and is not required to be wound up by reason of any event of withdrawal if, within 90 days after the withdrawal, all partners agree in writing to continue the business of the limited partnership and to the appointment of one or more additional general partners if necessary or desired; or

(4) entry of a decree of judicial dissolution under Section 802.

Commissioners' Comment

Section 801 merely collects in one place all of the events causing dissolution. Paragraph (3) is derived from Sections 9(1)(g) and 20 of the prior uniform law, but adds the 90-day grace period.

§ 802. Judicial Dissolution

On application by or for a partner the [here designate the proper court] court may decree dissolution of a limited partnership whenever it is not reasonably practicable to carry on the business in conformity with the partnership agreement.

Commissioners' Comment

Section 802 is new.

§ 803. Winding Up

Except as provided in the partnership agreement, the general partners who have not wrongfully dissolved a limited partnership or, if none, the limited partners, may wind up the limited partnership's affairs; but the [here designate the proper court] court may wind up the limited partnership's affairs upon application of any partner, his legal representative, or assignee.

Commissioners' Comment

Section 803 is new and is derived in part from Section 37 of the Uniform General Partnership Act.

§ 804. Distribution of Assets

Upon the winding up of a limited partnership, the assets shall be distributed as follows:

(1) to creditors, including partners who are creditors, to the extent otherwise permitted by law, in satisfaction of liabilities of the limited partnership other than liabilities for distributions to partners under Section 601 or 604;

(2) except as provided in the partnership agreement, to partners and former partners in satisfaction of liabilities for distributions under Section 601 or 604; and

(3) except as provided in the partnership agreement, to partners *first* for the return of their contributions and *secondly* respecting their partnership interests, in the proportions in which the partners share in distributions.

Commissioners' Comment

Section 804 revises Section 23 of the prior uniform law by providing that (1) to the extent partners are also creditors, other than in respect of their interests in the partnership, they share with other creditors, (2) once the partnership's obligation to make a distribution accrues, it must be paid before any other distributions of an "equity" nature are made, and (3) general and limited partners rank on the same level except as otherwise provided in the partnership agreement.

ARTICLE 9

FOREIGN LIMITED PARTNERSHIPS

§ 901. Law Governing

Subject to the Constitution of this State, (1) the laws of the state under which a foreign limited partnership is organized govern its organization and internal affairs and the liability of its limited partners, and (2) a foreign limited partnership may not be denied registration by reason of any difference between those laws and the laws of this State.

Commissioners' Comment

Section 901 is new.

§ 902. Registration

Before transacting business in this State, a foreign limited partnership shall register with the Secretary of State. In order to register, a foreign limited partnership shall submit to the Secretary of State, in duplicate, an application for registration as a foreign limited partnership, signed and sworn to by a general partner and setting forth:

(1) the name of the foreign limited partnership and, if different, the name under which it proposes to register and transact business in this State;

(2) the state and date of its formation;

(3) the general character of the business it proposes to transact in this State;

(4) the name and address of any agent for service of process on the foreign limited partnership whom the foreign limited partnership elects to appoint; the agent must be an individual resi-

dent of this State, a domestic corporation, or a foreign corporation having a place of business in, and authorized to do business in this State;

(5) a statement that the Secretary of State is appointed the agent of the foreign limited partnership for service of process if no agent has been appointed under paragraph (4) or, if appointed, the agent's authority has been revoked or if the agent cannot be found or served with the exercise of reasonable diligence;

(6) the address of the office required to be maintained in the State of its organization by the laws of that State or, if not so required, of the principal office of the foreign limited partnership; and

(7) If the certificate of limited partnership filed in the foreign limited partnership's state of organization is not required to include the names and business addresses of the partners, a list of the names and addresses.

Commissioners' Comment

Section 902 is new. It was thought that requiring a full copy of the certificate of limited partnership and all amendments thereto to be filed in each state in which the partnership does business would impose an unreasonable burden on interstate limited partnerships and that the information on file was sufficient to tell interested persons where they could write to obtain copies of these basic documents.

§ 903. Issuance of Registration

(a) If the Secretary of State finds that an application for registration conforms to law and all requisite fees have been paid, he shall:

(1) endorse on the application the word "Filed", and the month, day, and year of the filing thereof;

(2) file in his office a duplicate original of the application; and

(3) issue a certificate of registration to transact business in this State.

(b) The certificate of registration, together with a duplicate original of the application, shall be returned to the person who filed the application or his representative.

§ 904. Name

A foreign limited partnership may register with the Secretary of State under any name (whether or not it is the name under which it is registered in its state of organization) that includes without abbreviation the words "limited partnership" and that could be registered by a domestic limited partnership.

Commissioners' Comment

Section 904 is new.

§ 905. Changes and Amendments

If any statement in the application for registration of a foreign limited partnership was false when made or any arrangements or other facts described have changed, making the application inaccurate in any respect, the foreign limited partnership shall promptly file in the office of the Secretary of State a certificate, signed and sworn to by a general partner, correcting such statement.

Commissioners' Comment

Section 905 is new.

§ 906. Cancellation of Registration

A foreign limited partnership may cancel its registration by filing with the Secretary of State a certificate of cancellation signed and sworn to by a general partner. A cancellation does not terminate the authority of the Secretary of State to accept service of process on the foreign limited partnership with respect to [claims for relief] [causes of action] arising out of the transactions of business in this State.

Commissioners' Comment

Section 906 is new.

§ 907. Transaction of Business Without Registration

(a) A foreign limited partnership transacting business in this State may not maintain any action, suit, or proceeding in any court of this State until it has registered in this State.

(b) The failure of a foreign limited partnership to register in this State does not impair the validity of any contract or act of the foreign limited partnership or prevent the foreign limited partnership from defending any action, suit, or proceeding in any court of this State.

(c) A limited partner of a foreign limited partnership is not liable as a general partner of the foreign limited partnership solely by reason of having transacted business in this State without registration.

(d) A foreign limited partnership, by transacting business in this State without registration, appoints the Secretary of State as its agent for service of process with respect to [claims for relief] [causes of action] arising out of the transaction of business in this State.

Commissioners' Comment

Section 907 is new.

380

§ 908. Action by [Appropriate Official]

The [appropriate official] may bring an action to restrain a foreign limited partnership from transacting business in this State in violation of this Article.

Commissioners' Comment

Section 908 is new.

ARTICLE 10

DERIVATIVE ACTIONS

§ 1001. Right of Action

A limited partner may bring an action in the right of a limited partnership to recover a judgment in its favor if general partners with authority to do so have refused to bring the action or if an effort to cause those general partners to bring the action is not likely to succeed.

Commissioners' Comment

Section 1001 is new.

§ 1002. Proper Plaintiff

In a derivative action, the plaintiff must be a partner at the time of bringing the action and (1) at the time of the transaction of which he complains or (2) his status as a partner had devolved upon him by operation of law or pursuant to the terms of the partnership agreement from a person who was a partner at the time of the transaction.

Commissioners' Comment

Section 1002 is new.

§ 1003. Pleading

In a derivative action, the complaint shall set forth with particularity the effort of the plaintiff to secure initiation of the action by a general partner or the reasons for not making the effort.

Commissioners' Comment

Section 1003 is new.

§ 1004. Expenses

If a derivative action is successful, in whole or in part, or if anything is received by the plaintiff as a result of a judgment, compromise, or settlement of an action or claim, the court may award the plaintiff reasonable expenses, including reasonable attorney's fees, and shall direct him to remit to the limited partnership the remainder of those proceeds received by him.

Commissioners' Comment

Section 1004 is new.

ARTICLE 11

MISCELLANEOUS

§ 1101. Construction and Application

This Act shall be so applied and construed to effectuate its general purpose to make uniform the law with respect to the subject of this Act among states enacting it.

§ 1102. Short Title

This Act may be cited as the Uniform Limited Partnership Act.

§ 1103. Severability

If any provision of this Act or its application to any person or circumstance is held invalid, the invalidity does not affect other provisions or applications of the Act which can be given effect without the invalid provision or application, and to this end the provisions of this Act are severable.

§ 1104. Effective Date, Extended Effective Date and Repeal

Except as set forth below, the effective date of this Act is _____ and the following Acts [list prior limited partnership acts] are hereby repealed:

(1) The existing provisions for execution and filing of certificates of limited partnerships and amendments thereunder and cancellations thereof continue in effect until [specify time required to create central filing system], the extended effective date, and Sections 102, 103, 104, 105, 201, 202, 203, 204 and 206 are not effective until the extended effective date.

(2) Section 402, specifying the conditions under which a general partner ceases to be a member of a limited partnership, is not effective until the extended effective date, and the applicable provisions of existing law continue to govern until the extended effective date.

(3) Sections 501, 502 and 608 apply only to contributions and distributions made after the effective date of this Act.

(4) Section 704 applies only to assignments made after the effective date of this Act.

(5) Article 9, dealing with registration of foreign limited partnerships, is not effective until the extended effective date.

§ 1105. Rules for Cases Not Provided for in This Act

In any case not provided for in this Act the provisions of the Uniform Partnership Act govern.

III. SECURITIES

A. SECURITIES ACT OF 1933

15 U.S.C.A. §§ 77a et seq.

Contents

TITLE I

Short Title

SECTION 1. This act may be cited as the Securities Act of 1933.

Definitions

SEC. 2. When used in this title, unless the context otherwise requires—

(1) the term "security" means any note, stock, treasury stock, bond, debenture, evidence of indebtedness, certificate of interest or participation in any profit-sharing agreement, collateral-trust certificate, preorganization certificate or subscription, transferable share, investment contract, voting-trust certificate, certificate of deposit for a security, fractional undivided interest in oil, gas, or other mineral rights, or, in general, any interest or instrument commonly known as a "security," or any certificate of interest or participation in, temporary or interim certificate for, receipt for, guarantee of, or warrant or right to subscribe to or purchase, any of the foregoing.

(2) The term "person" means an individual, a corporation, a partnership, an association, a joint-stock company, a trust, any unincorporated organization, or a government or political subdivision thereof. As used in this paragraph the term "trust" shall include only a trust where the interest or interests of the beneficiary or beneficiaries are evidenced by a security.

(3) The term "sale" or "sell" shall include every contract of sale or disposition of a security or interest in a security, for value. The term "offer to sell", "offer for sale", or "offer" shall include every attempt or offer to dispose of, or solicitation of an offer to buy, a security or interest in a security, for value. The terms defined in this paragraph and

the term "offer to buy" as used in subsection (c) of section 5 shall not include preliminary negotiations or agreements between an issuer (or any person directly or indirectly controlling or controlled by an issuer, or under direct or indirect common control with an issuer) and any underwriter or among underwriters who are or are to be in privity of contract with an issuer (or any person directly or indirectly controlling or controlled by an issuer, or under direct or indirect common control with an issuer). Any security given or delivered with, or as a bonus on account of, any purchase of securities or any other thing, shall be conclusively presumed to constitute a part of the subject of such purchase and to have been offered and sold for value. The issue or transfer of a right or privilege, when originally issued or transferred with a security, giving the holder of such security the right to convert such security into another security of the same issuer or of another person, or giving a right to subscribe to another security of the same issuer or of another person, which right cannot be exercised until some future date, shall not be deemed to be an offer or sale of such other security; but the issue or transfer of such other security upon the exercise of such right of conversion or subscription shall be deemed a sale of such other security.

(4) The term "issuer" means every person who issues or proposes to issue any security; except that with respect to certificates of deposit, voting-trust certificates, or collateral-trust certificates, or with respect to certificates of interest or shares in an unincorporated investment trust not having a board of directors (or persons performing similar functions) or of the fixed, restricted management, or unit type, the term "issuer" means the person or persons performing the acts and assuming the duties of depositor or manager pursuant to the provisions of the trust or other agreement or instrument under which such securities are issued; except that in the case of an unincorporated association which provides by its articles for limited liability of any or all of its members, or in the case of a trust, committee, or other legal entity, the trustees or members thereof shall not be individually liable as issuers of any security issued by the association, trust, committee, or other legal entity; except that

with respect to equipment-trust certificates or like securities, the term "issuer" means the person by whom the equipment or property is or is to be used; and except that with respect to fractional undivided interests in oil, gas, or other mineral rights, the term "issuer" means the owner of any such right or of any interest in such right (whether whole or fractional) who creates fractional interests therein for the purpose of public offering.

(5) The term "Commission" means the Federal Trade Commission.

(6) The term "Territory" means Puerto Rico, Canal Zone, the Virgin Islands, and the insular possessions of the United States.

(7) The term "interstate commerce" means trade or commerce in securities or any transportation or communication relating thereto among the several States or between the District of Columbia or any Territory of the United States and any State or other Territory, or between any foreign country and any State, Territory, or the District of Columbia, or within the District of Columbia.

(8) The term "registration statement" means the statement provided for in section 6, and includes any amendment thereto and any report, document, or memorandum filed as part of such statement or incorporated therein by reference.

(9) The term "write" or "written" shall include printed, lithographed, or any means of graphic communication.

(10) The term "prospectus" means any prospectus, notice, circular, advertisement, letter, or communication, written or by radio or television, which offers any security for sale or confirms the sale of any security; except that (a) a communication sent or given after the effective date of the registration statement (other than a prospectus permitted under subsection (b) of section 10) shall not be deemed a prospectus if it is proved that prior to or at the same time with such communication a written prospectus meeting the requirements of subsection (a) of section 10 at the time of such communication was sent or given to the person to whom the communication was made, and (b) a notice, circular, advertisement, letter, or communication in respect of a security shall not be deemed to be a prospectus if it states from whom a

written prospectus meeting the requirements of section 10 may be obtained and, in addition, does no more than identify the security, state the price thereof, state by whom orders will be executed, and contain such other information as the Commission, by rules or regulations deemed necessary or appropriate in the public interest and for the protection of investors, and subject to such terms and conditions as may be prescribed therein, may permit.[1]

(11) The term "underwriter" means any person who has purchased from an issuer with a view to, or offers or sells for an issuer in connection with, the distribution of any security, or participates or has a direct or indirect participation in any such undertaking, or participates or has a participation in the direct or indirect underwriting of any such undertaking; but such term shall not include a person whose interest is limited to a commission from an underwriter or dealer not in excess of the usual and customary distributors' or sellers' commission. As used in this paragraph the term "issuer" shall include, in addition to an issuer, any person directly or indirectly controlling or controlled by the issuer, or any person under direct or indirect common control with the issuer.

(12) The term "dealer" means any person who engages either for all or part of his time, directly or indirectly, as agent, broker, or principal, in the business of offering, buying, selling, or otherwise dealing or trading in securities issued by another person.

(13) The term "insurance company" means a company which is organized as an insurance company, whose primary and predominant business activity is the writing of insurance or the re-insuring of risks underwritten by insurance companies, and which is subject to supervision by the insurance commissioner, or a similar official or agency of a State or territory or the District of Columbia; or any receiver or similar official or any liquidating agent for such company, in his capacity as such.

(14) The term "separate account" means an account established and maintained by an insurance company pursuant to the laws of any State or territory of the United States, the District of Columbia, or of Canada or any province thereof, under which income, gains and losses, whether or not realized, from assets allocated to such account, are, in accordance with the applicable contract, credited to or charged against such account without regard to other income, gains or losses of the insurance company.

(15) The term "accredited investor" shall mean—

(i) a bank as defined in section 3(a)(2) of the Act whether acting in its individual or fiduciary capacity; an insurance company as defined in section 2(13) of the Act: an investment company registered under the Investment Company Act of 1940 or a business development company as defined in section 2(a)(48) of that Act; a Small Business Investment Company licensed by the Small Business Administration; or an employee benefit plan, including an individual retirement account, which is subject to the provisions of the Employee Retirement Income Security Act of 1974, if the investment decision is made by a plan fiduciary, as defined in section 3(21) of such Act, which is either a bank, insurance company, or registered investment adviser; or

(ii) any person who, on the basis of such factors as financial sophistication, net worth, knowledge and experience in financial matters, or amount of assets under management qualifies as an accredited investor under rules and regulations which the Commission shall prescribe.

Exempted Securities

Sec. 3. (a) Except as hereinafter expressly provided, the provisions of this title shall not apply to any of the following classes of securities:

(1) Any security which, prior to or within sixty days after the enactment of this title, has been sold or disposed of by the issuer or bona fide offered to the public, but this exemption shall not apply to any new offering of any such security by an issuer or underwriter subsequent to such sixty days;

(2) Any security issued or guaranteed by the United States or any territory thereof, or by the District of Columbia, or by any State of the United States, or by any political subdivision of a State or Territory, or by any public instru-

mentality of one or more States or Territories, or by any person controlled or supervised by and acting as an instrumentality of the Government of the United States pursuant to authority granted by the Congress of the United States; or any certificate of deposit for any of the foregoing; or any security issued or guaranteed by any bank; or any security issued by or representing an interest in or a direct obligation of a Federal Reserve bank; or any interest or participation in any common trust fund or similar fund maintained by a bank exclusively for the collective investment and reinvestment of assets contributed thereto by such bank in its capacity as trustee, executor, administrator, or guardian; or any security which is an industrial development bond (as defined in section 103(c)(2) of the Internal Revenue Code of 1954) the interest on which is excludable from gross income under section 103(a)(1) of such Code if, by reason of the application of paragraph (4) or (6) of section 103(c) of such Code (determined as if paragraphs (4)(A), (5), and (7) were not included in such section 103(c)), paragraph (1) of such section 103(c) does not apply to such security; or any interest or participation in a single trust fund, or in a collective trust fund maintained by a bank, or any security arising out of a contract issued by an insurance company, which interest, participation, or security is issued in connection with (A) a stock bonus, pension, or profit-sharing plan which meets the requirements for qualification under section 401 of the Internal Revenue Code of 1954, (B) an annuity plan which meets the requirements for the deduction of the employer's contributions under section 404(a)(2) of such Code, or (C) a governmental plan as defined in section 414(d) of such Code which has been established by an employer for the exclusive benefit of its employees or their beneficiaries for the purpose of distributing to such employees or their beneficiaries the corpus and income of the funds accumulated under such plan, if under such plan it is impossible, prior to the satisfaction of all liabilities with respect to such employees and their beneficiaries, for any part of the corpus or income to be used for, or diverted to, purposes other than the exclusive benefit of such employees or their beneficiaries, other than any plan described in clause (A),

(B), or (C) of this paragraph (i) the contributions under which are held in a single trust fund or in a separate account maintained by an insurance company for a single employer and under which an amount in excess of the employer's contribution is allocated to the purchase of securities (other than interests or participations in the trust or separate account itself) issued by the employer or any company directly or indirectly controlling, controlled by, or under common control with the employer, (ii) which covers employees some or all of whom are employees within the meaning of section 401(c)(1) of such Code, or (iii) which is a plan funded by an annuity contract described in section 403(b) of such Code. The Commission, by rules and regulations or order, shall exempt from the provisions of section 5 of this title any interest or participation issued in connection with a stock bonus, pension, profit-sharing, or annuity plan which covers employees some or all of whom are employees within the meaning of section 401(c)(1) of the Internal Revenue Code of 1954, if and to the extent that the Commission determines this to be necessary or appropriate in the public interest and consistent with the protection of investors and the purposes fairly intended by the policy and provisions of this title. For the purposes of this paragraph, a security issued or guaranteed by a bank shall not include any interest or particpation in any collective trust fund maintained by a bank; and the term "bank" means any national bank, or any banking institution organized under the laws of any State, territory, or the District of Columbia, the business of which is substantially confined to banking and is supervised by the State or territorial banking commission or similar official; except that in the case of a common trust fund or similar fund, or a collective trust fund, the term "bank" has the same meaning as in the Investment Company Act of 1940.

(3) Any note, draft, bill of exchange, or bankers' acceptance which arises out of a current transaction or the proceeds of which have been or are to be used for current transactions, and which has a maturity at the time of issuance of not exceeding nine months, exclusive of days of grace, or any

renewal thereof the maturity of which is likewise limited;

(4) Any security issued by a person organized and operated exclusively for religious, educational, benevolent, fraternal, charitable, or reformatory purposes and not for pecuniary profit, and no part of the net earnings of which inures to the benefit of any person, private stockholder, or individual;

(5) Any security issued (A) by a savings and loan association, building and loan association, cooperative bank, homestead association, or similar institution, which is supervised and examined by State or Federal authority having supervision over any such institution, except that the foregoing exemption shall not apply with respect to any such security where the issuer takes from the total amount paid or deposited by the purchaser, by way of any fee, cash value or other device whatsoever, either upon termination of the investment at maturity or before maturity, an aggregate amount in excess of 3 per centum of the face value of such security; or (B) by (i) a farmer's cooperative organization exempt from tax under section 521 of the Internal Revenue Code of 1954, (ii) a corporation described in section 501(c)(16) of such Code and exempt from tax under section 501(a) of such Code, or (iii) a corporation described in section 501(c)(2) of such Code which is exempt from tax under section 501(a) of such Code and is organized for the exclusive purpose of holding title to property, collecting income therefrom, and turning over the entire amount thereof, less expenses, to an organization or corporation described in clause (i) or (ii);

(6) Any security issued by a motor carrier the issuance of which is subject to the provisions of section 214 of the Interstate Commerce Act, or any interest in a railroad equipment trust. For purposes of this paragraph "interest in a railroad equipment trust" means any interest in an equipment trust, lease, conditional sales contract or other similar arrangement entered into, issued, assumed, guaranteed by, or for the benefit of, a common carrier to finance the acquisition of rolling stock, including motive power.

(7) Certificates issued by a receiver or by a trustee or debtor in possession in a case under title 11 of the United States Code, with the approval of the court;

(8) Any insurance or endowment policy or annuity contract or optional annuity contract, issued by a corporation subject to the supervision of the insurance commissioner, bank commissioner, or any agency or officer performing like functions, of any State or Territory of the United States or the District of Columbia;

(9) Except with respect to a security exchanged in a case under title 11 of the United States Code, any security exchanged by the issuer with its existing security holders exclusively where no commission or other remuneration is paid or given directly or indirectly for soliciting such exchange;

(10) Except with respect to a security exchanged in a case under title 11 of the United States Code, any security which is issued in exchange for one or more bona fide outstanding securities, claims or property interests, or partly in such exchange and partly for cash, where the terms and conditions of such issuance and exchange are approved, after a hearing upon the fairness of such terms and conditions at which all persons to whom it is proposed to issue securities in such exchange shall have the right to appear, by any court, or by any official or agency of the United States, or by any State or Territorial banking or insurance commission or other governmental authority expressly authorized by law to grant such approval;

(11) Any security which is a part of an issue offered and sold only to persons resident within a single State or Territory, where the issuer of such security is a person resident and doing business within, or, if a corporation, incorporated by and doing business within, such State or Territory.

(b) The Commission may from time to time by its rules and regulations, and subject to such terms and conditions as may be prescribed therein, add any class of securities to the securities exempted as provided in this section, if it finds that the enforcement of this title with respect to such securities is not necessary in the public interest and for the protection of investors by reason of the small amount involved or the limited character of the public offering; but no issue of securities shall be exempted under this subsection where the aggregate amount at which such issue is offered to the public exceeds $5,000,000.

(c) The Commission may from time to time by its rules and regulations and subject to such terms and conditions as may be prescribed therein, add to the securities exempted as provided in this section any class of securities issued by a small business investment company under the Small Business Investment Act of 1958 if it finds, having regard to the purposes of that Act, that the enforcement of this Act with respect to such securities is not necessary in the public interest and for the protection of investors.

Exempted Transactions

SEC. 4. The provisions of section 5 shall not apply to—

(1) transactions by any person other than an issuer, underwriter, or dealer.

(2) transactions by an issuer not involving any public offering.

(3) transactions by a dealer (including an underwriter no longer acting as an underwriter in respect of the security involved in such transaction), except—

    (A) transactions taking place prior to the expiration of forty days after the first date upon which the security was bona fide offered to the public by the issuer or by or through an underwriter,

    (B) transactions in a security as to which a registration statement has been filed taking place prior to the expiration of forty days after the effective date of such registration statement or prior to the expiration of forty days after the first date upon which the security was bona fide offered to the public by the issuer or by or through an underwriter after such effective date, whichever is later (excluding in the computation of such forty days any time during which a stop order issued under section 8 is in effect as to the security), or such shorter period as the Commission may specify by rules and regulations or order, and

    (C) transactions as to securities constituting the whole or a part of an unsold allotment to or subscription by such dealer as a participant in the distribution of such securities by the issuer or by or through an underwriter.

With respect to transactions referred to in clause (B), if securities of the issuer have not previously been sold pursuant to an earlier effective registration statement the applicable period, instead of forty days, shall be ninety days, or such shorter period as the Commission may specify by rules and regulations or order.

(4) brokers' transactions executed upon customers' orders on any exchange or in the over-the-counter market but not the solicitation of such orders.

(5)(A) Transactions involving offers or sales of one or more promissory notes directly secured by a first lien on a single parcel of real estate upon which is located a dwelling or other residential or commercial structure, and participation interests in such notes—

    (i) where such securities are originated by a savings and loan association, savings bank, commercial bank, or similar banking institution which is supervised and examined by a Federal or State authority, and are offered and sold subject to the following conditions:

        (a) the minimum aggregate sales price per purchaser shall not be less than $250,000;

        (b) the purchaser shall pay cash either at the time of the sale or within sixty days thereof; and

        (c) each purchaser shall buy for his own account only; or

    (ii) where such securities are originated by a mortgagee approved by the Secretary of Housing and Urban Development pursuant to sections 203 and 211 of the National Housing Act, and are offered or sold subject to the three conditions specified in subparagraph (A)(i) to any institution described in such subparagraph or to any insurance company subject to the supervision of the insurance commissioner, or any agency or officer performing like function, of any State or territory of the United States or the District of Columbia, or the Federal Home Loan Mortgage Corporation, the Federal National Mortgage Association, or the Government National Mortgage Association.

(B) Transactions between any of the entities described in subparagraph (A)(i) or (A)(ii) hereof involving non-assignable contracts to buy or sell the foregoing securities which are to be completed within two years, where the seller of the foregoing securities pursuant to any such contract is one of the parties described in subparagraph (A)(i) or (A)(ii) who may originate such securities and the purchaser of such securities pursuant to any such contract is any institution described in subparagraph (A)(i) or any insurance company described in subparagraph (A)(ii), the Federal Home Loan Mortgage Corporation, Federal National Mortgage Association, or the Government National Mortgage Association and where the foregoing securities are subject to the three conditions for sale set forth in subparagraphs (A)(i)(a) through (c).

(C) The exemption provided by subparagraphs (A) and (B) hereof shall not apply to resales of the securities acquired pursuant thereto, unless each of the conditions for sale contained in subparagraphs (A)(i)(a) through (c) are satisfied.

(6) transactions involving offers or sales by an issuer solely to one or more accredited investors, if the aggregate offering price of an issue of securities offered in reliance on this paragraph does not exceed the amount allowed under section 3(b) of this title, if there is no advertising or public solicitation in connection with the transaction by the issuer or anyone acting on the issuer's behalf and if the issuer files such notice with the Commission as the Commission shall prescribe.

Prohibitions Relating to Interstate Commerce and the Mails

SEC. 5. (a) Unless a registration statement is in effect as to a security, it shall be unlawful for any person, directly or indirectly—

(1) to make use of any means or instruments of transportation or communication in interstate commerce or of the mails to sell such security through the use or medium of any prospectus or otherwise; or

(2) to carry or cause to be carried through the mails or in interstate commerce, by any means or instruments of transportation, any such security for the purpose of sale or for delivery after sale.

(b) It shall be unlawful for any person, directly or indirectly—

(1) to make use of any means or instruments of transportation or communication in interstate commerce or of the mails to carry or transmit any prospectus relating to any security with respect to which a registration statement has been filed under this title, unless such prospectus meets the requirements of section 10; or

(2) to carry or cause to be carried through the mails or in interstate commerce any such security for the purpose of sale or for delivery after sale, unless accompanied or preceded by a prospectus that meets the requirements of subsection (a) of section 10.

(c) It shall be unlawful for any person, directly or indirectly, to make use of any means or instruments of transportation or communication in interstate commerce or of the mails to offer to sell or offer to buy through the use or medium of any prospectus or otherwise any security, unless a registration statement has been filed as to such security, or while the registration statement is the subject of a refusal order or stop order or (prior to the effective date of the registration statement) any public proceeding or examination under section 8.

Court Review of Orders

SEC. 9. (a) Any person aggrieved by an order of the Commission may obtain a review of such order in the Court of Appeals of the United States, within any circuit wherein such person resides or has his principal place of business, or in the United States Court of Appeals for the District of Columbia, by filing in such court, within sixty days after the entry of such order, a written petition praying that the order of the Commission be modified or be set aside in whole or in part. A copy of such petition shall be forthwith transmitted by the clerk of the court to the Commission, and thereupon the Commission shall file in the court the record upon which the order complained of was entered, as provided in section 2112 of title 28, United States Code. No objection to the order of the Commission shall be considered by the court unless such objection shall have been urged before the Commission. The finding of the Commission as to the facts, if supported by evidence, shall be conclusive. If either party shall apply to the court for leave to adduce additional evidence, and shall show to the satisfaction of the court that such additional evidence is material and that there were reasonable grounds for failure to adduce such evidence in the hearing before the Commission, the court may order such additional evidence to be taken before the Commission and to be adduced upon the hearing in such manner and upon such terms and conditions as to the court may seem proper. The Commission may modify its findings as to the facts by reason of the additional evidence so taken, and it shall file such modified or new findings, which, if supported by evidence, shall be conclusive, and its recommendation, if any, for the modification or setting aside of the original order. The jurisdiction of the court shall be exclusive and its judgment and decree, affirming, modifying, or setting aside, in whole or in part, any order of the Commission, shall be final, subject to review by the Supreme Court of the United States upon certiorari or certification as provided in sections 239 and 240 of the Judicial Code, as amended (U.S.C., title 28, secs. 346 and 347).

(b) The commencement of proceedings under subsection (a) shall not, unless specifically ordered by the court, operate as a stay of the Commission's order.

Information Required in Prospectus

Sec. 10. (a) Except to the extent otherwise permitted or required pursuant to this subsection or subsections (c), (d), or (e) —

(1) a prospectus relating to a security other than a security issued by a foreign government or political subdivision thereof, shall contain the information contained in the registration statement, but it need not include the documents referred to in paragraphs (28) to (32), inclusive, of Schedule A;

(2) a prospectus relating to a security issued by a foreign government or political subdivision thereof shall contain the information contained in the registration statement, but it need not include the documents referred to in paragraphs (13) and (14) of Schedule B;

(3) notwithstanding the provisions of paragraphs (1) and (2) of this subsection (a) when a prospectus is used more than nine months after the effective date of the registration statement, the information contained therein shall be as of a date not more than sixteen months prior to such use, so far as such information is known to the user of such prospectus or can be furnished by such user without unreasonable effort or expense;

(4) there may be omitted from any prospectus any of the information required under this subsection (a) which the Commission may by rules or regulations designate as not being necessary or appropriate in the public interest or for the protection of investors.

(b) In addition to the prospectus permitted or required in subsection (a), the Commission shall by rules or regulations deemed necessary or appropriate in the public interest or for the protection of investors permit the use of a prospectus for the purposes of subsection (b) (1) of section 5 which omits in part or summarizes information in the prospectus specified in subsection (a). A prospectus permitted under this subsection shall, except to the extent the Commission by rules or regulations deemed necessary or appropriate in the public interest or for the protection of investors otherwise provides, be filed as part of the registration statement but shall not be deemed a part of such registration statement for the purposes of section 11. The Commission may at any time issue an order preventing or suspending the use of a prospectus permitted under this subsection (b), if it has reason to believe that such prospectus has not been filed (if required to be filed as part of the registration statement) or includes any untrue statement of a material fact or omits to state any material fact required to be stated therein or necessary to make the statements therein, in the light of the circumstances under which such prospectus is or is to be used, not misleading. Upon issuance of an order under this subsection, the Commission shall give notice of the issuance of such order and opportunity for hearing by personal service or the sending of confirmed telegraphic notice. The Commission shall vacate or modify the order at any time for good cause or if such prospectus has been filed or amended in accordance with such order.

(c) Any prospectus shall contain such other information as the Commission may by rules or regulations require as being necessary or appropriate in the public interest or for the protection of investors.

(d) In the exercise of its powers under subsections (a), (b), or (c), the Commission shall have authority to classify prospectuses according to the nature and circumstances of their use or the nature of the security, issue, issuer, or otherwise, and, by rules and regulations and subject to such terms and conditions as it shall specify therein, to prescribe as to each class the form and contents which it may find appropriate and consistent with the public interest and the protection of investors.

(e) The statements or information required to be included in a prospectus by or under authority of subsections (a), (b), (c), or (d), when written, shall be placed in a conspicuous part of the prospectus and, except as otherwise permitted by rules or regulations, in type as large as that used generally in the body of the prospectus.

(f) In any case where a prospectus consists of a radio or television broadcast, copies thereof shall be filed with the Commission under such rules and regulations as it shall prescribe. The Commission may by rules and regulations require the filing with it of forms and prospectuses used in connection with the offer or sale of securities registered under this title.

Civil Liabilities on Account of False Registration Statement

SEC. 11. (a) In case any part of the registration statement, when such part became effective, contained an untrue statement of a material fact or omitted to state a material fact required to be stated therein or necessary to make the statements therein not misleading, any person acquiring such security (unless it is proved that at the time of such acquisition he knew of such untruth or omission) may, either at law or in equity, in any court of competent jurisdiction, sue—

(1) every person who signed the registration statement;

(2) every person who was a director of (or person performing similar functions) or partner in, the issuer at the time of the filing of the part of the registration statement with respect to which his liability is asserted;

(3) every person who, with his consent, is named in the registration statement as being or about to become a director, person performing similar functions, or partner;

(4) every accountant, engineer, or appraiser, or any person whose profession gives authority to a statement made by him, who has with his consent been named as having prepared or certified any part of the registration statement, or as having prepared or certified any report or valuation which is used in connection with the registration statement, with respect to the statement in such registration statement, report, or valuation, which purports to have been prepared or certified by him;

(5) every underwriter with respect to such security.

If such person acquired the security after the issuer has made generally available to its security holders an earning statement covering a period of at least twelve months beginning after the effective date of the registration statement, then the right of recovery under this subsection shall be conditioned on proof that such person acquired the security relying upon such untrue statement in the registration statement or relying upon the registration statement and not knowing of such omission, but such reliance may be established without proof of the reading of the registration statement by such person.

(b) Notwithstanding the provisions of subsection (a) no person, other than the issuer, shall be liable as provided therein who shall sustain the burden of proof—

(1) that before the effective date of the part of the registration statement with respect to which his liability is asserted (A) he had resigned from or had taken such steps as are permitted by law to resign from, or ceased or

refused to act in, every office, capacity, or relationship in which he was described in the registration statement as acting or agreeing to act, and (B) he had advised the Commission and the issuer in writing that he had taken such action and that he would not be responsible for such part of the registration statement; or

(2) that if such part of the registration statement became effective without his knowledge, upon becoming aware of such fact he forthwith acted and advised the Commission, in accordance with paragraph (1), and, in addition, gave reasonable public notice that such part of the registration statement had become effective without his knowledge; or

(3) that (A) as regards any part of the registration statement not purporting to be made on the authority of an expert, and not purporting to be a copy of or extract from a report or valuation of an expert, and not purporting to be made on the authority of a public official document or statement, he had, after reasonable investigation, reasonable ground to believe and did believe, at the time such part of the registration statement became effective, that the statements therein were true and that there was no omission to state a material fact required to be stated therein or necessary to make the statements therein not misleading; and (B) as regards any part of the registration statement purporting to be made upon his authority as an expert or purporting to be a copy of or extract from a report or valuation of himself as an expert, (i) he had, after reasonable investigation, reasonable ground to believe and did believe, at the time such part of the registration statement became effective, that the statements therein were true and that there was no omission to state a material fact required to be stated therein or necessary to make the statements therein not misleading, or (ii) such part of the registration statement did not fairly represent his statement as an expert or was not a fair copy of or extract from his report or valuation as an expert; and (C) as regards any part of the registration statement purporting to be made on the authority of an expert (other than himself) or purporting to be a copy of or extract from a report or valuation of an expert (other than himself), he had no reasonable ground to believe and did not believe, at the time such part of the registration statement became effective, that the statements therein were untrue or that there was an omission to state a material fact required to be stated therein or necessary to make the statements therein not misleading, or that such part of the registration statement did not fairly represent the statement of the expert or was not a fair copy of or extract from the report or valuation of the expert; and (D) as regards any part of the registration statement purporting to be a statement made by an official person or purporting to be a copy of or extract from a public official document, he had no reasonable ground to believe and did not believe, at the time such part of the registration statement became effective, that the statements therein were untrue, or that there was an omission to state a material fact required to be stated therein or necessary to make the statements therein not misleading, or that such part of the registration statement did not fairly represent the statement made by the official person or was not a fair copy of or extract from the public official document.

(c) In determining, for the purpose of paragraph (3) of subsection (b) of this section, what constitutes reasonable investigation and reasonable ground for belief, the standard of reasonableness shall be that required of a prudent man in the management of his own property.

(d) If any person becomes an underwriter with respect to the security after the part of the registration statement with respect to which his liability is asserted has become effective, then for the purposes of paragraph (3) of subsection (b) of this section such part of the registration statement shall be considered as having become effective with respect to such person as of the time when he became an underwriter.

(e) The suit authorized under subsection (a) may be to recover such damages as shall represent the difference between the amount paid for the security (not exceeding the price at which the security was offered to the public) and (1) the value thereof as of the time such suit was brought, or (2) the price at which such security shall have been disposed of in the market before suit, or (3) the price at which such security shall have been disposed of after suit but before judgment if such damages shall be less than the damages representing the difference between the amount paid for the security (not exceeding the price at which the security was offered to the public) and the value thereof as of the time such suit was brought: Provided, that if the defendant proves that any portion or all of such damages represents other than the depreciation in value of such security resulting from such part of the registration statement, with respect to which his liability is asserted, not being true or omitting to state a material fact required to be stated therein or necessary to make the statements therein not misleading, such portion of or all such damages shall not be recoverable. In no event shall any underwriter (unless such underwriter shall have knowingly received from the issuer for acting as an underwriter some benefit, directly or indirectly, in which all other underwriters similarly situated did not share in proportion to their respective interests in the underwriting) be liable in any suit or as a consequence of suits authorized under subsection (a) for damages in excess of the total price at which the securities underwritten by him and distributed to the public were offered to the public. In any suit under this or any other section of this title the court may, in its discretion, require an undertaking for the payment of the costs of such suit, including reasonable attorney's fees, and if judgment shall be rendered against a party litigant, upon the motion of the other party litigant, such costs may be assessed in favor of such party litigant (whether or not such undertaking has been required) if the court believes the suit or the defense to have been without merit, in an amount sufficient to reimburse him for the reasonable expenses incurred by him, in connection with such suit, such costs to be taxed in the manner usually provided for taxing of costs in the court in which the suit was heard.

(f) All or any one or more of the persons specified in subsection (a) shall be jointly and severally liable, and every person who becomes liable to make any payment under this section may recover contribution as in cases of contract from any person who, if sued separately, would have been liable to make the same payment, unless the person who has become liable was, and the other was not, guilty of fraudulent misrepresentation.

(g) In no case shall the amount recoverable under this section exceed the price at which the security was offered to the public.

Civil Liabilities Arising in Connection With Prospectuses and Communications.

SEC. 12. Any person who—

(1) offers or sells a security in violation of section 5, or

(2) offers or sells a security (whether or not exempted by the provisions of section 3, other than paragraph (2) of subsection (a) thereof), by the use of any means or instruments of transportation or communication in interstate commerce or of the mails, by means of a prospectus or oral communication, which includes an untrue statement of a material fact or omits to state a material fact necessary in order to make the statements, in the light of the circumstances under which they were made, not misleading (the purchaser not knowing of such untruth or omission), and who shall not sustain the burden of proof that he did not know, and in the exercise of reasonable care could not have known, of such untruth or omission,

shall be liable to the person purchasing such security from him, who may sue either at law or in equity in any court of competent jurisdiction, to recover the consideration paid for such security with interest thereon, less the amount of any income received thereon, upon the tender of such security, or for damages if he no longer owns the security.

Limitation of Actions

SEC. 13. No action shall be maintained to enforce any liability created under section 11 or section 12

(2) unless brought within one year after the discovery of the untrue statement or the omission, or after such discovery should have been made by the exercise of reasonable diligence, or, if the action is to enforce a liability created under section 12 (1), unless brought within one year after the violation upon which it is based. In no event shall any such action be brought to enforce a liability created under section 11 or section 12 (1) more than three years after the security was bona fide offered to the public, or under section 12 (2) more than three years after the sale.

Contrary Stipulations Void

SEC. 14. Any condition, stipulation, or provision binding any person acquiring any security to waive compliance with any provision of this title or of the rules and regulations of the Commission shall be void.

Liability of Controlling Persons

SEC. 15. Every person who, by or through stock ownership, agency, or otherwise, or who, pursuant to or in connection with an agreement or understanding with one or more other persons by or through stock ownership, agency, or otherwise, controls any person liable under section 11 or 12, shall also be liable jointly and severally with and to the same extent as such controlled person to any person to whom such controlled person is liable, unless the controlling person had no knowledge of or reasonable grounds to believe in the existence of the facts by reason of which the liability of the controlled person is alleged to exist.

Fraudulent Interstate Transactions

SEC. 17. (a) It shall be unlawful for any person in the offer or sale of any securities by the use of any means or instruments of transportation or communication in interstate commerce or by the use of the mails, directly or indirectly—

(1) to employ any device, scheme, or artifice to defraud, or

(2) to obtain money or property by means of any untrue statement of a material fact or any omission to state a material fact necessary in order to make the statements made, in the light of the circumstances under which they were made, not misleading, or

(3) to engage in any transaction, practice, or course of business which operates or would operate as a fraud or deceit upon the purchaser.

(b) It shall be unlawful for any person, by the use of any means or instruments of transportation or communication in interstate commerce or by the use of the mails, to publish, give publicity to, or circulate any notice, circular, advertisement, newspaper, article, letter, investment service, or communication which, though not purporting to offer a security for sale, describes such security for a consideration received or to be received, directly or indirectly, from an issuer, underwriter, or dealer, without fully disclosing the receipt, whether past or prospective, of such consideration and the amount thereof.

(c) The exemptions provided in section 3 shall not apply to the provisions of this section.

State Control of Securities

SEC. 18. Nothing in this title shall affect the jurisdiction of the securities commission (or any agency or office performing like functions) of any State or Territory of the United States, or the District of Columbia, over any security or any person.

Jurisdiction of Offenses and Suits

SEC. 22. (a) The district courts of the United States, the United States courts of any Territory, and the United States District Court for the District of Columbia shall have jurisdiction of offenses and violations under this title and under the rules and regulations promulgated by the Commission in respect thereto, and concurrent with State and Territorial courts, of all suits in equity and actions at law brought to enforce any liability or duty created by this title. Any such suit or action may be brought in the district wherein the defendant is found or is an inhabitant or transacts business, or in the district where the offer or sale took place, if the defendant participated therein, and process in such cases may be served in any other district of which the defendant is an inhabitant or wherever the defendant may be found. Judgments and decrees so rendered shall be subject to review as provided in sections 128 and 240 of the Judicial Code, as amended (U. S. C., title 28, secs. 225 and 347). No case arising under this title and brought in any State court of competent jurisdiction shall be removed to any court of the United States. No costs shall be assessed for or against the Commission in any proceeding under this title brought by or against it in the Supreme Court or such other courts.

(b) In case of contumacy or refusal to obey a subpena issued to any person, any of the said United States courts, within the jurisdiction of which said person guilty of contumacy or refusal to obey is found or resides, upon application by the Commission may issue to such person an order requiring such person to appear before the Commission, or one of its examiners designated by it, there to produce documentary evidence if so ordered, or there to give evidence touching the matter in question; and any failure to obey such order of the court may be punished by said court as a contempt thereof.

Schedule A

(1) The name under which the issuer is doing or intends to do business;

(2) the name of the State or other sovereign power under which the issuer is organized;

(3) the location of the issuer's principal business office, and if the issuer is a foreign or territorial person, the name and address of its agent in the United States authorized to receive notice;

(4) the names and addresses of the directors or persons performing similar functions, and the chief executive, financial and accounting officers, chosen or to be chosen if the issuer be a corporation, association, trust, or other entity; of all partners, if the issuer be a partnership; and of the issuer, if the issuer be an individual; and of the promoters in the case of a business to be formed, or formed within two years prior to the filing of the registration statement;

(5) the names and addresses of the underwriters;

(6) the names and addresses of all persons, if any, owning of record or beneficially, if known, more than 10 per centum of any class of stock of the issuer, or more than 10 per centum in the aggregate of the outstanding stock of the issuer as of a date within twenty days prior to the filing of the registration statement;

(7) the amount of securities of the issuer held by any person specified in paragraphs (4), (5), and (6) of this schedule, as of a date within twenty days prior to the filing of the registration statement, and, if possible, as of one year prior thereto, and the amount of the securities, for which the registration statement is filed, to which such persons have indicated their intention to subscribe;

(8) the general character of the business actually transacted or to be transacted by the issuer;

(9) a statement of the capitalization of the issuer, including the authorized and outstanding amounts of its capital stock and the proportion thereof paid up, the number and classes of shares in which such capital stock is divided, par value thereof, or if it has no par value, the stated or assigned value thereof, a description of the respective voting rights, preferences, conversion and exchange rights, rights to dividends, profits, or capital of each class, with respect to each other class, including the retirement and liquidation rights or values thereof;

(10) a statement of the securities, if any, covered by options outstanding or to be created in connection with the security to be offered, together with the names and addresses of all persons, if any, to be allotted more than 10 per centum in the aggregate of such options;

(11) the amount of capital stock of each class issued or included in the shares of stock to be offered;

(12) the amount of the funded debt outstanding and to be created by the security to be offered, with a brief description of the date, maturity, and character of such debt, rate of interest, character of amortization provisions, and the security, if any, therefor. If substitution of any security is permissible, a summarized statement of the conditions under which such substitution is permitted.

If substitution is permissible without notice, a specific statement to that effect;

(13) the specific purposes in detail and the approximate amounts to be devoted to such purposes, so far as determinable, for which the security to be offered is to supply funds, and if the funds are to be raised in part from other sources, the amounts thereof and the sources thereof, shall be stated;

(14) the remuneration, paid or estimated to be paid, by the issuer or its predecessor, directly or indirectly, during the past year and ensuing year, to (a) the directors or persons performing similar functions, and (b) its officers and other persons, naming them wherever such remuneration exceeded $25,000 during any such year;

(15) the estimated net proceeds to be derived from the security to be offered;

(16) the price at which it is proposed that the security shall be offered to the public or the method by which such price is computed and any variation therefrom at which any portion of such security is proposed to be offered to any persons or classes of persons, other than the underwriters, naming them or specifying the class. A variation in price may be proposed prior to the date of the public offering of the security, but the Commission shall immediately be notified of such variation;

(17) all commissions or discounts paid or to be paid, directly or indirectly, by the issuer to the underwriters in respect of the sale of the security to be offered. Commissions shall include all cash, securities, contracts, or anything else of value, paid, to be set aside, disposed of, or understandings with or for the benefit of any other persons in which any underwriter is interested, made, in connection with the sale of such security. A commission paid or to be paid in connection with the sale of such security by a person in which the issuer has an interest or which is controlled or directed by, or under common control with, the issuer shall be deemed to have been paid by the issuer. Where any such commission is paid the amount of such commission paid to each underwriter shall be stated;

(18) the amount or estimated amounts, itemized in reasonable detail, of expenses, other than commissions specified in paragraph (17) of this schedule, incurred or borne by or for the account of the issuer in connection with the sale of the security to be offered or properly chargeable thereto, including legal, engineering, certification, authentication, and other charges;

(19) the net proceeds derived from any security sold by the issuer during the two years preceding the filing of the registration statement, the price at which such security was offered to the public, and the names of the principal underwriters of such security;

(20) any amount paid within two years preceding the filing of the registration statement or intended to be paid to any promoter and the consideration for any such payment;

(21) the names and addresses of the vendors and the purchase price of any property, or goodwill, acquired or to be acquired, not in the ordinary course of business, which is to be defrayed in whole or in part from the proceeds of the security to be offered, the amount of any commission payable to any person in connection with such acquisition, and the name or names of such person or persons, together with any expense incurred or to be incurred in connection with such acquisition, including the cost of borrowing money to finance such acquisition;

(22) full particulars of the nature and extent of the interest, if any, of every director, principal executive officer, and of every stockholder holding more than 10 per centum of any class of stock or more than 10 per centum in the aggregate of the stock of the issuer, in any property acquired, not in the ordinary course of business of the issuer, within two years preceding the filing of the registration statement or proposed to be acquired at such date;

(23) the names and addresses of counsel who have passed on the legality of the issue;

(24) dates of and parties to, and the general effect concisely stated of every material contract made, not in the ordinary course of business, which contract is to be executed in whole or in part at or after the filing of the registration statement or which contract has been made not more than two years before such filing. Any management contract or contract providing for special bonuses

or profit-sharing arrangements, and every material patent or contract for a material patent right, and every contract by or with a public utility company or an affiliate thereof, providing for the giving or receiving of technical or financial advice or service (if such contract may involve a charge to any party thereto at a rate in excess of $2,500 per year in cash or securities or anything else of value), shall be deemed a material contract;

(25) a balance sheet as of a date not more than ninety days prior to the date of the filing of the registration statement showing all of the assets of the issuer, the nature and cost thereof, whenever determinable, in such detail and in such form as the Commission shall prescribe (with intangible items segregated), including any loan in excess of $20,000 to any officer, director, stockholder or person directly or indirectly controlling or controlled by the issuer, or person under direct or indirect common control with the issuer. All the liabilities of the issuer in such detail and such form as the Commission shall prescribe, including surplus of the issuer showing how and from what sources such surplus was created, all as of a date not more than ninety days prior to the filing of the registration statement. If such statement be not certified by an independent public or certified accountant, in addition to the balance sheet required to be submitted under this schedule, a similar detailed balance sheet of the assets and liabilities of the issuer, certified by an independent public or certified accountant, of a date not more than one year prior to the filing of the registration statement, shall be submitted;

(26) a profit and loss statement of the issuer showing earnings and income, the nature and source thereof, and the expenses and fixed charges in such detail and such form as the Commission shall prescribe for the latest fiscal year for which such statement is available and for the two preceding fiscal years, year by year, or, if such issuer has been in actual business for less than three years, then for such time as the issuer has been in actual business, year by year. If the date of the filing of the registration statement is more than six months after the close of the last fiscal year, a statement from such closing date to the latest practicable date. Such statement shall show what the practice of the issuer has been during the three years or lesser period as to the character of the charges, dividends or other distributions made against its various surplus accounts, and as to depreciation, depletion, and maintenance charges, in such detail and form as the Commission shall prescribe, and if stock dividends or avails from the sale of rights have been credited to income, they shall be shown separately with a statement of the basis upon which the credit is computed. Such statement shall also differentiate between any recurring and nonrecurring income and between any investment and operating income. Such statement shall be certified by an independent public or certified accountant;

(27) if the proceeds, or any part of the proceeds, of the security to be issued is to be applied directly or indirectly to the purchase of any business, a profit and loss statement of such business certified by an independent public or certified accountant, meeting the requirements of paragraph (26) of this schedule, for the three preceding fiscal years, together with a balance sheet, similarly certified, of such business, meeting the requirements of paragraph (25) of this schedule of a date not more than ninety days prior to the filing of the registration statement or at the date such business was acquired by the issuer if the business was acquired by the issuer more than ninety days prior to the filing of the registration statement;

(28) a copy of any agreement or agreements (or, if identic agreements are used, the forms thereof) made with any underwriter, including all contracts and agreements referred to in paragraph (17) of this schedule;

(29) a copy of the opinion or opinions of counsel in respect to the legality of the issue, with a translation of such opinion, when necessary, into the English language;

(30) a copy of all material contracts referred to in paragraph (24) of this schedule, but no disclosure shall be required of any portion of any such contract if the Commission determines that disclosure of such portion would impair the value

of the contract and would not be necessary for the protection of the investors;

(31) unless previously filed and registered under the provisions of this title, and brought up to date, (a) a copy of its articles of incorporation, with all amendments thereof and of its existing bylaws or instruments corresponding thereto, whatever the name, if the issuer be a corporation; (b) copy of all instruments by which the trust is created or declared, if the issuer is a trust; (c) a copy of its articles of partnership or association and all other papers pertaining to its organization, if the issuer is a partnership, unincorporated association, joint-stock company, or any other form of organization; and

(32) a copy of the underlying agreements or indentures affecting any stock, bonds, or debentures offered or to be offered.

In case of certificates of deposit, voting trust certificates, collateral trust certificates, certificates of interest or shares in unincorporated investment trusts, equipment trust certificates, interim or other receipts for certificates, and like securities, the Commission shall establish rules and regulations requiring the submission of information of a like character applicable to such cases, together with such other information as it may deem appropriate and necessary regarding the character, financial or otherwise, of the actual issuer of the securities and/or the person performing the acts and assuming the duties of depositor or manager.

B. SELECTED SEC RULES AND FORMS UNDER THE SECURITIES ACT OF 1933

17 C.F.R. § 230.—1

Contents

GENERAL

GENERAL

* * *

Rule 144. Persons Deemed Not to Be Engaged in a Distribution and Therefore Not Underwriters

Preliminary Note to Rule 144

Rule 144 is designed to implement the fundamental purposes of the Act, as expressed in its preamble, "To provide full and fair disclosure of the character of the securities sold in interstate commerce and through the mails, and to prevent fraud in the sale thereof . . ." The rule is designed to prohibit the creation of public markets in securities of issuers concerning which adequate current information is not available to the public. At the same time, where adequate current information concerning the issuer is available to the public, the rule permits the public sale in ordinary trading transactions of limited amounts of securities owned by persons controlling, controlled by or under common control with the issuer and by persons who have acquired restricted securities of the issuer.

Certain basic principles are essential to an understanding of the requirement of registration in the Act:

1. If any person utilizes the jurisdictional means to sell any non-exempt security to any other person, the security must be registered unless a statutory exemption can be found for the transaction.

2. In addition to the exemptions found in Section 3, four exemptions applicable to transactions in securities are contained in Section 4. Three of these Section 4 exemptions are clearly not available to anyone acting as an "underwriter" of securities. (The fourth, found in Section 4(4), is available only to those who act as brokers under certain limited circumstances.) An understanding of the term "underwriter" is therefore important to anyone who wishes to determine whether or not an exemption from registration is available for his sale of securities.

The term underwriter is broadly defined in Section 2(11) of the Act to mean any person who has purchased from an issuer with a view to, or offers or sells for an issuer in connection with, the distribution of any security, or participates or has a direct or indirect participation in any such undertaking, or participates or has a participation in the direct or indirect underwriting of any such undertaking. The interpretation of this definition has traditionally focused on the words "with a view to" in the phrase "purchased from an issuer with a view to . . . distribution." Thus, an investment banking firm which arranges with an issuer for the public sale of its securities is clearly an "underwriter" under that Section. Individual investors who are not professionals in the securities business may also be "underwriters" within the meaning of that term as used in the Act if they act as links in a chain of transactions through which securities move from an issuer to the public. Since it is difficult to ascertain the mental state of the purchaser at the time of his acquisition, subsequent acts and circumstances have been considered to determine whether such person took with a view to distribution at the time of his acquisition. Emphasis has been placed on factors such as the length of time the person has held the securities and whether there has been an unforeseeable change in circumstances of the holder. Experience has shown, however, that reliance upon such factors as the above has not assured adequate protection of investors through the maintenance of informed trading markets and has led to uncertainty in the application of the registration provisions of the Act.

It should be noted that the statutory language of Section 2(11) is in the disjunctive. Thus, it is insufficient to conclude that a person is not an underwriter solely because he did not purchase securities from an issuer with a view to their distribution. It must also be established that the person is not offering or selling for an issuer in connection with the distribution of the securities, does not participate or have a direct or indirect participation in any such undertaking, and does not participate or have a participation in the direct or indirect underwriting of such an undertaking.

In determining when a person is deemed not to be engaged in a distribution several factors must be considered.

First, the purpose and underlying policy of the Act to protect investors requires that there be adequate current information concerning the issuer, whether the resales of securities by persons result in a distribution or are effected in trading transactions. Accordingly, the availability of the rule is conditioned on the existence of adequate current public information.

Secondly, a holding period prior to resale is essential, among other reasons, to assure that those persons who buy under a claim of a Section 4(2) exemption have assumed the economic risks of investment, and therefore are not acting as conduits for sale to the public of unregistered securities, directly or indirectly, on behalf of an issuer. It should be noted that there is nothing in Section 2(11) which places a time limit on a person's status as an underwriter. The public has the same need for protection afforded by registration whether the securities are distributed shortly after their purchase or after a considerable length of time.

A third factor, which must be considered in determining what is deemed not to constitute a "distribution," is the impact of the particular transaction or transactions on the trading markets. Section 4(1) was intended to exempt only routine trading transactions between individual investors with respect to securities already issued and not to exempt distributions by issuers or acts of other individuals who engage in steps necessary to such distributions. Therefore, a person reselling securities under Section 4(1) of the Act must sell the securities in such limited quantities and in such a manner as not to disrupt the trading markets. The larger the amount of securities involved, the more likely it is that such resales may involve methods of offering and amounts of compensation usually associated with a distribution rather than routine trading transac-

tions. Thus, solicitation of buy orders or the payment of extra compensation are not permitted by the rule.

In summary, if the sale in question is made in accordance with *all* of the provisions of the rule, as set forth below, any person who sells restricted securities shall be deemed not to be engaged in a distribution of such securities and therefore not an underwriter thereof. The rule also provides that any person who sells restricted or other securities on behalf of a person in a control relationship with the issuer shall be deemed not to be engaged in a distribution of such securities and therefore not to be an underwriter thereof, if the sale is made in accordance with *all* the conditions of the rule.

Rule 144.

(a) *Definitions.* The following definitions shall apply for the purposes of this rule.

(1) An "affiliate" of an issuer is a person that directly, or indirectly through one or more intermediaries, controls, or is controlled by, or is under common control with, such issuer.

(2) The term "person" when used with reference to a person for whose account securities are to be sold in reliance upon this rule includes, in addition to such person, all of the following persons:

(A) Any relative or spouse of such person, or any relative of such spouse, any one of whom has the same home as such person;

(B) Any trust or estate in which such person or any of the persons specified in (A) collectively own ten percent or more of the total beneficial interest or of which any of such persons serve as trustee, executor or in any similar capacity; and

(C) Any corporation or other organization (other than the issuer) in which such person or any of the persons specified in (A) are the beneficial owners collectively of ten percent or more of any class of equity securities or ten percent or more of the equity interest.

(3) The term restricted securities means securities that are acquired directly or indirectly from the issuer, or from an affiliate of the is-

suer, in a transaction or chain of transactions not involving any public offering, or securities acquired from the issuer that are subject to the resale limitations of Regulation D under the Act, or securities that are subject to the resale limitations of Regulation D and are acquired in a transaction or chain of transactions not involving any public offering.

(b) *Conditions to be Met.* Any affiliate or other person who sells restricted securities of an issuer for his own account, or any person who sells restricted or any other securities for the account of an affiliate of the issuer of such securities, shall be deemed not to be engaged in a distribution of such securities and therefore not to be an underwriter thereof within the meaning of Section 2(11) of the Act if all of the conditions of this rule are met.

(c) *Current Public Information.* There shall be available adequate current public information with respect to the issuer of the securities. Such information shall be deemed to be available only if either of the following conditions is met:

(1) *Filing of Reports.* The issuer has securities registered pursuant to Section 12 of the Securities Exchange Act of 1934, has been subject to the reporting requirements of Section 13 of that Act for a period of at least 90 days immediately preceding the sale of the securities and has filed all the reports required to be filed thereunder during the 12 months preceding such sale (or for such shorter period that the issuer was required to file such reports); or has securities registered pursuant to the Securities Act of 1933, has been subject to the reporting requirements of Section 15(d) of the Securities Exchange Act of 1934 for a period of at least 90 days immediately preceding the sale of the securities and has filed all the reports required to be filed thereunder during the 12 months preceding such sale (or for such shorter period that the issuer was required to file such reports). The person for whose account the securities are to be sold shall be entitled to rely upon a statement in whichever is the most recent report, quarterly or annual, required to be filed and filed by the issuer that such issuer has filed all reports required to be filed by Section 13 or 15(d) of the Securities Exchange Act of 1934 during the preceding 12

months (or for such shorter period that the issuer was required to file such reports) and has been subject to such filings requirements for the past 90 days, unless he knows or has reason to believe that the issuer has not complied with such requirements. Such person shall also be entitled to rely upon a written statement from the issuer that it has complied with such reporting requirements unless he knows or has reason to believe that the issuer has not complied with such requirements.

(2) *Other Public Information.* If the issuer is not subject to Section 13 or 15(d) of the Securities Exchange Act of 1934, there is publicly available the information concerning the issuer specified in clauses (1) to (14), inclusive, and clause (16) of paragraph (a)(4) of Rule 15c2–11 under that Act or, if the issuer is an insurance company, the information specified in Section 12(g)(2)(G)(i) of that Act.

(d) *Holding Period for Restricted Securities.* If the securities sold are restricted securities, the following provisions apply:

(1) *General Rule.* The person for whose account the securities are sold shall have been the beneficial owner of the securities for a period of at least two years prior to the sale and, if the securities were purchased, the full purchase price or other consideration shall have been paid or given at least two years prior to the sale.

(2) *Promissory Notes, Other Obligations or Installment Contracts.* Giving the person from whom the securities were purchased a promissory note or other obligation to pay the purchase price, or entering into an installment purchase contract with such person, shall not be deemed full payment of the purchase price unless the promissory note, obligation or contract—

(A) provides for full recourse against the purchaser of the securities;

(B) is secured by collateral, other than the securities purchased, having a fair market value at least equal to the purchase price of the securities purchased; and

(C) shall have been discharged by payment in full prior to the sale of the securities.

(3) *Short Sales, Puts or Other Options to Sell Securities.* In computing the two-year holding period the following periods shall be excluded:

(A) If the securities sold are equity securities, there shall be excluded any period during which the person for whose account they are sold had a short position in, or any put or other option to dispose of, any equity securities of the same class or any securities convertible into securities of such class; and

(B) If the securities sold are nonconvertible debt securities, there shall be excluded any period during which the person for whose account they are sold had a short position in, or any put or other option to dispose of, any nonconvertible debt securities of the same issuer.

(4) *Determination of Holding Period.* The following provisions shall apply for the purpose of determining the period securities have been held:

(A) *Stock Dividends, Splits and Recapitalizations.* Securities acquired from the issuer as a dividend or pursuant to a stock split, reverse split or recapitalization shall be deemed to have been acquired at the same time as the securities on which the dividend or, if more than one, the initial dividend was paid, the securities involved in the split or reverse split, or the securities surrendered in connection with the recapitalization;

(B) *Conversions.* If the securities sold were acquired from the issuer for a consideration consisting solely of other securities of the same issuer surrendered for conversion, the securities so acquired shall be deemed to have been acquired at the same time as the securities surrendered for conversion;

(C) *Contingent Issuance of Securities.* Securities acquired as a contingent payment of the purchase price of an equity interest in a business, or the assets of a business, sold to the issuer or an affiliate of the issuer shall be deemed to have been acquired at the time of such sale if the issuer or affiliate was then committed to issue the

securities subject only to conditions other than the payment of further consideration for such securities. An agreement entered into in connection with any such purchase to remain in the employment of, or not to compete with, the issuer or affiliate or the rendering of services pursuant to such agreement shall not be deemed to be the payment of further consideration for such securities.

(D) *Pledged Securities.* Securities which are bona fide pledged by any person other than the issuer when sold by the pledgee, or by a purchaser, after a default in the obligation secured by the pledge, shall be deemed to have been acquired when they were acquired by the pledgor, except that if the securities were pledged without recourse they shall be deemed to have been acquired by the pledgee at the time of the pledge or by the purchaser at the time of purchase.

> *Note.* Securities sold by the pledgee shall be aggregated with those sold by the pledgor, as provided in paragraph (e)(3)(B) below.

(E) *Gifts of Securities.* Securities acquired from any person, other than the issuer, by gift shall be deemed to have been acquired by the donee when they were acquired by the donor;

> *Note.* Securities sold by the donee shall be aggregated with those sold by the donor, as provided in paragraph (e) (3)(C) below.

(F) *Trusts.* Securities acquired from the settlor of a trust by the trust or acquired from the trust by the beneficiaries thereof shall be deemed to have been acquired when they were acquired by the settlor;

> *Note.* Securities sold by the trust shall be aggregated with those sold by the settlor of the trust, as provided in paragraph (e)(3)(D) below.

(G) *Estates.* Securities held by the estate of a deceased person or acquired from such an estate by the beneficiaries thereof shall be deemed to have been acquired when they were acquired by the deceased person, except that no holding period is required if the estate is not an affiliate of the issuer or if the securities are sold by a beneficiary of the estate who is not such an affiliate.

Notes. 1. Securities sold by the estate shall be aggregated with those sold by the deceased person, as provided in paragraph (e)(3)(E) below, if the estate is an affiliate of the issuer.

2. While there is no holding period or amount limitation for estates and beneficiaries thereof which are not affiliates of the issuer, paragraphs. (c), (f), (g), (h) and (i) of the rule apply to securities sold by such persons in reliance upon the rule.

(e) *Limitation on Amount of Securities Sold.* Except as hereinafter provided, the amount of securities which may be sold in reliance upon this rule shall be determined as follows:

(1) *Sales by Affiliates.* If restricted or other securities are sold for the account of an affiliate of the issuer, the amount of securities sold, together with all sales of restricted and other securities of the same class for the account of such person within the preceding three months, shall not exceed the greater of (i) one percent of the shares or other units of the class outstanding as shown by the most recent report or statement published by the issuer, or (ii) the average weekly volume of trading in such securities reported on all national securities exchanges and/or reported through the automated quotation system of a registered securities association during the four calendar weeks preceding the filing of the notice required by paragraph (h), or, if no such notice is required, the date of receipt of the order to execute the transaction by the broker or the date of execution of the transaction directly with a market maker, or (iii) the average weekly volume of trading in such securities reported through the consolidated transaction reporting system contemplated by Rule 17a–15 under the Securities Exchange Act of 1934 during the four-week period specified in subdivision (ii) of this subparagraph.

(2) *Sales by Persons Other than Affiliates.* The amount of restricted securities sold for the account of any person other than an affiliate of

the issuer, together with all other sales of restricted securities of the same class for the account of such person within the preceding three months, shall not exceed the amount specified in paragraphs (e)(1)(i), (1)(ii) or (1)(iii) of this section, whichever is applicable unless the conditions in paragraph (k) of this rule are satisfied.

(3) *Determination of Amount.* For the purpose of determining the amount of securities specified in paragraphs (e)(1) and (2) of this rule, the following provisions shall apply:

(i) Where both convertible securities and securities of the class into which they are convertible are sold, the amount of convertible securities sold shall be deemed to be the amount of securities of the class into which they are convertible for the purpose of determining the aggregate amount of securities of both classes sold;

(ii) The amount of securities sold for the account of a pledgee thereof, or for the account of a purchaser of the pledged securities, during any period of three months within two years after a default in the obligation secured by the pledge, and the amount of securities sold during the same three-month period for the account of the pledgor shall not exceed, in the aggregate, the amount specified in subparagraph (1) or (2) of this paragraph, whichever is applicable;

(iii) The amount of securities sold for the account of a donee thereof during any period of three months within two years after the donation, and the amount of securities sold during the same three-month period for the account of the donor, shall not exceed, in the aggregate, the amount specified in subparagraph (1) or (2) of this paragraph, whichever is applicable;

(iv) Where securities were acquired by a trust from the settlor of the trust, the amount of such securities sold for the account of the trust during any period of three months within two years after the acquisition of the securities by the trust, and the amount of securities sold during the same three-month period for the account of the settlor, shall not exceed, in the aggregate, the amount specified in subparagraph (1) or (2) of this paragraph, whichever is applicable;

(v) The amount of securities sold for the account of the estate of a deceased person, or for the account of a beneficiary of such estate, during any period of three months and the amount of securities sold during the same period for the account of the deceased person prior to his death shall not exceed, in the aggregate, the amount specified in subparagraph (1) or (2) of this paragraph, whichever is applicable, *Provided*, That no limitation on amount shall apply if the estate or beneficiary thereof is not an affiliate of the issuer;

(vi) When two or more affiliates or other persons agree to act in concert for the purpose of selling securities of an issuer, all securities of the same class sold for the account of all such persons during any period of three months shall be aggregated for the purpose of determining the limitation on the amount of securities sold;

(vi) Securities sold pursuant to an effective registration statement under the Act or pursuant to an exemption provided by Regulation A under the Act or in a transaction exempt pursuant to Section 4 of the Act and not involving any public offering need not be included in determining the amount of securities sold in reliance upon this rule.

(f) *Manner of Sale.* The securities shall be sold in "brokers' transactions" within the meaning of section 4(4) of the Act or in transactions directly with a "market maker," as that term is defined in section 3(a)(38) of the Securities Exchange Act of 1934, and the person selling the securities shall not (1) solicit or arrange for the solicitation of orders to buy the securities in anticipation of or in connection with such transaction, or (2) make any payment in connection with the offer or sale of the securities to any person other than the broker who executes the order to sell the securities. The requirements of this paragraph, however, shall not apply to securities sold for the account of the estate of a deceased person or for the account of a beneficiary of such estate provided the estate or beneficiary

thereof is not an affiliate of the issuer; nor shall they apply to securities sold for the account of any person other than an affiliate of the issuer, provided the conditions of paragraph (k) of this rule are satisfied.

(g) *Brokers' Transactions.* The term "brokers' transactions" in Section 4(4) of the Act shall for the purposes of this rule be deemed to include transactions by a broker in which such broker—

(1) does no more than execute the order or orders to sell the securities as agent for the person for whose account the securities are sold; and receives no more than the usual and customary broker's commission;

(2) neither solicits nor arranges for the solicitation of customers' orders to buy the securities in anticipation of or in connection with the transaction; provided, that the foregoing shall not preclude *(i)* inquiries by the broker of other brokers or dealers who have indicated an interest in the securities within the preceding 60 days, *(ii)* inquiries by the broker of his customers who have indicated an unsolicited bona fide interest in the securities within the preceding 10 business days; or *(iii)* the publication by the broker of bid and ask quotations for the security in an inter-dealer quotation system provided that such quotations are incident to the maintenance of a bona fide inter-dealer market for the security for the broker's own account and that the broker has published bona fide bid and ask quotations for the security in an inter-dealer quotation system on each of at least twelve days within the preceding thirty calendar days with no more than four business days in succession without such two-way quotations;

Note to Subparagraph g(2)(ii): The broker should obtain and retain in his files written evidence of indications of bona fide unsolicited interest by his customers in the securities at the time such indications are received.

(3) after reasonable inquiry is not aware of circumstances indicating that the person for whose account the securities are sold

is an underwriter with respect to the securities or that the transaction is a part of a distribution of securities of the issuer. Without limiting the foregoing, the broker shall be deemed to be aware of any facts or statements contained in the notice required by paragraph (h) below.

Notes. 1. The broker, for his own protection, should obtain and retain in his files a copy of the notice required by paragraph (h).

2. The reasonable inquiry required by paragraph (g)(3) above should include, but not necessarily be limited to, inquiry as to the following matters:

a. The length of time the securities have been held by the person for whose account they are to be sold. If practicable, the inquiry should include physical inspection of the securities;

b. The nature of the transaction in which the securities were acquired by such person;

c. The amount of securities of the same class sold during the past six months by all persons whose sales are required to be taken into consideration pursuant to paragraph (e) above;

d. Whether such person intends to sell additional securities of the same class through any other means;

e. Whether such person has solicited or made any arrangement for the solicitation of buy orders in connection with the proposed sale of securities;

f. Whether such person has made any payment to any other person in connection with the proposed sale of the securities; and

g. The number of shares or other units of the class outstanding, or the relevant trading volume.

(h) *Notice of Proposed Sale.* If the amount of securities to be sold in reliance upon the rule during any period of three months exceeds 500 shares or other units or has an aggregate sale price in excess of $10,000, three copies of a notice on Form 144 shall be filed with the Commission at its principal office in Washington, D.C.; and if such securities are admitted to trading on any national securities exchange, one copy of such notice shall also be transmitted to the principal exchange on which such securities are so admitted. The Form 144 shall be signed by the person for whose account the securities are to be sold and shall be transmitted for filing concurrently with either the placing with a broker of an order to execute a sale of securities in reliance upon this rule or the execution directly with a market maker of such a sale. Neither the filing of such notice nor the failure of the Commission to comment thereon shall be deemed to preclude the Commission from taking any action it deems necessary or appropriate with respect to the sale of the securities referred to in such notice. The requirements of this paragraph, however, shall not apply to securities sold for the account of any person other than an affiliate of the issuer, provided the conditions of paragraph (k) of this rule are satisfied.

(i) *Bona Fide Intention to Sell.* The person filing the notice required by paragraph (h) shall have a bona fide intention to sell the securities referred to therein within a reasonable time after the filing of such notice.

(j) *Non-exclusive Rule.* Although this rule provides a means for reselling restricted securities and securities held by affiliates without registration, it is not the exclusive means for reselling such securities in that manner. Therefore, it does not eliminate or otherwise affect the availability of any exemption for resales under the Securities Act that a person or entity may be able to rely upon.

(k) *Termination of Certain Restrictions on Sales of Restricted Securities by Persons Other than Affiliates.* The requirements of paragraphs (e), (f) and (h) of this rule shall not apply to restricted securities sold for the account of a person who is not an affiliate of the issuer at the time of the sale and has not been an affiliate during the preceding three months, provided the securities have been beneficially owned by the person for a period of at least three years prior to their sale. In computing the period for which securities have been beneficially owned for purposes of this provision, reference should be made to paragraph (d) of this rule.

Rule 145. Reclassifications of Securities, Mergers, Consolidations and Acquisitions of Assets

Preliminary Note to Rule 145

Rule 145 is designed to make available the protection provided by registration under the Securities Act of 1933, as amended (Act), to persons who are offered securities in a business combination of the type described in subparagraphs (a)(1), (2), and (3) of the Rule. The thrust of the Rule is that an "offer", "offer to sell", "offer for sale", or "sale" occurs when there is submitted to security holders a plan or agreement pursuant to which such holders are required to elect, on the basis of what is in substance a new investment decision, whether to accept a new or different security in exchange for their existing security. Rule 145 embodies the Commission's determination that such transactions are subject to the registration requirements of the Act, and that the previously existing "no-sale" theory of Rule 133 is no longer consistent with the statutory purposes of the Act. Rule 145 is effective for matters formally submitted for security holder vote or consent on or after January 1, 1973 except for those matters formally presented prior to that date to a governmental agency for approval, where such approval is required by law.

While Rule 133 is rescinded effective January 1, 1973, it will remain available for any transaction which, before that date, had been submitted to security holders for vote or consent, or which had been submitted formally to a governmental agency for approval where such approval was required by law. Rule 133 shall also remain available for resales of securities received by persons in any transaction for which Rule 133 was available.

In order to minimize the burdens of registration to the extent feasible, particularly for small businesses, the Commission has amended Form S–14 so that registration under the Securities Act may be effectuated through the use of the informational requirements under Regulation 14 A or 14C of the Exchange Act, which are generally less burdensome than those of the Securities Act.

Transactions for which statutory exemptions under the Act, including those contained in Sections 3(a)(9), 3(a)(10), 3(a)(11), and 4(2), are otherwise available are not affected by Rule 145.

Rule 145

Note 1: Reference is made to Rule 153A, describing the prospectus delivery required in a transaction of the type referred to in Rule 145.

Note 2: A reclassification of securities covered by Rule 145 would be exempt from registration pursuant to Sections 3(a)(9) or 3(a)(11) of the Act if the conditions of either of these sections are satisfied.

(a) *Transactions Within the Rule.* An "offer", "offer to sell", "offer for sale" or "sale" shall be deemed to be involved, within the meaning of Section 2(3) of the Act, so far as the security holders of a corporation or other person are concerned where, pursuant to statutory provisions of the jurisdiction under which such corporation or other person is organized, or pursuant to provisions contained in its certificate of incorporation or similar controlling instruments, or otherwise, there is submitted for the vote or consent of such security holders a plan or agreement for—

(1) *Reclassifications.* A reclassification of securities of such corporation or other person, other than a stock split, reverse stock split, or change in par value, which involves the substitution of a security for another security;

(2) *Mergers or Consolidations.* A statutory merger or consolidation or similar plan of acquisition in which securities of such corporation or other person held by such security holders will become or be exchanged for securities of any other person, except where the sole purpose of the transaction is to change an issuer's domicile; or

(3) *Transfers of Assets.* A transfer of assets of such corporation or other person, to another person in consideration of the issuance of securities of such other person or any of its affiliates, if:

(A) such plan or agreement provides for dissolution of the corporation or other person whose security holders are voting or consenting; or

(B) such plan or agreement provides for a pro rata or similar distribution of such securities to the security holders voting or consenting; or

(C) the board of directors or similar representatives of such corporation or other person, adopts resolutions relative to (A) or (B) above within one year after the taking of such vote or consent; or

(D) the transfer of assets is a part of a pre-existing plan for distribution of such securities, notwithstanding (A), (B) or (C), above.

(b) *Communications Not Deemed to be a "Prospectus" or "Offer to Sell"*. For the purpose of this rule, the term "prospectus" as defined in Section 2(10) of the Act and the term "offer to sell" in Section 5 of the Act shall not be deemed to include the following:

(1) Any written communication or other published statement which contains no more than the following information: the name of the issuer of the securities to be offered, or the person whose assets are to be sold in exchange for the securities to be offered, and the names of other parties to any transaction specified in paragraph (a); a brief description of the business of parties to such transaction; the date, time and place of the meeting of security holders to vote on or consent to any such transaction specified in paragraph (a); a brief description of the transaction to be acted upon and the basis upon which such transaction will be made; and any legend or similar statement required by State or federal law or administrative authority.

(2) Any written communication subject to and meeting the requirements of paragraph (a) of Rule 14a–12 under the Securities Exchange Act of 1934 and filed in accordance with paragraph (b) of that rule.

(c) *Persons and Parties Deemed to be Underwriters*. For purposes of this rule, any party to

any transaction specified in paragraph (a), other than the issuer, or any person who is an affiliate of such party at the time any such transaction is submitted for vote or consent, who publicly offers or sells securities of the issuer acquired in connection with any such transaction, shall be deemed to be engaged in a distribution and therefore to be an underwriter thereof within the meaning of Section 2(11) of the Act. The term "party" as used in this paragraph (c) shall mean the corporations, business entities, or other persons, other than the issuer, whose assets or capital structure are affected by the transactions specified in paragraph (a).

(d) *Resale Provisions for Persons and Parties Deemed Underwriters*. Notwithstanding the provisions of paragraph (c), a person or party specified therein shall not be deemed to be engaged in a distribution and therefore not to be an underwriter of registered securities acquired in a transaction specified in paragraph (a) of this section if: (1) such securities are sold by such person or party in accordance with the provisions of paragraphs (c), (e), (f) and (g) of * * * [Rule 144]; or (2) such person or party is not affiliated with the issuer and has held the securities for at least two years, and the issuer is subject to the periodic reporting requirements of sections 13 or 15(d) of the Securities Exchange Act of 1934, has been so subject for at least the preceding 12 months, and has filed all of the reports required to be filed under those sections during the preceding 12 months. The person or party selling securities under this paragraph (d)(2) shall be entitled to rely upon a statement in whichever is the most recent report filed by the issuer that such issuer has filed all of the reports to be under sections 13 or 15(d) of the Exchange Act during the preceding 12 months, unless such person or party has reason to believe that the issuer has not complied with such requirements.

(e) *Definition of "Person"*. The term "person" as used in paragraphs (c) and (d) of this rule, when used with reference to a person for whose account securities are to be sold, shall have the same meaning as the definition of that term in paragraph (a)(2) of Rule 144 under the Act.

Rule 147. "Part of an Issue," "Person Resident," and "Doing Business Within" for Purposes of Section 3(a)(11)

(a) *Transactions Covered*.

Offers, offers to sell, offers for sale and sales by an issuer of its securities made in accordance with all of the terms and conditions of this rule shall be deemed to be part of an issue offered and sold only to persons resident and doing business within such state or territory, within the meaning of Section 3(a)(11) of the Act.

(b) *Part of an Issue*.

(1) For purposes of this rule, all securities of the issuer which are part of an issue shall be offered, offered for sale or sold in accordance with all of the terms and conditions of this rule.

(2) For purposes of this rule only, an issue shall be deemed not to include offers, offers to sell, offers for sale or sales of securities of the issuer pursuant to the exemptions provided by Section 3 or Section 4(2) of the Act or pursuant to a registration statement filed under the Act, that take place prior to the six month period immediately preceding or after the six month period immediately following any offers, offers for sale or sales pursuant to this rule, *provided that*, there are during either of said six month periods no offers, offers for sale or sales of securities by or for the issuer of the same or similar class as those offered, offered for sale or sold pursuant to the rule.

NOTE: In the event that securities of the same or similar class as those offered pursuant to the rule are offered, offered for sale or sold less than six months prior to or subsequent to any offer, offer for sale or sale pursuant to this rule, see Preliminary Note 3 hereof, as to which offers, offers to sell, offers for sale, or sales are part of an issue.

(c) *Nature of the Issuer*.

The issuer of the securities shall at the time of any offers and the sales be a person resident and doing business within the state or territory in which all of the offers, offers to sell, offers for sale and sales are made.

(1) The issuer shall be deemed to be a resident of the state or territory in which:

(i) it is incorporated or organized, if a corporation, limited partnership, trust or other form of business organization that is organized under state or territorial law;

(ii) its principal office is located, if a general partnership or other form of business organization that is not organized under any state or territorial law;

(iii) his principal residence is located, if an individual.

(2) The issuer shall be deemed to be doing business within a state or territory if:

(i) the issuer derived at least 80% of its gross revenues and those of its subsidiaries on a consolidated basis;

(A) for its most recent fiscal year, if the first offer of any part of the issue is made during the first six months of the issuer's current fiscal year; or

(B) for the first six months of its current fiscal year or during the twelve month fiscal period ending with such six month period, if the first offer of any part of the issue is made during the last six months of the issuer's current fiscal year

from the operation of a business or of real property located in or from the rendering of services within such state or territory; provided, however, that this provision does not apply to any issuer which has not had gross revenues in excess of $5,000 from the sale of products or services or other conduct of its business for its most recent twelve month fiscal period; and

(ii) the issuer had at the end of its most recent semi-annual fiscal period prior to the first offer of any part of the issue, at least 80 percent of its assets and those of its subsidiaries on a consolidated basis located within such state or territory;

(iii) the issuer intends to use and uses at least 80% of the net proceeds to the issuer from sales made pursuant to this rule in connection with the operation of a business or of real property, the purchase of real property located in, or the rendering of services within such state or territory; and

    (iv) the principal office of the issuer is located within such state or territory.

(d) *Offerees and Purchasers; Person Resident.*

Offers, offers to sell, offers for sale and sales of securities that are part of an issue shall be made only to persons resident within the state or territory of which the issuer is a resident. For purposes of determining the residence of offerees and purchasers:

(1) A corporation, partnership, trust or other form of business organization shall be deemed to be a resident of a state or territory if, at the time of the offer and sale to it, it has its principal office within such state or territory.

(2) An individual shall be deemed to be a resident of a state or territory if such individual has, at the time of the offer and sale to him, his principal residence in the state or territory.

(3) A corporation, partnership, trust or other form of business organization which is organized for the specific purpose of acquiring part of an issue offered pursuant to this rule shall be deemed not to be a resident of a state or territory unless all of the beneficial owners of such organization are residents of such state or territory.

(e) *Limitation of Resales.*

During the period in which securities that are part of an issue are being offered and sold by the issuer, and for a period of nine months from the date of the last sale by the issuer of such securities, all resales of any part of the issue, by any person, shall be made only to persons resident within such state or territory.

    NOTES: 1. In the case of convertible securities resales of either the convertible security, or if it is converted, the underlying security, could be made during the period described in paragraph (e) only to persons resident within such state or territory. For purposes of this rule a conversion in reliance on Section 3(a)(9) of the Act does not begin a new period.

    2. Dealers must satisfy the requirements of Rule 15c2–11 under the Securities Exchange Act of 1934 prior to publishing any quotation for a security, or submitting any quotation for publication, in any quotation medium.

(f) *Precautions Against Interstate Offers and Sales.*

(1) The issuer shall, in connection with any securities sold by it pursuant to this rule:

    (i) place a legend on the certificate or other document evidencing the security stating that the securities have not been registered under the Act and setting forth the limitations on resale contained in paragraph (e);

    (ii) issue stop transfer instructions to the issuer's transfer agent, if any, with respect to the securities, or, if the issuer transfers its own securities, make a notation in the appropriate records of the issuer; and

    (iii) obtain a written representation from each purchaser as to his residence.

(2) The issuer shall, in connection with the issuance of new certificates for any of the securities that are part of the same issue that are presented for transfer during the time period specified in paragraph (e), take the steps required by subsections (f)(1)(i) and (ii).

(3) The issuer shall, in connection with any offers, offers to sell, offers for sale or sales by it pursuant to this rule, disclose, in writing, the limitations on resale contained in paragraph (e) and the provisions of subsections (f)(1)(i) and (ii) and subparagraph (f)(2).

           * * *

Rule 237. Exemption of Certain Securities Owned for Five Years

(a) *Securities exempted.* Subject to the terms and conditions of this rule, securities sold by any person, other than the issuer of the securities, an affiliate of such issuer or broker or dealer, shall be exempt from registration under the Act, provided all of the following conditions are met:

    (1) The issuer is incorporated or organized under the laws of the United States or

any State or Territory or the District of Columbia and has its principal business operations in the United States.

(2) The issuer has been actively engaged in business as a going concern during a period of at least the last five years.

(3) The securities sold have been beneficially owned by the person for a period of at least five years prior to the sale and, if the securities were purchased, the full purchase price or other consideration shall have been paid or given at least five years prior to the sale. Giving the person from whom the securities were purchased a promissory note or other obligation to pay the purchase price shall not be deemed to be payment of the purchase price until the note or other obligation has been discharged by payment in full.

(4) The securities are bona fide sold in negotiated transactions otherwise than through a broker or dealer.

(b) *Amount of securities exempted.* The gross proceeds from all securities of the issuer, its predecessors, and all of its affiliates, sold under this section by any person during any period of 1 year shall not exceed the lesser of the gross proceeds from the sale of 1 percent of the securities of the class outstanding or $50,000 in aggregate gross proceeds. Such amounts shall be reduced by the amount of the gross proceeds from any securities sold during such year pursuant to any other exemption under section 3(b) of the Act and the amount of the gross proceeds from securities of the same class sold in reliance upon Rule 144 of this chapter.

(c) *Filing of notice.* At least 10 days (Saturdays, Sundays and holidays excluded) prior to the sale of the securities there shall be filed with the Regional Office of the Commission for the region in which the issuer's principal business operations are conducted three copies of a notice on Form 237 which shall be signed by the selling security holder. A copy of such notice shall also be sent or given, at the same time, to the issuer of the securities.

(d) *Definition of terms.* The definitions contained in the Act and in Rule 405 thereunder shall apply to the terms in this rule. The following definition shall also apply:

Person. The term "person" when used with reference to a person who sells securities in reliance upon the exemption provided by this rule includes, in addition to such person, all of the following persons:

(1) Any relative or spouse of such person or any relative of such spouse, anyone of whom has the same home as such person;

(2) Any trust or estate in which such person or any of the persons specified in (a) collectively own ten percent or more of the total beneficial interest or of which any of such persons serve as trustee, executor or in any similar capacity; and

(3) Any corporation or other organization (other than the issuer) in which such person or any of the persons specified in (a) are the beneficial owners collectively of ten percent or more of any class of equity securities or ten percent or more of the equity interest.

REGULATION A—GENERAL EXEMPTION

Rule 251. Definitions of Terms Used in This Regulation

As used in this regulation, the following terms shall have the meaning indicated:

Affiliate. An "affiliate" of an issuer is a person controlling, controlled by or under common control with such issuer.

Parent. A "parent" of a specified person is an affiliate controlling such person directly, or indirectly through one or more intermediaries.

Predecessor. A "predecessor" of an issuer is (i) a person the major portion of whose assets have been acquired directly or indirectly by the issuer, or (ii) a person from which the issuer acquired directly or indirectly the major portion of its assets.

Promoter. The term "promoter" includes—

(*a*) Any person who, acting alone or in conjunction with one or more other persons, directly or indirectly takes the initiative in founding and organizing the business or enterprise of an issuer:

(*b*) Any person who, in connection with the founding or organizing of the business or enterprise of an issuer, directly or indirectly receives in consideration of services or property, or both services and property, 10 percent or more of any class of securities of the issuer or 10 percent or more of the proceeds from the sale of any class of securities. However, a person who receives such securities or proceeds either solely as underwriting commissions or solely in consideration of property shall not be deemed a promoter within the meaning of this paragraph if such person does not otherwise take part in founding and organizing the enterprise.

Province. A "Province" is any Province or Territory of Canada.

Resident. A "resident" of a specified country is an individual resident of such country or a corporation or other organization which is incorporated or organized under the laws of such country or any of its political subdivisions.

State. A "State" is any State, Territory or insular possession of the United States, or the District of Columbia.

Underwriter. The term "underwriter" shall have the meaning given in section 2(11) of the Act.

Rule 252. Securities Exempted

(*a*) Except as hereinafter provided in this regulation, securities issued by any of the following persons shall be exempt from registration under the Act if offered in accordance with the terms and conditions of this regulation:

(1) Any corporation, unincorporated association or trust (i) which is incorporated or organized under the laws of the United States or Canada or any State or Province thereof and (ii) which has or proposes to have its principal busi-

ness operations in the United States or Canada; or

(2) Any individual who is a resident of, and has or proposes to have his principal business operations in, any State or Province; or

(3) In the case of an offering to existing security holders on a pro rata basis pursuant to warrants or rights, any direct or indirect majority-owned subsidiary of any issuer specified in (1) above which has securities registered on a national securities exchange pursuant to the provisions of the Securities Exchange Act of 1934.

(*b*) No exemption under this regulation shall be available for any of the following securities:

(1) Fractional undivided interests in oil or gas rights as defined in Rule 300, or similar interests in other mineral rights;

(2) Securities of any investment company registered or required to be registered under the Investment Company Act of 1940.

(*c*) No exemption under this regulation shall be available for the securities of any issuer if such issuer, any of its predecessors or any affiliated issuer—

(1) Has filed a registration statement which is the subject of any proceeding or examination under section 8 of the Act, or is the subject of any refusal order or stop order entered thereunder within 5 years prior to the filing of the notification required by Rule 255;

(2) Is subject to pending proceedings under Rule 261 or any similar rule adopted under section 3(b) of the Act, or to an order entered thereunder within 5 years prior to the filing of such notification;

(3) Has been convicted within five years prior to the filing of such notification of any felony or misdemeanor in connection with the purchase or sale of any security or involving the making of any false filing with the Commission;

(4) Is subject to any order, judgment, or decree of any court of competent jurisdiction temporarily or preliminarily restraining or enjoining, or is subject to any order, judgment or decree of any court of competent jurisdiction, entered within five years prior to the filing of

such notification, permanently restraining or enjoining, such person from engaging in or continuing any conduct or practice in connection with the purchase or sale of any security or involving the making of any false filing with the Commission; or

(5) Is subject to a United States Postal Service false representation order entered under section 3005 of title 39, United States Code, within five years prior to the filing of the notification required by Rule 255; or is subject to a temporary restraining order or preliminary injunction entered under section 3007 of title 39, United States Code, with respect to conduct alleged to have violated section 3005 of title 39, United States Code.

This paragraph (c) of Rule 252 shall not apply to any order, judgment, or decree contemplated by paragraphs (1) through (5) hereunder because of its entry against any affiliated entity before the affiliation with the issuer arose, if the affiliated entity is not in control of the issuer and if the affiliated entity and the issuer are not under the common control of a third party who was in control of the affiliated entity at the time the order, judgment, or decree was entered against it.

(*d*) No exemption under this regulation shall be available for the securities of any issuer, if any of its directors, officers, general partners, or beneficial owners of ten percent or more of any class of its equity securities (beneficial ownership meaning the power to vote or direct the vote and/or the power to dispose or direct the disposition of such securities), any of its promoters presently connected with it in any capacity, any underwriter of the securities to be offered, or any partner, director, or officer of any such underwriter—

(1) Has been convicted within ten years prior to the filing of the notification required by Rule 255 of any felony or misdemeanor in connection with the purchase or sale of any security, involving the making of a false filing with the Commission, or arising out of the conduct of the business of an underwriter, broker, dealer, municipal securities dealer, or investment adviser;

(2) Is subject to any order, judgment, or decree of any court of competent jurisdiction temporarily or preliminarily enjoining or restraining, or is subject to any order, judgment, or decree of any court of competent jurisdiction, entered within five years prior to the filing of such notification, permanently enjoining or restraining such person from engaging in or continuing any conduct or practice in connection with the purchase or sale of any security, involving the making of a false filing with the Commission, or arising out of the conduct of the business of an underwriter, broker, dealer, municipal securities dealer, or investment adviser;

(3) Is subject to an order of the Commission entered pursuant to section 15(b), 15B(a), or 15B(c) of the Securities Exchange Act of 1934; or is subject to an order of the Commission entered pursuant to section 203(e) or (f) of the Investment Advisers Act of 1940;

(4) Is suspended or expelled from membership in, or suspended or barred from association with a member of, an exchange registered as a national securities exchange pursuant to section 6 of the Securities Exchange Act of 1934, an association registered as a national securities association under section 15A of the Securities Exchange Act of 1934, or a Canadian securities exchange or association for any act or omission to act constituting conduct inconsistent with just and equitable principles of trade; or

(5) Is subject to a United States Postal Service false representation order entered under section 3005 of title 39, United States Code, within five years prior to the filing of the notification required by Rule 255; or is subject to a restraining order or preliminary injunction entered under section 3007 of title 39, United States Code, with respect to conduct alleged to have violated section 3005 of title 39, United States Code.

(*e*) No exemption under this regulation shall be available for the securities of any issuer if any underwriter of such securities was, or was named as, an underwriter of any securities:

(1) Covered by any registration statement which is the subject of any pending proceeding or examination under section 8 of the Act, or is the subject of any refusal order or stop order entered thereunder within 5 years prior to the

filing of the notification required by Rule 255; or

(2) Covered by a filing which is subject to pending proceedings under Rule 261 or any similar rule adopted under section 3(b) of the Act, or to an order entered thereunder within 5 years prior to the filing of such notification.

(*f*) No exemption under this regulation shall be available for the securities of an issuer which is subject to the requirements of sections 13, 14, 15(d) of the Securities Exchange Act of 1934, unless such issuer has filed all reports required by those sections to be filed during the 12 calendar months preceding the filing of the notification required by Rule 255 (or for such shorter period that the issuer was required to file such reports).

(*g*) Paragraph (*c*), (*d*), (*e*) or (*f*) shall not apply to the securities of any issuer if the Commission determines, upon a showing of good cause, that it is not necessary under the circumstances that the exemption be denied. Any such determination by the Commission shall be without prejudice to any other action by the Commission in any other proceeding or matter with respect to the issuer or any other person.

Rule 253. Special Requirements for Certain Offerings

(*a*) The following provisions of this rule shall apply to any offering under this regulation of securities of any issuer which—

(1) was incorporated or organized within 1 year prior to the date of filing the notification required by Rule 255 and has not had a net income from operations; or

(2) was incorporated or organized more than 1 year prior to such date and has not had a net income from operations, of the character in which the issuer intends to engage, for at least one of the last 2 fiscal years.

(*b*) If the issuer conducts or proposes to conduct its principal business operations in Canada, the securities to be offered hereunder shall be qualified or made eligible for offering in the Province in which such operations are or will be conducted. The securities of any other issuer incorporated or organized under the laws of Canada or any Province thereof shall be qualified or made eligible for offering in the Province in which the issuer has its principal office or principal place of business in Canada. All securities subject to this paragraph shall be offered in the Province in which they are qualified or made eligible for offering, concurrently with the offering in the United States. Issuers engaged in extractive or manufacturing enterprises shall be deemed to have their principal business operations in the Province in which their principal plants or other properties are located.

(*c*) In computing the amount of securities which may be offered hereunder, there shall be included, in addition to the securities specified in Rule 254—

(1) All securities issued prior to the filing of the offering statement, or proposed to be issued, for a consideration consisting in whole or in part of assets or services and held by the person to whom issued; and

(2) All securities issued to and held by or proposed to be issued, pursuant to options or otherwise, to any director, officer or promoter of the issuer, or to any underwriter, dealer or security salesman:

Provided, That such securities need not be included to the extent that effective provision is made, by escrow arrangements or otherwise, to assure that none of such securities or any interest therein will be reoffered to the public within 1 year after the commencement of the offering hereunder and that any reoffering of such securities will be made in accordance with the applicable provisions of the Act.

(*d*) None of the securities to be offered hereunder shall be offered for the account of any person other than the issuer of such securities.

(*e*) Rule 257 shall not apply to any offering of securities under this regulation by any issuer which is subject to this rule.

Rule 254. Amount of Securities Exempted

(*a*) For determining the requisite amount:

(1) The aggregate offering price of all securities of the issuer offered or sold pursuant to this regulation and any other securities offered or

sold within one year prior to the commencement of the proposed offering pursuant to any other exemption under Section 3(b) of the Act or in violation of Section 5(a) of the Act shall not exceed the following amounts:

(i) $1,500,000 if the securities are offered or sold by or on behalf of the issuer, or by the estate of a decedent who owned the securities at death if offered within two years after the death of the decedent, or by affiliates of issuer; provided that the aggregate offering price of securities offered or sold by or on behalf of any one affiliate, other than an estate shall not exceed $100,000; and

(ii) $100,000 if the securities are offered or sold by or on behalf of any person other than the issuer or its affiliates; provided that the aggregate offering price of all such securities offered or sold by or on behalf of all such other persons shall not exceed $300,-000 and provided that the aggregate offering price of securities offered or sold by or on behalf of an estate pursuant to this paragraph and paragraph (i) above shall not exceed $500,000.

(2) When two or more persons agree to act in concert for the purpose of selling securities of the issuer, all securities of the same class sold for the account of all such persons during any 12-month period shall be aggregated for the purpose of determining the limitation on the amount of securities sold.

(3) The following definitions shall apply for the purposes of this rule:

(A) The term "securities of the issuer" shall include securities issued by any predecessor of the issuer or by any affiliate of the issuer which was organized or became such an affiliate within the past two years.

(B) The term "person" when used with reference to a person who offers securities in reliance upon the exemption provided by this rule includes, in addition to such person, all of the following persons:

(i) Any relative or spouse of such person, or any relative of such spouse, any one of whom has the same home as such person;

(ii) Any trust or estate in which such person or any of the persons specified in (i) collectively own ten percent or more of the total beneficial interest or of which any of such persons serve as trustee, executor or in any similar capacity; and

(iii) Any corporation or other organization (other than the issuer) in which such person or any of the persons specified in (i) are the beneficial owners collectively of ten percent or more of any class of equity securities or ten percent or more of the equity interest.

(b) The aggregate offering price of securities which have a determinable market value shall be computed upon the basis of such market value as determined from transactions or quotations on a specified date within 15 days prior to the date of filing the offering statement, or the offering price to the public, whichever is higher: *Provided*, That the aggregate gross proceeds actually received from the public for the securities offered hereunder shall not exceed the maximum aggregate offering price permitted in the particular case by paragraph (a) of this rule.

(c) Where securities which have no determinable market value are offered in exchange for outstanding securities, claims, property, or services, the aggregate offering price thereof shall be computed at the public offering price of securities of the same class for cash, or if no cash offering is to be made, then upon the basis of the value of the securities, claims, property or services to be received in exchange, as established by bona fide sales made within a reasonable time, or in the absence of such sales, upon the basis of the fair value of the securities, claims, property or services to be received in exchange, as determined by some accepted standard.

(d) The following securities need not be included in computing the amount of securities which may be offered under this regulation:

(1) Unsold securities the offering of which has been withdrawn with the consent of the Commission by amending the pertinent offering statement to reduce the amount stated therein as proposed to be offered;

(2) Securities acquired or to be acquired, otherwise than for distribution by a single holder of the majority of the outstanding voting stock of the issuer in connection with a pro rata offering to stockholders;

(3) In the case of an offering by an issuer to existing security holders on a pro rata basis pursuant to warrants or rights, that portion of the offering made outside of the United States and Canada;

(4) In the case of an offering of interests in an unincorporated theatrical production, interests in any affiliated unincorporated theatrical production; or

(5) In the case of an offering of interests in an unincorporated issuer organized to hold title to, lease, operate or improve specific real property, interests in any affiliated issuer organized to hold title to, lease, operate or improve other specific real property.

Rule 255. Filing of Offering Statement

(a) At least 10 days (Saturdays, Sundays and holidays excluded) prior to the date on which the initial offering or sale of any securities is to be made under this regulation, there shall be filed with the Regional Office of the Commission specified below five copies of the offering statement required by this Regulation which shall consist of Part I—Notification, Part II—Offering Circular, and Part III—Exhibits. The Commission may, however, in its discretion, authorize the commencement of the offering prior to the expiration of such 10-day period upon a written request for such authorization.

(b) The offering statement shall be signed by the issuer and each person, other than the issuer, for whose account any of the securities are to be offered. If the offering statement is signed by any person on behalf of any other person, evidence of authority to sign on behalf of such other person shall be filed with the offering statement, except where an officer of the is-

suer signs on behalf of the issuer. At the time of filing an offering statement, the applicant shall pay to the Commission at the Regional Office where the offering statement is filed a fee of $100.00, no part of which shall be refunded.

(c) The offering statement shall be filed with the Regional Office for the region in which the issuer's principal business operations are conducted or proposed to be conducted in the United States. The offering statement of any issuer having or proposing to have its principal business operations in Canada shall be filed with the Regional Office nearest the place where the issuer's principal business operations are conducted or proposed to be conducted, unless the offering is to be made through a principal underwriter located in the United States, in which case the offering statement shall be filed with the Regional Office for the region in which such underwriter has its principal office.

(d) An amendment to any part of the offering statement will necessitate the filing of an amended offering statement which shall be signed in the same manner as the original offering statement. Five copies of such amendment shall be filed with the same Regional Office as the original offering statement at least 10 days prior to any offering or sale of the securities subsequent to the filing of such amendment, or such shorter period as the Commission, in its discretion, may authorize upon a written request for such authorization.

(e) An offering statement or any other document filed as a part thereof may be withdrawn upon application unless the offering statement is subject to an order under Rule 261 at the time the application is filed or becomes subject to such an order within 15 days (Saturdays, Sundays and holidays excluded) thereafter, *Provided* That an offering statement may not be withdrawn after any of the securities proposed to be offered thereunder have been sold. Any such application shall be signed in the same manner and filed with the same Regional Office as the offering statement.

(f) The manually signed original (or in the case of duplicate originals, one duplicate original) of all offering statements, reports, or other documents filed shall be numbered sequentially (in addition to any internal numbering which otherwise may be present) by handwritten, typed, printed, or other legible form of notation from the cover page of the document through the last page of that document and any exhibits or attachments thereto. Further, the total number of pages contained in a numbered original shall be set forth on the first page of the document.

(*g*) Each offering statement shall contain an exhibit index, which should immediately precede the exhibits filed with such offering statement. The index shall list each exhibit filed and identify by handwritten, typed, printed, or other legible form of notation in the manually signed original, the page number in the sequential numbering system described in paragraph (*f*) of this section where such exhibit can be found or where it is stated that the exhibit is incorporated by reference. Further, the first page of the manually signed offering statement shall list the page in the filing where the exhibit index is located.

Rule 256. Filing and Use of the Offering Circular

(*a*) Except as provided in paragraph (*c*) of this rule and in Rule 257—

(1) No written offer of securities of any issuer shall be made under this regulation unless an offering circular containing the information specified in Part II of the offering statement is concurrently given or has previously been given to the person to whom the offer is made, or has been sent to such person under such circumstances that it would normally have been received by him at or prior to the time of such written offer; and

(2) No securities of such issuer shall be sold under this regulation unless such an offering circular is furnished to the person to whom the securities are expected to be sold at least 48 hours prior to the mailing of the confirmation of sale to such person, or is sent to such person under such circumstances that it would normally be received by him 48 hours prior to his receipt of confirmation of the sale; provided however, if the issuer is required to file reports pursuant to Section 13(a) or 15(d) of the Securities Ex-

change Act of 1934, as amended, the offering circular may be furnished with or prior to the confirmation of sale.

(*b*) In the case of transactions effected on a securities exchange, delivery of the offering circular (offering statement—Part II) shall be deemed to have been made if prior to such transactions a reasonable number of copies of the offering circular have been furnished to the exchange for delivery to any person or persons requesting copies thereof.

(*c*) Any written advertisement or other written communication, or any radio or television broadcast, which states from whom an offering circular containing the information specified in Part II of the offering statement may be obtained and in addition contains no more than the following information may be published, distributed or broadcast at or after the commencement of the public offering to any person prior to sending or giving such person a copy of such circular:

(1) the name of the issuer of such security;

(2) the title of the security, the amount being offered, and the per-unit offering price to the public;

(3) the identity of the general type of business of the issuer; and

(4) a brief statement as to the general character and location of its property.

(*d*) If the offering is not completed within nine months from the date of the offering circular (offering statement—Part II) a revised offering circular shall be prepared, filed and used in accordance with these rules as for an original offering circular, except that in the case of offerings under stock purchase, savings, stock option or other similar plans for the benefit of employees, if the offering is not completed within 12 months from the date of the offering circular, a revised offering circular shall be prepared, filed and used in accordance with these rules as for an original offering circular. In no event shall an offering circular be used which is false or misleading in light of the circumstances then existing.

(*e*) If the original offering circular (offering statement—Part II) is revised or amended, such revised or amended circular shall be filed as an amendment to the offering statement, as provided by Rule 255(d), with the appropriate Regional Office of the Commission at least 10 days prior to its use, or such shorter period as the Commission may, in its discretion, authorize upon a written request for such authorization.

(f) Sales by a dealer (including an underwriter no longer acting as an underwriter in respect of the security involved in such transaction) of securities of an issuer not subject, immediately prior to the time of filing an offering statement, to the provisions of section 13(a) or 15(d) of the Securities Exchange Act of 1934, as amended, offered pursuant to this regulation and taking place prior to the expiration of ninety days after the first date upon which the securities were bona fide offered to the public, shall not be exempt pursuant to this regulation unless: (1) the dealer furnishes a copy of the then current offering circular (offering statement—Part II) to the purchaser prior to or with the purchaser's receipt of the confirmation of the sale; or (2) the offering circular has previously been mailed or delivered to such purchaser. Failure by a dealer to comply with the provision of this subparagraph shall not otherwise affect the availability of the exemption for any other person, including the aggregate amount of securities exempted pursuant to Rule 254.

(g) The issuer or if there is an underwriter, the underwriter shall provide reasonable quantities of copies of the offering circular (offering statement—Part II) to any dealer on request prior to the expiration of ninety days after the first date upon which securities of such issuer were bona fide offered to the public pursuant to this regulation.

(h) An offering circular filed pursuant to paragraph (e) of this section may be distributed prior to the expiration of the 10-day waiting period for offerings provided for in Rule 255(a) and (d) and paragraph (e) of this rule and such distribution may be accompanied or followed by oral offers related thereto, provided the conditions in paragraphs (1) through (4) are met. For the purposes of this rule, any offering circular distributed prior to the expiration of the ten day waiting period is called a Preliminary Offering Circular. Such Preliminary Offering Circular may be used to meet the requirements of paragraph (a)(2) of Rule 256: *Provided,* That if a Preliminary Offering Circular is inaccurate or inadequate in any material respect, a revised Preliminary Offering Circular or an offering circular of the type referred to in paragraph (4) of this rule, shall be furnished to all persons to whom the securities are to be sold at least 48 hours prior to the mailing of any confirmation of sale to such persons, or shall be sent to such persons under such circumstances that it would normally be received by them 48 hours prior to their receipt of confirmation of the sale.

(1) Such Preliminary Offering Circular contains substantially the information required by this rule to be included in an offering circular, or contains substantially that information except for the omission of information with respect to the offering price, underwriting discounts or commissions, discounts or commissions to dealers, amount of proceeds, conversion rates, call prices, or other matters dependent upon the offering price. For issuers not subject to the reporting provisions under section 13(a) or 15(d) of the Securities Exchange Act of 1934, the disclosure on the outside front cover page of the Preliminary Offering Circular should include a bona fide estimate of the range of the maximum offering price and maximum number of shares or other units of securities to be offered or should include a bona fide estimate of the principal amount of debt securities to be offered.

(2) The outside front cover page of the Preliminary Offering Circular shall bear the caption "Preliminary Offering Circular," the date of its issuance, and the following statement which shall run along the left hand margin of the page and be printed perpendicular to the text, in boldface type at least as large as that used generally in the body of such offering circular;

An offering statement pursuant to Regulation A relating to these securities has been filed with the Securities and Exchange Commission. Information contained in this Preliminary Offering Circular is subject to completion or amendment. These securities may not be sold nor may offers to buy be accepted prior to the time an offerng circular which is not designated as a Preliminary Offering Circular is delivered. This Preliminary Offering Circular shall not constitute an offer to sell or the solicitation of an offer to buy nor shall there be any sales of these securities in any state in which such offer, solicitation or sale would be unlawful prior to registration or qualification under the securities laws of any such state.

(3) The Preliminary Offering Circular relates to a proposed public offering of securities which is to be sold by or through one or more underwriters who are broker-dealers registered under section 15 of the Securities Exchange Act of 1934, each of whom has furnished a signed Consent and Certification in the form prescribed as a condition to the use of such offering circular.

(4) An offering circular which contains all of the information specified in Part II of the offering statement and which is not designated as a Preliminary Offering Circular is furnished with or prior to delivery of the confirmation of sale to any person who has been furnished with a Preliminary Offering Circular pursuant to this paragraph.

Rule 257. Offerings Not in Excess of $100,000

Except as to issues specified in paragraph (*a*) of Rule 253 and issues of assessable stock, the offering circular (offering statement—Part II) need not be filed or used in connection with an offering of securities under this regulation if the aggregate offering price of all securities of the issuer, its predecessors and affiliates offered or sold without the use of such an offering circular does not exceed $100,000 computed in accordance with Rule 254, provided the following conditions are met:

(*a*) In addition to filing Part I—Notification and Part III—Exhibits, there shall be filed as an exhibit five copies of a statement setting forth the information (other than financial statements) required by Part II—Offering Circular of the offering statement.

(*b*) No advertisement, article or other communication published in any newspaper, magazine or other periodical and no radio or television broadcast in regard to the offering shall contain more than the following information:

(1) The name of the issuer of such security;

(2) The title of the security, amount offered, and the per-unit offering price to the public;

(3) The identity of the general type of business of the issuer;

(4) A brief statement as to the general character and location of its property; and

(5) By whom orders will be filled or from whom further information may be obtained.

Rule 258. Sales Material to Be Filed

Four copies of each of the following communications prepared or authorized by the issuer or anyone associated with the issuer, any of its affiliates or any principal underwriter for use in connection with the offering of any securities under this regulation shall be filed, with the office of the Commission with which the offering statement is filed, at least 5 days (exclusive of Saturdays, Sundays and holidays) prior to any use thereof, or such shorter period as the Commission, in its discretion, may authorize:

(*a*) Every advertisement, article or other communication proposed to be published in any newspaper, magazine or other periodical;

(*b*) The script of every radio or television broadcast; and

(*c*) Every letter, circular or other written communication proposed to be sent, given or otherwise communicated to more than 10 persons, except an offering circular (offering statement—Part II) filed pursuant to Rule 256(*e*).

Rule 259. Statement Required in All Offering Circulars

There shall be set forth on the cover page of every offering circular the following statement in capital letters printed in boldface roman type at least as large as ten-point modern type and at least two points leaded;

"THE UNITED STATES SECURITIES AND EXCHANGE COMMISSION DOES NOT PASS UPON THE MERITS OF OR GIVE ITS APPROVAL TO ANY SECURITIES OFFERED OR THE TERMS OF THE OFFERING, NOR DOES IT PASS UPON THE ACCURACY OR COMPLETENESS OF ANY OFFERING CIR-

CULAR OR OTHER SELLING LITERATURE. THESE SECURITIES ARE OFFERED PURSUANT TO AN EXEMPTION FROM REGISTRATION WITH THE COMMISSION; HOWEVER, THE COMMISSION HAS NOT MADE AN INDEPENDENT DETERMINATION THAT THE SECURITIES OFFERED HEREUNDER ARE EXEMPT FROM REGISTRATION."

Rule 260. Reports of Sales Hereunder

Within 30 days after the end of each 6-month period following the date of the original offering circular (offering statement—Part II) required by Rule 256, or of the statement required by Rule 257, the issuer or other person for whose account the securities are offered shall file with the Regional Office of the Commission with which the offering statement was filed four copies of a report on Form 2–A containing the information called for by that form. A final report shall be made upon completion or termination of the offering and may be made prior to the end of the 6-month period in which the last sale is made.

Rule 261. Suspension of Exemption

(a) The Commission may, at any time after the filing of an offering statement, enter an order temporarily suspending the exemption, if it has reason to believe that—

(1) No exemption is available under this regulation for the securities purported to be offered hereunder or any of the terms or conditions of this regulation have not been complied with, including failure to file any report as required by Rule 260.

(2) The offering statement or any other sales literature contains any untrue statement of a material fact or omits to state a material fact necessary in order to make the statements made, in the light of the circumstances under which they are made, not misleading;

(3) The offering is being made or would be made in violation of section 17 of the Act;

(4) Any event has occurred after the filing of the offering statement which would have rendered the exemption hereunder unavailable if it had occurred prior to such filing;

(5) Any person specified in paragraph (c) of Rule 252 has been indicted for any crime or offense of the character specified in subparagraph (3) thereof, or any proceeding has been initiated for the purpose of enjoining any such person from engaging in or continuing any conduct or practice of the character specified in subparagraph (4) of such paragraph;

(6) Any person specified in paragraph (d) of Rule 252 has been indicted for any crime or offense of the character specified in subparagraph (1) thereof, or any proceeding has been initiated for the purpose of enjoining any such person from engaging in or continuing any conduct or practice of the character specified in subparagraph (2) of such paragraph; or

(7) The issuer or any promoter, officer, director or underwriter has failed to cooperate, or has obstructed or refused to permit the making of an investigation by the Commission in connection with any offering made or proposed to be made hereunder.

(b) Upon the entry of an order under paragraph (a) of this rule, the Commission will promptly give notice to the persons on whose behalf the offering statement was filed (i) that such order has been entered, together with a brief statement of the reasons for the entry of the order, and (ii) that the Commission, upon receipt of a written request within 30 days after the entry of such order, will, within 20 days after the receipt of such request, set the matter down for hearing at a place to be designated by the Commission. If no hearing is requested and none is ordered by the Commission, the order shall become permanent on the 30th day after its entry and shall remain in effect unless or until it is modified or vacated by the Commission. Where a hearing is requested or is ordered by the Commission, the Commission will, after notice of and opportunity for such hearing, either vacate the order or enter an order permanently suspending the exemption.

(c) The Commission may at any time after notice of an opportunity for hearing, enter an order permanently suspending the exemption for any reason upon which it could have entered a temporary suspension order under paragraph (a) of this rule. Any such order shall remain in effect until vacated by the Commission.

(*d*) All notices required by this rule shall be given to the person or persons on whose behalf the offering statement was filed by personal service, registered or certified mail or confirmed telegraphic notice at the addresses of such persons given in the offering statement.

Rule 262. Consent to Service of Process

(*a*) If the issuer, any of its directors or officers, any person for whose account any of the securities are to be offered, or any underwriter of the securities to be offered, is not a resident of the United States, each such nonresident person shall, at the time of filing the offering statement required by Rule 255, furnish the Commission in a form prescribed by or acceptable to it, a written irrevocable consent and power of attorney which—

(1) Designates the Securities and Exchange Commission as an agent upon whom may be served any process, pleadings, or other papers in any civil suit or action brought against the person executing the consent and power of attorney or to which he has been joined as defendant or respondent, in any appropriate court in any place subject to the jurisdiction of the United States, where the cause of action (i) accrues on or after the effective date of this rule, and (ii) arises out of any offering made or purported to be made under this regulation or any purchase or sale of any security in connection therewith; and

(2) Stipulates and agrees that any such civil suit or action may be commenced by the service of process upon the Commission and the forwarding of a copy thereof as provided in paragraph (*b*) of this rule, and that the service as aforesaid of any such process, pleadings, or other papers upon the Commission shall be taken and held in all courts to be as valid and binding as if due personal service thereof had been made.

(*b*) Service of any process, pleadings or other papers on the Commission under this rule shall be made by delivering the requisite number of copies thereof to the Secretary of the Commission or to such other person as the Commission may authorize to act in its behalf. Whenever any process, pleadings or other papers as aforesaid are served upon the Commission, it shall promptly forward a copy thereof by registered or certified mail to the appropriate defendants at their last address of record filed with the Commission. The Commission shall be furnished a sufficient number of copies for such purpose, and one copy for its files.

Rule 263. Notice of Delayed or Suspended Offering and Sale

If within 3 business days after the issuer has received notice that the Commission has no further comments with respect to the offering statement a bona fide effort is not made to proceed with the offering and sale of the securities proposed to be offered under this regulation, or if the offering or sale of such securities is suspended by the issuer or any underwriter within 15 days after the issuer has received such notice, a notice of the delay or suspension, stating the reasons therefor, shall be filed by the issuer or underwriter with the Regional Office of the Commission with which the offering statement was filed, unless such information is set forth in the offering statement. Such notice shall be sent promptly by telegraph or air mail and if sent by telegraph shall be confirmed in writing within a reasonable time by the filing of a signed copy of the notice.

* * *

REGULATION C—REGISTRATION

Rule 405. Definitions of Terms

Unless the context otherwise requires, all terms used in this regulation, or in the forms for registration have the same meanings as in the Act and in the general rules and regulations. In addition, the following definitions apply, unless the context otherwise requires:

Affiliate. An "affiliate" of, or person "affiliated" with, a specified person, is a person that directly, or indirectly through one or more intermediaries, controls or is controlled by, or is under common control with, the person specified.

Amount. The term "amount," when used in regard to securities, means the principal amount if relating to evidences of indebtedness, the number of shares if relating to shares, and the number of units if relating to any other kind of security.

Associate. The term "associate," when used to indicate a relationship with any person, means (1) a corporation or organization (other than the registrant or a majority-owned subsidiary of the registrant) of which such person is an officer or partner or is, directly or indirectly, the beneficial owner of 10 percent or more of any class of equity securities, (2) any trust or other estate in which such person has a substantial beneficial interest or as to which such person serves as trustee or in a similar capacity, and (3) any relative or spouse of such person, or any relative of such spouse, who has the same home as such person or who is a director or officer of the registrant or any of its parents or subsidiaries.

Business Development Company. The term "business development company" refers to a company which has elected to be regulated as a business development company under sections 55 through 65 of the Investment Company Act of 1940.

Certified. The term "certified," when used in regard to financial statements, means examined and reported upon with an opinion expressed by an independent public or certified public accountant.

Charter. The term "charter" includes articles of incorporation, declarations of trust, articles of association or partnership, or any similar instrument, as amended, affecting (either with or without filing with any governmental agency) the organization or creation of an incorporated or unincorporated person.

Common Equity. The term "common equity" means any class of common stock or an equivalent interest, including but not limited to a unit of beneficial interest in a trust or a limited partnership.

Commission. The term "Commission" means the Securities and Exchange Commission.

Control. The term "control" (including the terms "controlling," "controlled by" and "under common control with") means the possession, direct or indirect, of the power to direct or cause the direction of the management and policies of a person, whether through the ownership of voting securities by contract, or otherwise.

Director. The term "director" mens any director of a corporation or any person performing similar functions with respect to any organization whether incorporated or unincorporated.

* * *

Employee. The term "employee" does not include a director, trustee, or officer.

Employee Benefit Plan. The term "employee benefit plan" means any purchase, savings, option, bonus, appreciation, profit sharing, thrift, incentive, pension or similar plan solely for employees, directors, trustees or officers.

Equity Security. The term "equity security" means any stock or similar security, certificate of interest or participation in any profit sharing agreement, preorganization certificate or subscription, transferable share, voting trust certificate or certificate of deposit for an equity security, limited partnership interest, interest in a joint venture, or certificate of interest in a business trust; or any security convertible, with or without consideration into such a security, or carrying any warrant or right to subscribe to or purchase such a security; or any such warrant or right; or any put, call, straddle, or other option or privilege of buying such a security from or selling such a security to another without being bound to do so.

Executive Officer. The term "executive officer," when used with reference to a registrant, means its president, any vice president of the registrant in charge of a principal business unit, division or function (such as sales, administration or finance), any other officer who performs a policy making function or any other person who performs similar policy making functions for the registrant. Executive officers of subsidiaries may be deemed executive officers of the registrant if they perform such policy making functions for the registrant.

Fiscal Year. The term "fiscal year" means the annual accounting period or, if no closing date has been adopted, the calendar year ending on December 31.

* * *

Managing underwriter. The term "managing underwriter" includes an underwriter (or underwriters) who, by contract or otherwise, deals with the registrant; organizes the selling effort; receives some benefit directly or indirectly in which all other underwriters similarly situated do not share in proportion to their respective interests in the underwriting; or represents any other underwriters in such matters as maintaining the records of the distribution, arranging the allotments of securities offered or arranging for appropriate stabilization activities, if any.

Material. The term "material," when used to qualify a requirement for the furnishing of information as to any subject, limits the information required to those matters to which there is a substantial likelihood that a reasonable investor would attach importance in determining whether to purchase the security registered.

* * *

Officer. The term "officer" means a president, vice president, secretary, treasurer or principal financial officer, comptroller or principal accounting officer, and any person routinely performing corresponding functions with respect to any organization whether incorporated or unincorporated.

Parent. A "parent" of a specified person is an affiliate controlling such person directly, or indirectly through one or more intermediaries.

Predecessor. The term "predecessor" means a person the major portion of the business and assets of which another person acquired in a single succession, or in a series of related successions in each of which the acquiring person acquired the major portion of the business and assets of the acquired person.

Principal Underwriter. The term "principal underwriter" means an underwriter in privity of contract with the issuer of the securities as to which he is underwriter, the term "issuer" having the meaning given in sections 2(4) and 2(11) of the Act.

Promoter. (1) The term "promoter" includes—

(i) Any person who, acting alone or in conjunction with one or more other persons, directly or indirectly takes initiative in founding and organizing the business or enterprise of an issuer; or

(ii) Any person who, in connection with the founding and organizing of the business or enterprise of an issuer, directly or indirectly receives in consideration of services or property, or both services and property, 10 percent or more of any class of securities of the issuer or 10 percent or more of the proceeds from the sale of any class of such securities. However, a person who receives such securities or proceeds either solely as underwriting commissions or solely in consideration of property shall not be deemed a promoter within the meaning of this paragraph if such person does not otherwise take part in founding and organizing the enterprise.

(2) All persons coming within the definition of "promoter" in paragraph (1) of this definition may be referred to as "founders" or "organ-

izers" or by another term provided that such term is reasonably descriptive of those persons' activities with respect to the issuer.

Prospectus. Unless otherwise specified or the context otherwise requires, the term "prospectus" means a prospectus meeting the requirements of section 10(a) of the Act.

Registrant. The term "registrant" means the issuer of the securities for which the registration statement is filed.

Share. The term "share" means a share of stock in a corporation or unit of interest in an unincorporated person.

* * *

Succession. The term "succession" means the direct acquisition of the assets comprising a going business, whether by merger, consolidation, purchase, or other direct transfer. The term does not include the acquisition of control of a business unless followed by the direct acquisition of its assets. The terms "succeed" and "successor" have meanings correlative to the foregoing.

* * *

Voting Securities. The term "voting securities" means securities the holders of which are presently entitled to vote for the election of directors.

* * *

FORM S-1

Registration Statement Under The Securities Act of 1933

GENERAL INSTRUCTIONS

I. Eligibility Requirements for Use of Form S-1

This Form shall be used for the registration under the Securities Act of 1933 ("Securities Act") of securities of all registrants for which no other form is authorized or prescribed, except that this Form shall not be used for securities of foreign governments or political sub-divisions thereof.

II. Application of General Rules and Regulations

A. Attention is directed to the General Rules and Regulations under the Securities Act, particularly those comprising Regulation C thereunder. That Regulation contains general requirements regarding the preparation and filing of the registration statement.

B. Attention is directed to Regulation S-K for the requirements applicable to the content of the nonfinancial statement portions of registration statements under the Securities Act. Where this Form directs the registrant to furnish information required by Regulation S-K and the item of Regulation S-K so provides, information need only be furnished to the extent appropriate.

III. Exchange Offers

If any of the securities being registered are to be offered in exchange for securities of any other issuer the prospectus shall also include the information which would be required by Item 11 if the securities of such other issuer were registered on this Form. There shall also be included the information concerning such securities of such other issuer which would be called for by Item 9 if such securities were being registered. In connection with this instruction, reference is made to Rule 409.

PART I. INFORMATION REQUIRED IN PROSPECTUS

Item 1. Forepart of the Registration Statement and Outside Front Cover Page of Prospectus

Set forth in the forepart of the registration statement and on the outside front cover page of the prospectus the information required by Item 501 of Regulation S-K.

Item 2. Inside Front and Outside Back Cover Pages of Prospectus

Set forth on the inside front cover page of the prospectus or, where permitted, on the outside back cover page, the information required by Item 502 of Regulation S–K.

Item 3. Summary Information, Risk Factors and Ratio of Earnings to Fixed Charges

Furnish the information required by Item 503 of Regulation S–K.

Item 4. Use of Proceeds

Furnish the information required by Item 504 of Regulation S–K.

Item 5. Determination of Offering Price

Furnish the information required by Item 505 of Regulation S–K.

Item 6. Dilution

Furnish the information required by Item 506 of Regulation S–K.

Item 7. Selling Security Holders

Furnish the information required by Item 507 of Regulation S–K.

Item 8. Plan of Distribution

Furnish the information required by Item 508 of Regulation S–K.

Item 9. Description of Securities to Be Registered

Furnish the information required by Item 202 of Regulation S–K.

Item 10. Interests of Named Experts and Counsel

Furnish the information required by Item 509 of Regulation S–K.

Item 11. Information With Respect to the Registrant

Furnish the following information with respect to the registrant:

(a) Information required by Item 101 of Regulation S–K, description of business;

(b) Information required by Item 102 of Regulation S–K, description of property;

(c) Information required by Item 103 of Regulation S–K, legal proceedings;

(d) Where common equity securities are being offered, information required by Item 201 of Regulation S–K, market price of and dividends on the registrant's common equity and related stockholder matters;

(e) Financial statements meeting the requirements of Regulation S–X;

(f) Information required by Item 301 of Regulation S–K, selected financial data;

(g) Information required by Item 302 of Regulation S–K, supplementary financial information;

(h) Information required by Item 303 of Regulation S–K, management's discussion and analysis of financial condition and results of operations;

(i) Information required by Item 304 of Regulation S–K, disagreements with accountants on accounting and financial disclosure;

(j) Information required by Item 401 of Regulation S–K, directors and executive officers;

(k) Information required by Item 402 of Regulation S–K, management remuneration and transactions; and

(*l*) Information required by Item 403 of Regulation S–K, security ownership of certain beneficial owners and management.

Item 12. Disclosure of Commission Position on Indemnification for Securities Act Liabilities

Furnish the information required by Item 510 of Regulation S–K.

PART II. INFORMATION NOT REQUIRED IN PROSPECTUS

Item 13. Other Expenses of Issuance and Distribution

Furnish the information required by Item 511 of Regulation S–K.

Item 14. Indemnification of Directors and Officers

Furnish the information required by Item 702 of Regulation S–K.

Item 15. Recent Sales of Unregistered Securities

Furnish the information required by Item 701 of Regulation S–K.

Item 16. Exhibits and Financial Statement Schedules

(a) Subject to the rules regarding incorporation by reference, furnish the exhibits as required by Item 601 of Regulation S–K.

(b) Furnish the financial statement schedules required by Regulation S–X, and item 11(a)(5) of this Form. These schedules shall be lettered or numbered in the manner described for exhibits in paragraph (a).

Item 17. Undertakings

Furnish the undertakings required by Item 512 of Regulation S–K.

FORM S–14

For Simplified Registration Procedure for Securities in Certain Transactions Under Rules 133 and 145

GENERAL INSTRUCTIONS

A. Rule as to Use of Form S–14.

Form S–14 and Form S–1 may be used for registration under the Securities Act of 1933 of securities to be issued in a transaction specified in paragraph (a) of Rule 145; provided, however, that Form S–14 shall not be so used unless the prospectus is delivered to the security holders whose vote or consent is solicited at least 20 days prior to the date on which the meeting of such security holders is held or the date on which the transaction is effectuated if no such meeting is held: provided further, that if applicable law of the jurisdiction permits the furnishing of a notice of the meeting or other action within less than the 20-day period specified herein, then compliance with such provisions of such law shall be deemed to satisfy this requirement. Form S–14 may also be used by persons and parties who may be deemed underwriters, for the registration of a public reoffering of securities issued in a transaction specified in paragraph (a) of Rule 145 or in a transaction specified in paragraph (a) of Rule 133 exempted by that rule prior to its rescission effective on or after January 1, 1973.

* * *

C. Compliance with Proxy or Information Rules.

(a) If a corporation or other person submits a proposal to its security holders entitled to vote on or consent to the proposed transaction of the character described in Rule 145, and such person's submission to its security holders is subject to Regulation 14A or 14C under the Securities Exchange Act of 1934, then the provisions of such regulations shall apply in all respects to such person's submission, except that copies of the preliminary and definitive proxy or information statement, form of proxy or other material filed as a part of the registration statement shall be deemed filed pursuant to such person's obligations under such regulations. All other soliciting material shall be filed in accordance with such regulations.

(b) If the proxy or information material sent to such security holders is not subject to Regulation 14A or 14C, all such material shall be filed as a part of the registration statement at the time the statement is filed or as an amendment thereto prior to the use of such material.

PART I. INFORMATION REQUIRED IN PROSPECTUS

Item 1. Forepart of Registration Statement and Outside Front Cover Page of Prospectus

Set forth on the outside front cover page of the prospectus the information required by Item 501 of Regulation S–K.

Instruction. The cross-reference sheet required by Item 501 shall show the location of the information required by proxy or information rules, as specified in Item 5 of this form.

Item 2. Inside Front and Outside Back Cover Pages of Prospectus

Set forth on the inside front cover page of the prospectus or, where permitted, on the outside back cover page, the information required by Item 502 of Regulation S–K.

Item 3. Summary Information, Risk Factors and Ratio of Earnings to Fixed Charges

Furnish the information required by Item 503 of Regulation S–K.

Item 4. Market Price of and Dividends on the Registrant's Common Equity and Related Stockholder Matters

Furnish the information required by Item 201 of Regulation S–K.

Item 5. Information Required by Proxy or Information Rules

(a) If the registrant or any other person which is a party to the transaction in which the securities to be registered are to be issued, is required to solicit proxies pursuant to Section 14 (a), or furnish information to security holders pursuant to Section 14(c), of the Securities Exchange Act of 1934 in regard to the transaction, the prospectus shall contain the information required to be included in, and may be in the form of, such proxy or information statement.

(b) If neither the registrant nor any other person which is a party to the transaction in which the securities to be registered are to be issued is required to solicit proxies pursuant to Section 14(a), or to furnish information to security holders pursuant to Section 14(c), of the Securities Exchange Act of 1934 in regard to the transaction, then the prospectus shall contain the information which would be required to be included in a proxy or information statement of the registrant if it were subject to Section 14(a) or 14(c) and may be in form of such a proxy or information statement.

Item. 6. Additional Information Required for Reoffering by Persons and Parties Deemed to be Underwriters

If any of the securities are to be reoffered to the public by any person or party who is deemed to be an underwriter thereof, within the meaning of Rule 145(c), the prospectus shall, at the time of such offering, include the following additional information which would then be required to be included in the prospectus by the appropriate registration form, other than Form S–14, to the extent that such information is not already included in the prospectus:

(a) Furnish the information required by Item 507 of Regulation S–K;

(b) Information with respect to the consummation of the Rule 145 transaction and any material developments in the business or affairs of the registrant subsequent to the transaction; and

(c) Any other information necessary to make the prospectus current, including financial statements of the registrant and any other party to the transaction.

Instruction. Information in response to Item 6(a) may be included to describe public reofferings proposed to be made, if such reofferings are subject only to consummation of the transaction described in Rule 145 (a).

Item. 7. Interests of Named Experts and Counsel

Furnish the information required by Item 509 of Regulation S–K.

Item 8. Disclosure of Commission Position on Indemnification for Securities Act Liabilities

Furnish the information required by Item 510 of Regulation S–K.

PART II. INFORMATION NOT REQUIRED IN PROSPECTUS

Item 9. Indemnification of Directors and Officers

Furnish the information required by Item 702 of Regulation S–K.

Item 10. Exhibits

Subject to the rules regarding incorporation by reference, furnish the exhibits required by Item 601 of Regulation S–K.

Item 11. Undertakings

Furnish the undertakings required by Item 512 of Regulation S–K.

FORM S–18

Registration Statement Under the Securities Act of 1933 for Certain Offerings Not in Exess of $5,000,000

GENERAL INSTRUCTIONS

I. Rule as to Use of Form S–18.

A. This form is to be used for the registration of securities not to exceed an aggregate offering price of $5 million which are to be sold for cash, installments for cash and/or cash assessments and assumptions by partners of partnership debt, by the registrant, or for the account of security holders in accordance with paragraph B, provided such registrant:

(1) Is organized under the laws of the United States or Canada or any State or Province thereof, and has or proposes to have its principal business operations in the United States, if a domestic issuer, or Canada or the United States if a Canadian issuer;

(2) Is not subject to the reporting provisions of the Securities Exchange Act of 1934 pursuant to Sections 12 or 15(d) of that Act;

(3) Is not an investment company;

(4) Is not an insurance company which is exempt from the provisions of Section 12 of the Securities Exchange Act of 1934 in reliance upon Section 12(g)(2)(G) thereof; and

(5) Is not a majority owned subsidiary of a registrant which does not meet the qualifications for use of the form, as specified herein.

B. This form may be used for the registration of securities to be sold for the account of any person other than the registrant, provided: (i) the aggregate offering price of such securities does not exceed $1.5 million and (ii) the aggregate offering price of such securities together with the aggregate offering price of any securities to be sold by the registrant does not exceed $5 million.

C. For purposes of computing the $5 million ceiling specified above, there shall be included in the aggregate offering price of the securities registered herein, the aggregate offering price of all securities sold: (i) by the registrant within one year prior to the commencement of the proposed offering in violation of Section 5(a) of the Securities Act; (ii) by the registrant within one year prior to the commencement of the proposed offering pursuant to a registration statement filed on Form S–18; and (iii) which would be deemed integrated with the proposed offering. In computing the $5 million ceiling, the aggregate price of all securities sold which fall in more than one of the above described categories need be counted only once.

D. Notwithstanding the provisions of paragraph (A)(2), a registrant which has had a prior offering on Form S–18 may, during the remainder of the fiscal year in which the prior registration statement was made effective, use the form to register additional securities until the offering limit as computed in paragraph C has been met.

II. Place of Filing.

A. At the election of the registrant, all registration statements on Form S–18 and related papers filed with the Commission shall be filed either at its principal office in Washington, D. C. or in the Regional Office for the region in which the registrant's principal business operations are conducted, or are proposed to be conducted. The registration statement of any registrant having or proposing to have its principal business operations in Canada may be filed with the Regional Office nearest the place where the registrant's principal business operations are conducted, or are proposed to be conducted: *Provided, however,* That if the offering is to be made through a principal underwriter located in the United

States, the offering statement may be filed with the Regional Office for the region in which such underwriter has its principal office. Such material may be filed by delivery to the Commission through the mails or otherwise. Questions concerning the appropriate place of filing may be directed to the Commission's Regional Offices.

B. The Commission will endeavor to process Form S–18 registration statements at the place of filing. However, due to workload or other special consideration, the Commission may refer processing to a different Commission office.

C. All post-effective amendments to the Form S–18 registration statement shall be filed in the office where the corresponding Form S–18 registration statement was declared effective.

PART I. INFORMATION REQUIRED IN PROSPECTUS

Item 1. Forepart of the Registration Statement and Outside Front Cover Page of Prospectus.

Set forth in the forepart of the registration statement and on the outside front cover page of the prospectus the information required by Item 501 of Regulation S–K.

Item 2. Inside Front and Outside Back Cover Pages of Prospectus.

Set forth on the inside front cover page of the prospectus or, where permitted, on the outside back cover page, the information required by Item 502 of Regulation S–K.

Item 3. Summary Information and Risk Factors.

Furnish the information required by Item 503 (a), (b), and (c) of Regulation S–K.

Item 4. Use of Proceeds.

Furnish the information required by Item 504 of Regulation S–K.

Item 5. Determination of Offering Price.

Furnish the information required by Item 505 of Regulation S–K.

Item 6. Dilution.

Furnish the information required by Item 506 of Regulation S–K.

Item 7. Selling Security Holders.

Furnish the information required by Item 507 of Regulation S–K.

Item 8. Plan of Distribution.

Furnish the information required by Item 508 of Regulation S–K, except the information specified in Item 508(c)(1), (3), and (d).

Item 9. Legal Proceedings.

Furnish the information required by Item 103 of Regulation S–K.

Item 10. Directors and Executive Officers.

Furnish the information required by Item 401 of Regulation S–K.

Item 11. Security Ownership of Certain Beneficial Owners and Management.

Furnish the information required by Item 403 of Regulation S–K.

Item 12. Description of the Securities To Be Registered.

Furnish the information required by Item 202 of Regulation S–K.

Item 13. Interest of Named Experts and Counsel.

Furnish the information required by Item 509 of Regulation S–K.

Item 14. Statement as to Indemnification.

Furnish the information required by Item 510 of Regulation S–K.

Item 15. Organization Within 5 Years.

If the registrant was organized within the past 5 years, furnish the following information:

(a) State the names of the promoters, the nature and amount of anything of value (including money, property, contracts, options or rights of any kind) received or to be received by each promoter directly or indirectly from the registrant, and the nature and amount of any assets, services or other consideration therefor received or to be received by the registrant. The term "promotor" is defined in Rule 405 under the Act.

(b) As to any assets acquired or to be acquired by the registrant from a promoter, state the amount at which acquired or to be acquired and the principle followed or to be followed in determining the amount. Identify the persons making the determination and state their relationship, if any, with the registrant or any promoter. If the assets were acquired by the promoter within two years prior to their transfer to the registrant, state the cost thereof to the promoter.

(c) List all parents of the registrant showing the basis of control and as to each parent, the percentage of voting securities owned or other basis of control by its immediate parent if any.

Instruction. Include the registrant and show the percentage of its voting securities owned or other basis of control by its immediate parent.

Item 16.   Description of Business.

(a) *General development of business.* Describe the general development of the business of the registrant, its subsidiaries and any predecessor(s) during the past five years, or such shorter period as the registrant may have been engaged in business. Information shall be disclosed for earlier periods if material to an understanding of the general development of the business.

(1) In describing developments, information shall be given as to matters such as the following: the year in which the registrant was organized and its form of organization; the nature and results of any bankruptcy, receivership or similar proceedings with respect to the registrant or any of its significant subsidiaries; the nature and results of any other material reclassification, merger or consolidation of the registrant or any of its significant subsidiaries; the acquisition or disposition of any material amount of assets otherwise than in the ordinary course of business; and any material changes in the mode of conducting the business.

Instruction: The following requirement in paragraph (2) applies only to registrants (including predecessors) which have not received revenue from operations during each of the three fiscal years immediately prior to the filing of the registration statement.

(2) Describe, if formulated, the registrant's plan of operation for the remainder of the fiscal year, if the registration statement is filed prior to the end of the registrant's second fiscal quarter. Describe, if formulated, the registrant's plan of operation for the remainder of the fiscal year and for the first six months of the next fiscal year if the registration statement is filed subsequent to the end of the second fiscal quarter. If such information is not available, the reasons for its not being available shall be stated. Disclosure relating to any plan should include such matters as:

(i) A statement in narrative form indicating the registrant's opinion as to the period of time that the proceeds from the offering will satisfy cash requirements and whether in the next six months it will be necessary to raise additional funds to meet the expenditures required for operating the business of the registrant. The specific reasons for such opinion shall be set forth and categories of expenditures and sources of cash resources shall be identified; however, amounts of expenditure and cash resources need not be provided. In addition, if the narrative statement is based on a cash budget, such budget should be furnished to the Commission as supplemental information, but not as a part of the registration statement.

(ii) An explanation of material product research and development to be performed during the period covered in the plan.

(iii) Any anticipated material acquisition of plant and equipment and the capacity thereof.

(iv) Any anticipated material changes in number of employees in the various departments such as research and development, production, sales or administration.

(v) Other material areas which may be peculiar to the registrant's business.

(b) *Narrative description of business.*

(1) Describe the business done and intended to be done by the registrant and its subsidiaries. Such description should include, if material to an understanding of the registrant's business, a discussion of:

(a) the principal products produced and services rendered and the principal markets for and methods of distribution of such products and services.

(b) the status of a product or service if the issuer has made public information about a new product or service which would require the investment of a material amount of the assets of the registrant or is otherwise material.

(c) the estimated amount spent during each of the last two fiscal years on company-sponsored research and development activities determined in accordance with generally accepted accounting principles. In addition, state the estimated dollar amount spent during each of such years on material customer-sponsored research activities relating to the development of new products, services or techniques or the improvement of existing products, services or techniques.

(d) the number of persons employed by the registrant indicating the number employed full time.

(e) the material effects that compliance with Federal, State and local provisions which have been enacted or adopted regulating the discharge of materials into the environment, or otherwise relating to the protection of the environment, may have upon the capital expenditures, earnings and competitive position of the registrant and its subsidiaries. The registrant shall disclose any material estimated capital expenditures for environmental control facilities for the remainder of its current fiscal year and for such further periods as the registrant may deem material.

(2) The registrant should also describe those distinctive or special characteristics of the registrant's operations or industry which may have a material impact upon the registrant's future financial performance. Examples of factors which might be discussed include dependence on one or a few major customers or suppliers (including suppliers of raw materials or financing), existing or probable governmental regulation, expiration of material labor contracts or patents, trademarks, licenses, franchises, concessions or royalty agreements, unusual competitive conditions in the industry, cyclicality of the industry and anticipated raw material or energy shortages to the extent management may not be able to secure a continuing source of supply.

(c) *Segment data.* If the registrant is required to include segment information in its financial statements, such information may be disclosed in the description of business or in the financial statements. If such information is included in the financial statements, an appropriate cross reference shall be included in the description of business.

Item 17. Description of Property.

State briefly the location and general character of the principal plants, and other materially important physical properties of the registrant and its subsidiaries. If any such property is not held in fee or is held subject to any major encumbrance, so state and briefly describe how held.

Instruction. What is required is information essential to an investor's appraisal of the securities being registered. Such information should be furnished as will reasonably inform investors as to the suitability, adequacy, productive capacity and extent of utilization of the facilities used in the enterprise. Detailed descriptions of the physical characteristics of individual properties or legal descriptions by metes and bounds are not required and should not be given.

* * *

Item 18. Interest of Management and Others in Certain Transactions.

Describe briefly any transactions during the previous two years or any presently proposed transactions, to which the registrant or any of its subsidiaries was or is to be a party, in which any of the following persons had or is to have a direct or indirect material interest, naming such person and stating his relationship to the issuer, the nature of his interest in the transaction and, where practicable, the amount of such interest:

(1) Any director or officer of the issuer;

(2) Any nominee for election as a director;

(3) Any security holder named in answer to Item 11; or

(4) Any relative or spouse of any of the foregoing persons, or any relative of such spouse, who has the same house as such persons or who is a director or officer of any parent or subsidiary of the registrant.

Instructions. 1. See Instruction 2 to Item 20(a)(1). No information need be given in response to this item as to any remuneration or other transaction reported in response to Item 20 or specifically excluded from Item 20.

431

2. No information need be given in answer to this item as to any transaction where:

(a) the rates or charges involved in the transaction are determined by competitive bids, or the transaction involves the rendering of services as a common or contract carrier, or public utility, at rates or charges fixed in conformity with law or governmental authority;

(b) the transaction involves services as a bank depositary of funds, transfer agent, registrar, trustee under a trust indenture, or similar services;

(c) the amount involved in the transaction or a series of similar transactions, including all periodic installments in the case if any lease or other agreement providing for periodic payments or installments, does not exceed $40,000; or

(d) the interest of the specified person arises solely from the ownership of securities of the issuer and the specified person receives no extra or special benefit not shared on a pro rata basis by all holders of securities of the class.

3. It should be noted that this item calls for disclosure of indirect, as well as direct, material interests in transactions. A person who has a position or relationship with a firm, corporation, or other entity, which engages in a transaction with the issuer or its subsidiaries may have an indirect interest in such transaction by reason of such position or relationship. However, a person shall be deemed not to have a material indirect interest in a transaction within the meaning of this item where:

(a) the interest arises only (i) from such person's position as a director of another corporation or organization (other than a partnership) which is a party to the transaction, or (ii) from the direct or indirect ownership by such person and all other persons specified in subparagraphs (1) through (3)

above, in the aggregate, of less than a 10 percent equity interest in another person (other than a partnership) which is a party to the transaction, or (iii) from both such position and ownership.

(b) the interest arises only from such person's position as a limited partner in a partnership in which he and all other persons specified in (1) through (4) above had an interest of less than 10 percent; or

(c) the interest of such person arises solely from the holding of an equity interest (including a limited partnership interest but excluding a general partnership interest) or a creditor interest in another person which is a party to the transaction with the issuer or any of its subsidiaries and the transaction is not material to such other person.

4. Include the name of each person whose interest in any transaction is described and the nature of the relationships by reason of which such interest is required to be described. The amount of the interest of any specified person shall be computed without regard to the amount of the profit or loss involved in the transaction. Where it is not practicable to state the approximate amount of the interest, the approximate amount involved in the transaction shall be disclosed.

5. Information should be included as to any material underwriting discounts and commissions upon the sale of securities by the registrant where any of the specified persons was or is to be a principal underwriter or is a controlling person, or member, of a firm which was or is to be a principal underwriter. Information need not be given concerning ordinary management fees paid by underwriters to a managing underwriter pursuant to an agreement among underwriters the parties to which do not include the registrant or its subsidiaries.

6. As to any transaction involving the purchase or sale of assets by or to the regis-

trant or any subsidiary, otherwise than in the ordinary course of business, state the cost of the assets to the purchaser and if acquired by the seller within two years prior to the transaction, the cost thereof to the seller.

7. Information shall be furnished in answer to this item with respect to transactions not excluded above which involve remuneration from the registrant or its subsidiaries, directly or indirectly, to any of the specified persons for services in any capacity usless the interest of such persons arises solely from the ownership individually and in the aggregate of less than 10% of any class of equity securities of another corporation furnishing the services to the registrant or its subsidiaries.

8. The foregoing instructions specify certain transactions and interests as to which information may be omitted in answering this item. There may be situations where, although the foregoing instructions do not expressly authorize nondisclosure, the interest of a specified person in the particular transaction or series of transactions is not a material interest. In that case, information regarding such interest and transaction is not required to be disclosed in response to this item. The materiality of any interest or transaction is to be determined on the basis of the significance of the information to investors in light of all of the circumstances of the particular transaction. The importance of the interest to the person having the interest, the relationship of the parties to the transaction to each other and the amount involved in the transaction are among the factors to be considered in determining the significance of the information to investors.

Item 19. Certain Market Information.

Furnish the information required by Item 201 (a)(2) of Regulation S–K.

Item 20. Remuneration of Directors and Officers.

(a) Furnish the following information in substantially the tabular form indicated as to all remuneration concerning the following persons for services in all capacities:

(i) each of the five highest paid persons who are officers or directors of the registrant whose aggregate remuneration exceeded $50,000, naming each such person.

(ii) all directors and officers of the registrant as a group, without naming them.

Name of individual or identity of group	Capacities in which remuneration was received	Aggregate remuneration

Instructions. 1. Information is to be included as to all options, securities, or other property given for services, annuity, pension, or retirement benefits; bonus or profit sharing plans; future remuneration; or personal benefits. In case of remuneration paid or to be paid otherwise than in cash, if it is impracticable to determine the cash value thereof, state in a note to the table the nature and amount thereof.

2. This item applies to any person who was a director or officer of the registrant at any time during the period specified. However, information need not be given for any portion of the period during which such person was not a director or officer of the registrant.

3. This item is to be answered on an accrual basis if practicable; if not so answered, state the basis used.

4. If the registrant has not completed a full fiscal year since its organization or if it acquired or is to acquire the majority of its assets from a predecessor within the current fiscal year, the information shall be given for the current fiscal year, estimating future payments, if necessary. To the extent that such remuneration is to be computed upon the basis of a percentage of profits, it will suffice to state such percentage without estimating the amount of such profits to be paid.

5. Personal benefits. Disclosure shall be provided as to the value of personal benefits which are not directly related to job performance, other than those provided to broad categories of employees and which do not discriminate in favor of officers or directors, furnished by the registrant or its subsidiaries directly or through third par-

433

ties to each of the specified persons and groups, or benefits furnished by the registrant or its subsidiaries to other persons which indirectly benefit the specified persons.

6. Information relating to any pension or retirement benefits need not be disclosed if the amounts to be paid are computed on an actuarial basis under any plan which provides for fixed benefits in the event of retirement at a specified age or after a specified number of years of service.

7. Information need not be included as to payments to be made for, or benefits to be received from, group life or accident insurance, group hospitalization or similar group payments or benefits. If it is impracticable to state the amount of remuneration payments proposed to be made, the aggregate amount set aside or accrued to date in respect of such payments should be stated.

(b) Furnish the following information as to options to purchase securities from the registrant or any of its subsidiaries which are outstanding as of a specified date not more than 30 days prior to the date of filing of the registration statement held by (1) each director and executive officer named in answer to paragraph (a), above, naming each such person, and (2) all directors and officers as a group without naming them:

(i) the title and amount of the securities called for by such options;

(ii) the purchase price of the securities called for and the expiration dates of such options; and

(iii) the market value of the securities called for by such options as of the latest practicable date.

> *Instructions.* 1. The term "options" as used in this item includes all options, warrants, and rights other than those issued to security holders on a pro rata basis.
>
> 2. The extension of options shall be deemed the granting of options within the meaning of this item.
>
> 3. Where the total market value of securities called for by all outstanding options as of the specified date referred to in this item does not exceed $10,000 for any direc-

tor or executive officer named in answer to paragraph (a), above, or $50,000 for all officers and directors as a group this item need not be answered with respect to options held by such person or group.

> 4. In case a number of options are outstanding having different prices and expiration dates, the options may be grouped by prices and date. If this produces more than five separate groups, then there may be shown only the range of the expiration dates and the average purchase prices, i.e., the aggregate purchase price of all securities of the same class called for by all outstanding options to purchase securities of that class divided by the number of securities of such class so called for.

Item 21. Financial Statements.

(a) General

(1) The financial statements of the registrant, or the registrant and its predecessors or any businesses to which the registrant is a successor, which are to be filed as part of the registration statement shall be prepared in accordance with generally accepted accounting principles (GAAP) in the United States or in the case of a Canadian registrant, a reconciliation to such U. S. GAAP shall be included in a note or schedule to the financial statements.

(2) Regulation S–X, Form and Content of Requirements for Financial Statements, shall not apply to the preparation of such financial statements, except that the report and qualifications of the independent accountant shall comply with the requirements of Article 2 of Regulation S–X, and registrants engaged in oil and gas producing activities shall follow the financial accounting and reporting standards specified in Article 4–10 of Regulation S–X with respect to such activities.

(3) The Commission may, upon the informal written request of the registrant, and where consistent with the protection of investors, permit the omission of one or more of the financial statements herein required or the filing in substitution therefor of appropriate statements of comparable character. The Commission may also by informal written notice require the filing of other financial statements in addition to, or in substitution for, the statements herein required

in any case where such statements are necessary or appropriate for as adequate presentation of the financial condition of any person whose financial statements are required, or whose statements are otherwise necessary for the protection of investors.

(b) Consolidated Balance Sheets

(1) The registrant and its subsidiaries consolidated shall file an audited balance sheet as of the end of the most recent fiscal year, or as of a date within 135 days of the date of filing the registration statement if the registrant (including predecessors) existed for a period less than one fiscal year.

(2) When the filing date of the registration statement falls after 134 days subsequent to the end of the registrant's most recent fiscal year a balance sheet as of an interim date within 135 days of the filing date also shall be included in the registration statement. Such balance sheet need not be audited and may be in condensed form.

(c) Consolidated Statements of Income, Changes in Financial Condition and Stockholder's Equity.

(1) There shall be filed for the registrant and its subsidiaries consolidated, statements of income, changes in financial position and stockholders equity for each of the two fiscal years preceding the date of the most recent audited balance sheet being filed (or for such shorter period as the registrant has been in business), and for the interim period, if any, between the end of the most recent fiscal year and the date of the most recent balance sheet being filed. These statements should be audited to the date of the most recent audited balance sheet being filed. Any interim financial statements may be in condensed form.

(2) If an income statement is filed for an interim period there shall also be filed, except for registrants in the development stage as defined by GAAP, an income statement for a comparable period of the prior year.

(3) In connection with any unaudited statement for an interim period a statement shall be made that all adjustments necessary to a fair statement of the results for such period have been included. If all such adjustments are of a normal recurring nature, a statement to that effect shall be made; otherwise, there shall be furnished information describing in appropriate detail the nature and amount of any adjustments other than normal recurring adjustments entering into the determination of the results shown.

* * *

PART II. INFORMATION NOT REQUIRED IN PROSPECTUS

Item 22. Indemnification of Directors and Officers.

Furnish the information called for Item 702 of Regulation S–K.

Item 23. Other Expenses of Issuance and Distribution.

Furnish the information called for by Item 511 of Regulation S–K.

Item 24. Recent Sales of Unregistered Securities.

Furnish the information called for by Item 701 of Regulation S–K.

Item 25. Exhibits.

Furnish the exhibits as required by Item 601 of Regulation S–K.

Item 26. Undertakings.

Furnish the undertakings required by Item 512 of Regulation S–K.

* * *

Rule 460. Distribution of Preliminary Prospectus

(a) Pursuant to the statutory requirement that the Commission in ruling upon requests for acceleration of the effective date of a registration statement shall have due regard to the adequacy of the information respecting the issuer theretofore available to the public, the Commission may consider whether the persons making the offering have taken reasonable steps to make the information contained in the registration statement conveniently available to underwriters and dealers who it is reasonably anticipated will be invited to participate in the distribution of the security to be offered or sold.

(b) As a minimum, reasonable steps to make the information conveniently available would involve the distribution, to each underwriter and dealer who it is reasonably anticipated will be invited to participate in the distribution of the security, a reasonable time in advance of the anticipated effective date of the registration statement, of as many copies of the proposed form of preliminary prospectus permitted by Rule 430 as appears to be reasonable to secure adequate distribution of the preliminary prospectus.

(c) The granting of acceleration will not be conditioned upon

(1) The distribution of a preliminary prospectus in any state where such distribution would be illegal; or

(2) The distribution of a preliminary prospectus (i) in the case of a registration statement relating solely to securities to be offered at competitive bidding, provided the undertaking in Item 512(d)(1) of Regulation S-K is included in the registration statement and distribution of prospectuses pursuant to such undertaking is made prior to the publication or distribution of the invitation for bids, or (ii) in the case of a registration statement relating to a security is-sued by a face-amount certificate company or a redeemable security issued by an open-end management company or unit investment trust if any other security of the same class is currently being offered or sold, pursuant to an effective registration statement by the issuer or by or through an underwriter, or (iii) in the case of an offering of subscription rights unless it is contemplated that the distribution will be made through dealers and the underwriters intend to make the offering during the stockholders' subscription period, in which case copies of the preliminary prospectus must be distributed to dealers prior to the effective date of the registration statement in the same fashion as is required in the case of other offerings through underwriters, or (iv) in the case of a registration statement pertaining to a security to be offered pursuant to an exchange offer or transaction described in Rule 145.

REGULATION D—LIMITED OFFERINGS

Preliminary Notes

1. The following rules relate to transactions exempted from the registration requirements of section 5 of the Securities Act of 1933 (the "Act"). Such transactions are not exempt from the antifraud, civil liability, or other provisions of the federal securities laws. Issuers are reminded of their obligation to provide such further material information, if any, as may be necessary to make the information required under this regulation, in light of the circumstances under which it is furnished, not misleading.

2. Nothing in these rules obviates the need to comply with any applicable state law relating to the offer and sale of securities. Regulation D is intended to be a basic element in a uniform system of federal-state limited offering exemptions consistent with the provisions of sections 18 and 19(c) of the Act. In those states that have adopted Regulation D, or any version of Regulation D, special attention should be directed to the applicable state laws and regulations, including those relating to registration of persons who receive remuneration in connection with the of-fer and sale of securities, to disqualification of issuers and other persons associated with offerings based on state administrative orders or judgments, and to requirements for filings of notices of sales.

3. Attempted compliance with any rule in Regulation D does not act as an exclusive election; the issuer can also claim the availability of any other applicable exemption. For instance, an issuer's failure to satisfy all the terms and conditions of Rule 506 shall not raise any presumption that the exemption provided by section 4(2) of the Act is not available.

4. These rules are available only to the issuer of the securities and not to any affiliate of that issuer or to any other person for resales of the issuer's securities. The rules provide an exemption only for the transactions in which the securities are offered or sold by the issuer, not for the securities themselves.

5. These rules may be used for business combinations that involve sales by virtue of Rule 145(a) or otherwise.

6. In view of the objectives of these rules and the policies underlying the Act, Regulation D is not available to any issuer for any transaction or chain of transactions that, although in technical compliance with these rules, is part of a plan or scheme to evade the registration provisions of the Act. In such cases, registration under the Act is required.

Rule 501. Definitions and Terms Used in Regulation D

As used in Regulation D, the following terms shall have the meaning indicated:

(a) *Accredited investor.* "Accredited investor" shall mean any person who comes within any of the following categories, or who the issuer reasonably believes comes within any of the following categories, at the time of the sale of the securities to that person:

(1) Any bank as defined in section 3(a)(2) of the Act whether acting in its individual or fiduciary capacity; insurance company as defined in section 2(13) of the Act; investment company registered under the Investment Company Act of 1940 or a business development company as defined in section 2(a)(48) of that Act; Small Business Investment Company licensed by the U. S. Small Business Administration under section 301(c) or (d) of the Small Business Investment Act of 1958; employee benefit plan within the meaning of Title I of the Employee Retirement Income Security Act of 1974, if the investment decision is made by a plan fiduciary, as defined in section 3(21) of such Act, which is either a bank, insurance company, or registered investment adviser, or if the employee benefit plan has total assets in excess of $5,000,000;

(2) Any private business development company as defined in section 202(a)(22) of the Investment Advisers Act of 1940;

(3) Any organization described in Section 501(c)(3) of the Internal Revenue Code with Total assets in excess of $5,000,000;

(4) Any director, executive officer, or general partner of the issuer of the securities being offered or sold, or any director, executive officer, or general partner of a general partner of that issuer;

(5) Any person who purchases at least $150,000 of the securities being offered, where the purchaser's total purchase price does not exceed 20 percent of the purchaser's net worth at the time of sale, or joint net worth with that person's spouse, for one or any combination of the following: (i) cash, (ii) securities for which market quotations are readily available, (iii) an unconditional obligation to pay cash or securities for which market quotations are readily available which obligation is to be discharged within five years of the sale of the securities to the purchaser, or (iv) the cancellation of any indebtedness owed by the issuer to the purchaser;

(6) Any natural person whose individual net worth, or joint net worth with that person's spouse, at the time of his purchase exceeds $1,000,000;

(7) Any natural person who had an individual income in excess of $200,000 in each of the two most recent years and who reasonably expects an income in excess of $200,000 in the current year; and

(8) Any entity in which all of the equity owners are accredited investors under paragraph (a)(1), (2), (3), (4), (6), or (7) of Rule 501.

(b) *Affiliate.* An "affiliate" of, or person "affiliated" with, a specified person shall mean a person that directly, or indirectly through one or more intermediaries, controls or is controlled by, or is under common control with, the person specified.

(c) *Aggregate offering price.* "Aggregate offering price" shall mean the sum of all cash, services, property, notes, cancellation of debt, or other consideration received by an issuer for issuance of its securities. Where securities are being offered for both cash and non-cash consideration, the aggregate offering price shall be based on the price at which the securities are offered for cash. If securities are not offered for cash, the aggregate offering price shall be based on the value of the consideration as established by bona fide sales of that consideration made within a reasonable time, or, in the absence of sales, on the fair value as determined by an accepted standard.

(d) *Business combination.* "Business combination" shall mean any transaction of the type specified in paragraph (a) of Rule 145 under the Act and any transaction involving the acquisition by one issuer, in exchange for all or a part of its own or its parent's stock, of stock of another issuer if, immediately after the acquisition, the acquiring issuer has control of the other issuer (whether or not it had control before the acquisition).

(e) *Calculation of number of purchasers.* For purposes of calculating the number of purchasers under Rule 505(b) and Rule 506(b) only, the following shall apply:

(1) The following purchasers shall be excluded:

(i) Any relative, spouse or relative of the spouse of a purchaser who has the same principal residence as the purchaser;

(ii) Any trust or estate in which a purchaser and any of the persons related to him as specified in paragraph (e)(1)(i) or (e)(1)(iii) of Rule 501 collectively have more than 50 percent of the beneficial interest (excluding contingent interests);

(iii) Any corporation or other organization of which a purchaser and any of the persons related to him as specified in paragraph (e)(1)(i) or (e)(1)(ii) of Rule 501 collectively are beneficial owners of more than 50 percent of the equity securities (excluding directors' qualifying shares) or equity interests; and

(iv) Any accredited investor.

(2) A corporation, partnership or other entity shall be counted as one purchaser. If, however, that entity is organized for the specific purpose of acquiring the securities offered and is not an accredited investor under paragraph (a)(8) of Rule 501, then each beneficial owner of equity securities or equity interests in the entity shall count as a separate purchaser for all provisions of Regulation D.

Note: The issuer must satisfy all the other provisions of Regulation D for all purchasers whether or not they are included in calculating the number of purchasers. Clients of an investment adviser or customers of a broker or dealer shall be considered the "purchasers" under Regulation D regardless of the amount of discretion given to the investment adviser or broker or dealer to act on behalf of the client or customer.

(f) *Executive officer.* "Executive officer" shall mean the president, any vice president in charge of a principal business unit, division or function (such as sales, administration or finance), any other officer who performs a policy making function, or any other person who performs similar policy making functions for the issuer. Executive officers of subsidiaries may be deemed executive officers of the issuer if they perform such policy making functions for the issuer.

(g) *Issuer.* The definition of the term "issuer" in section 2(4) of the Act shall apply, except that in the case of a proceeding under the Federal Bankruptcy Code, the trustee or debtor in possession shall be considered the issuer in an offering under a plan of reorganization, if the securities are to be issued under the plan.

(h) *Purchaser representative.* "Purchaser representative" shall mean any person who satisfies all of the following conditions or who the issuer reasonably believes satisfies all of the following conditions:

(1) Is not an affiliate, director, officer or other employee of the issuer, or beneficial owner of 10 percent or more of any class of the equity securities or 10 percent or more of the equity interest in the issuer, except where the purchaser is:

(i) A relative of the purchaser representative by blood, marriage or adoption and not more remote than a first cousin;

(ii) A trust or estate in which the purchaser representative and any persons related to him as specified in paragraph (h)(1)(i) or (h)(1)(iii) of Rule 501 collectively have more than 50 percent of the beneficial interest (excluding contingent interest) or of which the purchaser representative serves as trustee, executor, or in any similar capacity; or

(iii) A corporation or other organization of which the purchaser representative and any persons related to him as specified in paragraph (h)(1)(i) or (h)(1)(ii) of Rule 501 collectively are the beneficial owners of more than 50 percent of the equity securities (excluding directors' qualifying shares) or equity interests;

(2) Has such knowledge and experience in financial and business matters that he is capable of evaluating, alone, or together with other purchaser representatives of the purchaser, or together with the purchaser, the merits and risks of the prospective investment;

(3) Is acknowledged by the purchaser in writing, during the course of the transaction, to be his purchaser representative in connection with evaluating the merits and risks of the prospective investment; and

(4) Discloses to the purchaser in writing prior to the acknowledgment specified in paragraph (h)(3) of Rule 501 any material relationship between himself or his affiliates and the issuer or its affiliates that then exists, that is mutually understood to be contemplated, or that has existed at any time during the previous two years, and any compensation received or to be received as a result of such relationship.

Note 1: A person acting as a purchaser representative should consider the applicability of the registration and antifraud provisions relating to brokers and dealers under the Securities Exchange Act of 1934 ("Exchange Act") and relating to investment advisers under the Investment Advisers Act of 1940.

Note 2: The acknowledgment required by paragraph (h)(3) and the disclosure required by paragraph (h)(4) of Rule 501 must be made with specific reference to each prospective investment. Advance blanket acknowledgment, such as for "all securities transactions" or "all private placements," is not sufficient.

Note 3: Disclosure of any material relationships between the purchaser representa-

tive or his affiliates and the issuer or its affiliates does not relieve the purchaser representative of his obligation to act in the interest of the purchaser.

Rule 502. General Conditions to be Met

The following conditions shall be applicable to offers and sales made under Regulation D:

(a) *Integration.* All sales that are part of the same Regulation D offering must meet all of the terms and conditions of Regulation D. Offers and sales that are made more than six months before the start of a Regulation D offering or are made more than six months after completion of a Regulation D offering will not be considered part of that Regulation D offering, so long as during those six month periods there are no offers or sales of securities by or for the issuer that are of the same or a similar class as those offered or sold under Regulation D, other than those offers or sales of securities under an employee benefit plan as defined in Rule 405 under the Act.

Note: The term "offering" is not defined in the Act or in Regulation D. If the issuer offers or sells securities for which the safe harbor rule in paragraph (a) of Rule 502 is unavailable, the determination as to whether separate sales of securities are part of the same offering (*i.e.* are considered "integrated") depends on the particular facts and circumstances.

The following factors should be considered in determining whether offers and sales should be integrated for purposes of the exemptions under Regulation D:

(a) Whether the sales are part of a single plan of financing;

(b) Whether the sales involve issuance of the same class of securities;

(c) Whether the sales have been made at or about the same time;

(d) Whether the same type of consideration is received; and

(e) Whether the sales are made for the same general purpose. *See* Release No. 33–4552 (November 6, 1962).

(b) *Information requirements.*

(1) *When information must be furnished.*

(i) If the issuer sells securities either under Rule 504 or only to accredited investors, paragraph (b) of Rule 502 does not require that specific information be furnished to purchasers.

(ii) If the issuer sells securities under Rule 505 or Rule 506 to any purchaser that is not an accredited investor, the issuer shall furnish the information specified in paragraph (b)(2) of Rule 502 to all purchasers during the course of the offering and prior to sale.

(2) *Type of information to be furnished.*

(i) If the issuer is not subject to the reporting requirements of section 13 or 15(d) of the Exchange Act, the issuer shall furnish the following information, to the extent material to an understanding of the issuer, its business, and the securities being offered:

(A) *Offerings up to $5,000,000.* The same kind of information as would be required in Part I of Form S-18, except that only the financial statements for the issuer's most recent fiscal year must be certified by an independent public or certified accountant. If Form S-18 is not available to an issuer, then the issuer shall furnish the same kind of information as would be required in Part I of a registration statement filed under the Act on the form that the issuer would be entitled to use, except that only the financial statements for the most recent two fiscal years prepared in accordance with generally accepted accounting principles shall be furnished and only the financial statements for the issuer's most recent fiscal year shall be certified by an independent public or certified accountant. If an issuer, other than a limited partnership, cannot obtain audited financial statements without unreasonable effort or expense, then only the issuer's balance sheet, which shall be dated within 120 days of the start of the offering, must be audited. If the issuer is a limited partnership and cannot obtain the required financial statements without unreasonable effort or expense, it may furnish financial statements that have been prepared on the basis of federal income tax requirements and examined and reported on in accordance with generally accepted auditing standards by an independent public or certified accountant.

(B) *Offerings over $5,000,000.* The same kind of information as would be required in Part I of a registration statement filed under the Act on the form that the issuer would be entitled to use. If an issuer, other than a limited partnership, cannot obtain audited financial statements without unreasonable effort or expense, then only the issuer's balance sheet, which shall be dated within 120 days of the start of the offering, must be audited. If the issuer is a limited partnership and cannot obtain the required financial statements without unreasonable effort or expense, it may furnish financial statements that have been prepared on the basis of federal income tax requirements and examined and reported on in accordance with generally accepted auditing standards by an independent public or certified accountant.

(ii) If the issuer is subject to the reporting requirements of section 13 or 15(d) of the Exchange Act, the issuer shall furnish the information specified in paragraph (b)(2)(ii)(A) or (b)(2)(ii)(B), and in either event the information specified in paragraph (b)(2)(ii)(C) of Rule 502:

(A) The issuer's annual report to shareholders for the most recent fiscal year, if such annual report meets the requirements of Rule 14a-3 or Rule 14c-3 under the Exchange Act, the definitive proxy statement filed in connection with that annual report, and, if requested by the purchaser in writing, a copy of the issuer's most recent Form 10–K under the Exchange Act.

(B) The information contained in an annual report on Form 10–K under the Exchange Act or in a registration statement on Form S–1 under the Act or on Form 10 under the Exchange Act, whichever filing is the most recent required to be filed.

(C) The information contained in any reports or documents required to be filed by the issuer under sections 13(a), 14(a), 14(c), and 15(d) of the Exchange Act since the distribution or filing of the report or registration statement specified in paragraph (A) or (B), and a brief description of the securities being offered, the use of the proceeds from the offering, and any material changes in the issuer's affairs that are not disclosed in the documents furnished.

(iii) Exhibits required to be filed with the Commission as part of a registration statement or report, other than an annual report to shareholders or parts of that report incorporated by reference in a Form 10–K report, need not be furnished to each purchaser if the contents of the exhibits are identified and the exhibits are made available to the purchaser, upon his written request, prior to his purchase.

(iv) At a reasonable time prior to the purchase of securities by any purchaser that is not an accredited investor in a transaction under Rule 505 or Rule 506, the issuer shall furnish the purchaser a brief description in writing of any written information concerning the offering that has been provided by the issuer to any accredited investor. The issuer shall furnish any portion or all of this information to the purchaser, upon his written request, prior to his purchase.

(v) The issuer shall also make available to each purchaser at a reasonable time prior to his purchase of securities in a transaction under Rule 505 or Rule 506 the oppor-tunity to ask questions and receive answers concerning the terms and conditions of the offering and to obtain any additional information which the issuer possesses or can acquire without unreasonable effort or expense that is necessary to verify the accuracy of information furnished under paragraph (b)(2)(i) or (ii) of Rule 502.

(vi) For business combinations, in addition to information required by paragraph (b)(2) of Rule 502, the issuer shall provide to each purchaser at the time the plan is submitted to security holders, or, with an exchange, during the course of the transaction and prior to sale, written information about any terms or arrangements of the proposed transaction that are materially different from those for all other security holders.

(c) *Limitation on manner of offering.* Except as provided in Rule 504(b)(1), neither the issuer nor any person acting on its behalf shall offer or sell the securities by any form of general solicitation or general advertising, including, but not limited to, the following:

(1) Any advertisement, article, notice or other communication published in any newspaper, magazine, or similar media or broadcast over television or radio; and

(2) Any seminar or meeting whose attendees have been invited by any general solicitation or general advertising.

(d) *Limitations on resale.* Except as provided in Rule 504(b)(1), securities acquired in a transaction under Regulation D shall have the status of securities acquired in a transaction under section 4(2) of the Act and cannot be resold without registration under the Act or an exemption therefrom. The issuer shall exercise reasonable care to assure that the purchasers of the securities are not underwriters within the meaning of section 2(11) of the Act, which reasonable care shall include, but not be limited to, the following:

(1) Reasonable inquiry to determine if the purchaser is acquiring the securities for himself or for other persons;

(2) Written disclosure to each purchaser prior to sale that the securities have not been registered under the Act and, therefore, cannot be resold unless they are registered under the Act or unless an exemption from registration is available; and

(3) Placement of a legend on the certificate or other document that evidences the securities stating that the securities have not been registered under the Act and setting forth or referring to the restrictions on transferability and sale of the securities.

Rule 503. Filing of Notice of Sales

(a) The issuer shall file with the Commission five copies of a notice on Form D at the following times:

(1) No later than 15 days after the first sale of securities in an offering under Regulation D;

(2) Every six months after the first sale of securities in an offering under Regulation D, unless the final notice required by paragraph (a)(3) of Rule 503 has been filed; and

(3) No later than 30 days after the last sale of securities in an offering under Regulation D.

(b) If the offering is completed within the 15 day period described in paragraph (a)(1) of Rule 503 and if the notice is filed no later than the end of that period but after the completion of the offering, then only one notice need be filed to comply with paragraphs (a)(1) and (3) of Rule 503.

(c) One copy of every notice on Form D shall be manually signed by a person duly authorized by the issuer.

(d) If sales are made under Rule 505, the notice shall contain an undertaking by the issuer to furnish to the Commission, upon the written request of its staff, the information furnished by the issuer under Rule 502(b)(2) to any purchaser that is not an accredited investor.

(e) If more than one notice for an offering is required to be filed under paragraph (a) of Rule 503, notices after the first notice need only report the issuer's name and the information required by Part C and any material change in the facts from those set forth in Parts A and B of the first notice.

(f) A notice on Form D shall be considered filed with the Commission under paragraph (a) of Rule 503:

(1) As of the date on which it is received at the Commission's principal office in Washington, D.C.; or

(2) As of the date on which the notice is mailed by means of United States registered or certified mail to the Commission's Office of Small Business Policy, Division of Corporation Finance, at the Commission's principal office in Washington, D.C., if the notice is delivered to such office after the date on which it is required to be filed.

Rule 504. Exemption for Limited Offers and Sales of Securities Not Exceeding $500,000

(a) *Exemption.* Offers and sales of securities that satisfy the conditions in paragraph (b) of Rule 504 by an issuer that is not subject to the reporting requirements of section 13 or 15(d) of the Exchange Act and that is not an investment company shall be exempt from the provisions of section 5 of the Act under section 3(b) of the Act.

(b) *Conditions to be met.*

(1) *General conditions.* To qualify for exemption under Rule 504, offers and sales must satisfy the terms and conditions of Rules 501 through 503, except that the provisions of Rule 502(c) and (d) shall not apply to offers and sales of securities under Rule 504 that are made exclusively in one or more states each of which provides for the registration of the securities and requires the delivery of a disclosure document before sale and that are made in accordance with those state provisions.

(2) *Specific condition.*

(i) *Limitation on aggregate offering price.* The aggregate offering price for an offering of securities under Rule 504, as defined in Rule 501(c), shall not exceed $500,000, less the aggregate offering price for all securities sold within the twelve months before the start of and during the offering of securities under Rule 504 in reliance on any exemption under section 3(b) of the Act or in violation of section 5(a) of the Act.

Note 1: The calculation of the aggregate offering price is illustrated as follows:

Example 1. If an issuer sold $200,000 of its securities on June 1, 1982 under Rule 504 and an additional $100,000 on September 1, 1982, the issuer would be permitted to sell only $200,000 more under Rule 504 until June 1, 1983. Until that date the issuer must count both prior sales towards the $500,000 limit. However, if the issuer made its third sale on June 1, 1983, the issuer could then sell $400,000 of its securities because the June 1, 1982 sale would not be within the preceding twelve months.

Example 2. If an issuer sold $100,000 of its securities on June 1, 1982 under Rule 504 and an additional $4,500,000 on December 1, 1982 under Rule 505, the issuer could not sell any of its securities under Rule 504 until December 1, 1983. Until then the issuer must count the December 1, 1982 sale towards the limit of $500,000 within the preceding twelve months.

Note 2: If a transaction under Rule 504 fails to meet the limitation on the aggregate offering price, it does not affect the availability of Rule 504 for the other transactions considered in applying such limitation. For example, if the issuer in *Example 1* made its third sale on May 31, 1983, in the amount of $250,000, Rule 504 would not be available for that sale, but the exemption for the prior two sales would be unaffected.

Rule 505. Exemption for Limited Offers and Sales of Securities Not Exceeding $5,000,-000

(a) *Exemption.* Offers and sales of securities that satisfy the conditions in paragraph (b) of Rule 505 by an issuer that is not an investment company shall be exempt from the provisions of section 5 of the Act under section 3(b) of the Act.

(b) *Conditions to be met.*

(1) *General conditions.* To qualify for exemption under Rule 505, offers and sales must satisfy the terms and conditions of Rules 501 through 503.

(2) *Specific conditions.*

(i) *Limitation on aggregate offering price.* The aggregate offering price for an offering of securities under Rule 505, as defined in Rule 501(c), shall not exceed $5,000,000, less the aggregate offering price for all securities sold within the twelve months before the start of and during the offering of securities under Rule 505 in reliance on any exemption under section 3(b) of the Act or in violation of section 5(a) of the Act.

Note: The calculation of the aggregate offering price is illustrated as follows:

Example 1. If an issuer sold $2,000,000 of its securities on June 1, 1982 under Rule 505 and an additional $1,000,000 on September 1, 1982, the issuer would be permitted to sell only $2,000,000 more under Rule 505 until June 1, 1983. Until that date the issuer must count both prior sales towards the $5,000,000 limit. However, if the issuer made its third sale on June 1, 1983, the issuer could then sell $4,000,000 of its securities because the June 1, 1982 sale would not be within the preceding twelve months.

Example 2. If an issuer sold $500,000 of its securities on June 1, 1982 under Rule 504 and an additional $4,500,000 on December 1, 1982 under Rule 505, then the issuer could not sell any of its securities under Rule 505 until June 1, 1983. At that time it could sell an additional $500,000 of its securities.

(ii) *Limitation on number of purchasers.* The issuer shall reasonably believe that there are no more than 35 purchasers of securities from the issuer in any offering under Rule 505.

Note: See Rule 501(e) for the calculation of the number of purchasers and Rule 502(a) for what may or may not constitute an offering under this section.

(iii) *Disqualifications.* No exemption under Rule 505 shall be available for the securities of any issuer described in Rule 252(c), (d), (e), or (f) of Regulation A, except that for purposes of Rule 505 only:

(A) The term "filing of the notification required by Rule 255" as used in Rule 252(c), (d), (e) and (f) shall mean the first sale of securities under Rule 505;

(B) The term "underwriter" as used in Rule 252(d) and (e) shall mean a person that has been or will be paid directly or indirectly remuneration for solicitation of purchasers in connection with sales of securities under Rule 505; and

(C) Paragraph (b)(2)(iii) of Rule 505 shall not apply to any issuer if the Commission determines, upon a showing of good cause, that it is not necessary under the circumstances that the exemption be denied. Any such determination shall be without prejudice to any other action by the Commission in any other proceeding or matter with respect to the issuer or any other person.

Rule 506. Exemption for Limited Offers and Sales Without Regard to Dollar Amount of Offering

(a) *Exemption.* Offers and sales of securities by an issuer that satisfy the conditions in paragraph (b) of Rule 506 shall be deemed to be transactions not involving any public offering within the meaning of section 4(2) of the Act.

(b) *Conditions to be met.*

(1) *General conditions.* To qualify for exemption under Rule 506, offers and sales must satisfy all the terms and conditions of Rules 501 through 503.

(2) *Specific conditions.*

(i) *Limitation on number of purchasers.* The issuer shall reasonably believe that there are no more than 35 purchasers of securities from the issuer in any offering under Rule 506.

Note: See Rule 501(e) for the calculation of the number of purchasers and Rule 502(a) for what may or may not constitute an offering under Rule 506.

(ii) *Nature of purchasers.* The issuer shall reasonably believe immediately prior to making any sale that each purchaser who is not an accredited investor either alone or with his purchaser representative(s) has such knowledge and experience in financial and business matters that he is capable of evaluating the merits and risks of the prospective investment.

C. SECURITIES EXCHANGE ACT OF 1934

15 U.S.C.A. §§ 78a et seq.

Contents

TITLE I—REGULATION OF SECURITIES EXCHANGES

FOREIGN CORRUPT PRACTICES ACT OF 1977

TITLE I—REGULATION OF SECURITIES EXCHANGES

Short Title

SECTION 1. This act may be cited as the "Securities Exchange Act of 1934."

Necessity for Regulation as Provided in This Title

SECTION 2. For the reasons hereinafter enumerated, transactions in securities as commonly conducted upon securities exchanges and over-the-counter markets are affected with a national public interest which makes it necessary to provide for regulation and control of such transactions and of practices and matters related thereto, including transactions by officers, directors, and principal security holders, to require appropriate reports, to remove impediments to and perfect the mechanisms of a national market system for securities and a national system for the clearance and settlement of securities transactions and the safeguarding of securities and funds related thereto, and to impose requirements necessary to make such regulation and control reasonably complete and effective, in order to protect interstate commerce, the national credit, the Federal taxing power, to protect and make more effective the national banking system and Federal Reserve System, and to insure the maintenance of fair and honest markets in such transactions:

(1) Such transactions (a) are carried on in large volume by the public generally and in large part originate outside the States in which the exchanges and over-the-counter markets are located

and/or are effected by means of the mails and instrumentalities of interstate commerce; (b) constitute an important part of the current of interstate commerce; (c) involve in large part the securities of issuers engaged in interstate commerce; (d) involve the use of credit, directly affect the financing of trade, industry, and transportation in interstate commerce, and directly affect and influence the volume of interstate commerce; and affect the national credit.

(2) The prices established and offered in such transactions are generally disseminated and quoted throughout the United States and foreign countries and constitute a basis for determining and establishing the prices at which securities are bought and sold, the amount of certain taxes owing to the United States and to the several States by owners, buyers, and sellers of securities, and the value of collateral for bank loans.

(3) Frequently the prices of securities on such exchanges and markets are susceptible to manipulation and control, and the dissemination of such prices gives rise to excessive speculation, resulting in sudden and unreasonable fluctuations in the prices of securities which (a) cause alternately unreasonable expansion and unreasonable contraction of the volume of credit available for trade, transportation, and industry in interstate commerce, (b) hinder the proper appraisal of the value of securities and thus prevent a fair calculation of taxes owing to the United States and to the several States by owners, buyers, and sellers of securities, and (c) prevent the fair valuation of collateral for bank loans and/or obstruct the effective operation of the national banking system and Federal Reserve System.

(4) National emergencies, which produce widespread unemployment and the dislocation of trade, transportation, and industry, and which burden interstate commerce and adversely affect the general welfare, are precipitated, intensified, and prolonged by manipulation and sudden and unreasonable fluctuations of security prices and by excessive speculation on such exchanges and markets, and to meet such emergencies the Federal Government is put to such great expense as to burden the national credit.

Definitions and Application of Title

Section 3. (a) When used in this title, unless the context otherwise requires—

(1) The term "exchange" means any organization, association, or group of persons, whether incorporated or unincorporated, which constitutes, maintains, or provides a market place or facilities for bringing together purchasers and sellers of securities or for otherwise performing with respect to securities the functions commonly performed by a stock exchange as that term is generally understood, and includes the market place and the market facilities maintained by such exchange.

(2) The term "facility" when used with respect to an exchange includes its premises, tangible or intangible property whether on the premises or not, any right to the use of such premises or property or any service thereof for the purpose of effecting or reporting a transaction on an exchange (including, among other things, any system of communication to or from the exchange, by ticker or otherwise, maintained by or with the consent of the exchange), and any right of the exchange to the use of any property or service.

(3)(A) The term "member" when used with respect to a national securities exchange means (i) any natural person permitted to effect transactions on the floor of the exchange without the services of another person acting as broker, (ii) any registered broker or dealer with which such a natural person is associated, (iii) any registered broker or dealer permitted to designate as a representative such a natural person, and (iv) any other registered broker or dealer which agrees to be regulated by such exchange and with respect to which the exchange undertakes to enforce compliance with the provisions of this title, the rules and regulations thereunder, and its own rules. For purposes of sections 6(b)(1), 6(b)(4), 6(b)(6), 6(b)(7), 6(d), 17(d), 19(d), 19(e), 19(g), 19(h), and 21 of this title, the term "member" when used with respect to a national securities exchange also means, to the extent of the rules of the exchange specified by the Commission, any person required by the Commission to comply with such rules pursuant to section 6(f) of this title.

(B) The term "member" when used with respect to a registered securities association means any broker or dealer who agrees to be regulated by such association and with respect to whom the association undertakes to enforce compliance with the provisions of this title, the rules and regulations thereunder, and its own rules.

(4) The term "broker" means any person engaged in the business of effecting transactions in securities for the account of others, but does not include a bank.

(5) The term "dealer" means any person engaged in the business of buying and selling securities for his own account, through a broker or otherwise, but does not include a bank, or any person insofar as he buys or sells securities for his own account, either individually or in some fiduciary capacity, but not as a part of a regular business.

(6) The term "bank" means (A) a banking institution organized under the laws of the United States, (B) a member bank of the Federal Reserve System, (C) any other banking institution, whether incorporated or not, doing business under the laws of any State or of the United States, a substantial portion of the business of which consists of receiving deposits or exercising fiduciary powers similar to those permitted to national banks under section 11 (k) of the Federal Reserve Act, as amended, and which is supervised and examined by State or Federal authority having supervision over banks, and which is not operated for the purpose of evading the provisions of this title, and (D) a receiver, conservator, or other liquidating agent of any institution or firm included in clauses (A), (B), or (C) of this paragraph.

(7) The term "director" means any director of a corporation or any person performing similar functions with respect to any organization, whether incorporated or unincorporated.

(8) The term "issuer" means any person who issues or proposes to issue any security; except that with respect to certificates of deposit for securities, voting-trust certificates, or collateral-trust certificates, or with respect to certificates of

interest or shares in an unincorporated investment trust not having a board of directors or of the fixed, restricted management, or unit type, the term "issuer" means the person or persons performing the acts and assuming the duties of depositor or manager pursuant to the provisions of the trust or other agreement or instrument under which such securities are issued; and except that with respect to equipment-trust certificates or like securities, the term "issuer" means the person by whom the equipment or property is, or is to be, used.

(9) The term "person" means a natural person, company, government, or political subdivision, agency, or instrumentality of a government.

(10) The term "security" means any note, stock, treasury stock, bond, debenture, certificate of interest or participation in any profit-sharing agreement or in any oil, gas, or other mineral royalty or lease, any collateral-trust certificate, preorganization certificate or subscription, transferable share, investment contract, voting-trust certificate, certificate of deposit, for a security, or in general, any instrument commonly known as a "security"; or any certificate of interest or participation in, temporary or interim certificate for, receipt for, or warrant or right to subscribe to or purchase, any of the foregoing; but shall not include currency or any note, draft, bill of exchange, or banker's acceptance which has a maturity at the time of issuance of not exceeding nine months, exclusive of days of grace, or any renewal thereof the maturity of which is likewise limited.

(11) The term "equity security" means any stock or similar security; or any security convertible, with or without consideration, into such a security; or carrying any warrant or right to subscribe to or purchase such a security; or any such warrant or right; or any other security which the Commission shall deem to be of similar nature and consider necessary or appropriate, by such rules and regulations as it may prescribe in the public interest or for the protection of investors, to treat as an equity security.

(12) The term "exempted security" or "exempted securities" includes securities which are direct obligations of or obligations guaranteed as

to principal or interest by the United States; such securities issued or guaranteed by corporations in which the United States has a direct or indirect interest as shall be designated for exemption by the Secretary of the Treasury as necessary or appropriate in the public interest or for the protection of investors; municipal securities, as defined in section 3(a)(29) of this title; Provided, however, That municipal securities shall not be deemed to be "exempted securities" for the purposes of sections 15, 15A (except subsections (b)(6), (b)(11), and (g)(2) thereof), and 17A, of this title; any interest or participation in any common trust fund or similar fund maintained by a bank exclusively for the collective investment and reinvestment of assets contributed thereto by such bank in its capacity as trustee, executor, administrator, or guardian; any interest or participation in a collective trust fund maintained by a bank or in a separate account maintained by an insurance company which interest or participation is issued in connection with (A) a stock-bonus, pension, or profit-sharing plan which meets the requirements for qualification under section 401 of the Internal Revenue Code of 1954, or (B) an annuity plan which meets the requirements for the deduction of the employer's contribution under section 404(a)(2) of such Code, or (C) a governmental plan as defined in section 414(d) of such code which has been established by an employer for the exclusive benefit of its employees or their beneficiaries for the purpose of distributing to such employees or their beneficiaries the corpus and income of the funds accumulated under such plan, if under such plan it is impossible, prior to the satisfaction of all liabilities with respect to such employees and their beneficiaries, for any part of the corpus or income to be used for, or diverted to, purposes other than the exclusive benefit of such employees or their beneficiaries, other than any plan described in clause (A), (B), or (C) of this paragraph (i) which covers employees some or all of whom are employees within the meaning of section 401(c) of such Code, or (ii) which is a plan funded by an annuity contract described in section 403(b) of such Code; and such other securities (which may include, among others, unregistered securities, the market in which is predominantly intrastate) as the Commission may, by such rules and regulations as it deems consistent with the public interest and the protection of investors, either unconditionally or upon specified terms and conditions or for stated periods, exempt from the operation of any or more provisions of this title which by their terms do not apply to an "exempted security" or to "exempted securities."

(13) The terms "buy" and "purchase" each include any contract to buy, purchase, or otherwise acquire.

(14) The terms "sale" and "sell" each include any contract to sell or otherwise dispose of.

(15) The term "Commission" means the Securities and Exchange Commission established by section 4 of this title.

(16) The term "State" means any State of the United States, the District of Columbia, Puerto Rico, the Canal Zone, the Virgin Islands, or any other possession of the United States.

(17) The term "interstate commerce" means trade, commerce, transportation, or communication among the several States, or between any foreign country and any State, or between any State and any place or ship outside thereof. The term includes intrastate use of (A) any facility of a national securities exchange or of a telephone or other interstate means of communication, or (B) any other interstate instrumentality.

(18) The term "person associated with a broker or dealer" or "associated person of a broker or dealer" means any partner, officer, director, or branch manager of such broker or dealer (or any person occupying a similar status or performing similar functions), or any person directly or indirectly controlling, controlled by, or under common control with such broker or dealer, or any employee of such broker or dealer, except that any person associated with a broker or dealer whose functions are solely clerical or ministerial shall not be included in the meaning of such term for purposes of section 15(b) of this title (other than paragraph (6) thereof).

(19) The terms "investment company," "affiliated person," "insurance company," "separate account", and "company" have the same meanings as in the Investment Company Act of 1940.

(20) The terms "investment adviser" and "underwriter" have the same meanings as in the Investment Advisers Act of 1940.

* * *

(26) The term "self-regulatory organization" means any national securities exchange, registered securities association, or registered clearing agency, or (solely for purposes of sections 19(b), 19(c), and 23(b) of this title) the Municipal Securities Rulemaking Board established by section 15B of this title.

* * *

(34) The term "appropriate regulatory agency" means—

* * *

(i) the Comptroller of the Currency, in the case of a national bank or a bank operating under the Code of Law for the District of Columbia.

(ii) the Board of Governors of the Federal Reserve System, in the case of any other member bank of the Federal Reserve System.

(iii) the Federal Deposit Insurance Corporation, in the case of any other bank the deposits of which are insured in accordance with the Federal Deposit Insurance Act; and

(iv) the Commission in the case of all other persons.

* * *

(38) The term "market maker" means any specialist permitted to act as a dealer, any dealer acting in the capacity of block positioner, and any dealer who, with respect to a security, holds himself out (by entering quotations in an inter-dealer communications system or otherwise) as being willing to buy and sell such security for his own account on a regular or continuous basis.

(39) A person is subject to a "statutory disqualification" with respect to membership or participation in, or association with a member of, a self-regulatory organization, if such person—

(A) has been and is expelled or suspended from membership or participation in, or barred or suspended from being associated with a member of, any self-regulatory organization;

(B) is subject to an order of the Commission denying, suspending for a period not exceeding twelve months, revoking his registration as a broker, dealer, or municipal securities dealer, or barring his being associated with a broker, dealer, or municipal securities dealer;

(C) by his conduct while associated with a broker, dealer, or municipal securities dealer, has been found to be a cause of any effective suspension, expulsion, or order of the character described in subparagraph (A) or (B) of this paragraph, and in entering such a suspension, expulsion, or order, the Commission or any such self-regulatory organization shall have jurisdiction to find whether or not any person was a cause thereof;

(D) has associated with him any person who is known, or in the exercise of reasonable care should be known, to him to be a person described by subparagraph (A), (B), or (C) of this paragraph; or

(E) has committed or omitted any act enumerated in subparagraph (D) or (E) of paragraph (4) of section 15(b) of this title, has been convicted of any offense specified in subparagraph (B) of such paragraph (4) within ten years of the date of the filing of an application for membership or participation in, or to become associated with a member of, such self-regulatory organization, is enjoined from any action, conduct, or practice specified in subparagraph (C) of such paragraph (4), has willfully made or caused to be made in any application for membership or participation in, or to become associated with a member of, a self-regulatory organization, report required to be filed with a self-regulatory organization, or proceeding before a self-regulatory organization, any statement which was at the time, and in the light of the circumstances under which it was made, false or misleading with respect to any material fact, or has omitted to state in any such application, report, or proceeding any material fact which is required to be stated therein.

(b) The Commission and the Board of Governors of the Federal Reserve System, as to matters within their respective jurisdictions, shall have power by rules and regulations to define technical, trade, accounting, and other terms used in this title, consistently with the provisions and purposes of this title.

* * *

Securities and Exchange Commission

SECTION 4. (a) There is hereby established a Securities and Exchange Commission (hereinafter referred to as the "Commission") to be composed of five commissioners to be appointed by the President by and with the advice and consent of the Senate. Not more than three of such commissioners shall be members of the same political party, and in making appointments members of different political parties shall be appointed alternately as nearly as may be practicable. No commissioner shall engage in any other business, vocation, or employment than that of serving as commissioner, nor shall any commissioner participate, directly or indirectly, in any stock-market operations or transactions of a character subject to regulation by the Commission pursuant to this title. Each Commissioner shall hold office for a term of five years and until his successor is appointed and has qualified, except that he shall not so continue to serve beyond the expiration of the next session of Congress subsequent to the expiration of said fixed term of office, and except (1) any Commissioner appointed to fill a vacancy occurring prior to the expiration of the term for which his predecessor was appointed shall be appointed for the remainder of such term, and (2) the terms of office of the Commissioners first taking office after the enactment of this title shall expire as designated by the President at the time of nomination, one at the end of one year, one at the end of two years, one at the end of three years, one at the end of four years, and one at the end of fiive years, after the date of the enactment of this title.

(b) The Commission is authorized to appoint and fix the compensation of such officers, attorneys, examiners, and other experts as may be necessary for carrying out its functions under this Act, without regard to the provisions of other laws applicable to the employment and compensation of officers and employees of the United States, and the Commission may, subject to the civil-service laws, appoint such other officers and employees as are necessary in the execution of its functions and fix their salaries in accordance with the Classification Act of 1923, as amended.

Transactions on Unregistered Exchanges

SECTION 5. It shall be unlawful for any broker, dealer, or exchange, directly or indirectly, to make use of the mails or any means or instrumentality of interstate commerce for the purpose of using any facility of an exchange within or subject to the jurisdiction of the United States to effect any transaction in a security, or to report any such transaction, unless such exchange (1) is registered as a national securities exchange under section 6 of this title, or (2) is exempted from such registration upon application by the exchange because, in the opinion of the Commission, by reason of the limited volume of transactions effected on such exchange, it is not practicable and not necessary or appropriate in the public interest or for the protection of investors to require such registration.

National Securities Exchanges

SECTION 6. (a) An exchange may be registered as a national securities exchange under the terms and conditions hereinafter provided in this section and in accordance with the provisions of section 19(a) of this title, by filing with the Commission an application for registration in such form as the Commission, by rule, may prescribe containing the rules of the exchange and such other information and documents as the Commission, by rule, may prescribe as necessary or appropriate in the public interest or for the protection of investors.

(b) An exchange shall not be registered as a national securities exchange unless the Commission determines that—

(1) Such exchange is so organized and has the capacity to be able to carry out the purposes of this title and to comply, and (subject to any rule or order of the Commission pursuant to section 17(d) or 19(g)(2) of this title) to enforce compliance by its members and persons associated with its members, with the provisions of this title, the rules and regulations thereunder, and the rules of the exchange.

(2) Subject to the provisions of subsection (c) of this section, the rules of the exchange provide that any registered broker or dealer or natural person associated with a registered broker or dealer may become a member of such exchange and any person may become associated with a member thereof.

(3) The rules of the exchange assure a fair representation of its members in the selection of its directors and administration of its affairs and provide that one or more directors shall be representative of issuers and investors and not be associated with a member of the exchange, broker, or dealer.

(4) The rules of the exchange provide for the equitable allocation of reasonable dues, fees, and other charges among its members and issuers and other persons using its facilities.

(5) The rules of the exchange are designed to prevent fraudulent and manipulative acts and practices, to promote just and equitable principles of trade, to foster cooperation and coordination with persons engaged in regulating, clearing, settling, processing information with respect to, and facilitating transactions in securities, to remove impediments to and perfect the mechanism of a free and open market and a national market system, and, in general, to protect investors and the public interest; and are not designed to permit unfair discrimination between customers, issuers, brokers, or dealers, or to regulate by virtue of any authority conferred by this title matters not related to the purposes of this title or the administration of the exchange.

(6) The rules of the exchange provide that (subject to any rule or order of the Commission pursuant to section 17(d) or 19 (g)(2) of this title) its members and persons associated with its members shall be appropriately disciplined for violation of the provisions of this title, the rules or regulations thereunder, or the rules of the exchange, by expulsion, suspension, limitation of activities, functions, and operations, fine, censure, being suspended or barred from being associated with a member, or any other fitting sanction.

(7) The rules of the exchange are in accordance with the provisions of subsection (d) of this section, and in general, provide a fair procedure for the disciplining of members and persons associated with members, the denial of membership to any person seeking membership therein, the barring of any person from becoming associated with a member thereof, and the prohibition or limi-

tation by the exchange of any person with respect to access to services offered by the exchange or a member thereof.

(8) The rules of the exchange do not impose any burden on competition not necessary or appropriate in furtherance of the purposes of this title.

(c)(1) A national securities exchange shall deny membership to (A) any person, other than a natural person, which is not a registered broker or dealer or (B) any natural person who is not, or is not associated with, a registered broker or dealer.

(2) A national securities exchange may, and in cases in which the Commission, by order, directs as necessary or appropriate in the public interest or for the protection shall, deny membership to any registered broker or dealer or natural person associated with a registered broker or dealer, and bar from becoming associated with a member any person, who is subject to a statutory disqualification. * * *

* * *

(d)(1) In any proceeding by a national securities exchange to determine whether a member or person associated with a member should be disciplined (other than a summary proceeding pursuant to paragraph (3) of this subsection), the exchange shall bring specific charges, notify such member or person of, and give him an opportunity to defend against, such charges, and keep a record. * * *

* * *

(e)(1) On and after the date of enactment of the Securities Acts Amendments of 1975, no national securities exchange may impose any schedule or fix rates of commissions, allowances, discounts, or other fees to be charged by its members: * * *

* * *

(f) The Commission, by rule or order, as it deems necessary or appropriate in the public interest and for the protection of investors, to maintain fair and orderly markets, or to assure equal regulation, may require—

(1) any person not a member or a designated representative of a member of a national securities exchange effecting transactions on such exchange without the services of another person acting as a broker, or

(2) any broker or dealer not a member of a national securities exchange effecting transactions on such exchange on a regular basis,

to comply with such rules of such exchange as the Commission may specify.

Prohibition Against Manipulation of Security Prices

SECTION 9. (a) It shall be unlawful for any person, directly or indirectly, by the use of the mails or any means or instrumentality of interstate commerce, or of any facility of any national securities exchange, or for any member of a national securities exchange—

(1) For the purpose of creating a false or misleading appearance of active trading in any security registered on a national securities exchange, or a false or misleading appearance with respect to the market for any such security, (A) to effect any transaction in such security which involves no change in the beneficial ownership thereof, or (B) to enter an order or orders for the purchase of such security with the knowledge that an order or orders of substantially the same size, at substantially the same time and at substantially the same price, for the sale of any such security, has been or will be entered by or for the same or different parties, or (C) to enter any order or orders for the sale of any such security with the knowledge that an order or orders of substantially the same size, at substantially the same time, and at substantially the same price, for the purchase of such security, has been or will be entered by or for the same or different parties.

(2) To effect, alone or with one or more other persons, a series of transactions in any security

registered on a national securities exchange creating actual or apparent active trading in such security or raising or depressing the price of such security, for the purpose of inducing the purchase or sale of such security by others.

(3) If a dealer or broker, or other person selling or offering for sale or purchasing or offering to purchase the security, to induce the purchase or sale of any security registered on a national securities exchange by the circulation or dissemination in the ordinary course of business of information to the effect that the price of any such security will or is likely to rise or fall because of market operations of any one or more persons conducted for the purpose of raising or depressing the prices of such security.

(4) If a dealer or broker, or other person selling or offering for sale or purchasing or offering to purchase the security, to make, regarding any security registered on a national securities exchange, for the purpose of inducing the purchase or sale of such security, any statement which was at the time and in the light of the circumstances under which it was made, false or misleading with respect to any material fact, and which he knew or had reasonable ground to believe was so false or misleading.

(5) For a consideration, received directly or indirectly from a dealer or broker, or other person selling or offering for sale or purchasing or offering to purchase the security, to induce the purchase or sale of any security registered on a national securities exchange by the circulation or dissemination of information to the effect that the price of any such security will or is likely to rise or fall because of the market operations of any one or more persons conducted for the purpose of raising or depressing the price of such security.

(6) To effect either alone or with one or more other persons any series of transactions for the purchase and/or sale of any security registered on a national securities exchange for the purpose of pegging, fixing, or stabilizing the price of such security in contravention of such rules and regulations as the Commission may prescribe as necessary or appropriate in the public interest or for the protection of investors.

(b) It shall be unlawful for any person to effect, by use of any facility of a national securities exchange, in contravention of such rules and regulations as the Commission may prescribe as necessary or appropriate in the public interest or for the protection of investors—

(1) any transaction in connection with any security whereby any party to such transaction acquires any put, call, straddle, or other option or privilege of buying the security from or selling the security to another without being bound to do so; or

(2) any transaction in connection with any security with relation to which he has, directly or indirectly, any interest in any such put, call, straddle, option, or privilege; or

(3) any transaction in any security for the account of any person who he has reason to believe has, and who actually has, directly or indirectly, any interest in any such put, call, straddle, option, or privilege with relation to such security.

(c) It shall be unlawful for any member of a national securities exchange directly or indirectly to endorse or guarantee the performance of any put, call, straddle, option, or privilege in relation to any security registered on a national securities exchange, in contravention of such rules and regulations as the Commission may prescribe as necessary or appropriate in the public interest or for the protection of investors.

(d) The terms "put", "call", "straddle", "option", or "privilege" as used in this section shall not include any registered warrant, right, or convertible security.

(e) Any person who willfully participates in any act or transaction in violation of subsection (a), (b), or (c) of this section, shall be liable to any person who shall purchase or sell any security at a price which was affected by such act or transaction, and the person so injured may sue in law or in equity in any court of competent jurisdiction to recover the damages sustained as a result of any such act or transaction. In any such suit the court may, in its discretion, require an undertaking for the payment of the costs of such suit, and assess reasonable costs, including reasonable attorneys' fees, against either party litigant.

Every person who becomes liable to make any payment under this subsection may recover contribution as in cases of contract from any person who, if joined in the original suit, would have been liable to make the same payment. No action shall be maintained to enforce any liability created under this section, unless brought within one year after the discovery of the facts constituting the violation and within three years after such violation.

(f) The provisions of this section shall not apply to an exempted security.

Regulation of the Use of Manipulative and Deceptive Devices

SECTION 10. It shall be unlawful for any person, directly or indirectly, by the use of any means or instrumentality of interstate commerce or of the mails, or of any facility of any national securities exchange—

(a) To effect a short sale, or to use or employ any stop-loss order in connection with the purchase or sale, of any security registered on a national securities exchange, in contravention of such rules and regulations as the Commission may prescribe as necessary or appropriate in the public interest or for the protection of investors.

(b) To use or employ, in connection with the purchase or sale of any security registered on a national securities exchange or any security not so registered, any manipulative or deceptive device or contrivance in contravention of such rules and regulations as the Commission may prescribe as necessary or appropriate in the public interest or for the protection of investors.

Registration Requirements for Securities

SECTION 12. (a) It shall be unlawful for any member, broker, or dealer to effect any transaction in any security (other than an exempted security) on a national securities exchange unless a registration is effective as to such security for such exchange in accordance with the provisions of this title and the rules and regulations thereunder.

(b) A security may be registered on a national securities exchange by the issuer filing an application with the exchange (and filing with the Commission such duplicate originals thereof as the Commission may require), which application shall contain—

(1) Such information, in such detail, as to the issuer and any person directly or indirectly controlling or controlled by, or under direct or indirect common control with, the issuer, and any guarantor of the security as to principal or interest or both, as the Commission may by rules and regulations require, as necessary or appropriate in the public interest or for the protection of investors, in respect of the following:

(A) the organization, financial structure and nature of the business;

(B) the terms, position, rights, and privileges of the different classes of securities outstanding;

(C) the terms on which their securities are to be, and during the preceding three years have been, offered to the public or otherwise;

(D) the directors, officers, and underwriters, and each security holder of record holding more than 10 per centum of any class of any equity security of the issuer (other than an exempted security), their remuneration and their interests in the securities of, and their material contracts with, the issuer and any person directly or indirectly controlling or controlled by, or under direct or indirect common control with, the issuer;

(E) remuneration to others than directors and officers exceeding $20,000 per annum;

(F) bonus and profit-sharing arrangements;

(G) management and service contracts;

(H) options existing or to be created in respect of their securities;

(I) material contracts, not made in the ordinary course of business, which are to be executed in whole or in part at or after the filing of the application or which were made not more than 2 years before such filing, and every material patent or contract for a material patent right shall be deemed a material contract;

(J) balance sheets for not more than the three preceding fiscal years, certified if required by the rules and regulations of the Commission by independent public accountants;

(K) profit and loss statements for not more than the three preceding fiscal years, certified if required by the rules and regulations of the Commission by independent public accountants; and

(L) any further financial statements which the Commission may deem necessary or appropriate for the protection of investors.

(2) Such copies of articles of incorporation, by-laws, trust indentures, or corresponding documents by whatever name known, underwriting arrangements, and other similar documents of, and voting trust agreements with respect to, the issuer and any person directly or indirectly controlling or controlled by, or under direct or indirect common control with, the issuer as the Commission may require as necessary or appropriate for the proper protection of investors and to insure fair dealing in the security.

(3) Such copies of material contracts, referred to in paragraph (1) (I) above, as the Commission may require as necessary or appropriate for the proper protection of investors and to insure fair dealing in the security.

(c) If in the judgment of the Commission any information required under subsection (b) is inapplicable to any specified class or classes of issuers, the Commission shall require in lieu thereof the submission of such other information of comparable character as it may deem applicable to such class of issuers.

(d) If the exchange authorities certify to the Commission that the security has been approved by the exchange for listing and registration, the registration shall become effective thirty days after the receipt of such certification by the Com-

mission or within such shorter period of time as the Commission may determine. A security registered with a national securities exchange may be withdrawn or stricken from listing and registration in accordance with the rules of the exchange and, upon such terms as the Commission may deem necessary to impose for the protection of investors, upon application by the issuer or the exchange to the Commission; whereupon the issuer shall be relieved from further compliance with the provisions of this section and section 13 of this title and any rules or regulations under such sections as to the securities so withdrawn or stricken. An unissued security may be registered only in accordance with such rules and regulations as the Commission may prescribe as necessary or appropriate in the public interest or for the protection of investors.

(e) Notwithstanding the foregoing provisions of this section, the Commission may by such rules and regulations as it deems necessary or appropriate in the public interest or for the protection of investors, permit securities listed on any exchange at the time the registration of such exchange as a national securities exchange becomes effective, to be registered for a period ending not later than July 1, 1935, without complying with the provisions of this section.

(f) (1) Notwithstanding the foregoing provisions of this section, any national securities exchange, subject to the terms and conditions hereinafter set forth—

(A) may continue unlisted trading privileges to which a security had been admitted on such exchange prior to July 1, 1964;

(B) upon application to and approval of such application by the Commission, may extend unlisted trading privileges to any security listed and registered on any other national securities exchange; and

(C) upon application to and approval of such application by the Commission, may extend unlisted trading privileges to any security registered pursuant to section 12 of this title or which would be required to be so registered except for the exemption from registration provided in subsection (g)(2) (B) or (g)(2)(G) of that section.

If an extension of unlisted trading privileges to a security is based upon its listing and registration on another national securities exchange, such privileges shall continue in effect only so long as such security remains listed and registered on a national securities exchange.

* * *

(g)(1) Every issuer which is engaged in interstate commerce, or in a business affecting interstate commerce, or whose securities are traded by use of the mails or any means or instrumentality of interstate commerce shall—

(A) within one hundred and twenty days after the last day of its first fiscal year ended after the effective date of this subsection on which the issuer has total assets exceeding $1,000,000 and a class of equity security (other than an exempted security) held of record by seven hundred and fifty or more persons; and

(B) within one hundred and twenty days after the last day of its first fiscal year ended after two years from the effective date of this subsection on which the issuer has total assets exceeding $1,000,000 and a class of equity security (other than an exempted security) held of record by five hundred or more but less than seven hundred and fifty persons,

register such security by filing with the Commission a registration statement (and such copies thereof as the Commission may require) with respect to such security containing such information and documents as the Commission may specify comparable to that which is required in an application to register a security pursuant to subsection (b) of this section. Each such registration statement shall become effective sixty days after filing with the Commission or within such shorter period as the Commission may direct. Until such registration statement becomes effective it shall not be deemed filed for the purposes of section 18 of this title. Any issuer may register any class of equity security not required to be registered by filing a registration statement pursuant to the provisions of this paragraph. The Commission is authorized to extend the date upon which any issuer or class of issuers is required to register a security pursuant to the provisions of this paragraph.

(2) The provisions of this subsection shall not apply in respect of—

(A) any security listed and registered on a national securities exchange.

(B) any security issued by an investment company registered pursuant to section 8 of the Investment Company Act of 1940.

(C) any security, other than permanent stock, guaranty stock, permanent reserve stock, or any similar certificate evidencing nonwithdrawable capital, issued by a savings and loan association, building and loan association, cooperative bank, homestead association, or similar institution, which is supervised and examined by State or Federal authority having supervision over any such institution.

(D) any security of an issuer organized and operated exclusively for religious, educational, benevolent, fraternal, charitable, or reformatory purposes and not for pecuniary profit, and no part of the net earnings of which inures to the benefit of any private shareholder or individual.

(E) any security of an issuer which is a "cooperative association" as defined in the Agricultural Marketing Act, approved June 15, 1929, as amended, or a federation of such cooperative associations, if such federation possesses no greater powers or purposes than cooperative associations so defined.

(F) any security issued by a mutual or cooperative organization which supplies a commodity or service primarily for the benefit of its members and operates not for pecuniary profit, but only if the security is part of a class issuable only to persons who purchase commodities or services from the issuer, the security is transferable only to a successor in interest or occupancy of premises serviced or to be served by the issuer, and no dividends are payable to the holder of the security.

(G) any security issued by an insurance company if all of the following conditions are met:

(i) Such insurance company is required to and does file an annual statement with the Commissioner of Insurance (or other officer or agency performing a similar function) of its domiciliary State, and such annual statement conforms to that prescribed by the National Association of Insurance Commissioners or in the determination of such State commissioner, officer or agency substantially conforms to that so prescribed.

(ii) Such insurance company is subject to regulation by its domiciliary State of proxies, consents, or authorizations in respect of securities issued by such company and such regulation conforms to that prescribed by the National Association of Insurance Commissioners.

(iii) After July 1, 1966, the purchase and sales of securities issued by such insurance company by beneficial owners, directors, or officers of such company are subject to regulation (including reporting) by its domiciliary State substantially in the manner provided in section 16 of this title.

(H) any interest or participation in any collective trust funds maintained by a bank or in a separate account maintained by an insurance company which interest or participation is issued in connection with (i) a stock-bonus, pension, or profit-sharing plan which meets the requirements for qualification under section 401 of the Internal Revenue Code of 1954, or (ii) an annuity plan which meets the requirements for deduction of the employer's contribution under section 404(a)(2) of such Code.

(3) The Commission may by rules or regulations or, on its own motion, after notice and opportunity for hearing, by order, exempt from this subsection any security of a foreign issuer, including any certificate of deposit for such a security, if the Commission finds that such exemption is in the public interest and is consistent with the protection of investors.

(4) Registration of any class of security pursuant to this subsection shall be terminated ninety days, or such shorter period as the Commission may determine, after the issuer files a certification with the Commission that the number of holders of record of such class of security is reduced to less than three hundred persons.

* * *

(h) The Commission may by rules and regulations, or upon application of an interested person, by order, after notice and opportunity for hearing, exempt in whole or in part any issuer or class of issuers from the provisions of subsection (g) of this section or from section 13, 14, or 15(d), or may exempt from section 16 any officer, director, or beneficial owner of securities of any issuer, any security of which is required to be registered pursuant to subsection (g) hereof, upon such terms and conditions and for such period as it deems necessary or appropriate, if the Commission finds, by reason of the number of public investors, amount of trading interest in the securities, the nature and extent of the activities of the issuer, income or assets of the issuer or otherwise, that such action is not inconsistent with the public interest or the protection of investors.

* * *

(i) In respect of any securities issued by banks the deposits of which are insured in accordance with the Federal Deposit Insurance Act or institutions the accounts of which are insured by the Federal Savings and Loan Insurance Corporation, the powers, functions, and duties vested in the Commission to administer and enforce sections 12, 13, 14(a), 14(c), 14(d), 14(f), and 16, (1) with respect to national banks and banks operating under the Code of Law for the District of Columbia are vested in the Comptroller of the Currency, (2) with respect to all other member banks of the Federal Reserve System are vested in the Board of Governors of the Federal Reserve System, (3) with respect to all other insured banks are vested in the Federal Deposit Insurance Corporation, and (4) with respect to institutions the accounts of which are insured by the Federal Savings and Loan Insurance Corporation are vested in the Federal Home Loan Bank Board. The Comptroller of the Currency, the Board of Governors of the Federal Reserve System, the Federal Deposit Insurance Corporation, and the Federal Home Loan Bank Board shall have the power to make such rules and regulations as may be necessary for the execution of the functions vested in them as provided in this subsection. In carrying out their responsibilities under this subsection, the agencies named in the first sentence of this subsection shall issue substantially similar regulations to regulations and rules issued by the Commission under sections 12, 13, 14(a), 14(c), 14(d), 14(f), and 16, unless they find that implementation of substantially similar regulations with respect to insured banks and insured institutions are not necessary or appropriate in the public interest or for protection of investors, and publish such findings, and the detailed reasons therefor, in the Federal Register. Such regulations of the above-named agencies, or the reasons for failure to publish such substantially similar regulations to those of the Commission, shall be published in the Federal Register within 120 days of the date of enactment of this subsection, and, thereafter, within 60 days of any changes made by the Commission in its relevant regulations and rules.

(j) The Commission is authorized, by order, as it deems necessary or appropriate for the protection of investors to deny, to suspend the effective date of, to suspend for a period not exceeding twelve months, or to revoke the registration of a security, if the Commission finds, on the record after notice and opportunity for hearing, that the issuer of such security has failed to comply with any provision of this title

or the rules and regulations thereunder. No member of a national securities exchange, broker, or dealer shall make use of the mails or any means or instrumentality of interstate commerce to effect any transaction in, or to induce the purchase or sale of, any security the registration of which has been and is suspended or revoked pursuant to the preceding sentence.

(k) If in its opinion the public interest and the protection of investors so require, the Commission is authorized summarily to suspend trading in any security (other than an exempted security) for a period not exceeding ten days, or with the approval of the President, summarily to suspend all trading on any national securities exchange or otherwise, in securities other than exempted securities, for a period not exceeding ninety days. No member of a national securities exchange, broker, or dealer shall make use of the mails or any means or instrumentality of interstate commerce to effect any transaction in, or to induce the purchase or sale of, any security in which trading is so suspended.

(l) It shall be unlawful for an issuer, any class of whose securities is registered pursuant to this section or would be required to be so registered except for the exemption from registration provided by subsection (g)(2)(B) or (g)(2)(G) of this section, by the use of any means or instrumentality of interstate commerce, or of the mails, to issue, either originally or upon transfer, any of such securities in a form or with a format which contravenes such rules and regulations as the Commission may prescribe as necessary or appropriate for the prompt and accurate clearance and settlement of transactions in securities. The provisions of this subsection shall not apply to variable annuity contracts or variable life policies issued by an insurance company or its separate accounts.

(m) The Commission is authorized and directed to make a study and investigation of the practice of recording the ownership of securities in the records of the issuer in other than the name of the beneficial owner of such securities and to determine (1) whether such practice is consistent with the purposes of this title, with particular reference to subsection (g) of this section and sections 13, 14, 15(d), 16, and 17A, and (2) whether steps can be taken to facilitate communications between issuers and the beneficial owners of their securities while at the same time retaining the benefits of such practice. The Commission shall report to the Congress its preliminary findings within six months after the date of enactment of the Securities Acts Amendments of 1975, and its final conclusions and recommendations within one year of such date.

Periodical and Other Reports

Section 13. (a) Every issuer of a security registered pursuant to section 12 of this title shall file with the Commission, in accordance with such rules and regulations as the Commission may prescribe as necessary or appropriate for the proper protection of investors and to insure fair dealing in the security—

(1) such information and documents (and such copies thereof) as the Commission shall require to keep reasonably current the information and documents required to be included in or filed with an application or registration statement filed pursuant to section 12, except that the Commission may not require the filing of any material contract wholly executed before July 1, 1962.

(2) such annual reports (and such copies thereof), certified if required by the rules and regulations of the Commission by independent public accountants, and such quarterly reports (and such copies thereof), as the Commission may prescribe.

Every issuer of a security registered on a national securities exchange shall also file a duplicate original of such information, documents, and reports with the exchange.

(b)(1) The Commission may prescribe, in regard to reports made pursuant to this title, the form or forms in which the required information shall be set forth, the items or details to be shown in the balance sheet and the earning statement, and the methods to be followed in the preparation of reports, in the appraisal or valuation of assets and liabilities, in the determination of depreciation and depletion, in the differentiation of recurring and nonrecurring income, in the differentiation of investment and operating income, and in the preparation, where the Commission deems it necessary or desirable, of separate and/or consolidated balance sheets or income accounts of any person directly or indirectly controlling or controlled by the issuer, or any person under direct or indirect common control with the issuer; but in the case of the reports of any person whose methods of accounting are prescribed under the provisions of any law of the United States, or any rule or regulation thereunder, the rules and regulations of the Commission with respect to reports shall not be inconsistent with the requirements imposed by such law or rule or regulation in respect of the same subject matter (except that such rules and regulations of the Commission may be inconsistent with such requirements to the extent that the Commission determines that the public interest or the protection of investors so requires).

(2) Every issuer which has a class of securities registered pursuant to section 12 of this title and every issuer which is required to file reports pursuant to section 15(d) of this title shall—

(A) make and keep books, records, and accounts, which, in reasonable detail, accurately and fairly reflect the transactions and dispositions of the assets of the issuer; and

(B) devise and maintain a system of internal accounting controls sufficient to provide reasonable assurances that—

(i) transactions are executed in accordance with management's general or specific authorization;

(ii) transactions are recorded as necessary (I) to permit preparation of financial statements in conformity with generally accepted accounting principles or any other criteria applicable to such statements, and (II) to maintain accountability for assets;

(iii) access to assets is permitted only in accordance with management's general or specific authorization; and

(iv) the recorded accountability for assets is compared with the existing assets at reasonable intervals and appropriate action is taken with respect to any differences.

(3)(A) With respect to matters concerning the national security of the United States, no duty or liability under paragraph (2) of this subsection shall be imposed upon any person acting in cooperation with the head of any Federal department or agency responsible for such matters if such act in cooperation with such head of a department or agency was done upon the specific, written directive of the head of such department or agency pursuant to Presidential authority to issue such directives. Each directive issued under this paragraph shall set forth the specific facts and circumstances with respect to which the provisions of this paragraph are to be invoked. Each such directive shall, unless renewed in writing, expire one year after the date of issuance.

(B) Each head of a Federal department or agency of the United States who issues a directive pursuant to this paragraph shall maintain a complete file of all such directives and shall, on October 1 of each year, transmit a summary of matters covered by such directives in force at any time during the previous year to the Permanent Select Committee on Intelligence of the House of Representatives and the Select Committee on Intelligence of the Senate.

(c) If in the judgment of the Commission any report required under subsection (a) is inapplicable to any specified class or classes of issuers, the Commission shall require in lieu thereof the submission of such reports of comparable character as it may deem applicable to such class or classes of issuers.

(d) (1) Any person who, after acquiring directly or indirectly the beneficial ownership of any equity security of a class which is registered pursuant to section 12 of this title, or any equity security of an insurance company which would have been required to be so registered except for the exemption contained in section 12(g)(2)(G) of this title, or any equity security issued by a closed-end investment company registered under the Investment Company Act of 1940, is directly or indirectly the beneficial owner of more than 5 percentum of such class shall, within ten days after such acquisition, send to the issuer of the security at its principal executive office, by registered or certified mail, send to each exchange where the security is traded, and file with the Commission, a statement containing such of the following information, and such additional information, as the Commission may by rules and regulations prescribe as necessary or appropriate in the public interest or for the protection of investors—

(A) the background, and identity, residence, and citizenship of, and the nature of such beneficial ownership by, such person and all other persons by whom or on whose behalf the purchases have been or are to be effected;

(B) the source and amount of the funds or other consideration used or to be used in making the purchases, and if any part of the purchase price or proposed purchase price is represented or is to be represented by funds or other consideration borrowed or otherwise obtained for the purpose of acquiring, holding, or trading such security, a description of the transaction and the names of the parties thereto, except that where a source of funds is a loan made in the ordinary course of business by a bank, as defined in section 3(a)(6) of this title, if the person filing such statement so requests, the name of the bank shall not be made available to the public;

(C) if the purpose of the purchases or prospective purchases is to acquire control of the business of the issuer of the securities, any plans or proposals which such persons may have to liquidate such issuer, to sell its assets to or merge it with any other persons, or to make any other major change in its business or corporate structure;

(D) the number of shares of such security which are beneficially owned, and the number of shares concerning which there is a right to acquire, directly or indirectly, by (i) such person, and (ii) by each associate of such person, giving the name and address of each such associate; and

(E) information as to any contracts, arrangements, or understandings with any person with respect to any securities of the issuer, including but not limited to transfer of any of the securities, joint ventures, loan or option arrangements, puts or calls, guaranties of loans, guaranties against loss or guaranties of profits, division of losses or profits, or the giving or withholding of proxies, naming the persons with whom such contracts, arrangements, or understandings have been entered into, and giving the details thereof.

(2) If any material change occurs in the facts set forth in the statements to the issuer and the exchange, and in the statement filed with the Commission, an amendment shall be transmitted to the issuer and the exchange and shall be filed with the Commission, in accordance with such rules and regulations as the Commission may prescribe as necessary or appropriate in the public interest or for the protection of investors.

(3) When two or more persons act as a partnership, limited partnership, syndicate, or other group for the purpose of acquiring, holding, or disposing of securities of an issuer, such syndicate or group shall be deemed a "person" for the purposes of this subsection.

(4) In determining, for purposes of this subsection, any percentage of a class of any security, such class shall be deemed to consist of the amount of the outstanding securities of such class, exclusive of any securities of such class held by or for the account of the issuer or a subsidiary of the issuer.

(5) The Commission, by rule or regulation or by order, may permit any person to file in lieu of the statement required by paragraph (1) of this subsection or the rules and regulations thereunder, a notice stating the name of such person, the number of shares of any equity securities subject to paragraph (1) which are owned by him, the date of their acquisition and such other information as the Commission may specify, if it appears to the Commission that such securities were acquired by such person in the ordinary course of his business and were not acquired for the purpose of and do not have the effect of changing or influencing the control of the issuer nor in connection with or as a participant in any transaction having such purpose or effect.

(6) The provisions of this subsection shall not apply to—

(A) any acquisition or offer to acquire securities made or proposed to be made by means of a registration statement under the Securities Act of 1933;

(B) any acquisition of the beneficial ownership of a security which, together with all other acquisitions by the same person of securities of the same class during the preceding twelve months, does not exceed 2 per centum of that class;

(C) any acquisition of an equity security by the issuer of such security;

(D) any acquisition or proposed acquisition of a security which the Commission, by rules or regulations or by order, shall exempt from the provisions of this subsection as not entered into for the purpose of, and not having the effect of, changing or influencing the control of the issuer or otherwise as not comprehended within the purposes of this subsection.

(e) (1) It shall be unlawful for an issuer which has a class of equity securities registered pursuant to section 12 of this title, or which is a closed-end investment company registered under the Investment Company Act of 1940, to purchase any equity security issued by it if such purchase is in contravention of such rules and regulations as the Commission, in the public interest or for the protection of investors, may adopt (A) to define acts and practices which are fraudulent, deceptive, or manipulative, and (B) to prescribe means reasonably designed to prevent such acts and practices. Such rules and regulations may require such issuer to provide holders of equity securities of such class with such information relating to the reasons for such purchase, the source of funds, the number of shares to be purchased, the price to be paid for such securities, the method of purchase, and such additional information, as the Commission deems necessary or appropriate in the public interest or for the protection of investors, or which the Commission deems to be material to a determination whether such security should be sold.

(2) For the purpose of this subsection, a purchase by or for the issuer or any person controlling, controlled by, or under common control with the issuer, or a purchase subject to control of the issuer or any such person, shall be deemed to be a purchase by the issuer. The Commission shall have power to make rules and regulations implementing this paragraph in the public interest and for the protection of investors, including exemptive rules and regulations covering situations in which the Commission deems it unnecessary or inappropriate that a purchase of the type described in this paragraph shall be deemed to be a purchase by the issuer for purposes of some or all of the provisions of paragraph (1) of this subsection.

(f) (1) Every institutional investment manager which uses the mails, or any means or instrumentality of interstate commerce in the course of its business as an institutional investment manager and which exercises investment discretion with respect to accounts holding equity securities of a class described in section 13(d)(1) of this title having an aggregate fair market value on the last trading day in any of the preceding twelve months of at least $100,000,000 or such lesser amount (but in no case less than $10,000,000) as the Commission, by rule, may determine, shall file reports with the Commission in such form, for such periods, and at such times after the end of such periods as the Commission, by rule, may prescribe, but in no event shall such reports be filed for periods longer than one year or shorter than one quarter. Such reports shall include for each such equity security held on the last day of the reporting period by accounts (in aggregate or by type as the Commission, by rule, may prescribe) with respect to which the institutional investment manager exercises investment discretion (other than securities held in amounts which the Commission, by rule, determines to be insignificant for purposes of this subsection), the name of the issuer and the title, class, CUSIP number, number of shares or principal amount, and aggregate fair market value of each such security. Such reports may also include for accounts (in aggregate or by type) with respect to which the institutional investment manager exercises investment discretion such of the following information as the Commission, by rule, prescribes—

(A) the name of the issuer and the title, class, CUSIP number, number of shares or principal amount, and aggregate fair market value or cost or amortized cost of each other security (other than an exempted security) held on the last day of the reporting period by such accounts;

(B) the aggregate fair market value or cost or amortized cost of exempted securities (in aggregate or by class) held on the last day of the reporting period by such accounts;

(C) the number of shares of each equity security of a class described in section 13(d)(1) of this title held on the last day of the reporting period by such accounts with respect to which the institutional investment manager possesses sole or shared authority to exercise the voting rights evidenced by such securities;

(D) the aggregate purchases and aggregate sales during the reporting period of each security (other than an exempted security) effected by or for such accounts; and

(E) with respect to any transaction or series of transactions having a market value of at least $500,000 or such other amount as the Commission, by rule, may determine, effected during the reporting period by or for such accounts in any equity security of a class described in section 13(d)(1) of this title—

(i) the name of the issuer and the title, class, and CUSIP number of the security;

(ii) the number of shares or principal amount of the security involved in the transaction;

(iii) whether the transaction was a purchase or sale;

(iv) the per share price or prices at which the transaction was effected;

(v) the date or dates of the transaction;

(vi) the date or dates of the settlement of the transaction;

(vii) the broker or dealer through whom the transaction was effected;

(viii) the market or markets in which the transaction was effected; and

(ix) such other related information as the Commission, by rule, may prescribe.

* * *

(5)(A) For purposes of this subsection the term "institutional investment manager" includes any person, other than a natural person, investing in or buying and selling securities for its own account, and any person exercising investment discretion with respect to the account of any other person.

* * *

(g)(1) Any person who is directly or indirectly the beneficial owner of more than 5 per centum of any security of a class described in subsection (d)(1) of this section shall send to the issuer of the security and shall file with the Commission a statement setting forth, in such form and at such time as the Commission may, by rule, prescribe—

(A) such person's identity, residence, and citizenship; and

(B) the number and description of the shares in which such person has an interest and the nature of such interest.

(2) If any material change occurs in the facts set forth in the statement sent to the issuer and filed with the Commission, an amendment shall be transmitted to the issuer and shall be filed with the Commission, in accordance with such rules and regulations as the Commission may prescribe as necessary or appropriate in the public interest or for the protection of investors.

(3) When two or more persons act as a partnership, limited partnership, syndicate, or other group for the purpose of acquiring, holding, or disposing of securities of an issuer, such syndicate or group shall be deemed a "person" for the purposes of this subsection.

(4) In determining, for purposes of this subsection, any percentage of a class of any security, such class shall be deemed to consist of the amount of the outstanding securities of such class, exclusive of any securities of such class held by or for the account of the issuer or a subsidiary of the issuer.

(5) In exercising its authority under this subsection, the Commission shall take such steps as it deems necessary or appropriate in the public interest or for the protection of investors (A) to achieve centralized reporting of information regarding ownership, (B) to avoid unnecessarily duplicative reporting by and minimize the compliance burden on persons required to report, and (C) to tabulate and promptly make available the information con-

tained in any report filed pursuant to this subsection in a manner which will, in the view of the Commission, maximize the usefulness of the information to other Federal and State agencies and the public.

(6) The Commission may, by rule or order, exempt, in whole or in part, any person or class of persons from any or all of the reporting requirements of this subsection as it deems necessary or appropriate in the public interest or for the protection of investors.

(h) The Commission shall report to the Congress within thirty months of the date of enactment of this subsection with respect to (1) the effectiveness of the ownership reporting requirements contained in this title and (2) the desirability and the feasibility of reducing or otherwise modifying the 5 per centum threshold used in subsections (d)(1) and (g)(1) of this section, giving appropriate consideration to—

(A) the incidence of avoidance of reporting by beneficial owners using multiple holders of record;

(B) the cost of compliance to persons required to report;

(C) the cost to issuers and others of processing and disseminating the reported information;

(D) the effect of such action on the securities markets, including the system for the clearance and settlement of securities transactions;

(E) the benefits to investors and to the public;

(F) any bona fide interests of individuals in the privacy of their financial affairs;

(G) the extent to which such reported information gives or would give any person an undue advantage in connection with activities subject to sections 13(d) and 14 (d) of this title;

(H) the need for such information in connection with the administration and enforcement of this title; and

(I) such other matters as the Commission may deem relevant, including the information obtained pursuant to section 13 (f) of this title.

* * *

Proxies

SECTION 14. (a) It shall be unlawful for any person, by the use of the mails or by any means or instrumentality of interstate commerce or of any facility of a national securities exchange or otherwise, in contravention of such rules and regulations as the Commission may prescribe as necessary or appropriate in the public interest or for the protection of investors, to solicit or to permit the use of his name to solicit any proxy or consent or authorization in respect of any security (other than an exempted security) registered pursuant to section 12 of this title.

(b) It shall be unlawful for any member of a national securities exchange, or any broker or dealer registered under this title, in contravention of such rules and regulations as the Commission may prescribe as necessary or appropriate in the public interest or for the protection of investors, to give, or to refrain from giving a proxy, consent, or authorization in respect of any security registered pursuant to section 12 of this title and carried for the account of a customer.

(c) Unless proxies, consents, or authorizations in respect of a security registered pursuant to section 12 of this title are solicited by or on behalf of the management of the issuer from the holders of record of such security in accordance with the rules and regulations prescribed under subsection (a) of this section, prior to any annual or other meeting of the holders of such security, such issuer shall, in accordance with rules and regulations prescribed by the Commission, file with the Commission and transmit to all holders of record of such security information substantially equivalent to the information which would be required to be transmitted if a solicitation were made, but no information shall be required to be filed or transmitted pursuant to this subsection before July 1, 1964.

(d) (1) It shall be unlawful for any person, directly or indirectly, by use of the mails or by any means or instrumentality of interstate commerce or of any facility of a national securities exchange or otherwise, to make a tender offer for, or a request or invitation for tenders of, any class of any equity security which is registered pursuant to section 12 of this title, or any equity security of an insurance company which would have been required to be so registered except for the exemption contained in section 12(g)(2)(G) of this title, or any equity security issued by a closed-end investment company registered under the Investment Company Act of 1940, if, after consummation thereof, such person would, directly or indirectly, be the beneficial owner of more than 5 per centum of such class, unless at the time copies of the offer or request or invitation are first published or sent or given to security holders such person has filed with the Commission a statement containing such of the information specified in section 13(d) of this title, and such additional information as the Commission may by rules and regulations prescribe as necessary or appropriate in the public interest or for the protection of investors. All requests or invitations for tenders or advertisements making a tender offer or requesting or inviting tenders of such a security shall be filed as a part of such statement and shall contain such of the information contained in such statement as the Commission may by rules and regulations prescribe. Copies of any additional material soliciting or requesting such tender offers subsequent to the initial solicitation or request shall contain such information as the Commission may by rules and regulations prescribe as necessary or appropriate in the public interest or for the protection of investors, and shall be filed with the Commission not later than the time copies of such material are first published or sent or given to security holders. Copies of all statements, in the form in which such material is furnished to security holders and the Commission, shall be sent to the issuer not later than the date such material is first published or sent or given to any security holders.

(2) When two or more persons act as a partnership, limited partnership, syndicate, or other group for the purpose of acquiring, holding, or disposing of securities of an issuer, such syndicate or group shall be deemed a "person" for purposes of this subsection.

(3) In determining, for purposes of this subsection, any percentage of a class of any security, such class shall be deemed to consist of the amount of the outstanding securities of such class, exclusive of any securities of such class held by or for the account of the issuer or a subsidiary of the issuer.

(4) Any solicitation or recommendation to the holders of such a security to accept or reject a tender offer or request or invitation for tenders shall be made in accordance with such rules and regulations as the Commission may prescribe as necessary or appropriate in the public interest or for the protection of investors.

(5) Securities deposited pursuant to a tender offer or request or invitation for tenders may be withdrawn by or on behalf of the depositor at any time until the expiration of seven days after the time definitive copies of the offer or request or invitation are first published or sent or given to security holders, and at any time after sixty days from the date of the original tender offer or request or invitation, except as the Commission may otherwise prescribe by rules, regulations, or order as necessary or appropriate in the public interest or for the protection of investors.

(6) Where any person makes a tender offer, or request or invitation for tenders, for less than all the outstanding equity securities of a class, and where a greater number of securities is deposited pursuant thereto within ten days after copies of the offer or request or invitation are first published or sent or given to security holders than such person is bound or willing to take up and pay for, the securities taken up shall be taken up as nearly as may be pro rata, disregarding fractions, according to the number of securities deposited by each depositor. The provisions of this subsection shall also apply to securities deposited within ten days after notice of an increase in the consideration offered to security holders, as described in paragraph (7), is first published or sent or given to security holders.

(7) Where any person varies the terms of a tender offer or request or invitation for tenders

before the expiration thereof by increasing the consideration offered to holders of such securities, such person shall pay the increased consideration to each security holder whose securities are taken up and paid for pursuant to the tender offer or request or invitation for tenders whether or not such securities have been taken up by such person before the variation of the tender offer or request or invitation.

(8) The provisions of this subsection shall not apply to any offer for, or request or invitation for tenders of, any security—

(A) if the acquisition of such security, together with all other acquisitions by the same person of securities of the same class during the preceding twelve months, would not exceed 2 per centum of that class;

(B) by the issuer of such security; or

(C) which the Commission, by rules or regulations or by order, shall exempt from the provisions of this subsection as not entered into for the purpose of, and not having the effect of, changing or influencing the control of the issuer or otherwise as not comprehended within the purposes of this subsection.

(e) It shall be unlawful for any person to make any untrue statement of a material fact or omit to state any material fact necessary in order to make the statements made, in the light of the circumstances under which they are made, not misleading, or to engage in any fraudulent, deceptive, or manipulative acts or practices, in connection with any tender offer or request or invitation for tenders, or any solicitation of security holders in opposition to or in favor of any such offer, request, or invitation. The Commission shall, for the purposes of this subsection, by rules and regulations define, and prescribe means reasonably designed to prevent, such acts and practices as are fraudulent, deceptive, or manipulative.

(f) If, pursuant to any arrangement or understanding with the person or persons acquiring securities in a transaction subject to subsection (d) of this section or subsection (d) of section 13

of this title, any persons are to be elected or designated as directors of the issuer, otherwise than at a meeting of security holders, and the persons so elected or designated will constitute a majority of the directors of the issuer, then, prior to the time any such person takes office as a director, and in accordance with rules and regulations prescribed by the Commission, the issuer shall file with the Commission, and transmit to all holders of record of securities of the issuer who would be entitled to vote at a meeting for election of directors, information substantially equivalent to the information which would be required by subsection (a) or (c) of this section to be transmitted if such person or persons were nominees for election as directors at a meeting of such security holders.

Directors, Officers, and Principal Stockholders

SECTION 16. (a) Every person who is directly or indirectly the beneficial owner of more than 10 per centum of any class of any equity security (other than an exempted security) which is registered pursuant to section 12 of this title, or who is a director or an officer of the issuer of such security, shall file, at the time of the registration of such security on a national securities exchange or by the effective date of a registration statement filed pursuant to section 12(g) of this title, or within ten days after he becomes such beneficial owner, director, or officer, a statement with the Commission (and, if such security is registered on a national securities exchange, also with the exchange) of the amount of all equity securities of such issuer of which he is the beneficial owner, and within ten days after the close of each calendar month thereafter, if there has been a change in such ownership during such month, shall file with the Commission (and if such security is registered on a national securities exchange, shall also file with the exchange), a statement indicating his ownership at the close of the calendar month and such changes in his ownership as have occurred during such calendar month.

(b) For the purpose of preventing the unfair use of information which may have been obtained by such beneficial owner, director, or officer by reason of his relationship to the issuer, any profit realized by him from any purchase and sale, or any sale and purchase, of any equity security of such issuer (other than an exempted security) within any period of less than six months, unless such security was acquired in good faith in connection with a debt previously contracted, shall inure to and be recoverable by the issuer, irrespective of any intention on the part of such beneficial owner, director, or officer in entering into such transaction of holding the security purchased or of not repurchasing the security sold for a period exceeding six months. Suit to recover such profit may be instituted at law or in equity in any court of competent jurisdiction by the issuer, or by the owner of any security of the issuer in the name and in behalf of the issuer if the issuer shall fail or refuse to bring such suit within sixty days after request or shall fail diligently to prosecute the same thereafter; but no such suit shall be brought more than two years after the date such profit was realized. This subsection shall not be construed to cover any transaction where such beneficial owner was not such both at the time of the purchase and sale, or the sale and purchase, of the security involved, or any transaction or transactions which the Commission by rules and regulations may exempt as not comprehended within the purpose of this subsection.

(c) It shall be unlawful for any such beneficial owner, director, or officer, directly or indirectly, to sell any equity security of such issuer (other than an exempted security), if the person selling the security or his principal (1) does not own the security sold, or (2) if owning the security, does not deliver it against such sale within twenty days thereafter, or does not within five days after such sale deposit it in the mails or other usual channels of transportation; but no person shall be deemed to have violated this subsection if he proves that notwithstanding the exercise of good faith he was unable to make such delivery or deposit within such time, or that to do so would cause undue inconvenience or expense.

(d) The provisions of subsection (b) of this section shall not apply to any purchase and sale, or sale and purchase, and the provisions of subsection (c) of this section shall not apply to any sale, of an equity security not then or theretofore held by him in an investment account, by a dealer in the ordinary course of his business and incident to the establishment or maintenance by him of a primary or secondary market (otherwise than on a national securities exchange or an exchange exempted from registration under section 5 of this title) for such security. The Commission may, by such rules and regulations as it deems necessary or appropriate in the public interest, define and prescribe terms and conditions with respect to securities held in an investment account and transactions made in the ordinary course of business and incident to the establishment or maintenance of a primary or secondary market.

(e) The provisions of this section shall not apply to foreign or domestic arbitrage transactions unless made in contravention of such rules and regulations as the Commission may adopt in order to carry out the purposes of this section.

Accounts and Records, Reports, Examinations of Exchanges, Members, and Others

Section 17. (a) (1) Every national securities exchange, member thereof, broker or dealer who transacts a business in securities through the medium of any such member, registered securities association, registered broker or dealer, registered municipal securities dealer, registered securities information processor, registered transfer agent, and registered clearing agency and the Municipal Securities Rulemaking Board shall make and keep for prescribed periods such records, furnish such copies thereof, and make and disseminate such reports as the Commission, by rule, prescribes as necessary or appropriate in the public interest, for the protection of investors, or otherwise in furtherance of the purposes of this title.

(2) Every registered clearing agency shall also make and keep for prescribed periods such records, furnish such copies thereof, and make and disseminate such reports, as the appropriate regulatory agency for such clearing agency, by rule, prescribes as necessary or appropriate for the safeguarding of securities and funds in the custody or control of such clearing agency or for which it is responsible.

(3) Every registered transfer agent shall also make and keep for prescribed periods such records, furnish such copies thereof, and make such reports as the appropriate regulatory agency for such transfer agent, by rule, prescribes as necessary or appropriate in furtherance of the purposes of section 17A of this title.

(b) All records of persons described in subsection (a) of this section are subject at any time, or from time to time, to such reasonable periodic, special, or other examinations by representatives of the Commission and the appropriate regulatory agency for such persons as the Commission or the appropriate regulatory agency for such persons deems necessary or appropriate in the public interest, for the protection of investors, or otherwise in furtherance of the purposes of this title: Provided, however, That the Commission shall, prior to conducting any such examination of a registered clearing agency, registered transfer agent, or registered municipal securities dealer for which it is not the appropriate regulatory agency, give notice to the appropriate regulatory agency for such clearing agency, transfer agent, or municipal securities dealer of such proposed examination and consult with such appropriate regulatory agency concerning the feasibility and desirability of coordinating such examination with examinations conducted by such appropriate regulatory agency with a view to avoiding unnecessary regulatory duplication or undue regulatory burdens for such clearing agency, transfer agent, or municipal securities dealer. Nothing in the proviso to the preceding sentence shall be construed to impair or limit (other than by the requirement of prior consultation) the power of the Commission under this subsection to examine any clearing agency, transfer agent, or municipal securities dealer or to affect in any way the power of the Commission under any other provision of this title or otherwise to inspect, examine, or investigate any such clearing agency, transfer agent, or municipal securities dealer.

* * *

(e)(1)(A) Every registered broker or dealer shall annually file with the Commission a balance sheet and income statement certified by an independent public accountant, prepared on a calendar or fiscal year basis, and such other financial statements (which shall, as the Commission specifies, be certified) and information concerning its financial condition as the Commission, by rule, may prescribe as necessary or appropriate in the public interest or for the protection of investors.

(B) Every registered broker and dealer shall annually send to its customers its certified balance sheet and such other financial statements and information concerning its financial condition as the Commission, by rule, may prescribe pursuant to subsection (a) of this section.

* * *

Liability for Misleading Statements

SECTION 18. (a) Any person who shall make or cause to be made any statement in any application, report, or document filed pursuant to this title or any rule or regulation thereunder or any undertaking contained in a registration statement as provided in subsection (d) of section 15 of this title, which statement was at the time and in the light of the circumstances under which it was made false or misleading with respect to any material fact, shall be liable to any person (not knowing that such statement was false or misleading) who, in reliance upon such statement, shall have purchased or sold a security at a price which was affected by such statement, for damages caused by such reliance, unless the person sued shall prove that he acted in good faith and had no knowledge that such statement was false or misleading. A person seeking to enforce such liability may sue at law or in equity in any court of competent jurisdiction. In any such suit the court may, in its discretion, require an undertaking for the payment of the costs of such suit, and assess reasonable costs, including reasonable attorneys' fees, against either party litigant.

(b) Every person who becomes liable to make payment under this section may recover contribution as in cases of contact from any person who, if joined in the original suit, would have been liable to make the same payment.

(c) No action shall be maintained to enforce any liability created under this section unless brought within one year after the discovery of the facts constituting the cause of action and within three years after such cause of action accrued.

Unlawful Representations

SECTION 26. No action or failure to act by the Commission or the Board of Governors of the Federal Reserve System, in the administration of this title shall be construed to mean that the particular authority has in any way passed upon the merits of, or given approval to, any security or any transaction or transactions therein, nór shall such action or failure to act with regard to any statement or report filed with or examined by such authority pursuant to this title or rules and regulations thereunder, be deemed a finding by such authority that such statement or report is true and accurate on its face or that it is not false or misleading. It shall be unlawful to make, or cause to be made, to any prospective purchaser or seller of a security any representation that any such action or failure to act by any such authority is to be so construed or has such effect.

Jurisdiction of Offenses and Suits

SECTION 27. The district courts of the United States, the United States District Court for the District of Columbia, and the United States courts of any Territory or other place subject to the jurisdiction of the United States shall have exclusive jurisdiction of violations of this title or the rules and regulations thereunder, and of all suits in equity and actions at law brought to enforce any liability or duty created by this title or the rules and regulations thereunder. Any criminal proceeding may be brought in the district wherein any act or transaction constituting the violation occurred. Any suit or action to enforce any liability or duty created by this title or rules and regulations thereunder, or enjoin any violation of such title or rules and regulations, may be

brought in any such district or in the district wherein the defendant is found or is an inhabitant or transacts business, and process in such cases may be served in any other district of which the defendant is an inhabitant or wherever the defendant may be found. Judgments and decrees so rendered shall be subject to review as provided in sections 128 and 240 of the Judicial Code, as amended (U.S.C., title 28, secs. 225 and 347). No costs shall be assessed for or against the Commission in any proceeding under this title brought by or against it in the Supreme Court or such other courts.

Effect on Existing Law

SECTION 28. (a) The rights and remedies provided by this title shall be in addition to any and all other rights and remedies that may exist at law or in equity; but no person permitted to maintain a suit for damages under the provisions of this title shall recover, through satisfaction of judgment in one or more actions, a total amount in excess of his actual damages on account of the act complained of. Nothing in this title shall affect the jurisdiction of the securities commission (or any agency or officer performing like functions) of any State over any security or any person insofar as it does not conflict with the provisions of this title or the rules and regulations thereunder.

(b) Nothing in this title shall be construed to modify existing law with regard to the binding effect (1) on any member of or participant in any self-regulatory organization of any action taken by the authorities of such organization to settle disputes between its members or participants, (2) on any municipal securities dealer or municipal securities broker of any action taken pursuant to a procedure established by the Municipal Securities Rulemaking Board to settle disputes between municipal securities dealers and municipal securities brokers, or (3) of any action described in paragraph (1) or (2) on any person who has agreed to be bound thereby.

(c) The stay, setting aside, or modification pursuant to section 19(e) of this title of any disciplinary sanction imposed by a self-regulatory organization or a member thereof, person associated with a member, or participant therein, shall not affect the validity or force of any action taken as a result of such sanction by the self-regulatory organization prior to such stay, setting aside, or modification: Provided, That such action is not inconsistent with the provisions of this title or the rules or regulations thereunder. The rights of any person acting in good faith which arise out of any such action shall not be affected in any way by such stay, setting aside, or modification.

(d) No State or political subdivision thereof shall impose any tax on any change in beneficial or record ownership of securities effected through the facilities of a registered clearing agency or registered transfer agent or any nominee thereof or custodian therefor or upon the delivery or transfer of securities to or through or receipt from such agency or agent or any nominee thereof or custodian therefor, unless such change in beneficial or record ownership or such transfer or delivery or receipt would otherwise be taxable by such State or political subdivision if the facilities of such registered clearing agency, registered transfer agent, or any nominee thereof or custodian therefor were not physically located in the taxing State or political subdivision. No State or political subdivision thereof shall impose any tax on securities which are deposited in or retained by a registered clearing agency, registered transfer agent, or any nominee thereof or custodian therefor, unless such securities would otherwise be taxable by such State or political subdivision if the facilities of such registered clearing agency, registered transfer agent, or any nominee thereof or custodian therefor were not physically located in the taxing State or political subdivision.

(e)(1) No person using the mails, or any means or instrumentality of interstate commerce, in the exercise of investment discretion with respect to an account shall be deemed to have acted unlawfully or to have breached a fiduciary duty under State or Federal law un-

less expressly provided to the contrary by a law enacted by the Congress or any State subsequent to the date of enactment of the Securities Acts Amendments in 1975 solely by reason of his having caused the account to pay a member of an exchange, broker, or dealer an amount of commission for effecting a securities transaction in excess of the amount of commission another member of an exchange, broker, or dealer would have charged for effecting that transaction, if such person determined in good faith that such amount of commission was reasonable in relation to the value of the brokerage and research services provided by such member, broker, or dealer, viewed in terms of either that particular transaction or his overall responsibilities with respect to the accounts as to which he exercises investment discretion. This subsection is exclusive and plenary insofar as conduct is covered by the foregoing, unless otherwise expressly provided by contract: Provided, however, That nothing in this subsection shall be construed to impair or limit the power of the Commission under any other provision of this title or otherwise.

(2) A person exercising investment discretion with respect to an account shall make such disclosure of his policies and practices with respect to commissions that will be paid for effecting securities transactions, at such times and in such manner, as the appropriate regulatory agency, by rule, may prescribe as necessary or appropriate in the public interest or for the protection of investors.

(3) For purposes of this subsection a person provides brokerage and research services insofar as he—

(A) furnishes advice, either directly or through publications or writings, as to the value of securities, the advisability of investing in, purchasing, or selling securities, and the availability of securities or purchasers or sellers of securities;

(B) furnishes analyses and reports concerning issuers, industries, securities, economic factors and trends, portfolio strategy, and the performance of accounts; or

(C) effects securities transactions and performs functions incidental thereto (such as clearance, settlement, and custody) or required in connection therewith by rules of the Commission or a self-regulatory organization of which such person is a member or person associated with a member or in which such person is a participant.

FOREIGN CORRUPT PRACTICES ACT OF 1977

Foreign Corrupt Practices by Domestic Concerns

SECTION 104.   (a) It shall be unlawful for any domestic concern, other than an issuer which is subject to section 30A of the Securities Exchange Act of 1934, or any officer, director, employee, or agent of such domestic concern or any stockholder thereof acting on behalf of such domestic concern, to make use of the mails or any means or instrumentality of interstate commerce corruptly in furtherance of an offer, payment, promise to pay, or authorization of the payment of any money, or offer, gift, promise to give, or authorization of the giving of anything of value to—

(1) any foreign official for purposes of—

(A) influencing any act or decision of such foreign official in his official capacity, including a decision to fail to perform his official functions; or

(B) inducing such foreign official to use his influence with a foreign government or instrumentality thereof to affect or influence any act or decision of such government or instrumentality,

in order to assist such domestic concern in obtaining or retaining business for or with, or directing business to, any person;

(2) any foreign political party or official thereof or any candidate for foreign political office for purposes of—

(A) influencing any act or decision of such party, official, or candidate in its or his official capacity, including a decision to fail to perform its or his official functions; or

(B) inducing such party, official, or candidate to use its or his influence with a foreign government or instrumentality thereof to affect or influence any act or decision of such government or instrumentality,

in order to assist such domestic concern in obtaining or retaining business for or with, or directing business to, any person; or

(3) any person, while knowing or having reason to know that all or a portion of such money or thing of value will be offered, given, or promised, directly or indirectly, to any foreign official, to any foreign political party or official thereof, or to any candidate for foreign political office, for purposes of—

(A) influencing any act or decision of such foreign official, political party, party official, or candidate in his or its official capacity, including a decision to fail to perform his or its official functions; or

(B) inducing such foreign official, political party, party official, or candidate to use his or its influence with a foreign government or instrumentality thereof to affect or influence any act or decision of such government or instrumentality,

in order to assist such domestic concern in obtaining or retaining business for or with, or directing business to, any person.

(b)(1)(A) Except as provided in subparagraph (B), any domestic concern which violates subsection (a) shall, upon conviction, be fined not more than $1,000,000.

(B) Any individual who is a domestic concern and who willfully violates subsection (a) shall, upon conviction, be fined not more than $10,000, or imprisoned not more than five years, or both.

(2) Any officer or director of a domestic concern, or stockholder acting on behalf of such domestic concern, who willfully violates subsection (a) shall, upon conviction, be fined not more than $10,000, or imprisoned not more than five years, or both.

(3) Whenever a domestic concern is found to have violated subsection (a) of this section, any employee or agent of such domestic concern who is a United States citizen, national, or resident or is otherwise subject to the jurisdiction of the United States (other than an officer, director, or stockholder acting on behalf of such domestic concern), and who willfully carried out the act or practice constituting such violation shall, upon conviction, be fined not more than $10,000, or imprisoned not more than five years, or both.

(4) Whenever a fine is imposed under paragraph (2) or (3) of this subsection upon any officer, director, stockholder, employee, or agent of a domestic concern, such fine shall not be paid, directly or indirectly, by such domestic concern.

(c) Whenever it appears to the Attorney General that any domestic concern, or officer, director, employee, agent, or stockholder thereof, is engaged, or is about to engage, in any act or practice constituting a violation of subsection (a) of this section, the Attorney General may, in his discretion, bring a civil action in an appropriate district court of the United States to enjoin such act or practice, and upon a proper showing a permanent or temporary injunction or a temporary restraining order shall be granted without bond.

(d) As used in this section:

(1) The term "domestic concern" means (A) any individual who is a citizen, national, or resident of the United States; or (B) any corporation, partnership, association, joint-stock company, business trust, unincorporated organization, or sole proprietorship which has its principal place of business in the United States, or which is organized under the laws of a State of the United States or a territory, possession, or commonwealth of the United States.

(2) The term "foreign official" means any officer or employee of a foreign government or any department, agency, or instrumentality thereof, or any person acting in an official capacity for or on behalf of any such government or department, agency, or instrumentality. Such term does not include any employee of a foreign government or any department, agency, or instrumentality thereof whose duties are essentially ministerial or clerical.

(3) The term "interstate commerce" means trade, commerce, transportation, or communication among the several States, or between any foreign country and any State or between any State and any place or ship outside thereof. Such term includes the intrastate use of (A) a telephone or other interstate means of communication, or (B) any other interstate instrumentality.

D. SELECTED SEC RULES AND FORMS UNDER SECURITIES EXCHANGE ACT OF 1934

17 C.F.R. § 240.——

Contents

DEFINITIONS

MANIPULATION AND DECEPTION

REPORTS BY BENEFICIAL OWNERS

REPURCHASES BY ISSUERS

REPORTS BY INSTITUTIONAL MANAGERS

SECURITIES

SOLICITATION OF PROXIES

TENDER OFFERS

OVER–THE–COUNTER MARKETS

DEFINITIONS

Rule 3b–2.   Definition of "Officer"

The term "officer" means a president, vice president, secretary, treasury or principal financial officer, comptroller or principal accounting officer, and any person routinely performing corresponding functions with respect to any organization whether incorporated or unincorporated.

MANIPULATION AND DECEPTION

Rule 10b–4.   Short Tendering of Securities

(a) It shall constitute a "manipulative or deceptive device or contrivance" as used in Section 10(b) of the Act for any person, in response to an offer for, or to a request or invitation for tenders of, any security,

(1) to tender any security for his own account unless (A) he owns the security or, (B) he owns a security convertible into or exchangeable for, or owns an option, warrant or right to purchase the tendered security, intends to acquire the tendered security, by conversion, exchange, or exercise of such option, warrant or right to the extent necessary to deliver the tendered security, and, upon the acceptance of his tender, he does convert, exchange, or exercise such option, warrant or right to the extent necessary to deliver the tendered security, *Provided, however,* that if he tenders a security on the basis of his ownership of an option to purchase such security, he shall have reason to believe that the maker or writer of the option has title to and possession of such security and will promptly deliver it upon exercise of the option; or,

(2) to tender or guarantee the tender of any security on behalf of another person, unless (A) such security is in the possession of the person making the tender or giving the guarantee, or (B) the person making the tender or giving the guarantee, upon information furnished by the person on whose behalf the tender or guarantee is made, has reason to believe that such person owns the security tendered and, as soon as possible, without undue inconvenience or expense, will deliver the security for the purpose of the tender to the person making the tender or giving the guarantee, or (C) the person on whose behalf the tender or guarantee is made owns a security convertible into, or exchangeable for, or owns an option, warrant or right to purchase the tendered security and the person making the tender has reason to believe that such other person intends to acquire the tendered security, by the conversion, exchange, or exercise of such option, warrant or right to the extent necessary to deliver the tendered security. *Provided, however,* that if the tender or guarantee of the tender of a security is made on the basis of the ownership of an option to purchase such security, the person making the tender or guarantee shall have reason to believe that the maker or writer of the option has title to and possession of such security and will promptly deliver it upon exercise of the option.

(b) For the purposes of this section, a person shall be deemed to own a security if (1) he or his agent has title to it; or (2) he has purchased, or has entered into an unconditional contract, binding on both parties thereto, to purchase it but has not yet received it; or (3) he owns a security convertible into or exchangeable for it and has tendered such security for conversion or exchange; or (4) he has an option to purchase or acquire it and has exercised such option; or (5) he has rights or warrants to subscribe to it and has exercised such rights or warrants. *Provided, however,* that a person shall be deemed to own securities only to the extent that he has a net long position in such securities.

Rule 10b–5.   Employment of Manipulative and Deceptive Devices

It shall be unlawful for any person, directly or indirectly, by the use of any means or instrumentality of interstate commerce, or of the mails, or of any facility of any national securities exchange,

(1) to employ any device, scheme, or artifice to defraud,

(2) to make any untrue statement of a material fact or to omit to state a material fact necessary in order to make the statements made, in the light of the circumstances under which they were made, not misleading. or

(3) to engage in any act, practice, or course of business which operates or would operate as a fraud or deceit upon any person,

in connection with the purchase or sale of any security.

Rule 10b-6. Prohibitions Against Trading by Persons Interested in a Distribution

(a) It shall constitute a "manipulative or deceptive device or contrivance" as used in section 10(b) of the Act for any person,

(1) who is an underwriter or prospective underwriter in a particular distribution of securities, or

(2) who is the issuer or other person on whose behalf such a distribution is being made, or

(3) who is a broker, dealer, or other person who has agreed to participate or is participating in such a distribution, directly or indirectly, by the use of any means or instrumentality of interstate commerce, or of the mails, or of any facility of any national securities exchange, either alone or with one or more other persons, to bid for or purchase for any account in which he has a beneficial interest, any security which is the subject of such distribution, or any security of the same class and series, or any right to purchase any such security, or to attempt to induce any person to purchase any such security or right until after he has completed his participation in such distribution: *Provided, however,* That this rule shall not prohibit (1) transactions in connection with the distribution effected otherwise than on a securities exchange with the issuer or other person or persons on whose behalf such distribution is being made or among underwriters, prospective underwriters, or other persons who have agreed to participate or are participating in such distribution; (2) unsolicited privately negotiated purchases, each involving a substantial amount of such security, effected neither on a securities exchange nor from or through a broker or dealer; or (3) purchases by an issuer effected more than 40 days after the commencement of the distribution for the purpose of satisfying a sinking fund or similar obligation to which it is subject; or (4) odd-lot transactions (and the off-setting round-lot transactions hereinafter referred to) by a person registered as an odd-lot dealer in such security on a national securities exchange who offsets such odd-lot transactions in such security by round-lot transactions as promptly as possible; or (5) brokerage transactions not involving solicitation of the customer's order; or (6) offers to sell or the solicitation of offers to buy the securities being distributed (including securities or rights acquired in stabilizing) or securities or rights offered as principal by the person making such offer to sell or solicitation; or (7) the exercise of any right or conversion privilege to acquire any security; or (8) stabilizing transactions not in violation of . . . [Rule 10b-7]; or (9) bids for or purchases of rights not in violation of . . . [Rule 10b-8]; or (10) transactions effected on a national securities exchange in accordance with the provisions of a plan filed by such exchange under . . . [Rule 10b-2(d)] and declared effective by the Commission; or (11) purchases or bids by an underwriter, prospective underwriter or dealer otherwise than on a securities exchange, 10 or more business days prior to the proposed commencement of such distribution (or 5 or more business days in the case of unsolicited purchases), if none of such purchases or bids are for the purpose of creating actual, or apparent, active trading in or raising the price of such security. In the case of securities offered pursuant to an effective registration statement under the Securities Act of 1933 the distribution shall not deemed to commence for purposes of this clause (11) prior to the effective date of the registration statement.

(b) The distribution of a security (1) which is immediately exchangeable for or convertible into another security, or (2) which entitles the holder thereof immediately to acquire another security, shall be deemed to include a distribution of such other security within the meaning of this rule.

(*c*) The following shall be applicable for the purposes of this rule:

(1) The term "underwriter" means a person who has agreed with an issuer or other person on whose behalf a distribution is to be made (A) to purchase securities for distribution or (B) to distribute securities for or on behalf of such issuer or other person or (C) to manage or supervise a distribution of securities for or on behalf of such issuer or other person.

(2) The term "prospective underwriter" means a person (A) who has agreed to submit or has submitted a bid to become an underwriter of securities as to which the issuer, or other person on whose behalf the distribution is to be made, has issued a public invitation for bids, or (B) who has reached an understanding, with the issuer or other person on whose behalf a distribution is to be made, that he will become an underwriter, whether or not the terms and conditions of the underwriting have been agreed upon.

(3) A person shall be deemed to have completed his participation in a particular distribution as follows: (A) the issuer or other person on whose behalf such distribution is being made, when such distribution is completed; (B) an underwriter, when he has distributed his participation, including all other securities of the same class acquired in connection with the distribution, and any stabilization arrangements and trading restrictions with respect to such distribution to which he is a party have been terminated; (C) any other person, when he has distributed his participation. A person, including an underwriter or dealer, shall be deemed for purposes of this paragraph (c)(3) to have distributed securities acquired by him for investment.

(4) The term "plan" shall include any bonus, profit-sharing, pension, retirement, thrift, savings, incentive, stock purchase, stock ownership, stock appreciation, stock option, dividend reinvestment or similar plan for employees or shareholders of an issuer or its subsidiaries.

(*d*) The provisions of this rule shall not apply to any of the following securities: (1) "exempted securities" as defined in Section 3(a)(12) of the Act, including securities issued, or guaranteed both as to principal and interest, by the International Bank for .Reconstruction and

Development; or (2) face-amount certificates issued by a face-amount certificate company, or redeemable securities issued by an open-end management company or a unit investment trust. Any terms used in clause (2) of this paragraph (d) which are defined in the Investment Company Act of 1940 shall have the meanings specified in such Act.

(*e*) The provisions of this section shall not apply to any distribution of securities by an issuer or a subsidiary of an issuer to employees or shareholders of the issuer or its subsidiaries, or to a trustee or other person acquiring such securities for the account of such employees or shareholders pursuant to a plan, as that term is defined in paragraph (c)(4) of this section.

(*f*) If the provisions of this section would apply to bids for or purchases of any equity security pursuant to an issuer tender offer, as that term is defined in Rule 13e–4(a)(2) under the Act, or to a tender offer subject to section 14(d) of the act and the rules applicable thereto, solely because the issuer has outstanding securities which are immediately convertible into, or exchangeable or exercisable for, the security for which the tender offer is to be made, such provisions shall not apply to such bids and purchases if such bids and purchases are subject to and made in accordance with the provisions of Rule 13e–4 or section 14(d) and the rules applicable thereto.

(*g*) This rule shall not prohibit any transaction or transactions if the Commission, upon written request or upon its own motion, exempts such transaction or transactions, either unconditionally or on specified terms and conditions, as not constituting a manipulative or deceptive device or contrivance comprehended within the purpose of this rule.

REPORTS BY BENEFICIAL OWNERS

Rule 13d–1. Filing of Schedules 13D and 13G

(a) Any person who, after acquiring directly or indirectly the beneficial ownership of any equity security of a class which is specified in paragraph (d) of this section, is directly or indirectly the beneficial owner of more than 5 percent of such class shall, within 10 days after such acquisition, send to the issuer of the security at its principal executive office, by registered or certified mail, and to each exchange where the security is traded, and file with the Commission, a statement containing the information required by Schedule 13D. Six copies of the statement, including all exhibits, shall be filed with the Commission.

(b)(1) A person who would otherwise be obligated under paragraph (a) of this section to file a statement on Schedule 13D may, in lieu thereof, file with the Commission, within 45 days after the end of the calendar year in which such person became so obligated, six copies, including all exhibits, of a short form statement on Schedule 13G and send one copy each of such schedule to the issuer of the security at its principal executive office, by registered or certified mail, and to the principal national securities exchange where the security is traded: *Provided,* That it shall not be necessary to file a Schedule 13G unless the percentage of the class of equity security specified in paragraph (d) of this section beneficially owned as of the end of the calendar year is more than 5 percent: *And provided further,* That:

(i) Such person has acquired such securities in the ordinary course of his business and not with the purpose nor with the effect of changing or influencing the control of the issuer, nor in connection with or as a participant in any transaction having such purpose or effect, including any transaction subject to Rule 13d–3(b);

* * *

(2) Any person relying on Rules 13d–1(b)(1) and 13d–2(b) shall, in addition to filing any statements required thereunder, file a statement on Schedule 13G, within ten days after the end of the first month in which such person's direct or indirect beneficial ownership exceeds ten percent of a class of equity securities specified in Rule 13d–1(c) * * *

(3)(i) Notwithstanding paragraphs (b)(1) and (2) of this section and Rule 13d–2(b) a person shall immediately become subject to Rules 13d–1(a) and 13d–2(a) and shall promptly, but not more than 10 days later, file a statement on Schedule 13D if such person:

(A) Has reported that it is the beneficial owner of more than five percent of a class of equity

securities in a statement on Schedule 13G pursuant to paragraph (b)(1) or (b)(2) of this section, or is required to report such acquisition but has not yet filed the schedule;

(B) Determines that it no longer has acquired or holds such securities in the ordinary course of business or not with the purpose nor with the effect of changing or influencing the control of the issuer, nor in connection with or as a participant in any transaction having such purpose or effect, including any transaction subject to Rule 13d–3(b); and

(C) Is at that time the beneficial owner of more than five percent of a class of equity securities described in Rule 13d–1(c).

(ii) For the ten day period immediately following the date of the filing of a Schedule 13D pursuant to this paragraph (b)(3), such person shall not: (A) Vote or direct the voting of the securities described in paragraph (b)(3)(i)(A); nor, (B) Acquire an additional beneficial ownership interest in any equity securities of the issuer of such securities, nor of any person controlling such issuer.

(4) Any person who has reported an acquisition of securities in a statement on Schedule 13G pursuant to paragraph (b)(1) or (b)(2) of this section and thereafter ceases to be a person specified in paragraph (b)(1)(ii) of this section shall immediately become subject to Rules 13d–1(a) and 13d–2(a) and shall file, within ten days thereafter a statement on Schedule 13D, in the event such person is a beneficial owner at that time of more than five perecent of the class of equity securities.

(c) Any person who, as of December 31, 1978, or as of the end of any calendar year thereafter, is directly or indirectly the beneficial owner of more than 5 percent of any equity security of a class specified in paragraph (d) of this section and who is not required to file a statement under paragraph (a) of this section by virtue of the exemption provided by Section 13(d)(6)(A) or (B) of the Act, or because such beneficial ownership was acquired prior to December 22, 1970, or because such person otherwise (except for the exemption provided by Section 13(d)(6)(c) of the Act) is not required to file such statement, shall, within 45 days after the end of the calendar year in which such person became obligated to report under this paragraph, send to the issuer of the security at its principal executive office, by registered or certified mail, and file with the Commission a statement containing the information required by Schedule 13G. Six copies of the statement, including all exhibits, shall be filed with the Commission.

* * *

Rule 13d-2 Filing of Amendments to Schedule 13D or 13G.

(a) Schedule 13D—If any material change occurs in the facts set forth in the statement required by Rule 13d-1(a), including, but not limited to, any material increase or decrease in the percentage of the class beneficially owned, the person or persons who were required to file such statement shall promptly file or cause to be filed with the Commission and send or cause to be sent to the issuer at its principal executive office, by registered or certified mail, and to each exchange on which the security is traded an amendment disclosing such change. An acquisition or disposition of beneficial ownership of securities in an amount equal to one percent or more of the class of securities shall be deemed "material" for purposes of this rule; acquisitions or dispositions of less than such amounts may be material, depending upon the facts and circumstances. Six copies of each such amendment shall be filed with the Commission.

(b) Schedule 13G—Notwithstanding paragraph (a) of this rule, and provided that the person or persons filing a statement pursuant to Rule 13d-1(b) continue to meet the requirements set forth therein, any person who has filed a short form statement on Schedule 13G shall amend such statement within forty-five days after the end of each calendar year to reflect, as of the end of the calendar year, any changes in the information reported in the previous filing on that Schedule, or if there are no changes from the previous filing a signed statement to that effect under cover of Schedule 13G. Six copies of such amendment, including all exhibits, shall be filed with the Commission and one each sent, by registered or certified mail, to the issuer of the security at its principal executive office and

to the principal national securities exchange where the security is traded. Once an amendment has been filed reflecting beneficial ownership of five percent or less of the class of securities, no additional filings are required unless the person thereafter becomes the beneficial owner of more than five percent of the class and is required to file pursuant to Rule 13d-1.

Rule 13d-3. Determination of Beneficial Owner

(a) For the purposes of section 13(d) and 13(g) of the Act a beneficial owner of a security includes any person who, directly or indirectly, through any contract, arrangement, understanding, relationship, or otherwise has or shares:

(1) *Voting power* which includes the power to vote, or to direct the voting of, such security; and/or

(2) *Investment power* which includes the power to dispose, or to direct the disposition, of such security.

(b) Any person who, directly or indirectly, creates or uses a trust, proxy, power of attorney, pooling arrangement or any other contract, arrangement, or device with the purpose or effect of divesting such person of beneficial ownership of a security or preventing the vesting of such beneficial ownership as part of a plan or scheme to evade the reporting requirements of section 13(d) or 13(g) of the Act shall be deemed for purposes of such section to be the beneficial owner of such security.

(c) All securities of the same class beneficially owned by a person, regardless of the form which such beneficial ownership takes, shall be aggregated in calculating the number of shares beneficially owned by such person.

(d) Notwithstanding the provisions of paragraphs (a) and (c) of this rule:

(1)(i) A person shall be deemed to be the beneficial owner of a security, subject to the provisions of paragraph (b) of this rule, if that person has the right to acquire beneficial ownership of such security, as defined in Rule 13d-3(a), within sixty days, including but not limited to any right acquired: (A) through the exercise of any option, warrant or right; (B) through

479

the conversion of a security; (C) pursuant to the power to revoke a trust, discretionary account, or similar arrangement; or (D) pursuant to the automatic termination of a trust, discretionary account or similar arrangement; provided, however, any person who acquires a security or power specified in paragraphs (A), (B) or (C), above, with the purpose or effect of changing or influencing the control of the issuer, or in connection with or as a participant in any transaction having such purpose or effect, immediately upon such acquisition shall be deemed to be the beneficial owner of the securities which may be acquired through the exercise or conversion of such security or power. Any securities not outstanding which are subject to such options, warrants, rights or conversion privileges shall be deemed to be outstanding for the purpose of computing the percentage of outstanding securities of the class owned by such person but shall not be deemed to be outstanding for the purpose of computing the percentage of the class by any other person.

(ii) Paragraph (i) remains applicable for the purpose of determining the obligation to file with respect to the underlying security even though the option, warrant, right or convertible security is of a class of equity security, as defined in Rule 13d–1(c), and may therefore give rise to a separate obligation to file.

(2) A member of a national securities exchange shall not be deemed to be a beneficial owner of securities held directly or indirectly by it on behalf of another person solely because such member is the record holder of such securities and, pursuant to the rules of such exchange, may direct the vote of such securities, without instruction, on other than contested matters or matters that may affect substantially the rights or privileges of the holders of the securities to be voted, but is otherwise precluded by the rules of such exchange from voting without instruction.

(3) A person who in the ordinary course of his business is a pledgee of securities under a written pledge agreement as to which there has been a default shall not be deemed to be the beneficial owner of such pledged securities until the pledgee has taken all formal steps necessary which are required to declare such default and determines that the power to vote or to direct the vote or to dispose or to direct the disposition of such pledged securities will be exercised: *Provided,* That:

(i) The pledge agreement is bona fide, does not grant the power to vote or to direct the vote or to dispose or to direct the disposition of such pledged securities to the pledgee prior to default, and was not entered into with the purpose nor with the effect of changing or influencing the control of the issuer, nor in connection with any transaction having such purpose or effect, including any transaction subject to Rule 13d–3(b); and

(ii) The pledgee is a person specified in Rule 13d–1(b)(1)(ii).

(4) A person engaged in business as an underwriter of securities who acquires securities through his participation in good faith in a firm commitment underwriting registered under the Securities Act of 1933 shall not be deemed to be the beneficial owner of such securities until the expiration of forty days after the date of such acquisition.

Rule 13d–4. Disclaimer of Beneficial Ownership

Any person may expressly declare in any statement filed that the filing of such statement shall not be construed as an admission that such person is, for the purposes of section 13(d), or 13(g) of the Act, the beneficial owner of any securities covered by the statement.

Rule 13d–5 Acquisition of Securities.

(a) A person who becomes a beneficial owner of securities shall be deemed to have acquired such securities for purposes of section 13(d)(1) of the Act, whether such acquisition was through purchase or otherwise. However, executors or administrators of a decedent's estate generally will be presumed not to have acquired beneficial ownership of the securities in the decedent's estate until such time as such executors or administrators are qualified under local law to perform their duties.

(b)(1) When two or more persons agree to act together for the purpose of acquiring, holding, voting or disposing of equity securities of an issuer, the group formed thereby shall be deemed to have acquired beneficial ownership, for purposes of sections 13(d) and 13(g) of the Act, as of the date of such agreement, of all equity securities of that issuer beneficially owned by any such persons.

(2) Notwithstanding the previous paragraph, a group shall be deemed not to have acquired any equity securities beneficially owned by the other members of the group solely by virtue of their concerted actions relating to the purchase of equity securities directly from an issuer in a transaction not involving a public offering: *Provided,* That:

(i) All the members of the group are persons specified in Rule 13d–1(b)(1)(ii);

(ii) The purchase is in the ordinary course of each member's business and not with the purpose nor with the effect of changing or influencing control of the issuer, nor in connection with or as a participant in any transaction having such purpose or effect, including any transaction subject to Rule 13d–3(b);

(iii) There is no agreement among, or between any members of the group to act together with respect to the issuer or its securities except for the purpose of facilitating the specific purchase involved; and

(iv) The only actions among or between any members of the group with respect to the issuer or its securities subsequent to the closing date of the non-public offering are those which are necessary to conclude ministerial matters directly related to the completion of the offer or sale of the securities.

Rule 13d–6. Exemption of Certain Acquisitions

The acquisition of securities of an issuer by a person who, prior to such acquisition, was a beneficial owner of more than five percent of the outstanding securities of the same class as those acquired shall be exempt from section 13(d) of the Act: *Provided,* That:

(a) The acquisition is made pursuant to preemptive subscription right in an offering made to all holders of securities of the class to which the preemptive subscription rights pertain;

(b) Such person does not acquire additional securities except through the exercise of his pro rata share of the preemptive subscription rights; and

(c) The acquisition is duly reported if required, pursuant to section 16(a) of the Act and the rules and regulations thereunder.

Rule 13d–7 Fees for filing Schedules 13D or 13G.

The initial Schedule 13D or 13G filed by a person shall be accompanied by a fee of $100 payable to the Commission, no part of which shall be refunded. No fees shall be required with respect to the filing of any amended Schedule 13D or 13G: *Provided, however,* That once an amendment has been filed reflecting beneficial ownership of 5 percent or less of such class, an additional fee of $100 shall be paid with the next filing of that person which reflects ownership of more than 5 percent thereof.

Schedule 13D. Information to Be Included in Statements Filed Pursuant to Rule 13d–1 (a) and Amendments Thereto Filed Pursuant to Rule 13d–2(a)

Item 1. Security and Issuer

State the title of the class of equity securities to which this statement relates and the name and address of the principal executive offices of the issuer of such securities.

Item 2. Identity and Background

If the person filing this statement or any person enumerated in Instruction C of this statement is a corporation, general partnership, limited partnership, syndicate or other group of persons, state its name, the state or other place of its organization, its principal business, the address of its principal business, the address of its principal office and the information required by (d) and (e) of this Item. If the person filing this statement or any person enumerated in Instruction C is a natural person, provide the information specified in (a) through (f) of this Item with respect to such person(s).

(a) Name;

(b) Residence or business address;

(c) Present principal occupation or employment and the name, principal business and address of any corporation or other organization in which such employment is conducted;

(d) Whether or not, during the last five years, such person has been convicted in a criminal proceeding (excluding traffic violations or similar misdemeanors) and, if so, give the dates, nature of conviction, name and location of court, any penalty imposed, or other disposition of the case;

(e) Whether or not, during the last five years, such person was a party to a civil proceeding of a judicial or administrative body of competent jurisdiction and as a result of such proceeding was or is subject to a judgment, decree or final order enjoining future violations of, or prohibiting or mandating activities subject to, federal or state securities laws or finding any violation with respect to such laws; and, if so, identify and describe such proceedings and summarize the terms of such judgment, decree or final order; and

(f) Citizenship.

Item 3. Source and Amount of Funds or Other Consideration

State the source and the amount of funds or other consideration used or to be used in making the purchases, and if any part of the purchase price is or will be represented by funds or other consideration borrowed or otherwise obtained for the purpose of acquiring, holding, trading or voting the securities, a description of the transaction and the names of the parties thereto. Where material, such information should also be provided with respect to prior acquisitions not previously reported pursuant to this regulation. If the source of all or any part of the funds is a loan made in the ordinary course of business by a bank, as defined in Section 3(a)(6) of the Act, the name of the bank shall not be made available to the public if the person at the time of filing the statement so requests in writing and files such request, naming such bank, with the Secretary of the Commission. If the securities were acquired other than by purchase, describe the method of acquisition.

Item 4. Purpose of Transaction

State the purpose or purposes of the acquisition of securities of the issuer. Describe any plans or proposals which the reporting persons may have which relate to or would result in:

(a) The acquisition by any person of additional securities of the issuer, or the disposition of securities of the issuer;

(b) An extraordinary corporate transaction, such as a merger, reorganization or liquidation, involving the issuer or any of its subsidiaries;

(c) A sale or transfer of a material amount of assets of the issuer or any of its subsidiaries;

(d) Any change in the present board of directors or management of the issuer, including any plans or proposals to change the number or term of directors or to fill any existing vacancies on the board;

(e) Any material change in the present capitalization or dividend policy of the issuer;

(f) Any other material change in the issuer's business or corporate structure, including but not limited to, if the issuer is a registered closed-end investment company, any plans or proposals to make any changes in its investment policy for which a vote is required by section 13 of the Investment Company Act of 1940;

(g) Changes in the issuer's charter, bylaws or instruments corresponding thereto or other actions which may impede the acquisition of control of the issuer by any person:

(h) Causing a class of securities of the issuer to be delisted from a national securities exchange or to cease to be authorized to be quoted in an inter-dealer quotation system of a registered national securities association;

(i) A class of equity securities of the issuer becoming eligible for termination of registration pursuant to Section 12(g)(4) of the Act; or

(j) Any action similar to any of those enumerated above.

Item 5. Interest in Securities of the Issuer

(a) State the aggregate number and percentage of the class of securities identified pursuant to Item 1 (which may be based on the number of securities outstanding as contained in the most recently available filing with the Commission by the issuer unless the filing person has reason to believe such information is not current) beneficially owned (identifying those shares which there is a right to acquire) by each person named in Item 2. The above mentioned information should also be furnished with respect to persons who, together with any of the persons named in Item 2, comprise a group within the meaning of Section 13(d)(3) of the Act;

(b) For each person named in response to paragraph (a), indicate the number of shares as to which there is sole power to vote or to direct the vote, shared power to vote or to direct the vote, sole power to dispose or to direct the disposition, or shared power to dispose or to direct the disposition. Provide the applicable information required by Item 2 with respect to each person with whom the power to vote or to direct the vote or to dispose or direct the disposition is shared;

(c) Describe any transactions in the class of securities reported on that were effected during the past sixty days or since the most recent filing on Schedule 13D, whichever is less, by the persons named in response to paragraph (a).

Instruction. The description of a transaction required by Item 5(c) shall include, but not necessarily be limited to: (1) the identity of the person covered by Item 5(c) who effected the transaction; (2) the date of the transaction; (3) the amount of securities involved; (4) the price per share or unit; and (5) where and how the transaction was effected.

(d) If any other person is known to have the right to receive or the power to direct the receipt of dividends from, or the proceeds from the sale of, such securities, a statement to that effect should be included in response to this item and, if such interest relates to more than five percent of the class, such person should be identified. A listing of the shareholders of an investment company registered under the Investment Company Act of 1940 or the beneficiaries of an employee benefit plan, pension fund or endowment fund is not required.

(e) If applicable, state the date on which the reporting person ceased to be the beneficial owner of more than five percent of the class of securities.

Instruction. For computations regarding securities which represent a right to acquire an underlying security, see Rule 13d–3(d)(1) and the note thereto.

Item 6. Contracts, Arrangements, Understandings or Relationships With Respect to Securities of the Issuer

Describe any contracts, arrangements, understandings or relationships (legal or otherwise) among the persons named in Item 2 and between such persons and any person with respect to any securities of the issuer, including but not limited to transfer or voting of any of the securities, finder's fees, joint ventures, loan or option arrangements, put or calls, guarantees of profits, division of profits or loss, or the giving or withholding of proxies, naming the persons with whom such contracts, arrangements, understandings or relationships have been entered into. Include such information for any of the securities that are pledged or otherwise subject to a contingency the occurrence of which would give another person voting power or investment power over such securities except that disclosure of standard default and similar provisions contained in loan agreements need not be included.

Item 7. Material to be Filed as Exhibits

The following shall be filed as exhibits: copies of written agreements relating to the filing of joint acquisition statements as required by Rule 13d–1(f) and copies of all written agreements, contracts, arrangements, understandings, plans or proposals relating to (1) the borrowing of funds to finance the acquisition as disclosed in Item 3; (2) the acquisition of issuer control, liquidation, sale of assets, merger, or change in business or corporate structure or any other matter as disclosed in Item 4; and (3) the transfer or voting of the securities, finder's fees, joint ventures, options, puts, calls, guarantees of loans, guarantees against loss or of profit, or the giving or withholding of any proxy as disclosed in Item 6.

REPURCHASES BY ISSUERS

Rule 13e–1. Purchase of Securities by Issuer Thereof

When a person other than the issuer makes a tender offer for, or request or invitation for tenders of, any class of equity securities of an issuer subject to Section 13(e) of the Act, and such person has filed a statement with the Commission pursuant to Rule 14d–1 and the issuer has received notice thereof, such issuer shall not thereafter, during the period such tender offer, request or invitation continues, purchase any equity securities of which it is the issuer unless it has complied with both of the following conditions:

(a) The issuer has filed with the Commission eight copies of a statement containing the information specified below with respect to the proposed purchases:

(1) The title and amount of securities to be purchased, the names of the persons or classes of persons from whom, and the market in which, the securities are to be purchased, including the name of any exchange on which the purchase is to be made;

(2) The purpose for which the purchase is to be made and whether the securities are to be retired, held in the treasury of the issuer or otherwise disposed of, indicating such disposition; and

(3) The source and amount of funds or other consideration used or to be used in making the purchases, and if any part of the purchase price or proposed purchase price is represented by funds or other consideration borrowed or otherwise obtained for the purpose of acquiring, holding, or trading the securities, a description of the transaction and the names of the parties thereto.

(b) The issuer has at any time within the the past six months sent or given to its equity security holders the substance of the information contained in the statement required by subparagraph (a).

Provided, however, that any issuer making such purchases which commenced prior to July 30,

1968 shall, if such purchases continue after such date comply with the provisions of this rule on or before August 12, 1968.

Rule 13e-2.   (Proposed) Purchases of Certain Equity Securities by the Issuer and Others.

(a) Definitions. Unless the context otherwise requires, all terms used in this rule shall have the same meaning as in the Act. In addition, unless the context otherwise requires, the following definitions shall apply:

(1) The term "affiliate" means any person that directly or indirectly controls, is controlled by, or is under common control with, the issuer;

(2) The term "affiliated purchaser" means

(i) A person acting with the issuer for the purpose of acquiring the issuer's securities; or

(ii) A person who controls the issuer's purchases of such securities, whose purchases are controlled by the issuer, or whose purchases are under common control with those of the issuer; or

(iii) A person who controls the issuer by means of his ownership of the issuer's securities; or

(iv) Any affiliate that is not a natural person;

Provided, however, That the term "affiliated purchaser" shall not include a broker, dealer, or other person solely by reason of his making Rule 13e–2 bids or effecting Rule 13e–2 purchases on behalf of the issuer and for its account;

(3) The term "Section 13(e) issuer" means an issuer that has a class of equity securities registered pursuant to section 12 of the Act or that is a closed-end investment company registered under the Investment Company Act of 1940;

(4) The term "Section 15(d) issuer" means an issuer that is required to file periodic reports pursuant to section 15(d) of the Act;

(5) The term "Rule 13e–2 purchase" means a purchase of common stock or preferred stock of a Section 13(e) issuer, or a Section 15(d) issuer, by or for the issuer or any affiliate or affiliated purchaser, but does not include

(i) Any purchase of common stock or preferred stock of a Section 13(e) issuer if the class of such stock is not registered pursuant to section 12 of the Act;

(ii) Any purchase of common stock or preferred stock of a Section 15(d) issuer if the class of such stock has not been the subject of a registration statement that has become effective pursuant to the Securities Act of 1933, or if the class is held of record by fewer than 300 persons; or

(iii) Any purchase of a security effected by or for an issuer plan if the transaction is effected by an agent independent of the issuer;

(6) The term "Rule 13e-2 bid" means

(i) A bid for securities that, if accepted, or

(ii) A limit order to purchase securities that, if executed, would result in a Rule 13e-2 purchase;

(7) The term "issuer plan" means any bonus, profit-sharing, pension, retirement, thrift, savings, incentive, stock purchase, stock option, stock ownership, dividend reinvestment or similar plan for employees or security holders of the issuer or any affiliate;

(8) The term "agent independent of the issuer" means a trustee or other person who is independent of the issuer. The agent shall be deemed to be independent of the issuer only if

(i) The agent is not an affiliate of the issuer; and

(ii) Neither the issuer nor any affiliate has any direct or indirect control or influence over the times when, or the prices at which, the independent agent may purchase the issuer's common stock or preferred stock for the issuer plan, the amounts of the security to be purchased, the manner in which the security is to be purchased, or the selection of a broker or dealer (other than the independent agent itself) through which purchases may be executed; *Provided, however,* That the issuer or affiliate will not be deemed to have such control or influence solely because it has the power to revise not more than once in any six-month period the

basis for determining the amount of its contributions to the issuer plan or the basis for determining the frequency of its allocations to the issuer plan;

(9) The term "consolidated system" means the consolidated transaction reporting system contemplated by Rule 11Aa3-1;

(10) The term "reported security" means any security as to which last sale information is reported in the consolidated system;

(11) The term "exchange traded security" means any security, except a reported security, that is listed, or admitted to unlisted trading privileges, on a national securities exchange;

(12) The term "NASDAQ security" means any security, except a reported security, as to which bid and offer quotations are reported in the automated quotation system ("NASDAQ") operated by the National Association of Securities Dealers, Inc. ("NASD");

(13) The term "trading volume" means

(i) With respect to a reported security, the average daily trading volume for each security reported in the consolidated system in the four calendar weeks preceding the week in which the Rule 13e-2 purchase is to be effected or the Rule 13e-2 bid is to be made;

(ii) With respect to an exchange traded security, the average of the aggregate daily trading volume, including the daily trading volume reported on all exchanges on which the security is traded and, if such security is also a NASDAQ security, the daily trading volume for such security made available by the NASD, for the four calendar weeks preceding the week in which the Rule 13e-2 purchase is to be effected or the Rule 13e-2 bid is to be made; and

(iii) With respect to a NASDAQ security that is not an exchange traded security, the average daily trading volume for such security made available by the NASD for the four calendar weeks preceding the week in which the Rule 13e-2 purchase is to be effected or the Rule 13e-2 bid is to be made;

Provided, however, that such trading volume under paragraph (a)(13)(i), (ii) and (iii) shall not include any Rule 13e–2 purchases by or for the issuer or any affiliated purchaser, and shall not include any amount of shares acquired pursuant to the exercise by the issuer or affiliated purchaser of listed call options.

(14) The term "purchase price" means the price paid per share

(i) For a reported security, or an exchange traded security on a national securities exchange, exclusive of any commission paid to a broker acting as agent, or commission equivalent, mark-up, or differential paid to a dealer;

(ii) For a NASDAQ security, or a security that is not a reported security or a NASDAQ security, otherwise than on a national securities exchange, inclusive of any commission equivalent, mark-up, or differential paid to a dealer;

(15) The term "round lot" means 100 shares or other customary unit of trading for a security;

(16A) The term "block" means a quantity of stock that either

(i) Has an aggregate purchase price of not less than (A) $50,000 if the purchase price per share is less than $10, (B) $75,000 if the purchase price per share is at least $10 but less than $20, (C) $125,000 if the purchase price per share is at least $20 but less than $35, (D) $175,000 if the purchase price per share is at least $35 but less than $50, or (E) $200,000 if the purchase price per share is $50 or more; or

(ii) Is at least 20 round lots of the security and totals 150 percent or more of the trading volume for that security or, in the event that trading volume data are unavailable, is at least 20 round lots of the security and totals at least one-tenth of one percent (.001) of the outstanding shares of the security, exclusive of any shares owned by any affiliate;

Provided, however, That a block under paragraph (a)(16)(i) and (ii) shall not include any

amount that a broker or a dealer has assembled or accumulated for the purpose of sale or resale to the issuer or to any affiliated purchaser; or any amount that a broker or dealer has sold short to the issuer or affiliated purchaser if the issuer or affiliated purchaser knows or has reason to know that the sale was a short sale; and shall not include any amount of shares acquired pursuant to the exercise by the issuer or affiliated purchaser of listed call options;

(16B) The term "block" means a quantity of stock that either

(i) Has a purchase price of $200,000 or more; or

(ii) Is at least 5,000 shares and has a purchase price of at least $50,000; or

(iii) Is at least 20 round lots of the security and totals 150 percent or more of the trading volume for that security or, in the event that trading volume data are unavailable, is at least 20 round lots of the security and totals at least one-tenth of one percent (.001) of the outstanding shares of the security, exclusive of any shares owned by any affiliate;

Provided, however, that a block under paragraph (a)(16)(i), (ii) and (iii) shall not include any amount that a broker or a dealer has assembled or accumulated for the purpose of sale or resale to the issuer or to any affiliated purchaser; or any amount that a broker or dealer has sold short to the issuer or affiliated purchaser if the issuer or affiliated purchaser knows or has reason to know that the sale was a short sale; and shall not include any amount of shares acquired pursuant to the exercise by the issuer or affiliated purchaser of listed call options.

(b) *Application to section 13(e) issuers and certain other persons.*

(1) It shall constitute a fraudulent, deceptive, or manipulative act or practice within the meaning of section 13(e) of the Act for a Section 13(e) issuer, for an affiliate or an affiliated purchaser of such issuer, or for a broker, a dealer, or any other person acting for such an issuer or affiliate or affiliated purchaser, in connection

with a Rule 13e–2 purchase, or with a Rule 13e–2 bid, effected or made by or for such issuer or affiliate or affiliated purchaser

(i) To employ any device, scheme, or artifice to defraud any person;

(ii) To make any untrue statement of a material fact or to omit to state a material fact necessary in order to make the statements made, in the light of the circumstances under which they were made, not misleading; or

(iii) To engage in any act, practice, or course of business which operates or would operate as a fraud or deceit upon any person.

(2) As a means reasonably designed to prevent fraudulent, deceptive, or manipulative acts or practices in connection with a Rule 13e–2 purchase, or with a Rule 13e–2 bid, it shall be unlawful, by the use of any means or instrumentality of interstate commerce or of the mails

(i) For any Section 13(e) issuer, or for any affiliated purchaser of such an issuer, to effect a Rule 13e–2 purchase or to make or cause to be made a Rule 13e–2 bid unless that issuer or affiliated purchaser complies with paragraphs (d) and (e) of this section; *Provided, however,* That the issuer or affiliated purchaser shall be deemed not to have violated paragraphs (e)(2), (e)(3), or (e)(4) of this section if a violation occurred solely by reason of the conduct of a broker, dealer, or other person acting for it if the issuer or affiliated purchaser did not know or have reason to know that the broker, dealer, or other person was engaging or would engage in such conduct, and if the issuer or affiliated purchaser had taken reasonable steps to assure that the broker, dealer, or other person would comply with paragraphs (e)(2), (e)(3), and (e)(4) of this section.

(ii) For any broker, dealer, or other person acting for a Section 13(e) issuer, or for an affiliated purchaser of such an issuer, to effect any Rule 13e–2 purchase or to make or cause to be made any Rule 13e–2 bid that

he knows or has reason to know is a Rule 13e–2 purchase or a Rule 13e–2 bid unless that broker, dealer, or other person complies with paragraphs (e)(2), (e)(3), and (e)(4) of this section; *Provided, however,* That the broker, dealer, or other person shall be deemed not to have violated paragraphs (e)(2), (e)(3), and (e)(4) of this section if a violation occurred solely by reason of the conduct of the Section 13(e) issuer or affiliated purchaser if the broker, dealer, or other person did not know or have reason to know that such issuer or affiliated purchaser was engaging or would engage in such conduct.

(c) *Application to section 15(d) issuer or any affiliated purchaser of such issuer.*

It shall be unlawful as a fraudulent, deceptive, or manipulative act or practice for any Section 15(d) issuer, or for any affiliated purchaser of such an issuer, to effect a Rule 13e–2 purchase or to make or cause to be made any Rule 13e–2 bid unless that issuer or affiliated purchaser complies with paragraph (d) of this rule.

(d) *Disclosure of certain information.*

(1) A person who is required to comply with paragraph (d) shall not effect a Rule 13e–2 purchase, or a series of Rule 13e–2 purchases, that seeks the acquisition of more than two percent of the outstanding shares of any class of common stock or preferred stock within any 12-month period, unless disclosure is made of the following information in a manner reasonably calculated to inform investors before any such Rule 13e–2 purchase is effected, or any Rule 13e–2 bid that could result in any such Rule 13e–2 purchase is made:

(i) The estimated time at which, or time period during which, the purchase or purchases are proposed to be effected;

(ii) The maximum number of shares of the security proposed to be purchased or the maximum amount of funds or other consideration to be expanded;

(iii) The purpose or purposes to be achieved through acquisition of the shares to be purchased; and

(iv) Any plan or proposal that relates to, or would result in, the disposition of the shares to be purchased.

(2) A person who is required by paragraph (d)(1) if this section to disclose the information described therein shall also disclose that information, before any Rule 13e-2 purchase is effected, or any Rule 13e-2 bid is made, to each national securities exchange on which the securities to be purchased are registered and listed for trading and to the NASD if the securities to be purchased are authorized for quotation in NASDAQ.

(3) A person who is required to comply with paragraph (e) of this section shall disclose to any broker, dealer, or other person acting on his behalf in connection with a Rule 13e-2 purchase that the transaction is a Rule 13e-2 purchase and that it must be effected in accordance with paragraph (e) of this section.

(e) *Purchasing requirements.*

(1) *One broker or dealer.* A person required to comply with paragraph (e)(1) shall not effect any Rule 13e-2 purchase or purchases with a dealer, or from or through more than one broker on any single day, nor shall such person make or cause to be made any Rule 13e-2 bid to any dealer, or through more than one broker on any single day;

Provided, however, That

(i) If a broker is not used on a day, Rule 13e-2 purchases may be effected with, and Rule 13e-2 bids may be made to, a single dealer on that day;

(ii) This paragraph (e)(1) shall not apply to Rule 13e-2 purchases that are not solicited by or on behalf of that person; and

(iii) Where Rule 13e-2 purchases or Rule 13e-2 bids are made by or on behalf of more than one affiliated purchaser (or the issuer and one or more affiliated purchasers) on a single day, this paragraph (e)(1) shall apply to all such bids and purchases in the aggregate.

(2) *Time limitations.* A person required to comply with paragraph (e)(2) shall not effect any Rule 13e-2 purchase from or through a broker or dealer

(i) In a reported security for which the principal market is a national securities exchange, (A) if such purchase would constitute the opening transaction in the security reported in the consolidated system; or (B) during the period commencing one-half hour before the scheduled close or trading in the principal market for the security and ending with the termination of the period in which last sale prices are reported in the consolidated system;

(ii) In a reported security for which the principal market is not on a national securities exchange, (A) if such purchase would constitute the opening transaction in the security reported in the consolidated system; or (B) during the one-half hour before the termination of the period in which last sale prices are reported in the consolidated system;

(iii) On a national securities exchange, in any exchange traded security, (A) if the Rule 13e-2 bid would constitute the opening bid for the security on such exchange; or (B) during the one-half hour before the scheduled close of trading on the exchange;

(iv) Otherwise than on a national securities exchange in any NASDAQ security unless a current independent bid quotation for the security is reported in Level 2 of NASDAQ.

(3) *Price limitations.* A person required to comply with paragraph (e)(3) shall neither effect any Rule 13e-2 purchase from or through a broker or dealer at a purchase price, nor make nor cause to be made any Rule 13e-2 bid at a price

(i) For a reported security, higher than the published bid, as that term is defined in Rule 11Ac1-1(a)(9) under the Act, that is the highest current independent published bid or the last independent sale price reported in the consolidated system, whichever is higher;

(ii) On a national securities exchange, for an exchange traded security, higher than the highest current independent bid quotation or the last independent sale price on that exchange, whichever is higher;

(iii) Otherwise than on a national securities exchange, for a NASDAQ security, higher than the lowest current independent offer quotations reported in Level 2 of NASDAQ; or

(iv) Otherwise than on a national securities exchange, for a security that is not a reported security or a NASDAQ security, higher than the lowest current independent offer quotation, determined on the basis of reasonable inquiry.

(4) *Volume limitations.* A person required to comply with paragraph (e)(4) shall not effect from or through a broker or dealer any Rule 13e-2 purchase, other than a block purchase, or any purchase through the exercise of an exchange listed call option

(i) Of a reported security, an exchange traded security or a NASDAQ security, in an amount that, when added to the amounts of all other Rule 13e-2 purchases and purchases through the exercise of an exchange listed call option effected by or for the issuer or any affiliated purchaser on that day, exceeds the higher of (A) one round lot or (B) the number of round lots closest to 15 percent of the trading volume for the security;

(ii) Of any other security, in an amount that, (A) when added to the amounts of all other Rule 13e-2 purchases and purchases through the exercise of an exchange listed call option effected by or for the issuer or any affiliated purchaser on that day, exceeds one round lot and (B) when added to the amounts of all other Rule 13e-2 purchases and purchases through the exercise of an exchange listed call option effected by or for the issuer or any affiliated purchaser during that day and the preceding six calendar days, exceeds 1/20th of one percent (0.-0005) of the outstanding shares of the security, exclusive of shares known to be owned beneficially by affiliates.

(f) Paragraph (e) of this section shall not apply to a bid or purchase that is:

(1) Subject to, and made in compliance with, Rule 10b-7 under the Act;

(2) By the issuer and is subject to, and made in compliance with, Rule 13e-1 under the Act;

(3) Pursuant to a tender offer that is subject to, and made in compliance with, Rule 13e-4 under the Act;

(4) Pursuant to a tender offer that is subject to, and made in compliance with, section 14(d) of the Act and the rules and regulations thereunder;

(5) Pursuant to the call or redemption of any security in accordance with the terms and conditions of its governing instrument or instruments;

(6) Pursuant to a merger, acquisition, or similar transaction involving a recapitalization;

(7) A bid for or purchase of securities of a dissenting shareholder who has asserted rights of appraisal with respect to his shares;

(8) Made to satisfy mandatory sinking fund obligations that must be satisfied not more than one year from the time such bids or purchases are made;

(9) A bid for or purchase of any fractional interest in a security, evidenced by a scrip certificate, order form, or similar document;

(10) A bid for or purchase of securities from an employee upon termination of the employment relationship, or from a former employee of the issuer or of any wholly-owned subsidiary thereof, or from the estate of such employee, pursuant to any right or obligation to purchase such securities established in connection with the employment of, or the sale of such securities to, the employee; and

(11) A bid for or purchase of any security that is not traded on a national securities exchange and with respect to which the issuer thereof does not know or have reason to know that any dealer acts as market maker if neither the purchaser nor any person acting on his behalf has engaged in any solicitation in connection with the transaction.

(g) The Commission may, upon written request or upon its own motion, exempt any Rule 13e-2 bid or Rule 13e-2 purchase from one or more paragraphs of this section, either unconditionally or upon specified terms or conditions, as not comprehended within the intended meaning and purpose of this section or of such paragraph or paragraphs.

Rule 13e-3. Going Private Transactions by Certain Issuers or Their Affiliates

(a) *Definitions.* Unless indicated otherwise or the context requires, all terms used in this section and in Schedule 13E-3 shall have the same meaning as in the Act or elsewhere in the General Rules and Regulations thereunder. In addition, the following definitions apply:

(1) An "affiliate" of an issuer is a person that directly or indirectly through one or more intermediaries controls, is controlled by, or is under common control with such issuer. For the purposes of this section only, a person who is not an affiliate of an issuer at the commencement of such person's tender offer for a class of equity securities of such issuer will not be deemed an affiliate of such issuer prior to the stated termination of such tender offer and any extensions thereof;

(2) The term "purchase" means any acquisition for value including, but not limited to, (i) any acquisition pursuant to the dissolution of an issuer subsequent to the sale or other disposition of substantially all the assets of such issuer to its affiliate, (ii) any acquisition pursuant to a merger, (iii) any acquisition of fractional interests in connection with a reverse stock split, and (iv) any acquisition subject to the control of an issuer or an affiliate of such issuer;

(3) A "Rule 13e-3 transaction" is any transaction or series of transactions involving one or more of the transactions described in paragraph (a)(3)(i) of this section which has either a reasonable likelihood or a purpose of producing, either directly or indirectly, any of the effects described in paragraph (a)(3)(ii) of this section;

(i) The transactions referred to in paragraph (a)(3) of this section are:

(A) A purchase of any equity security by the issuer of such security or by an affiliate of such issuer;

(B) A tender offer for or request or invitation for tenders of any equity security made by the issuer of such class of securities or by an affiliate of such issuer; or

(C) A solicitation subject to Regulation 14A of any proxy, consent or authorization of, or a distribution subject to Regulation 14C of information statements to, any equity security holder by the issuer of the class of securities or by an affiliate of such issuer, in connection with: a merger, consolidation, reclassification, recapitalization, reorganization or similar corporate transaction of an issuer or between an issuer (or its subsidiaries) and its affiliate; a sale of substantially all the assets of an issuer to its affiliate or group of affiliates; or a reverse stock split of any class of equity securities of the issuer involving the purchase of fractional interests.

(ii) The effects referred to in paragraph (a) (4) of this section are:

(A) Causing any class of equity securities of the issuer which is subject to section 12(g) or section 15(d) of the Act to be held of record by less than 300 persons; or

(B) Causing any class of equity securities of the issuer which is either listed on a national securities exchange or authorized to be quoted in an inter-dealer quotation system of a registered national securities association to be neither listed on any national securities exchange nor authorized to be quoted on an inter-dealer quotation system of any registered national securities association.

(4) An "unaffiliated security holder" is any security holder of an equity security subject to a Rule 13e-3 transaction who is not an affiliate of the issuer of such security.

(b) *Application of Section to an Issuer (or an Affiliate of Such Issuer) Subject to Section 12 of the Act.*

(1) It shall be a fraudulent, deceptive or manipulative act or practice, in connection with a Rule 13e-3 transaction, for an issuer which has a class of equity securities registered pursuant to Section 12 of the Act or which is a closed-end investment company registered under the Investment Company Act of 1940, or an affiliate of such issuer, directly or indirectly.

(i) To employ any device, scheme or artifice to defraud any person;

(ii) To make any untrue statement of a material fact or to omit to state a material fact necessary in order to make the statements made, in light of the circumstances under which they were made, not misleading; or

(iii) To engage in any act, practice or course of business which operates or would operate as a fraud or deceit upon any person.

(2) As a means reasonably designed to prevent fraudulent, deceptive or manipulative acts or practices in connection with any Rule 13e-3 transaction, it shall be unlawful for an issuer which has a class of equity securities registered pursuant to Section 12 of the Act, or an affiliate of such issuer, to engage, directly or indirectly, in a Rule 13e-3 transaction unless:

(i) Such issuer or affiliate complies with the requirements of paragraphs (d), (e) and (f) of this Section; and

(ii) The Rule 13e-3 transaction is not in violation of paragraph (b)(1) of this section.

(c) *Application of Section to an Issuer (or an Affiliate of Such Issuer) Subject to Section 15(d) of the Act.*

(1) It shall be unlawful as a fraudulent, deceptive or manipulative act or practice for an issuer which is required to file periodic reports pursuant to Section 15(d) of the Act, or an affiliate of such issuer, to engage, directly or indirectly, in a Rule 13e-3 transaction unless such issuer or affiliate complies with the requirements of paragraphs (d), (e) and (f) of this section.

(2) An issuer or affiliate which is subject to paragraph (c)(1) of this section and which is soliciting proxies or distributing information statements in connection with a transaction described in paragraph (a)(3)(i)(A) of this section may elect to use the timing procedures for conducting a solicitation subject to Regulation 14A or a distribution subject to Regulation 14C in complying with paragraphs (d), (e) and (f) of this section, *provided that* if an election is made, such solicitation or distribution is conducted in accordance with the requirements of the respective regulations, including the filing of preliminary copies of soliciting materials or an information statement at the time specified in Regulation 14A or 14C, respectively.

(d) *Material Required to be Filed.*

The issuer or affiliate engaging in a Rule 13e-3 transaction shall, in accordance with the General Instructions to the Rule 13e-3 Transaction Statement on Schedule 13E-3:

(1) File with the Commission eight copies of such schedule, including all exhibits thereto;

(2) Report any material change in the information set forth in such schedule by promptly filing with the Commission eight copies of an amendment on such schedule; and

(3) Report the results of the Rule 13e-3 transaction by filing with the Commission promptly but no later than ten days (ten business days if Rule 13e-4 is applicable) after the termination of such transaction eight copies of a final amendment to such schedule.

(e) *Disclosure of Certain Information.*

(1) The issuer or affiliate engaging in the Rule 13e-3 transaction, in addition to any other information required to be disclosed pursuant to any other applicable rule or regulation under the federal securities laws, shall disclose to security holders of the class of equity securities which is the subject of the transaction, in the manner prescribed by paragraph (f) of this section, the information required by Items 1, 2, 3, 4, 5, 6, 10, 11, 12, 13, 14, 15 and 16 of Schedule 13e-3, or a fair and adequate summary thereof, and Items 7, 8 and 9 and include in the document which contains such information the exhibit required by Item 17(e) of such Schedule. If the Rule 13e-3 transaction involves (i) a transaction subject to Regulation 14A or 14C of the Act, (ii) the registration of securities pursuant to the Securities Act of 1933 and the General Rules and Regulations promulgated thereunder, or (iii) a tender offer subject to Regulation 14D or Rule 13e-4, such information shall be included in the proxy statement, the information statement, the registration statement or the tender offer for or request or invitation for tenders of securities published, sent or given to security holders, respectively.

(2) If any material change occurs in the information previously disclosed to security holders of the class of equity securities which is the subject of the transaction, the issuer or affiliate shall promptly disclose such change to such secur-

ity holders in the manner prescribed by paragraph (f)(iii) of this section.

(3) Any document transmitted to such security holders which contains the information required by paragraph (e)(1) of this section shall:

(i) set forth prominently the information required by Items 7, 8 and 9 of the Rule 13e-3 Transaction Statement on Schedule 13E-3 in a Special Factors section to be included in the forepart of such document; and

(ii) set forth on the outside front cover page, in capital letters printed in bold face roman type at least as large as ten point modern type and at least two points leaded, the statement in paragraph (e)(3)(ii)(A) of this section, if the Rule 13e-3 transaction does not involve a prospectus, or the statement in paragraph (e)(3)(ii)(B) of this section, if the Rule 13e-3 transaction involves a prospectus, and in the latter case such statement shall be used in lieu of that required by Item 501(c)(5) of Regulation S-K.

(A) THIS TRANSACTION HAS NOT BEEN APPROVED OR DISAPPROVED BY THE SECURITIES AND EXCHANGE COMMISSION NOR HAS THE COMMISSION PASSED UPON THE FAIRNESS OR MERITS OF SUCH TRANSACTION NOR UPON THE ACCURACY OR ADEQUACY OF THE INFORMATION CONTAINED IN THIS DOCUMENT. ANY REPRESENTATION TO THE CONTRARY IS UNLAWFUL.

(B) NEITHER THIS TRANSACTION NOR THESE SECURITIES HAVE BEEN APPROVED OR DISAPPROVED BY THE SECURITIES AND EXCHANGE COMMISSION, THE COMMISSION HAS NOT PASSED UPON THE FAIRNESS OR MERITS OF THIS TRANSACTION NOR UPON THE ACCURACY OR ADEQUACY OF THE INFORMATION CONTAINED IN THIS PROSPECTUS. ANY REPRESENTATION TO THE CONTRARY IS UNLAWFUL.

Instructions. 1. Negative responses to any item of Schedule 13E-3 need not be included in the information disseminated to security holders unless otherwise indicated.

2. Although the financial information necessary to present a fair and adequate summary of

Item 14 of Schedule 13E-3 may vary depending on the facts and circumstances involved, the following historical and pro forma summary financial information normally will be sufficient for purposes of paragraph (e) of this section:

(a) Summary financial information equivalent to that required by paragraph (e) of Guide 59 of the Guides for Preparation and Filing of Registration Statements for (i) the two most recent fiscal years and (ii) the latest year-to-date interim period and corresponding interim period of the preceding year;

(b) Ratio of earnings to fixed charges for the same periods required by 2(a) above;

(c) Book value per share as of the most recent fiscal year end and as of the date of the latest interim balance sheet; and

(d) If material, pro forma data for the summarized financial information described in 2(a), (b), and (c) above, disclosing the effect of the transaction, should be provided for the most recent fiscal year and latest year-to-date interim period.

If the information required by Item 14 is summarized, appropriate instructions should be included stating how more complete financial information can be obtained.

(f) *Dissemination of disclosure.* (1) If the Rule 13e-3 transaction involves a purchase as described in paragraph (a)(3)(i)(A) of this section or a vote, consent, authorization, or distribution of information statements as described in paragraph (a)(3)(i)(C) of this section, the issuer or affiliate engaging in the Rule 13e-3 transaction shall:

(i) Provide the information required by paragraph (e) of this section: (A) in accordance with the provisions of any applicable federal or state law, but in no event later than 20 days prior to: any such purchase; any such vote, consent or authorization; or with respect to the distribution of information statements, the meeting date, or if corporate action is to be taken by means of the written authorization or consent of security holders, the earliest date on which corporate action may be taken, (B) to each person who is a record holder of a class of equity security subject to the Rule 13e-3 transaction as of a date not more than 20 days prior to the date of dissemination of such information.

(ii) If the issuer or affiliate knows that securities of the class of securities subject to the Rule 13e–3 transaction are held of record by a broker, dealer, bank or voting trustee or their nominees, such issuer or affiliate shall (unless Rule 14a–3(d) or 14c–7 is applicable) furnish the number of copies of the information required by paragraph (e) of this section that are requested by such persons (pursuant to inquiries by or on behalf of the issuer or affiliate), instruct such persons to forward such information to the beneficial owners of such securities in a timely manner and undertake to pay the reasonable expenses incurred by such persons in forwarding such information; and

(iii) Promptly disseminate disclosure of material changes to the information required by paragraph (d) of this section in a manner reasonably calculated to inform security holders.

(2) If the Rule 13e–3 transaction is a tender offer or a request or invitation for tenders of equity securities which is subject to Regulation 14D or Rule 13e–4, the tender offer containing the information required by paragraph (e) of this section, and any material change with respect thereto, shall be published, sent or given in accordance with Regulation 14D or Rule 13e–4, respectively, to security holders of the class of securities being sought by the issuer or affiliate.

(g) *Exceptions.* This section shall not apply to:

(1) Any Rule 13e–3 transaction by or on behalf of a person which occurs within one year of the date of termination of a tender offer in which such person was the bidder and became an affiliate of the issuer as a result of such tender offer *provided* that the consideration offered to unaffiliated security holders in such Rule 13e–3 transaction is at least equal to the highest consideration offered during such tender offer and *provided further* that:

(i) If such tender offer was made for any or all securities of a class of the issuer;

(A) Such tender offer fully disclosed such person's intention to engage in a Rule 13e–3 transaction, the form and effect of such trans-

action and, to the extent known, the proposed terms thereof; and

(B) Such Rule 13e–3 transaction is substantially similar to that described in such tender offer; or

(ii) If such tender offer was made for less than all the securities of a class of the issuer:

(A) Such tender offer fully disclosed a plan of merger, a plan of liquidation or a similar binding agreement between such person and the issuer with respect to a Rule 13e–3 transaction; and

(B) Such Rule 13e–3 transaction occurs pursuant to the plan of merger, plan of liquidation or similar binding agreement disclosed in the bidder's tender offer.

(2) Any Rule 13e–3 transaction in which the security holders are offered or receive only an equity security *provided* That:

(i) such equity security has substantially the same rights as the equity security which is the subject of the Rule 13e–3 transaction including, but not limited to, voting, dividends, redemption and liquidation rights except that this requirement shall be deemed to be satisfied if unaffiliated security holders are offered common stock;

(ii) such equity security is registered pursuant to section 12 of the Act or reports are required to be filed by the issuer thereof pursuant to section 15(d) of the Act; and

(iii) if the security which is the subject of the Rule 13e–3 transaction was either listed on a national securities exchange or authorized to be quoted in an inter-dealer quotation system of a registered national securities association, such equity security is either listed on a national securities exchange or authorized to be quoted in an inter-dealer quotation system of a registered national securities association.

(3) Transactions by a holding company registered under the Public Utility Holding Company Act of 1935 in compliance with the provisions of that Act;

(4) Redemptions, calls or similar purchases of an equity security by an issuer pursuant to specific provisions set forth in the instrument(s)

creating or governing that class of equity securities; or

(5) Any solicitation by an issuer with respect to a plan of reorganization under Chapter X of the Bankruptcy Act, as amended, if made after the entry of an order approving such plan pursuant to section 174 of that Act and after, or concurrently with, the transmittal of information concerning such plan as required by section 175 of the Act.

Rule 13e-4. Tender Offers by Issuers

(a) *Definitions.* Unless the context otherwise requires, all terms used in this section and in Schedule 13E-4 shall have the same meaning as in the Act or elsewhere in the General Rules and Regulations thereunder. In addition, the following definitions shall apply:

(1) The term "issuer" means any issuer which has a class of equity security registered pursuant to section 12 of the Act, or which is required to file periodic reports pursuant to section 15(d) of the Act, or which is a closed-end investment company registered under the Investment Company Act of 1940.

(2) The term "issuer tender offer" refers to a tender offer for, or a request or invitation for tenders of, any class of equity security, made by the issuer of such class of equity security or by an affiliate of such issuer.

(3) The term "business day" means any day, other than Saturday, Sunday or a federal holiday, on which the principal office of the Commission at Washington, D. C. is scheduled to be open for business. In computing any time period under this section, the date of commencement of the issuer tender offer shall be included.

(4) The term "commencement" means the date an issuer tender offer is first published, sent or given to security holders.

(5) The term "termination" means the date after which securities may not be tendered pursuant to an issuer tender offer.

(6) The term "security holders" means holders of record and beneficial owners of securities of the class of equity security which is the subject of an issuer tender offer.

(7) The term "security position listing" means, with respect to the securities of any issuer held by a registered clearing agency in the name of the clearing agency or its nominee, a list of those participants in the clearing agency on whose behalf the clearing agency holds the issuer's securities and of the participants' respective positions in such securities as of a specified date.

(b)(1) It shall be a fraudulent, deceptive or manipulative act or practice, in connection with an issuer tender offer, for an issuer or an affiliate of such issuer, in connection with an issuer tender offer:

(i) to employ any device, scheme or artifice to defraud any person;

(ii) to make any untrue statement of a material fact or to omit to state a material fact necessary in order to make the statements made, in the light of the circumstances under which they were made, not misleading; or

(iii) to engage in any act, practice or course of business which operates or would operate as a fraud or deceit upon any person.

(2) As a means reasonably designed to prevent fraudulent, deceptive or manipulative acts or practices in connection with any issuer tender offer, it shall be unlawful for an issuer or an affiliate of such issuer to make an issuer tender offer unless:

(i) such issuer or affiliate complies with the requirements of paragraphs (c), (d), (e) and (f) of this section; and

(ii) the issuer tender offer is not in violation of paragraph (b)(1) of this section.

(c) *Material Required to be Filed.* The issuer or affiliate making the issuer tender offer shall, in accordance with the General Instructions to the Issuer Tender Offer Statement on Schedule 13E-4:

(1) File with the Commission ten copies of such schedule, including all exhibits thereto, prior to or as soon as practicable on the date of commencement of the issuer tender offer;

(2) Report any material change in the information set forth in such schedule by promptly filing with the Commission ten copies of an amendment on such schedule;

(3) Report the results of the issuer tender offer by filing with the Commission no later than ten business days after the termination of the issuer tender offer ten copies of a final amendment to such schedule.

(d) *Disclosure of Certain Information.*

(1) The issuer or affiliate making the issuer tender offer shall publish, send or give to security holders in the manner prescribed in paragraph (e)(1) of this section a statement containing the following information:

(i) the scheduled termination date of the issuer tender offer and whether it may be extended;

(ii) the specified dates prior to which, and after which, persons who tender securities pursuant to the issuer tender offer may withdraw their securities pursuant to paragraph (f)(2) of this section;

(iii) if the issuer tender offer is for less than all the securities of a class, the exact dates of the period during which securities will be accepted on a pro rata basis pursuant to paragraph (f)(3) of this section and the manner in which securities will be accepted for payment and in which securities may be withdrawn; and

(iv) the information required by Items 1 through 8 of Schedule 13E–4 for a fair and adequate summary thereof: *Provided, however,* That if the issuer tender offer involves the registration of securities pursuant to the Securities Act of 1933 and the General Rules and Regulations promulgated thereunder, any prospectus relating to such securities shall include all of the information, not otherwise required to be included therein, required by this paragraph.

(2) If any material change occurs in the information previously disclosed to security holders, the issuer or affiliate shall disclose promptly such change in the manner prescribed by paragraph (e)(2) of this section.

If the information required by Item 7 is summarized, appropriate instructions should be included stating how more complete financial information can be obtained.

(3) If an issuer or an affiliate publishes, sends or gives the issuer tender offer to security holders by means of a summary publication in the manner prescribed in paragraph (e)(1)(iii) of this section, the summary advertisement shall not contain a transmittal letter pursuant to which securities which are sought in the issuer tender offer may be tendered, and shall disclose only the following information:

(i) the identity of the issuer or affiliate making the issuer tender offer;

(ii) the amount and class of securities being sought and the price being offered;

(iii) the information required by paragraphs (d)(1)(i)–(iii) of this section;

(iv) a statement of the purpose of the issuer tender offer;

(v) appropriate instructions for security holders regarding how to obtain promptly, at the expense of the issuer or affiliate making the issuer tender offer, the statement required by paragraph (d)(1) of this section; and

(vi) a statement that the information contained in the statement required by paragraph (d)(1) of this section is incorporated by reference.

(e) *Dissemination of Tender Offers.*

(1) The issuer or affiliate making the issuer tender offer will be deemed to have published, sent or given the issuer tender offer to security holders if such issuer or affiliate complies fully with one or more of the following methods of dissemination. Depending on the facts and circumstances involved, and for purposes of paragraphs (e)(1)(i) and (e)(1)(iii) of this section, adequate publication of the issuer tender offer may require publication in a newspaper with a national circulation or may require only publication in a newspaper with metropolitan or regional circulation or many require publication in a combination thereof.

(i) *Dissemination of cash issuer tender offers by long-form publication:*

By making adequate publication in a newspaper or newspapers, on the date of commencement of the issuer tender offer, of the statement required by paragraph (d)(1) of this section.

(ii) *Dissemination of any issuer tender offer by use of shareholder and other lists:*

(A) By mailing the statement required by paragraph (d)(1) of this section to each security holder whose name appears on the most recent shareholder list of the issuer;

(B) By contacting each participant named on the most recent security position listing of any clearing agency within the possession or access of the issuer or affiliate making the tender offer, and making inquiry of each such participant as to the approximate number of beneficial owners of the securities for which the issuer tender offer is made which are held by such participant;

(C) By furnishing to each such participant a sufficient number of copies of the statement required by paragraph (d)(1) of this section for transmittal to the beneficial owners; and

(D) By agreeing to reimburse promptly each such participant for reasonable expenses incurred by it in forwarding such statement to the beneficial owners.

(iii) *Dissemination of certain cash issuer tender offers by summary publication:*

(A) If the issuer tender offer is not subject to Rule 13e–3, by making adequate publication in a newspaper or newspapers, on the date of commencement of the issuer tender offer, of a summary advertisement containing the information required by paragraph (d)(3) of this section; and

(B) By mailing or otherwise furnishing promptly the statement required by paragraph (d)(1) of this section and a transmittal letter to any security holder who requests either a copy of such statement or a transmittal letter.

(2) If a material change occurs in the information published, sent or given to security holders, the issuer or affiliate shall disseminate promptly disclosure of such change in a manner reasonably calculated to inform security holders of such change.

(f) *Manner of Making Tender Offer.*

(1) The issuer tender offer, unless withdrawn, shall remain open until the expiration of at least fifteen business days from its commencement.

(2) The issuer or affiliate making the issuer tender offer shall permit securities tendered pursuant to the issuer tender offer to be withdrawn

(i) at any time until the expiration of ten business days from the commencement of the issuer tender offer;

(ii) if not yet accepted for payment, at any time until the expiration of seven business days from the date another tender offer for securities of the same class is first published, sent or given to security holders, pursuant to Section 14(d)(1) of the Act or otherwise; and

(iii) if not yet accepted for payment, after the expiration of forty business days from the commencement of the issuer tender offer.

(3) The issuer or affiliate making the issuer tender offer shall accept tendered securities as nearly as practicable on a pro rata basis (disregarding fractions) according to the amount of securities tendered by each security holder if the amount of securities tendered within ten business days (or such longer period as may be specified) from the commencement of the issuer tender offer exceeds the amount of securities that will be accepted. The provisions of this paragraph shall also apply to securities tendered within ten business days (or such longer period as may be specified) from the date notice of an increase in the consideration offered to security holders, as described in paragraph (f)(4) of this section, is first published, sent or given to security holders: *Provided, however,* That this provision shall not prohibit the issuer or affiliate making the issuer tender offer from

(i) accepting all securities tendered by persons who own, beneficially or of record, an aggregate of not more than a specified number which is less than one hundred shares of such security and who tender all their securities, before prorating securities tendered by others, or, in the case of a tender offer limited to such persons, accepting tendered securities by lot; or

(ii) accepting by lot securities tendered by security holders who tender all securities held by them and who, when tendering their securities, elect to have either all or none or at least a minimum amount or none accepted, if the issuer or affiliate first accepts all securities tendered by security holders who do not so elect;

(4) In the event the issuer or affiliate making the issuer tender offer increases the consideration offered after the issuer tender offer has commenced, such issuer or affiliate shall pay such increased consideration to all security holders whose tendered securities are accepted for payment by such issuer or affiliate.

(5) The issuer or affiliate making the tender offer shall either pay the consideration offered, or return the tendered securities, promptly after the termination or withdrawal of the tender offer.

(6) Until the expiration of at least ten business days after the date of termination of the issuer tender offer, neither the issuer nor any affiliate shall make any purchases, otherwise than pursuant to the tender offer, of:

(i) any security which is the subject of the issuer tender offer, or any security of the same class and series, or any right to purchase any such securities; and

(ii) in the case of an issuer tender offer which is an exchange offer any security being offered pursuant to such exchange offer, or any security of the same class and series, or any right to purchase any such security.

(g) This section shall not apply to:

(1) Calls or redemptions of any security in accordance with the terms and conditions of its governing instruments;

(2) Offers to purchase securities evidenced by a scrip certificate, order form or similar document which represents a fractional interest in a share of stock or similar security;

(3) Offers to purchase securities pursuant to a statutory procedure for the purchase of dissenting security holders' securities;

(4) Any tender offer which is subject to section 14(d) of the Act; or

(5) Any other transaction or transactions, if the Commission, upon written request or upon its own motion, exempts such transaction or transactions, either unconditionally, or on specified terms and conditions, as not constituting a fraudulent, deceptive or manipulative act or practice comprehended within the purpose of this section.

REPORTS BY INSTITUTIONAL MANAGERS

Rule 13f–1. Reporting by Institutional Investment Managers of Information With Respect to Accounts Over Which They Exercise Investment Discretion

(a) Every institutional investment manager which exercises investment discretion with respect to accounts holding section 13(f) securities, as defined in paragraph (c) of this section, having an aggregate fair market value on the last trading day of any month of any calendar year of at least $100,000,000 shall file a report on Form 13F with the Commission within 45 days after the last day of such calendar year and within 45 days after the last day of each of the first three calendar quarters of the subsequent calendar year.

(b) For the purposes of this rule, "investment discretion" has the meaning set forth in section 3(a)(35) of the Act. An institutional investment manager shall also be deemed to exercise "investment discretion" with respect to all accounts over which any person under its control exercises investment discretion.

(c) For purposes of this rule "section 13(f) securities" shall mean equity securities of a class described in section 13(d)(1) of the Act that are admitted to trading on a national securities exchange or quoted on the automated quotation system of a registered securities association. In determining what classes of securities are section 13(f) securities, an institutional investment manager may rely on the most recent list of such securities published by the Commission pursuant to section 13(f)(3) of the Act. Only securities of a class on such list shall be counted in determining whether an institutional investment manager must file a report under this rule and only those securities shall be reported in such report. Where a person controls the issuer of a class of equity securities which are "section 13(f) securities" as defined in this rule, those securities shall not be deemed to be "section 13(f) securities" with respect to the controlling person, provided that such person does not otherwise exercise investment discretion with respect to accounts with fair market value of at least $100,000,000 within the meaning of paragraph (a) of this section.

* * *

FORM 8–K

CURRENT REPORT

**Pursuant to Section 13 or 15(d) of The Securities Exchange Act of 1934
for the Month of _ _ _ _ _ _ _ _ _ _ , 19_ _**

GENERAL INSTRUCTIONS

A. Rule as to Use of Form 8–K

B. Events to be Reported and Time for Filing of Reports

1. A report of this form is required to be filed upon the occurrence of any one or more of the events specified in Items 1–4 and 6 of this form. Reports of events specified in those items are to be filed within 15 days after the occurrence of the earliest such event reported.

2. Since a report on this form pursuant to Item 5 is optional, there is correspondingly no mandatory time for filing. Registrants are encouraged, however, to file promptly after the occurrence of any event therein reported.

3. If substantially the same information as that required by this form has been previously reported by the registrant, an additional report of the informatiom on this form need not be made. The term "previously reported" is defined in Rule 12b–2.

4. When considering current reporting on this form, particularly of other events of importance pursuant to Item 5, registrants should have due regard for the accuracy, completeness and currency of the information in registration statements filed under the Securities Act of 1933 which incorporate by reference information in reports filed pursuant to the Securities Exchange Act of 1934, including reports on this form.

* * *

F. Incorporation by Reference

If the registrant makes available to its stockholders or otherwise publishes, within the period prescribed for filing the report, a press release or other document or statement containing information meeting some or all of the requirements of this form, the information called for may be incorporated by reference to such published document or statement, in answer or partial answer to any item or items of this form, provided copies thereof are filled as an exhibit to the report on this form.

Item 1. Changes in Control of Registrant.

(a) If, to the knowledge of management, a change in control of the registrant has occurred, state the name of the person(s) who acquired such control; the amount and the source of the consideration used by such person(s); the basis of the control; the date and a description of the transaction(s) which resulted in the change in control; the percentage of voting securities of the registrant now beneficially owned directly or indirectly by the person(s) who acquired control; and the identity of the person(s) from whom control was assumed. If the source of all or any part of the consideration used is a loan made in the ordinary course of business by a bank as defined by Section 3(a)(6) of the Act, the identity of such bank shall be omitted provided a request for confidentiality has been made pursuant to Section 13(d)(1)(B) of the Act by the person(s) who acquired control. In lieu thereof, the material shall indicate that disclosure of the identity of the bank has been so omitted and filed separately with the Commission.

(b) Furnish the information required by Item 403(c) of Regulation S–K.

> *Instructions.* 1. State the terms of any loans or pledges obtained by the new control group for the purpose of acquiring control, and the names of the lenders or pledgees.

> 2. Any arrangements or understandings among members of both the former and new control groups and their associates with respect to election of directors or other matters should be described.

(b) Describe any contractual arrangements, including any pledge of securities of the registrant, or any of its parents, known to the management, the operation of the terms of which may at a subsequent date result in a change in control of the registrant.

Instruction. Paragraph (b) does not require a description of ordinary default provisions contained in the charter, trust indentures or other governing instruments relating to securities of the registrant.

Item 2. Acquisition or Disposition of Assets.

If the registrant or any of its majority-owned subsidiaries has acquired or disposed of a significant amount of assets, otherwise than in the ordinary course of business, furnish the following information:

(a) The date and manner of acquisition or disposition and a brief description of the assets involved, the nature and amount of consideration given or received therefor, the principle followed in determining the amount of such consideration, the identity of the persons from whom the assets were acquired or to whom they were sold and the nature of any material relationship between such persons and the registrant or any of its affiliates, any director or officer of the registrant, or any associate of such director or officer. If the transaction being reported is an acquisition, identify the source(s) of the funds used unless all or any part of the consideration used is a loan made in the ordinary course of business by a bank as defined by Section 3(a)(6) of the Act in which the identity of such bank shall be omitted provided a request for confidentiality has been made pursuant to Section 13(d)(1) (B) of the Act. In lieu thereof, the material shall indicate that the identity of the bank has been so omitted and filed separately with the Commission.

(b) If any assets so acquired by the registrant or its subsidiaries constituted plant, equipment or other physical property, state the nature of the business in which the assets were used by the persons from whom acquired and whether the registrant intends to continue such use or intends to devote the assets to other purposes, indicating such other purposes.

* * *

Item 3. Bankruptcy or Receivership.

If a receiver, fiscal agent or similar officer has been appointed for a registrant or its parent, in a proceeding under the Bankruptcy Act or in any other proceeding under State or Federal law in which a court or governmental agency has assumed jurisdiction over substantially all of the assets or business of the registrant or its parent, or if such jurisdiction has been assumed by leaving the existing directors and officers in possession but subject to the supervision and orders of a court or governmental body, identify the proceeding, the court or governmental body, the date jurisdiction was assumed, the identity of the receiver, fiscal agent or similar officer and the date of his appointment.

* * *

Item 4. Changes in Registrant's Certifying Accountant.

If an independent accountant who was previously engaged as the principal accountant to audit the registrant's financial statements resigns (or indicates he declines to stand for re-election after the completion of the current audit) or is dismissed as the registrant's principal accountant, or another independent accountant is engaged as principal accountant, or another independent accountant on whom the principal accountant expressed reliance in his report regarding a significant subsidiary resigns (or formally indicates he declines to stand for re-election after the completion of the current audit) or is dismissed or another independent accountant is engaged to audit that subsidiary:

(a) State the date of such resignation (or declination to stand for re-election), dismissal or engagement.

(b) State whether in connection with the audits of the two most recent fiscal years and any subsequent interim period preceding such resignation, dismissal or engagement there were any disagreements with the former accountant on any matter of accounting principles or practices, financial statement disclosure, or auditing scope or procedure, which disagreements if not resolved to the satisfaction of the former accountant would have caused him to make reference in connection with his report to the subject matter of the disagreement(s); also, describe each such disagreement. The disagreements required to be reported in response to the preceding sentence include both those resolved to the former accountant's satisfaction and those not resolved to the former accountant's satisfaction. Disagreements contemplated by this rule are those which occur at the decision-making level; i. e., between personnel of the registrant responsible for presentation of its financial statements and personnel of the accounting firm responsible for rendering its report.

(c) State whether the principal accountant's report on the financial statements for any of the past two years contained an adverse opinion or a disclaimer of opinion or was qualified as to uncertainty, audit scope, or accounting principles; also describe the nature of each such adverse opinion, disclaimer of opinion, or qualification.

(d) The registrant shall request the former accountant to furnish the registrant with a letter addressed to the Commission stating whether he agrees with the statements made by the registrant in response to this item and, if not, stating the respects in which he does not agree. The registrant shall file copies of the former accountant's letter as an exhibit to the report on this form. If the former accountant's letter is unavailable at the time of filing, it shall be filed within thirty days thereafter.

(e) State whether the decision to change accountants was recommended or approved by:

(1) any audit or similar committee of the Board of Directors, if the issuer has such a committee; or

(2) the Board of Directors, if the issuer has no such committee.

Item 5.   Other Events.

The registrant may, at its option, report under this item any events, with respect to which information is not otherwise called for by this form, that the registrant deems of importance to security holders.

Item 6.   Resignations of Registrant's Directors.

(a) If a director has resigned or declined to stand for re-election to the board of directors since the date of the last annual meeting of shareholders because of a disagreement with the registrant on any matter relating to the registrant's operations, policies or practices, and if the director has furnished the registrant with a letter describing such disagreement and requesting that the matter be disclosed, the registrant shall state the date of such resignation or declination to stand for re-election and summarize the director's description of the disagreement.

(b) If the registrant believes that the description provided by the director is incorrect or incomplete, it may include a brief statement presenting its views of the disagreement.

(c) The registrant shall file a copy of the director's letter as an exhibit with all copies of the form 8–K required to be filed pursuant to general Instruction E.

* * *

FORM 10–K

Annual Report Pursuant to Section 13 or 15(d) of
The Securities Exchange Act of 1934

GENERAL INSTRUCTIONS

A. Rule as to Use of Form 10–K.

This Form shall be used for annual reports pursuant to section 13 or 15(d) of the Securities Exchange Act of 1934 (the "Act") for which no other form is prescribed. Reports on this form shall be filed within 90 days after the end of the fiscal year covered by the report. However, all schedules required by Article 12 of Regulation S–X may, at the option of the registrant, be filed as an amendment to the report not later than 120 days after the end of the fiscal year covered by the report. Such amendment shall be filed under cover of Form 8.

* * *

D. Signature and Filing of Report

(1) Three complete copies of the report, including financial statements, financial statement schedules, exhibits, and all other papers and documents filed as a part thereof, and five additional copies which need not include exhibits, shall be filed with the Commission. At least one complete copy of the report, including financial statements, financial statement schedules, exhibits, and all other papers and documents filed as a part thereof, shall be filed with each exchange on which any class of securities of the registrant is registered. At least one complete copy of the report filed with the Commission and one such copy filed with each exchange shall be manually signed. Copies not manually signed shall bear typed or printed signatures.

(2)(a) The report shall be signed by the registrant, and on behalf of the registrant by its principal executive officer or officers, its principal financial officer, its controller or principal accounting officer, and by at least the majority of the board of directors or persons performing similar functions. Where the registrant is a limited partnership, the report shall be signed by the majority of the board of directors of any corporate general partner who signs the report. (b) The name of each person who signs the report shall be typed or printed beneath his signature. Any person who occupies more than one of the specified positions shall indicate each capacity in which he signs the report. Attention is directed to Rule 12b–11 concerning manual signatures and signatures pursuant to powers of attorney.

* * *

G. Information to be Incorporated by Reference

(1) Attention is directed to Rule 12b–23 which provides for the incorporation by reference of information contained in certain documents in answer or partial answer to any item of a report.

(2) The information called for by Parts I and II of this Form (Items 1 through 9 or any portion thereof) may, at the registrant's option, be incorporated by reference from the registrant's annual report to security holders furnished to the Commission pursuant to Rule 14a–3(b) or Rule 14C–3(b) or from the registrant's annual report to security holders, even if not furnished to the Commission pursuant to Rule 14a–3(b) or Rule 14c–3(a), provided such annual report contains the information required by Rule 14a–3.

Note.—In order to fulfill the requirements of Part I of Form 10–K, the incorporated portion of the annual report to security holders must contain the information required by Items 1–3 of Form 10–K, to the extent applicable.

(3) The information called for by Part III (Items 10, 11 and 12) shall be incorporated by reference from the registrant's definitive proxy statement (filed or to be filed pursuant to Regulation 14A) or definitive information statement (filed or to be filed pursuant to Regulation 14C) which involves the election of directors, if such definitive proxy statement or information statement is filed with the Commission not later than 120 days after the end of the fiscal year covered by the Form 10–K. However, if such definitive proxy or information statement is not filed with the Commission in the 120-day period, the Items comprising the Part III information must be filed as part of the Form 10–K, or as an amendment to the Form 10–K under cover of Form 8, not later than the end of the 120-day period. It should be noted that the information regarding executive officers required by Item 401 of Regulation S–K may be included in Part I of Form 10–K under an appropriate caption. See Instruction 4 to Item 401(b) of Regulation S–K.

* * *

H. Integrated Reports to Security Holders

Annual reports to security holders may be combined with the required information of Form 10–K and will be suitable for filing with the Commission if the following conditions are satisfied:

(1) The combined report contains full and complete answers to all items required by Form 10–K. When responses to a certain item of required disclosure are separated within the combined report, an appropriate cross-reference should be made. If the information required by

Part III of Form 10–K is omitted by virtue of General Instruction G, a definitive proxy or information statement shall be filed.

(2) The cover page and the required signatures are included. As appropriate, a cross-reference sheet should be filed indicating the location of information required by the items of the Form.

I. Registrants Filing on Form S–18.

If the registrant is subject to the reporting requirements of Section 15(d) of the Exchange Act and such obligation arises solely because the registrant has filed a registration statement on Form S–18 which has become effective during the last fiscal year, the registrant may comply with the disclosure requirements of Form S–18 Item 6, Description of Business: Item 10, Remuneration of Directors and Officers; and Item 13, Interest of Management and Others in Certain Transactions, in lieu of complying with the disclosure requirements of Item 1, Business, and Item 11, Management Remuneration and Transactions, herein. Item 6 of this Form, Selected Financial Data, may be omitted at the election of such registrant.

* * *

PART I. [SEE GENERAL INSTRUCTION G(2)]

Item 1. Business.

Furnish the information required by Item 101 of Regulation S–K, except that the discussion of the development of the registrant's business need only include developments since the beginning of the fiscal year for which this report is filed.

Item 2. Properties.

Furnish the information required by Item 102 of Regulation S–K.

Item 3. Legal Proceedings.

(a) Furnish the information required by Item 103 of Regulation S–K.

(b) As to any proceeding that was terminated during the fourth quarter of the fiscal year covered by this report, furnish information similar to that required by Item 103 of Regulation S–K, including the date of termination and a description of the disposition thereof with respect to the registrant and its subsidiaries.

Item 4. Submission of Matters to a Vote of Security Holders.

If any matter was submitted during the fourth quarter of the fiscal year covered by this report to a vote of security holders, through the solicitation of proxies or otherwise, furnish the following information:

(a) The date of the meeting and whether it was an annual or special meeting.

(b) If the meeting involved the election of directors, the name of each director elected at the meeting and the name of each other director whose term of office as a director continued after the meeting.

(c) A brief description of each other matter voted upon at the meeting and the number of affirmative votes and the number of negative votes cast with respect to each such matter.

(d) A description of the terms of any settlement between the registrant and any other participant (as defined in Rule 14a–11 of Regulation 14A under the Act) terminating any solicitation subject to Rule 14a–11, including the cost or anticipated cost to the registrant.

Instructions. 1. If any matter has been submitted to a vote of security holders otherwise than at a meeting of such security holders, corresponding information with respect to such submission shall be furnished. The solicitation of any authorization or consent (other than a proxy to vote at a stockholders' meeting) with respect to any matter shall be deemed a submission of such matter to a vote of security holders within the meaning of this item.

2. Paragraph (a) need be answered only if paragraph (b) or (c) is required to be answered.

3. Paragraph (b) need not be answered if (i) proxies for the meeting were solicited pursuant to Regulation 14A under the Act, (ii) there was no solicitation in opposition to the management's nominees as listed in the proxy statement, and (iii) all of such nominees were elected. If the registrant did not solicit proxies and the board of directors as previously reported to the Commission was re-elected in its entirety, a

statement to that effect in answer to paragraph (b) will suffice as an answer thereto.

4. Paragraph (c) need not be answered as to procedural matters or as to the selection or approval of auditors.

5. If the registrant has furnished to its security holders proxy soliciting material containing the information called for by paragraph (d), the paragraph may be answered by reference to the information contained in such material.

6. If the registrant has published a report containing all of the information called for by this item, the item may be answered by a reference to the information contained in such report.

PART II. [SEE GENERAL INSTRUCTION G(2)]

Item 5. Market for Registrant's Common Equity and Related Stockholder Matters.

Furnish the information required by Item 201 of Regulation S–K.

Item 6. Selected Financial Data.

Furnish the information required by Item 301 of Regulation S–K.

Item 7. Management's Discussion and Analysis of Financial Condition and Results of Operation.

Furnish the information required by Item 303 of Regulation S–K.

Item 8. Financial Statements and Supplementary Data.

Furnish financial statements meeting the requirements of Regulation S–X, and the supplementary financial information required by Item 302 of Regulation S–K. Financial statements of the registrant and its subsidiaries consolidated [as required by Rule 14a–3(b)] shall be filed under this item. Other financial statements and schedules required under Regulation S–X may be filed as "Financial Statement Schedules" pursuant to Item 13, Exhibits, Financial Statement Schedules, and Reports on Form 8–K, of this Form.

Item 9. Disagreements on Accounting and Financial Disclosure.

Furnish the information required by Item 304 of Regulation S–K.

PART III. [SEE GENERAL INSTRUCTION G(3)]

Item 10. Directors and Executive Officers of the Registrant.

Furnish the information required by Item 401 of Regulation S–K.

Item 11. Management Remuneration and Transactions.

Furnish the information required by Item 402 of Regulation S–K.

Item 12. Security Ownership of Certain Beneficial Owners and Management.

Furnish the information required by Item 403 of Regulation S–K.

PART IV.

Item 13. Exhibits, Financial Statement Schedules, and Reports on Form 8–K.

(a) List the following documents filed as a part of the report:

1. All financial statements;

2. Those financial statement schedules required to be filed by Item 8 of this Form, and by paragraph (d) below.

(3) Those exhibits required by Item 601 of Regulation S–K, and by paragraph (c) below. Where any financial statement, financial statement schedule, or exhibit is incorporated by reference, the incorporation by reference shall be set forth in the list required by this item. For purposes of all rules concerning incorporation by reference a financial statement schedule shall constitute an "exhibit." See Rule 12b–23.

(c) Registrants shall file, as exhibits to this Form, the exhibits required by Item 601 of Regulation S–K.

FORM 10-Q

For Quarterly Reports Under Section 13 or 15(d) of the Securities Exchange Act of 1934

GENERAL INSTRUCTIONS

A. Rule as to Use of Form 10-Q.

(a) Form 10-Q shall be used for quarterly reports under Section 13 or 15(d) of the Securities Exchange Act of 1934, filed pursuant to Rule 13a–13 or Rule 15d–13.

(b) A report on this form shall be filed within 45 days after the end of each of the first three fiscal quarters of each fiscal year. No report need be filed for the fourth quarter of any fiscal year.

* * *

E. Integrated Reports to Security Holders.

Quarterly reports to security holders may be combined with the required information of Form 10-Q and will be suitable for filing with the Commission if the following conditions are satisfied:

1. The combined report contains full and complete answers to all items required by Part I of this form. When responses to a certain item of required disclosure are separated within the combined report, an appropriate cross-reference should be made.

2. If not included in the combined report, the cover page, appropriate responses to Part II, and the required signatures shall be included in the Form 10-Q. Additionally, as appropriate, a cross-reference sheet should be filed indicating the location of information required by the items of the form.

F. Filed Status of Information Presented.

1. Pursuant to Rule 13a–13(d) and Rule 15d–13(d), the information presented in satisfaction of the requirements of Items 1 and 2 of Part I of this form, whether included directly in a report on this form, incorporated therein by reference from a report, document or statement filed as an exhibit to Part I of this form pursuant to Instruction D(1) above, included in an integrated report pursuant to Instruction E above, or contained in a statement regarding computation of per share earnings or a letter regarding a change in accounting, principles filed as an exhibit to Part I pursuant to Item 601 of Regulation S–K, except as provided by Instruction F(2) below, shall not be deemed filed for the purpose of Section 18 of the Act or otherwise subject to the liabilities of that section of the Act but shall be subject to the other provisions of the Act.

2. Information presented in satisfaction of the requirements of this form other than those of Items (1) and (2) of Part I shall be deemed filed for the purpose of Section 18 of the Act; except that, where information presented in response to Item (1) or (2) of Part I (or as an exhibit thereto) is also used to satisfy Part II requirements through incorporation by reference, only that portion of Part I (or exhibit thereto) consisting of the information required by Part II shall be deemed so filed.

PART I. FINANCIAL INFORMATION

Item 1. Financial Statements.

Provide the information required by Rule 10–01 of Regulation S–X.

Item 2. Management's Discussion and Analysis of Financial Condition and Results of Operations.

Furnish the information required by Item 303 of Regulation S–K.

PART II. OTHER INFORMATION

Item 1. Legal Proceedings.

Furnish the information required by Item 103 of Regulation S–K. As to such proceedings which have been terminated during the period covered by the report provide similar information, including the date of termination and a description of the disposition thereof with respect to the registrant and its subsidiaries.

Instruction. A legal proceeding need only be reported in the 10–Q filed for the quarter in which it first became a reportable event and in subsequent quarters in which there have been material developments. Subsequent Form 10–Q filings in the same fiscal year in which a legal proceeding or a material development is reported should reference any previous reports in that year.

Item 2.   Changes in Securities.

(a) If the constituent instruments defining the rights of the holders of any class of registered securities have been materially modified, give the title of the class of securities involved and state briefly the general effect of such modification upon the rights of holders of such securities.

(b) If the rights evidenced by any class of registered securities have been materially limited or qualified by the issuance or modification of any other class of securities, state briefly the general effect of the issuance or modification of such other class of securities upon the rights of the holders of the registered securities.

Instruction. Working capital restrictions and other limitations upon the payment of dividends are to be reported hereunder.

Item 3.   Defaults upon Senior Securities.

(a) If there has been any material default in the payment of principal, interest, a sinking or purchase fund installment, or any other material default not cured within 30 days, with respect to any indebtedness of the registrant or any of its significant subsidiaries exceeding 5 percent of the total assets of the registrant and its consolidated subsidiaries, identify the indebtedness and state the nature of the default. In the case of such a default in the payment of principal, interest, or a sinking or purchase fund installment, state the amount of the default and the total arrearage on the date of filing this report.

Instruction. This paragraph refers only to events which have become defaults under the governing instruments, *i. e.*, after the expiration of any period of grace and compliance with any notice requirements.

(b) If any material arrearage in the payment of dividends has occurred or if there has been any other material delinquency not cured within 30 days, with respect to any class of preferred stock of the registrant which is registered or which ranks prior to any class of registered securities, or with respect to any class of preferred stock of any significant subsidiary of the registrant, give the title of the class and state the nature of the arrearage or delinquency. In the case of an arrearage in the payment of dividends, state the amount and the total arrearage on the date of filing this report.

Instruction. Item 3 need not be answered as to any default or arrearage with respect to any class of securities all of which is held by, or for the account of, the registrant or its totally held subsidiaries.

Item 4.   Submission of Matters to a Vote of Security Holders.

If any matter has been submitted to a vote of security holders, through the solicitation of proxies or otherwise, furnish the following information:

(a) The date of the meeting and whether it was an annual or special meeting.

(b) If the meeting involved the election of directors, state the name of each director elected at the meeting and the name of each other director whose term of office as a director continued after the meeting.

(c) A brief description of each other matter voted upon at the meeting and state the number of affirmative votes and the number of negative report.

(d) Describe the terms of any settlement between the registrant and any other participant (as defined in Rule 14a–11 of Regulation 14A under the Act) terminating any solicitation subject to Rule 14a–11, including the cost or anticipated cost to the registrant.

Instructions. 1. If any matter has been submitted to a vote of security holders otherwise than at a meeting of such security holders, corresponding information with respect to such submission shall be furnished. The solicitation of any authorization or consent (other than a proxy to vote at a stockholders' meeting) with respect to any matter shall be deemed a submission of such matter to a vote of security holders within the meaning of this item.

2. Paragraph (a) need be answered only if paragraph (b) or (c) is required to be answered.

3. Paragraph (b) need not be answered if (i) proxies for the meeting were solicited pursuant to Regulation 14 under the Act, (ii) there was no solicitation in opposition to the management's nominees as listed in the proxy statement, and (iii) all of such nominees were elected. If the registrant did not solicit proxies and the board of directors as previously reported to the Commission was re-elected in its entirety, a statement to that effect in answer to paragraph (b) will suffice as an answer thereto.

4. Paragraph (c) need not be answered as to procedural matters or as to the selection or approval of auditors.

5. If the registrant has furnished to its security holders proxy soliciting material containing the information called for by paragraph (d), the paragraph may be answered by reference to the information contained in such material.

6. If the registrant has published a report containing all of the information called for by this item, the item may be answered by a reference to the information contained in such report.

* * *

Item 5. Other Information.

The registrant may, at its option, report under this item any information, not previously reported in a report on Form 8–K, with respect to which information is not otherwise called for by this form. If disclosure of such information is made under this item, it need not be repeated in a report on Form 8–K which would otherwise be required to be filed with respect to such information or in a subsequent report on Form 10–Q.

Item 6. Exhibits and Reports on Form 8–K.

(a) Furnish the exhibit required by Item 60 of Regulation S–K.

(b) Reports on Form 8–K. State whether any reports on Form 8–K have been filed during the quarter for which this report is filed, listing the items reported, any financial statements filed, and the dates of any such reports.

SOLICITATION OF PROXIES

Rule 14a–1. Definitions

Unless the context otherwise requires, all terms used in this regulation have the same meanings as in the Act or elsewhere in the General Rules and Regulations thereunder. In addition, the following definitions apply unless the context otherwise requires:

(a) *Associate.* The term "associate" used to indicate a relationship with any person, means (1) any corporation or organization (other than the issuer or a majority owned subsidiary of the issuer) of which such person is an officer or partner or is, directly or indirectly, the beneficial owner of 10 percent or more of any class of equity securities, (2) any trust or other estate in which such person has a substantial beneficial interest or as to which such person serves as trustee or in a similar fiduciary capacity, and (3) any relative or spouse of such person, or any relative of such spouse, who has the same home as such person or who is a director or officer of the issuer or any of its parents or subsidiaries.

(b) *Issuer.* The term "issuer" means the issuer of the securities in respect of which a proxy is solicited.

(c) *Last fiscal year.* The term "last fiscal year" of the issuer means the last fiscal year of the issuer ending prior to the date of the meeting for which proxies are to be solicited.

(d) *Proxy.* The term "proxy" includes every proxy, consent or authorization within the meaning of Section 14(a) of the Act. The consent or authorization may take the form of failure to object or to dissent.

(e) *Proxy statement.* The term "proxy statement" means the statement required by Rule 14a–3(a), whether or not contained in a single document.

(f) *Solicitation.* (1) The terms "solicit" and "solicitation" include—

(i) any request for a proxy whether or not accompanied by or included in a form of proxy;

(ii) any request to execute or not to execute, or to revoke, a proxy; or

(iii) the furnishing of a form of proxy or other communication to security holders under circumstances reasonably calculated to result in the procurement, withholding or revocation of a proxy.

(2) The terms do not apply, however, to the furnishing of a form of proxy to a security holder upon the unsolicited request of such security holder, the performance by the issuer of acts required by . . . Rule 14a–7, or the performance by any person of ministerial acts on behalf of a person soliciting a proxy.

Rule 14a–2. Solicitations to Which Rules 14a–3 to 14a–12 Apply

Rules 14a–3 to 14a–12 apply to every solicitation of a proxy with respect to securities registered pursuant to section 12 of the Act, whether or not trading in such securities has been suspended, except that:

(a) Rules 14a–3 to 14a–12 do not apply to the following:

(1) Any solicitation by a person in respect to securities carried in his name or in the name of his nominee (otherwise than as voting trustee) or held in his custody, if such person—

(i) Receives no commission or remuneration for such solicitation, directly or indirectly, other than reimbursement of reasonable expenses.

(ii) Furnishes promptly to the person solicited a copy of all soliciting material with respect to the same subject matter or meeting received from all persons who shall furnish copies thereof for such purpose and who shall, if requested, defray the reasonable expenses to be incurred in forwarding such material, and

(iii) In addition, does no more than impartially instruct the person solicited to forward a proxy to the person, if any, to whom the person solicited desires to give a proxy, or impartially request from the person solicited instructions as to the authority to be conferred by the proxy and state that a proxy will be given if no instructions are received by a certain date.

(2) Any solicitation by a person in respect of securities of which he is the beneficial owner;

(3) Any solicitation involved in the offer and sale of securities registered under the Securities Act of 1933: *Provided,* That this paragraph shall not apply to securities to be issued in any

transaction of the character specified in paragraph (a) of Rule 145 under that Act;

(4) Any solicitation with respect to a plan of reorganization under Chapter X of the Bankruptcy Act, as amended, if made after the entry of an order approving such plan pursuant to section 174 of said Act and after, or concurrently with, the transmittal of information concerning such plan as required by section 175 of said Act;

(5) Any solicitation which is subject to Rule 62 under the Public Utility Holding Company Act of 1935; and

(6) Any solicitation through the medium of a newspaper advertisement which informs security holders of a source from which they may obtain copies of a proxy statement, form of proxy and any other soliciting material and does no more than (i) name the issuer, (ii) state the reason for the advertisement, and (iii) identify the proposal or proposals to be acted upon by security holders.

(b) Rules 14a–3 to 14a–8 and Rules 14a–10 to 14a–12 do not apply to the following:

(1) Any solicitation made otherwise than on behalf of the issuer where the total number of persons solicited is not more than ten; and

(2) The furnishing of proxy voting advice by any person (the "advisor") to any other person with whom the advisor has a business relationship, if:

(i) The advisor renders financial advice in the ordinary course of his business;

(ii) The advisor discloses to the recipient of the advice any significant relationship with the issuer or any of its affiliates, or a shareholder proponent of the matter on which advice is given, well as any material interest of the advisor in such matter;

(iii) The advisor receives no special commission or remuneration for furnishing the proxy voting advice from any person other than a recipient of the advice and other persons who receive similar advice under this subsection; and

(iv) The proxy voting advice is not furnished on behalf of any person soliciting proxies or on behalf of a participant in an election subject to the provisions of Rule 14a–11.

Rule 14a–3. Information to Be Furnished to Security Holders

(a) No solicitation subject to this regulation shall be made unless each person solicited is concurrently furnished or has previously been furnished with a written proxy statement containing the information specified in Schedule 14A or with a written proxy statement included in a registration statement filed under the Securities Act of 1933 on Form S–15 and containing the information specified in such Form.

(b) If the solicitation is made on behalf of the issuer, and relates to an annual meeting of security holders at which directors are to be elected, each proxy statement furnished pursuant to paragraph (a) shall be accompanied or preceded by an annual report to security holders as follows:

(1) The report shall include, for the registrant and its subsidiaries consolidated, audited balance sheets as of the end of the two most recent fiscal years and audited statements of income and changes in financial position for each of the three most recent fiscal years prepared in accordance with Regulation S–X, except that the provisions of Article 3, other than §§ 210.3–06(e), shall not apply and only substantial compliance with Articles 6 and 9 is required. Any financial statement schedules or exhibits or separate financial statements which may otherwise be required in filings with the Commission may be omitted. Investment companies registered under the Investment Company Act of 1940 need include financial statements only for the last fiscal year except for statements of changes in net assets which are to be filed for the two most recent fiscal years. If the financial statements of the registrant and its subsidiaries consolidated in the annual report filed or to be filed with the Commission are not required to be audited, the financial statements required by this paragraph may be unaudited.

* * *

(2) Financial statements and notes thereto shall be presented in roman type at least as large and as legible as 10-point modern type. If necessary for convenient presentation, the financial statements may be in roman type as large and as legible as 8-point modern type. All type shall be leaded at least 2-point.

(3) The report shall contain the supplementary financial information required by Item 302 of Regulation S–K.

(4) The report shall contain information concerning disagreements with accountants on accounting and financial disclosure required by Item 304 of Regulation S–K.

(5)(i) The report shall contain the selected financial data required by Item 301 of Regulation S–K.

(ii) The report shall contain management's discussion and analysis of financial condition and results of operations required by Item 303 of Regulation S–K.

(6) The report shall contain a brief description of the business done by the issuer and its subsidiaries during the most recent fiscal year which will, in the opinion of management, indicate the general nature and scope of the business of the issuer and its subsidiaries.

(7) The report shall contain information relating to the issuer's industry segments, classes of similar products or services, foreign and domestic operations and export sales required by paragraphs (b), (c)(1)(i) and (d) of Item 101 of Regulation S–K.

> **Note:** Paragraph (b)(11) of this section permits the information required by this paragraph to be set forth in any form deemed suitable by management.

(8) The report shall identify each of the issuer's directors and executive officers, and shall indicate the principal occupation or employment of each such person and the name and principal business of any organization by which such person is employed.

(9) The report shall contain the market price of and dividends on the issuer's common equity and related stock holder matters required by Item 201 of Regulation S–K.

(10) Management's proxy statement, or the report, shall contain an undertaking in bold face or otherwise reasonably prominent type to provide without charge to each person solicited, on the written request of any such person, a copy of the issuer's annual report on Form 10–K including the financial statements and the finan-

cial statement schedules, required to be filed with the Commission pursuant to Rule 13a–1 under the Act for the issuer's most recent fiscal year, and shall indicate the name and address of the person to whom such a written request is to be directed. In the discretion of management, an issuer need not undertake to furnish without charge copies of all exhibits to its Form 10–K provided that the copy of the annual report on Form 10–K furnished without charge to requesting security holders is accompanied by a list briefly describing all the exhibits not contained therein and indicating that the issuer will furnish any exhibit upon the payment of a specified reasonable fee which fee shall be limited to the issuer's reasonable expenses in furnishing such exhibit. If the issuer's annual report to security holders complies with all of the disclosure requirements of Form 10–K and is filed with the Commission in satisfaction of its Form 10–K filing requirements, such issuer need not furnish a separate Form 10–K to security holders who receive a copy of such annual report.

Note: Pursuant to the undertaking required by paragraph (b)(10) of this section, an issuer shall furnish a copy of its annual report on Form 10–K to a beneficial owner of its securities upon receipt of a written request from such person. Each request must set forth a good faith representation that, as of the record date for the annual meeting of the issuer's security holders, the person making the request was a beneficial owner of securities entitled to vote at such meeting.

(11) Subject to the foregoing requirements, the report may be in any form deemed suitable by management and the information required by paragraphs (b)(5) to (b)(10) of this section may be presented in an appendix or other separate section of the report, provided that the attention of security holders is called to such presentation.

(12) Paragraphs (b)(5) through (b)(11) of this section shall not apply to an investment company registered under the Investment Company Act of 1940. Subject to the requirements of paragraphs (b)(1) through (b)(4) of this section, the annual report to security holders of such invest-

ment company may be in any form deemed suitable by management.

(c) Seven copies of the report sent to security holders pursuant to this rule shall be mailed to the Commission, solely for its information, not later than the date on which such report is first sent or given to security holders or the date on which preliminary copies of solicitation material are filed with the Commission pursuant to Rule 14a–6(a), whichever date is later. The report is not deemed to be "soliciting material" or to be "filed" with the Commission or subject to this regulation otherwise than as provided in this rule, or to the liabilities of Section 18 of the Act, except to the extent that the issuer specifically requests that it be treated as a part of the proxy soliciting material or incorporates it in the proxy statement or other filed report by reference.

Note: To assist the staff, managements of issuers are requested to indicate in a letter transmitting to the Commission copies of their annual reports to shareholders or in a separate letter at or about the time the annual report is furnished to the Commission, whether the financial statements in the report reflect a change from the preceding year in any accounting principles or practices or in the method of applying any such principles or practices.

(d) If the issuer knows that securities of any class entitled to vote at a meeting with respect to which the issuer intends to solicit proxies, consents or authorization are held of record by a broker, dealer, bank or voting trustee, or their nominees, the issuer shall inquire of such record holder whether other persons are the beneficial owners of such securities and, if so, the number of copies of the proxy and other soliciting material and, in the case of an annual meeting at which directors are to be elected, the number of copies of the annual report to security holders, necessary to supply such material to such beneficial owners. The issuer shall supply such record holder with additional copies in such quantities, assembled in such form and at such a place, as the record holder may reasonably request in order to address and send one copy of each to each beneficial owner of securities so held and shall, upon the request of such record holder, pay its reasonable expenses for completing the mailing of such material to security holders to whom the material is sent.

Note 1: If the issuer's list of security holders indicates that some of its securities are registered in the name of "Cede & Co.", a nominee for the Depository Trust Company, or in the name of a nominee for any central certificate depository system, an issuer shall make appropriate inquiry of the central depository system and thereafter of the participants in such a system who may hold on behalf of a beneficial owner, and shall comply with the above paragraph with respect to any such participant.

Note 2: The requirement for sending an annual report to security holders of record having the same address will be satisfied by sending at least one report to a holder of record at that address provided that those holders of record to whom a report is not sent agree thereto in writing. This procedure is not available to issuers, however, where banks, broker-dealers, and other persons hold securities in nominee accounts or "street names" on behalf of beneficial owners, and such persons are not relieved of any obligation to obtain or send such annual report to the beneficial owners.

Note 3: The attention of issuers is called to the fact that broker-dealers have an obligation pursuant to applicable self-regulatory requirements to obtain and forward annual reports and proxy soliciting materials in a timely manner to beneficial owners for whom such broker-dealers hold securities.

(e) An annual report to security holders prepared on an integrated basis pursuant to General Instruction H to Form 10-K, may also be submitted in satisfaction of this rule. When filed as the annual report on Form 10-K, responses to the Items of that form are subject to section 18 of the Act notwithstanding paragraph (c).

Rule 14a-4. Requirements as to Proxy

(a) The form of proxy (1) shall indicate in bold-face type whether or not the proxy is solicited on behalf of the issuer's board of directors or, if provided other than by a majority of the board of directors, shall indicate in bold-face type the identity of the persons on whose behalf the solicitation is made; (2) shall provide a specifically designated blank space for dating the proxy card; and (3) shall identify clearly and impartially each matter or group of related matters intended to be acted upon, whether proposed by the issuer or by security holders. No reference need be made, however, to proposals as to which discretionary authority is conferred pursuant to paragraph (c) of this section.

(b)(1) Means shall be provided in the form of proxy whereby the person solicited is afforded an opportunity to specify by boxes a choice between approval or disapproval of, or abstention with respect to, each matter or group of related matters referred to therein as intended to be acted upon, other than elections to office. A proxy may confer discretionary authority with respect to matters as to which a choice is not specified by the security holder provided that the form of proxy states in bold-face type how it is intended to vote the shares represented by the proxy in each such case.

(2) A form of proxy which provides for the election of directors shall set forth the names of persons nominated for election as directors. Such form of proxy shall clearly provide any of the following means for security holders to withhold authority to vote for each nominee:

    (i) a box opposite the name of each nominee which may be marked to indicate that authority to vote for such nominee is withheld; or

    (ii) an instruction in bold-face type which indicates that the security holder may withhold authority to vote for any nominee by lining through or otherwise striking out the name of any nominee; or

    (iii) designated blank spaces in which the shareholder may enter the names of nominees with respect to whom the shareholder chooses to withhold authority to vote; or

    (iv) any other similar means, provided that clear instructions are furnished indicating how the shareholder may withhold authority to vote for any nominee.

Such form of proxy also may provide a means for the security holder to grant authority to vote for the nominees set forth, as a group, provided that there is a similar means for the security holder to withhold authority to vote for such group of nominees. Any such form of proxy which is executed by the security holder in such manner as not to withhold authority to vote for the election of any nominee shall be deemed to grant such authority, provided that the form of proxy so states in bold-face type.

Instructions. 1. Paragraph (2) does not apply in the case of a merger, consolidation or other plan if the election of directors is an integral part of the plan.

2. If applicable state law gives legal effect to votes cast against a nominee, then in lieu of, or in addition to, providing a means for security holders to withhold authority to vote, the issuer should provide a similar means for security holders to vote against each nominee.

(c) A proxy may confer discretionary authority to vote with respect to any of the following matters:

(1) Matters which the persons making the solicitation do not know, a reasonable time before the solicitation, are to be presented at the meeting, if a specific statement to that effect is made in the proxy statement or form of proxy;

(2) Approval of the minutes of the prior meeting if such approval does not amount to ratification of the action taken at that meeting;

(3) The election of any person to any office for which a bona fide nominee is named in the proxy statement and such nominee is unable to serve or for good cause will not serve.

(4) Any proposal omitted from the proxy statement and form of proxy pursuant to Rule 14a-8 or 14a-9.

(5) Matters incident to the conduct of the meeting.

(d) No proxy shall confer authority (1) to vote for the election of any person to any office for which a bona fide nominee is not named in the proxy statement, or (2) to vote at any annual meeting other than the next annual meeting (or any adjournment thereof) to be held after the date on which the proxy statement and form of proxy are first sent or given to security holders. A person shall not be deemed to be a bona fide nominee and he shall not be named as such unless he has consented to being named in the proxy statement and to serve if elected.

(e) The proxy statement or form of proxy shall provide, subject to reasonable specified conditions, that the shares represented by the proxy will be voted and that where the person solicited specifies by means of a ballot provided pursuant to paragraph (b) a choice with respect to any matter to be acted upon, the shares will be voted in accordance with the specifications so made.

Rule 14a-5. Presentation of Information in Proxy Statement

(a) The information included in the proxy statement shall be clearly presented and the statements made shall be divided into groups according to subject matter and the various groups of statements shall be preceded by appropriate headings. The order of items and sub-items in the schedule need not be followed. Where practicable and appropriate, the information shall be presented in tabular form. All amounts shall be stated in figures. Information required by more than one applicable item need not be repeated. No statement need be made in response to any item or sub-item which is inapplicable.

(b) Any information required to be included in the proxy statement as to terms of securities or other subject matter which from a standpoint of practical necessity must be determined in the future may be stated in terms of present knowledge and intention. To the extent practicable, the authority to be conferred concerning each such matter shall be confined within limits reasonably related to the need for discretionary authority. Subject to the foregoing, information which is not known to the persons on whose behalf the solicitation is to be made and which it is not reasonably within the power of such persons to ascertain or procure may be omitted, if a brief statement of the circumstances rendering such information unavailable is made.

(c) There may be omitted from the proxy statement any information contained in any other proxy soliciting material which has been furnished to each person solicited in connection with the same meeting or subject matter if a clear reference is made to the particular document containing such information.

(d) All printed proxy statements shall be in roman type at least as large and as legible as 10-point modern type, except that to the extent necessary for convenient presentation financial statements and other tabular data, but not the notes thereto, may be in roman type at least as large and as legible as 8-point modern type. All such type shall be leaded at least 2 points.

(e) All proxy statements shall disclose on the first page thereof the complete mailing address, including zip code, of the principal executive offices of the issuer and the approximate date on which the proxy statement and form of proxy are first sent or given to security holders.

(f) All proxy statements shall disclose, under an appropriate caption, the date by which proposals of security holders intended to be presented at the next annual meeting must be received by the issuer for inclusion in the issuer's proxy statement and form of proxy relating to that meeting, such date to be calculated in accordance with the provisions of rule 14a–8(a)(3)(i). If the date of the next annual meeting is subsequently advanced by more than 30 calendar days or delayed by more than 90 calendar days from the date of the annual meeting to which the proxy statement relates, the issuer shall, in a timely manner, inform security holders of such change, and the date by which proposals of security holders must be received, by any means reasonably calculated to so inform them.

Rule 14a–6. Material Required to Be Filed

(a) Five preliminary copies of the proxy statement and form of proxy and any other soliciting material to be furnished to security holders concurrently therewith shall be filed with the Commission at least 10 days prior to the date definitive copies of such material are first sent or given to security holders, or such shorter period prior to that date as the Commission may authorize upon a showing of good cause therefor. In computing the 10-day period the filing date of the preliminary material is to be counted as the first day and the 11th day is the date on which definitive material may be mailed to security holders.

Note. The officials responsible for the preparation of the preliminary material should make every effort to verify the accuracy and completeness of the information required by the applicable rules. The preliminary material should be filed with the Commission at the earliest practicable date. It should be accompanied by a letter, over the signature of an officer of the company or its counsel, stating whether the current preliminary material merely reflects an updating of the prior year's material (e. g., changes in the board of directors or nominees for election to the board) or includes changes of a material nature. All changes from the previously filed material should be identified in an accompanying marked copy of the proxy statement. If a change is material, the letter should include any explanatory comment which may be of assistance in the expeditious processing of the material.

(b) Five preliminary copies of any additional soliciting material, relating to the same meeting or subject matter, furnished to security holders subsequent to the proxy statement shall be filed with the Commission at least 2 days (exclusive of Saturdays, Sundays, and holidays) prior to the date copies of such material are first sent or given to security holders, or such shorter period prior to such date as the Commission may authorize upon a showing of good cause therefor.

(c) Eight definitive copies of the proxy statement, form of proxy and all other soliciting material, in the form in which such material is furnished to security holders, shall be filed with, or mailed for filing to, the Commission not later than the date such material is first sent or given to any security holders. Three copies of such material shall at the same time be filed with, or mailed for filing to, each national securities exchange upon which any class of securities of the issuer is listed and registered.

Note. The definitive material filed with the Commission should be accompanied by a letter indicating any material changes which have been made therein, other than those made in response to the staff's comments and, whenever possible, should also be accompanied by a marked copy of the definitive material indicating all changes made therein.

(d) If the solicitation is to be made in whole or in part by personal solicitation, three copies of all written instructions or other material which discusses or reviews, or comments upon the merits of, any matter to be acted upon and which is furnished to the individuals making the actual solicitation for their use directly or indirectly in connection with the solicitation shall be filed with the Commission by the person on whose behalf the solicitation is made at least five days prior to the date copies of such material are first sent or given to such individuals, or such shorter period prior to that date as the Commission may authorize upon a showing of good cause therefor.

(e) All copies of material filed pursuant to paragraph (a) or (b) of this section shall be clearly marked "Preliminary Copies" shall be for the information of the Commission only and shall not be deemed available for public inspection before definitive material has been filed with the Commission except that such material may be disclosed to any department or agency of the United States Government and to the Congress and the Commission may make such inquiries or investigation in regard to the material as may be necessary for an adequate review thereof by the Commission. All preliminary material filed pursuant to paragraph (a) or (b) of this section shall be accompanied by a statement of the date on which definitive copies thereof filed pursuant to paragraph (c) of this section are intended to be released to security holders. All definitive material filed pursuant to paragraph (c) of this section shall be accompanied by a statement of the date on which copies of such material have been released to security holders, or, if not released, the date on which copies thereof are intended to be released. All material filed pursuant to paragraph (d) of this section shall be accompanied by a statement of the date on which copies thereof are intended to be released to the individuals who will make the actual solicitation.

(f) Copies of replies to inquiries from security holders requesting further information and copies of communications which do no more than request that forms of proxy theretofore solicited

be signed and returned need not be filed pursuant to this section.

Note. Where preliminary copies of material are filed with the Commission pursuant to this rule, the printing of definitive copies for distribution to security holders should be deferred until the comments of the Commission's staff have been received and considered.

(g) Notwithstanding the provisions of paragraphs (a) and (b) of this section and of Rule 14a–11(e), copies of soliciting material in the form of speeches, press releases and radio or television scripts may, but need not, be filed with the Commission prior to use or publication. Definitive copies, however, shall be filed with or mailed for filing to the Commission as required by paragraph (c) of this section not later than the date such material is used or published. The provisions of paragraphs (a) and (b) of this section and of Rule 14a–11(e) shall apply, however, to any reprints or reproductions of all or any part of such material.

(h) Where any proxy statement, form of proxy or other material filed pursuant to this section is amended or revised, two of the copies of such amended or revised material filed pursuant to this section (or in the case of investment companies registered under the Investment Company Act of 1940, three of such copies) shall be marked to indicate clearly and precisely the changes effected therein. If the amendment or revision alters the text of the material the changes in such text shall be indicated by means of underscoring or in some other appropriate manner.

(i) At the time of filing the preliminary proxy solicitation material, the persons upon whose behalf the solicitation is made, other than companies registered under the Investment Company Act of 1940, or where an application or declaration under the Public Utility Holding Company Act of 1935 is involved, shall pay to the Commission the following applicable fee: (1) For preliminary proxy material which solicits proxies for election of directors or other business for which a stockholder vote is necessary, but apparently no controversy is involved, a fee of $125; (2) for proxy material where a contest as set forth in Rule 14a-11 is involved, a fee of $500 from each party to the controversy; and (3) for proxy material involving acquisitions or mergers, a fee of $1,000. Where both companies involved in the acquisition or merger must file proxy material with the Commission, each shall pay $500 of the fee. There shall be no refunds.

(j) Notwithstanding the foregoing provisions of this section, any proxy statement, form of proxy or other soliciting material included in a registration statement filed under the Securities Act of 1933 on Form S-14, or Form S-15, shall be deemed filed both for the purposes of that Act and for the purposes of this section, but separate copies of such material need not be furnished pursuant to this section nor shall any fee be required under paragraph (i) of this section. However, any additional soliciting material used after the effective date of the registration statement on Form S-14 or Form S-15 shall be filed in accordance with this section but separate copies of such material need not be filed as an amendment of such registration statement.

Rule 14a-7. Mailing Communications for Security Holders

If the issuer has made or intends to make any solicitation subject to Rules 14a-1 to 14a-10, the issuer shall perform such of the following acts as may be duly requested in writing with respect to the same subject matter or meeting by any security holder who is entitled to vote on such matter or to vote at such meeting and who shall defray the reasonable expenses to be incurred by the issuer in the performance of the act or acts requested.

(a) The issuer shall mail or otherwise furnish to such security holder the following information as promptly as practicable after the receipt of such request:

(1) A statement of the approximate number of holders of record of any class of securities, any of the holders of which have been or are to be solicited on behalf of the issuer, or any group of such holders which the security holder shall designate.

(2) If the issuer has made or intends to make, through bankers, brokers or other persons any solicitation of the beneficial owners of securities of any class, a statement of the approximate number of such beneficial owners, or any group of such owners which the security holder shall designate.

(3) An estimate of the cost of mailing a specified proxy statement, form of proxy or other communication to such holders, including insofar as known or reasonably available, the estimated handling and mailing costs of the bankers, brokers or other persons specified in subparagraph (2) of this paragraph.

(b)(1) Copies of any proxy statement, form of proxy or other communication furnished by the security holder shall be mailed by the issuer to such of the holders of record specified in paragraph (a)(1) of this section as the security holder shall designate. The issuer shall also mail to each banker, broker, or other person specified in paragraph (a)(2) of this section a sufficient number of copies of such proxy statement, form of proxy or other communication as will enable the banker, broker, or other person to furnish a copy thereof to each beneficial owner solicited or to be solicited through him.

(2) Any such material which is furnished by the security holder shall be mailed with reasonable promptness by the issuer after receipt of a tender of the material to be mailed of envelopes or other containers therefor and of postage or payment for postage. The issuer need not, however, mail any such material which relates to any matter to be acted upon at an annual meeting of security holders prior to the earlier of (i) a day corresponding to the first date on which the issuer proxy solicited material was released to security holders in connection with the last annual meeting of security holders, or (ii) the first day on which solicitation is made on behalf of the issuer. With respect to any such material which relates to any matter to be acted upon by security holders otherwise than at an annual meeting, such material need not be mailed prior to the first day on which solicitation is made on behalf of the issuer.

(3) The issuer shall not be responsible for such proxy statement, form of proxy or other communication.

(c) In lieu of performing the acts specified in paragraphs (a) and (b) of this section, the issuer may at its option, furnish promptly to such security holder a reasonably current list of the names and addresses of such of the holders of record specified in paragraph (a)(1) of this section as the security holder shall designate, and a list of the names and addresses of such of the bankers, brokers or other persons specified in paragraph (a)(2) of this section as the security holder shall designate together with a statement of the approximate number of beneficial owners solicited or to be solicited through each such banker, broker or other person and a schedule of the handling and mailing costs of each such banker, broker or other person if such schedule has been supplied to the issuer. The foregoing information shall be furnished promptly upon the request of the security holder or at daily or other reasonable intervals as it becomes available to the issuer.

Rule 14a–8. Proposals of Security Holders

(a) If any security holder of an issuer notifies the issuer of his intention to present a proposal for action at a forthcoming meeting of the issuer's security holders, the issuer shall set forth the proposal in its proxy statement and identify it in its form of proxy and provide means by which security holders can make the specification required by Rule 14a–4(b). Notwithstanding the foregoing, the issuer shall not be required to include the proposal in its proxy statement or form of proxy unless the security holder (hereinafter, the "proponent") has complied with the requirements of this paragraph and paragraphs (b) and (c) of this section:

(1) *Eligibility.* At the time he submits the proposal, the proponent shall be a record or beneficial owner of a security entitled to be voted at the meeting on his proposal, and he shall continue to own such security through the date on which the meeting is held. If the issuer requests documentary support for a proponent's claim that he is a beneficial owner of a voting security of the issuer, the proponent shall furnish appropri-

ate documentation within 10 business days after receiving the request. In the event the issuer includes the proponent's proposal in its proxy soliciting materials for the meeting and the proponent fails to comply with the requirement that he continuously be a voting security holder through the meeting date, the issuer shall not be required to include any proposals submitted by the proponent in its proxy soliciting materials for any meeting held in the following two calendar years.

(2) *Notice.* The proponent shall notify the issuer in writing of his intention to appear personally at the meeting to present his proposal for action. The proponent shall furnish the requisite notice at the time he submits the proposal, except that if he was unaware of the notice requirement at that time he shall comply with it within 10 business days after being informed of it by the issuer. If the proponent, after furnishing in good faith the notice required by this provision, subsequently determines that he will be unable to appear personally at the meeting, he shall arrange to have another security holder of the issuer present his proposal on his behalf at the meeting. In the event the proponent or his proxy fails, without good cause, to present the proposal for action at the meeting, the issuer shall not be required to include any proposals submitted by the proponent in its proxy soliciting materials for any meeting held in the following two calendar years.

(3) *Timeliness.* The proponent shall submit his proposal sufficiently far in advance of the meeting so that it is received by the issuer within the following time periods:

(i) *Annual Meetings.* A proposal to be presented at an annual meeting shall be received by the issuer at its principal executive offices not less than 90 days in advance of the date of the issuer's proxy statement released to security holders in connection with the previous year's annual meeting of security holders, except that if no annual meeting was held in the previous year or the date of the annual meeting has been changed by more than 30 calendar days from the date contemplated at the time of the previous year's proxy statement, a proposal shall be received by the issuer a reasonable time before the solicitation is made.

(ii) *Other Meetings.* A proposal to be presented at any meeting other than an annual meeting shall be received a reasonable time before the solicitation is made.

> **Note.** In order to curtail controversy as to the date on which a proposal was received by the management, it is suggested that proponents submit their proposals by Certified Mail-Return Receipt Requested.

(4) *Number and Length of Proposals.* The proponent may submit a maximum of two proposals of not more than 300 words each for inclusion in the issuer's proxy materials for a meeting of security holders. If the proponent fails to comply with either of these requirements, or if he fails to comply with the 200-word limit on supporting statements mentioned in paragraph (b) of this section, he shall be provided the opportunity by the issuer to reduce within 10 business days, the items submitted by him to the limits required by this rule.

(b) If the issuer opposes any proposal received from a proponent, it shall also, at the request of the proponent, include in its proxy statement a statement of the proponent of not more than 200 words in support of the proposal, which statement shall not include the name and address of the proponent. The statement and request of the proponent shall be furnished to the issuer at the time that the proposal is furnished, and the issuer shall not be responsible for such statement. The proxy statement shall also include either the name and address of the proponent or a statement that such information will be furnished by the issuer or by the Commission to any person, orally or in writing as requested, promptly upon the receipt of any oral or written request therefor. If the name and address of the proponent are omitted from the proxy statement, they shall be furnished to the Commission at the time of filing the management's preliminary proxy material pursuant to Rule 14a-6(a).

(c) The issuer may omit a proposal and any statement in support thereof from its proxy statement and form of proxy under any of the following circumstances:

(1) The proposal is, under the laws of the issuer's domicile, not a proper subject for action by security holders;

> **Note.** A proposal that may be improper under the applicable state law when framed as a mandate or directive may be proper when framed as a recommendation or request.

(2) If the proposal would, if implemented, require the issuer to violate any state law or federal law of the United States, or any law of any foreign jurisdiction, to which the issuer is subject, except that this provision shall not apply with respect to any foreign law compliance with which would be violative of any state law or federal law of the United States;

(3) If the proposal or the supporting statement is contrary to any of the Commission's proxy rules and regulations, including Rule 14a-9, which prohibits false or misleading statements in proxy soliciting materials;

(4) If the proposal relates to the enforcement of a personal claim or the redress of a personal grievance against the issuer, or any other person;

(5) If the proposal deals with a matter that is not significantly related to the issuer's business;

(6) If the proposal deals with a matter that is beyond the issuer's power to effectuate;

(7) If the proposal deals with a matter relating to the conduct of the ordinary business operations of the issuer;

(8) If the proposal relates to an election to office;

(9) If the proposal is counter to a proposal to be submitted by the issuer at the meeting;

(10) If the proposal has been rendered moot;

(11) If the proposal is substantially duplicative of a proposal previously submitted to the issuer by another proponent, which proposal will be included in the issuer's proxy materials for the meeting;

(12) If substantially the same proposal has previously been submitted to security holders in the issuer's proxy statement and form of proxy relating to any annual or special meeting of security holders held within the preceding

5 calendar years, it may be omitted from the issuer's proxy materials relating to any meeting of security holders held within 3 calendar years after the latest such previous submission: *Provided*, That—(i) If the proposal was submitted at only one meeting during such preceding period, it received less than 3 percent of the total number of votes cast in regard thereto; or

(ii) If the proposal was submitted at only two meetings during such preceding period, it received at the time of its second submission less than 6 percent of the total number of votes cast in regard thereto; or

(iii) If the proposal was submitted at three or more meetings during such preceding period, it received at the time of its latest submission less than 10 percent of the total number of votes cast in regard thereto; and

(13) If the proposal relates to specific amounts of cash or stock dividends.

(d) Whenever the issuer asserts, for any reason, that a proposal and any statement in support thereof received from a proponent may properly be omitted from its proxy statement and form of proxy, it shall file with the Commission, not later than 50 days prior to the date the preliminary copies of the proxy statement and form of proxy are filed pursuant to Rule 14a-6(a), or such shorter period prior to such date as the Commission or its staff may permit, five copies of the following items: (1) The proposal; (2) any statement in support thereof as received from the proponent; (3) a statement of the reasons why the issuer deems such omission to be proper in the particular case; and (4) where such reasons are based on matters of law, a supporting opinion of counsel. The issuer shall at the same time, if it has not already done so, notify the proponent of its intention to omit the proposal from its proxy statement and form of proxy and shall forward to him a copy of the statement of reasons why the management deems the omission of the proposal to be proper and a copy of such supporting opinion of counsel.

(e) If the issuer intends to include in the proxy statement a statement in opposition to a proposal received from a proponent, it shall, not later than ten calendar days prior to the date the preliminary copies of the proxy statement and form of proxy are filed pursuant to Rule 14a-6(a), or, in the event that the proposal must be revised to be includable, not later than five calendar days after receipt by the issuer of the revised proposal, promptly forward to the proponent a copy of the statement in opposition to the proposal.

In the event the proponent believes that the statement in opposition contains materially false or misleading statements within the meaning of Rule 14a-9 and the proponent wishes to bring this matter to the attention of the Commission, the proponent should promptly provide the staff with a letter setting forth the reasons for this view and at the same time promptly provide the issuer with a copy of such letter.

Rule 14a-9.   **False or Misleading Statements**

(a) No solicitation subject to this regulation shall be made by means of any proxy statement, form of proxy, notice of meeting or other communication, written or oral, containing any statement which, at the time and in the light of the circumstances under which it is made, is false or misleading with respect to any material fact, or which omits to state any material fact necessary in order to make the statements therein not false or misleading or necessary to correct any statement in any earlier communication with respect to the solicitation of a proxy for the same meeting or subject matter which has become false or misleading.

(b) The fact that a proxy statement, form of proxy or other soliciting material has been filed with or examined by the Commission shall not be deemed a finding by the Commission that such material is accurate or complete or not false or misleading, or that the Commission has passed upon the merits of or approved any statement contained therein or any matter to be acted upon by security holders. No representation contrary to the foregoing shall be made.

Note. The following are some examples of what, depending upon particular facts and circumstances, may be misleading within the meaning of this section:

(a) Predictions as to specific future market values.

(b) Material which directly or indirectly impugns character, integrity or personal reputation, or directly or indirectly makes charges concerning improper, illegal or immoral conduct or associations, without factual foundation.

(c) Failure to so identify a proxy statement, form of proxy and other soliciting material as to clearly distinguish it from the soliciting material of any other person or persons soliciting for the same meeting or subject matter.

(d) Claims made prior to a meeting regarding the results of a solicitation.

* * *

Rule 14a-10. Prohibition of Certain Solicitations

No person making a solicitation which is subject to Rules 14a-1 to 14a-10 shall solicit:

(a) any undated or post-dated proxy, or

(b) any proxy which provides that it shall be deemed to be dated as of any date subsequent to the date on which it is signed by the security holder.

Rule 14a-11. Special Provisions Applicable to Election Contests

(a) *Solicitations to which this section applies.* This section applies to any solicitation subject to Rules 14a-1 to 14a-11 by any person or group of persons for the purpose of opposing a solicitation subject to Rules 14a-1 to 14a-11 by any other person or group of persons with respect to the election or removal of directors at any annual or special meeting of security holders.

(b) *Participant or participant in a solicitation.* For purposes of this rule the terms "participant" and "participant in a solicitation" include the following:

(1) The issuer;

(2) Any director of the issuer, and any nominee for whose election as a director proxies are solicited;

(3) Any committee or group which solicits proxies, any member of such committee or group,

and any person whether or not named as a member who acting alone or with one or more other persons directly or indirectly takes the initiative, or engages, in organizing, directing, or arranging for the financing of, any such committee or group;

(4) Any person who finances or joins with another to finance the solicitation of proxies, except persons who contribute not more than $500 and who are not otherwise participants;

(5) Any person who lends money or furnishes credit or enters into any other arrangements, pursuant to any contract or understanding with a participant, for the purpose of financing or otherwise inducing the purchase, sale, holding or voting of securities of the issuer by any participant or other persons, in support of or in opposition to a participant; except that such terms do not include a bank, broker or dealer who, in the ordinary course of business, lends money or executes orders for the purchase or sale of securities and who is not otherwise a participant; and

(6) Any other person who solicits proxies. The foregoing terms do not, however, include (i) any person or organization retained or employed by a participant to solicit security holders and whose activities are limited to the performance of his duties in the course of such employment; (ii) any person who merely transmits proxy soliciting material or performs other ministerial or clerical duties; (iii) any person employed by a participant in the capacity of attorney, accountant, or advertising public relations or financial adviser, and whose activities are limited to the performance of his duties in the course of such employment; (iv) any person regularly employed as an officer or employee of the issuer or any of its subsidiaries who is not otherwise a participant; or (v) any officer or director of, or any person regularly employed by, any other participant, if such officer, director or employee is not otherwise a participant.

(c) *Filing of information required by Schedule 14B.* (1) No solicitation subject to this section shall be made by any person other than the issuer unless at least five business days prior thereto, or such shorter period as the Commission may authorize upon a showing of good cause therefor, there has been filed, with the Commission and with each national securities exchange upon which any security of the issuer is listed and registered, by or on behalf of each participant in such solicitation, a statement in triplicate containing the information specified by Schedule 14B.

(2) Within five business days after a solicitation subject to this section is made by the issuer, or such longer period as the Commission may authorize upon a showing of good cause therefor, there shall be filed, with the Commission and with each national securities exchange upon which any security of the issuer is listed and registered, by or on behalf of each participant in such a solicitation, other than the issuer, a statement in triplicate containing the information specified by Schedule 14B.

(3) If any solicitation on behalf of the issuer or any other person has been made, or if proxy material is ready for distribution, prior to a solicitation subject to this section in opposition thereto, a statement in triplicate containing the information specified in Schedule 14B shall be filed by or on behalf of each participant in such prior solicitation, other than the issuer, as soon as reasonably practicable after the commencement of the solicitation in opposition thereto, with the Commission and with each national securities exchange on which any security of the issuer is listed and registered.

(4) If, subsequent to the filing of the statements required by paragraphs (c)(1), (2), and (3) of this section, additional persons become participants in a solicitation subject to this section, there shall be filed, with the Commission and each appropriate exchange, by or on behalf of each such person a statement in duplicate containing the information specified by Schedule 14B, within three business days after such person becomes a participant, or such longer period as the Commission may authorize upon a showing of good cause therefor.

(5) If any material change occurs in the facts reported in any statement filed by or on behalf of any participant, and appropriate amendment to such statement shall be filed promptly with the Commission and each appropriate exchange.

(6) Each statement and amendment thereto filed pursuant to this paragraph shall be part of the official public files of the Commission and for purposes of this regulation shall be deemed a communication subject to the provisions of Rule 14a-9.

(d) *Solicitations prior to furnishing required written proxy statement.* Notwithstanding the provisions of Rule 14a-3(a), a solicitation subject to this section may be made prior to furnishing security holders a written proxy statement containing the information specified in Schedule 14A with respect to such solicitation: *Provided, That—*

(1) The statements required by paragraph (c) of this section are filed by or on behalf of each participant in such solicitation.

(2) No form of proxy is furnished to security holders prior to the time the written proxy statement required by Rule 14a-3(a) is furnished to security holders: *Provided, however, That* this paragraph (d)(2) shall not apply where a proxy statement then meeting the requirements of Schedule 14A has been furnished to security holders by or on behalf of the person making the solicitation.

(3) At least the information specified in Items 2(a) and 3(a) of the statement required by paragraph (c) of this section to be filed by each participant, or an appropriate summary thereof, is included in each communication sent or given to security holders in connection with the solicitation.

(4) A written proxy statement meeting the requirements of this regulation is sent or given to security holders at the earliest practicable date.

(e) *Solicitations prior to furnishing required written proxy statement; filing requirements.* Three copies of any soliciting material proposed to be sent or given to security holders prior to the furnishing of the written proxy statement required by Rule 14a-3(a) shall be filed with the Commission in preliminary form, at least five business days prior to the date definitive copies of such material are first sent or given to security holders, or such shorter period as the Commission may authorize upon a showing of good cause therefor.

(f) *Application of this section to annual report.* Notwithstanding the provisions of Rule 14a–3(b) and (c) three copies of any portion of the annual report referred to in Rule 14a–3(b) which comments upon or refers to any solicitation subject to this section, or to any participant in any such solicitation, other than the solicitation by the issuer, shall be filed with the Commission as proxy material subject to Rule 14a–1 to 14a–11. Such portion of the annual report shall be filed with the Commission in preliminary form at least five business days prior to the date copies of the report are first sent or given to security holders.

(g) *Application of Rule 14a–6.* The provisions of paragraphs (c), (d), (e), (f) and (g) of Rule 14a–6 shall apply to the extent pertinent, to soliciting material subject to paragraphs (e) and (f) of this section.

(h) *Use of reprints or reproductions.* In any solicitation subject to this section, soliciting material which includes, in whole or part, any reprints or reproductions of any previously published material shall:

(1) State the name of the author and publication, the date of prior publication, and identify any person who is quoted without being named in the previously published material.

(2) Except in the case of a public official document or statement, state whether or not the consent of the author and publication has been obtained to the use of the previously published material as proxy soliciting material.

(3) If any participant using the previously published material, or anyone on his behalf, paid, directly or indirectly, for the preparation or prior publication of the previously published material, or has made or proposes to make any payments or give any other consideration in connection with the publication or republication of such material, state the circumstances.

Rule 14a–12. Solicitation Prior to Furnishing Required Proxy Statement

(a) Notwithstanding the provisions of Rule 14a–3(a), a solicitation (other than one subject

to Rule 14a–11) may be made prior to furnishing security holders a written proxy statement meeting the requirements of Rule 14a–3(a) if—

(1) The solicitation is made in opposition to a prior solicitation or an invitation for tenders or other publicized activity, which if successful, could reasonably have the effect of defeating the action proposed to be taken at the meeting;

(2) No form of proxy is furnished to security holders prior to the time the written proxy statement required by Rule 14a–3(a) is furnished to security holders: *Provided, however,* That this paragraph (a)(2) shall not apply where a proxy statement then meeting the requirements of Rule 14a–3(a) has been furnished to security holders by or on behalf of the person making the solicitation;

(3) The identity of the person or persons by or on whose behalf the solicitation is made and a description of their interests direct or indirect, by security holdings or otherwise, are set forth in each communication sent or given to security holders in connection with the solicitation, and

(4) A written proxy statement meeting the requirements of this regulation is sent or given to security holders at the earliest practicable date.

(b) Three copies of any soliciting material proposed to be sent or given to security holders prior to the furnishing of the written proxy statement required by Rule 14a–3(a) shall be filed with the Commission in preliminary form at least 5 business days prior to the date definitive copies of such material are first sent or given to security holders, or such shorter period as the Commission may authorize upon a showing of good cause therefor.

Schedule 14A. Information Required in Proxy Statement

Notes. A. Where any item calls for information with respect to any matter to be acted upon and such matter involves other matters with respect to which information is called for by other items of this schedule, the information called for by such other items shall also be given. For example, a merger, consolidation, or acquisition or disposition of assets specified in Item 14, in which the security holders to be solicited will become or continue to be security holders of the surviving or acquiring company, shall be deemed to involve the election of directors if any person who will serve as a director of such company was not elected to such office by security holders of the issuer of the securities in respect of which proxies are to be solicited. In such case, Items 6 and 7 shall be answered with respect to each such person who will serve as a director of the surviving or acquiring company.

B. Where any item calls for information with respect to any matter to be acted upon at the meeting, such item need be answered in the issuer's soliciting material only with respect to proposals to be made by or on behalf of the issuer.

C. Except as otherwise specifically provided, where any item calls for information for a specified period in regard to directors, officers or other persons holding specified positions or relationships, the information shall be given in regard to any person who held any of the specified positions or relationships at any time during the period. However, information need not be included for any portion of the period during which such person did not hold any such position or relationship provided a statement to that effect is made.

Item 1.   Revocability of Proxy

State whether or not the person giving the proxy has the power to revoke it. If the right of revocation before the proxy is exercised is limited or is subject to compliance with any formal procedure, briefly describe such limitation or procedure.

Item 2.   Dissenters' Rights of Appraisal

Outline briefly the rights of appraisal or similar rights of dissenters with respect to any matter to be acted upon and indicate any statutory procedure required to be followed by dissenting security holders in order to perfect such rights. Where such rights may be exercised only within a limited time after the date of adoption of a proposal, the filing of a charter amendment or other similar act, state whether the persons solicited will be notified of such date.

Instruction. Indicate whether a security holder's failure to vote against a proposal will constitute a waiver of his appraisal or similar rights and whether a vote against a proposal will be deemed to satisfy any notice requirements under State law with respect to appraisal rights. If the State law is unclear, state what position will be taken in regard to these matters.

Item 3.   Persons Making the Solicitation

(a) *Solicitations not subject to Rule 14a–11* (1) If the solicitation is made by the issuer, so state. Give the name of any director of the issuer who has informed the issuer in writing that he intends to oppose any action intended to be taken by the issuer and indicate the action which he intends to oppose.

(2) If the solicitation is made otherwise than by the issuer, so state and give the names of the persons by whom and on whose behalf it is made.

(3) If the solicitation is to be made otherwise than by the use of the mails, describe the methods to be employed. If the solicitation is to be made by specially engaged employees or paid solicitors, state (i) the material features of any contract or arrangement for such solicitation and identify the parties, and (ii) the cost or anticipated cost thereof.

(4) State the names of the persons by whom the cost of solicitation has been or will be borne, directly or indirectly.

(b) *Solicitations subject to Rule 14a–11.* (1) State by whom the solicitation is made and describe the methods employed and to be employed to solicit security holders.

(2) If regular employees of the issuer or any other participant in a solicitation have been or are to be employed to solicit security holders, describe the class or classes of employees to be so employed, and the manner and nature of their employment for such purpose.

(3) If specially engaged employees, representatives or other persons have been or are to be employed to solicit security holders, state (i) the material features of any contract or arrangement for such solicitation and identify the parties (ii) the cost or anticipated cost thereof, and (iii) the approximate number of such employees or employees of any other person (naming such other person) who will solicit security holders.

(4) State the total amount estimated to be spent and the total expenditures to date for, in furtherance of, or in connection with the solicitation of security holders.

(5) State by whom the cost of the solicitation will be borne. If such cost to be borne initially by any person other than the issuer, state whether reimbursement will be sought from the issuer, and, if so, whether the question of such reimbursement will be submitted to a vote of security holders.

(6) If any such solicitation is terminated pursuant to a settlement between the issuer and any other participant in such solicitation, describe the terms of such settlement, including the cost or anticipated cost thereof to the issuer.

Instructions. 1. With respect to solicitations subject to Rule 14a–11, costs and expenditures within the meaning of this item 3 shall include fees for attorneys, accountants, public relations or financial advisers, solicitors, advertising, printing, transportation, litigation and other costs incidental to the solicitation, except that the issuer may exclude the amount of such costs represented by the amount normally expended for a solicitation for an election of directors in the absence of a contest, and costs represented by salaries and wages of regular employees and officers, provided a statement to the effect is included in the proxy statement.

2. The information required pursuant to paragraph (6) of item 3(b) should be included in any amended or revised proxy statement or other soliciting materials relating to the same meeting or subject matter furnished to security holders by the issuer subsequent to the date of settlement.

Item 4. Interest of Certain Persons in Matters to be Acted Upon

(a) *Solicitations not subject to Rule 14a–11.* Describe briefly any substantial interest, direct or indirect, by security holdings or otherwise, of each of the following persons in any matter to be acted upon, other than elections to office:

(1) If the solicitation is made on behalf of issuer, each person who has been a director or officer of the issuer at any time since the beginning of the last fiscal year.

(2) If the solicitation is made otherwise than on behalf of issuer, each person on whose behalf the solicitation is made.

Any person who would be a participant in a solicitation for purposes of Rule 14a–11 as defined in paragraph (b)(3), (4), (5) and (6) thereof shall be deemed a person on whose behalf the solicitation is made for purposes of this paragraph (a).

(3) Each nominee for election as a director of the issuer.

(4) Each associate of the foregoing persons.

Instruction. Except in the case of a solicitation subject to this regulation made in opposition to another solicitation subject to this regulation, this sub-item (a) shall not apply to any interest arising from the ownership of securities of the issuer where the security holder receives no extra or special benefit not shared on a pro rata basis by all other holders of the same class.

(b) *Solicitations subject to Rule 14a–11.* (1) Describe briefly any substantial interest, direct or indirect, by security holdings or otherwise, of each participant as defined in Rule 14a–11(b)(2), (3), (4), (5) and (6), in any matter to be acted upon at the meeting, and include with respect to each participant the information, or a fair and adequate summary thereof, required by Items 2(a), 2(d), 3, 4(b) and 4(c) of Schedule 14B.

(2) With respect to any person, other than a director or officer of the issuer acting solely in that capacity, who is a party to an arrangement or understanding pursuant to which a nominee for election as director is proposed to be elected, describe any substantial interest, direct or indirect, by security holdings or otherwise, that he has in any matter to be acted upon at the meeting, and furnish the information called for by Item 4(b) and (c) of Schedule 14B.

Item 5. Voting Securities and Principal Holders Thereof

(a) State as to each class of voting securities of the issuer entitled to be voted at the meeting, the number of shares outstanding and the number of votes to which each class is entitled.

(b) Give the date as of which the record of security holders entitled to vote at the meeting will be determined. If the right to vote is not limited to security holders of record on that date, indicate the conditions under which other security holders may be entitled to vote.

(c) If action is to be taken with respect to the election of directors and if the persons solicited have cumulative voting rights: (1) Make a statement that they have such rights, (2) briefly describe such rights, (3) state briefly the conditions precedent to the exercise thereof, and (4) if discretionary authority to cumulate votes is solicited, so indicate.

(d) Furnish the information required by Item 403(a) of Regulation S–K, to the extent known by the persons on whose behalf the solicitation is made.

(e) Furnish the information required by Item 403(b) of Regulation S–K.

(f) If, to the knowledge of the persons on whose behalf the solicitation is made, a change in control of the issuer has occurred since the beginning of its last fiscal year, state the name of the person(s) who acquired such control, the amount and the source of the consideration used by such person or persons; the basis of the control, the date and a description of the transaction(s) which resulted in the change of control and the percentage of voting securities of the issuers now beneficially owned directly or indirectly by the person(s) who acquired control; and the identity of the person(s) from whom control was assumed. If the source of all or any part of the consideration used is a loan made in the ordinary course of business by a bank as defined by section 3(a)(6) of the Act, the identity of such bank shall be omitted provided a request for confidentiality has been made pursuant to section 13(d)(1)(B) of the Act by the person(s) who acquired control. In lieu thereof, the material shall indicate that the identity of the bank has been so omitted and filed separately with the Commission.

Instructions. 1. State the terms of any loans or pledges obtained by the new control group for the purpose of acquiring control, and the names of the lenders or pledgees.

2. Any arrangements or understandings among members of both the former and new control groups and their associates with respect to election of directors or other matters should be described.

(g) Furnish the information required by Item 403(c) of Regulation S–K.

Item 6. Directors and Executive Officers

If action is to be taken with respect to election of directors, furnish the following information, in tabular form to the extent practicable, with respect to each person nominated for election as a director and each person whose term of office will continue after the meeting. However, if the solicitation is made on behalf of persons other than the issuer, the information required need be furnished only as to nominees of the persons making the solicitation.

(a) The information required by Item 401 of Requisition S–K.

(b) With respect to issuers other than investment companies registered under the Investment Company Act of 1940, describe any of the following relationships which exist:

(1) If the nominee or director has during the past five years had a principal occupation or employment with any of the issuer's parents, subsidiaries or other affiliates.

(2) If the nominee or director is related to an executive officer of any of the issuer's parents, subsidiaries or other affiliates by blood, marriage or adoption (except relationships more remote than first cousin);

(3) If the nominee or director is, or has within the last two full fiscal years been, an officer, directors or employee of, or owns, or has within the last two full fiscal years owned, directly or indirectly, in excess of 1 percent equity interest in any firm, corporation or other business or professional entity:

(i) Which has made payments to the issuer or its subsidiaries for property or services during the issuer's last full fiscal year in excess of 1 percent of the issuer's consolidated gross revenues for its last full fiscal year;

(ii) Which proposes to make payments to the issuer or its subsidiaries for property or services during the current fiscal year in excess of 1 percent of the issuer's consolidated gross revenues for its last full fiscal year;

(iii) To which the issuer or its subsidiaries was indebted at any time during the issuer's last fiscal year in an aggregate amount in excess of 1 percent of the issuer's total consolidated assets at the end of such fiscal year, or $5,000,000, whichever is less;

(iv) To which the issuer or its subsidiaries has made payments for property or services during such entity's last fiscal year in excess of 1 percent of such entity's consolidated gross revenues for its last full fiscal year;

(v) To which the issuer or its subsidiaries proposes to make payments for property or services during such entity's current fiscal year in excess of 1 percent of such entity's consolidated gross revenues for its last full fiscal year;

(vi) In order to determine whether payments made or proposed to be made exceed 1 percent of the consolidated gross revenues of any entity other than the issuer for such entity's last full fiscal year, it is appropriate to rely on information provided by the nominee or director;

(vii) In calculating payments for property and services the following may be excluded:

(A) Payments where the rates or charges involved in the transaction are determined by competitive bids, or the transaction involves the rendering of services as a public utility at rates or charges fixed in conformity with law or governmental authority;

(B) Payments which arise solely from the ownership of securities of the issuer and no extra or special benefit not shared on a pro rata basis by all holders of the class of securities is received;

(viii) In calculating indebtedness for purposes of subparagraph (iii) above, debt securities which have been publicly offered, admitted to trading on a national securities exchange, or quoted on the automated quotation system of a registered securities association may be excluded.

(4) That the nominee or director is a member or employee of, or is associated with, a law firm which the issuer has retained in the last two full fiscal years or proposes to retain in the current fiscal year;

(5) That the nominee or director is a director, partner, officer or employee of any investment banking firm which has performed services for the issuer other than as a participating underwriter in a syndicate in the last two full fiscal years or which the issuer proposes to have performed services in the current year; or

(6) That the nominee or director is a control person of the issuer (other than solely as a director of the issuer).

(7) In addition, the issuer should disclose any other relationships it is aware of between the director or nominee and issuer or its management which are substantially similar in nature and scope to those relationships listed above.

> **Note.** In the Commission's view, where significant business or personal relationships exist between the director or nominee and the issuer or its management, including, but not limited to, those as to which disclosure would be required pursuant to item 6(b), characterization of a director or nominee by any "label" connoting a lack of relationship to the issuer and its management may be materially misleading.

(c) With respect to investment companies registered under the Investment Company Act of 1940, indicate by an asterisk any nominee or director who is or would be an "interested person" within the meaning of section 2(a)(19) of the Investment Company Act of 1940 and briefly describe the relationships by reason of which such person is deemed an "interested person."

(d)(1) State whether or not the issuer has standing audit, nominating and compensation committees of the Board of Directors, or committees performing similar functions. If the issuer has such committees, however designated, identify each committee member, state the number of committee meetings held by each such committee during the last fiscal year and describe briefly the functions performed by such committees. In the case of investment companies registered under the Investment Company Act of 1940, indicate by an asterisk whether that member is an "interested person" as defined in section 2(a)(19) of that Act. Information concerning compensation committees is not required of registered investment companies whose management functions are performed by external managers.

(2) If the issuer has a nominating or similar committee, state whether the committee will consider nominees recommended by shareholders and, if so, describe the procedures to be followed by shareholders in submitting such recommendations.

(e) State the total number of meetings of the board of directors (including regularly scheduled and special meetings) which were held during the last full fiscal year. Name each incumbent director who during the last full fiscal year attended fewer than 75 percent of the aggregate of (1) the total number of meetings of the board of directors (held during the period for which he has been a director) and (2) the total number of meetings held by all committees of the board on which he served (during the periods that he served).

(f) If a director has resigned or declined to stand for re-election to the board of directors since the date of the last annual meeting of shareholders because of a disagreement with the issuer on any matter relating to the issuer's operations, policies or practices, and if the director has furnished the issuer with a letter describing such disagreement and requesting that the matter be disclosed, the issuer shall state the date of resignation or declination to stand for re-election and summarize the director's description of the disagreement.

If the issuer believes that the description provided by the director is incorrect or incomplete, it may include a brief statement presenting its views of the disagreement.

(g) With respect to those classes of voting stock which participated in the election of directors at the most recent meeting at which directors were elected:

(1) State in an introductory paragraph the percentage of shares present at the meeting and voting or withholding authority to vote in the election of directors; and (2) disclose in tabular format, following such introductory paragraph, the percentage of total shares cast for and withheld from the vote for or, where applicable, cast against, each nominee, which, respectively, were voted for and withheld from the vote for, or voted against, such nominee. When groups of classes or series of classes voted together in the election of a director or directors, they shall be treated as a single class for the purpose of the preceding sentence.

Instructions. 1. Calculate the percentage of shares present at the meeting and voting or withholding authority to vote in the election of directors, referred to in paragraph g(1), by dividing the total shares cast for and withheld from the vote for or, where applicable, voted against, the director in respect of whom the highest aggregate number of shares was cast by the total number of shares outstanding which were eligible to vote as of the record date for the meeting.

2. No information need be given in response to item 6(g) unless, with respect to any class of voting stock (or group of classes which voted together), 5% or more of the total shares cast for and withheld from the vote for or, where applicable, cast against any nominee were withheld from the vote for or cast against such nominee.

3. If an issuer elects less than the entire board of directors annually, disclosure is required as to all directors if 5% or more of the total shares cast for and withheld from, the vote for, or, where applicable, cast against any incumbent director were withheld from, or cast against the vote for such director at the meeting at which he was most recently elected.

4. No information need be given in response to item 6(g) if the issuer has previously furnished to its security holders a report of the results of the most recent meeting of security holders at which directors were elected which includes: (1) a description of each matter voted upon at the meeting and a statement of the percentage of the shares voting which were voted for and against each such matter; and (2) the information which would be called for by this item 6(g).

If an issuer has previously furnished such results to its security holders, this fact should be set forth in the issuer's cover letter accompanying the filing of preliminary proxy materials with the Commission.

Item 7.   Remuneration of Directors and Executive Officers

(See Note C at the beginning of Schedule 14A.)

Furnish the information required by Item 402, and Instruction 4 to Item 103 of Regulation S–K, if action is to be taken with regard to (i) the election of directors, (ii) any bonus, profit sharing or other remuneration plan, contract or arrangement in which any director, nominee for election as a director, or officer of the issuer will participate, (iii) any pension or retirement plan in which any such person will participate or (iv) the granting or extension to any such person of any options, warrants or rights to purchase any securities, other than warrants or rights issued to security holders as such, on a pro rata basis. However, if the solicitation is made on behalf of persons other than the issuer, the information required need be furnished only as to nominee of the persons making the solicitation and associates of such nominees.

Item 8.   Relationship with Independent Public Accountants

If the solicitation is made on behalf of the issuer and relates to an annual meeting of security holders at which directors are to be elected, or financial statements are included pursuant to Item 15, furnish the following information describing the issuer's relationship with its independent public accountants:

(a) The name of the principal accountant selected or being recommended to shareholders for election, approval or ratification for the current year. If no accountant has been selected or recommended, so state and briefly describe the reasons therefor.

(b) The name of the principal accountant for the fiscal year most recently completed if different from the accountant selected or recommended for the current year or if no accountant has yet been selected or recommended for the current year.

(c) If a change or changes in accountants have taken place since the date of the proxy statement for the most recent annual meeting of shareholders, and if in connection with such change(s) a disagreement between the accountant and issuer has been reported or was required to be reported on Form 8–K or in the accountant's letter filed as an exhibit thereto, the disagreement shall be described. Prior to filing the preliminary proxy materials with the Commission which contains or amends such description, the issuer shall furnish the description of the disagreement to any accountant with whom a disagreement has been or was required to be reported. If that accountant believes that the description of the disagreement is incorrect or incomplete, he may include a brief statement, ordinarily expected not to exceed 200 words, in the proxy statement presenting his view of the disagreement. This statement shall be submitted to the issuer within ten business days of the date the accountant receives the issuer's description.

(d) The proxy statement shall indicate whether or not representatives of the principal accountants for the current year and for the most recently completed fiscal year are expected to be present at the stockholders' meeting with the opportunity to make a statement if they desire to do so and whether or not such representatives are expected to be available to respond to appropriate questions.

(e) If any change in accountants has taken place since the date of the proxy statement for the most recent annual meeting of shareholders, state whether such change was recommended or approved by:

(1) Any audit or similar committee of the Board of Directors, if the issuer has such a committee; or

(2) The Board of Directors, if the issuer has no such committee.

Item 9.   Bonus, Profit Sharing and Other Remuneration Plans

If action is to be taken with respect to any bonus, profit sharing or other remuneration plan, furnish the following information:

(a) Describe briefly the material features of the plan, identify each class of persons who will participate therein, indicate the approximate number of persons in each such class and state the basis of such participation.

(b) State separately the amounts which would have been distributable under the plan during the last fiscal year of the issuer (1) to directors and officers and (2) to employees if the plan had been in effect.

(c) State the name and position with the issuer of each person specified in Item 402(a) of Regulation S–K, who will participate in the plan and the amount which each such person would have received under the plan for the last fiscal year of the issuer if the plan had been in effect.

(d) Furnish such information, in addition to that required by this item and Item 402 of Regulation S–K, as may be necessary to describe adequately the provisions already made pursuant to all bonus, profit sharing, pension, retirement, stock option, stock purchase, deferred compensation, or other remuneration or incentive plans, now in effect or in effect within the past five years for (i) each director or officer named in answer to Item 402(a) of Regulation S–K, who may participate in the plan to be acted upon, (ii) all present directors and officers of the issuer as a group, if any director or officer may participate in the plan and (iii) all employees, if employees may participate in the plan.

(e) If the plan to be acted upon can be amended otherwise than by a vote of stockholders, to increase the cost thereof to the issuer or to alter the allocation of the benefits as between the groups specified in (b), state the nature of the amendments which can be so made.

Instructions. 1. The term "plan" as used in the item means any plan as defined in Instruction 7 to Item 402(a) of Regulation S–K.

2. If action is to be taken with respect to the amendment or modification of an existing plan, the item shall be answered with respect to the plan as proposed to be amended or modified and shall indicate any material differences from the existing plan.

3. The following instructions shall apply to paragraph (d):

(a) Information need only be given with respect to benefits received or set aside within the past 5 years.

(b) Information need not be included as to payments made for, or benefits to be received from, group life or accident insurance, group hospitalization or similar group payments or benefits.

(c) If action is to be taken with respect to any plan in which directors or officers may participate, the information called for in Item 402(d)(1) and (2) of Regulation S–K, shall be furnished for the last five fiscal years of the issuer and any period subsequent to the end of the latest such fiscal year, in aggregate amounts for the entire period for each such person and group. If any named person, or any other director or officer, purchased securities through the exercise of options during such period, state the aggregate amount of securities of that class sold during the period by such named person and by such named person and such other directors and officers as a group. The information called for by this Instruction 3(c) is in lieu of the information since the beginning of the issuer's last fiscal year called for by Item 402(d)(1) and (2) of Regulation S–K. If employees may participate in the plan to be acted upon, state the aggregate amount of securities called for by all options granted to employees during the five-year period and, if the options were other than "restricted" or "qualified" stock options or options granted pursuant to an "employee stock purchase plan", as the quoted terms are defined in sections 422 through 424 of the Internal Revenue Code, state that fact and the weighted average option price per share. The information called for by this instruction may be furnished in the form of the table illustrated in Item 402 of Regulation S–K.

4. If the plan to be acted upon is set forth in a written document, three copies thereof shall be filed with the Commission at the time preliminary copies of the proxy statement and form of proxy are filed pursuant to paragraph (a) of Rule 14a–6.

Item 10. Pension and Retirement Plans

If action is to be taken with respect to any pension or retirement plan, furnish the following information:

(a) Describe briefly the material features of the plan, identify each class of persons who will be entitled to participate therein, indicate the approximate number of persons in each such class and state the basis of such participation.

(b) State (1) the approximate total amount necessary to fund the plan with respect to past services, the period over which such amount is to be paid and the estimated annual payments necessary to pay the total amount over such period, (2) the estimated annual payment to be made with respect to current services and (3) the amount of such annual payments to be made for the benefit of (i) directors and officers and (ii) employees.

(c) State (1) the name and position with the issuer of each person specified in Item 402(a) of Regulation S–K, who will be entitled to participate in the plan, (2) the amount which would have been paid or set aside by the issuer and its subsidiaries for the benefit of such person for the last fiscal year of the issuer if the plan had been in effect, and (3) the amount of the annual benefit estimated to be payable to such person in the event of retirement at normal retirement date.

(d) Furnish such information, in addition to that required by this item and Item 402 of Regulation S–K, as may be necessary to describe adequately the provisions already made pursuant to all bonus, profit sharing, pension, retirement, stock option, stock purchase, deferred compensation or other remuneration or incentive plans, now in effect or in effect within the past five years, for (i) each director or officer named in answer to Item 402(a) of Regulation S–K, who may participate in the plan to be acted upon; (ii) all present directors and officers of the issuer as a group, if any director or officer may participate in the plan; and (iii) all employees, if employees may participate in the plan.

(e) If the plan to be acted upon can be amended otherwise than by a vote of stockholders to increase the cost thereof to the issuer or alter the allocation of the benefits as between the groups specified in (b)(3), state the nature of the amendments which can be so made.

Instructions. 1. The term "plan" as used in this item means any plan as defined in Instruction 7 to Item 402(a) of Regulation S–K. Instruction 2 to Item 9 shall apply to this item.

2. The information called for by paragraph (b)(3) or (c)(2) need not be given as to payments made on an actuarial basis pursuant to any group pension plan which provides for fixed benefits in the event of retirement at a specified age or after a specified number of years of service.

3. Instruction 3 to Item 9 shall apply to paragraph (d) of this item.

4. If the plan to be acted upon is set forth in a written document, three copies thereof shall be filed with the Commission at the time preliminary copies of the proxy statement and form of proxy are filed pursuant to paragraph (a) of Rule 14a–6.

Item 11. Options, Warrants or Rights

If action is to be taken with respect to the granting or extension of any options, warrants or rights to purchase securities of the issuer or any subsidiary, furnish the following information:

(a) State (i) the title and amount of securities called for or to be called for by such options, warrants or rights; (ii) the prices, expiration dates and other material conditions upon which the options, warrants or rights may be exercised; (iii) the consideration received or to be received by the issuer or subsidiary for the granting of extension of the options, warrants or rights; (iv) the market value of the securities called for or to be called for by the options, warrants or rights as of the latest practicable date, and (v) in the case of options, the Federal income tax consequences of the issuance and exercise of such options to the recipient and to the issuer.

(b) State separately the amount of options, warrants or rights received or to be received by the following persons, naming each such person: (i) each director or officer named in answer to Item 402(a) of Regulation S–K, (ii) each nominee for election as a director of the issuer, (iii) each associate of such directors, officers or nominees; and (iv) each other person who received or is to receive 5 percent of such options, warrants or rights. State also the total amount of such options, warrants or rights received or to be received by all directors and officers of the issuer as a group, without naming them.

(c) Furnish such information, in addition to that required by this item and Item 402 of Regulation S–K, as may be necessary to describe adequately the provisions already made pursuant to all bonus, profit sharing, pension, retirement, stock option, stock purchase, deferred compensation, or other remuneration or incentive plans, now in effect or in effect within the past five years, for (i) each director or officer named in answer to Item 402(a) of Regulation S–K, who may participate in the plan to be acted upon; (ii) all present directors and officers of the issuer as a group, if any director or officer may participate in the plan; and (iii) all employees, if employees may participate in the plan.

Instructions. 1. The term "plan" as used in this item means any plan as defined in Instruction 7 to Item 402(a) of Regulation S–K.

2. Paragraphs (b) and (c) do not apply to warrants or rights to be issued to security holders as such on a pro rata basis.

3. Instruction 3 to Item 9 shall apply to paragraph (c) of this item.

4. If the options described in answer to this item are issued pursuant to a plan which is set forth in a written document, three copies thereof shall be filed with the Commission at the time preliminary copies of the proxy statement and form of proxy are filed pursuant to paragraph (a) of Rule 14a–6.

> **Note.** The Commission should be informed, as supplemental information, when the proxy statement in preliminary form is filed, as to when the options, warrants or rights and the shares called for thereby will be registered under the Securities Act of 1933, or if such registration is not contemplated the section of the Act or rule of the Commission under which exemption from such registration is claimed and the facts relied upon to make the exemption available.

Item 12. Authorization or Issuance of Securities Otherwise Than for Exchange

If action is to be taken with respect to the authorization or issuance of any securities otherwise than for exchange for outstanding securities of the issuer, furnish the following information:

(a) State the title and amount of securities to be authorized or issued.

(b) Furnish a description of the securities such as would be required to be furnished in an application on the appropriate form for their registration on a national securities exchange. If the terms of the securities cannot be stated or estimated with respect to any or all of the securities to be authorized, because no offering thereof is contemplated in the proximate future, and if no further authorization by security holders for the issuance thereof is to be obtained, it should be stated that the terms of the securities to be authorized, including dividend or interest rates, conversion prices, voting rights, redemption prices, maturity dates, and similar matters will be determined by the board of directors. If the securities are additional shares of common stock of a class outstanding, the description may be omitted except for a statement of the preemptive rights, if any. Where the statutory provisions with respect to preemptive rights are so indefinite or complex that they cannot be stated in summarized form, it will suffice to make a statement in the form of an opinion of counsel as to the existence and extent of such rights.

(c) Describe briefly the transaction in which the securities are to be issued, including a statement as to (1) the nature and approximate amount of consideration received or to be received by the issuer, and (2) the approximate amount devoted to each purpose so far as determinable for which the net proceeds have been or are to be used. If it is impracticable to describe the transaction in which the securities are to be issued, state the reason, indicate the purpose of the authorization of the securities, and state whether further authorization for the issuance of the securities by a vote of security holders will be solicited prior to such issuance.

(d) If the securities are to be issued otherwise than in a general public offering for cash, state the reasons for the proposed authorization or issuance and the general effect thereof upon the rights of existing security holders.

Item 13. Modification or Exchange of Securities.

If action is to be taken with respect to the modification of any class of securities of the issuer, or the issuance or authorization for issuance of securities of the issuer in exchange for outstanding securities of the issuer, furnish the following information:

(a) If outstanding securities are to be modified, state the title and amount thereof. If securities are to be issued in exchange for outstanding securities, state the title and amount of securities to be so issued, the title and amount of outstanding securities to be exchanged therefor and the basis of the exchange.

(b) Describe any material differences between the outstanding securities and the modified or new securities in respect of any of the matters concerning which information would be required in the description of the securities in an application on the appropriate form for their registration on a national securities exchange.

(c) State the reasons for the proposed modification or exchange and the general effect thereof upon the rights of existing security holders.

(d) Furnish a brief statement as to arrears in dividends or as to defaults in principal or interest in respect to the outstanding securities which are to be modified or exchanged and such other information as may be appropriate in the particular case to disclose adequately the nature and effect of the proposed action.

(e) Outline briefly any other material features of the proposed modification or exchange. If the plan of proposed action is set forth in a written document, file copies thereof with the Commission in accordance with Rule 14a–6.

Instruction. If the existing security is presently listed and registered on a national securities exchange, state whether it is intended to apply for listing and registration of the new or reclassified security on such exchange or any other exchange. If it is not intended to make such application, state the effect of the termination of such listing and registration.

Item 14. Mergers, Consolidations, Acquisitions and Similar Matters

Furnish the following information if action is to be taken with respect to any plan for (i) the merger or consolidation of the issuer into or with any other person or of any other person into or with the issuer, (ii) the acquisition by the issuer or any of its security holders of securities of another issuer, (iii) the acquisition by the issuer of any other going business or of the assets thereof, (iv) the sale or other transfer of all or any substantial part of the assets of the issuer, or (v) the liquidation or dissolution of the issuer:

(a) Outline briefly the material features of the plan. State the reasons therefor and the general effect thereof upon the rights of existing security holders. If the plan is set forth in a written document, file three copies thereof with the Commission at the time preliminary copies of the proxy statement and form of proxy are filed pursuant to Rule 14a–6(a).

(b) Furnish the following information as to the issuer and each person which is to be merged into the issuer or into or with which the issuer is to be merged or consolidated or the business or assets of which are to be acquired or which is the issuer of securities to be acquired by the issuer in exchange for all or a substantial part of its assets or to be acquired by security holders of the issuer. What is required is information essential to an investor's appraisal of the action proposed to be taken.

(1) Describe briefly the business of such person. Information is to be given regarding pertinent matters such as the nature of the products or services, methods of production, markets, methods of distribution and the sources and supply of raw materials.

(2) State the location and describe the general character of the plants and other important physical properties of such person. The description is to be given from an economic and business standpoint, as distinguished from a legal standpoint.

(3) Furnish a brief statement as to dividends in arrears or defaults in principal or interest in respect of any securities of the issuer or of such person, and as to the effect of the plan thereon and such other information as may be appropriate in the particular case to disclose adequately the nature and effect of the proposed action.

(4) Furnish a tabulation in columnar form showing the existing and the pro forma capitalization.

(5) Furnish in columnar form for each of the last 5 fiscal years a historical summary of earnings and show per share amounts of net earnings, dividends declared for each year and book value per share at the end of the latest period.

(6) Furnish in columnar form for each of the last 5 fiscal years a combined pro forma summary of earnings, as appropriate in the circumstances, indicating the aggregate and per share earnings for each such year and the pro forma book value per share at the end of the latest period. If the transaction establishes a new basis of accounting for assets of any of the persons included therein, the pro forma summary of earnings shall be furnished only for the most recent fiscal year and interim period and shall reflect appropriate pro forma adjustments resulting from such new basis of accounting.

(7) To the extent material for the exercise of prudent judgment in regard to the matter to be acted upon, furnish the historical and pro forma earnings data sepcified in (5) and (6) above for interim periods of the current and prior fiscal years, if available.

(8) Furnish the information relating to the issuer's industry segments, classes of similar products or services, foreign and domestic operations and export sales required by paragraphs (b), (c) (1)(f) and (d) of Item 101 of Regulation S–K.

Instructions. 1. The earnings per share and dividends per share amounts required by paragraphs (b)(5) and (6) shall be presented in tabular form where appropriate and equated to a common basis in exchange transactions.

2. Include comparable data for any additional fiscal years necessary to keep the summary from being misleading. Subject to appropriate variation to conform to the nature of the business or the purpose of the offering, the following items shall be included: net sales or operating revenues; cost of goods sold or operating expenses (or gross profit); interest charges; income taxes; net income; special items, and net income and special items. The summary shall reflect the retroactive adjustment of any material items affecting the comparability of the results.

3. In connection with any unaudited summary for an interim period or periods between the end of the last fiscal year and the balance sheet date, and any comparable unaudited prior period, a statement shall be made that all adjustments necessary to a fair statement of the results for such interim period or periods have been included. In addition, there shall be furnished in such cases, as supplemental information but not as a part of the proxy statement, a letter describing in detail the nature and amount of any adjustments, other than normal recurring accruals, entering into the determination of the results shown.

4. Paragraph (b) shall not apply if the plan described in answer to paragraph (a) involves only the issuer and one or more of its totally held subsidiaries.

(c) As to each class of securities of the issuer, or of any person specified in paragraph (b), which is admitted to dealing on a national securities exchange or with respect to which a market otherwise exists, and which will be materially affected by the plan, state the high and low sale prices (or, in the absence of trading in a particular period, the range of the bid and asked prices) for each quarterly period within two years. This information may be omitted if the plan involves merely the liquidation or dissolution of the issuer.

Item 15. Financial Information

(a) If action is to be taken with respect to any matter specified in Item 12, 13 or 14 above, furnish the financial statements required by Regulation S–X. One copy of the definitive proxy statement filed with the Commission shall include a manually signed copy of the accountant's certificate. If financial statements required by Regulation S–X are furnished, also furnish the supplementary financial information required by Item 302 of Regulation S–K, information concerning disagreements with accountants on accounting and financial disclosure required by Item 304 of Regulation S–K, and management's discussion and analysis of financial condition and results of operations required by Item 303 of Regulation S–K.

(b) In the usual case, financial statements are deemed material to the exercise of prudent judgment where the matter to be acted upon is the authorization or issuance of a material amount of senior securities, but are not deemed material where the matter to be acted upon is the authorization or issuance of common stock otherwise than in an exchange, merger, consolidation, acquisition or similar transaction.

(c) Financial statements may be omitted with respect to a plan described in answer to Item 14(a) if the plan involves only the issuer and one or more of its totally-held subsidiaries.

(d) Notwithstanding the provisions of Regulation S–X, no schedules other than those prepared in accordance with Rules 12–15, 12–28 and 12–29 of that regulation need be furnished in the proxy statement.

(e) The proxy statement may incorporate by reference any financial statements contained in an annual report sent to security holder pursuant to Rule 14a–3 with respect to the same meeting as that to which the proxy statement relates, provided such financial statements substantially meet the requirements of this item.

(f) The financial statements of an acquired company not subject to the reporting provisions of the Exchange Act required to be furnished pursuant to Regulation S–X shall be certified to the extent practicable. However, if the proxy statement is to be included in a filing on Form S–14 and if any of the securities are to be reoffered to the public by any person who is deemed to be an underwriter thereof, within the meaning of Rule 145(c), the financial statements of the acquired business must be certified for three years or must comply with the requirements of Securities Act Release No. 4950.

Item 16. Acquisition or Disposition of Property

If action is to be taken with respect to the acquisition or disposition of any property, furnish the following information:

(a) Describe briefly the general character and location of the property.

(b) State the nature and amount of consideration to be paid or received by the issuer or any subsidiary. To the extent practicable, outline briefly the facts bearing upon the question of the fairness of the consideration.

(c) State the name and address of the transferer or transferee, as the case may be, and the nature of any material relationship of such person to the issuer or any affiliate of the issuer.

(d) Outline briefly any other material features of the contract or transaction.

Item 17. Restatement of Accounts

If action is to be taken with respect to the restatement of any asset, capital, or surplus account of the issuer, furnish the following information:

(a) State the nature of the restatement and the date as of which it is to be effective.

(b) Outline briefly the reasons for the restatement and for the selection of the particular effective date.

(c) State the name and amount of each account (including any reserve accounts) affected by the restatement and the effect of the restatement thereon. Tabular presentation of the amounts shall be made when appropriate, particularly in the case of recapitalizations.

(d) To the extent practicable, state whether and the extent, if any, to which, the restatement will, as of the date thereof, alter the amount available for distribution to the holders of equity securities.

Item 18. Action with Respect to Reports

If action is to be taken with respect to any report of the issuer or of its directors, officers or committees or any minutes of meeting of its stockholders, furnish the following information:

(a) State whether or not such action is to constitute approval or disapproval of any of the matters referred to in such reports or minutes.

(b) Identify each of such matters which it is intended will be approved or disapproved, and furnish the information required by the appropriate item or items of this schedule with respect to each such matter.

Item 19. Matters Not Required to be Submitted

If action is to be taken with respect to any matter which is not required to be submitted to a vote of security holders, state the nature of such matter, the reasons for submitting it to a vote of security holders and what action is intended to be taken by the issuer in the event of a negative vote on the matter by the security holders.

Item 20. Amendment of Charter, Bylaws of Other Documents

If action is to be taken with respect to any amendment of the issuer's charter, bylaws or other documents as to which information is not required above, state briefly the reasons for and the general effect of such amendment.

Instruction. Where the matter to be acted upon is the classification of directors, state whether vacancies which occur during the year may be filled by the board of directors to serve only until the next annual meeting or may be so filled for the remainder of the full term.

Item 21. Other Proposed Action

If action is to be taken with respect to any matter not specifically referred to above, describe briefly the substance of each such matter in substantially the same degree of detail as is required by Items 5 to 20, inclusive, above.

Item 22. Vote Required for Approval

As to each matter which is to be submitted to a vote of security holders, other than elections to office or the selection or approval of auditors, state the vote required for its approval.

Schedule 14B. Information to Be Included in Statements Filed by or on Behalf of a Participant (Other than the Issuer) pursuant to Rule 14a–11(c)

Instructions. 1. The item numbers and captions of the items shall be included but the text of the items may be omitted if the answers thereto are so prepared as to indicate clearly the coverage of the items. Answer every item. If an item is inapplicable or the answer is in the negative, so state. The information called for by Items 2(a) and 3(a) or a fair summary thereof is required to be included in all preliminary soliciting by Rule 14a–11(d)(3).

2. If the participant is a partnership, corporation, association or other business entity, the information called for by Item 2, 3 and 4(b) and (c) shall be given with respect to each partner, officer and director of such entity, and each person controlling such entity, who is not a participant.

Item 1. Issuer

State the name and address of the issuer.

Item 2. Identity and Background

(a) State the following:

(1) Your name and business address.

(2) Your present principal occupation or employment and the name, principal business and address of any corporation or other organization in which such employment is carried on.

(b) State the following:

(1) Your residence address.

(2) Information as to all material occupations, positions, offices or employments during the last ten years, giving starting and ending dates of each and the name, principal business and address of any business corporation or other business organization in which each such occupation, position, office or employment was carried on.

(c) State whether or not you are or have been a participant in any other proxy contest involving this or other issuers within the past ten years. If so, identify the principals, the subject matter and your relationship to the parties and the outcome.

(d) State whether or not, during the past ten years, you have been convicted in a criminal proceeding (excluding traffic violations or similar misdemeanors) and, if so, give dates, nature of conviction, name and location of court, and penalty imposed or other disposition of the case. A negative answer to this sub-item need not be included in the proxy statement or other proxy soliciting material.

Item 3. Interests in Securities of the Issuer

(a) State the amount of each class of securities of the issuer which you own beneficially, directly or indirectly.

(b) State the amount of each class of securities of the issuer which you own of record but not beneficially.

(c) State with respect to all securities of the issuer purchased or sold within the past 2 years, the dates on which they were purchased or sold and the amount purchased or sold on each such date.

(d) If any part of the purchase price or market value of any of the shares specified in paragraph (c) is represented by funds borrowed or otherwise obtained for the purpose of acquiring or holding such securities, so state and indicate the amount of the indebtedness as of the latest practicable date. If such funds were borrowed or obtained otherwise than pursuant to a margin account or bank loan in the regular course of business of a bank, broker or dealer, briefly describe the transaction, and state the names of the parties.

(e) State whether or not you are, or were within the past year, a party to any contract, arrangements or understandings with any person with respect to any securities of the issuer, including, but not limited to joint ventures, loan or option arrangements, puts or calls, guarantees against loss or guarantees of profit, division of losses or profits, or the giving or withholding of proxies. If so, name the parties to such contracts, arrangements or understandings and give the details thereof.

(f) State the amount of securities of the issuer owned beneficially, directly or indirectly, by each of your associates and the name and address of each such associate.

(g) State the amount of each class of securities of any parent or subsidiary of the issuer which you own beneficially, directly or indirectly.

Instruction. For purposes of this item, beneficial ownership shall be determined in accordance with Rule 13d–3 under the Act (Rule 13d–3).

Item 4. Further Matters

(a) Describe the time and circumstances under which you became a participant in the solicitation and state the nature and extent of your activities or proposed activities as a participant.

(b) Furnish for yourself and your associates the information required by Item 402(f) of Regulation S–K.

(c) State whether or not you or any of your associates have any arrangement or understanding with any person—

(1) With respect to any future employment by the issuer or its affiliates; or

(2) With respect to any future transactions to which the issuer or any of its affiliates will or may be a party.

If so, describe such arrangement or understanding and state the names of the parties thereto.

(d) State the total amount contributed and proposed to be contributed by you in furtherance of the solicitation, directly or indirectly, if such amount exceeds or will exceed $500 in the aggregate.

Rule 14b–1. Obligation of Registered Brokers in Connection With the Prompt Forwarding of Certain Communications to Beneficial Owners

A broker registered under Section 15 of the Act shall:

(a) Respond to an inquiry made in accordance with Rule 14a–3(d) by or on behalf of an issuer soliciting proxies, consents or authorization by promptly indicating, by means of a search card or otherwise, the approximate number of its customers who are beneficial owners of the issuer's securities that are held of record by the broker or its nominees; and

(b) Upon receipt of the proxy, other proxy soliciting material and/or annual reports to security holders and of assurances that its reasonable expenses shall be paid by the issuer, forward such materials promptly to such customers.

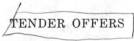

TENDER OFFERS

Rule 14d–1. Scope of and Definitions Applicable to Regulations 14D and 14E

(a) *Scope.* Regulation 14D (Rules 14d–1 through 14d–101) shall apply to any tender offer which is subject to section 14(d)(1) of the Act, including, but not limited to, any tender offer for securities of a class described in that section which is made by an affiliate of the issuer of such class. Regulation 14E (Rules 14e–1 and 14e–2) shall apply to an tender offer for securities (other than exempted securities) unless otherwise noted therein.

(b) *Definitions.* Unless the context otherwise requires, all terms used in Regulation 14D and Regulation 14E have the same meaning as in the Act and in Rule 12b–2 promulgated thereunder. In addition, for purposes of sections 14(d) and 14(e) of the Act and Regulations 14D and 14E, the following definitions apply:

(1) The term "bidder" means any person who makes a tender offer or on whose behalf a tender offer is made: *Provided, however,* That the term does not include an issuer which makes a tender offer for securities of any class of which it is the issuer;

(2) The term "subject company" means any issuer of securities which are sought by a bidder pursuant to a tender offer;

(3) The term "security holders" means holders of record and beneficial owners of securities which are the subject of a tender offer;

(4) The term "beneficial owner" shall have the same meaning as that set forth in Rule 13d–3: *Provided, however,* That, except with respect to Rule 14d–3, Rule 14d–9(d) and Item 6 of Schedule 14D–1, the term shall not include a person who does not have or share investment power or who is deemed to be a beneficial owner by virtue of Rule 13d–3(d)(1);

(5) The term "tender offer material" means:

(i) The bidder's formal offer, including all the material terms and conditions of the tender offer and all amendments thereto;

(ii) The related transmittal letter (whereby securities of the subject company which are sought in the tender offer may be transmitted to the bidder or its depositary) and all amendments thereto; and

(iii) Press releases, advertisements, letters and other documents published by the bidder or sent or given by the bidder to security holders which, directly or indirectly, solicit, invite or request tenders of the securities being sought in the tender offer;

(6) The term "business day" means any day, other than Saturday, Sunday or a federal holiday, and shall consist of the time period from 12:01 a. m. through 12:00 midnight Eastern time. In computing any time period under section 14(d)(5) or section 14(d)(6) of the Act or under Regulation 14D or Regulation 14E, the date of the event which begins the running of such time period shall be included *except that* if such event occurs on other than a business day such period shall begin to run on and shall include the first business day thereafter; and

(7) The term "security position listing" means, with respect to securities of any issuer held by a registered clearing agency in the name of the clearing agency or its nominee, a list of those participants in the clearing agency on whose behalf the clearing agency holds the issuer's securities and of the participants' respective positions in such securities as of a specified date.

Rule 14d–2. Date of Commencement of a Tender Offer

(a) *Commencement.* A tender offer shall commence for the purposes of section 14(d) of the Act and the rules promulgated thereunder at 12:01 a. m. on the date when the first of the following events occurs:

(1) The long form publication of the tender offer is first published by the bidder pursuant to Rule 14d–4(a)(1);

(2) The summary advertisement of the tender offer is first published by the bidder pursuant to Rule 14d–4(a)(2);

(3) The summary advertisement or the long form publication of the tender offer is first published by the bidder pursuant to Rule 14d–4(a)(3);

(4) Definitive copies of a tender offer, in which the consideration offered by the bidder consists of securities registered pursuant to the Securities Act of 1933, are first published or sent or given by the bidder to security holders; or

(5) The tender offer is first published or sent or given to security holders by the bidder by any means not otherwise referred to in paragraphs (a)(1) through (a)(4) of this section.

(b) *Public announcement.* A public announcement by a bidder through a press release, newspaper advertisement or public statement which includes the information in paragraph (c) of this section with respect to a tender offer in which the consideration consists solely of cash and/or securities exempt from registration under section 3 of the Securities Act of 1933 shall be deemed to constitute the commencement of a tender offer under paragraph (a)(5) of this section except that such tender offer shall not be deemed to be first published or sent or given to security holders by the bidder under paragraph (a)(5) of this section on the date of such public announcement if within five business days of such public announcement, the bidder either:

(1) Makes a subsequent public announcement stating that the bidder has determined not to continue with such tender offer, in which event paragraph (a)(5) of this section shall not apply to the initial public announcement; or

(2) Complies with Rule 14d-3(a) and contemporaneously disseminates the disclosure required by Rule 14d-6 to security holders pursuant to Rule 14d-4 or otherwise in which event:

(i) The date of commencement of such tender offer under paragraph (a) of this section will be determined by the date the information required by Rule 14d-6 is first published or sent or given to security holders pursuant to Rule 14d-4 or otherwise; and

(ii) Notwithstanding paragraph (b)(2)(i) of this section, section 14(d)(7) of the Act shall be deemed to apply to such tender offer from the date of such public announcement.

(c) *Information.* The information referred to in paragraph (b) of this section is as follows:

(1) The identity of the bidder;

(2) The identity of the subject company; and

(3) The amount and class of securities being sought and the price or range of prices being offered therefor.

(d) *Announcements not resulting in commencement.* A public announcement by a bidder through a press release, newspaper advertisement or public statement which only discloses the information in paragraphs (d)(1) through (d)(3) of this section concerning a tender offer in which

the consideration consists solely of cash and/or securities exempt from registration under section 3 of the Securities Act of 1933 shall not be deemed to constitute the commencement of a tender offer under paragraph (a)(5) of this section.

(1) The identity of the bidder;

(2) The identity of the subject company; and

(3) A statement that the bidder intends to make a tender offer in the future for a class of equity securities of the subject company which statement does not specify the amount of securities of such class to be sought or the consideration to be offered therefor.

(e) *Announcement made pursuant to Rule 135.* A public announcement by a bidder through a press release, newspaper advertisement or public statement which discloses only the information in Rule 135(a)(4) concerning a tender offer in which the consideration consists solely or in part of securities to be registered under the Securities Act of 1933 shall not be deemed to constitute the commencement of a tender offer under paragraph (a)(5) of this section: *Provided,* That such bidder files a registration statement with respect to such securities promptly after such public announcement.

Rule 14d-3. Filing and Transmission of Tender Offer Statement

(a) *Filing and transmittal.* No bidder shall make a tender offer if, after consummation thereof, such bidder would be the beneficial owner of more than 5 percent of the class of the subject company's securities for which the tender offer is made, unless as soon as practicable on the date of the commencement of the tender offer such bidder:

(1) Files with the Commission ten copies of a Tender Offer Statement on Schedule 14D–1 (Rule 14d–100), including all exhibits thereto;

(2) Hand delivers a copy of such Schedule 14D–1, including all exhibits thereto:

(i) To the subject company at its principal executive office; and

(ii) To any other bidder, which has filed a Schedule 14D–1 with the Commission relating to a tender offer which has not yet terminated for the same class of securities of the subject company, at such bidder's principal executive office or at the address of the person authorized to receive notices and communications (which is disclosed on the cover sheet of such other bidder's Schedule 14D-1);

(3) Gives telephonic notice of the information required by Rule 14d-6(e)(2)(i) and (ii) and mails by means of first class mail a copy of such Schedule 14D-1, including all exhibits thereto:

(i) To each national securities exchange where such class of the subject company's securities is registered and listed for trading (which may be based upon information contained in the subject company's most recent Annual Report on Form 10-K filed with the Commission unless the bidder has reason to believe that such information is not current) which telephonic notice shall be made when practicable prior to the opening of each such exchange; and

(ii) To the National Association of Securities Dealers, Inc. ("NASD") if such class of the subject company's securities is authorized for quotation in the NASDAQ interdealer quotation system.

(b) *Additional materials.* The bidder shall file with the Commission ten copies of any additional tender offer materials as an exhibit to the Schedule 14D-1 required by this section, and if a material change occurs in the information set forth in such Schedule 14D-1, ten copies of an amendment to Schedule 14D-1 (each of which shall include all exhibits other than those required by Item 11(a) of Schedule 14D-1) disclosing such change and shall send a copy of such additional tender offer material or such amendment to the subject company and to any exchange and/or the NASD, as required by paragraph (a) of this section, promptly but not later than the date such additional tender offer material or such change is first published or sent or given to security holders.

(c) *Certain announcements.* Notwithstanding the provisions of paragraph (b) of this section, if the additional tender offer material or an amendment to Schedule 14D-1 discloses only the number of shares deposited to date, and/or announces an extension of the time during which shares may be tendered, then the bidder may file such tender offer material or amendment and send a copy of such tender offer material or amendment to the subject company, any exchange and/or the NASD, as required by paragraph (a) of this section, promptly after the date such tender offer material is first published or sent or given to security holders.

Rule 14d-4. Dissemination of Certain Tender Offers

(a) *Materials deemed published or sent or given.* A tender offer in which the consideration consists solely of cash and/or securities exempt from registration under section 3 of the Securities Act of 1933 shall be deemed "published or sent or given to security holders" within the meaning of section 14(d)(1) of the Act if the bidder complies with all of the requirements of any one of the following sub-paragraphs: *Provided, however,* That any such tender offers may be published or sent or given to security holders by other methods, but with respect to summary publication, and the use of stockholder lists and security position listings pursuant to Rule 14d-5, paragraphs (a)(2) and (a)(3) of this section are exclusive.

(1) *Long-form publication.* The bidder makes adequate publication in a newspaper or newspapers of long-form publication of the tender offer.

(2) *Summary publication.* (i) If the tender offer is not subject to Rule 13e-3, the bidder makes adequate publication in a newspaper or newspapers of a summary advertisement of the tender offer; and

(ii) Mails by first class mail or otherwise furnishes with reasonable promptness the bidder's tender offer materials to any security holder who requests such tender offer materials pursuant to the summary advertisement or otherwise.

(3) *Use of stockholder lists and security position listings.* Any bidder using stockholder lists and security position listings pursuant to Rule 14d-5 shall comply with paragraphs (a)(1) or (a)(2) of this section on or prior to the date of the bidder's request for such lists or listing pursuant to Rule 14d-5(a).

(b) *Adequate publication.* Depending on the facts and circumstances involved, adequate publication of a tender offer pursuant to this section may require publication in a newspaper with a national circulation or may only require publication in a newspaper with metropolitan or regional circulation or may require publication in a combination thereof: *Provided, however,* That publication in all editions of a daily newspaper with a national circulation shall be deemed to constitute adequate publication.

(c) *Publication of changes.* If a tender offer has been published or sent or given to security holders by one or more of the methods enumerated in paragraph (a) of this section, a material change in the information published or sent or given to security holders shall be promptly disseminated to security holders in a manner reasonably designed to inform security holders of such change; *Provided, however,* That if the bidder has elected pursuant to rule 14d–5(f)(1) of this section to require the subject company to disseminate amendments disclosing material changes to the tender offer materials pursuant to Rule 14d–5, the bidder shall disseminate material changes in the information published or sent or given to security holders at least pursuant to Rule 14d–5.

Rule 14d–5. Dissemination of Certain Tender Offers by the Use of Stockholder Lists and Security Position Listings

(a) *Obligations of the subject company.* Upon receipt by a subject company at its principal executive offices of a bidder's written request, meeting the requirements of paragraph (e) of this section, the subject company shall comply with the following sub-paragraphs.

(1) The subject company shall notify promptly transfer agents and any other person who will assist the subject company in complying with the requirements of this section of the receipt by the subject company of a request by a bidder pursuant to this section.

(2) The subject company shall promptly ascertain whether the most recently prepared stockholder list, written or otherwise, within the access of the subject company was prepared as of a date earlier than ten business days before the date of the bidder's request and, if so, the subject company shall promptly prepare or cause to be prepared a stockholder list as of the most recent practicable date which shall not be more

than ten business days before the date of the bidder's request.

(3) The subject company shall make an election to comply and shall comply with all of the provisions of either paragraph (b) or paragraph (c) of this section. The subject company's election once made shall not be modified or revoked during the bidder's tender offer and extensions thereof.

(4) No later than the second business day after the date of the bidder's request, the subject company shall orally notify the bidder, which notification shall be confirmed in writing, of the subject company's election made pursuant to paragraph (a)(3) of this section. Such notification shall indicate (i) the approximate number of security holders of the class of securities being sought by the bidder and, (ii) if the subject company elects to comply with paragraph (b) of this section, appropriate information concerning the location for delivery of the bidder's tender offer materials and the approximate direct costs incidental to the mailing to security holders of the bidder's tender offer materials computed in accordance with paragraph (g)(2) of this section.

(b) *Mailing of tender offer materials by the subject company.* A subject company which elects pursuant to paragraph (a)(3) of this section to comply with the provisions of this paragraph shall perform the acts prescribed by the following subparagraphs.

(1) The subject company shall promptly contact each participant named on the most recent security position listing of any clearing agency within the access of the subject company and make inquiry of each such participant as to the approximate number of beneficial owners of the subject company securities being sought in the tender offer held by each such participant.

(2) No later than the third business day after delivery of the bidder's tender offer materials pursuant to paragraph (g)(1) of this section, the subject company shall begin to mail or cause to be mailed by means of first class mail a copy of the bidder's tender offer materials to each person whose name appears as a record holder of the class of securities for which the offer is made on the most recent stockholder list referred to in paragraph (a)(2) of this section. The subject

company shall use its best efforts to complete the mailing in a timely manner but in no event shall such mailing be completed in a substantially greater period of time than the subject company would complete a mailing to security holders of its own materials relating to the tender offer.

(3) No later than the third business day after the delivery of the bidder's tender offer materials pursuant to paragraph (g)(1) of this section, the subject company shall begin to transmit or cause to be transmitted a sufficient number of sets of the bidder's tender offer materials to the participants named on the security position listings described in paragraph (b)(1) of this section. The subject company shall use its best efforts to complete the transmittal in a timely manner, but in no event shall such transmittal be completed in a substantially greater period of time than the subject company would complete a transmittal to such participants pursuant to security position listings of clearing agencies of its own material relating to the tender offer.

(4) The subject company shall promptly give oral notification to the bidder, which notification shall be confirmed in writing, of the commencement of the mailing pursuant to paragraph (b)(2) of this section and of the transmittal pursuant to paragraph (b)(3) of this section.

(5) During the tender offer and any extension thereof the subject company shall use reasonable efforts to update the stockholder list and shall mail or cause to be mailed promptly following each update a copy of the bidder's tender offer materials (to the extent sufficient sets of such materials have been furnished by the bidder) to each person who has become a record holder since the later of (i) the date of preparation of the most recent stockholder list referred to in paragraph (a)(2) of this section or (ii) the last preceding update.

(6) If the bidder has elected pursuant to paragraph (f)(1) of this section to require the subject company to disseminate amendments disclosing material changes to the tender offer materials pursuant to this section, the subject company, promptly following delivery of each such amendment, shall mail or cause to be mailed a copy of each such amendment to each record holder whose name appears on the shareholder list described in paragraphs (a)(2) and (b)(5) of this section and shall transmit or cause to be transmitted sufficient copies of such amendment to each participant named on security position listings who received sets of the bidder's tender offer materials pursuant to paragraph (b)(3) of this section.

(7) The subject company shall not include any communication other than the bidder's tender offer materials or amendments thereto in the envelopes or other containers furnished by the bidder.

(8) Promptly following the termination of the tender offer, the subject company shall reimburse the bidder the excess, if any, of the amounts advanced pursuant to paragraph (f)(3)(iii) over the direct cost incidental to compliance by the subject company and its agents in performing the acts required by this section computed in accordance with paragraph (g)(2) of this section.

(c) *Delivery of stockholder lists and security position listings.* A subject company which elects pursuant to paragraph (a)(3) of this section to comply with the provisions of this paragraph shall perform the acts prescribed by the following subparagraphs.

(1) No later than the third business day after the date of the bidder's request, the subject company shall furnish to the bidder at the subject company's principal executive office a copy of the names and addresses of the record holders on the most recent stockholder list referred to in paragraph (a)(2) of this section and a copy of the names and addresses of participants identified on the most recent security position listing of any clearing agency which is within the access of the subject company.

(2) If the bidder has elected pursuant to paragraph (f)(1) of this section to require the subject company to disseminate amendments disclosing material changes to the tender offer materials, the subject company shall update the stockholder list by furnishing the bidder with the name and address of each record holder named on the stockholder list, and not previously furnished to the bidder, promptly after such information becomes available to the subject company during the tender offer and any extensions thereof.

(d) *Liability of subject company and others.* Neither the subject company nor any affiliate or agent of the subject company nor any clearing agency shall be:

(1) Deemed to have made a solicitation or recommendation respecting the tender offer within the meaning of section 14(d)(4) based solely upon the compliance or noncompliance by the subject company or any affiliate or agent of the subject company with one or more requirements of this section;

(2) Liable under any provision of the Federal securities laws to the bidder or to any security holder based solely upon the inaccuracy of the current names or addresses on the stockholder list or security position listing, unless such inaccuracy results from a lack of reasonable care on the part of the subject company or any affiliate or agent of the subject company;

(3) Deemed to be an "underwriter" within the meaning of section (2)(11) of the Securities Act of 1933 for any purpose of that Act or any rule or regulation promulgated thereunder based solely upon the compliance or noncompliance by the subject company or any affiliate or agent of the subject company with one or more of the requirements of this section;

(4) Liable under any provision of the Federal securities laws for the disclosure in the bidder's tender offer materials, including any amendment thereto, based solely upon the compliance or noncompliance by the subject company or any affiliate or agent of the subject company with one or more of the requirements of this section.

(e) *Content of the bidder's request.* The bidder's written request referred to in paragraph (a) of this section shall include the following:

(1) The identity of the bidder;

(2) The title of the class of securities which is the subject of the bidder's tender offer;

(3) A statement that the bidder is making a request to the subject company pursuant to paragraph (a) of this section for the use of the stockholder list and security position listings for the purpose of disseminating a tender offer to security holders;

(4) A statement that the bidder is aware of and will comply with the provisions of paragraph (f) of this section;

(5) A statement as to whether or not it has elected pursuant to paragraph (f)(1) of this section to disseminate amendments disclosing material changes to the tender offer materials pursuant to this section; and

(6) The name, address and telephone number of the person whom the subject company shall contact pursuant to paragraph (a)(4) of this section.

(f) *Obligations of the bidder.* Any bidder who requests that a subject company comply with the provisions of paragraph (a) of this section shall comply with the following subparagraphs.

(1) The bidder shall make an election whether or not to require the subject company to disseminate amendments disclosing material changes to the tender offer materials pursuant to this section, which election shall be included in the request referred to in paragraph (a) of this section and shall not be revocable by the bidder during the tender offer and extensions thereof.

(2) With respect to a tender offer subject to section 14(d)(1) of the Act in which the consideration consists solely of cash and/or securities exempt from registration under section 3 of the Securities Act of 1933, the bidder shall comply with the requirements of Rule 14d-4(a)(3).

(3) If the subject company elects to comply with paragraph (b) of this section,

(i) The bidder shall promptly deliver the tender offer materials after receipt of the notification from the subject company as provided in paragraph (a)(4) of this section;

(ii) The bidder shall promptly notify the subject company of any amendment to the bidder's tender offer materials requiring compliance by the subject company with paragraph (b)(6) of this section and shall promptly deliver such amendment to the subject company pursuant to paragraph (g)(1) of this section;

(iii) The bidder shall advance to the subject company an amount equal to the approximate cost of conducting mailings to security holders computed in accordance with paragraph (g)(2) of this section;

(iv) The bidder shall promptly reimburse the subject company for the direct costs incidental to compliance by the subject company and its agents in performing the acts required by this section computed in accordance with paragraph (g)(2) of this section which are in excess of the amount advanced pursuant to paragraph (f)(2)(iii) of this section; and

(v) The bidder shall mail by means of first class mail or otherwise furnish with reasonable promptness the tender offer materials to any security holder who requests such materials.

(4) If the subject company elects to comply with paragraph (c) of this section,

(i) The subject company shall use the stockholder list and security position listings furnished to the bidder pursuant to paragraph (c) of this section exclusively in the dissemination of tender offer materials to security holders in connection with the bidder's tender offer and extensions thereof;

(ii) The bidder shall return the stockholder lists and security position listings furnished to the bidder pursuant to paragraph (c) of this section promptly after the termination of the bidder's tender offer;

(iii) The bidder shall accept, handle and return the stockholder lists and security position listings furnished to the bidder pursuant to paragraph (c) of this section to the subject company on a confidential basis;

(iv) The bidder shall not retain any stockholder list or security position listing furnished by the subject company pursuant to paragraph (c) of this section, or any copy thereof, nor retain any information derived from any such list or listing or copy thereof after the termination of the bidder's tender offer;

(v) The bidder shall mail by means of first class mail, at its own expense, a copy of its tender offer materials to each person whose identity appears on the stockholder list as furnished and updated by the subject company pursuant to paragraphs (c)(1) and (c)(2) of this section;

(vi) The bidder shall contact the participants named on the security position listing of any clearing agency, make inquiry of each participant as to the approximate number of sets of tender offer materials required by each such participant, and furnish, at its own expense, sufficient sets of tender offer materials and any amendment thereto to each such participant for subsequent transmission to the beneficial owners of the securities being sought by the bidder;

(vii) The bidder shall mail by means of first class mail or otherwise furnish with reasonable promptness the tender offer materials to any security holder who requests such materials; and

(viii) The bidder shall promptly reimburse the subject company for direct costs incidental to compliance by the subject company and its agents in performing the acts required by this section computed in accordance with paragraph (g)(2) of this section.

(g) *Delivery of materials, computation of direct costs.*

(1) Whenever the bidder is required to deliver tender offer materials or amendments to tender offer materials, the bidder shall deliver to the subject company at the location specified by the subject company in its notice given pursuant to paragraph (a)(4) of this section a number of sets of the materials or of the amendment, as the case may be, at least equal to the approximate number of security holders specified by the subject company in such notice, together with appropriate envelopes or other containers therefor: *Provided, however,* That such delivery shall be deemed not to have been made unless the bidder has complied with paragraph (f)(3)(iii) of this section at the time the materials or amendments, as the case may be, are delivered.

(2) The approximate direct cost of mailing the bidder's tender offer materials shall be computed by adding (i) the direct cost incidental to the mailing of the subject company's last annual report to shareholders (excluding employee time), less the costs of preparation and printing of the report, and postage, plus (ii) the amount of first class postage required to mail the bidder's tender offer materials. The approximate direct costs incidental to the mailing of the amendments to the bidder's tender offer materials shall be computed by adding (iii) the estimated direct costs of preparing mailing labels, of updating shareholder lists and of third party handling charges plus (iv) the amount of first class postage required to mail the bidder's amendment. Direct costs incidental to the mailing of the bidder's tender offer materials and amendments thereto

when finally computed may include all reasonable charges paid by the subject company to third parties for supplies or services, including costs attendant to preparing shareholder lists, mailing labels, handling the bidder's materials, contacting participants named on security position listings and for postage, but shall exclude indirect costs, such as employee time which is devoted to either contesting or supporting the tender offer on behalf of the subject company. The final billing for direct costs shall be accompanied by an appropriate accounting in reasonable detail.

Rule 14d–6. Disclosure Requirements With Respect to Tender Offers

(a) *Information required on date of commencement.*

(1) *Long-form publication.* If a tender offer is published, sent or given to security holders on the date of commencement by means of long-form publication pursuant to Rule 14d–4(a)(1), such long-form publication shall include the information required by paragraph (e)(1) of this section.

(2) *Summary publication.* If a tender offer is published, sent or given to security holders on the date of commencement by means of summary publication pursuant to Rule 14d–4(a)(2),

(i) The summary advertisement shall contain and shall be limited to, the information required by paragraph (e)(2) of this section; and

(ii) The tender offer materials furnished by the bidder upon the request of any security holder shall include the information required by paragraph (e)(1) of this section.

(3) *Use of stockholder lists and security position listings.* If a tender offer is published or sent or given to security holders on the date of commencement by the use of stockholder lists and security position listings pursuant to Rule 14d–4(a)(3),

(i) Either (A) the summary advertisement shall contain, and shall be limited to the information required by paragraph (e)(2) of this section, or (B) if long form publication of the tender offer is made, such long form publication shall include the information required by paragraph (e)(1) of this section; and

(ii) The tender offer materials transmitted to security holders pursuant to such lists and security position listings and furnished by the bidder upon the request of any security holder shall include the information required by paragraph (e)(1) of this section.

(4) *Other tender offers.* If a tender offer is published or sent or given to security holders other than pursuant to Rule 14d–4(a), the tender offer materials which are published or sent or given to security holders on the date of commencement of such offer shall include the information required by paragraph (e)(1) of this section.

(b) *Information required in summary advertisement made after commencement.* A summary advertisement published subsequent to the date of commencement of the tender offer shall include at least the information specified in paragraphs (e)(1)(i)–(iv) and (e)(2)(iv) of this section.

(c) *Information required in other tender offer materials published after commencement.* Except for summary advertisements described in paragraph (b) of this section and tender offer materials described in paragraphs (a)(2)(ii) and (a)(3)(ii) of this section, additional tender offer materials published, sent or given to security holders subsequent to the date of commencement shall include the information required by paragraphs (e)(1) and may omit any of the information required by paragraphs (e)(1)(v)–(viii) of this section which has been previously furnished by the bidder in connection with the tender offer.

(d) *Material changes.* A material change in the information published or sent or given to security holders shall be promptly disclosed to security holders in additional tender offer materials.

(e) *Information to be included.*

(1) *Long-form publication and tender offer materials.* The information required to be disclosed by paragraphs (a)(1), (a)(2)(ii), (a)(3)(i)(B) and (a)(4) of this section shall include the following:

(i) The identity of the holder;

(ii) The identity of the subject company;

(iii) The amount of class of securities being sought and the type and amount of consideration being offered therefor;

(iv) The scheduled expiration date of the tender offer, whether the tender offer may be extended and, if so, the procedures for extension of the tender offer;

(v) The exact dates prior to which, and after which, security holders who deposit their securities will have the right to withdraw their securities pursuant to section 14(d)(5) of the Act and Rule 14d-7 and the manner in which shares will be accepted for payment and in which withdrawal may be effected;

(vi) If the tender offer is for less than all the outstanding securities of a class of equity securities and the bidder is not obligated to purchase all of the securities tendered, the period or periods, and in the case of the period from the commencement of the offer, the date of the expiration of such period during which the securities will be taken up pro rata pursuant to Section 14(d)(6) of the Act or Rule 14d-8, and the present intention or plan of the bidder with respect to the tender offer in the event of an oversubscription by security holders;

(vii) The disclosure required by Items 1(c); 2 (with respect to persons other than the bidder, excluding sub-items (b) and (d)); 3; 4; 5; 6; 7; 8; and 10 of Schedule 14D-1 or a fair and adequate summary thereof; *Provided, however,* That negative responses to any such item or sub-item or Schedule 14D-1 need not be included; and

(viii) The disclosure required by Item 9 of Schedule 14D-1 or a fair and adequate summary thereof. (Under normal circumstances, the following summary financial information for the period covered by the financial information furnished in response to Item 9 will be a sufficient summary. If the information required by Item 9 is summarized, appropriate instructions shall be included stating how complete financial information can be obtained).

Income Statement:

    Net sales and operating revenues and other revenues
    Income before extraordinary items
    Net income

Balance sheet (at end of period):
    Working capital
    Total assets
    Total assets less deferred research and development charges and excess cost of assets acquired over book value
    Total indebtedness
    Shareholders' equity
Per Share
    Income per common share before extraordinary items
    Extraordinary items
    Net income per common share (and common share equivalents if applicable)
    Net income per share on a fully diluted basis

(2) *Summary publication.* The information required to be disclosed by paragraphs (a)(2)(i) and (a)(3)(i)(A) of this section in a summary advertisement is as follows:

(i) The information required by paragraph (e)(1)(i) through (vi) of this section;

(ii) If the tender offer is for less than all the outstanding securities of a class of equity securities, a statement as to whether the purpose or one of the purposes of the tender offer is to acquire or influence control of the business of the subject company;

(iii) A statement that the information required by paragraph (e)(1)(vii) of this section is incorporated by reference into the summary advertisement;

(iv) Appropriate instructions as to how security holders may obtain promptly, at the bidder's expense, the bidder's tender offer materials; and

(v) In a tender offer published or sent or given to security holders by the use of stockholder lists and security position listings pursuant to Rule 14d-4(a)(3), a statement that a request is being made for such lists and listings and that tender offer materials will be mailed to record holders and will be furnished to brokers, banks and similar persons whose name appears or whose nominee appears on the list of stockholders or, if applicable, who are listed as participants in a clearing agency's security position listing for subsequent transmittal to beneficial owners of such securities.

(3) *No transmittal letter.* Neither the initial summary advertisement nor any subsequent summary advertisement shall include a transmittal letter (whereby securities of the subject company which are sought in the tender offer may be transmitted to the bidder or its depository) or any amendment thereto.

Rule 14d–7. Additional Withdrawal Rights

(a) *Rights.* In addition to the provisions of section 14(d)(5) of the Act, any person who has deposited securities pursuant to a tender offer has the right to withdraw any such securities during the following periods:

(1) At any time until the expiration of fifteen business days from the date of commencement of such tender offer; and

(2) On the date and until the expiration of ten business days following the date of commencement of another bidder's tender offer other than pursuant to Rule 14d–2(b) for securities of the same class *provided that* the bidder has received notice or otherwise has knowledge of the commencement of such other tender offer and, *Provided further,* That withdrawal may only be effected with respect to securities which have not been accepted for payment in the manner set forth in the bidder's tender offer prior to the date such other tender offer is first published, sent or given to security holders.

(b) *Computation of time periods.* The time periods for withdrawal rights pursuant to this section shall be computed on a concurrent, as opposed to a consecutive, basis.

(c) *Knowledge of competing offer.* For the purposes of this section, a bidder shall be presumed to have knowledge of another tender offer, as described in paragraph (a)(2) of this section, on the date such bidder receives a copy of the Schedule 14D–1 pursuant to Rule 14d–2 from such other bidder.

(d) *Notice of withdrawal.* Notice of withdrawal pursuant to this section shall be deemed to be timely upon the receipt by the bidder's depositary of a written notice of withdrawal specifying the name(s) of the tendering stockholder(s), the number or amount of the securities to be withdrawn and the name(s) in which the certificate(s) is (are) registered, if different from that of the tendering security holder(s). A bidder may impose other reasonable requirements, including certificate numbers and a signed request for withdrawal accompanied by a signature guarantee, as conditions precedent to the physical release of withdrawn securities.

Rule 14d–8. Exemption From Statutory Pro Rata Requirement

The limited pro rata provisions of section 14(d)(6) of the Act shall not apply to any tender offer for less than all the outstanding securities of the class for which the tender offer is made to the extent that the bidder provides in the tender offer materials disseminated to security holders on the date of commencement of the tender offer that in the event more securities are deposited during the period(s) described in paragraphs (a) and/or (b) of this section than the bidder is bound or willing to accept for payment, all securities deposited during such period(s) will be accepted for payment as nearly as practicable on a pro rata basis, disregarding fractions, according to the number of securities deposited by each depositor.

(a) Any period which exceeds ten days from the date of commencement of the tender offer.

(b) Any period which exceeds ten days from the date that notice of an increase in the consideration offered is first published, sent or given to security holders.

Rule 14d–9. Solicitation / Recommendation Statements With Respect to Certain Tender Offers

(a) *Filing and transmittal of recommendation statement.* No solicitation or recommendation to security holders shall be made by any person described in paragraph (d) of this section with respect to a tender offer for such securities unless as soon as practicable on the date such solicitation or recommendation is first published or sent or given to security holders such person complies with the following subparagraphs.

(1) Such person shall file with the Commission eight copies of a Tender Offer Solicitation/Rec-

ommendation Statement on Schedule 14D-9, including all exhibits thereto; and

(2) If such person is either the subject company or an affiliate of the subject company,

(i) Such person shall hand deliver a copy of the Schedule 14D-9 to the bidder at its principal office or at the address of the person authorized to receive notices and communications (which is set forth on the cover sheet of the bidder's Schedule 14D-1 filed with the Commission; and

(ii) Such person shall give telephonic notice (which notice to the extent possible shall be given prior to the opening of the market) of the information required by Items 2 and 4(a) of Schedule 14D-9 and shall mail a copy of the Schedule to each national securities exchange where the class of securities is registered and listed for trading and, if the class is authorized for quotation in the NASDAQ interdealer quotation system, to the National Association of Securities Dealers, Inc. ("NASD").

(3) If such person is neither the subject company nor an affiliate of the subject company,

(i) Such person shall mail a copy of the schedule to the bidder at its principal office or at the address of the person authorized to receive notices and communications (which is set forth on the cover sheet of the bidder's Schedule 14D-1 filed with the Commission); and

(ii) Such person shall mail a copy of the Schedule to the subject company at its principal office.

(b) *Amendments.* If any material change occurs in the information set forth in the Schedule 14D-9 required by this section, the person who filed such Schedule 14D-9 shall:

(1) File with the Commission eight copies of an amendment on Schedule 14D-9 disclosing such change promptly, but not later than the date such material is first published, sent or given to security holders; and

(2) Promptly deliver copies and give notice of the amendment in the same manner as that specified in paragraph (a)(2) or paragraph (a)(3) of this section, whichever is applicable; and

(3) Promptly disclose and disseminate such change in a manner reasonably designed to inform security holders of such change.

(c) *Information required in solicitation or recommendation.* Any solicitation or recommendation to holders of a class of securities referred to in section 14(d)(1) of the Act with respect to a tender offer for such securities shall include the name of the person making such solicitation or recommendation and the information required by Items 1, 2, 3(b), 4, 6, 7 and 8 of Schedule 14D-9 or a fair and adequate summary thereof: *Provided, however,* That such solicitation or recommendation may omit any of such information previously furnished to security holders of such class of securities by such person with respect to such tender offer.

(d) *Applicability.*

(1) Except as is provided in paragraphs (d)(2) and (e) of this section, this section shall only apply to the following persons:

(i) The subject company, any director, officer, employee, affiliate or subsidiary of the subject company;

(ii) An record holder or beneficial owner of any security issued by the subject company, by the bidder, or by any affiliate of either the subject company or the bidder; and

(iii) Any person who makes a solicitation or recommendation to security holders on behalf of any of the foregoing or on behalf of the bidder other than by means of a solicitation or recommendation to security holders which has been filed with the Commission pursuant to this section or Rule 14d-3.

(2) Notwithstanding paragraph (d)(1) of this section, this section shall not apply to the following persons:

(i) A bidder who has filed a Schedule 14D-1 pursuant to Rule 14d-3;

(ii) Attorneys, banks, brokers, fiduciaries or investment advisers who are not participating in a tender offer in more than a ministerial capacity and who furnish information and/or advice regarding such tender offer to their customers or clients on the unsolicited request of such customers or clients or solely pursuant to a contract or a relationship providing for advice to the customer or client to whom the information and/or advice is given.

(e) *Stop-look-and-listen communication.* This section shall not apply to the subject company with respect to a communication by the subject company to its security holders which only:

(1) Identifies the tender offer by the bidder;

(2) States that such tender offer is under consideration by the subject company's board of directors and/or management;

(3) States that on or before a specified date (which shall be no later than 10 business days from the date of commencement of such tender offer) the subject company will advise such security holders of (i) whether the subject company recommends acceptance or rejection of such tender offer; expresses no opinion and remains neutral toward such tender offer; or is unable to take a position with respect to such tender offer and (ii) the reason(s) for the position taken by the subject company with respect to the tender offer (including the inability to take a position); and

(4) Requests such security holders to defer making a determination whether to accept or reject such tender offer until they have been advised of the subject company's position with respect thereto pursuant to paragraph (e)(3) of this section.

(f) *Statement of management's position.* A statement by the subject company of its position with respect to a tender offer which is required to be published or sent or given to security holders pursuant to Rule 14e-2 shall be deemed to constitute a solicitation or recommendation within the meaning of this section and section 14(d)(4) of the Act.

Schedule 14D-1. Tender Offer Statement Pursuant to Section 14(d)(1) of the Securities Exchange Act of 1934

* * *

Item 1. Security and Subject Company

(a) State the name of the subject company and the address of its principal executive offices;

(b) State the exact title and the number of shares outstanding of the class of equity securities being sought (which may be based upon information contained in the most recently available filing with the Commission by the subject company unless the bidder has reason to believe such information is not current), the exact

amount of such securities being sought and the consideration being offered therefor; and

(c) Identify the principal market in which such securities are traded and state the high and low sales prices for such securities in such principal market (or, in the absence thereof, the range of high and low bid quotations) for each quarterly period during the past two years.

Item 2. Identity and Background

If the person filing this statement or any person enumerated in Instruction C of this statement is a corporation, partnership, limited partnership, syndicate or other group of persons, state its name, the state or other place of its organization, its principal business, the address of its principal office and the information required by (e) and (f) of this Item. If the person filing this statement or any person enumerated in Instruction C is a natural person, provide the information specified in (a) through (g) of this Item with respect to such person(s).

(a) Name;

(b) Residence or business address;

(c) Present principal occupation or employment and the name, principal business and address of any corporation or other organization in which such employment or occupation is conducted;

(d) Material occupations, positions, offices or employments during the last 5 years, giving the starting and ending dates of each and the name, principal business and address of any business corporation or other organization in which such occupation, position, office or employment was carried on;

Instruction. If a person has held various positions with the same organization, or if a person holds comparable positions with multiple related organizations, each and every position need not be specifically disclosed.

(e) Whether or not, during the last 5 years, such person has been convicted in a criminal proceeding (excluding traffic violations or similar misdemeanors) and, if so, give the dates, nature of conviction, name and location of court, and penalty imposed or other disposition of the case;

Instruction. While a negative answer to this sub-item is required in this schedule, it need not be furnished to security holders.

(f) Whether or not, during the last 5 years, such person was a party to a civil proceeding of a judicial or administrative body of competent jurisdiction and as a result of such proceeding was or is subject to a judgment, decree or final order enjoining future violations of, or prohibiting activities subject to federal or state securities laws or finding any violation of such laws; and, if so, identify and describe such proceeding and summarize the terms of such judgment, decree or final order; and

Instruction. While a negative answer to this sub-item is required in this schedule, it need not be furnished to security holders.

(g) Citizenship(s).

Item 3. Past Contacts, Transactions or Negotiations with the Subject Company

(a) Briefly state the nature and approximate amount (in dollars) of any transaction, other than those described in Item 3(b) of this schedule, which has occurred since the commencement of the subject company's third full fiscal year preceding the date of this schedule, between the person filing this schedule (including those persons enumerated in Instruction C of this schedule) and:

(1) the subject company or any of its affiliates which are corporations: *Provided, However,* That no disclosure need be made with respect to any transaction if the aggregate amount involved in such transaction was less than one percent of the subject company's consolidated revenues (which may be based upon information contained in the most recently available filing with the Commission by the subject company, unless the bidder has reason to believe otherwise) (i) for the fiscal year in which such transaction occurred or, (ii) for the portion of the current fiscal year which has occurred, if the transaction occurred in such year; and

(2) the executive officers, directors or affiliates of the subject company which are not corporations if the aggregate amount involved in such transaction or in a series of similar transactions,

including all periodic installments in the case of any lease or other agreement providing for periodic payments or installments, exceeds $40,-000.

(b) Describe any contacts, negotiations or transactions which have occurred since the commencement of the subject company's third full fiscal year preceding the date of this schedule between the bidder or its subsidiaries (including those persons enumerated in Instruction C of this schedule) and the subject company or its affiliates concerning: a merger, consolidation or acquisition; a tender offer or other acquisition of securities; an election of directors; or a sale or other transfer of a material amount of assets.

Item 4. Source and Amount of Funds or Other Consideration

(a) State the source and the total amount of funds or other consideration for the purchase of the maximum number of securities for which the tender offer is being made.

(b) If all or any part of such funds or other consideration are or are expected to be, directly or indirectly, borrowed for the purpose of the tender offer:

(1) Provide a summary of each loan agreement or arrangement containing the identity of the parties, the term, the collateral, the stated and effective interest rates, and other material terms or conditions relative to such loan agreement; and

(2) Briefly describe any plans or arrangements to finance or repay such borrowings, or if no such plans or arrangements have been made, make a statement to that effect.

(c) If the source of all or any part of the funds to be used in the tender offer is a loan made in the ordinary course of business by a bank as defined by section 3(a)(6) of the Act, the name of such bank shall not be made available to the public if the person filing the statement so requests in writing and files such request, naming such bank, with the Secretary of the Commission.

Item 5. Purpose of the Tender Offer and Plans or Proposals of the Bidder

State the purpose or purposes of the tender offer for the subject company's securities. Describe any plans or proposals which relate to or would result in:

(a) An extraordinary corporate transaction, such as a merger, reorganization or liquidation, involving the subject company or any of its subsidiaries;

(b) A sale or transfer of a material amount of assets of the subject company or any of its subsidiaries;

(c) Any change in the present board of directors or management of the subject company including, but not limited to, any plans or proposals to change the number or the term of directors or to fill any existing vacancies on the board;

(d) Any material change in the present capitalization or dividend policy of the subject company;

(e) Any other material change in the subject company's corporate structure or business, including, if the subject company is a registered closed-end investment company, any plans or proposals to make any changes in its investment policy for which a vote would be required by section 13 of the Investment Company Act of 1940;

(f) Causing a class of securities of the subject company to be delisted from a national securities exchange or to cease to be authorized to be quoted in an inter-dealer quotation system of a registered national securities association; or

(g) A class of equity securities of the subject company becoming eligible for termination of registration pursuant to section 12(g)(4) of the Act.

Item 6. Interest in Securities of the Subject Company

(a) State the aggregate number and percentage of the class represented by such shares (which may be based on the number of shares outstanding as contained in the most recently available filing with the Commission by the subject company unless the bidder has reason to believe such information is not current), beneficially owned (identifying those shares for which there is a right to acquire) by each person

named in Item 2 of this schedule and by each associate and majority-owned subsidiary of such person giving the name and address of any such associate or subsidiary.

(b) Describe any transaction in the class of securities reported on that was effected during the past 60 days by the persons named in response to paragraph (a) of this item or by any executive officer, director or subsidiary of such person.

Instructions. 1. The description of a transaction required by Item 6(b) shall include, but not necessarily be limited to: 1) the identity of the person covered by Item 6(b) who effected the transactions; 2) the date of the transaction; 3) the amount of securities involved; 4) the price per share; and 5) where and how the transaction was effected.

2. If the information required by Item 6(b) of this schedule is available to the bidder at the time this statement is initially filed with the Commission pursuant to Rule 14d–3(a)(1), such information should be included in such initial filing. However, if such information is not available to the bidder at the time of such initial filing, it shall be filed with the Commission promptly but in no event later than two business days after the date of such filing and, if material, shall be disclosed in a manner reasonably designed to inform security holders. The procedure specified by this instruction is provided for the purpose of maintaining the confidentiality of the tender offer in order to avoid possible misuse of inside information.

Item 7. Contracts, Arrangements, Understandings or Relationships with Respect to the Subject Company's Securities

Describe any contract, arrangement, understanding or relationship (whether or not legally enforceable) between the bidder (including those persons enumerated in Instruction C to this schedule) and any person with respect to any securities of the subject company, (including, but not limited to, any contract, arrangement, understanding or relationship concerning the transfer or the voting of any of such securities, joint ventures, loan or option arrangements, puts or calls, guaranties of loans, guaranties against loss, or the giving or withholding of proxies) naming the persons with whom such contracts, arrangements, understandings or relationships have been entered into and giving the material provisions thereof. Include such information for any of such securities that are pledged or otherwise subject to a contingency, the occurrence of which would give another person the power to direct the voting or disposition of such securities, except that disclosure of standard default and similar provisions contained in loan agreements need not be included.

Item 8. Persons Retained, Employed or to be Compensated

Identify all persons and classes of persons employed, retained or to be compensated by the bidder, or by any person on the bidder's behalf, to make solicitations or recommendations in connection with the tender offer and describe briefly the terms of such employment, retainer or arrangement for compensation.

Item 9. Financial Statements of Certain Bidders

Where the bidder is other than a natural person and the bidder's financial condition is material to a decision by a security holder of the subject company whether to sell, tender or hold securities being sought in the tender offer, furnish current, adequate financial information concerning the bidder *Provided* That if the bidder is controlled by another entity which is not a natural person and has been formed for the purpose of making the tender offer, furnish current, adequate financial information concerning such parent.

Instructions. 1. The facts and circumstances concerning the tender offer, particularly the terms of the tender offer, may influence a determination as to whether disclosure of financial information is material. However, once the materiality requirement is applicable, the adequacy of the financial information will depend primarily on the nature of the bidder.

In order to provide guidance in making this determination, the following types of financial information will be deemed adequate for purposes of this item for the type of bidder specified: (a) financial statements prepared in compliance with Form 10 as amended for a domestic bidder which is otherwise eligible to use such form; and (b) financial statements prepared in compliance with Form 20–F for a foreign bidder which is otherwise eligible to use such form.

2. If the bidder is subject to the periodic reporting requirements of sections 13(a) or 15 (d) of the Act, financial statements contained in any document filed with the Commission may be incorporated by reference in this schedule solely for the purposes of this schedule *Provided* That such financial statements substantially meet the requirements of this item; an express statement is made that such financial statements are incorporated by reference; the matter incorporated by reference is clearly identified by page, paragraph, caption or otherwise; and an indication is made where such information may be inspected and copies obtained. Financial statements which are required to be presented in comparative form for two or more fiscal years or periods shall not be incorporated by reference unless the material incorporated by reference includes the entire period for which the comparative data is required to be given.

3. If the bidder is not subject to the periodic reporting requirements of the Act, the financial statements required by this item need not be audited if such audited financial statements are not available or obtainable without unreasonable cost or expense and a statement is made to that effect disclosing the reasons therefor.

Item 10. Additional Information

If material to a decision by a security holder whether to sell, tender or hold securities being sought in the tender offer, furnish information as to the following:

(a) Any present or proposed material contracts, arrangements, understandings or relationships between the bidder or any of its executive officers, directors, controlling persons or subsidiaries and the subject company or any of its executive officers, directors, controlling persons or subsidiaries (other than any contract, arrangement or understanding required to be disclosed pursuant to Items 3 or 7 of this schedule);

(b) To the extent known by the bidder after reasonable investigation, the applicable regulatory requirements which must be complied with or approvals which must be obtained in connection with the tender offer;

(c) The applicability of anti-trust laws;

(d) The applicability of the margin requirements of section 7 of the Act and the regulations promulgated thereunder;

(e) Any material pending legal proceedings relating to the tender offer including the name and location of the court or agency in which the proceedings are pending, the date instituted, the principal parties thereto and a brief summary of the proceedings; and

Instruction. In connection with this sub-item, a copy of any document relating to a major development (such as pleadings, an answer, complaint, temporary restraining order, injunction, opinion, judgment or order) in a material pending legal proceeding should be promptly furnished to the Commission on a supplemental basis.

(f) Such additional material information, if any, as may be necessary to make the required statements, in light of the circumstances under which they are made, not materially misleading.

Item 11. Material to be Filed as Exhibits

Furnish a copy of:

(a) Tender offer material which is published, sent or given to security holders by or on behalf of the bidder in connection with the tender offer;

(b) Any loan agreement referred to in Item 4 of this schedule;

Instruction. The identity of any bank which is a party to a loan agreement need not be disclosed if the person filing the statement has requested that the identity of such bank not be made available to the public pursuant to Item 4 of this schedule.

(c) Any document setting forth the terms of any contracts, arrangements, understandings or relationships referred to in Item 7 or 10(a) of this schedule;

(d) Any written opinion prepared by legal counsel at the bidder's request and communicated to the bidder pertaining to the tax consequences of the tender offer;

(e) In an exchange offer where securities of the bidder have been or are to be registered under the Securities Act of 1933, the prospectus containing the information required to be included therein by Rule 432 of that Act;

(f) If any oral solicitations of security holders is to be made by or on behalf of the bidder, any written instruction, form or other material which is furnished to the persons making the actual oral solicitation for their use, directly or indirectly, in connection with the tender offer.

Schedule 14D–9. Solicitation/Recommendation Statement Pursuant to Section 14(d)(4) of the Securities Exchange Act of 1934

Instructions. Eight copies of this statement, including all exhibits, should be filed with the Commission.

General Instructions: A. The item numbers and captions of the items shall be included but the text of the items is to be omitted. The answers to the items shall be so prepared as to indicate clearly the coverage of the items without referring to the text of the items. Answer every item. If an item is inapplicable or the answer is in the negative so state.

B. Information contained in exhibits to the statement may be incorporated by reference in answer or partial answer to any item or sub-item of the statement unless it would render such answer misleading, incomplete, unclear or confusing. Material incorporated by reference shall be clearly identified in the reference by page, paragraph, caption or otherwise. An express statement that the specified matter is incorporated by reference shall be made at the particular place in the statement where the information is required. A copy of any information or a copy of the pertinent pages of a document containing such information which is incorporated by reference shall be submitted with this statement as an exhibit and shall be deemed to be filed with the Commission for all purposes of the Act.

Item 1. Security and Subject Company

State the title of the class of equity securities to which this statement relates and the name and the address of the principal executive offices of the subject company.

Item 2. Tender Offer of the Bidder

Identify the tender offer to which this statement relates, the name of the bidder and the address of its principal executive offices or, if the bidder is a natural person, the bidder's residence or business address (which may be based on the bidder's Schedule 14D–1 filed with the Commission).

Item 3. Identity and Background

(a) State the name and business address of the person filing this statement.

(b) If material, describe any contract, agreement, arrangement or understanding and any actual or potential conflict of interest between the person filing this statement or its affiliates and: (1) the subject company, its executive officers, directors or affiliates; or (2) the bidder, its executive officers, directors or affiliates.

Instruction. If the person filing this statement is the subject company and if the materiality requirement of Item 3(b) is applicable to any contract, agreement, arrangement or understanding between the subject company or any affiliate of the subject company and any executive officer or director of the subject company, it shall not be necessary to include a description thereof in this statement, or in any solicitation or recommendation published, sent or given to security holders if such information, or information which does not differ materially from such information, has been disclosed in any proxy statement, report or other communication sent within one year of the filing date of this statement by the subject company to the then holders of the securities and has been filed with the Commission: *Provided* That this statement and the solicitation or recommendation published, sent or given to security holders shall contain specific reference to such proxy statement, report or other communication and that a copy of the pertinent portion(s) thereof is filed as an exhibit to this statement.

Item 4. The Solicitation or Recommendation

(a) State the nature of the solicitation or the recommendation. If this statement relates to a recommendation, state whether the person filing this statement is advising security holders of the securities being sought by the bidder to accept or reject the tender offer or to take other action with respect to the tender offer and, if so, furnish a description of such other action being recommended. If the person filing this statement is the subject company and a recommendation is not being made, state whether the subject company is either expressing no opinion and is remaining neutral toward the tender offer or is unable to take a position with respect to the tender offer.

(b) State the reason(s) for the position (including the inability to take a position) stated in (a) of this Item.

Instruction. Conclusory statements such as "The tender offer is in the best interest of shareholders," will not be considered sufficient disclosure in response to Item 4(b).

Item 5. Persons Retained, Employed or to Be Compensated

Identify any person or class of persons employed, retained or to be compensated by the person filing this statement or by any person on its behalf, to make solicitations or recommendations to security holders and describe briefly the terms of such employment, retainer or arrangement for compensation.

Item 6. Recent Transactions and Intent with Respect to Securities

(a) Describe any transaction in the securities referred to in Item 1 which was effected during the past 60 days by the person(s) named in response to Item 3(a) and by any executive officer, director, affiliate or subsidiary of such person(s).

(b) To the extent known by the person filing this statement, state whether the persons referred to in Item 6(a) presently intend to tender to the bidder, sell or hold securities of the class of securities being sought by the bidder which are held of record or beneficially owned by such persons.

Item 7. Certain Negotiations and Transactions by the Subject Company

(a) If the person filing this statement is the subject company, state whether or not any negotiation is being undertaken or is underway by the subject company in response to the tender offer which relates to or would result in:

(1) An extraordinary transaction such as a merger or reorganization, involving the subject company or any subsidiary of the subject company;

(2) A purchase, sale or transfer of a material amount of assets by the subject company or any subsidiary of the subject company;

(3) A tender offer for or other acquisition of securities by or of the subject company; or

(4) Any material change in the present capitalization or dividend policy of the subject company.

Instruction. If no agreement in principle has yet been reached, the possible terms of any transaction or the parties thereto need not be disclosed if in the opinion of the Board of Directors of the subject company such disclosure would jeopardize continuation of such negotiations. In such event, disclosure that negotiations are being undertaken or are underway and are in the preliminary stages will be sufficient.

(b) Describe any transaction, board resolution, agreement in principle, or a signed contract in response to the tender offer, other than one described pursuant to Item 3(b) of this statement, which relates to or would result in one or more of the matters referred to in Item 7(a)(1), (2), (3) or (4).

Item 8. Additional Information to Be Furnished

Furnish such additional information, if any, as may be necessary to make the required statements, in light of the circumstances under which they are made, not materially misleading.

Item 9. Material to Be Filed as Exhibits

Furnish a copy of:

(a) Any written solicitation or recommendation which is published or sent or given to security holders in connection with the solicitation or recommendation referred to in Item 4.

(b) If any oral solicitation or recommendation to security holders is to be made by or on behalf of the person filing this statement, any written instruction, or other material which is furnished to the persons making the actual oral solicitation or recommendation for their use, directly or indirectly, in connection with the solicitation or recommendation.

(c) Any contract, agreement, arrangement or understanding described in Item 3(b) or the pertinent portion(s) of any proxy statement, report or other communication referred to in Item 3(b).

Rule 14e-1. Unlawful Tender Offer Practices

As a means reasonably designed to prevent fraudulent, deceptive or manipulative acts or practices within the meaning of section 14(e) of the Act, no person who makes a tender offer shall:

(a) Hold such tender offer open for less than twenty business days from the date such tender offer is first published or sent or given to security holders: *Provided, however,* That this paragraph shall not apply to a tender offer by the issuer of the class of securities being sought which is not made in anticipation of or in response to another person's tender offer for securities of the same class.

(b) Increase the offered consideration or the dealer's soliciting fee to be given in a tender offer unless such tender offer remains open for at least ten business days from the date that notice of such increase is first published, sent or given to security holders: *Provided, however,* That this paragraph shall not apply to a tender offer by the issuer of the class of securities being sought which is not made in anticipation of or in response to another person's tender offer for securities of the same class.

(c) Fail to pay the consideration offered or return the securities deposited by or on behalf of security holders promptly after the termination or withdrawal of a tender offer;

(d) Extend the length of a tender offer without issuing a notice of such extension by press release or other public announcement, which notice shall include disclosure of the approximate number of securities deposited to date and shall be issued no later than the earlier of (i) 9:00 a. m. Eastern time, on the next business day after the scheduled expiration date of the offer or (ii), if the class of securities which is the subject of the tender offer is registered on one or more national securities exchanges, the first opening of any one of such exchanges on the next business day after the scheduled expiration date of the offer.

Rule 14e-2. Position of Subject Company With Respect to a Tender Offer

(a) *Position of subject company.* As a means reasonably designed to prevent fraudulent, deceptive or manipulative acts or practices within the meaning of section 14(e) of the Act, the subject company, no later than 10 business days from the date the tender offer is first published or sent or given, shall publish, send or give to security holders a statement disclosing that the subject company:

(1) Recommends acceptance or rejection of the bidder's tender offer;

(2) Expresses no opinion and is remaining neutral toward the bidder's tender offer; or

(3) Is unable to take a position with respect to the bidder's tender offer.
Such statement shall also include the reason(s) for the position (including the inability to take a position) disclosed therein.

(b) *Material change.* If any material change occurs in the disclosure required by paragraph (a) of this section, the subject company shall promptly publish, send or give a statement disclosing such material change to security holders.

Rule 14e-3. Transactions in Securities on the Basis of Material, Nonpublic Information in the Context of Tender Offers

(a) If any person has taken a substantial step or steps to commence, or has commenced, a tender offer (the "offering person"), it shall constitute a fraudulent, deceptive or manipulative act or practice within the meaning of section 14(e) of the Act for any other person who is in possession of material information relating to such tender offer which information he knows or has reason to know is nonpublic and which he knows or has reason to know has been acquired directly or indirectly from (1) the offering person, (2)

the issuer of the securities sought or to be sought by such tender offer, or (3) any officer, director, partner or employee or any other person acting on behalf of the offering person or such issuer, to purchase or sell or cause to be purchased or sold any of such securities or any securities convertible into or exchangeable for any such securities or any option or right to obtain or to dispose of any of the foregoing securities, unless within a reasonable time prior to any purchase or sale such information and its source are publicly disclosed by press release or otherwise.

(b) A person other than a natural person shall not violate paragraph (a) of this section if such person shows that:

(1) The individual(s) making the investment decision on behalf of such person to purchase or sell any security described in paragraph (a) or to cause any such security to be purchased or sold by or on behalf of others did not know the material, nonpublic information; and

(2) Such person had implemented one or a combination of policies and procedures, reasonable under the circumstances, taking into consideration the nature of the person's business, to ensure that individual(s) making investment decision(s) would not violate paragraph (a), which policies and procedures may include, but are not limited to, (i) those which restrict any purchase, sale and causing any purchase and sale of any such security or (ii) those which prevent such individual(s) from knowing such information.

(c) Notwithstanding anything in paragraph (a) to the contrary, the following transactions shall not be violations of paragraph (a) of this section:

(1) Purchase(s) of any security described in paragraph (a) by a broker or by another agent on behalf of an offering person; or

(2) Sale(s) by any person of any security described in paragraph (a) to the offering person.

(d)(1) As a means reasonably designed to prevent fraudulent, deceptive or manipulative acts or practices within the meaning of section 14(e) of the Act, it shall be unlawful for any person described in paragraph (d)(2) of this section to communicate material, nonpublic information relating to a tender offer to any other person under circumstances in which it is reasonably foreseeable that such communication is likely to result in a violation of this section except that this paragraph shall not apply to a communication made in good faith,

(i) To the officers, directors, partners or employees of the offering person, to its advisors or to other persons, involved in the planning, financing, preparation or execution of such tender offer;

(ii) To the issuer whose securities are sought or to be sought by such tender offer, to its officers, directors, partners, employees or advisors or to other persons, involved in the planning, financing, preparation or execution of the activities of the issuer with respect to such tender offer; or

(iii) To any person pursuant to a requirement of any statute or rule or regulation promulgated thereunder.

(d)(2) The persons referred to in paragraph (d)(1) of this section are:

(i) The offering person or its officers, directors, partners, employees or advisors;

(ii) The issuer of the securities sought or to be sought by such tender offer or its officers, directors, partners, employees or advisors;

(iii) Anyone acting on behalf of the persons in paragraph (d)(2)(i) or the issuer or persons in paragraph (d)(2)(ii); and

(iv) Any person in possession of material information relating to a tender offer which information he knows or has reason to know is nonpublic and which he knows or has reason to know has been acquired directly or indirectly from any of the above.

Rule 14f-1 Change in Majority of Directors.

If, pursuant to any arrangement or understanding with the person or persons acquiring securities in a transaction subject to sections 13(d) or 14(d) of the Act, any persons are to be elected or designated as directors of the issuer, otherwise than at a meeting of security holders, and the persons so elected or designated will constitute a majority of the directors of the issuer,

then, not less than 10 days prior to the date any such person takes office as a director, or such shorter period prior to that date as the Commission may authorize upon a showing of good cause therefor, the issuer shall file with the Commission and transmit to all holders of record of securities of the issuer who would be entitled to vote at a meeting for election of directors, information substantially equivalent to the information which would be required by Items 5(a), (d), (e), and (f), 6, and 7 of Schedule 14A of Regulation 14A to be transmitted if such person or persons were nominees for election as directors at a meeting of such security holders. Eight copies of such information shall be filed with the Commission.

OVER–THE–COUNTER MARKETS
* * *

Rule 15c2–11. Initiation or Resumption of Quotations Without Specified Information

(a) It shall be a fraudulent, manipulative, and deceptive practice within the meaning of Section 15(c)(2) of the Act, for a broker or dealer to publish any quotation for a security or, directly or indirectly, to submit any such quotation for publication, in any quotation medium (as defined in this rule) unless:

(1) the issuer has filed a registration statement under the Securities Act of 1933 which became effective less than 90 calendar days prior to the day on which such broker or dealer publishes or submits the quotation to the quotation medium, *provided* that such registration statement has not thereafter been the subject of a stop order which is still in effect when the quotation is published or submitted, and such broker or dealer has in his records a copy of the prospectus specified by Section 10(a) of the Securities Act of 1933; or

(2) the issuer has filed a notification under Regulation A under the Securities Act of 1933 which became effective less than 40 calendar days prior to the day on which such broker or dealer publishes or submits the quotation to the quotation medium, *provided* that the offering circular provided for under Regulation A has not thereafter become the subject of a suspension

order which is still in effect when the quotation is published or submitted, and such broker or dealer has in his records a copy of such offering circular; or

(3)(A) the issuer is required to file reports pursuant to Section 13 or 15(d) of the Act, or is the issuer of a security covered by Section 12 (g)(2)(B) or (G) of the Act, and

(B) the broker or dealer has a reasonable basis for believing that the issuer is current in filing the reports required to be filed at regular intervals pursuant to Section 13 of 15(d) of the Act, or, in the case of insurance companies exempted from Section 12(g) of the Act by subparagraph 12(g)(2)(G) thereof, the annual statement referred to in Section 12(g)(2)(G)(i) of the Act; and

(C) the broker or dealer has in his records the issuer's most recent annual report filed pursuant to Section 13 of 15(d) of the Act, or the annual statement in the case of an insurance company not subject to Section 12(g) of the Act, together with any other reports required to be filed at regular intervals under such provisions of the Act which have been filed by the issuer after such annual report or annual statement; or

(4) such broker or dealer has in his records, and shall make reasonably available upon request to any person expressing an interest in a proposed transaction in the security with such broker or dealer, the following information (which shall be reasonably current in relation to the day the quotation is submitted), which he has no reasonable basis for believing is not true and correct or reasonably current, and which was obtained by him from sources which he has a reasonable basis for believing are reliable: (1) the exact name of the issuer and its predecessor (if any); (2) the address of its principal executive offices; (3) the state of incorporation, if it is a corporation; (4) the exact title and class of the security; (5) the par or stated value of the security; (6) the number of shares or total amount of the securities outstanding as of the end of the issuer's most recent fiscal year; (7) the name and address of the transfer agent; (8) the nature of the issuer's business; (9) the nature of products or services offered; (10) the nature and extent of the issuer's facilities; (11) the name of the

chief executive officer and members of the board of directors; (12) the issuer's most recent balance sheet and profit and loss and retained earnings statements; (13) similar financial information for such part of the two preceding fiscal years as the issuer or its predecessor has been in existence; (14) whether the broker or dealer or any associated persons is affiliated, directly or indirectly with the issuer; (15) whether the quotation is being published or submitted on behalf of any other broker or dealer, and, if so, the name of such broker or dealer; and, (16) whether the quotation is being submitted or published directly or indirectly on behalf of the issuer, or any director, officer or any person, directly or indirectly the beneficial owner of more than 10 per cent of the outstanding units or shares of any equity security of the issuer, and, if so, the name of such person, and the basis for any exemption under the federal securities laws for any sales of such securities on behalf of such person. If such information is made available to others upon request pursuant to the subparagraph, such delivery, unless otherwise represented, shall not constitute a representation by such broker or dealer that such information is true and correct, but shall constitute a representation by such broker or dealer that the information is reasonably current in relation to the day the quotation is submitted, that he has no reasonable basis for believing the information is not true and correct, and that the information was obtained from sources which he has a reasonable basis for believing are reliable.

(b) With respect to any security the quotation of which is within the provisions of this rule, the broker or dealer submitting or publishing such quotation shall maintain in his records information regarding all circumstances involved in the submission of publication of such quotation, including the identity of the person or persons for whom the quotation is being submitted or published and any information regarding the transaction provided to the broker or dealer by such person or persons.

(c) The broker or dealer shall maintain in writing as part of his records the information described in paragraphs (a) and (b), and any other information (including adverse information) regarding the issuer which comes to his knowledge or possession before the publication or submission of the quotation, and preserve such records for the periods specified in Rule 17a–4.

(d) For any security of an issuer included in paragraph (a)(4), the broker or dealer submitting the quotation shall furnish to the inter-dealer quotation system (as defined below), in such form as such system shall prescribe, at least 2 days before the quotation is published or submitted, the information regarding the security and the issuer which such broker or dealer is required to maintain pursuant to said paragraph (a)(4).

(e) For purposes of this rule:

(1) "Quotation medium" shall mean any "inter-dealer quotation system" or any publication or electronic communications network or other device which is used by brokers or dealers to make known to others their interest in transactions in any security, including offers to buy or sell at a stated price or otherwise, or invitations of offers to buy or sell.

(2) "inter-dealer quotation system" shall mean any system of general circulation to brokers or dealers which regularly disseminates quotations of identified brokers or dealers.

(3) except as otherwise specified in this rule, "quotation" shall mean any bid or offer at a specified price with respect to a security.

(f) The provisions of this rule shall not apply to:

(1) the publication or submission of a quotation respecting a security admitted to trading on a national securities exchange and which is traded on such an exchange on the same day as, or on the business day next preceding, the day the quotation is published or submitted.

(2) the publication or submission of a quotation for securities of foreign issuers exempt from Section 12(g) of the Act by reason of compliance with the provisions of Rule 12g3–2(b).

(3) the publication or submission of a quotation respecting a security which has been the subject of both bid and ask quotations in an inter-dealer quotation system at specified prices on each of at least twelve days within the previous thirty calendar days, with no more than four business days in succession without such a two-way quotation.

* * *

(g) The requirement in subparagraph (a)(4) that the information with respect to the issuer be "reasonably current" will be presumed to be satisfied, unless the broker or dealer has information to the contrary, if:

(1) the balance sheet is as of a date less than 16 months before the publication or submission of the quotation, the statements of profit and loss and retained earnings are for the 12 months preceding the date of such balance sheet, and if such balance sheet is not as of a date less than 6 months before the publication or submission of the quotation, it shall be accompanied by additional statements of profit and loss and retained earnings for the period from the date of such balance sheet to a date less than 6 months before the publication or submission of the quotation.

(2) other information regarding the issuer specified in subparagraph (a)(4) is as of a date within 12 months prior to the publication or submission of the quotation.

(h) This rule shall not prohibit any publication or submission of any quotation if the Commission, upon written request or upon its own motion, exempts such quotation either unconditionally or on specified terms and conditions, as not constituting a fraudulent, manipulative or deceptive practice comprehended within the purpose of this rule.

†